Houston's Hermann Park

Number Sixteen:
Sara and John Lindsey Series in the Arts and Humanities

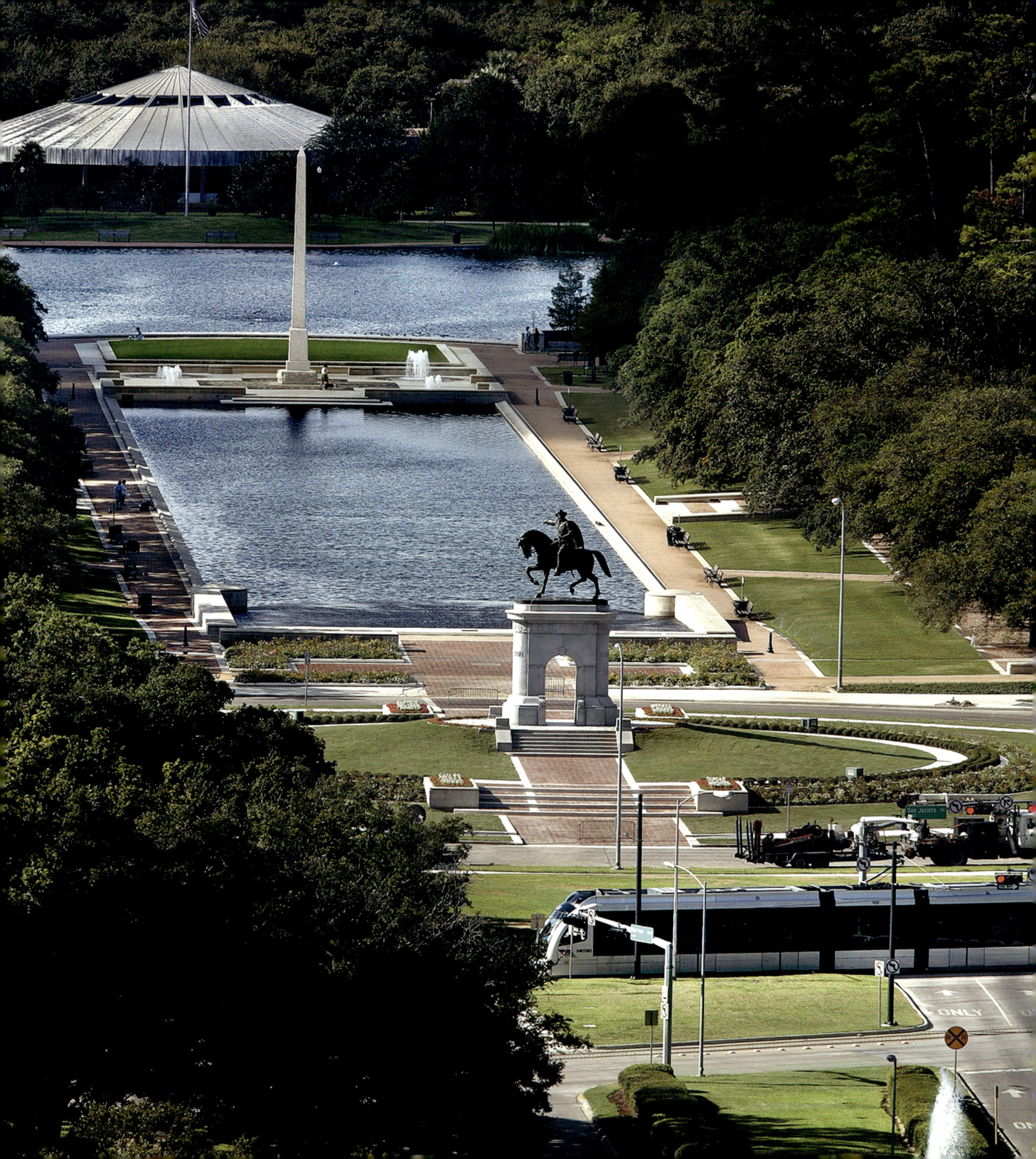

Houston's Hermann Park

A Century of Community

BARRIE SCARDINO BRADLEY

Foreword by Stephen Fox *Afterword by* Doreen Stoller

TEXAS A&M UNIVERSITY PRESS | COLLEGE STATION

Manufactured in South Korea,
through Four Colour Print Group

First edition

The paper used in this book meets the minimum requirements
of the American National Standard for Permanence
of Paper for Printed Library Materials, Z39.48-1984.
Binding materials have been chosen for durability.
∞

Library of Congress Cataloging-in-Publication Data

Bradley, Barrie Scardino, 1945–
Houston's Hermann Park : A century of community / by Barrie Scardino Bradley ; foreword by Stephen Fox ; afterword by Doreen Stoller.—1st ed.
p. cm.—(Sara and John Lindsey series in the arts and humanities ; no. 16)
Includes bibliographical references and index.
ISBN 978-1-62349-036-2 (cloth : alk. paper) 1. Hermann Park (Houston, Tex.)—History. 2. Houston (Tex.)—History. I. Title. II. Series: Sara and John Lindsey series in the arts and humanities ; no. 16.
F394.H87H473 2013
976.4'1411—dc23
2013008407

Frontispiece: Heart of the Park, aerial view, 2004. Photograph by David Schmoll, courtesy Hermann Park Conservancy.

Contents

Houston's Hermann Park

Foreword

The Hermann Park Conservancy chose to celebrate the centennial of the founding of Hermann Park in 1914 by commissioning Barrie Bradley to write a history of the park. Her splendid book names the significant personalities, dates the pivotal events, and pictures the historical stages through which Hermann Park took on its familiar shape and substance. As her text makes clear, the park's founding as a gift of George H. Hermann and its initial improvement under the guiding hand of the landscape architect and city planner George E. Kessler occurred as part of a broader pattern of civic development that gave Houston a range of cultural institutions it had not possessed in the nineteenth century: a public library, opened in 1904 (and supplemented by a second public library accessible to African American Houstonians in 1913); the William M. Rice Institute (now Rice University), opened in 1912; a symphony orchestra, founded in 1913 (although not established permanently until 1931); the Museum of Fine Arts, Houston, which opened in 1924; and the pair of public universities that opened as junior colleges in 1926, the University of Houston and Texas Southern University. Hermann Park reflected the remarkable energy, ambitiousness, and foresight that Houston exhibited in the ten-year period before the United States entered the First World War, when the Texas Company, the Gulf Oil Company, and Anderson, Clayton and Company moved their headquarters to Houston. Also during this period, the Humble Oil and Refining Company was organized in Houston, the Houston Ship Channel opened, and the City of Houston's Board of Park Commissioners sponsored preparation of Houston's first city plan in 1912 and 1913. Although Houston became notorious in the second half of the twentieth century as the largest US city to repudiate city planning, this inclination was not evident in the first decades of the twentieth century. Hermann Park's spatial integration with the Main Boulevard civic arena, much of it planned by Kessler in conjunction with the development of the park, attests to the commitment of Houstonians during the Progressive Era to the principles and methods of rational and responsible city building.

Barrie Bradley's text enables readers to understand when and why this optimistic vision faltered, even as such important new institutions as the Houston Zoo, Miller Theatre, and the Houston Museum of Natural Science were organized in the park, and as Houston's modest network of public parks grew into a system with the acquisition of Memorial Park in 1924 and construction of linear parks along the channels of Buffalo Bayou and Brays Bayou in the second half of the 1920s. Economic cycles and the divergent outlooks of succeeding generations of civic leaders meant that the period after the Second World War was not characterized by the same sorts of visions that prevailed in the 1910s and 1920s. The city's sale of one-quarter of Hermann Park's territory in 1943 to provide a site for the Texas Medical Center was symptomatic of this changed state of mind, which treated public space as expendable. The extent to which parking lots commenced to eat into the natural fabric of Hermann Park in the third quarter of the twentieth century represented the "Houstonization" of the park's green space. Even the well-intentioned practice of adding new attractions to the park in the 1970s and 1980s was too frequently achieved by enclosing additional park space and subtracting green space for yet more parking.

Houston's Hermann Park: A Century of Community identifies the steps through which this troubling state of affairs started being reversed in the 1980s. The imaginative interventions promoted by Drexel Turner of Rice University's School of Architecture and of the Rice Design Alliance, through its design competition of 1992 for rehabilitating the park's central axis, the formation of what is now the Hermann Park Conservancy, and the leadership provided by its executive directors—Mary Anne Piacentini, Patricia Winn, Roksan Okan-Vick, and Doreen Stoller—allied with the brilliant planning and masterful advocacy of the Philadelphia landscape architect Laurie Olin, transformed the landscape of Hermann Park by the turn of the twenty-first century. The superlative caliber of public space design and its refined execution have renewed Hermann Park, not just materially but metaphysically as well. The inspiring work of the conservancy in collaboration with the City of Houston's Parks and Recreation Department advances a new model of public space management. The public-private partnership between the conservancy and the city, initially sanctioned by Mayor Bob Lanier and supported by his successors, mayors Lee P. Brown, Bill White, and Annise Parker, has been efficacious for advancing ambitious public improvement projects that agencies of Houston's city government are not empowered to promote on their own.

Although critics voice concern about the agendas, responsibility, and accountability of the private partners in public-private partnerships, the directors of the Hermann Park Conservancy have shown themselves to be exemplars of public service as they seek to equip Hermann Park with the public space infrastructure to welcome and accommodate the exceptionally culturally diverse city that Houston had become by the turn of the twenty-first century. Barrie Bradley, who has personally participated in these endeavors for the last thirty-three years, gives us the historical perspective to reflect on the commitment of the City of Houston, the Hermann Park Conservancy, and the philanthropists who have funded these projects to protecting, maintaining, and sustaining Hermann Park as one of, if not the, most important public spaces in Houston.

Stephen Fox
Fellow of the Anchorage Foundation of Texas

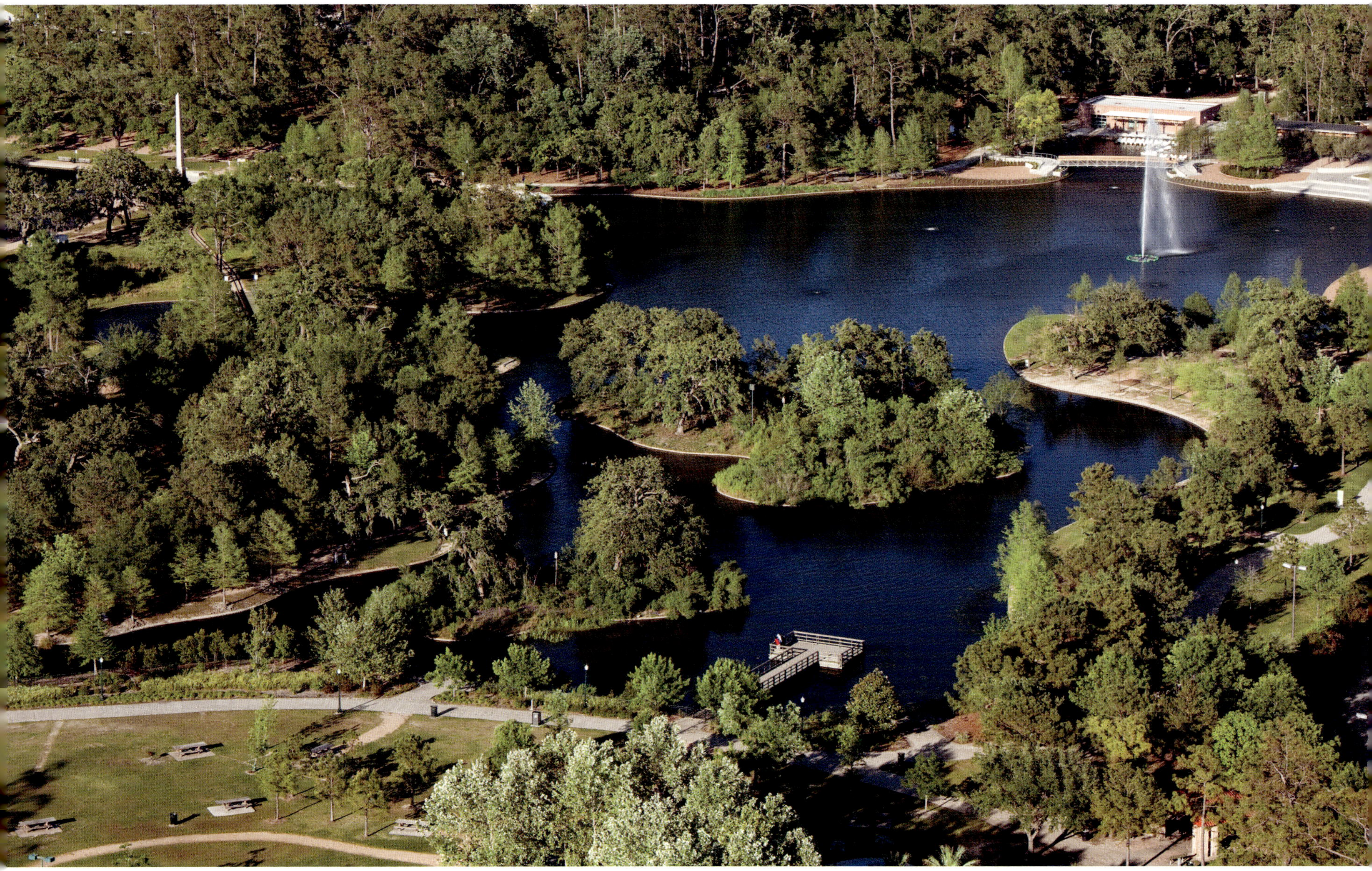

McGovern Lake, Hermann Park, aerial view, 2012. Courtesy Hermann Park Conservancy.

Preface

The story of Hermann Park, like that of a great institution or a great city, is the story of individuals who had the exceptional foresight, political power, and social commitment to achieve their goals. The men and women who dreamed, financed, approved, designed, built, and renewed Hermann Park are as important to the history and understanding of the park as the gardens and trees. This book attempts to identify and applaud those people who stand out in the history of Hermann Park. This park has experienced cycles of appreciation and neglect, but at the age of one hundred, it is a flagship urban American park enjoyed by millions each year and nurtured by the Hermann Park Conservancy and the City of Houston Parks and Recreation Department.

Hermann Park has grown with Houston, now the fourth largest city in the United States. Once located in a rural setting at the edge of town, the park today is a vibrant urban space that provides respite and enjoyment through both the institutions it holds—Miller Outdoor Theatre, the Houston Zoo, the Hermann Park Golf Course, and the Houston Museum of Natural Science—and through the variety of places one can explore in the park—McGovern Lake, the Bayou Parkland, the Carruth Playground, the Japanese Garden, the Centennial Gardens, picnic areas, and hidden trails. *Houston's Hermann Park* hopes to capture the special character of the park and its significance in Houston. The park is not only appreciated by those who live in Houston, but it has also become a place sought out by tourists and the families of those who come to the Texas Medical Center for treatment. The medical center, the largest in the world, was built next to Hermann Park on land that was, until the mid-1940s, part of the park.

Houston's Hermann Park was commissioned by the Hermann Park Conservancy to celebrate the centennial of the park in 2014. My friend and colleague Jay Baker approached me in 2010, on behalf of the board of directors, about writing this book. Meetings began with a small book committee of the Conservancy board: Ann Kennedy (chairman of the board from 2010 to 2014), Jay Baker, Sanford Criner, Jane Anderson Curtis, and Karen Rozzell. Other board members were willing to sit through long interviews: Jay Baker, Jane Curtis, Susan Keeton, Christopher Knapp, Marley Lott, Kunio Minami, and Marvin Taylor. Kathrine McGovern and Sara Lindsey also provided valuable input. Mrs. McGovern opened my eyes to the birds of Hermann Park, and Mrs. Lindsey suggested the title. I am especially grateful to Stephen Fox for his patience in answering unending questions, for reading the manuscript and making beneficial suggestions, and finally, for his scholarship, on which much of this work is based.

Laurie Olin was extraordinarily generous with his time, his drawings and photographs, and his insights during two lovely days I spent in Philadelphia. Without him and his role in the renewal of Hermann Park there would be no cause for a centennial celebration of the park, or, indeed, no impetus for this book. We all owe him and his colleagues a huge debt of appreciation.

From the beginning Doreen Stoller, executive director of the Conservancy, has been my soundboard, source of information, and advocate. In addition she and her husband Dan Pierre read early drafts, made good suggestions, and proofread final drafts. Special thanks to them both. Rick Dewees, Hermann Park Administrator for the Houston Parks and Recreation Department, was the source of innumerable facts, information, and documents—and he taught me about Google Earth's time machine. Members of the Hermann Park Conservancy staff have also been helpful: horticulturalist Barbara Jo Harwell (conservation director), Mike Johnson (project manager), Meghan Miller (director of development), Eliza Wright and her successor Adrienne Saxe (marketing managers), and Caroline Urquhart (administrative assistant).

Staff members of the Houston Metropolitan Research Center at the Houston Public Library, my primary source of information and historic photographs, have been especially accommodating, and I would particularly like to thank Joel Draut (photographic archivist), Laney Dwyer (architectural archivist), Timothy Ronk (archivist), and Elizabeth Sargent (acting director). Mary Daniels, archivist at the Frances

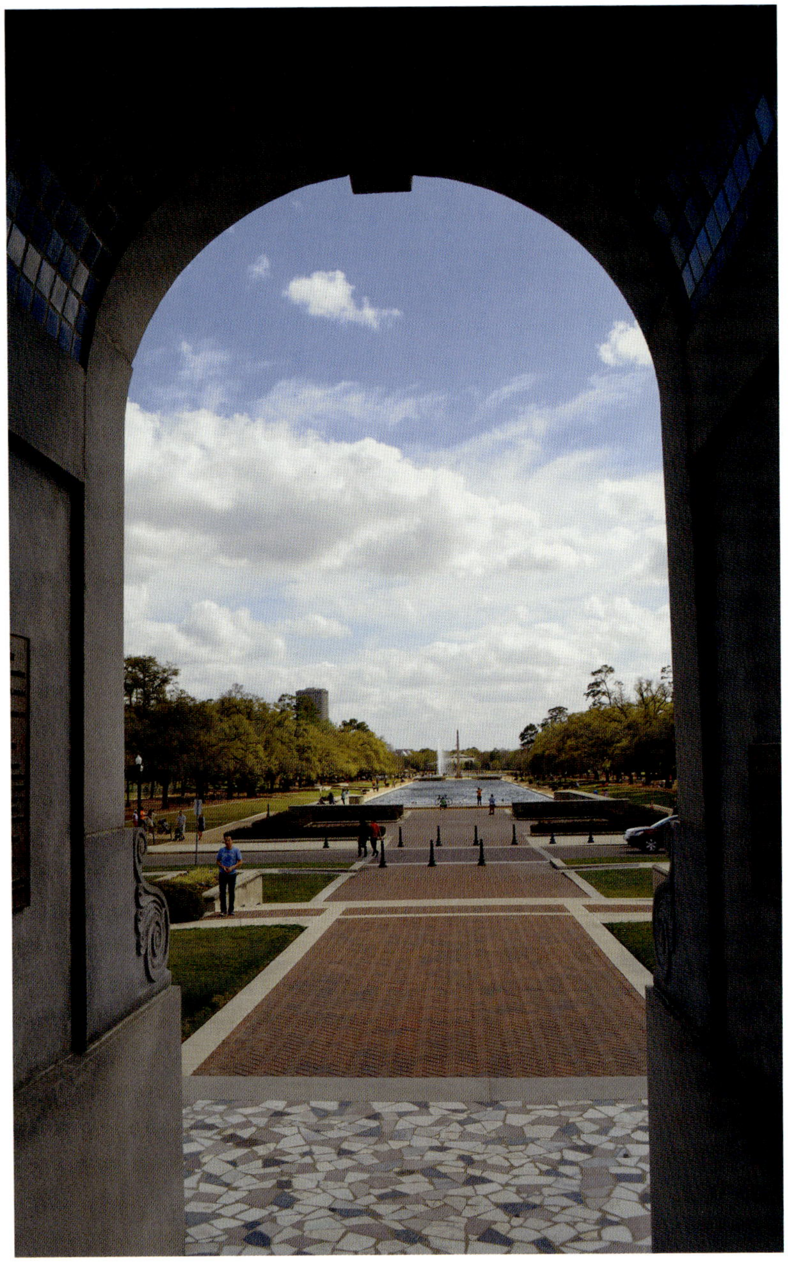

Heart of the Park viewed through Sam Houston Arch, 2013. Photograph by B. S. Bradley.

Loeb Library Special Collections, Harvard University, and David Butros of the State Historical Society of Missouri, Research Center-Kansas City, were both helpful in obtaining information and photographs from their collections. Lee Pecht, Rice University Archivist and Director of Special Collections, provided access to the collections in the Woodson Research Center at Rice. His associates Amanda Focke and Dara Flinn were helpful in retrieving images. Thank you also to Brian Hill, public relations director at the Houston Zoo, for providing images and information. Likewise Philip Montgomery, Archivist, and Alethea Drexler at the John P. McGovern Historical Collections and Research Center, Houston Academy of Medicine, Texas Medical Center Library, gave assistance in locating some important photographs. They led me to Lindsey Klingensmith at Memorial-Hermann Hospital, who informed me of the sad news that the George Hermann diary had been lost when the hospital was flooded by Tropical Storm Allison in 2001.

Along with the directors of the Hermann Park Conservancy, I am very pleased that Texas A&M University Press decided to publish *Houston's Hermann Park*. I thank Mary Lenn Dixon, editor-in-chief, director Charles Backus, who believed in the project and, with Mary Lenn, guided the manuscript through to acceptance, Mary Ann Jacob, design manager, Thom Lemmons, managing editor, Katie Cowart, and my old friend Gayla Christiansen, who will assure that someone besides this inner circle reads the book.

Friends of mine and of Hermann Park have been generous with their advice, expertise, and time, particularly Craig Minor of Minor Design Group, Ben Hulsey and Jim Winn of the Houston Audubon Society, Charles Tapley, FAIA, Ray Bailey, FAIA, of Bailey Architects, and Jim Furr, FAIA, of Gensler. Special appreciation goes to my supportive husband Jerry W. Bradley, English professor and advanced grammar guru. Thanks to you all, remembered and neglected, who helped produce this book to celebrate the 100th anniversary of our great Hermann Park.

Barrie Scardino Bradley

PART I

Then

CHAPTER ONE

Before Hermann Park

1836–1909

To see cities in terms of their open spaces is to begin to understand their form, their nature, and the dynamic of their economic life.[1]

—August Heckscher, 1982

Hermann Park is Houston's most significant urban space, and its history parallels the development of Houston into a major American city in the twentieth century. Founded in 1836, Houston was superimposed on a flat, grass plain interrupted by forested strips along its streams and bayous. These waterways were, and are, the area's only natural topographical features, and they determined the physical shape of the city. During the mid-nineteenth century the town remained a frontier settlement, then grew relatively slowly with commerce downtown, residential neighborhoods to the south and west, and railroad and industrial quarters to the north and east. Houston's early leaders focused their energy and political influence on commercial development and water and rail connections to markets beyond the Houston area. They apparently felt no need to set aside public recreational space, nor was there any city-owned property that could be developed for parks.

During the Civil War, Houston's economy was sustained in part by such clever merchants as William Marsh Rice and T. W. House, who found markets for local cotton in Mexico. Their ships were able to move around Union blockades to the Mexican port of Matamoros. Therefore, after the war, Houston's economic fortunes rebounded quickly, and Reconstruction was a relatively mild episode focused on political rather than economic recovery. Because local resources were restricted during the war, no construction of consequence took place until the mid-1860s, when building resumed at a rapid pace.

Thomas Howe Scanlan (1832–1906), an Irish immigrant, Unionist, and Houston's Reconstruction mayor, advocated the purchase of land for three municipal parks as early as 1871 to avoid, he said, the high price of land in the future.[2] Scanlan's administration was focused on municipal improvements and modernization. However, he was subsequently criticized for the large amount of money spent on construction of an ambitious new City Hall and Market House in 1872. It burned down without adequate insurance in 1876, exacerbating the city government's problems of meeting its financial obligations after the onset of the international economic depression caused by a financial crisis during the Panic of 1873. The city's substantial debt at this time precluded the purchase of parkland.

History of Houston Parks

The most significant landscape development in Houston during the Reconstruction period was the establishment of Glenwood Cemetery in 1871 on the north bank of Buffalo Bayou just west of town.[3] Although it was private property owned by investors in the Houston Cemetery Company, who purchased 50 acres for the initial cemetery site, in many respects Glenwood became Houston's first public park. It was planned as a "garden cemetery" with curving lanes and picturesque vistas, a radical departure from Houston's earlier cemeteries with rows of gravestones laid out in a grid pattern. The streetcar line was extended from downtown to Glenwood, which increased access to its beautiful grounds and made it a destination for middle-class Houston families out for a Sunday picnic. Glenwood Cemetery, for a time, sufficed as Houston's main public open space.

Houston's only downtown park was Courthouse Square. The three Harris County courthouses, built at intervals between 1837 and 1884, occupied only part of the square, leaving the perimeter of the site for

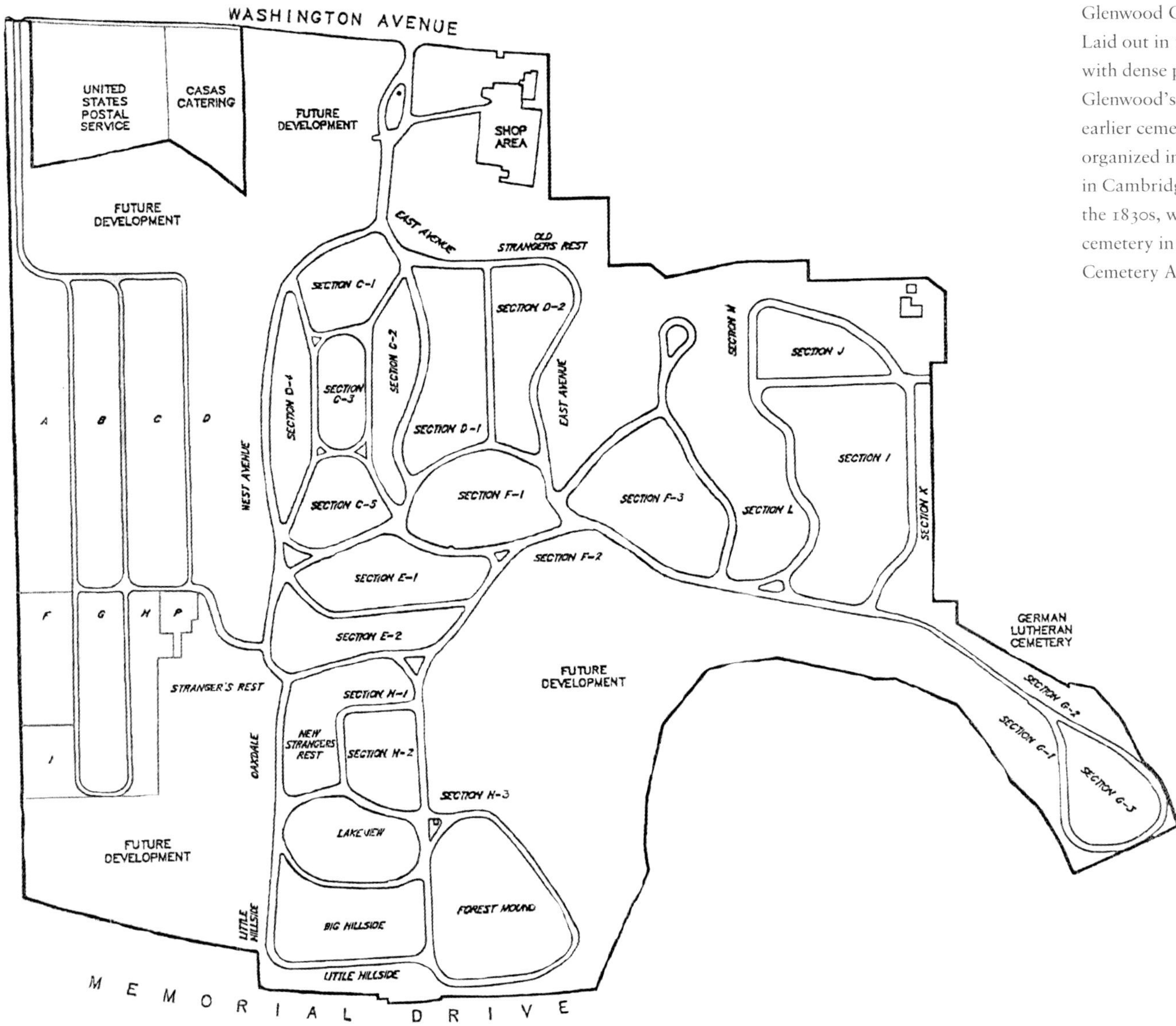

Glenwood Cemetery, early diagram. Laid out in 1871 as a "garden cemetery" with dense plantings and winding paths, Glenwood's design was a departure from earlier cemetery plans with tombstones organized in rows. Mt. Auburn Cemetery in Cambridge, Massachusetts, platted in the 1830s, was the first such picturesque cemetery in America. Source: Glenwood Cemetery Archives.

public use. The county installed gaslights, planted trees, placed iron benches in the shade under the trees, and erected an iron fence around the whole square. An 1882 report noted that Courthouse Square was a "popular resort for wives and children, as it is the only public square in the city."[4] This circumstance ended when foundations were laid in 1883 for a larger courthouse that nearly filled the block.

A significant post-Civil War park was established with the acquisition of a 10-acre outlot in the Third Ward for Emancipation Park. Although the Emancipation Proclamation had been signed on January 1, 1863, slavery was not legally abolished until Congress passed the 13th Amendment to the US Constitution on January 3, 1865.[5] The State of Texas ratified this amendment on June 19, 1865—a day celebrated in Texas ever since as Juneteenth. Freed slaves in Houston held celebrations at various locations until 1872 when the site bound by Elgin, Dowling, Hutchins, and Tuam became available. Prominent Houstonian John F. Dickson,[6] in a letter to the editor of the *Houston Daily Post* in 1910, exhorted the City of Houston to refrain from taking the park for back taxes. In his letter Dickson recounted and defended the history of the Emancipation Park as a place where black citizens had for decades held ownership and celebrated Juneteenth. In this letter he says: "The property was given to the negroes by Marshall C. Wellborn and Sarah J. Wellborn, his wife, on July 10, 1872, to enable them to congregate on their own ground for such amusement and recreation as they desired (much as the Sam Houston park is now used exclusively by whites)."[7]

In a conflicting story, recorded in 1936, Willie Parker Chestnutt noted: "Growing tired of this procedure [searching every year for a different site to celebrate Juneteenth], in the year 1872, Richard Allen, with

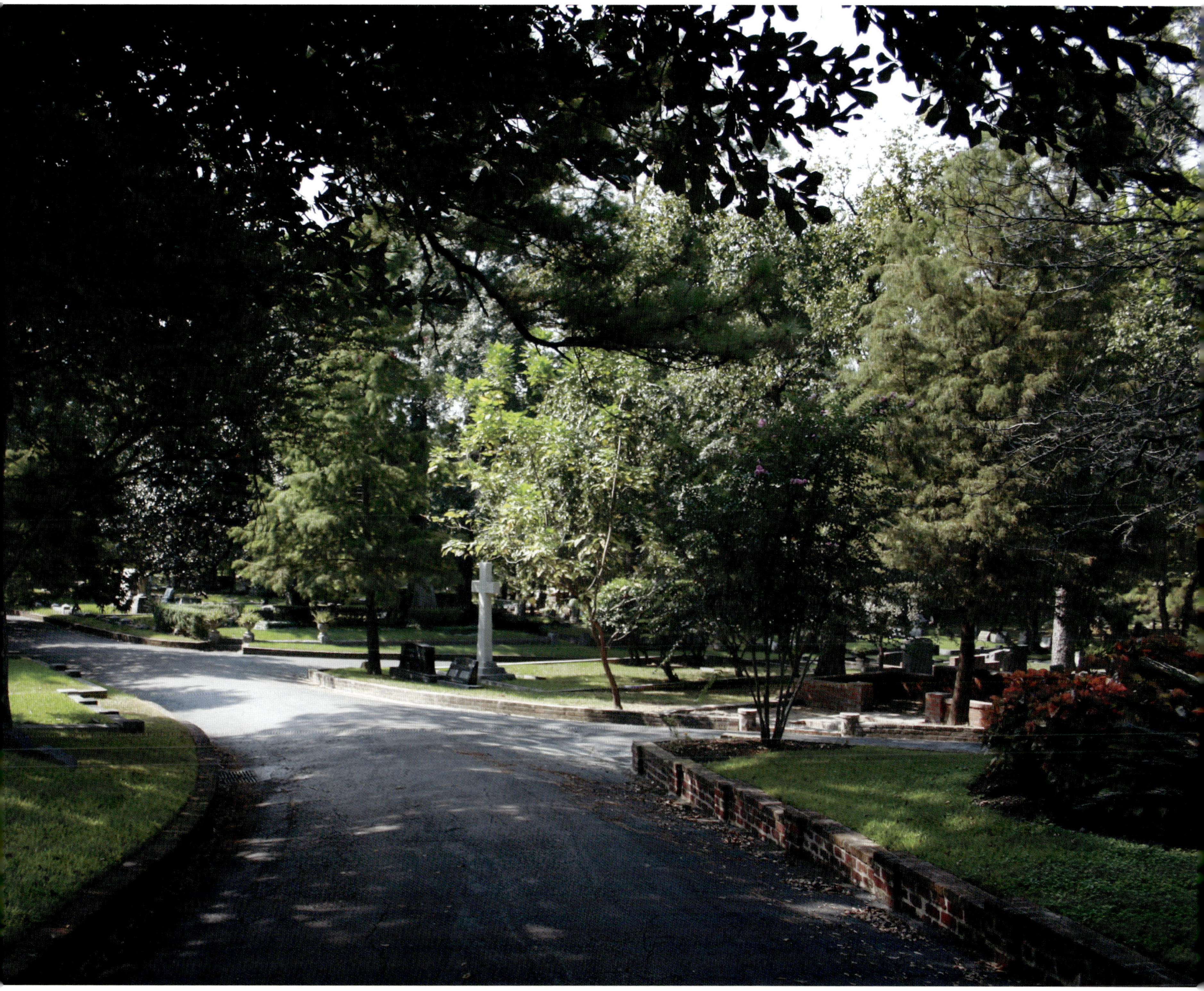

Glenwood Cemetery, 2525 Washington Avenue, 2012. Photograph by B. S. Bradley.

the Rev. Jack Yates, and Alias Dibbrels as associated, decided to buy a place of their own."[8] Chestnutt continued that the price of $1,000 was to be paid in yearly installments, however, "these men faced the problem of continued payments on the property which they had bought on the installment plan without funds." To help raise the money, they sold concessions for refreshment stands and rented the property to carnival companies, classifying the park as rental property in the eyes of the city. As a result Judge James R. Masterson agreed to take a mortgage on the property so the taxes could be paid, but receiving no payments on the mortgage, he foreclosed. In 1916, according to Chestnutt, Mayor Ben Campbell lifted the mortgage "and the property was made a part of the city to relieve the burden of taxes and provide for its upkeep."

Most likely the Wellborns[9] owned the property and signed it over to a group of trustees without receiving full payment, thus Dickson credits them with donating the property.[10] Emancipation Park was the only public park in Houston black citizens were allowed to use until the 1950s.[11] The park received a Texas Historical marker in 2008, and the *Houston Chronicle* announced plans in 2011 for an $18 million capital campaign to refurbish the park and construct new sports facilities.[12]

In 1885 the *Galveston Daily News* reported on the development of Brashear Park, which was privately owned but propitiously located on the Glenwood streetcar line just beyond the cemetery. Brashear was being developed "into a handsome suburban landscape with pools, ponds, and cool and shady nooks for the public to enjoy."[13] The land, acquired by Mrs. Isaac (Sarah) Brashear in 1872,[14] was purchased by the City of Houston in 1900 and was eventually incorporated into the parkway along Memorial Drive, as was part of the area known then as Vick's Park. The Vick family, three brothers who came from Tennessee about 1880, bought land along the north bank of Buffalo Bayou between what is now Studemont and Waugh, where they had a cattle farm and built houses for railroad and factory workers to rent. Louis Aulbach described the scene in the 1890s: "Houston residents escaped the hectic pace and the heat of summer in the city by spending a relaxing day in the park. . . . Picnicing among the shady trees along Buffalo Bayou was popular. So was canoeing the bayou and paddling on Vick's Lake. The bayou swimming hole in Vick's Park was considered to be one of the city's best."[15]

Like Glenwood Cemetery, Brashear Park, Vick's Park, and Magnolia Park became destinations for outings. Magnolia Park, a residential development east of Houston, was laid out in 1890 on a wooded 1,374-acre site on Harrisburg Road across Brays Bayou from Harrisburg 7 miles downstream from Houston. Thomas M. Brady, who owned the land, named the community for the 3,750 magnolias planted there by the developers. Marguerite Johnston documents several of Houston's nineteenth-century pleasure grounds, including Magnolia Park, where families went by railroad, streetcars, buggies, or on horseback for pas-

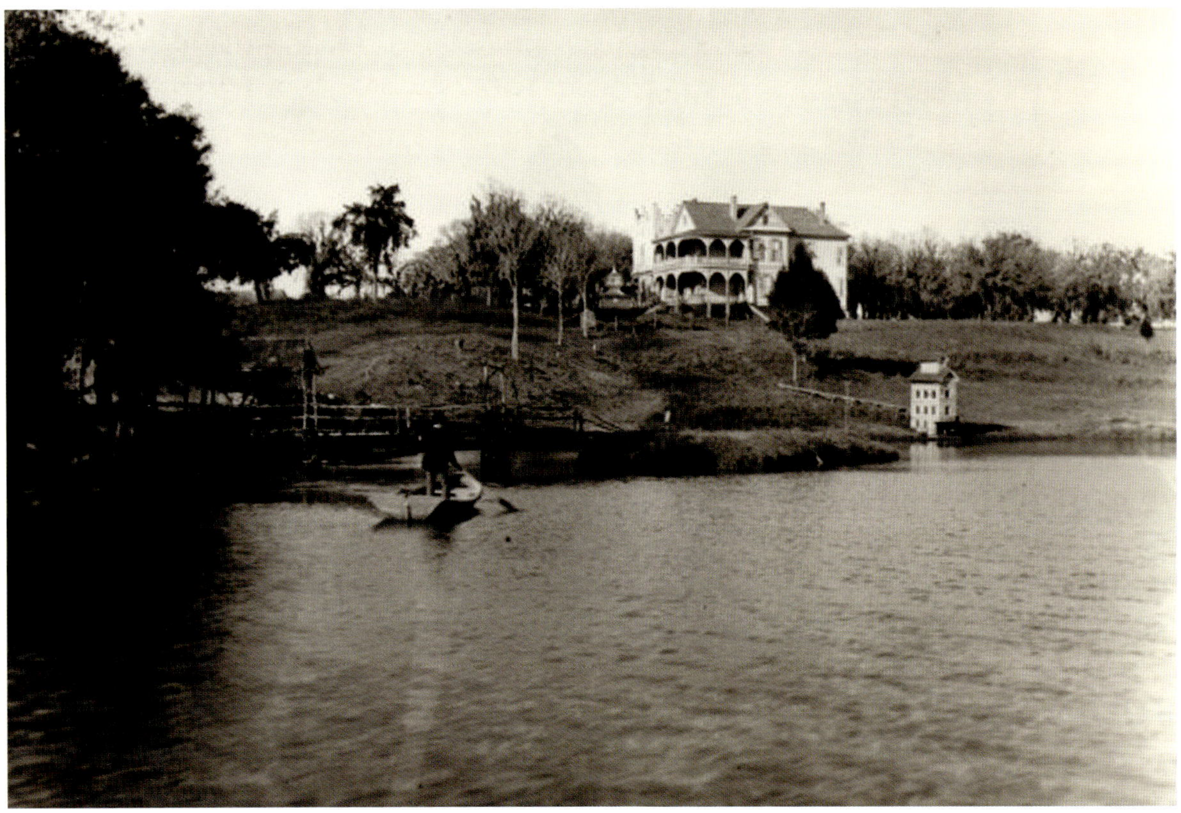

Vick's Park, c. 1900. Located on the north bank of Buffalo Bayou between what is now Studemont Street and Waugh Drive, Vick's Park was a popular recreation spot, where canoeing was a common pastime on Vick's Lake. The house was most likely the residence of one of the three Vick brothers who owned the property. Courtesy Houston Metropolitan Research Center, Houston Public Library.

toral scenery outside of the city: the Old Fairgrounds, Merkel's Grove, Volkfest Park, and, on Galveston Bay, Sylvan Beach.[16]

Perhaps the most popular late nineteenth-century park was Coombs Park (sometimes called Forest Park). In 1893 Eden L. Coombs, the partner of J. J. Sweeney in both a jewelry company and the Sweeney and Coombs Opera House, in 1893 bought a 64-acre tract in Houston Heights on White Oak Bayou for the establishment of an amusement park.[17] Heights historian, Sister Agatha, describes it as being "in the flamboyant style of Coney Island's heyday."[18] The park included a racetrack, a small lake with alligators, a zoo of sorts, and, most famously, the Heights Natatorium, which continued in operation until 1927. Coombs died in 1900, and the park was gradually sold off for residential development. Coombs might have designed his park, which does have an interesting configuration with the bayou running through it. An 1895 map shows a plan with trails, both rectilinear and meandering, around wooded areas. Coombs Park was not professionally landscaped, nor did it incorporate gardens. However, with the natatorium and bicycle track, it did provide recreational opportunities.

None of these late nineteenth-century parks was city-owned. They were business operations intended to make profits. In terms of clientele they conformed to the pattern of market segmentation based on socioeconomic status, ethnicity, and race. Recreational, amusement, and sporting facilities began to appear in these privately owned parks

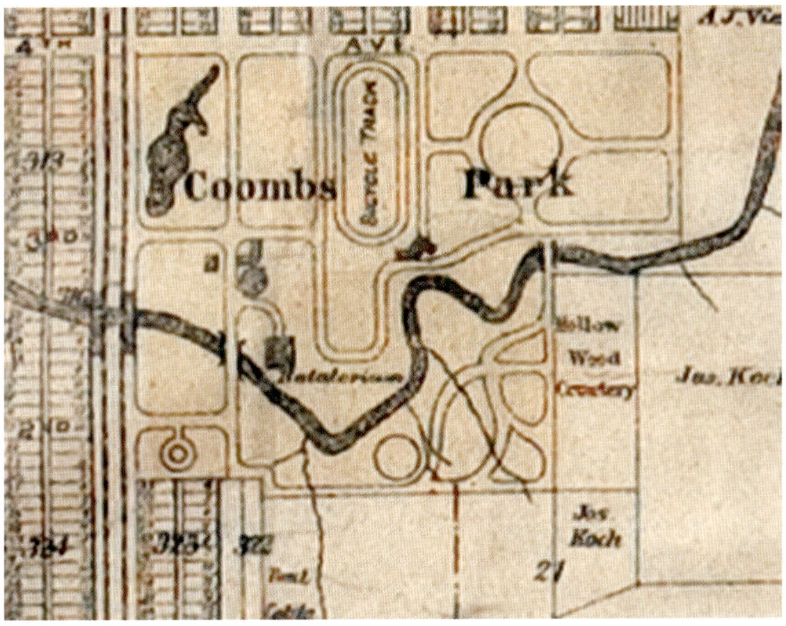

Coombs Park Plan, 1895. Houston had several such privately owned parks during the late nineteenth and early twentieth century that were commercial enterprises, open to the public for an entrance fee. Source: Whitty & Stott Engineers, *Map of City of Houston and Environs,* 1895. Courtesy Houston Metropolitan Research Center, Houston Public Library.

as these activities assumed greater importance in American social life in the 1880s and 1890s. As Houston began to grow at an increasingly rapid pace, these areas became one focus of more intensive real estate development, whetting a growing local appetite for more recreational opportunities. In the midst of urban expansion, the city government emerged as the institution better able to ensure permanent open recreational space within or nearby new residential additions.

Sarah Brashear's son, Samuel H. Brashear (1866–1941), was elected mayor in 1898, and the next year he appointed Houston's first park committee. Three aldermen plus Mayor Brashear were assigned the task of developing a comprehensive network of parks for Houston.[19] Only the purchases of the small Brashear Park, near Glenwood Cemetery, and of City Park, now called Sam Houston Park, were accomplished before Mayor Brashear resigned in 1900. On the south side of Buffalo Bayou, in what is now downtown Houston, Sam Houston Park sits on a 20-acre site purchased on June 21, 1899, for $26,000.[20] In the bargain came the historically significant Kellum-Noble House (1847), which was the headquarters of the Parks Department for a time. The park was picturesquely landscaped with winding paths, a rustic bridge over a stream with a water mill, and small ponds constructed in 1907 by city prisoners.[21] Other features included a bandstand and children's playground.

Sam Houston Park contained not only quaint landscape features but a number of monuments and artifacts, almost all connected to Civil War events and heroes, installed between 1905 and 1907 during the initial improvements in the park. These included the *Alexander Hodge Memorial* (1905), a granite monument to an American Revolution hero; the bell of the *Harriet Lane*, a federal gunboat captured in the Battle of Galveston in 1863; a Civil War cannon; the *Dick Dowling Memorial* (1905), a granite monument by Frank Teich honoring a Texas Civil War hero (now in Hermann Park); a granite boulder commemorating Terry's Texas Rangers (1906), the 8th Texas cavalry during the Civil War; *The Spirit of the Confederacy* (1907), an allegorical bronze figure by Louis Amateis; *Brownie* (1907), a bronze drinking fountain in the shape of a whimsical elf (now in Hermann Park); and the *Cenotaph to the Unknown Soldier* (1920), honoring missing World War I soldiers.

In 1914 the city purchased additional land for the park for $19,675.[22] Sam Houston Park was also home of Houston's first zoo—a collection of rabbits, raccoons, Mexican eagles, a black bear, a great horned owl, capuchin monkeys, prairie dogs, various birds, and an alligator pond. In 1920 the federal government donated a bison named Earl to the City of Houston; Earl lived for a while in the Sam Houston Park menagerie, prompting many to realize it was time to create a proper zoo.[23] In 1921 the city purchased an assortment of snakes, birds, and alligators and in 1922 moved all of these animals to a fence-enclosed area in Hermann Park, beginning what became the Houston Zoological Gardens, now the Houston Zoo.

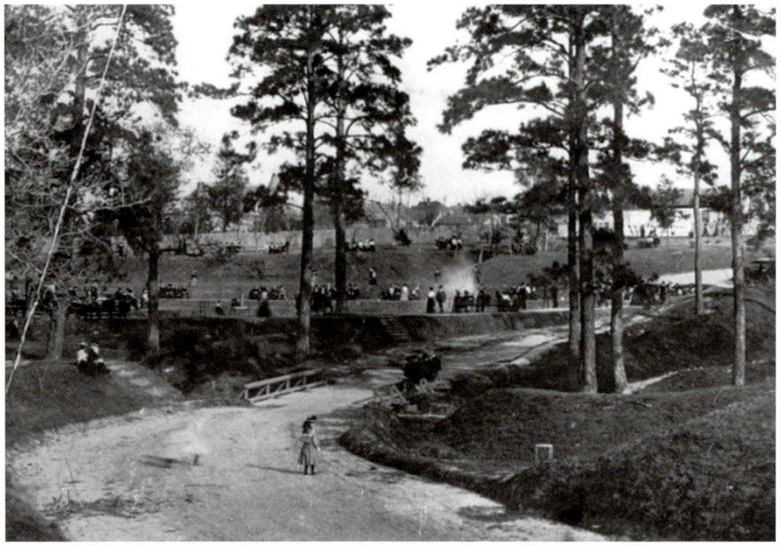

Sam Houston Park, c 1900. The City of Houston's first public park is located on the western edge of downtown Houston. Today it contains several historic houses moved from other parts of Houston and maintained by the Heritage Society. Courtesy Houston Metropolitan Research Center, Houston Public Library.

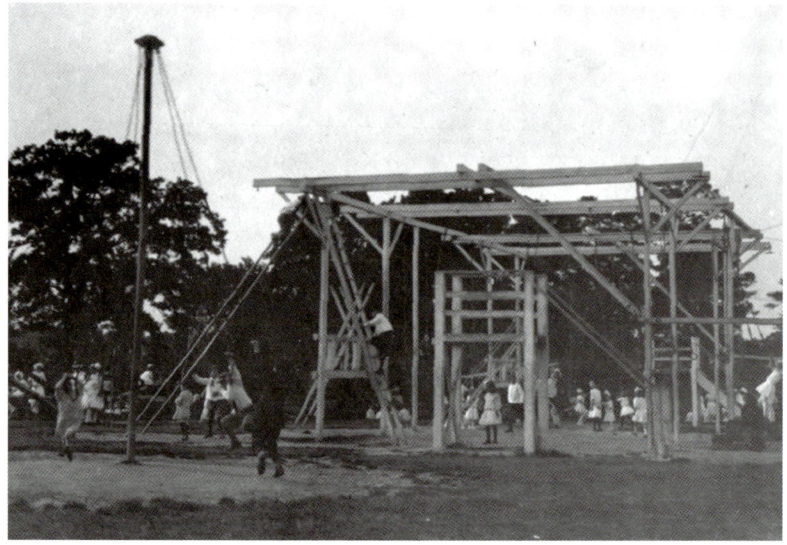

Sam Houston Park Playground, 1913, where children are playing on the latest in jungle gym equipment similar to wooden climbing and swinging structures built in Hermann Park in the 1920s. Photograph by Arthur C. Comey, courtesy Frances Loeb Library Special Collections, Harvard University.

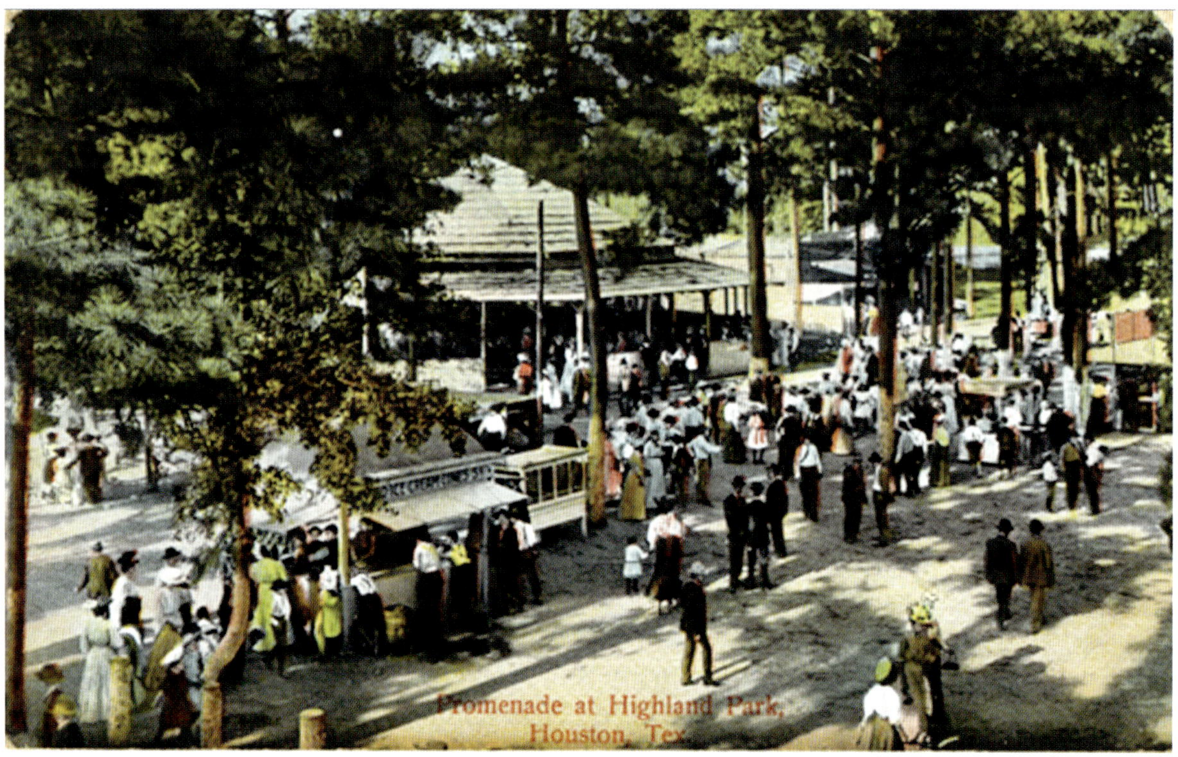

"Promenade at Highland Park," 1909. Courtesy Houston Metropolitan Research Center, Houston Public Library (187-0170).

Highland Park, Houston's second oldest park was developed in 1903 by the Houston Electric Company on a 30-acre tract between Houston Avenue and Little White Oak Bayou. An artificial lake was created by a dam across the bayou. Amenities such as a boathouse, restaurant, dance pavilion, and carnival rides attracted thousands of Houstonians. The City of Houston acquired the park in 1911 and renamed it Woodland Park in 1914. It is still maintained, although reduced in size because of Interstate 45.

Influences on American Parks

By 1910 Houston leaders were well aware that many American cities had an urban park patterned after New York's Central Park, designed by Frederick Law Olmsted (1822–1903). Although Olmsted is often referred to as the father of landscape design in America, this title should be reserved for the writer and horticulturalist Andrew Jackson Downing (1815–1852), who significantly influenced Olmsted's approach to landscape design. Downing, in turn, owed some of his theories and sensibilities to the Scottish botanist and cemetery designer John Claudius Loudon (1783–1843). Loudon was a prolific writer and began to receive notice after his *Encyclopedia of Gardening* was published in 1832. In reaction to the "gardenless" form of sweeping landscapes, introduced to England by Lancelot "Capability" Brown (1716–1783) and his successor, Sir Humphrey Repton (1752–1818), Loudon advocated a "gardenesque" approach where individual plants, preferably exotic ones, were introduced to give form to a landscape without mimicking nature as Brown and Repton had done. Loudon introduced the term *landscape architecture*, which was taken up by A. J. Downing, who published *A Treatise on the Theory and Practice of Landscape Gardening, Adapted to North America* in 1841 and the best-seller *Cottage Residences* in 1842.[24] In his preface to *Cottage Residences*, Downing explains that by *residences* he means both the house and its grounds, and in that volume he published over a dozen landscape plans that show meandering foot paths, curving carriage drives, wooded areas, and formal gardens.

Downing was a Romantic, a talented designer, and an imaginative thinker. He advocated lawns and shapely trees as essential elements for parks and, if possible, water. He helped construct a distinctive American version of picturesque Victorian architecture and landscapes, which led to the curvilinear plans and free-form landscapes of Olmsted and Vaux. After publishing *Architecture of Country Houses* in 1850, Downing visited Europe, where he toured English country houses and their seemingly boundless landscapes and innumerable parks. When he returned to the United States, he brought with him a new partner, the young English architect Calvert Vaux (1824–1895). In 1851, writing in reaction to London parks he had visited, Downing wrote in the *Horticulturist:*

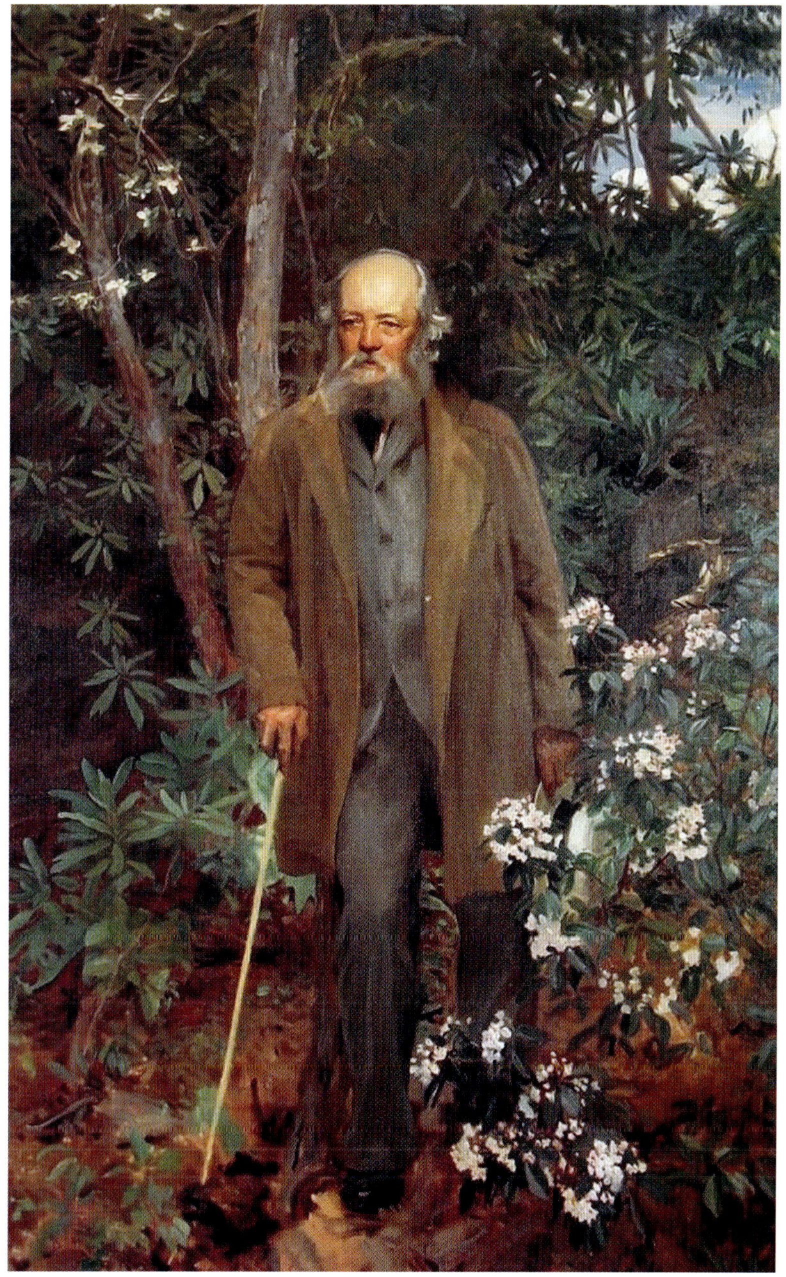

Frederick Law Olmsted (1895, John Singer Sargent). George W. Vanderbilt II commissioned Sargent to paint Olmsted and architect Richard Morris Hunt at Biltmore House, Asheville, North Carolina, the year house and grounds were completed. Shortly after this portrait was painted he retired from public life and died eight years later in 1913. Olmsted is buried in Old North Cemetery, Hartford, Connecticut. Source: John Singer Sargent Virtual Gallery.

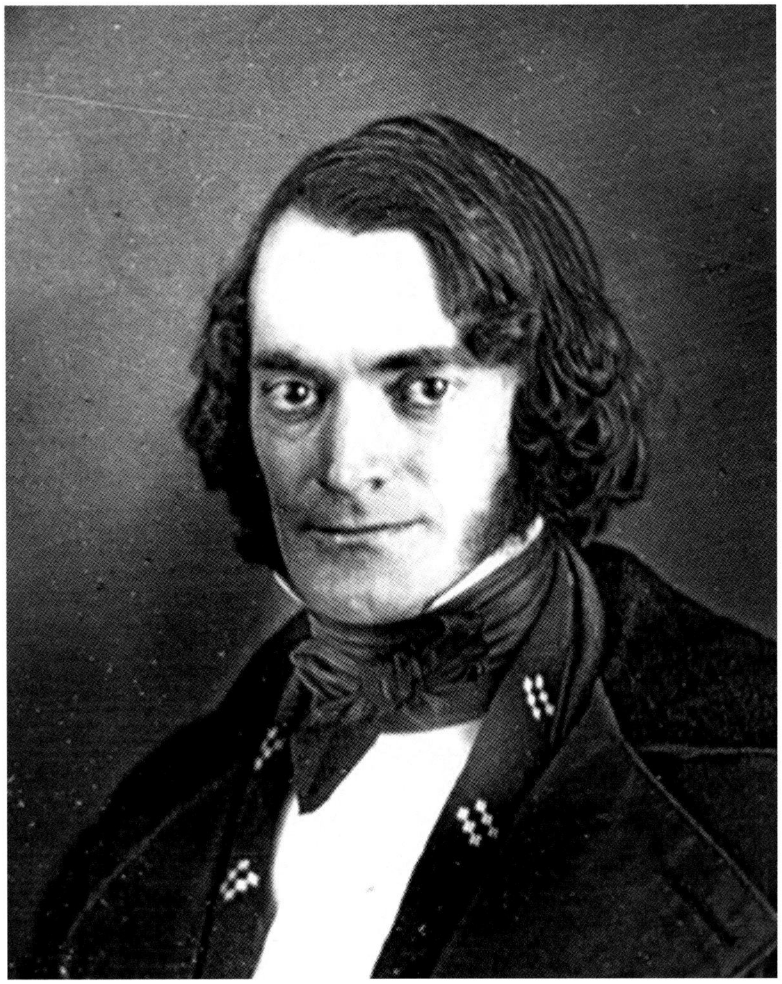

Andrew Jackson Downing (1815–1852) created the intellectual atmosphere that significantly influenced Olmsted and other landscape designers in the second half of the nineteenth century. Courtesy: Athenaeum of Philadelphia.

We only regret that the people of our large cities, generally, cannot see, with their own eyes, the beauty and realize the advantages of such parks in the midst of towns. New York, for instance, now one of the largest cities in the world, has no public park whatever, no breathing place, no grounds for the exercise and refreshment of her jaded citizens—for to call the little yards of land, covered with turf, and planted with trees, in various parts of the town, parks, is as much a misnomer as it would be to spread one's handkerchief down on the floor of the rotunda of the capitol, and call it a carpet. The fact is, Americans generally have no conception of the value, extent, or importance to the people of large cities of public parks—and among the good results that will grow out of the World's Fair in London [1851], will be that of showing thousands of them, Hyde Park, where the Crystal Palace stands—a building that covers twenty acres, and *appears* to take up as little room there, as if it were in an oak opening in Illinois.[25]

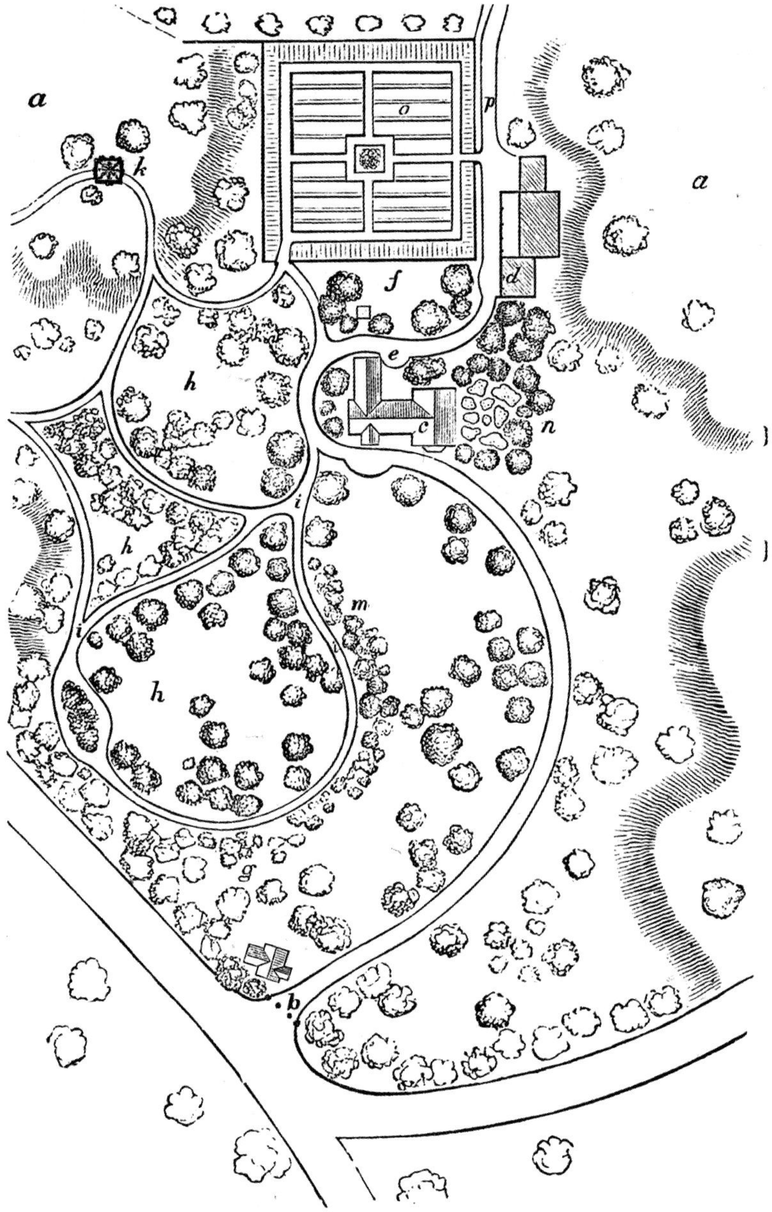

[Fig. 60.]

Landscape Plan (1842, A. J. Downing). Downing was an early advocate of landscapes that combined formal and informal gardens, parterres, and woodlands. Source: Andrew Jackson Downing, *Victorian Cottage Residences* (figure 60).

US cities, in the process of industrialization, had done a poor job of creating "breathing spaces" for recreation. Most European public parks developed from pleasure grounds and hunting parks associated with royal palaces—a legacy the United States did not possess. Older, eastern US cities had commons (established for common grazing of animals) and military parade grounds leftover from the seventeenth and eighteenth centuries. But these generally lacked the scale and scenic landscape features built into nineteenth-century

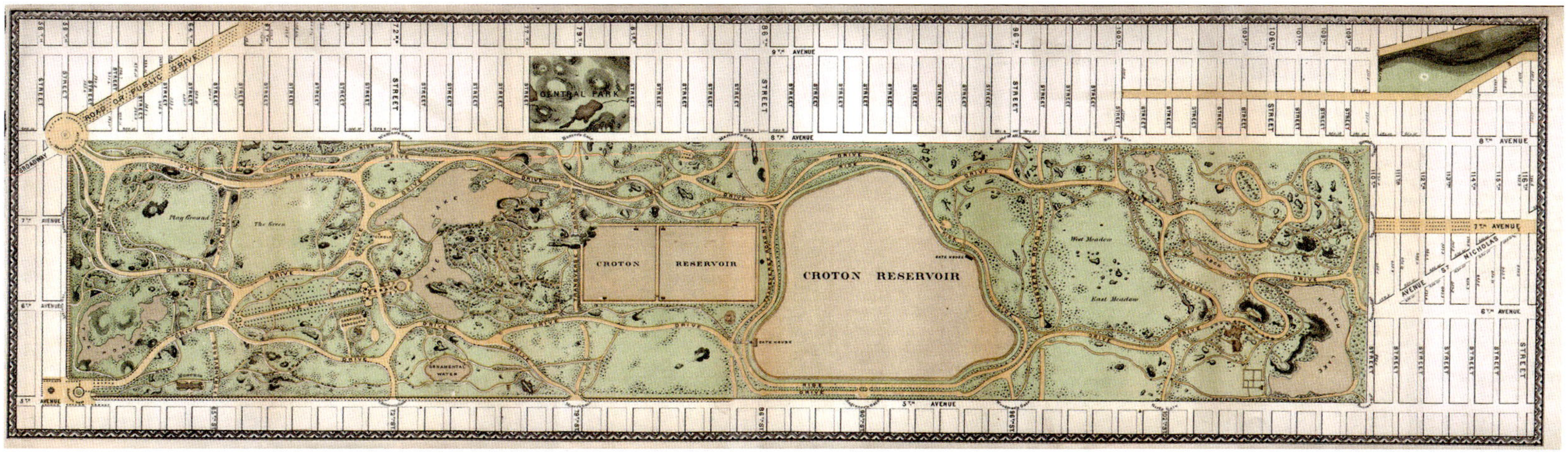

Central Park Map, 1868. Based on an original drawing by Frederick Law Olmsted, this map illustrates park design that became in vogue during the late nineteenth century following Downing's caveat that landscapes from residential gardens to great urban parks must include an interesting variety of spaces including formal allées, water features, winding foot and carriage paths, and, for large parks, institutions. Source: *Thirteenth Annual Report of the Board of Commissioners of the Central Park*, after Vaux and Olmstead 1863 plan.

parks designed by or under the influence of Frederick Law Olmsted and his contemporaries.

Downing's accidental death in a steamboat explosion on the Hudson River in 1852 left Vaux on his own. But in 1857 he approached Olmsted, whom Downing had known and whose writings Vaux admired, to collaborate in a competition to design a public park on 843 acres of city-owned property in upper Manhattan. Olmsted and Vaux won the Central Park competition of 1857 and worked for years refining their plan and supervising construction in the park. After the widespread publication of Central Park's success, commissions came to the firm from all over the United States for the planning of parks, parkways, estates, campuses, and subdivisions. After a Civil War hiatus, Olmsted and Vaux worked together again as Olmsted, Vaux and Company until 1872, when Olmsted went out on his own. One of Olmsted's last projects was the planning of the vast grounds of McLean Psychiatric Hospital in Belmont, Massachusetts. Two years after its completion in 1895, Olmsted moved in as a patient and remained there until his death in 1903.[26] Frederick Law Olmsted left over 60,000 manuscript pages, numerous publications, and an astounding number of completed landscape projects throughout the United States.[27]

Although historians have tended to treat the City Beautiful Movement, which blossomed after the World's Columbian Exposition of 1893 in Chicago, as antithetical to Olmsted's project of Romantic reform through landscape architecture, the City Beautiful Movement was sustained by the "moral environmentalism," of which Olmsted wrote, and his outspoken advocacy for public parks that could provide not only beautiful settings but also places where people of all walks of life could enjoy a respite from the clamorous city. The American middle class could not afford the private gardens and country estates of the wealthy but needed, Olmsted believed, recreational havens from commercial and industrial sectors that had infiltrated American cities.

Before his meteoric landscape career, Frederick Law Olmsted, among other pursuits, worked as a journalist and was dispatched on several trips, including one to Texas in 1854. In *A Journey Through Texas* Olmsted described the Houston landscape:

> Houston, at the head of the navigation of Buffalo Bayou, has had for many years the advantage of being the point of transhipment of a great part of the merchandise that enters or leaves the State. It shows many agreeable signs of the wealth accumulated in homelike, retired residences, its large and good hotel, its well-supplied shops and its shaded streets. . . . The country around it is low and flat, and generally covered by pines. . . . In the bayou bottoms near by, we noticed many magnolias, now in full glory of bloom, perfuming delicately the whole atmosphere.[28]

CHAPTER TWO

Houston Gets a Park

1910–1914

Central Park is wonderful. I wish my town of Houston had one like it.
Perhaps they will some day.[1]

—George H. Hermann, 1885

By the time the City Beautiful Movement and the Progressive Movement, of which it was a part, reached the consciousness of Houstonians, Olmsted had died, but his ideals had not. Local advocates of City Beautiful, like their counterparts elsewhere, hoped to mobilize political and economic power to create beautiful, spacious, and orderly cities with healthy open spaces. City Beautiful's theoretical basis was that beautification could create a harmonious social order and thus enhance the quality of life in America's cities. This philosophy was a refinement of the Progressive Movement's attempt to improve the harsh working and living conditions of urban industrial workers in the Northeast and Midwest by pushing for laws regulating tenement housing, child labor, and working conditions for women.[2] Architectural Historian Stephen Fox best explained the connection between the City Beautiful Movement and Hermann Park:

> Hermann Park was one of the chief reasons that Houston became involved in efforts at city planning during the second decade of the twentieth century. Not only was the park itself a focus of civic improvement and beautification, but the properties surrounding it—largely undeveloped when the park was acquired—seemed to present an exceptional opportunity for those citizens concerned about Houston's future to achieve an example of integrated city planning, resulting in a civic environment that was rational, healthy, and beautiful.[3]

Picking up where Mayor Brashear left off in 1900, Mayor Horace Baldwin Rice (1861–1929), a progressive reformer, appointed a Board of Park Commissioners in 1910 to advise on the development of a park system for Houston. The chairman was Edwin B. Parker (1868–1929) a lawyer and partner in the firm of Baker, Botts, Parker and Garwood. Parker's ten-acre estate, The Oaks, contained a prairie-style house designed by Sanguinet & Staats of Fort Worth in 1909.[4] Horticulture and gardening were Parker's avocation, and a newspaper report in 1909 makes clear why Parker was a good choice to head the park commission.

> Mr. Parker . . . lays not so much stress on the house itself as he does on his scheme for beautifying the surroundings. . . . In this Mr. Parker will be in his element. . . . In the front there will be nothing but the giant [oak] trees that are now standing there. The lawn will be sodded and carefully kept always. But in the rear of the house and to the Baldwin Street side is where the most beautiful profusion of plants and flowers are planned. It is contemplated that all sorts of shrubbery will be planted here, with due consideration being given always to its hardihood and its beautifying attributes. Walks will wind about through a veritable Eden.[5]

Sadie Gwin Blackburn gives an extensive description of the landscaping at The Oaks, noting that the landscaper, Arthur James Seiders of Austin, went to California to study estate gardens and parks there and returned with a train-car load of plants for The Oaks. On the grounds were a sunken garden, a pergola, raised beds, gravel paths, a rustic arbor, and a Japanese-style teahouse beyond which were a sweet gum grove, cutting gardens, chicken yards, and vegetable beds.[6] Although Parker's estate was extraordinary for Houston, other private gardens often were described in local newspapers and in the magazine *Progressive Houston*, published by the city from 1909 to 1912 to inform and influence Houstonians.[7]

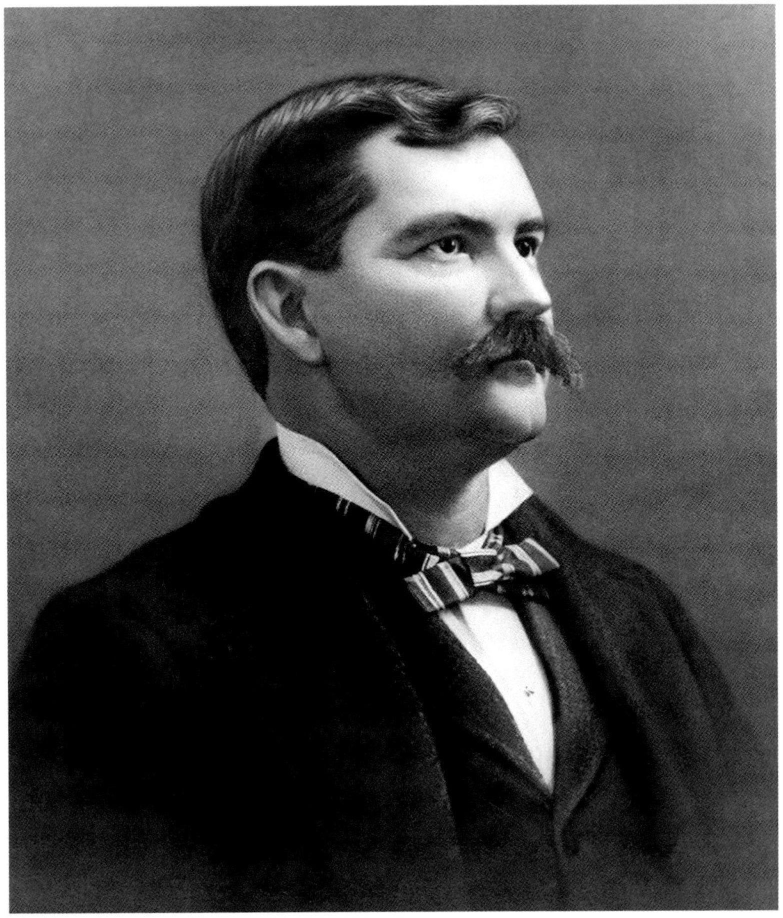

Mayor H. Baldwin Rice (1861–1929) appointed the first Board of Park Commissioners in 1910. Source: *City Book of Houston*, 1925. Courtesy Houston Metropolitan Research Center, Houston Public Library (157-379).

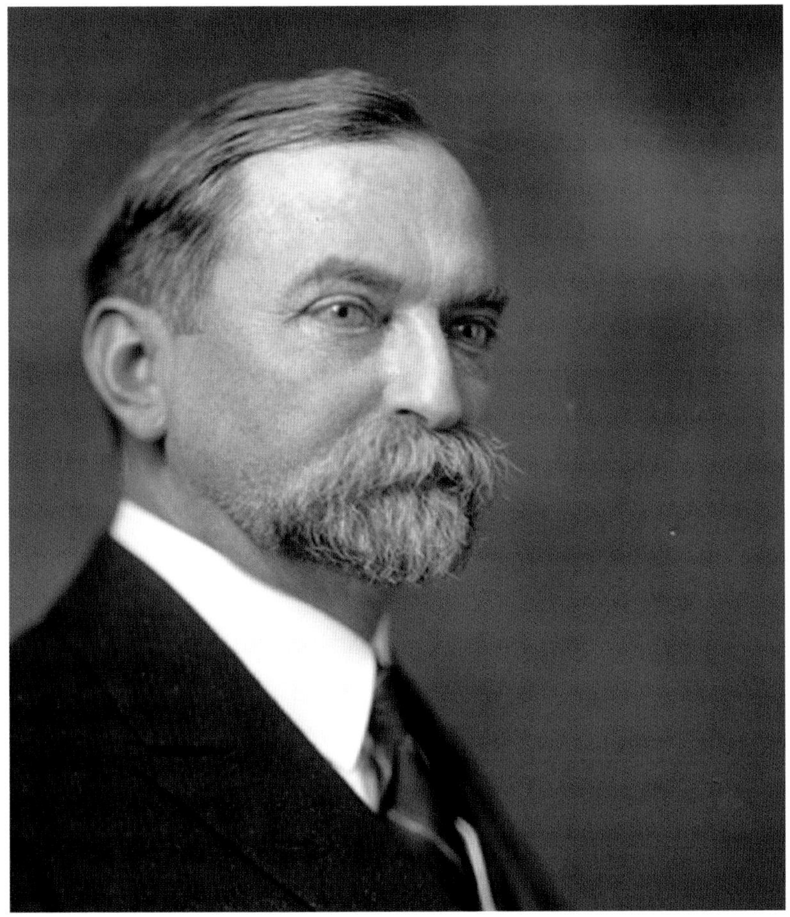

Edwin B. Parker (1868–1929), a partner in the firm Baker, Botts, Parker and Garwood and landscape enthusiast, was the first chairman of the Board of Park Commissioners. Courtesy Houston Metropolitan Research Center, Houston Public Library.

The second member of Mayor Rice's park commission was William A. Wilson, a real estate developer and community leader who would serve as president of the Chamber of Commerce in 1922.[8] Wilson developed the middle-income subdivision of Woodland Heights in 1907 on a 106-acre tract of high ground near White Oak Bayou. He planted hundreds of live oaks and sycamores along the streets and sidewalks that lined his 60-block subdivision. Wilson knew that good landscaping would enhance his development.[9] Clearly Wilson, like Parker, understood the principles and goals of the City Beautiful Movement that were to guide the work of Houston's Board of Park Commissioners.

George Henry Hermann

The most significant member of the Park Commission would prove to be George Henry Hermann (1843–1914). Hermann was born August 6, 1843, in Houston to Verina "Fannie" Michel (1805–1863) and John Hermann (1791–1862), who had emigrated from the Swiss Alpine town of Davos, the highest city in Europe. John Hermann had been to confectioner's school in Paris, from which he immigrated to the United States in 1821 after fighting with Napoleon at Waterloo. He returned to Davos in 1825 to marry. Both Hermanns were from well-to-do Swiss families, but they arrived in Houston after a time in Veracruz, Mexico, with very little money. Mrs. Hermann pawned some of her jewelry, and they were able to establish what is thought to have been the first bakery in Houston in 1838, on Main Street between Commerce and Franklin.[10] The bakery prospered, supplying bread to the steamboats coming and going on Buffalo Bayou, and in 1842 they purchased nine of the twelve lots in block 146 from S. S. Tompkins.[11] Eventually they also owned the entire city block surrounded by Walker, Smith, McKinney, and Brazos streets. In 1843 they built a two-story frame house at the corner of Smith and McKinney, facing Smith, in which George Henry was born and grew up.[12] Leaving the bakery business, John Hermann established various enterprises including a dairy and wagon yard, but his focus became real estate. By the time of his death, John Hermann owned extensive property in Houston, including most of the South End acreage on which Hermann Park is located.

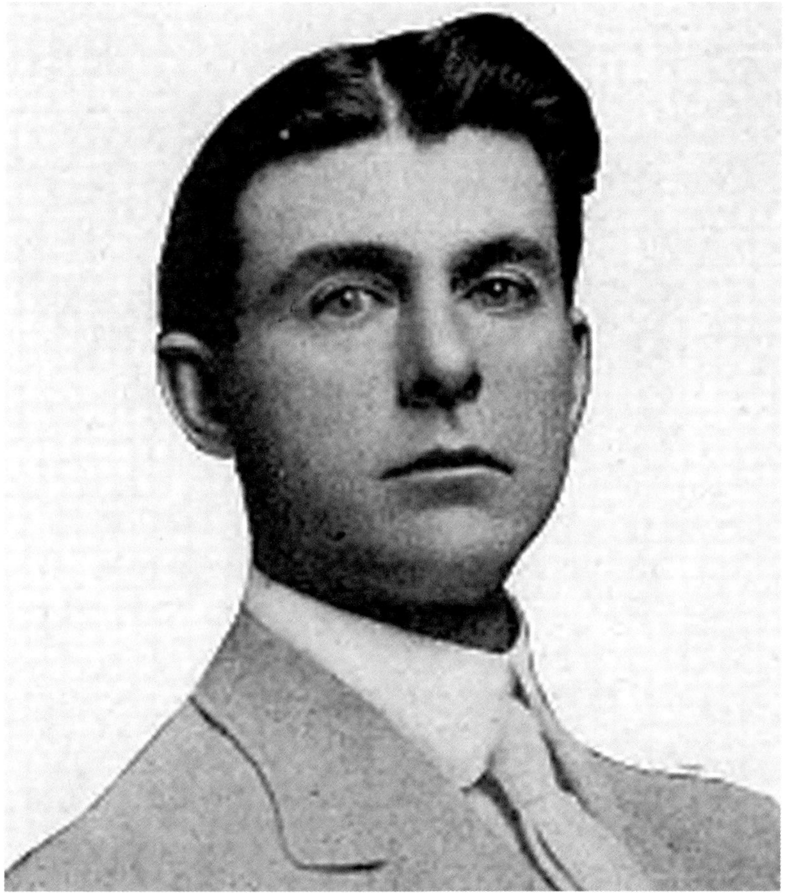

William A. Wilson (1864–1928) founded the William A. Wilson Realty Company in 1898 and developed the Houston subdivisions of Woodland Heights (1907) and Eastwood (1913). He built the largest house in Woodland Heights for his own family at 205 Bayland Avenue in 1910, which is now a registered Houston Protected Landmark. Wilson was an early advocate for city planning and public landscaping and was known for the many trees he planted in residential areas throughout Houston. Source: *Houston*, July 1922. Courtesy Houston Metropolitan Research Center, Houston Public Library.

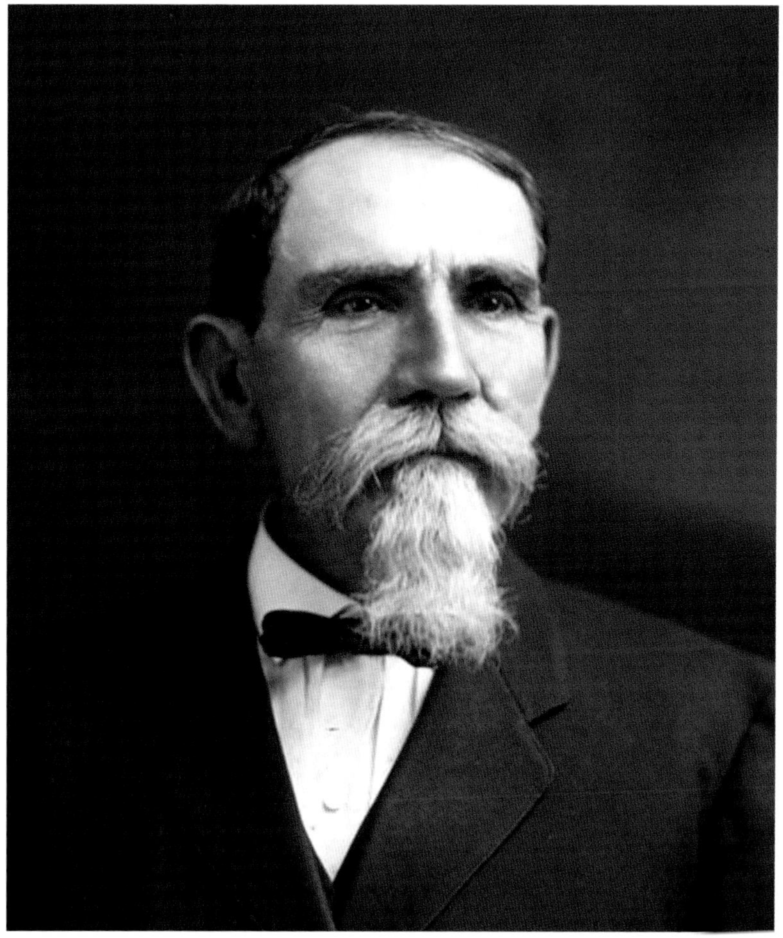

George Henry Hermann (1843–1914), c. 1890. This is the only known formal portrait of Hermann. Courtesy Houston Metropolitan Research Center, Houston Public Library (114-1461).

When the Hermanns arrived in Houston, they had three sons: George, Louis, and John. George accidentally shot and killed himself while hunting in 1840, and when a new son was born three years later, they named him after his brother who had died. George Henry grew up playing ball in the streets, running errands for his father, and riding the horses at Welch's Blacksmith Shop, his favorite pastime. He attended William Andrews' private school on Travis Street, where he was apparently an indifferent scholar and never finished high school.[13] His handwritten letters and diary show that his grammar and spelling were deficient.[14]

In the fall of 1861, at the age of eighteen, George joined the 26th Texas Cavalry (Bray's Regiment) and fought for the Confederacy in both Texas and Louisiana during the Civil War. He returned home in 1864 to find both his parents had died. He and his brothers asked T. M. Bagby and Henry F. Fisher to divide their parents' estate. Bagby and Fisher allotted the south half of block 146 to John and the north half of the block to Louis. George received lots in the adjoining block and a tract of 370 acres in the Joseph Gamble Survey, where he apparently operated a sawmill, one of his first ventures after returning from the war.[15] John (d. 1872) and Louis (d. 1869) never married; both died leaving their property to George, the sole heir of the Hermann properties. All five members of the Hermann family are buried in Glenwood Cemetery (except the first son, George).[16]

Immediately after the war, in addition to his lumber business (later called Brays Bayou Lumber Co.),[17] Hermann went to work for George Iams, a storekeeper for Francis R. Lubbock, governor of Texas from 1861 to 1863. But in 1870 he began driving cattle for McDonald's Beef Packery, riding the trail to Fort Worth and Abilene, Kansas, and, for the

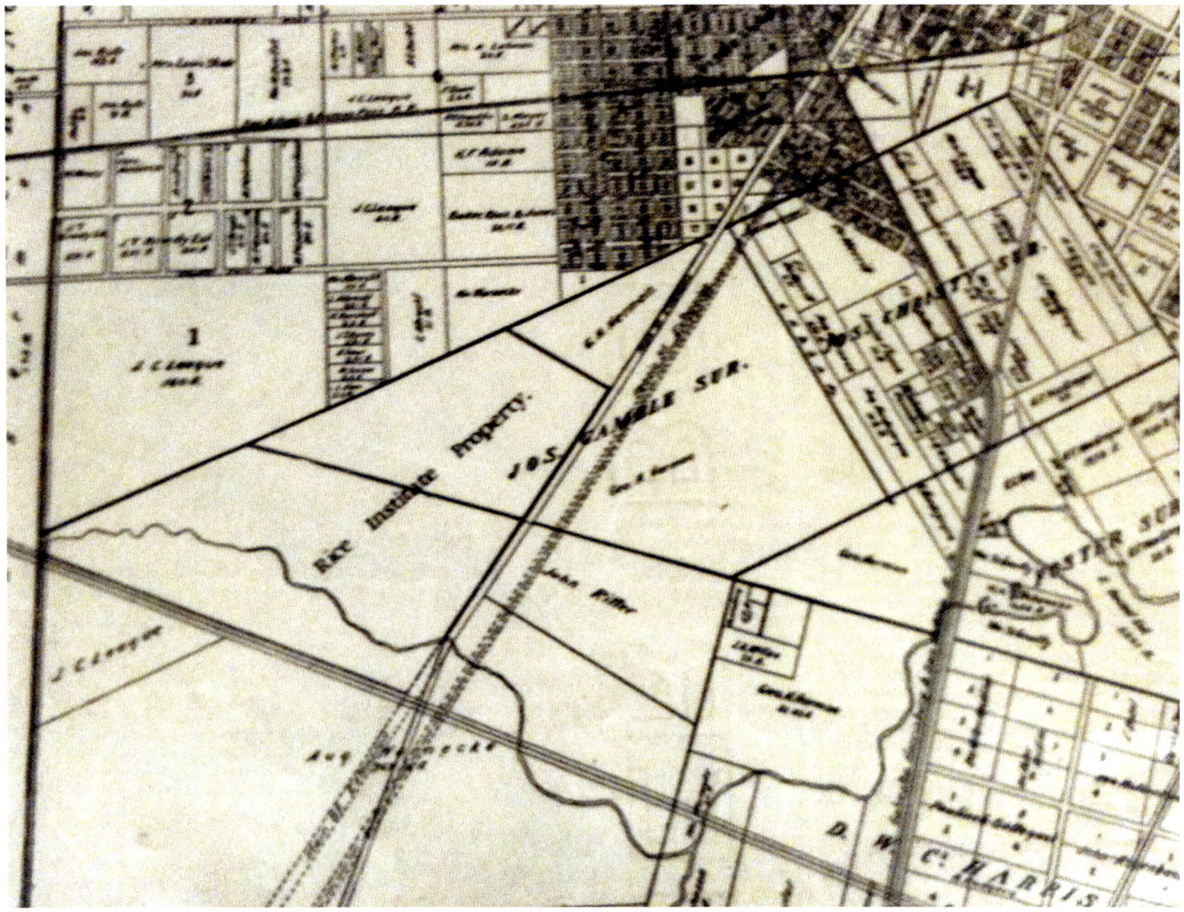

Houston Map, 1910, shows George Hermann's south end holdings that he donated to the City of Houston for Hermann Park in 1914. Source: *Map of the City of Houston and Vicinity,* Texas Map & Blueprint Co., 1910. Courtesy Houston Metropolitan Research Center, Houston Public Library.

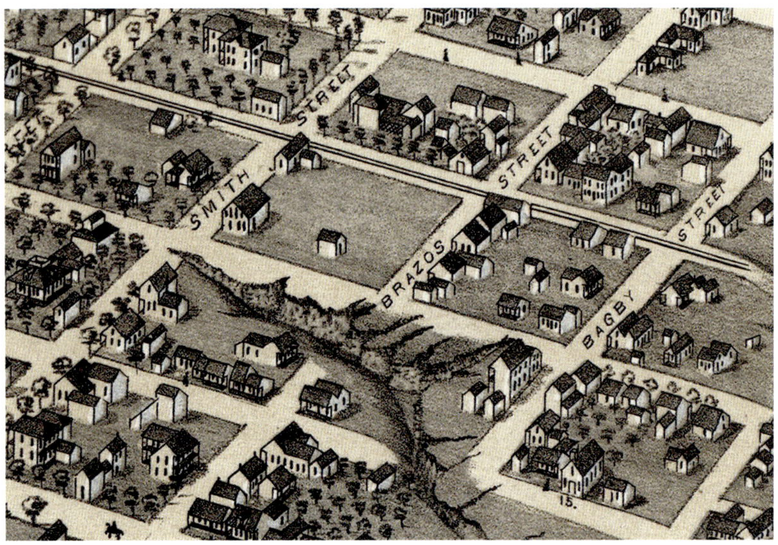

George Hermann's childhood home and neighborhood, 1873. The house, located on the southeast corner of Smith and McKinney, was a two-story frame building with outbuildings. This block (No. 146) was bequeathed by Hermann to the City of Houston and is now the site of Hermann Square in front of City Hall. Source: *Koch's Bird's Eye View of Houston,* 1873. Courtesy Houston Metropolitan Research Center, Houston Public Library.

rest of his life, he considered himself first and foremost a cattleman. Hermann returned to Houston in 1872 and formed a partnership with W. J. and Julius J. Settegast to buy and sell both cattle and real estate.[18] By 1885 he had saved enough money to travel to Europe, probably the only extravagance of his life. He hoped to meet his Swiss cousins and to see London and Paris. On this trip he kept a diary, which, in addition to recording his adventures, noted every penny he spent. From Houston he took the train to Washington, then New York. On Sunday, May 10, he visited Central Park, begrudging the twenty-five cents he spent to ride a hansom cab around the park. In his diary he wrote: "Central Park is wonderful. I wish my town of Houston had one like it. Perhaps they will some day."[19] After his grand tour of England, France, and Switzerland, Hermann returned in early 1886 and began buying property more aggressively in and around Houston.

Hermann's most astute investment came from what he considered an act of charity at the time. Hermann owned a team of horses and an "ambulance" buggy for which he had little use because he preferred riding his horse, Leo. A friend, Jim Hargraves, admired the team and buggy and expressed his desire to own such a rig; Hermann offered to sell him his. Hargraves did not have the cash but offered in exchange

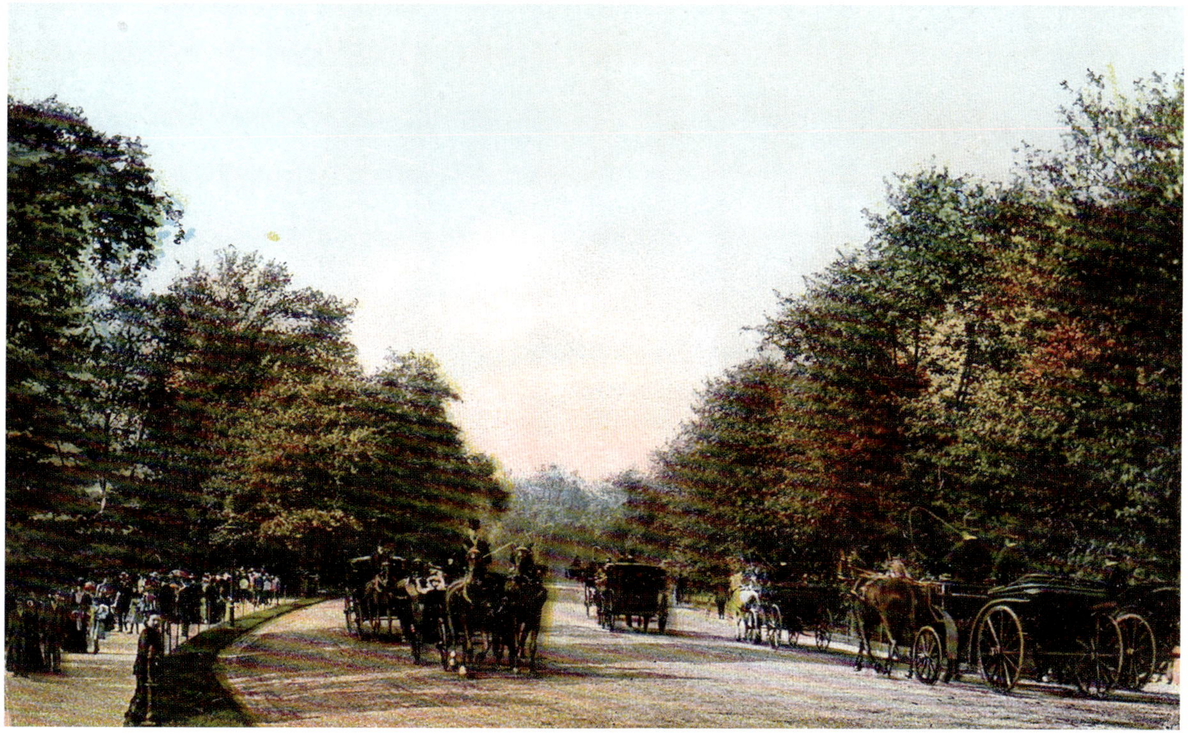

Central Park, New York City, c. 1890, as George Hermann would have seen it. Courtesy private collection.

land he owned in north Harris County, which neither of them thought was worth very much. Hermann accepted the deal and figured he paid about thirty-five cents an acre in the exchange. This land turned out to be in the middle of the extremely productive Humble oil field, where oil was discovered in 1904.[20] This investment made the already prosperous George Hermann a millionaire.

Hermann had lived with the family of T. J. Ewing since at least 1880, when Ewing lived on block 146 at 902 Smith at Walker, the address of the old Hermann house where George had been born.[21] At his death Hermann's property included large holdings on the west side of downtown: block 146 (which Hermann left to the City of Houston for Hermann Square in front of the present City Hall), most of block 149 (now the site of Houston City Hall), all of block 152 and adjoining property (now site of the Hobby Center, which Hermann left to the city as the site for Hermann Hospital), and various other lots in downtown Houston. By 1905 Hermann and the Ewing family had moved to a new house, possibly built and paid for by Hermann but owned by Ewing, at 117 San Felipe (now West Dallas, site of Allen Center). Hermann, it was rumored, lived in only one room of the house, giving the rest over to the Ewings for his board.[22] The bond between George Hermann and the Ewings extended beyond life. Hermann (d. 1914) and Thomas Jefferson Ewing (d. 1911) co-owned the plot in Glenwood Cemetery in which the Hermann family and several Ewings are buried. In his will George Hermann made generous provisions for the Ewing family, and T. J. Ewing, Jr. was one of his executors.[23]

By all accounts George Hermann was a humble but generous man. He chewed tobacco, wore the worn-out clothes of a cattleman most of the time, and lived a Spartan and frugal life. His attorney, J. W. Lockett, spoke of his frequent visits to the poor and sick and his constant concern for others. He was not a member of any church and never owned an automobile but rode his horse, Leo, everywhere he went. Hermann also bequeathed to George H. Getchell (possibly named after Hermann) his gold watch and a life estate in a town lot (where Getchell presumably lived), as well as income-producing property. Getchell was the son of Ellen (or Ella) Getchell, who is listed in Houston city directories as "colored." She lived on McKinney between Bagby and Brazos, property that Hermann owned; she was probably a longtime family employee.[24] Hermann's reserved personality, his modest personal habits, and his lack of education gave him a reputation as an eccentric. The *Houston Daily Post* published a description with which all other accounts of Hermann's personality and character agree:

> A plain citizen, he is a man without pomp or ostentation. Quiet. Reserved. Modest. Prompted by no motives or self-glorification, acting solely for the public weal, realizing through the absence in his own early life of those youthful pleasures which he hopes to bring to thousands of people in the years to come, George H. Hermann has done that which

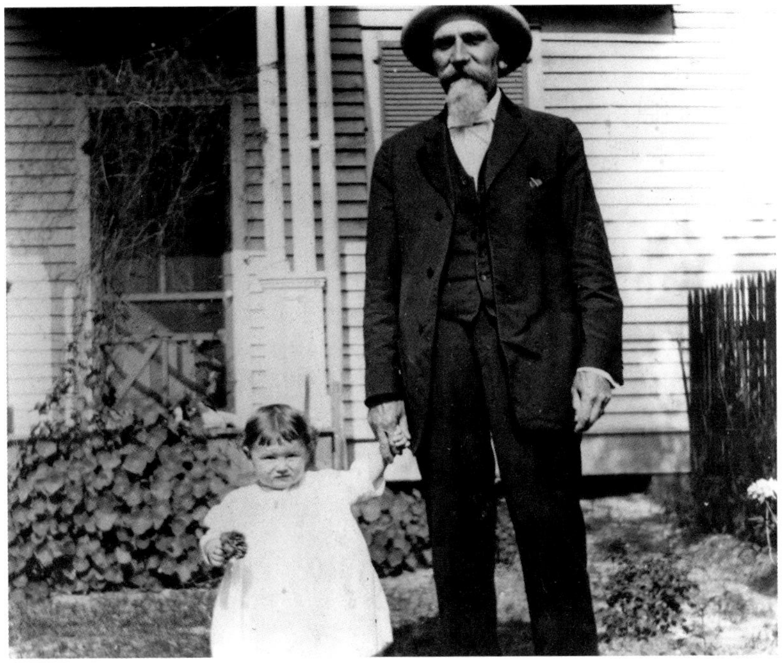

George Hermann, c. 1913, presumably with Melva Ewing (1912–1982), daughter of Thomas Jefferson Ewing, Jr., and May Melvina Price Ewing. Courtesy John P. McGovern Historical Collections and Research Center, Houston Academy of Medicine, Texas Medical Center Library.

> in the hearts of the people will place him in the foremost rank of public benefactors and make his name a household word.[25]

Hermann was in poor health during his latter years and, as a result, began to take great interest in hospitals. In 1891 he urged construction of a charity hospital and offered Harris County a choice of two different sites that he was willing to donate for the hospital. On February 18, 1898, he actually donated a plot east of downtown bound by Texas, Capitol, Hutchins, and Broadway (now Dowling). When the county had not built or even planned a hospital there, the land reverted to Hermann's ownership.[26] In his will Hermann specified another location for his hospital, block 152 and several surrounding blocks in the adjacent Hathaway Addition, a tract on the west of downtown along Buffalo Bayou. It is interesting to speculate that, if Hermann Hospital had been built in either of these locations, the Texas Medical Center might have ended up downtown, either sprawling out on the east side or along what is now Allen Parkway. Such an occurrence would have left Hermann Park intact, twice its present size.[27]

Hermann made several visits to John Kellog's Battle Creek Sanitarium in Michigan where the general goal was to restore a patient's health through a high-fiber, low-fat diet, fresh air, and exercise—an early twentieth-century spa of sorts.[28] He also went to Johns Hopkins Hospital in 1907 for "a major operation" and, in case he died, left a copy of his will with Beverly D. Harris, an officer at the South Texas Bank. After Hermann's return to Houston, Harris gave the will back to Hermann, who wrote a new will dated July 12, 1910, and again left it at South Texas Bank, where he did not regularly do business. After Hermann's death from pancreatic cancer in 1914, a frantic search for what was thought to be the 1907 will ended when Harris recognized one of Hermann's keys and found the 1910 will in a discarded set of old safety deposit boxes.[29] In this will Hermann left the 285-acre parcel for Hermann Park that he had already deeded to the City of Houston before his death. After a lengthy description of the property, Hermann's will states, "The said lands are to be used as a Public park and to be known and called 'The George Hermann Park'" (see appendix 3). It is significant that Hermann had decided in 1910 or earlier that a large, new public park would be established on his south end holdings.[30]

Aware that he was dying, Hermann arranged to donate property for Hermann Park to the city in early 1914. This was surely done at the urging of the mayor, park commissioners, and others who wanted an opportunity to salute Hermann and honor him for his life-long generosity. On May 30 in Mayor Ben Campbell's office at City Hall, only a few witnesses, including J. W. Lockett and J. W. Maxcy, were present when Hermann signed over the deed with the remarks: "This is the happiest day of my life," and "I thank God that I am able to do this." In the first paragraph of the deed, Hermann wrote that he was giving the park "in consideration of my desire to promote the general welfare of the City of Houston, and the health, comfort and happiness of the citizens thereof."[31] The 285 acres of the Hermann donation were bound by La Branch (had it extended through the park) on the west, what is now Hermann Drive on the north, Almeda Road on the east, and Bellaire (now Holcombe) Boulevard on the south.

Elaborate plans had already been made for a grand celebration to acknowledge Hermann's gift on Sunday, June 7, 1914, at the City Auditorium. Both the *Houston Post* and the *Houston Chronicle* ran several-page features about Hermann, the park donation, the speeches, and those attending the celebration. Over eight hundred people were present to hear master of ceremonies E. B. Parker and several others give speeches, including Thomas H. Stone's presentation "Go Thou and Do Likewise," Rice professor Stockton Axson on "Parks: Their Educational Value," and Leon Sonfield on "Parks and the People." The Rev. William States Jacobs, pastor of the First Presbyterian Church, made the presentation address, after which Mayor Campbell gave brief remarks accepting the parkland on behalf of the City of Houston. Finally Hermann himself gave a short speech (see appendix 2).[32] The three o'clock ceremony was preceded by a lengthy reception during which Hermann shook hundreds of hands. Hermann made the following comments to a *Houston Chronicle* reporter.

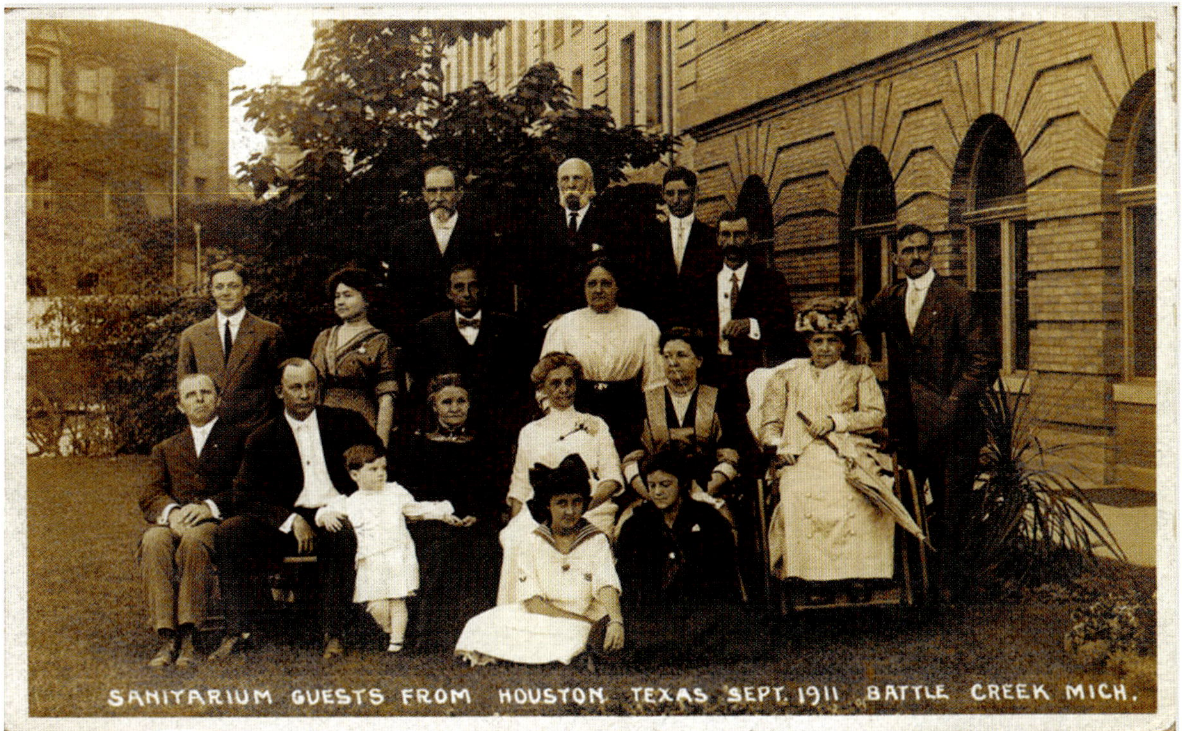

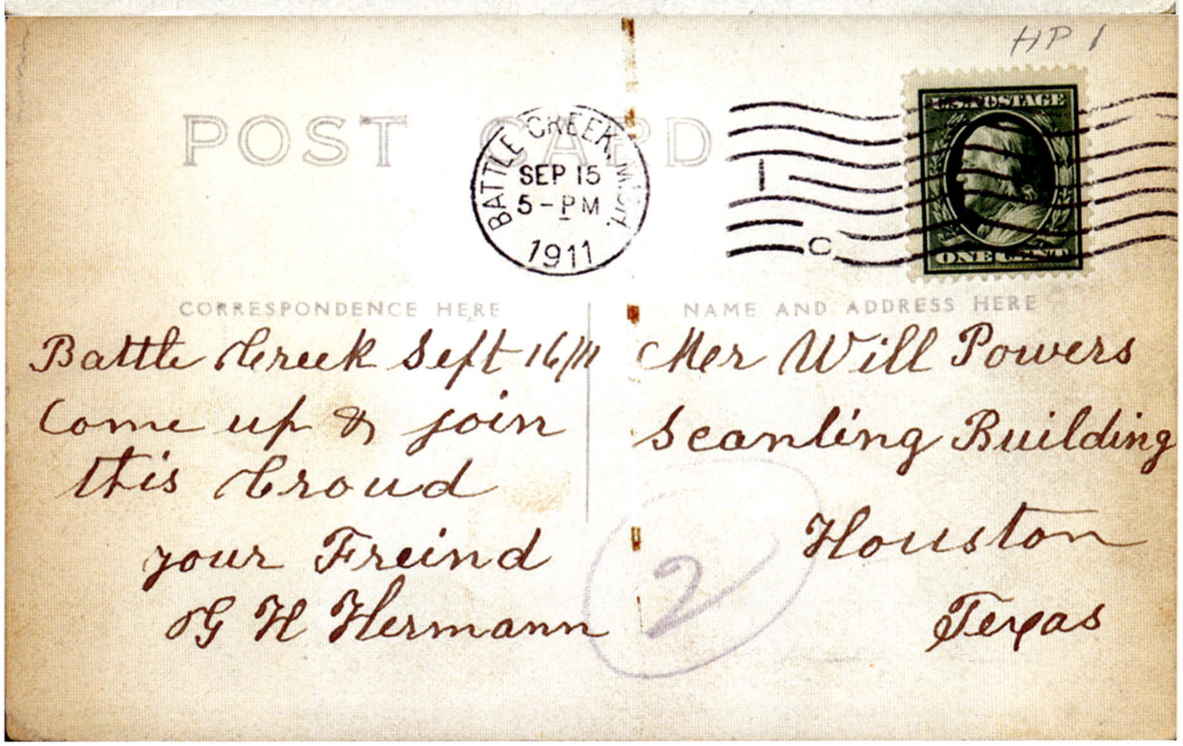

Battle Creek Sept 16/11
Come up & join
this croud
your Freind
G H Hermann

Mr Will Powers
Scanling Building
Houston
Texas

George Hermann with a group of Houstonians at Battle Creek Sanitarium, September 1911. Courtesy John P. McGovern Historical Collections and Research Center, Houston Academy of Medicine, Texas Medical Center Library.

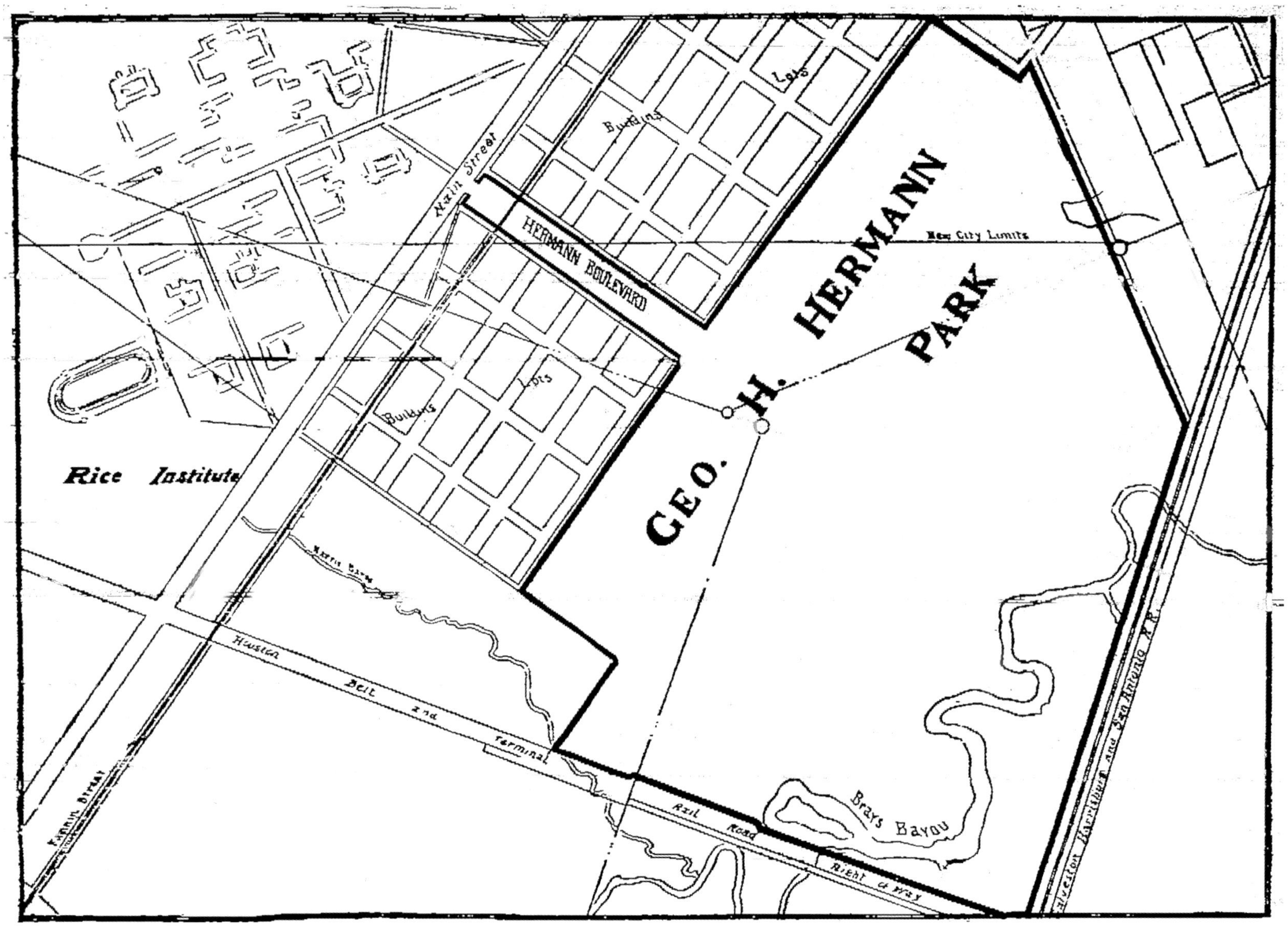

Initial plan for Hermann Park drawn by Houston city engineer J. W. Maxcy in consultation with George Hermann, June 1914. Courtesy Houston Metropolitan Research Center, Houston Public Library.

> I believe it is the duty of all property owners to have some thought of the general welfare and happiness of the people in their community. Although a man may acquire a legal right to a big tract of land, the general public has a right to some consideration. There are too many property owners who look upon their holding from too selfish a viewpoint. If it is necessary for park purposes to condemn certain property for the public good, the land owner should not complain, because the rights of the general public are in reality greater than those of the individual.[33]

These views alone would have made Hermann an excellent park commissioner.

The Comey Report

In February 1912 Mayor Rice's three-man Board of Park Commissioners, Hermann, Wilson, and Parker, retained at their own expense Arthur Coleman Comey (1886–1954), a young landscape architect from Cambridge, Massachusetts, to prepare a park master plan for Houston. Comey had graduated cum laude from Harvard at the age of twenty-one in 1907 with a degree in landscape architecture. One of his professors, Frederick Law Olmsted, Jr., helped Comey obtain his first two positions: as a park planner in Dixon, Illinois, and as Superintendent of Parks in Utica, New York. In 1911 Comey returned to Cambridge and began a practice as a "consultant on city planning." That same year he received

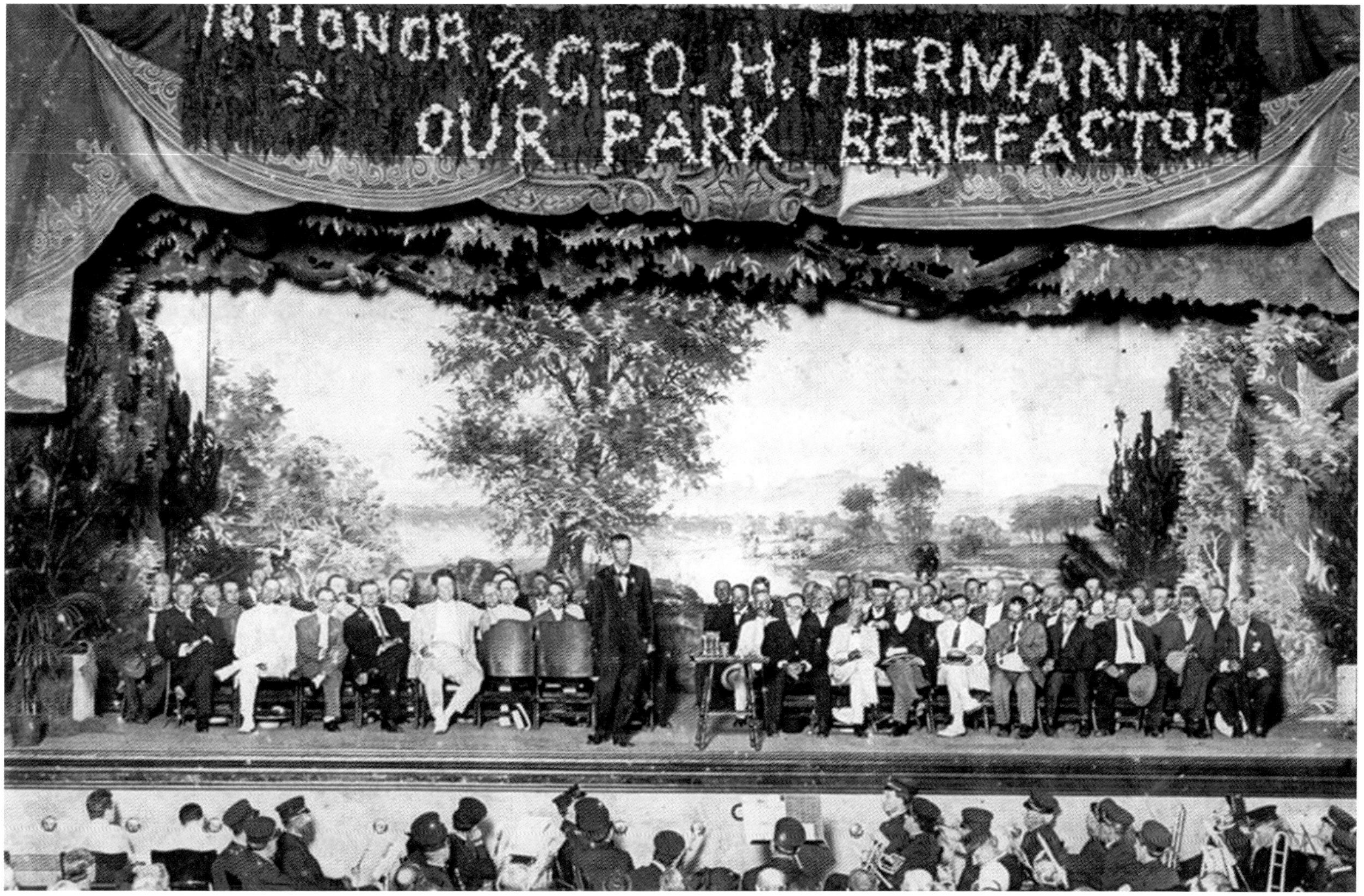

Hermann Park's donation celebration honoring George Hermann, June 7, 1914, in the City Auditorium (current site of Jones Hall). Hermann is seated on the first row just to the right of the speaker. Courtesy John P. McGovern Historical Collections and Research Center, Houston Academy of Medicine, Texas Medical Center Library.

notice for an article he wrote proposing maximum building height and bulk regulations.[34] His Houston commission was his first.[35] It is not clear how he came to the notice of the Houston Park Commissioners or why they took their chances with such an inexperienced planner.

Comey visited Houston in the spring of 1912 and began to gather data about population, park acreage, neighborhoods, commercial and industrial activity, and growth potential. During this visit he took several dozen photographs, including one of the pine stand near Brays Bayou on Hermann's land.[36] In July 1912 during the investigative phase of Comey's work, a $250,000 park bond was approved by Houstonians to acquire and improve parkland. On March 1, 1913, Comey delivered his report, which was published as *Houston, Tentative Plans for Its Development: Report to the Houston Park Commission*.[37] Comey began his introduction: "The twentieth century is an age of cities." He continues with what might be an apology for the City Beautiful Movement, recounting what is wrong with American cities and some general prescriptions for improvement. Of the relatively young city, he concludes: "Houston's problems can now be dealt with before the serious mistakes are made which have hampered so many American cities." Two paragraphs later he continues: "But Houston is far behind other progressive cities in certain respects, notably in its park system, and should act at once to remedy these conditions."[38] Comey was emphatic that the backbone of a park system in Houston should be the banks of its bayous. "The bayous are natural parks already."[39]

Comey's study, the first city planning document in Houston's history, laid the groundwork for specific plans that followed it, especially the establishment of Hermann Park. In his report Comey stressed the need for a large park in Houston that he called Pines Park as part of his

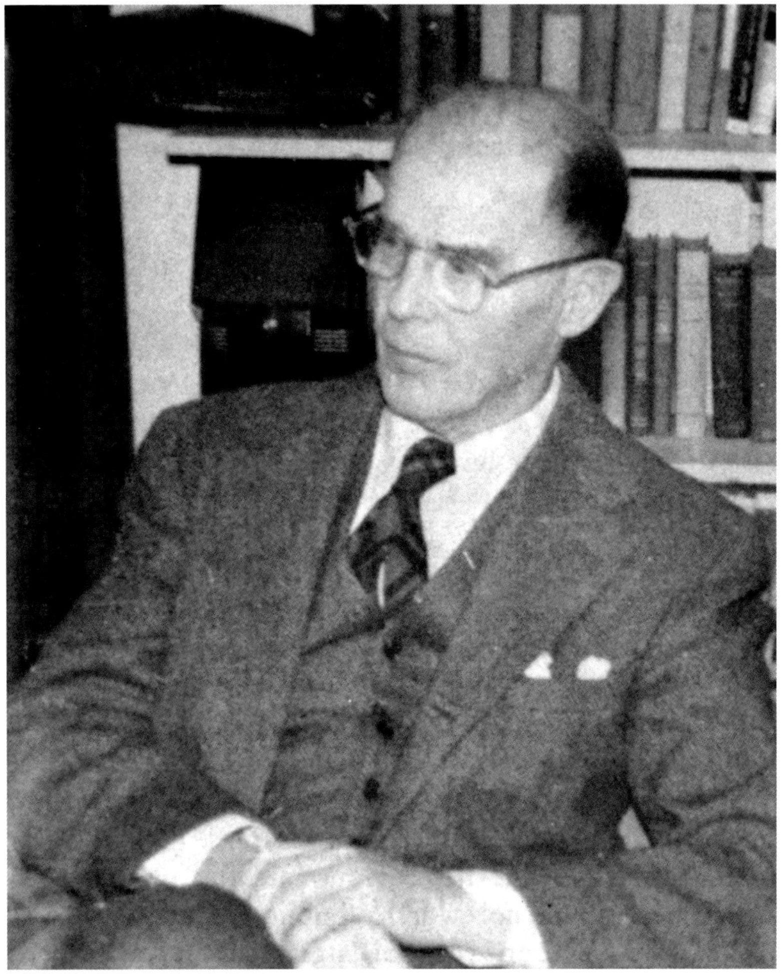

Arthur Coleman Comey (1886–1954), a young landscape planner from Cambridge, Massachusetts, produced Houston's first planning report in 1913 that recommended the placement of a major park in the South End. Source: *Landscape Architecture*, 1954, 44:3.

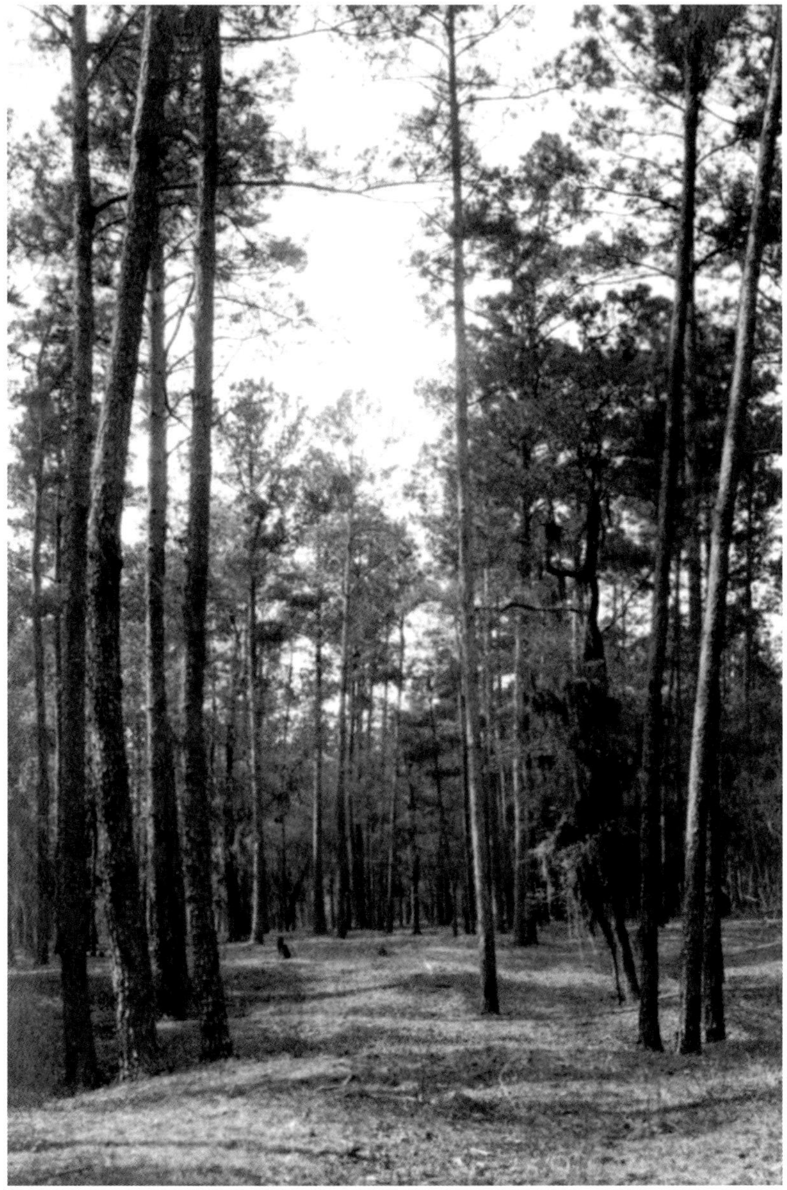

Pine Stand near Brays Bayou, 1913, located on Hermann's property that became part of Hermann Park. Photograph by Arthur C. Comey, courtesy Frances Loeb Library Special Collections, Harvard University.

proposed inner park system. "The most desirable location for such a park at present appears to be south of the city and east of Main Street where there is a fine stand of pine woods extending to Bray's Bayou. The open land on the south-western side of this woods may . . . later be of use for athletic fields, etc."[40] This is a precise description of George Hermann's property, which Comey shows as a large public park on his mapped proposal. Comey would have been aware that Hermann had planned (at least since his 1910 will) to give this land to the city, but Comey respectfully refrained from calling it Hermann Park before any official announcement had been made.

Comey's recommendation for the establishment of Pines Park was made as part of his proposal for a system of inner and outer park corridors along the bayous, new parkway drives, tree-shaded boulevards, the expansion of existing parks and school grounds, establishment of small neighborhood parks, and a civic center downtown. The report also dealt with street and railroad configurations, building height regulations, and other engineering matters that Comey considered essential to the development of Houston into a first-rate city. Of interest is Comey's plan for a recreation center proposal that could be built in Hermann Park. It shows an outdoor gymnasium for women and girls and a much larger one for men and boys flanking a field house with separate indoor swimming pools and locker rooms for men and women. Courts for basketball and tennis, fields for baseball, football, and volleyball, a running track, a children's playground with a wading pool, and a concert terrace are

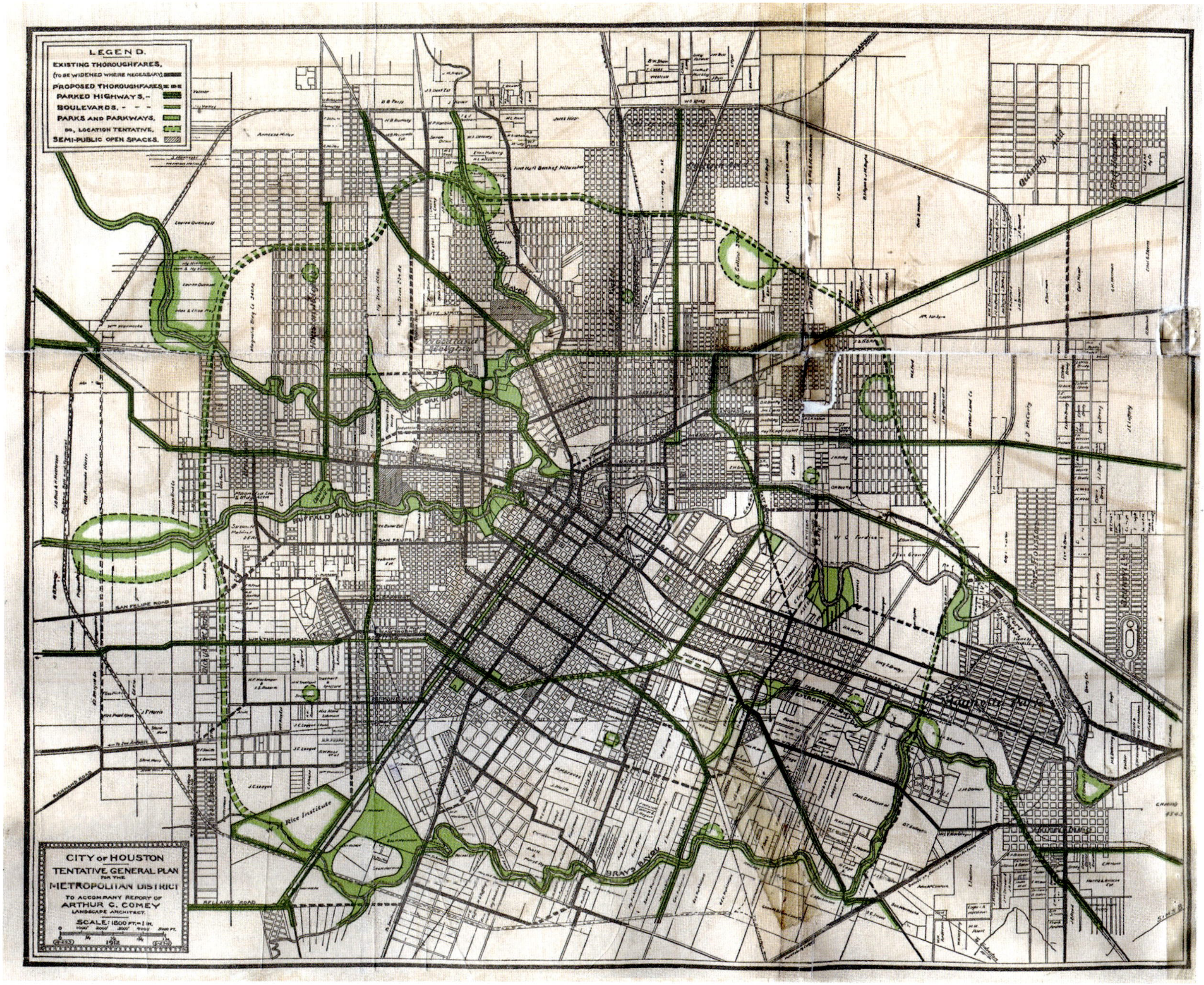

Map of Houston on which Comey delineated his proposal for a citywide park system proposed (green) including the acreage (lower left) that became Hermann Park. Source: Arthur C. Comey, *Houston: Tentative General Plan for its Development*, 1913.

all surrounded by rows of trees. Other proposals include references to, photographs of, and ordinances from other cities as examples Houston might follow. Tables, diagrams, and plans are scattered throughout the eighty-three-page report providing statistics as well as projections concerning the growth of Houston, which Comey underestimated. He predicted that the population in 1960 would be 717,751; it was 938,219. Although no attempt was made to adopt the Comey Report as policy, it was a seminal document that influenced planning efforts through the early 1940s.

The Maxcy Plan

John W. Maxcy, a civil engineer who held the post of Houston City Engineer and had laid out Sam Houston Park in 1899, created the initial plan for development of the 285 acres of Hermann Park, working

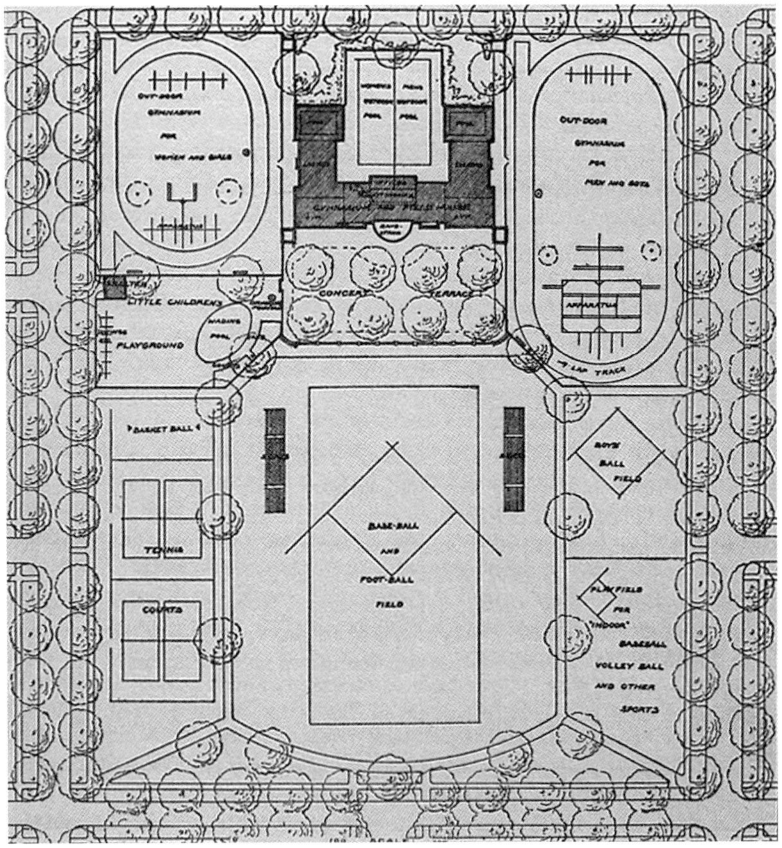

"Houston, Tentative Plan for a Recreation Center" shows Comey's idea for an athletic area in Hermann Park. George Hermann believed that exercise facilities should be part of a public park. Source: Arthur C. Comey, *Houston: Tentative Plans for Its Development*, 1913.

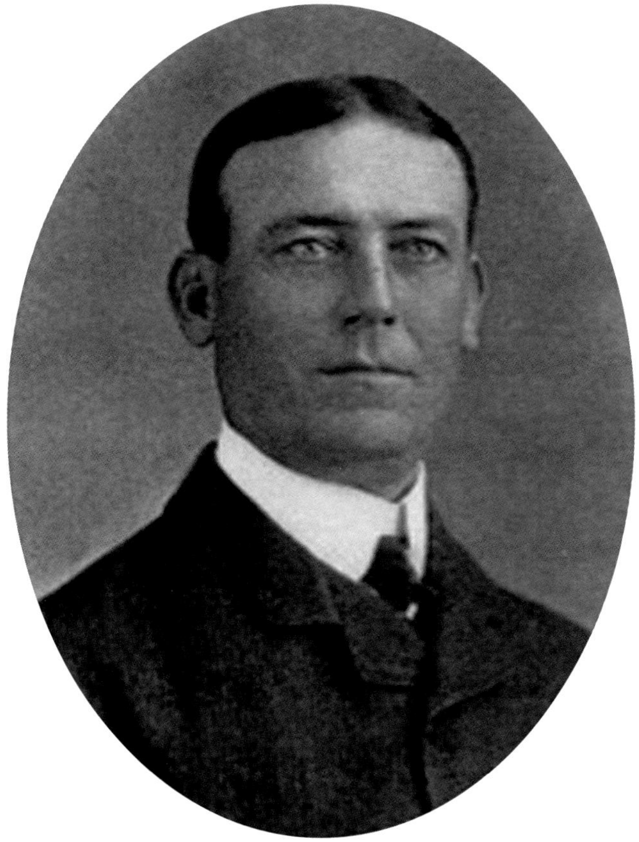

John Wharton Maxcy (c. 1865–c. 1945) was the civil engineer who worked with Hermann on initial plans for Hermann Park. Source: *Standard Blue Book of Houston*, 1908. Courtesy Houston Metropolitan Research Center, Houston Public Library.

closely with George Hermann. A *Houston Daily Post* report on the plan for the new park noted, "As if to emphasize the fact that Mr. Hermann had long since decided upon the magnificent endowment it became known that he has definite views for the beautification and utilization of the park and the ideas he has formulated will be the basis upon which it will be developed."[41] The article continues to describe in detail the elements of the park that Hermann envisioned. "The predominant theme will be playgrounds, plenty of room for everybody and cool and shady places for rest and recreation. Amusements for young and old will not be overlooked and they will be of great variety. It is the desire of Mr. Hermann to make it a thing of beauty as well as useful to the public." The account continues:

> There will be baseball and football fields, tennis grounds, golf links, croquet grounds, bowling greens and an athletic field. Open-air swimming pools will be constructed containing shower baths, dressing rooms and modern conveniences of all sorts. There will be a wading pool and general playgrounds for children of all sizes. Many other outdoor games will be provided for. Among the most beautiful features of the park are the large number of beautiful shade trees and the sinuous Brays bayou, which winds through the heart of the property. This will be widened and worked into a beautiful waterway and will be utilized for the purpose of drainage, fishing and for canoeing and other aquatic sports. . . . All of these plans are now being elaborated by John W. Maxcy, to whom Mr. Hermann has outlined the general plan of development.[42]

The Maxcy plan showed the major entrance to the park from Main Street that would extend to La Branch via a wide "Hermann Boulevard" directly across from Entrance Two of the Rice Institute. Hermann owned the five blocks between the initial Hermann Park boundary and Main Street, and it is a mystery why he did not include this parcel in the land gift for the park. On the first published drawing of the park, this area is laid out in blocks for residential development, so perhaps Hermann was planning to develop them himself. Fortunately the City of Houston was able to purchase this contiguous piece from the Hermann Estate in 1915. In Maxcy's plan Brays Bayou was to be

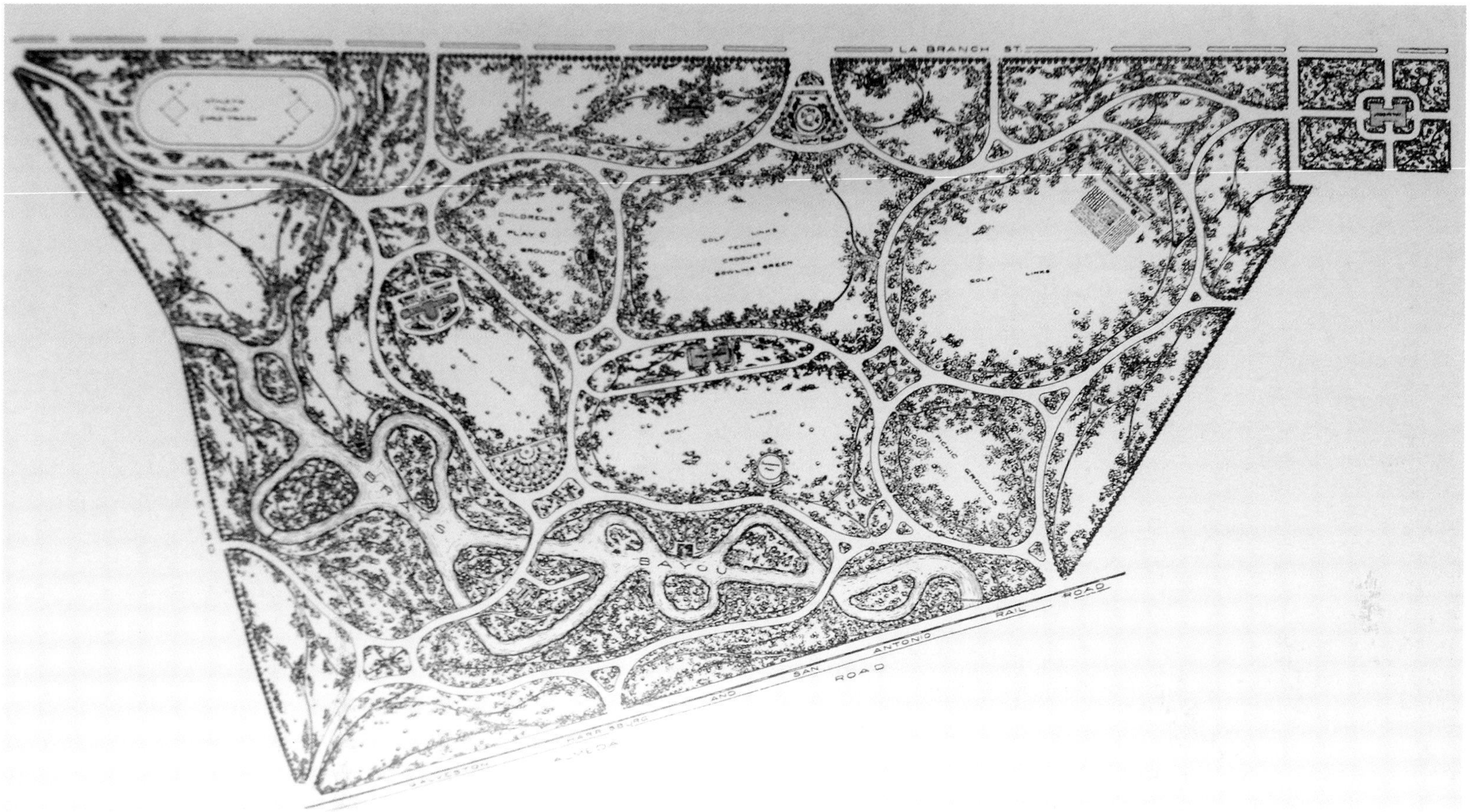

Maxcy Plan for Hermann Park, 1914, included a picnic area, golf course, tennis courts, a croquet lawn, and bowling green as well as athletic fields, a conservatory, gardens, and a children's playground. Brays Bayou is rechanneled to create small islands. George Hermann worked with Maxcy on this plan, and it demonstrates Hermann's concern that athletic areas be part of the park. When the southwest section was sold for the Texas Medical Center, the fields and gyms that might have been included became impossible. Source: *Illustrated City Book of Houston*, 1915. Courtesy Houston Metropolitan Research Center, Houston Public Library.

rechanneled into a more winding waterway with a series of wooded islands. Drives were laid out in a curvilinear pattern that encircled a children's playground, picnic grounds, and an eighteen-hole golf course that would cover most of the park's central area west of the bayou. A large oval athletic field with two baseball diamonds at either end occupied the far corner of the park at the intersection of Bellaire Boulevard and La Branch. Maxcy included just three or four small gardens in his plan, making athletic pursuits the primary focus of the park.[43] Before the Maxcy plan was published several influential Houstonians were already looking for a nationally known landscape architect and planner.

Shortly after the Hermann Park donation celebration on June 7, Hermann left for Johns Hopkins Hospital in Baltimore. On July 24, 1914, he wrote his friend Will Powers from St. Agnes Hospital in Baltimore[44] complaining about his stomach ailments. On September 12 he wrote Powers again, this time from the Battle Creek Sanitarium in Michigan, noting that he had been there over a month after being treated at Johns Hopkins Hospital for five weeks. In this letter he said that, if he didn't get better in a week or two, he would go back to Baltimore, which he did, dying there a little over a month later on Wednesday, October 21, 1914.[45]

Hermann's body, in a plain oak casket, returned to Houston by train, arriving Saturday, October 24 and met by a delegation headed by the mayor.[46] For two days Hermann's body lay in state at the house he had shared with the Ewings, where a private service was held at noon on October 27 before the huge public funeral at the City Auditorium.[47] By proclamation of the mayor and city council, all schools and businesses were closed the afternoon of the funeral, and flags throughout the city flew at half-staff. All seats in the auditorium were filled for the funeral, including 266 honorary pallbearers who were named in the *Houston Chronicle*.[48] The Rev. William States Jacobs conducted the funeral service, throughout which the City Hall bell tolled, and, afterwards, a

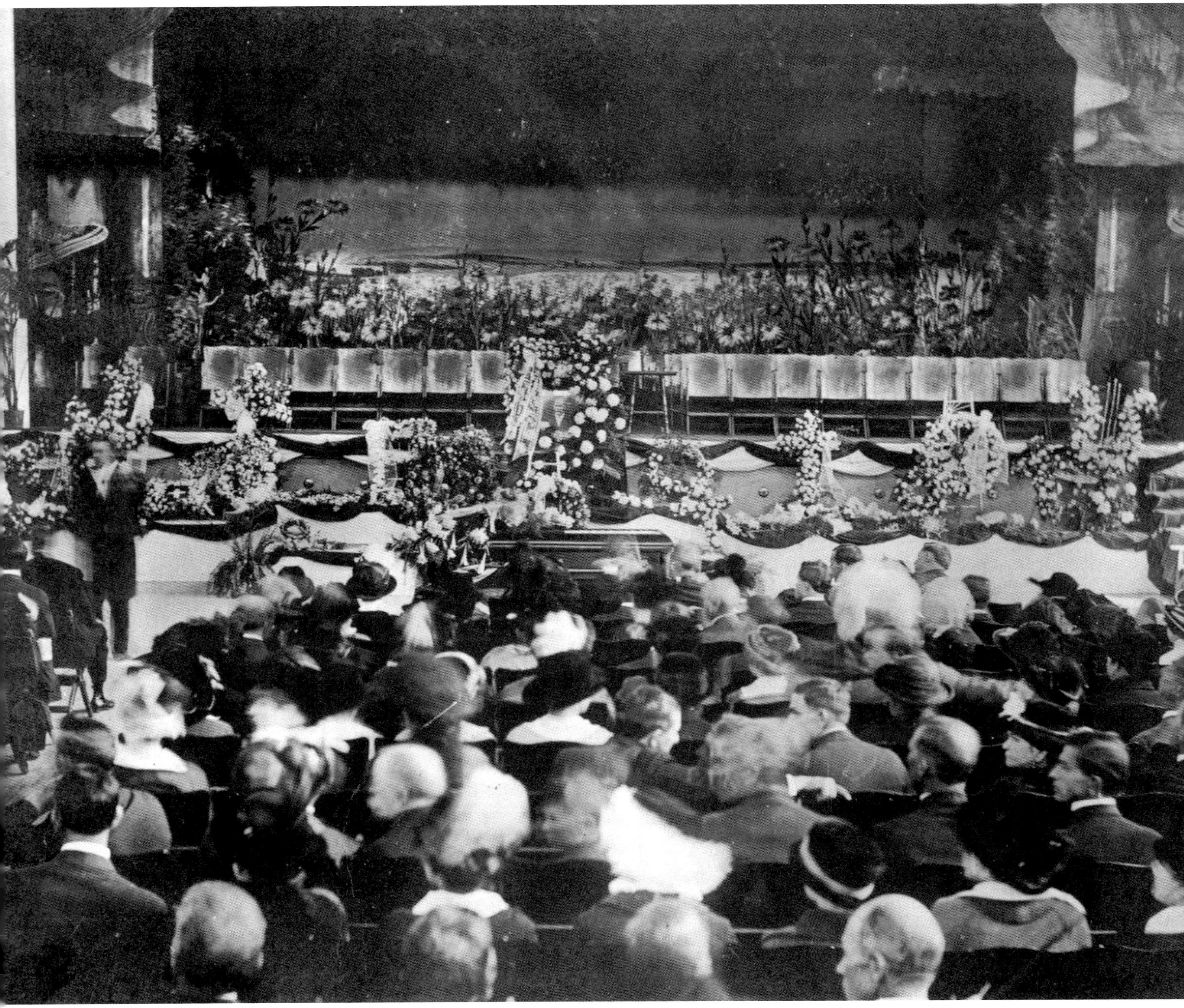

George Hermann's public funeral, October 27, 1914, at the City Auditorium was held after a private service at the T. J. Ewing House where Hermann lived. A portrait of Hermann was placed over the casket, surrounded by floral tributes. On stage empty chairs awaited the many dignitaries that spoke of Hermann's life and generosity. Schools and offices were closed the afternoon of the funeral. Courtesy John P. McGovern Historical Collections and Research Center, Houston Academy of Medicine, Texas Medical Center Library.

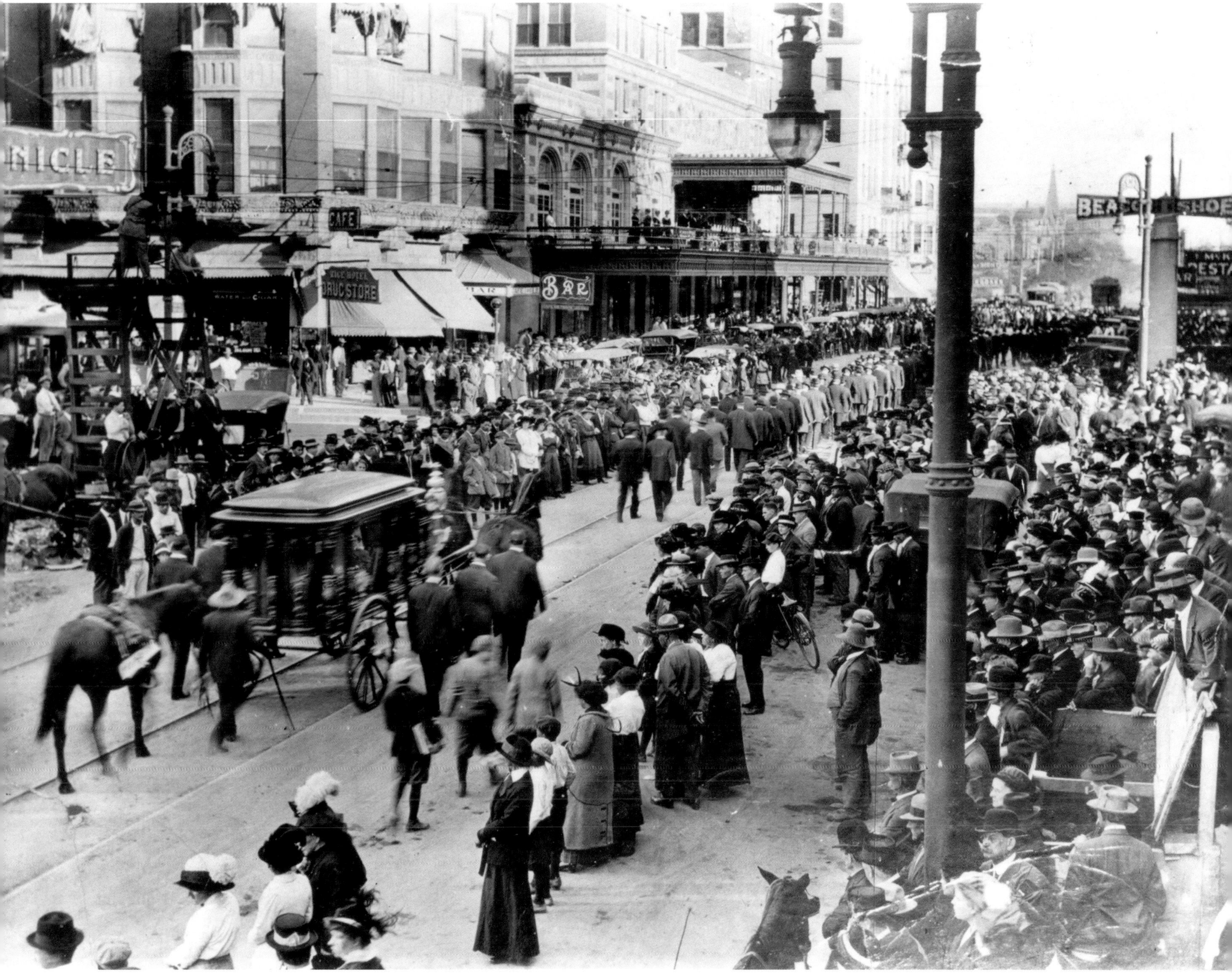

George Hermann's long, parade-like funeral procession, seen here passing the Rice Hotel, moved east on Texas Avenue from the City Auditorium to Washington Avenue, where streetcars waited to take mourners to Glenwood Cemetery. Dugan, Hermann's manservant, led Hermann's riderless horse, Leo, behind the horse-drawn hearse. Courtesy Houston Metropolitan Research Center, Houston Public Library (114–2196).

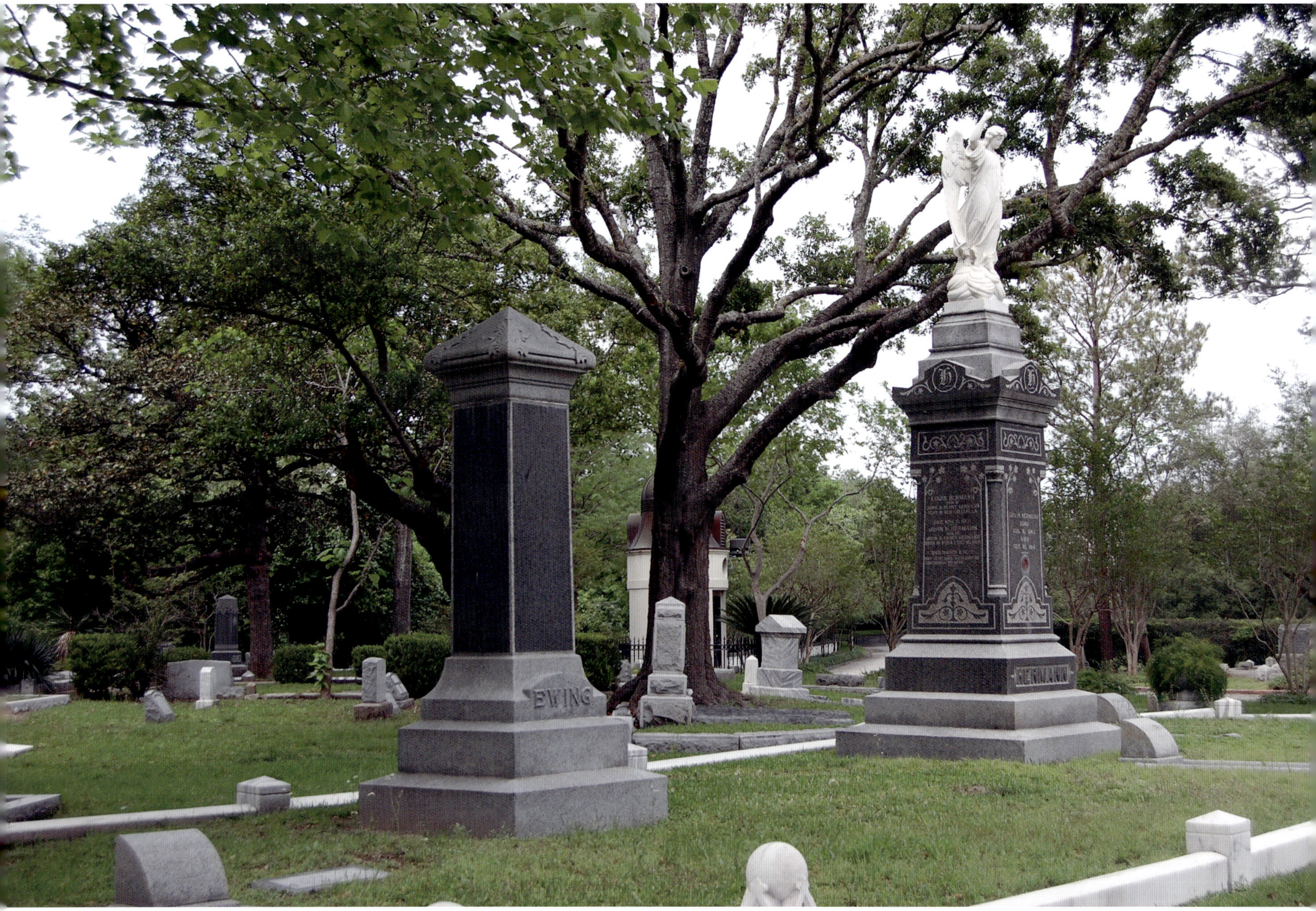

Hermann–Ewing Plot, Glenwood Cemetery, 2012. George Hermann was buried with his parents, Fannie and John Hermann, and two brothers, John M. and Louis Hermann. T. J. Ewing co-owned Lot 103 in Section C with George Hermann. Hermann's tall, gray granite monument crowned by an angel is inscribed "Geo H. Hermann Born Aug 6, 1843 Died Oct 21,1914." It contains a "Citizen of the Republic of Texas" medallion, 2007. The Ewing monument is in the foreground. Photograph by B. S. Bradley.

twenty-one-gun salute fired as the funeral procession to Glenwood Cemetery was formed. Hermann's casket, draped with a Confederate Flag and white roses, was placed in a horse-drawn hearse. Published reports made the funeral cortege sound like a parade. Mounted police, fifty uniformed firemen, contingents from organizations of which Hermann had been a member, and a military band led the mile-long procession. Hermann's horse, Leo, was led riderless by Hermann's manservant, Dugan, following behind the hearse. Hundreds more walked up Texas to Main, turned on Franklin, and continued to Washington Avenue, where a dozen streetcars stood ready to transport those who chose not to walk the rest of the way to Glenwood. Hermann was buried next to his parents and brothers.[49]

CHAPTER THREE

The Kessler Plan

1915–1923

Kessler demonstrated a pronounced facility for reconciling the requirements of ceremoniousness and informality in his design.[1]

—Stephen Fox, 1983

Before George Hermann died, and even before he publicly donated the site for Hermann Park, Houston oilman J. S. Cullinan was lobbying for a particular landscape architect to plan the park. In April 1914, on a train trip from Kansas City to Dallas, Cullinan met and was impressed with the renowned St. Louis landscape architect George Edward Kessler. At that time they discussed the need for planning in Houston. Cullinan then orchestrated a carefully thought out plan to convince Mayor Campbell and the park commissioners to retain Kessler. On May 23, 1914, Cullinan wrote to Kessler noting that he had been in discussions with "some of our people, including Mayor Campbell" concerning the need for local city planning. In that letter he more or less dismissed the 1913 Comey Plan by saying "a report was made by some engineer [Comey] to the previous administration," but, Cullinan stressed, no commitments had yet been made by Campbell to hire anyone to work on the new park.[2] Cullinan cleverly copied some very powerful Houstonians on this letter and subsequent correspondence with both Kessler and Campbell, creating allies in his efforts to have Kessler hired by the City of Houston.[3] The fact that Kessler was working in the rival cities of Fort Worth and Dallas also probably helped tip the scale in his favor. By January 1915 the Board of Park Commissioners had made arrangements with Kessler to come to Houston.[4] Cullinan had succeeded in convincing the mayor and Board of Park Commissioners (Parker, Wilson, and Sterling Meyer, who replaced Hermann) to retain "the exceptionally well qualified" Kessler. Cullinan's willingness to personally pay some of Kessler's initial expenses did not hurt either.[5] Although it would have been easier and a more obvious choice to have John Maxcy prepare a new plan including all of the park area or recall Arthur Comey, Maxcy and Comey were not considered after Cullinan began his campaign for Kessler. Although he had been in Houston only ten years, Cullinan's wealth and power, and the respect he garnered locally were considerable, and Kessler ultimately was hired.

Cullinan and Shadyside

Joseph Stephen Cullinan (1860–1937), one of eight children, was born in Pennsylvania to Irish immigrant parents. He began working in oilfields there at the age of fourteen, and, from 1882 to 1895, he worked for Standard Oil, which he left to form his own business, Petroleum Ironworks. After oil was discovered in Corsicana, Texas, in 1894, Cullinan served as a consultant to those involved in the Corsicana fields and eventually moved his family to Corsicana. There he constructed the first refinery west of the Mississippi River in 1899. He moved his operations to Beaumont in 1901 after the Spindletop discovery and founded the Texas Company (Texaco) there in 1902. After he moved the Texas Company to Houston in 1905, several other companies followed over the next decade, and by 1913 twelve oil companies were headquartered in Houston; Humble Oil Company (Exxon) followed in 1917.[6] Cullinan's impact on his adopted city was profound not only because his decision to move his company to Houston helped establish it as the oil capital, but he also became a key supporter of the development of the Houston Ship Channel and was president of the Chamber of Commerce from 1913 to 1919, the period during which many planning decisions concerning the future of Houston were made, including the development of Hermann Park.[7] Cullinan is remembered in Houston for his many accomplishments, but his daughter Nina recalled his great patriotism.

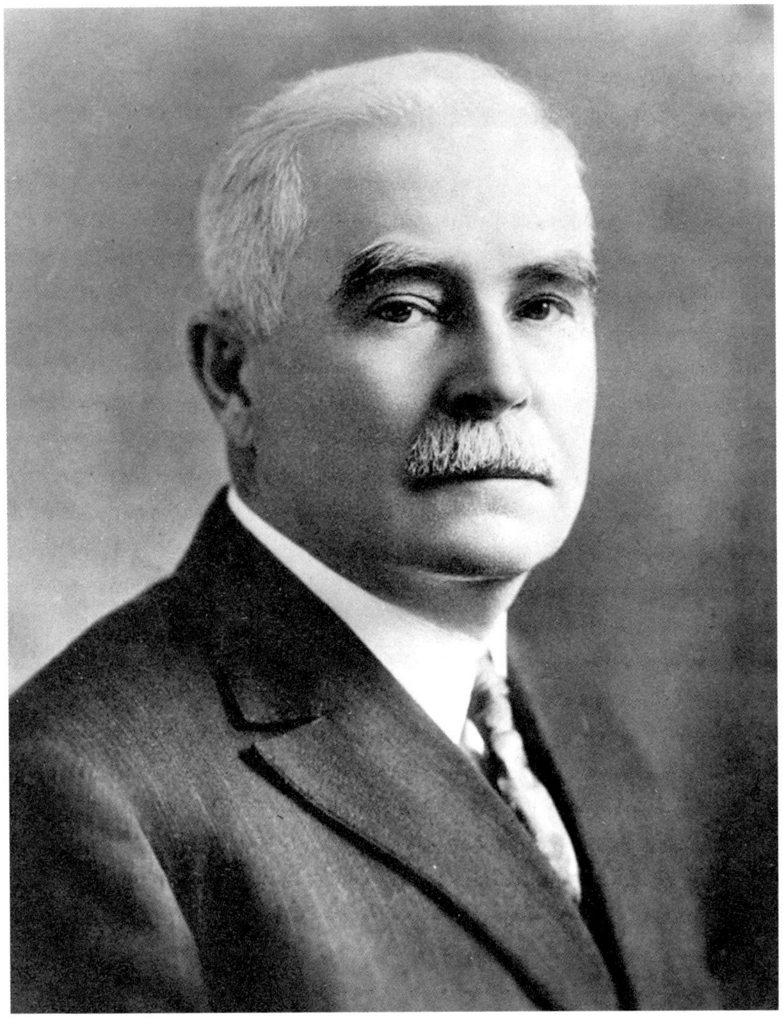

Joseph Stephen Cullinan (1860–1937), founder of the Texas Company (Texaco), was an early advocate for Hermann Park and contributed considerable personal resources to its development. He was instrumental in the commissioning of George Kessler to design Hermann Park and probably paid Kessler's initial fees and expenses. Courtesy Houston Metropolitan Research Center, Houston Public Library (69-1).

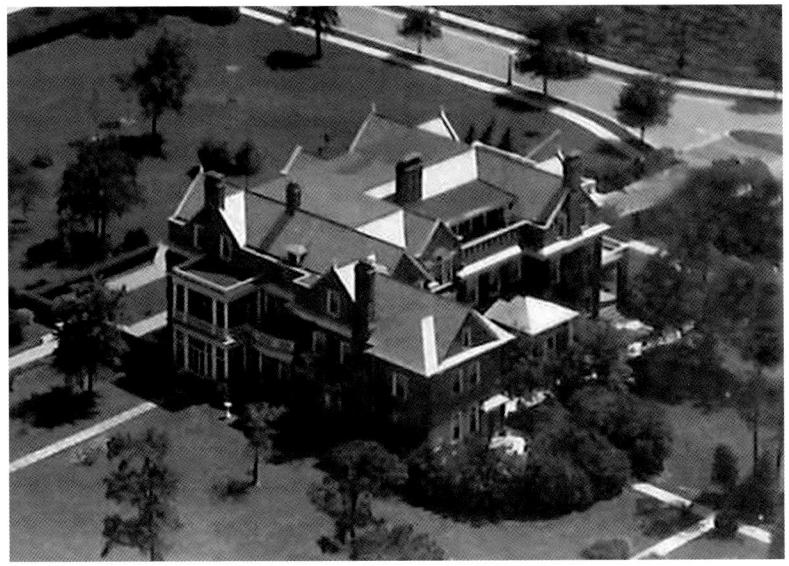

The Lucie Halm and J. S. Cullinan House, 2 Remington Lane, Shadyside, was completed in 1919 to the plans of the established St. Louis architect James P. Jamison (1867–1941). Frank Heidelberg was the builder. The Cullinan House was bought by Oveta and William P. Hobby and demolished by Mrs. Hobby in 1973. Courtesy State Historical Society of Missouri, Research Center-Kansas City.

He frequently handed out copies of the Bill of Rights and the US Constitution to people on the street.[8]

Before two other influential citizens, William Clifford Hogg (1875–1930) and his brother Michael Hogg (1885–1941), began to develop property along Buffalo Bayou into Houston's most elite residential community, River Oaks,[9] Cullinan purchased a 38-acre tract just north of the Rice Institute and west of George Hermann's park tract. Cullinan learned that Hermann, in addition to the land he was planning to donate for Hermann Park, owned a triangular piece of property on the west side of Main Street, which Hermann was holding to ensure it was developed to enhance the civic potential of the area around the park and university. Hermann died before any transaction with Cullinan was completed, but in February 1916 Cullinan purchased the property from the Hermann Estate.[10] He named his subdivision Shadyside and retained George Kessler to create twenty-four large lots along two boulevards, Longfellow Lane and Remington Lane. Cullinan offered these lots to his friends and business associates, who bought them and built large country houses in a range of eclectic architectural styles. Cullinan's own house, the first constructed in Shadyside (1916–1919, demolished 1973), was designed by the St. Louis architect James P. Jamieson as an English country house.[11]

The Rice Institute

Hermann need not have been concerned about the quality of the neighborhood near his proposed park. With the Rice Institute, Hermann Park, and then Shadyside, the South End civic arena developed into a remarkable area, which it remains today. The Rice campus was the first component of this South End precinct to begin improvements. Cram Goodhue & Ferguson's general plan for Rice's 295 acres, across Main Street from the Hermann Park site, was adopted in 1910. Construction began in 1910, and classes began in 1912. Edgar Odell Lovett (1871–1957), Rice's first president, gave an opening address called "The Meaning of the New Institution," which was published in 1915.[12] In a footnote Lovett writes, "With engaging frankness Mr. Hermann told me that he had been influenced in making this disposition of his property [Hermann Park and a site for a charity hospital] by the example of Wil-

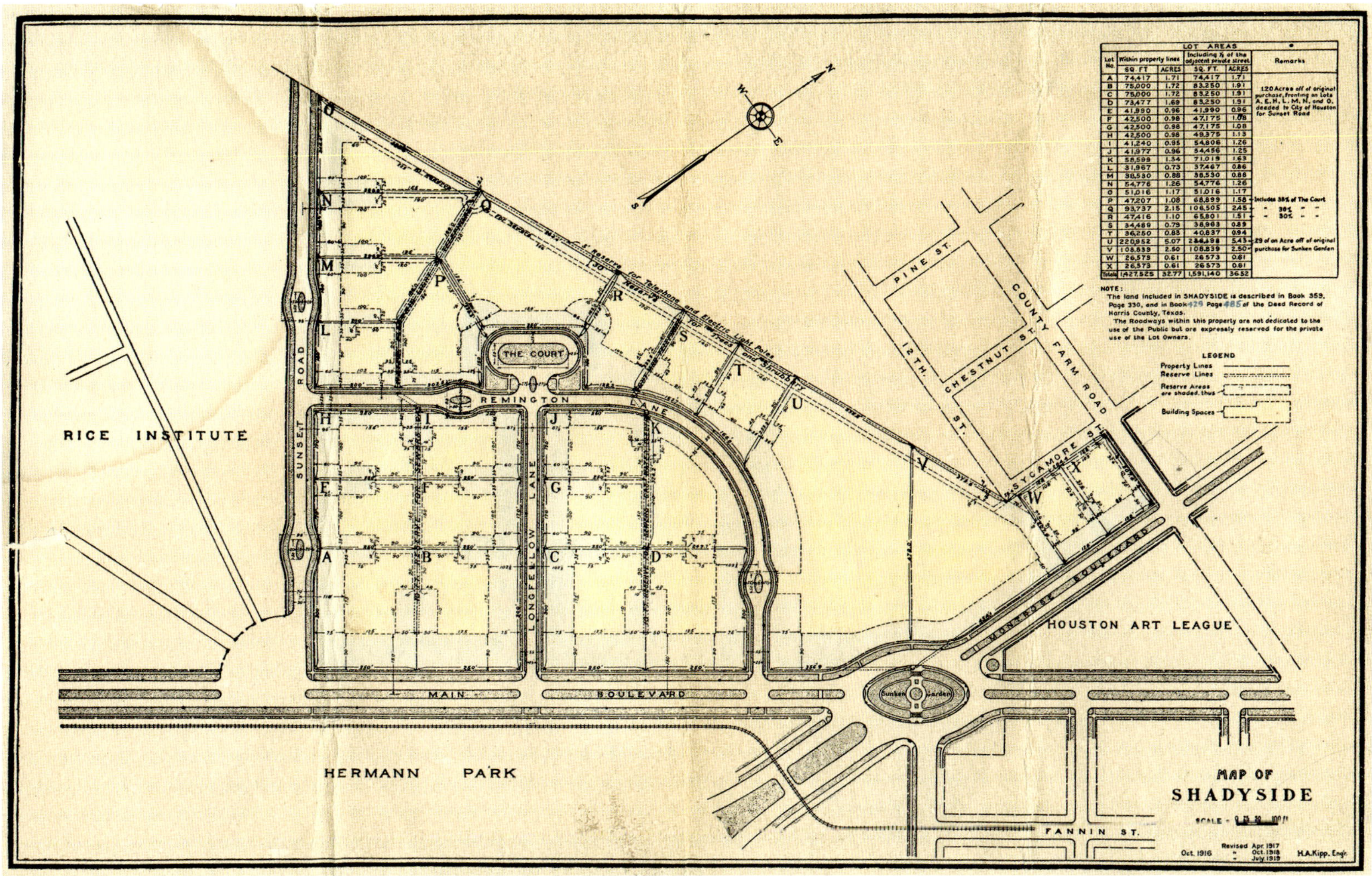

Shadyside, designed in 1916 by George Kessler at the behest of J. S. Cullinan, was platted according to this plan. Cullinan sold the large lots to his friends and business associates, on which they built some of Houston's grandest houses. Courtesy Houston Metropolitan Research Center, Houston Public Library (118).

liam Marsh Rice and the plans of the trustees of the Institute. Thus, in addition to a university for all the people, this city of homes and schools and churches is to have a great public park." The layout of Rice created a strong central axis on the diagonal from Main Street, a strategy Kessler also used for the Hermann Park entrance. The architecture and landscaping of Rice, like that of Shadyside, gave Houston an extraordinary new sense of possibility about how it might reimagine itself.[13]

The Museum of Fine Arts

The fourth component of Houston's City Beautiful sector on the edge of town was the Museum of Fine Arts. George Hermann had arranged, in an agreement with Mrs. Corinne Abercrombie Waldo in 1913, the gift of a triangular site at Main and Montrose to the Houston Art League for a museum. Cullinan also took an interest in this project and purchased the remainder of the tract for the museum as well as helped finance improvements to the property. The Art League took possession of the property in 1917, but it was not until after World War I that construction began on the first public art museum in Texas.[14] The central block of the Museum of Fine Arts, designed by William Ward Watkin, professor of architecture at Rice, with Ralph Adams Cram as consulting architect, was completed in 1924. Will C. Hogg raised the funds to build the flanking wings in 1926.[15] Indeed, despite his premature death, Hermann's hope that the area around Hermann Park be Houston's City Beautiful showcase, a civic monument to the Progressive Era and the benefits of careful planning, was realized.

George Edward Kessler

Even with the cooperation of a progressive city government, Hermann, Cullinan, Hogg, and others, including James A. Baker Jr. (chairman of the board of the Rice Institute), could not have been successful at

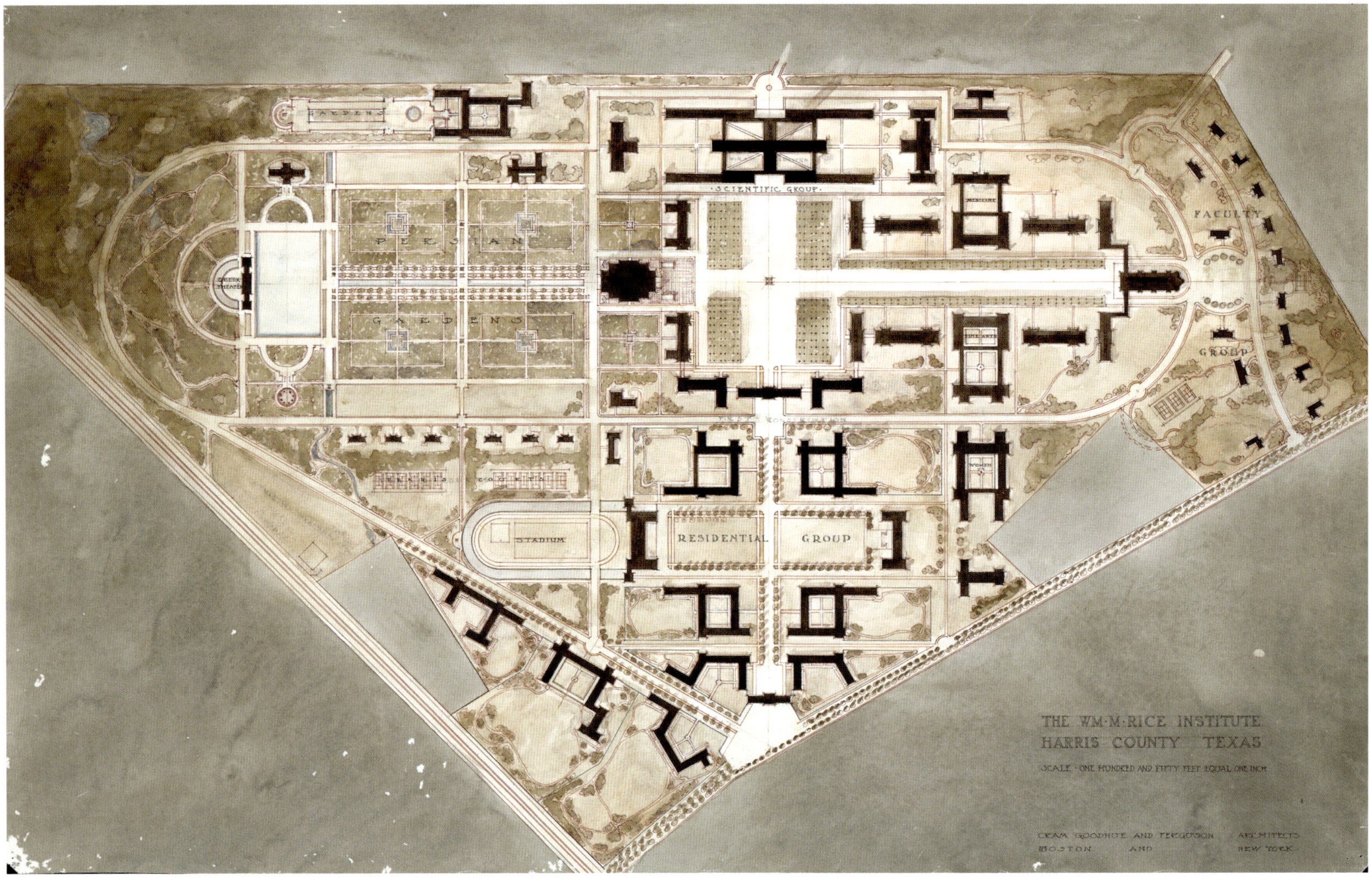

Rice Institute Plan (1911, Cram, Goodhue & Ferguson). Rice was the first institution in what became Houston's South End cultural district. George Hermann told Rice president Edward Odell Lovett that the establishment of the university prompted him to donate his South End property for a public park to enhance the character of this area. Courtesy Woodson Research Center, Fondren Library, Rice University.

creating this special Houston precinct had it not been for the talents of George E. Kessler (1862–1923). Born in the small, picturesque mountain town of Frankenhausen, Germany, George was the son of Ernst Edward Kessler and Adolphe Clotilde Zetzsche. Edward, the father, was the eldest son of a landed family who expected him to become manager of the family estates—a job for which he was ill-suited. After several business failures, the family sponsored the Kesslers' new start in America. In 1865 Edward and Clotilde sailed for New York with their two children—George, age three, and Antoinette, age eighteen. Following the pattern of many German immigrants, they left the East Coast for opportunity in the Midwest. Going first to St. Louis, then Hannibal, then Racine, Wisconsin, the Kesslers finally settled in Dallas, where Frederick, Edward's younger brother, joined them. The brothers invested in a cotton plantation, apparently without financial success. During their time in Dallas, Clotilde taught French and art, while as a teenager George worked as a "cash boy" (bill collector) for another German immigrant, Alex Sanger, at Sanger Brothers Department Store.[16]

In 1878 the family scattered. George's uncle Frederick moved to Galveston and was said to have been the first landscape gardener there. For a short time he was the keeper of Cedar Grove Park, a private garden, then became the proprietor of a saloon and boarding house. Frederick died in the Galveston Storm of 1900,[17] but his interest in landscaping probably influenced his nephew George's choice of career. Clotilde, determined that her son not end up like his disappointed "artistic" father, consulted with her family in Germany and, in 1878, returned there with George and Antoinette. Family resources and the preeminence of German educational institutions made this an easy choice, and George embarked on a rigorous and diverse German education.[18]

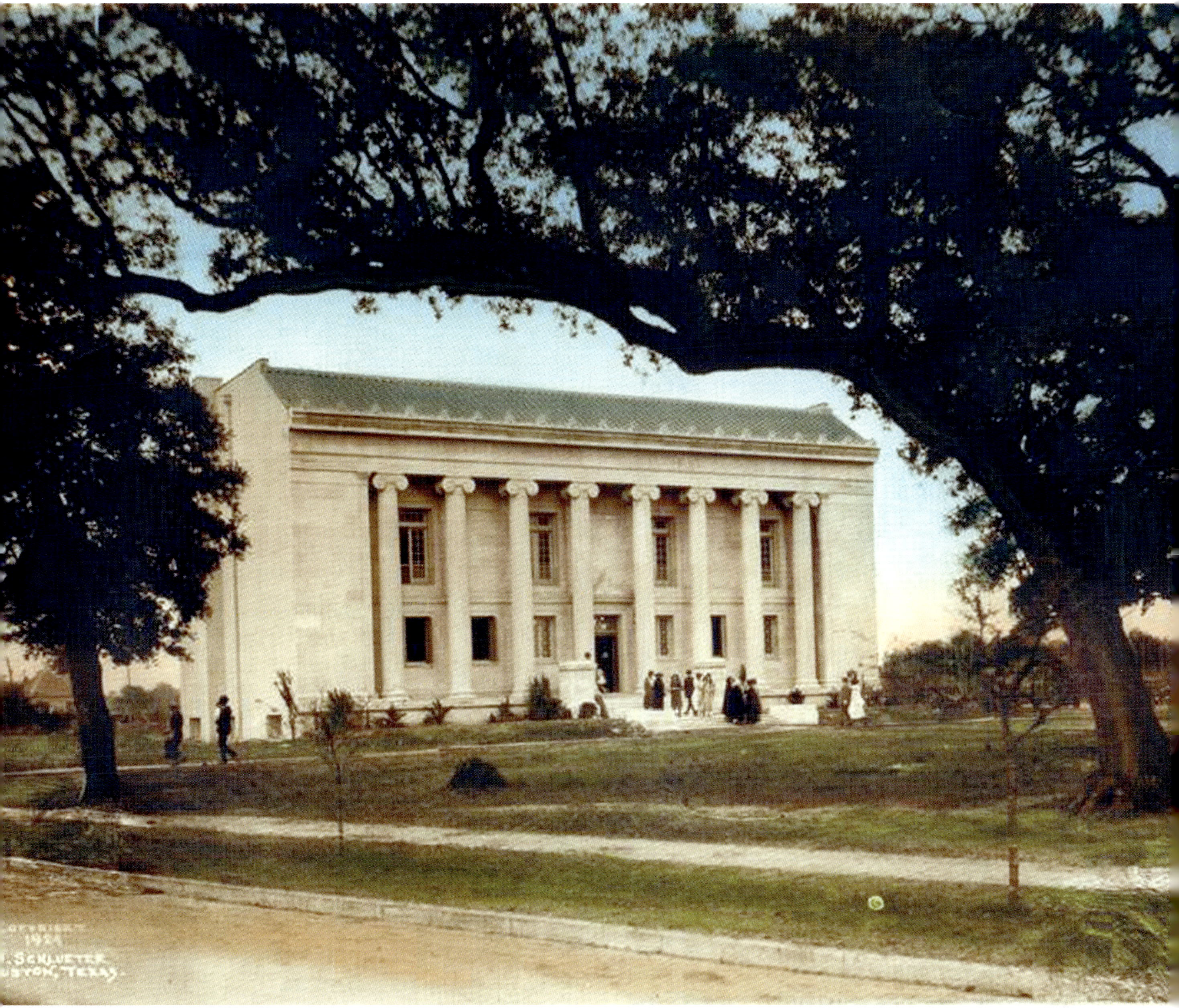

Museum of Fine Arts, Houston, 1001 Bissonnet Street, 1924, before the side wings were added in 1926. William Ward Watkin, architecture professor at Rice, designed the museum. Photograph by Frank J. Schlueter. Courtesy Houston Metropolitan Research Center, Houston Public Library (RG05-404).

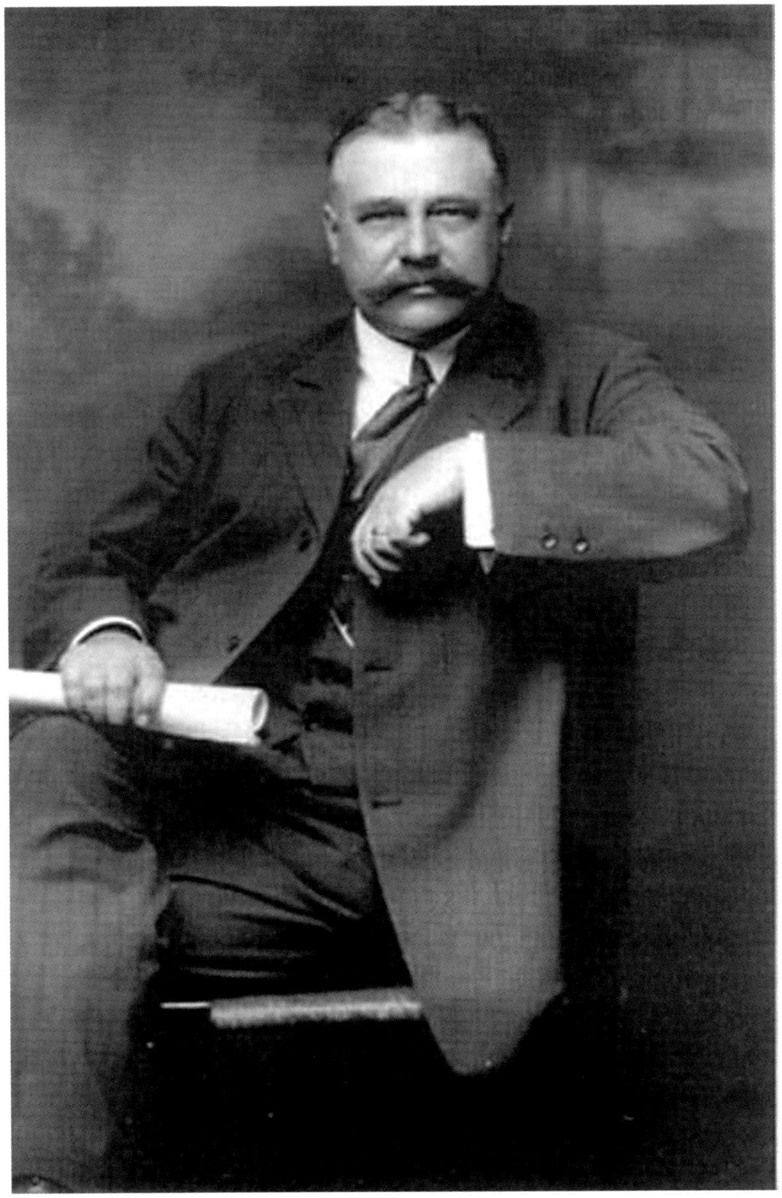

George Edward Kessler (1862–1923), c. 1910, landscape architect of Hermann Park, designed a large number of parks, cemeteries, and residential landscapes in the Midwest. After creating master plans for Kansas City, St. Louis, Dallas, and Fort Worth (among many other cities), he was commissioned by the City of Houston to design a park system and Houston's premier park space—Hermann Park. Source: *Landmarks* Association of St. Louis.

Back in Thuringia near his hometown, Kessler began his studies at age sixteen in a private school for landscape gardening at the Grand Ducal Gardens in Weimar. In contrast to Dallas, Weimar was a thousand-year-old town with a tradition of garden design based on the formal styles of France and Italy. Many of the great gardens of nineteenth-century Germany had been designed by students of the renowned French landscape architect, Andre Le Notre (1613–1700), principal designer for Louis XIV and mastermind behind the gardens at Versailles. Kessler would have studied these and later German parks and gardens with parterres, terraced gardens, long canals, and water cascades. Germany, at the time of Kessler's three years abroad, also had late eighteenth- and early nineteenth-century naturalistic gardens inspired by the great English landscape designers. In Weimar Kessler studied botany, forestry, and landscape design and worked in the city's parks surveying and planting as assistant to the garden inspector, Julius Hartwig, and estate gardener, Armin Sckell.[19]

Kessler's biographer, Kurt Culbertson, noted that Hartwig lived in a cottage at the edge of Park an der Ilm, which had been laid out in part by the poet Johann Wolfgang Goethe (1749–1832) between 1778 and 1833. Culbertson observed: "Goethe lived in the park for six years, living in the Garden House on the right bank of the Ilm and cultivating the small garden of his own design. Here Kessler would experience first hand the potential of urban waterways to enrich and enliven the public life of a city. Repeatedly in his own career as a park planner, Kessler would call upon cities to preserve and improve their streams and rivers as essential parts of a city's open space system."[20] When Kessler began his work in Houston, Comey had already suggested that parklands should be created along the bayous, a suggestion with which Kessler agreed and would implement in Houston.

In addition to his studies in Weimar, Kessler had other experiences that would inform his forty-year career as a landscape planner. He worked for a time with Haage and Schmidt, a major German plant nursery in Erfurt that now serves as the campus of the Erfurt School of Landscape Architecture. Kessler attended the famous University of Jena to study civil engineering. His sister, Antoinette, followed him to Jena and studied landscape art and design there. Culbertson believes that the most important part of Kessler's German education came in Potsdam, where he received further training in the Gärtner Lehranstalt, a famous garden school founded in 1824. In Potsdam he also studied with Theodore Neitner, author of the primary treatise on roses, at the Neue Garden. Kessler received further instruction at Berlin's Charlottenburg Polytechnnicum, the premier horticultural library in Germany. After his formal studies Kessler spent several months traveling through central and western Europe, including France and England, where he became familiar with the international trends in landscape design and planning on a grand scale in places such as the gardens of Paris and

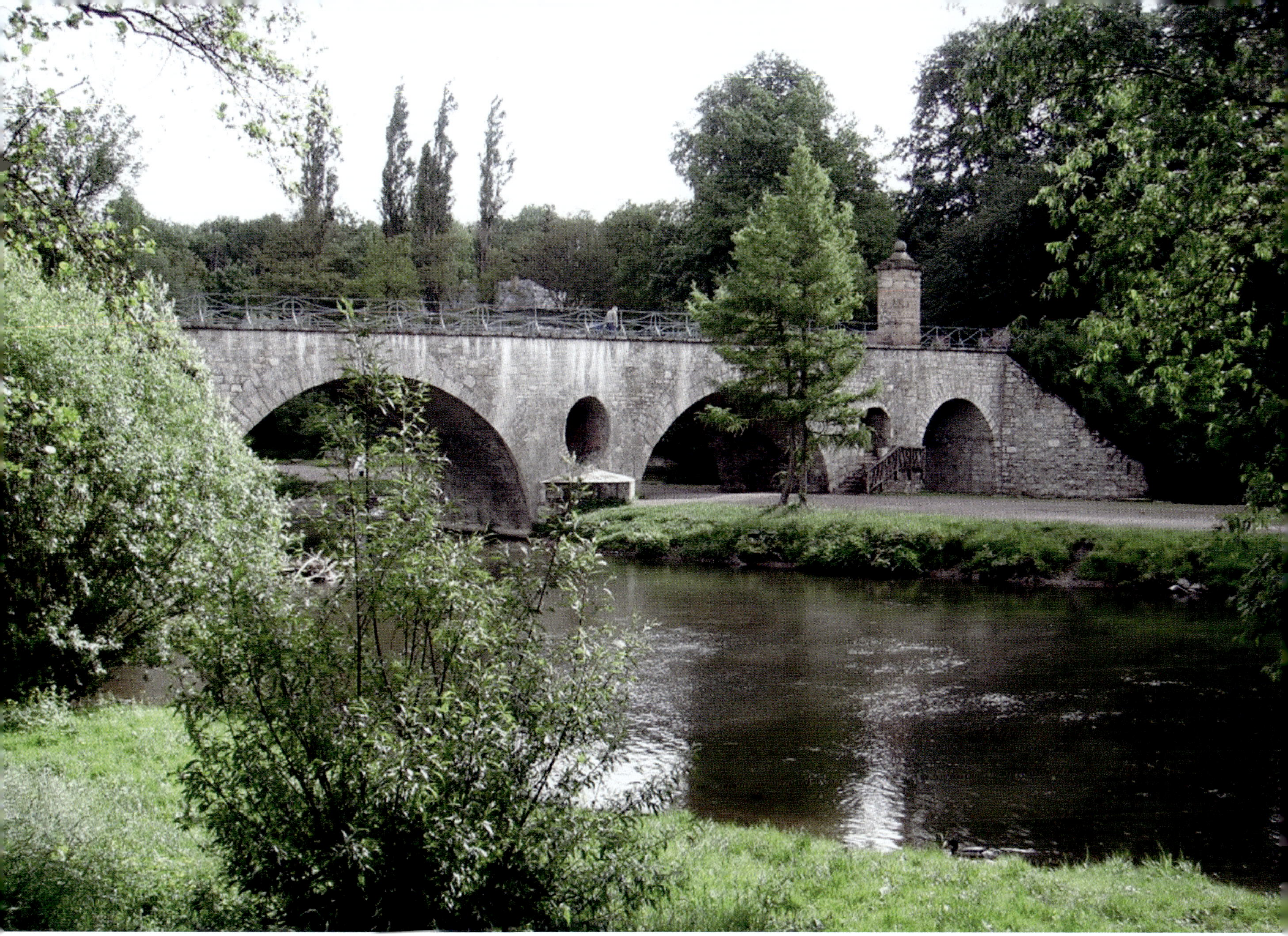

Park an der Ilm, 2009, Weimar, Germany, where George Kessler received training and experience in landscape design during his three-year study in Germany, 1878–1881. Photograph by Hardy Ernst. Source: http://www.goethe-gesellschaft-gunzenhausen.org/archiv2005.htm.

Hyde Park in London, where he saw carriage and foot paths popular in nineteenth-century parks as well as a prominent water feature, the "serpentine river."[21]

Kessler, with his mother and sister, returned to New York in October 1881 where he became familiar with Central Park, Frederick Law Olmsted's masterpiece begun in 1858. At this time there were few landscape architects in the United States. Most had been trained as architects, apprenticed with gardeners, or were horticulturalists knowledgeable about plants but without any design background. Kessler, educated as he had been in Europe, was an exception and in a position to find good employment. In a letter to Frederick Law Olmsted of January 22, 1882, Kessler introduced himself, elucidated his studies and travels, and inquired about job possibilities at the new arboretum in Boston.

In a second letter to Olmsted on February 15, Kessler mentions the possibility of obtaining a position in Central Park and reveals that, since November, he had been working for A. LeMoult in the Bowery, overseeing the greenhouse, seed and grass stock, and decorating concert halls. With this letter he enclosed some sample drawings.[22] In early March Olmsted's response was less than encouraging, advising Kessler to "free yourself from German associations, not because they are not excellent but because you have been too much confined in your education to them and they are likely to cramp your capabilities and limit your influence

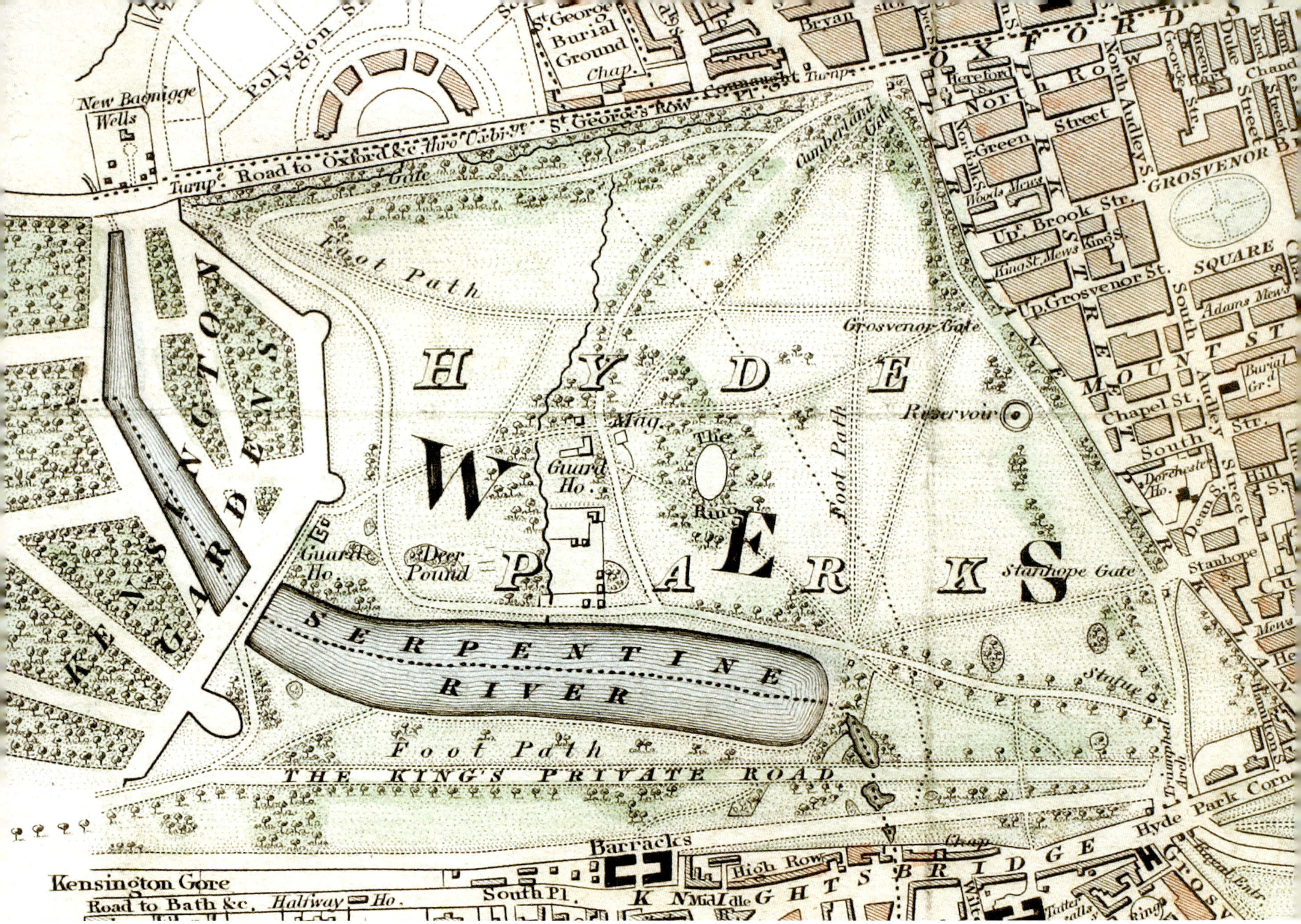

Hyde Park, London, 1833, developed from a royal hunting estate into a public park, is interesting to compare to American parks. Hyde Park appears less planned and lacks the variety of spaces American park designers incorporated in their parks. Source: Hyde Park section of "Improved map of London for 1833," engraved by W. Schmollinger, London. http://en.wikipedia.org/wiki/File:Hyde_Park_London_from_1833_Schmollinger_map.jpg.

and opportunities."[23] This—his German heritage—may be a clue as to why Kessler was not embraced by the East Coast landscapers and was not invited to become a founding member of the American Landscape Society. Olmsted did mention at the end of his long letter to Kessler that a railway company in Missouri was looking for someone to take charge of an excursion ground. On March 23, Kessler informed Olmsted that he, Kessler, was taking the position with the railroad.

In 1883 Kessler moved to Kansas City and began work for the Kansas City, Fort Scott & Gulf Railroad to create Merriam Park in Merriam, Kansas, just across the river from Kansas City, Missouri. This was Kessler's first documented project, but his reputation as a landscape architect and planner grew rapidly.[24] Between 1883 and 1900 Kessler completed twenty-four large projects, mostly in Missouri, for parks, cemeteries, and large residential gardens. Beginning in the 1890s he distinguished himself by designing a park and boulevard system for Kansas City, and in 1900 created a similar project for Memphis. It was clear that George Kessler had become the Midwestern heir of Frederick Law Olmsted as America entered its most intensive phase of the City Beautiful Movement. Arthur Comey, on the other hand, received most of his commissions in New England and New York, where Kessler did not work.[25]

When the Louisiana Purchase Exposition in St. Louis, organized to celebrate the one-hundredth anniversary of the Louisiana Purchase

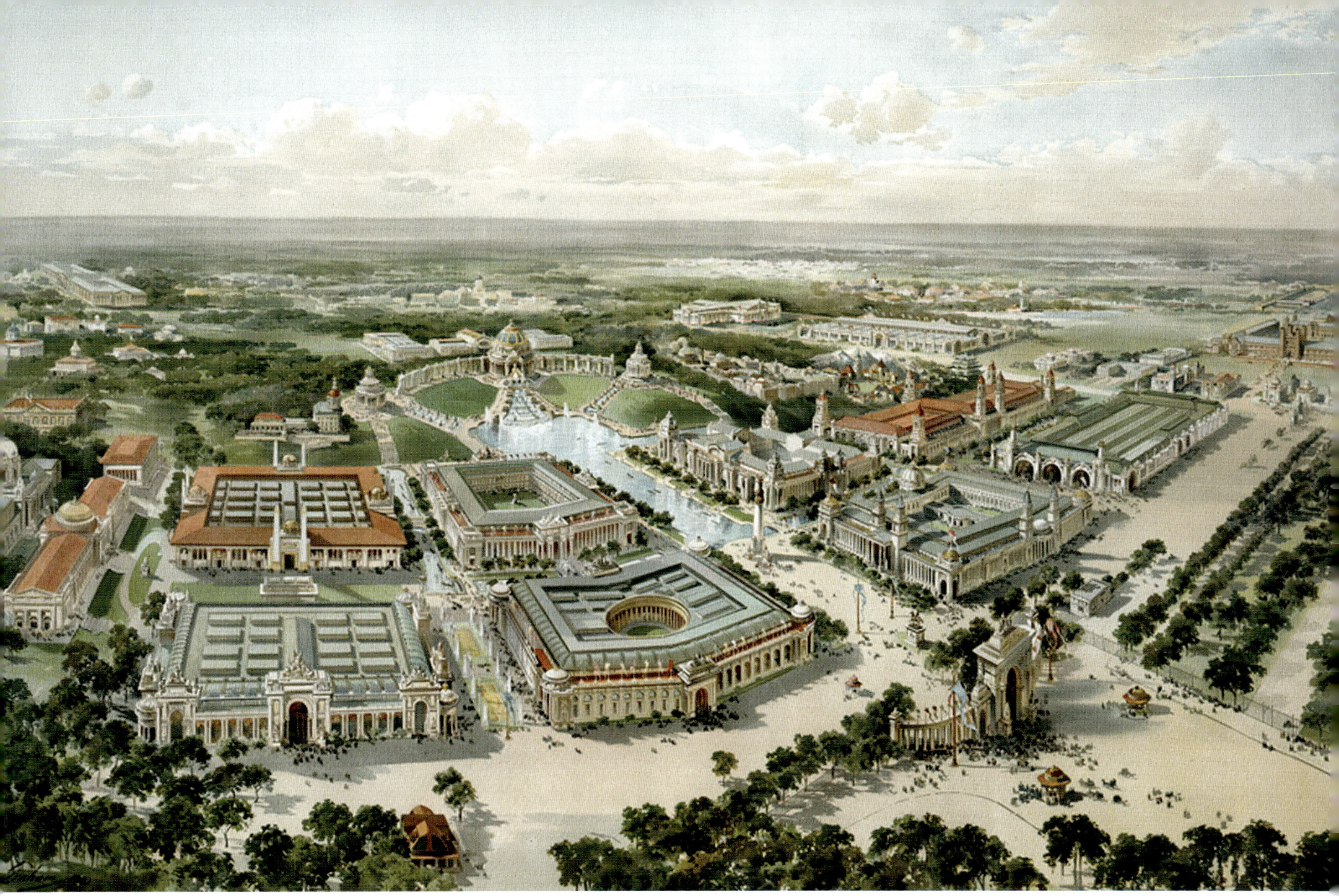

"World's Fair, St. Louis, 1904," chromolithography by Gray Lithographic Company, possibly the work of Charles S. Graham (1852–1911), a prolific sketch artist who worked for *Harper's Weekly*. This bird's-eye view shows the central section of the exposition grounds, which were planned by George Kessler. Source: Missouri History Museum, Photographs and Prints Collection. Courtesy private collection (facsimile).

(1803), was in the planning stages, Kessler was hired in 1900 to plan and landscape the 1,200-acre fair grounds in Forest Park. For this project Kessler moved to St. Louis and remained a resident there the rest of his life. Kessler dramatically changed the park: wetlands were drained and converted into water features with five connected lakes, curvilinear roads and pathways were installed, and thousands of trees were planted. Today, like Hermann Park, Forest Park is home to several institutions and recreational facilities. Far larger than Hermann Park, Forest Park has not only a zoo, science center, and amphitheater, but the St. Louis Art Museum and the Missouri History Museum, housed in buildings constructed for the exposition.

The St. Louis exposition was a larger version of Chicago's 1893 World's Fair, planned by Frederick Law Olmsted. Both featured grand Beaux Arts buildings, curving drives, water features, and elaborate gardens. The St. Louis fair site, at 1,200 acres, was almost twice the size of Chicago's 630 acres. Kessler's layout was similar to Olmsted's, with wide promenades, reflection pools, and fountains, but the architecture (1,500 buildings) was more nuanced and diverse. This project gained Kessler valuable experience and a national reputation as a planner and landscape architect. During his career Kessler completed an extensive body of work (over 230 documented projects), and he served as an advisor to numerous park boards and city planning departments. He was one of the founders of the American Institute of Planners in 1917 and was a member of the National Council of Fine Arts. During World War I he was a member of a committee of sixteen architects who planned military camps in the United States, including Camp Logan in Houston.

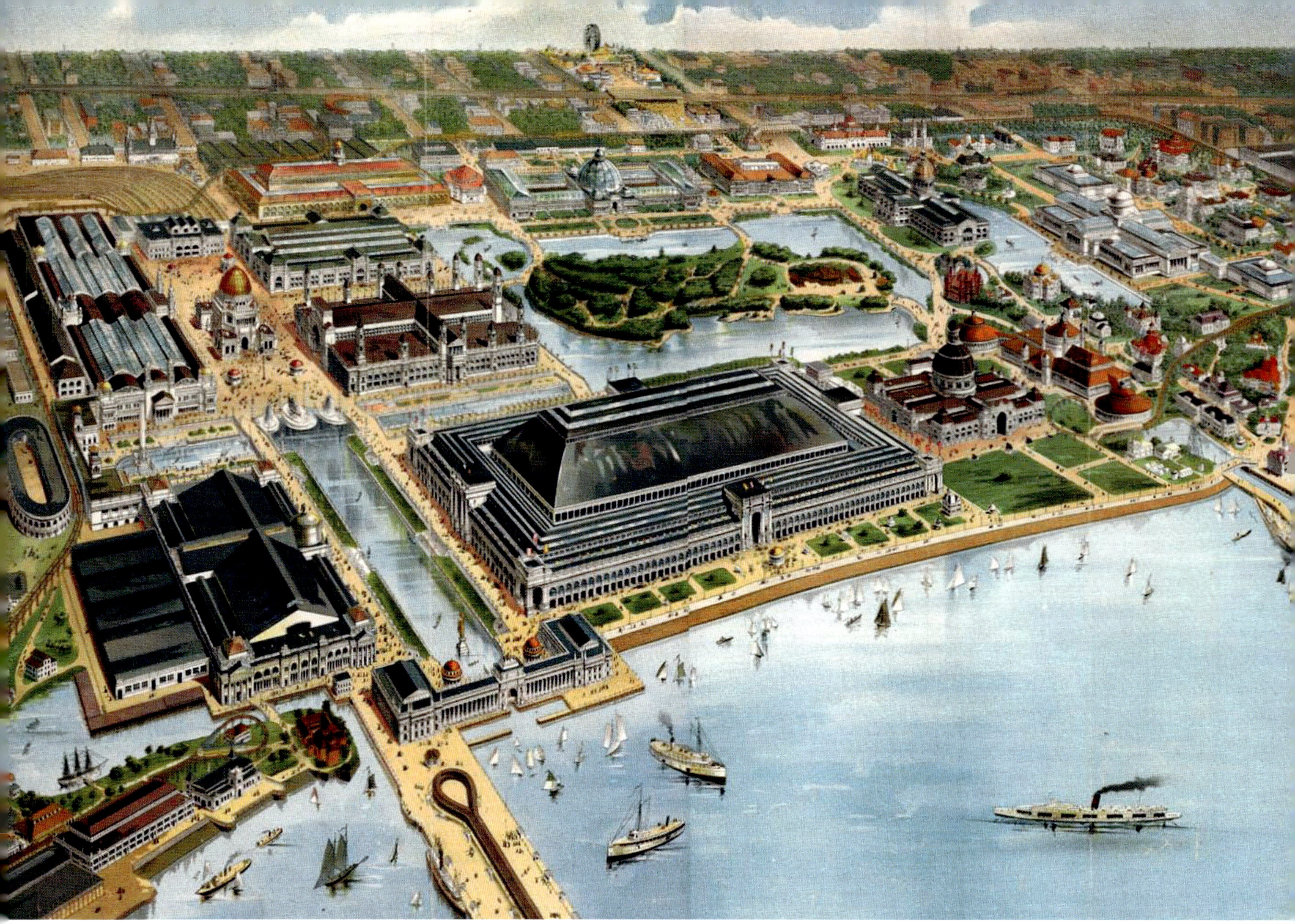

"Bird's-Eye View of the World's Columbian Exposition, Chicago, 1893," published by Rand McNally & Co., 1893. Frederick Law Olmsted planned the grounds of the exposition and set a standard followed by Kessler ten years later in St. Louis. Source: Division of Maps, Library of Congress. Courtesy private collection (facsimile).

Before Cullinan met Kessler in 1914, Kessler had completed plans for park and boulevard systems for Kansas City, Indianapolis, Syracuse, Cincinnati, Fort Worth, Denver, Pensacola, East St. Louis, Oklahoma City, Fort Wayne, Hamilton, Ohio, St. Joseph, Missouri, South Bend, and Dallas.[26] This list shows how popular civic planning was in the newer midwestern cities that competed to hire Kessler. These large projects were in addition to the many parks, university campuses, residential subdivisions, and private gardens produced by the Kessler office. Cullinan would not have encountered much, if any, opposition in recommending Kessler to take up where Comey had left off and to plan Hermann Park.

The Board of Park Commissioners, after securing the services of Kessler, organized an official dedication and opening of Hermann Park on July 4, 1915.[27] This was prior to the purchase of the crucial 122.5 acres between the park's west boundary and Main Street. Mayor Campbell had been in negotiation with the Hermann Estate to purchase this property for expansion of the park for $245,000 with generous terms. Others, no doubt willing to pay a much higher price, were also trying to buy this property for residential development, but the estate trustees decided to sell to the city.[28] The Kessler plan therefore incorporated 409.5 acres, which included Hermann's initial gift of 285 acres and an additional two acres that the Hermann Estate transferred to the city in late 1915.[29]

The Kessler Plan

Kessler made several trips to Houston, including one in September 1916 when he presented his plan to the mayor and park commissioners.[30] Unfortunately only one ink-on-linen Kessler drawing, "Plan for North & Principal Entrance," dated 1916, survives. It shows the entrance sequence from the intersection of Main Street and Montrose Boulevard, where Kessler placed a traffic circle containing a sunken garden (now site of the Mecom Fountain), through the Grand Basin (now McGovern Lake) to a long, formally landscaped arbor or pavilion behind the lake. An esplanaded boulevard is shown on the other side of this pavilion that connects with a smaller path or road corresponding to "Hermann Boulevard" on the Maxcy Plan leading to the Rice Institute's "Entrance Two. A picnic area (now "Playground for All Children") is designated near Main Street along this path. Other features on the Kessler plan include a shelter house east of the entrance, landscaped entrance gardens leading to a monument circle (now the site of the Sam Houston Monument), a reflecting pool set amid sectored lawns, and semicircular picnic grounds fronting another lawn that provides a vista to the lake and boat landing. A semicircular outdoor amphitheater (eventually the site of Miller Theatre) connects to the reflection pool and roads through radiating paths. These curving roads, or carriage drives as they were labeled then, meander through woodlands and structure circulation in the park.

Not indicated on the Kessler entrance plan are the recreational areas and ball fields that were so important to George Hermann. However, these would have been planned for the outer reaches of the park as Kessler's successors, Hare & Hare, later proposed. The most problematic omission was the lack of any provision for automobiles. This initial plan was very much of the nineteenth century, when, even by 1900, automobiles were rare in Houston. In 1910 the Houston Police Department purchased its first automobile and created a traffic squad indicating that, even after only one decade, automobiles had begun to create problems.[31] And by 1916 cars were vying with horses and carriages for space on the roads and places to park. Into the twenty-first century, sufficient parking has been one of the most difficult problems faced by Hermann Park and its conservators.

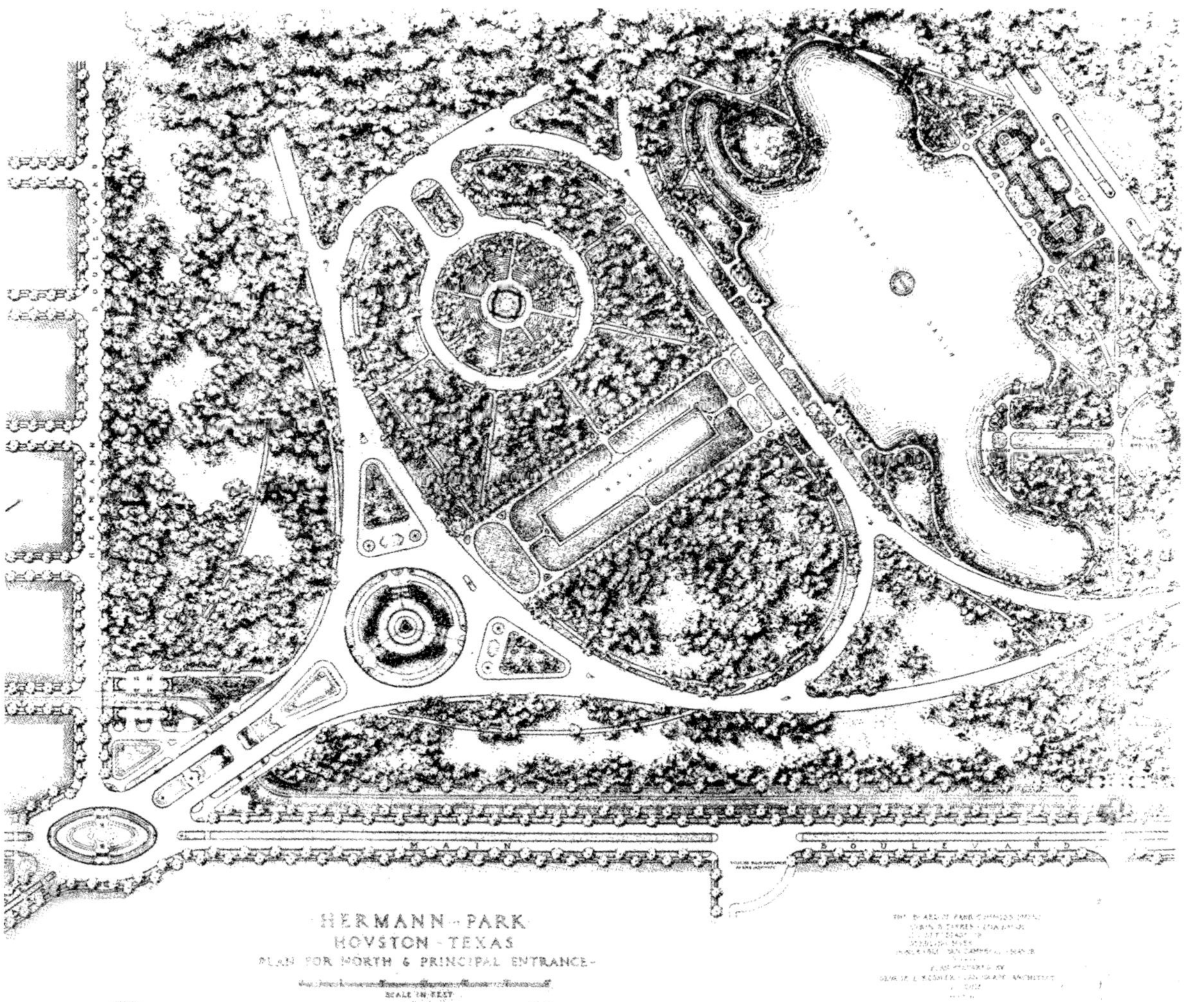

Hermann Park, Houston Texas, Plan for North and Principal Entrance (1916, George Kessler). This, the only surviving Kessler drawing, shows Hermann Park's entry sequence with primary access to the park on the diagonal, a sunken garden, a landscaped grand boulevard, a monument circle, a reflection pool, and lake. An outdoor terraced theater in the round (location of Miller Outdoor Theatre) is also indicated on this plan. Courtesy Houston Metropolitan Research Center, Houston Public Library (RGD 26).

Kessler's Hermann Park plan demonstrates his ability to blend formal elements with the naturalistic style of English landscapes, and, in his one drawing, his careful attention to sight lines, pulling the eye across a series of elements to a distant finishing point is evident. Kessler was able to balance open areas with wooded areas, natural or planted to look natural. This plan shows that it was Kessler who was responsible for the staggered rows of live oak trees on what he called Main Boulevard. They are now mature and frame the loveliest drive in Houston. A city map published in 1917 shows the great triple lobed layout that Kessler envisioned.

Stephen Fox described the Kessler Plan as follows:

> Kessler demonstrated a practical skill for reconciling the requirements of ceremony and informality in his design. The principal axis marked the ceremonial space of the park. Yet beyond the allée of trees flanking the reflecting basin, trees conformed to no fixed order in their location. The north and south embankments of the Grand Basin were part of the space of the axis. But the east and west shores (which were not) were eroded by canals and lagoons that broke down the sense of strict boundary and led to small-scale dells.[32]

It is interesting to compare Kessler's 1916 plan for Hermann Park with his 1901 plan for Overton Park in Memphis. The earlier Overton Park plan showed a less elaborate entrance, perpendicular to the tree-lined Poplar Boulevard, with an esplanade drive into the park terminating at a monument circle with a drive curving slightly to the left. There were no extended sight lines or formal elements beyond the entrance. Overton Park, at 342 acres, is comparable in size to Hermann Park (409.5 acres), but it features some of the same characteristics: meadows, curvilinear carriage drives and foot paths through the woods, a formless lake, a stream running through it, and an intrusive transportation artery.[33] However, it is clear that fifteen years after his plan for Overton Park, Kessler's design skill had matured. The Hermann Park plan is a much more sophisticated layout despite the challenge of a flat site, including the exceptional sight-line sequence along the central axis, one of the features that makes Hermann Park so distinctive. Kessler did give Overton Park corner entries like those Olmsted used often, including in Central Park and Brooklyn's Prospect Park. Prospect Park, built in 1867, is older and larger (585 acres) than Overton and Hermann parks, but it contains elements that Kessler employed in his park plans decades later. The diagonal entry sequence and landscaped oval at the entrance to Prospect Park are also present in Hermann Park.

In Hermann Park Kessler also incorporated features not derived from Olmsted but popular at the beginning of the twentieth century. He was fond of sunken gardens and used them in contrast to forested and informal areas of his parks. Kessler's Paseo Sunken Garden in Kansas City shows what he might have envisioned for the finished product at the entrance to Hermann Park. Sunken gardens, usually two to four feet below grade, were devised to provide a heightened perspective so that those slowly walking or riding by in carriages could appreciate the intricacies of the parterres and flowerbed arrangements.

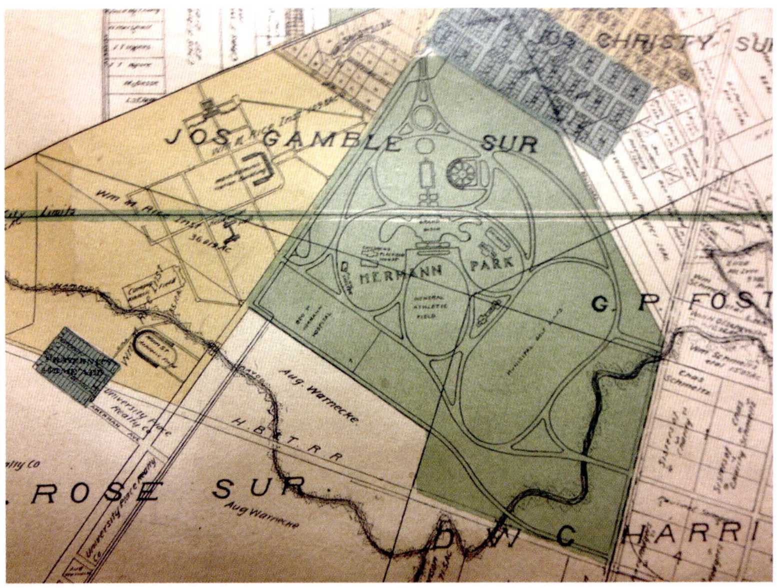

Map section, City of Houston, 1917, showing (in green) Hermann Park with a diagram of park roads and labeled areas that indicate Kessler's complete plan for the park. Note that the city limits at the time bisected the park and the Rice Institute. Source: "City of Houston Texas, 1917," pub. Houston Title Guaranty Co., R. B. Baer & M.E. Holland. Courtesy Houston Metropolitan Research Center, Houston Public Library.

Brock and Kipp

Two individuals who worked for the City of Houston were instrumental in the realization of initial improvements to Hermann Park. The first, Clarence Lockwood Brock (1880–1946), was a native of Michigan who moved to Houston in 1905. He was one of the founders of the Houston Museum and Scientific Society in 1909, which sought "to establish and maintain a free institution for the people, for education and science." He was appointed the superintendent (director) of City Parks in 1913, a position he held for thirty years until 1943 when the Parks Department was reorganized. In 1929 Brock, still director of the Parks Department, became the first director of the Houston Museum of Natural Science. In Hermann Park Brock supervised plantings, including hundreds of young live oak trees along Main Street and around the reflecting pool in the park. Brock was also a mineral collector, and he later established the American Mineral Exchange in Houston. He is typical of the many accomplished and energetic people who settled in Houston in the early years of the twentieth century and had a significant impact on its future. He, like many accomplished Houstonians, is buried in Glenwood Cemetery.[34]

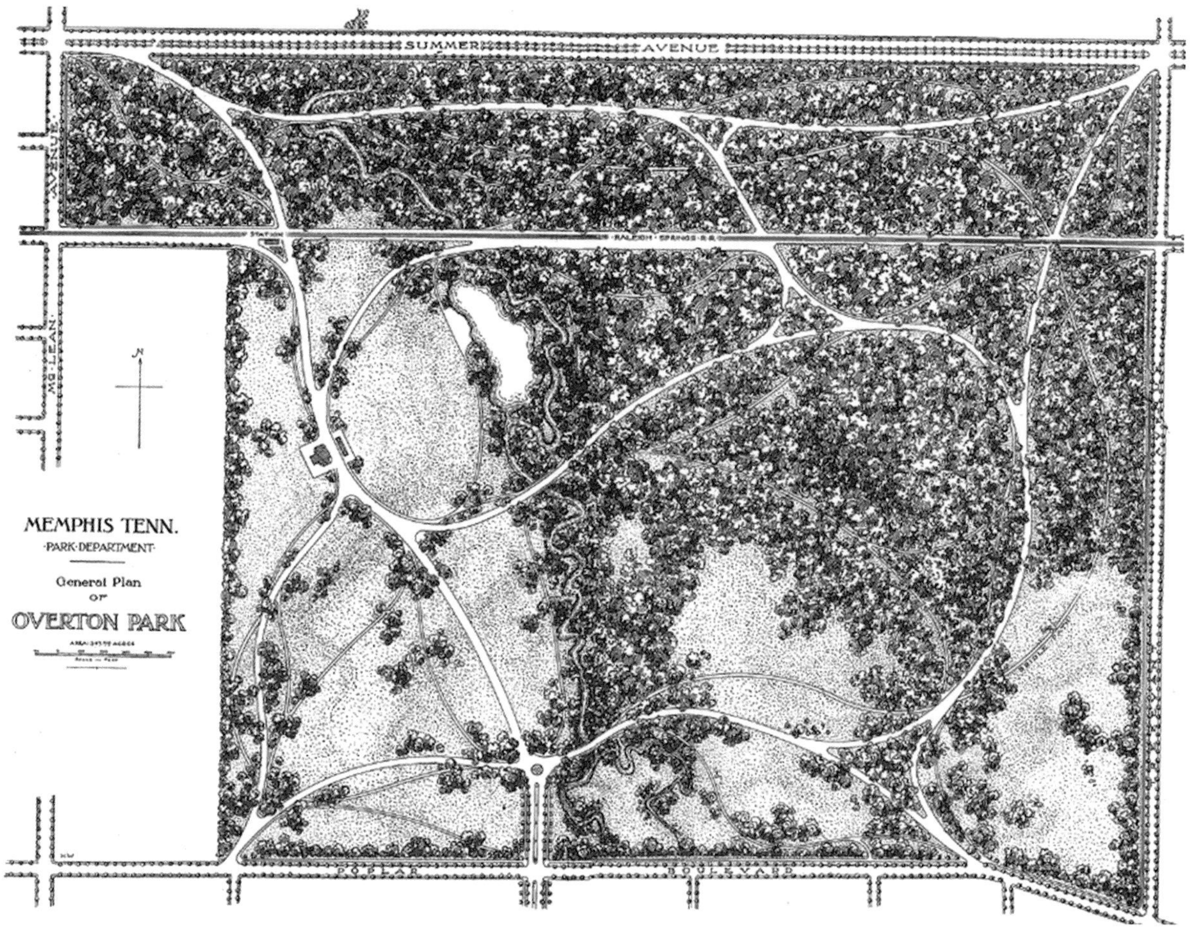

"General Plan of Overton Park," Memphis, Tennessee (1901, George Kessler) is related in layout to Kessler's more sophisticated plan for Houston's park, designed fifteen years later. Source: Citizens to Preserve Overton Park website www.overtonpark-forever.org.

The second individual crucial to the implementation of the Kessler Plan was Herbert A. Kipp (1884–1968), a civil engineer who came to Houston as an official of the US Department of Agriculture to advise on drainage plans for the city. In 1915 Kipp was appointed the Houston City Engineer.[35] He made the working drawings for Kessler's improvements to Hermann Park in 1916 and 1917 and supervised infrastructure improvements as Brock supervised plantings. By 1917 the major roadways of the park had been graded, a shelter house built, some wooden playground equipment installed, and the reflection pool had been laid out. In 1917 plans for a nine-hole golf course were prepared.[36] Drawings by Kipp for the City of Houston Parks Department survive, including one for the steps of the Sunken Garden dated January 1917, indicating that this element was not installed until 1917. Another Kipp drawing was for the new layout of "Hermann Avenue" along the northeast boundary of the park dated May 1917.[37] Kipp remained in Houston the rest of his life and is remembered not only for his work in Hermann Park but also as the planner of River Oaks and the Texas Medical Center. The Herbert A. and Elizabeth N. Kipp Memorial Aquarium at the Houston Zoo in Hermann Park is named for Kipp, whose bequest to the city was used to build the aquarium.

The US entrance into World War I on April 6, 1917, brought an end to further civic projects, and the $250,000 bond issue for parks had been exhausted. The proposed golf course was not built, and few improvements occurred in the park for the next three years. One article, in April 1920, was written to support an unsuccessful proposal to make Hermann Park the site of the Houston Fair and Exposition Grounds, but it also gave an assessment of the park at that time:

> Hermann Park as it stands now is a plot of ground containing 420 acres of undeveloped land—undeveloped except for the roadway that winds through it and a few minor improvements. There has been no appreciable development of the park within the last two years. . . . Hermann Park should contain a municipal golf course, municipal base-ball diamonds and tennis courts, and, above all, the tourists' camping grounds should be developed at the earliest possible moment. A thoroughly equipped camping ground, with the necessary facilities for the comfort and convenience of the tourists, would be a great boon to our city and would be the means of advertising Houston all over the continent. One of the first things that should be done is the construction of a suitable gate at the entrance of the park. . . . In its present condition, there is nothing there to indicate the existence of a public park.[38]

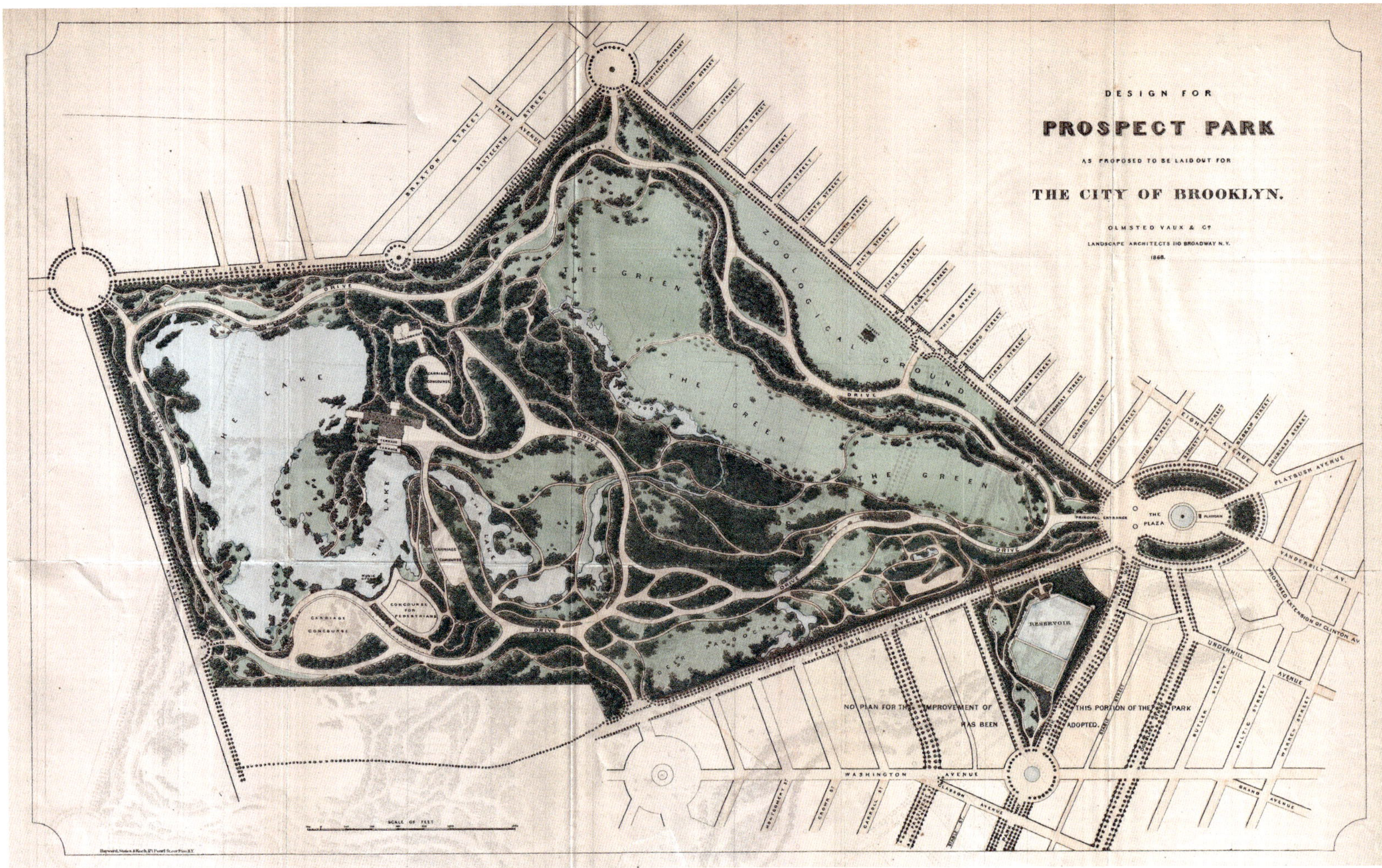

"Design for Prospect Park as proposed to be laid out for The City of Brooklyn" (1867, Olmsted Vaux & Co.) shows some elements employed by Kessler for Hermann Park such as the diagonal entrance, meandering drives and paths, a free-form lake, and a zoo. Source: City of New York Parks and Recreation department website http://www.nycgovparks.org /about/history/olmsted-parks.

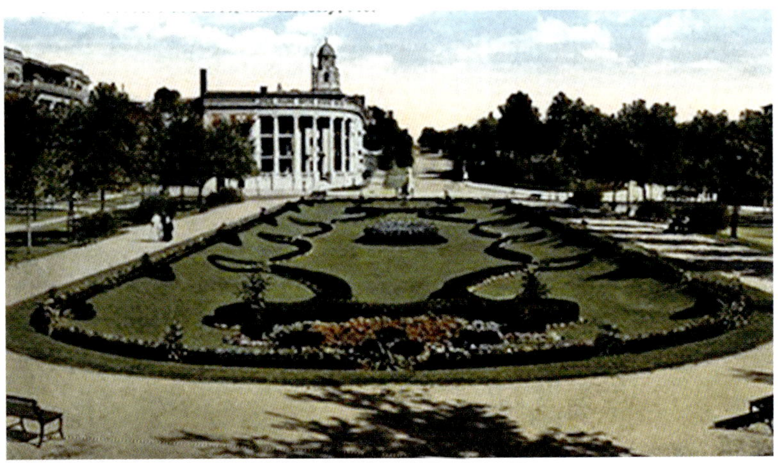

Paseo Sunken Garden, Kansas City (1906, George Kessler), shows an earlier version of the popular sunken gardens that Kessler often incorporated in his landscape plans. Courtesy private collection.

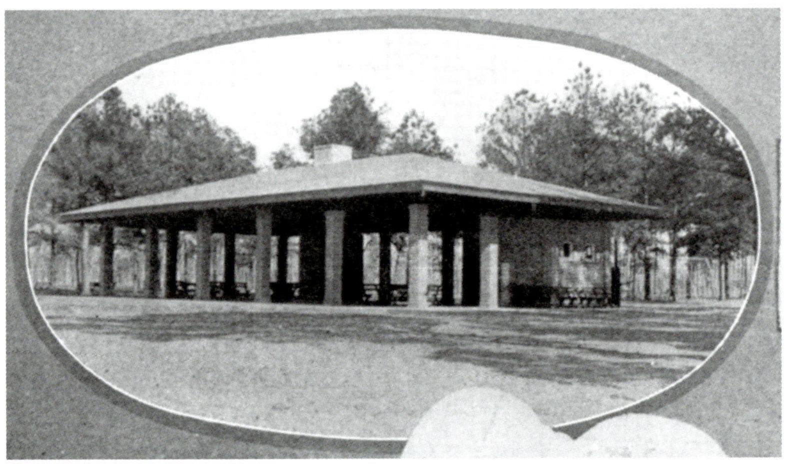

Shelter House (1916), the first structure in Hermann Park, was located to the left of the entrance, where the Houston Museum of Natural Science is today. It contained a huge fireplace in the center. Source: *Illustrated City Book of Houston, 1925*. Courtesy Houston Metropolitan Research Center, Houston Public Library.

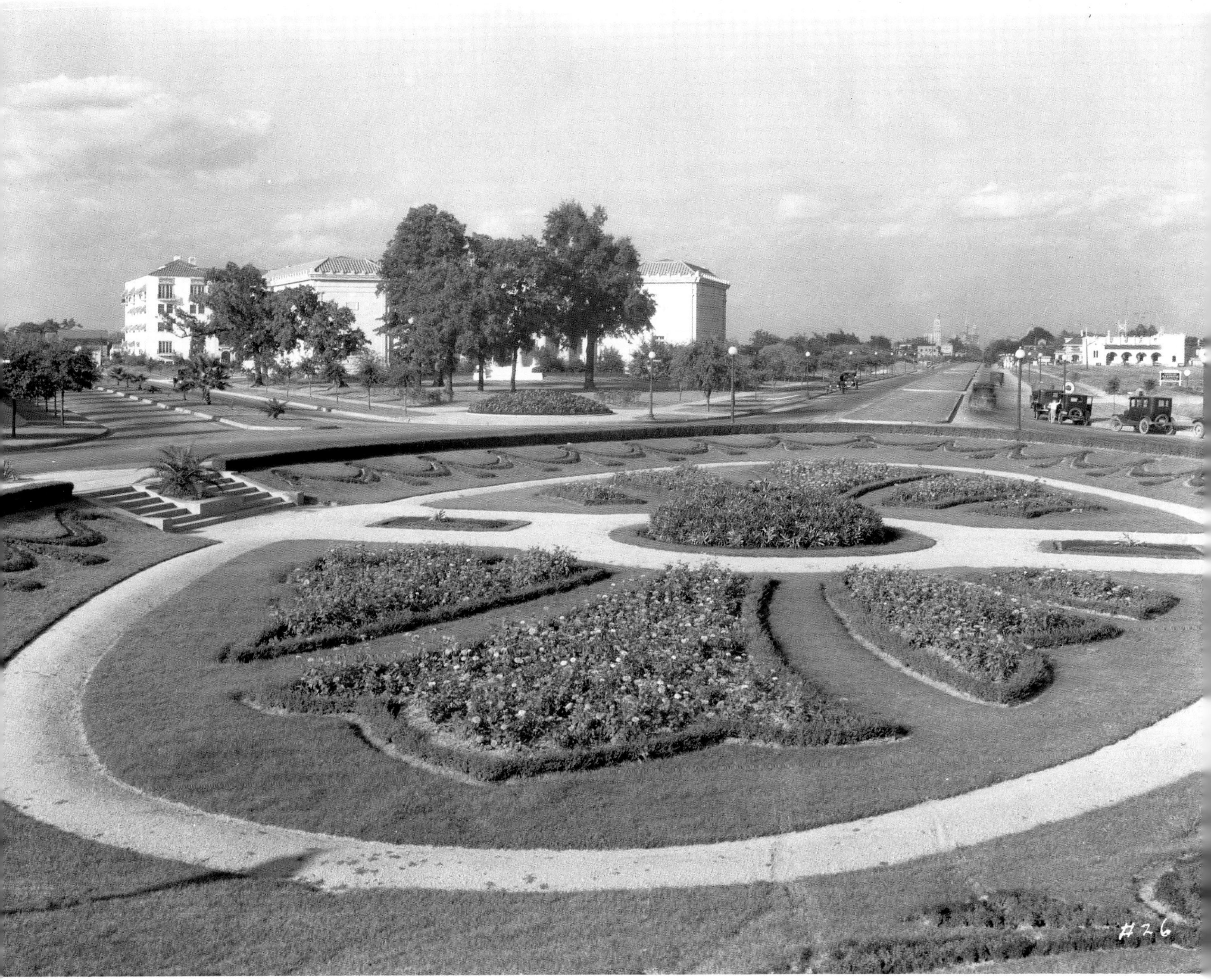

Sunken Garden, c. 1930, with the Museum of Fine Arts in the background, looking north down Main Street with Montrose Boulevard stretching off to the left. Courtesy Houston Metropolitan Research Center, Houston Public Library (334-825).

A more official description of the park was published in October 1920: "While only a portion of the park has been improved for park purposes, the entire area, with its tropical vegetation and magnificent pine trees, comprises a scene of great beauty. In the improved portion of the park is a pleasing shelter house, play equipment, drinking fountains, electric lights, and motor tourist camp sites."[39]

Memorial Oaks

Neither article mentioned the donation of over two hundred live oak trees by Will Hogg in memory of Houston soldiers who had died in World War I. In late spring 1920 the War Mothers of Houston planted these memorial oaks along what is now Cambridge Drive, where it curved through Hermann Park. A bronze nameplate was placed at the foot of each tree inscribed with the name of one of Houston's fallen soldiers. The nameplates were all eventually stolen or inadvertently buried, and many of the trees were taken down with later zoo expansions.[40]

The first indication of seriously renewed interest in Hermann Park came from J. S. Cullinan in the fall of 1921, when he wrote that he had been told by Brock that the trails and bridle paths through the park had not been "fully determined," but that Kessler was expected to visit Houston soon, and Brock anticipated that the paths would be "worked out in final form" then. Once Kessler planned the pathways, Brock promised that he would begin "clearing for the bridle paths and putting in rustic bridges that will permit crossing the bayou." Cullinan went on to say that he would be willing "to provide the funds against tax collections or otherwise." The purpose of these small steps, Cullinan said, was to "stimulate interest in the park at a very nominal investment."[41] Two months later Cullinan wrote Brock: "In walking through Hermann Park for the purpose of locating prospective foot trails and saddle paths, I was greatly impressed with the work that is being done under your direction."[42]

Oscar F. Holcombe (1888–1968) was elected mayor of Houston in 1921 and brought with him a commitment to civic improvements. Holcombe, a lumberman and real estate developer, served eleven nonconsecutive terms as mayor for a total of twenty-two years between 1921 and 1957, and during that time he was aggressive about increasing the city's boundaries and improving public services, including the park system. In 1922 Holcombe appointed the first City Planning Commission and reinstituted the Board of Park Commissioners, which had lapsed during World War I.[43]

Miller Memorial Theatre

In 1919, two years before Holcombe took office, mining engineer and cotton broker Jesse Wright Miller died, leaving property to the City of Houston for municipal purposes. The city sold that property for $50,000 to Miller's sister, Alma Miller Womack, who was a member of the Park Board. Finally, in 1921 with Mayor Holcombe's prodding, the City Council authorized use of profits from that sale to build the Miller Memorial Theatre on the site Kessler had set aside for a concert pavilion. William Ward Watkin designed the theatre as a neoclassical proscenium flanked by twenty limestone columns, ten on each side.[44] Tom Tellepsen, founder of Tellepsen Construction Company, was the contractor, and Kipp and Brock managed the project. The theatre was dedicated on May 12, 1923, with an extravagant produc-

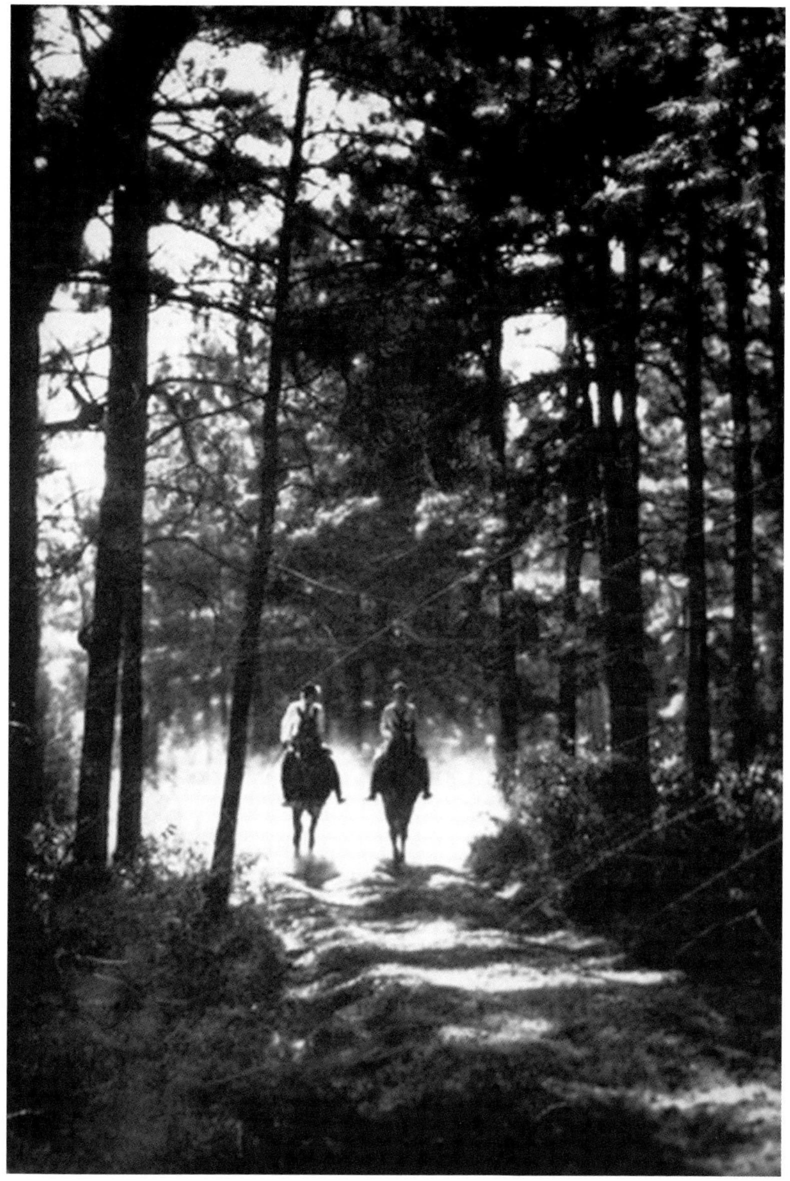

Bridle Path, Hermann Park, c. 1925. Stables at the corner of Almeda and Hermann Drive provided horses for rides through Hermann Park along designated bridle trails for over fifty years. Courtesy Houston Metropolitan Research Center, Houston Public Library.

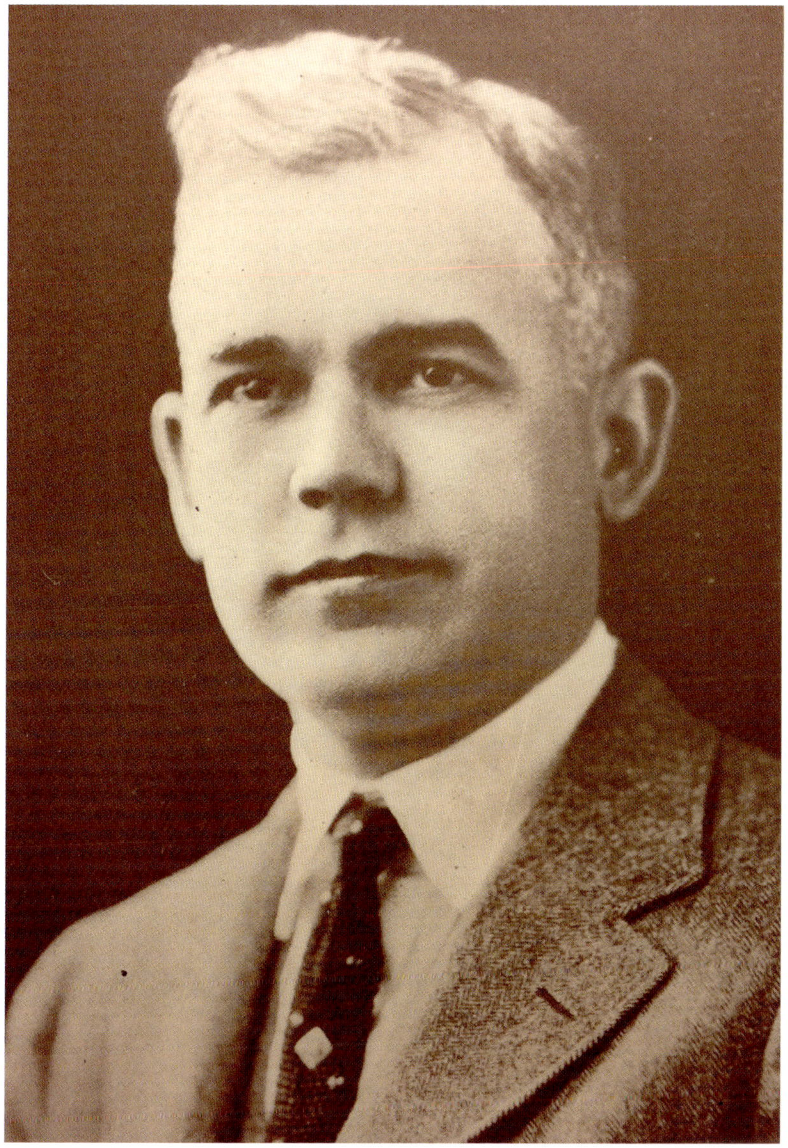

Mayor Oscar Holcombe (1888–1968) served a total of twenty-two years as mayor of Houston, and under his leadership city planning, parks, and public services all improved in Houston. Source: *Illustrated City Book of Houston, 1925*. Courtesy Houston Metropolitan Research Center, Houston Public Library.

tion called "Springtimes of Our Nation," a pageant with 2,500 performers. The dedication plaque read: "To the Arts of Music, Poetry, Drama and Oratory, by which the striving spirit of man seeks to interpret the words of God. This theatre of the City of Houston is permanently dedicated."[45] Not only was the Miller Theatre the location of various evening performances, it was a popular setting for dramatic daytime pageants and amateur performances. By 1925 Miller Theatre had been extensively wired for stage lighting and power for a curtain hoister. A "service box for attaching moving picture machines" was also installed.[46]

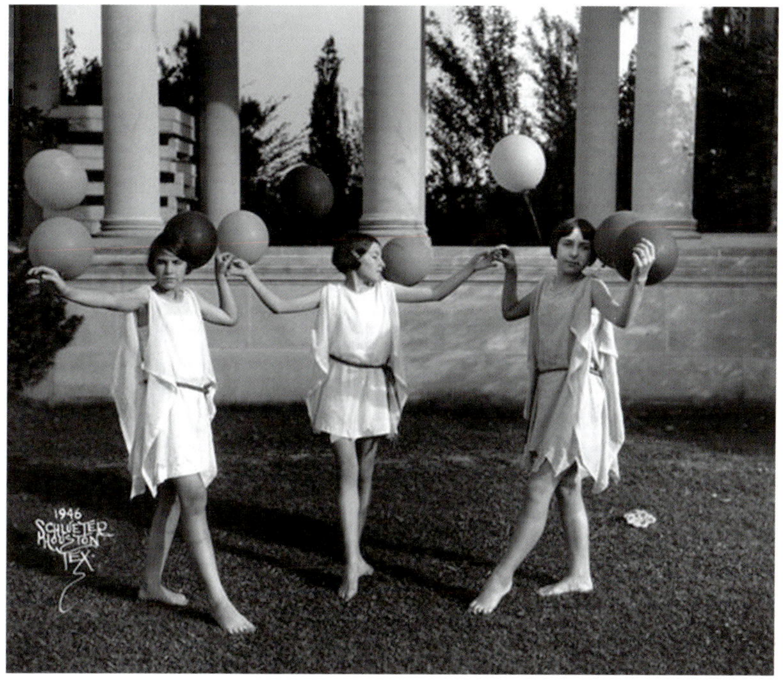

Young girls dancing with balloons at Miller Theatre, 1946. Miller Theatre's classical proscenium and colonnade were used for many types of performances, including theater, ballet, choral music, and pageants. Photograph by Frank J. Schlueter. Courtesy Houston Metropolitan Research Center, Houston Public Library (100-493).

William Ward Watkin (1886–1952) was born in Boston, grew up in Pennsylvania, and attended the University of Pennsylvania, studying architecture under the French-born architect Paul Philippe Cret, an advocate of classical architecture. Following graduation in 1908, Watkin spent a year on a European grand tour then returned to work for the Boston firm of Cram, Goodhue & Ferguson, architects of the Rice Institute. When construction began on the initial buildings at Rice in the summer of 1910, Watkin was sent to Houston by the firm as onsite supervisor.[47] He remained at Rice to begin an architecture department and was responsible for a number of significant buildings in the Hermann Park area, including the Chemistry Building (1922–1925) and Cohen House (1927) at Rice, the Edward Albert Palmer Memorial Chapel (1927), the Harry C. Wiess House (1920, now the Rice President's House) and the Frederick A. Heitmann House (1922–1923) in Cullinan's Shadyside neighborhood, and the Museum of Fine Arts (1924, 1926).[48] Watkin became an influential Houstonian, not only through the architects he trained at Rice, but also through his many residential and institutional projects, including the celebrated Julia Ideson Building of the Houston Public Library (1926 with Cram & Ferguson and Louis A. Glover) and the neo-Gothic Trinity Episcopal Church (1917–1919 with Cram & Ferguson). Watkin's work left a distinctive mark on Houston architecture, particularly in the Rice-

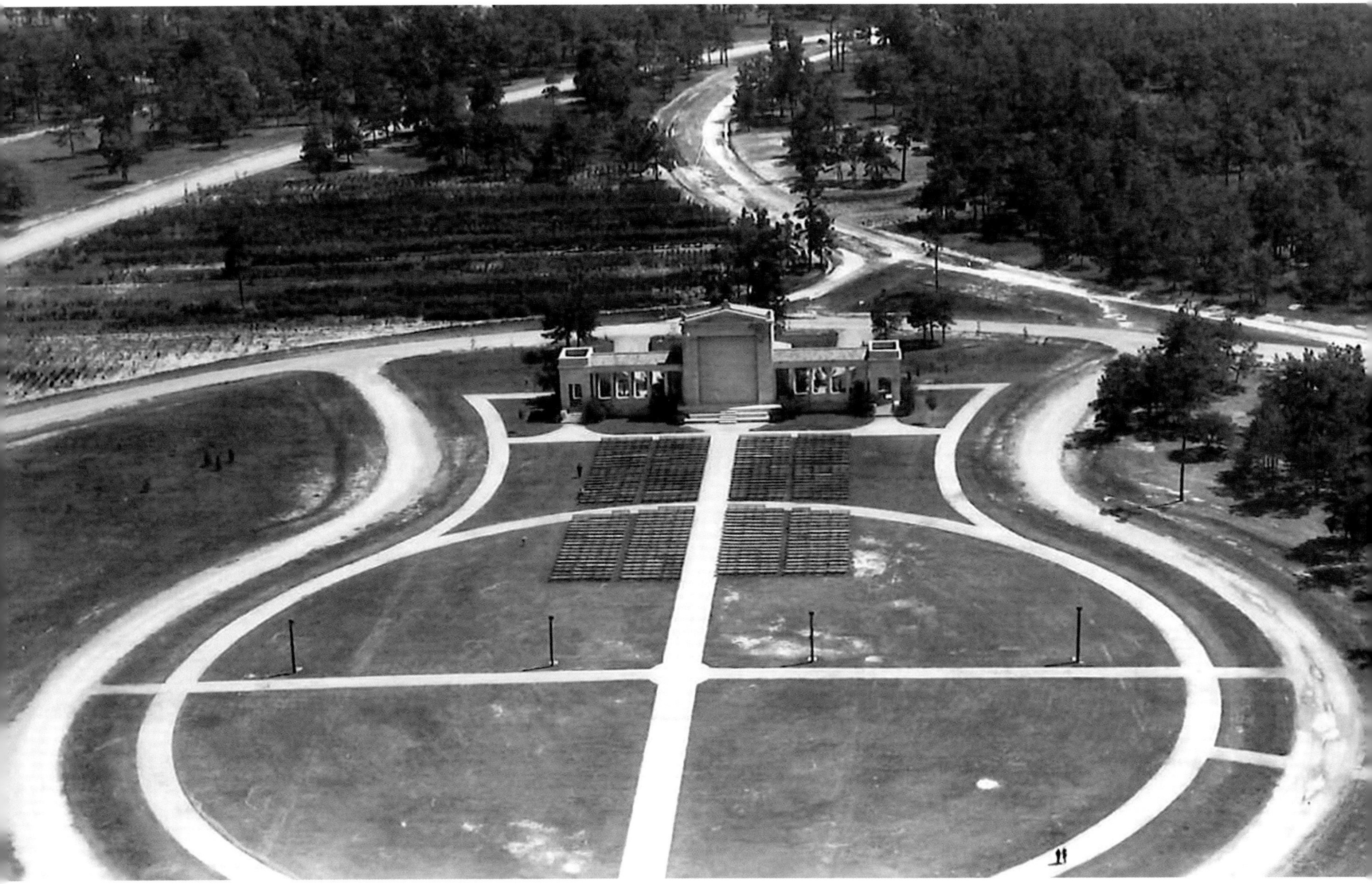

Miller Memorial Theatre (1923, William Ward Watkin), aerial view, c. 1926, shows the classically designed proscenium and colonnade built of Indiana limestone, as well as bench seating, delineated footpaths around the theater, and outdoor lights. The cleared but unimproved carriage drives are shown as they existed in the mid-1920s, meandering through dense pine stands. Courtesy State Historical Society of Missouri, Research Center-Kansas City.

Hermann Park neighborhood. He was definitely one of the noteworthy individuals who helped realize Hermann's and Kessler's dreams of building a beautiful, graceful precinct of which Hermann Park would be the hub.

Municipal Golf Course

During the planning of Miller Theatre in 1922, Clarence Brock laid out a new Automobile Tourist Camp for 150 cars "with water, electric lights, telephones, and other conveniences" a short distance from the Shelter House at the entrance to the park.[49] The site was likely where the Museum of Natural History and Centennial Gardens are today. But the camp was short-lived; it does not appear on any drawings of the park after 1929. Construction of an eighteen-hole golf course also began in 1922. Houston stockbroker and golfing enthusiast George V. Rotan and the engineer David M. Duller designed the Municipal Golf Course.[50] Located in the northernmost lobe of Kessler's plan, sixteen of the eighteen holes opened in July 1923 with a public dedication.[51] A cottage-like clubhouse with lockers, showers, and a golf

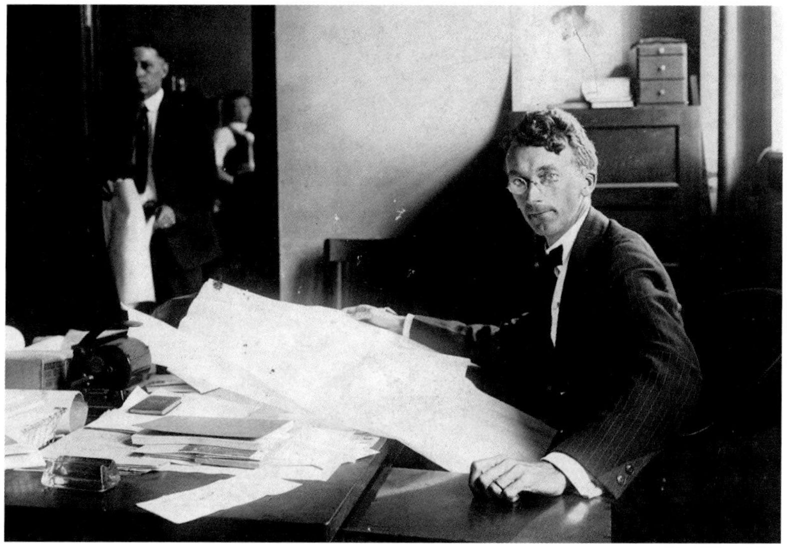

William Ward Watkin (1886–1952), first head of the architecture department at the Rice Institute, is pictured in his private architectural office in the Scanlan Building downtown, c. 1930. Watkin designed many notable buildings in the South End, including the first Miller Memorial Theatre and the Museum of Fine Arts. Courtesy Woodson Research Center, Fondren Library, Rice University.

shop was built with private donations. Greens fees were twenty-five cents, and the average number of daily players in the summer and fall of 1923 was two hundred.[52] One extraordinary feature of Houston's first public golf course was its grass greens; the majority of American golf courses at that time used sand. Today the golf course continues to be a popular park amenity, which delays any arguments for removing the course from Hermann Park in favor of more passive use of the park property.

A 1922 aerial view of the park shows Miller Theatre with an outdoor seating area in front, the golf course, but few other improvements other than the roadways. The photograph also shows Hermann Hospital under construction across from the Rice Institute; the future site of the Museum of Fine Arts below the sunken garden across Montrose Boulevard from Shadyside is also evident. The importance of the aggregate of a first-class residential enclave, a university, and an art museum across from Hermann Park cannot be overstated. Had Houston grown eastward, as some expected, and these important institutions and neighborhoods been built elsewhere, Hermann Park might not have received the community support to grow over the last century into the preeminence it enjoys today.

Kessler was still in the picture in 1922. In November of that year Mayor Holcombe assigned him a new project: to prepare plans for a permanent exposition site on 125 acres in the Sixth Ward along Buffalo Bayou that the city earlier had purchased for this purpose.[53] Kessler never completed these plans nor was this exposition plan realized. How-

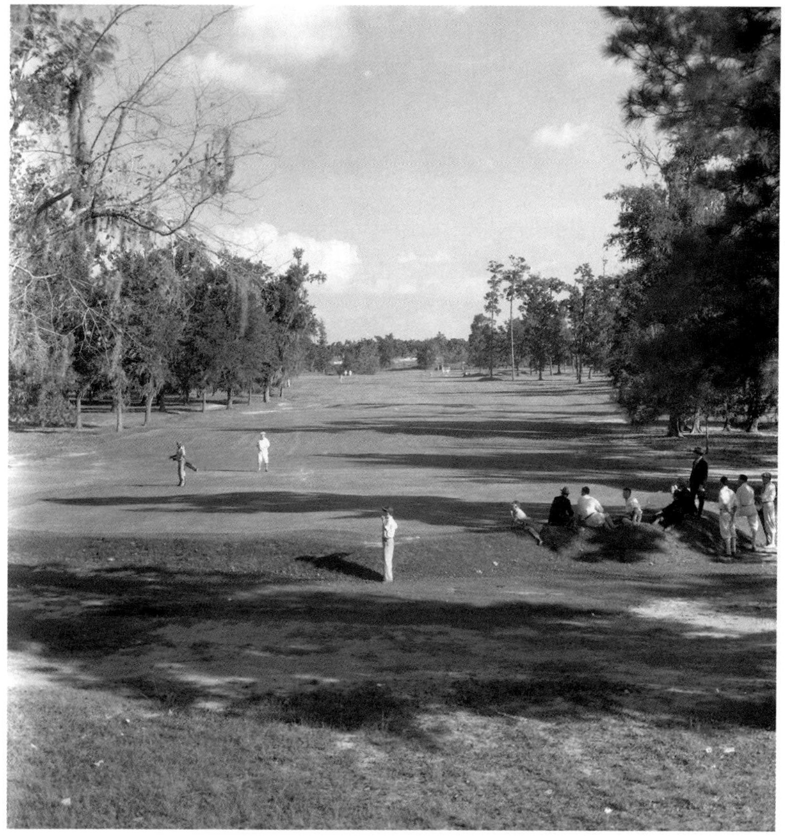

Municipal Golf Course, Hermann Park, c. 1923. The wide, straight fairways and small greens of the original course have been reconfigured with a more complex and challenging layout. Courtesy Houston Metropolitan Research Center, Houston Public Library (334-874).

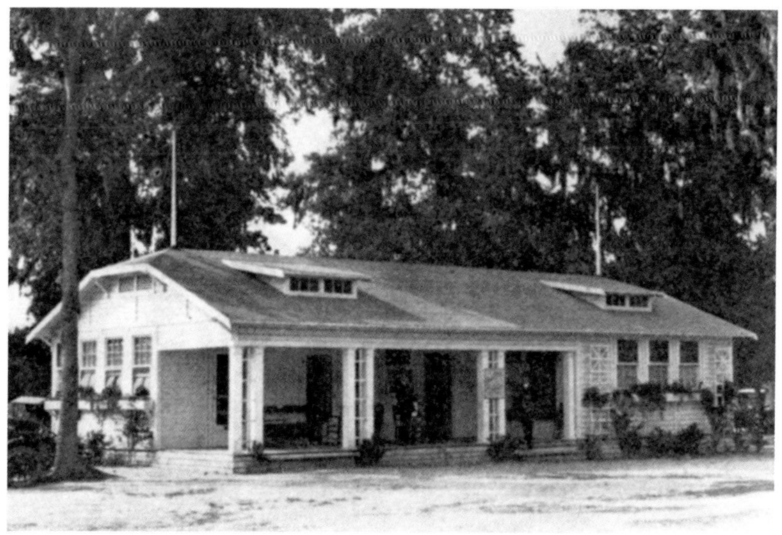

Hermann Park Golf Clubhouse, 1925. This, the first clubhouse in the park, was demolished in 1933 for a new, larger Spanish-style clubhouse built in 1933 on the same site. Source: *Illustrated City Book*, 1925. Courtesy Houston Metropolitan Research Center, Houston Public Library.

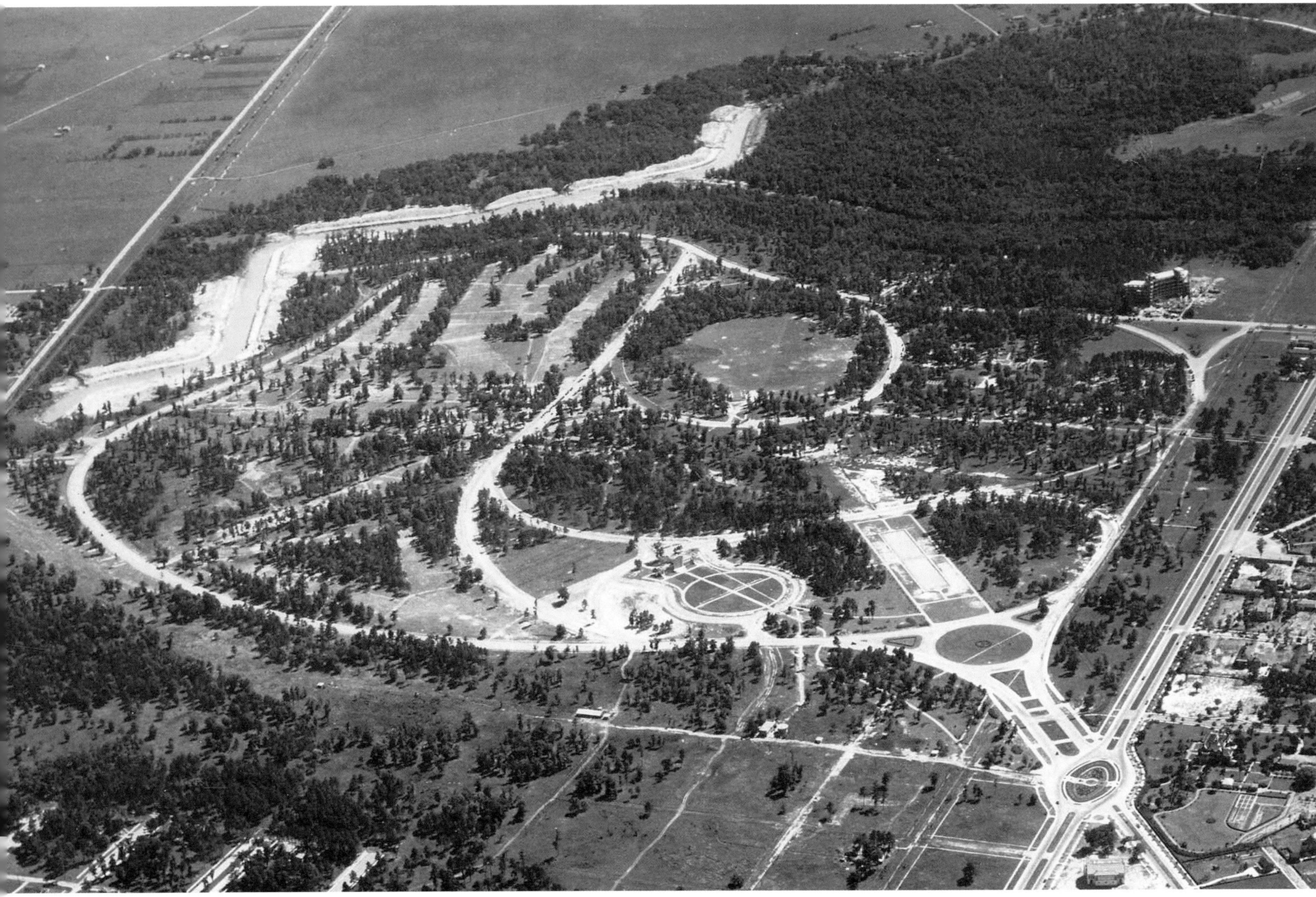

Hermann Park aerial view, 1922. This photograph shows the park before excavation of the lake, construction of the zoo, and other projects that were delayed until Hare & Hare began renewed work on the park in 1924. The dense wooded area at the top right is where the Texas Medical Center is today. Courtesy Houston Parks and Recreation Department.

ever, as this and other projects reveal, Houston was ready to resume its planning and parkland initiatives. Unfortunately, George Kessler died on March 20, 1923. He left seminal work in Houston that still resonates with planners and those working on Hermann Park improvements. When Kessler's offices were closed, virtually all his drawings were either destroyed or distributed to clients. The remaining papers were donated to the Missouri Historical Society in St. Louis. Today the Kessler Society of Kansas City champions his work.[54]

CHAPTER FOUR

Hare & Hare

1924–1951

The people of Houston and their officials will have to decide whether they are building a great city or merely a great population.[1]

—S. Herbert Hare, 1929

The Kansas City landscape architecture firm Hare & Hare inherited most of George Kessler's clients. The senior partner, Sidney J. Hare (1860–1938), knew and admired Kessler, for whom he had worked in the Kansas City engineer's office between 1881 and 1886. Sid Hare had no formal training, but as a high school student he studied horticulture, surveying, and geology, which qualified him to work for the city engineer as a surveyor, draftsman, and photographer. Hare was inspired by Kessler to pursue landscape design as a profession. In 1896 Sid Hare resigned his city job and accepted a position as the superintendent of Forest Hill Cemetery. The following year at the Association of American Cemetery Superintendents convention in Cleveland, he established himself as an authority on cemetery design, and in 1901 he delivered a paper on the cemetery as botanical garden, bird sanctuary, and arboretum. In his five years at Forest Hill, Hare assembled one of the most comprehensive collections of trees and shrubs in the Midwest. In 1902 Sidney J. Hare established a private practice in landscape architecture with the specialty of cemetery design.[2]

Sid Hare's son, S. Herbert Hare (1888–1960), followed in his father's footsteps but received the academic training necessary to put the family firm in the forefront of the new profession of landscape architecture. Herbert Hare attended Harvard's School of Architecture in 1908 where he, like Arthur Comey (who graduated one year before Herbert Hare's matriculation), studied under Frederick Law Olmsted, Jr. Hare did not complete his Master's Degree but returned to Kansas City in 1910 to enter his father's firm, which then became Hare & Hare. Throughout his career Herbert Hare was actively involved with the profession, publishing and lecturing on landscape planning and design. He was a fellow of both the American Institute of Park Executives and the American Society of Landscape Architects and served as the director of the American Institute of Planners and vice president and president of the American Society of Landscape Architects.[3]

In Kansas City before Kessler's death, Hare & Hare worked with him on many projects, and when Kessler died, the two firms were collaborating on a plan for the new town of Longview, Washington, evidence that Hare & Hare had moved into city planning as an important aspect of its practice. The appointment of Hare & Hare to finish George Kessler's Kansas City commissions "was a measure of Kessler's respect and trust of the Hare and Hare firm."[4] Houston's Board of Park Commissioners and Planning Commission followed Kansas City's lead and hired Hare & Hare in 1923 to take up where Kessler had left off. Herbert Hare was put in charge of the Houston work, and from the beginning he paid careful attention to the plans envisioned by Comey and particularly Kessler for a citywide park system and its central component, Hermann Park.[5]

Zoological Gardens

Hare & Hare's first project in Hermann Park was the Zoological Gardens. In 1921 the City of Houston had begun to move its animals, including Earl the buffalo, from Sam Houston Park to Hermann Park. Hare & Hare's ink-on-linen "Plan for Zoological Garden in Hermann Park," dated 1924, called for the main entrance to the zoo to be on axis with Montrose Boulevard, the entry sequence, and the reflection pool in the central lobe of Kessler's plan. Even though Kessler's plan shows this section of the park as "athletic fields," Herbert Hare wrote in one report that Kessler stipulated this area for the zoo before he died in 1923.[6] The Hare & Hare plan called for a wide oval drive circumscribing the center of the zoo area with three outlying triangular "parks" for deer, bison, and a new golf clubhouse (which was not built there). Several footpath entries are shown on this plan, but the main entrance was intended for an area behind Kessler's "pavilion and refectory" at the lip of the Grand Basin. The entrance today lies in the same location, but it sits to the east and behind the Kipp Aquarium. Beyond the entrance, Hare & Hare planned a line of three rectangular reflection pools flanked by a double row of live oak trees. Beyond these allées a building for the Museum of Natural History was stipulated on the west and an aquarium on the east. This pedestrian concourse terminated at the lion house.

Most of the early zoo consisted of open-air exhibits set in an informal network of curvilinear paths. Hare & Hare obviously worked closely with zookeeper Hans Nagel (?–1941) to provide particular spaces for the animals already housed in the park and for those he hoped to acquire, and Herbert Hare designated these areas on his plan. Areas were specified for alligators, hogs, sea lions, goats and sheep, ruminants, camels, yaks, raccoons, opossums, pheasants, birds, bear dens, small mammals, ducks, and more. Inside the oval, Hare called out a few small service buildings, ponds, and cages. Outside of the oval, in addition to the deer and bison tracts, he laid out a pony track.

Although the Zoological Gardens opened on December 1, 1924, it is clear from a 1926 aerial photograph that the new zoo designed by Hare & Hare was incomplete. The photograph shows the double row of baby live oak trees and outlines of the rectangular reflection pools. The first four structures had been built at the four corners of the central portion of the zoo: the Bird House in the upper left; the Primate House, the zoo's first building, completed in 1925,[7] in the upper right; the enclosure for Hans (named for the zookeeper) and Nellie the elephants in the lower left; and a general animal shelter building with a fanciful gable in the lower right behind a large cylindrical cage built for circus-like animal shows.

The large building under construction at the center left of the aerial zoo photograph is the aviary. Completed in 1926, the "flying cage," as it was called, was the largest structure in the zoo. Although Hurricane Carla destroyed the aviary's wire superstructure in 1961, the concrete faux bois sculptures, designed by Dionicio Rodriguez (c. 1891–1955) remain.[8] These include a fountain, logs, ledges, and rock bordering a shallow pond. In 2005, based on the prominence of Rodriguez, a distinguished Mexican-American sculptor from San Antonio, the aviary at the Houston Zoo was listed on the National Register of Historic Places.[9] Rodriguez's dramatic tree sculpture in Hermann Park inspired a painting called *The Bird Haunt* by the Houston artist and teacher Ola McNeil Davidson (1884–1976). The painting was featured on the cover of *Civics for Houston* magazine in 1928.[10] This area that once housed a variety of bird life is now the flamingo habitat filled with pink Chilean flamingos and the surviving Rodriguez sculptures. After completion of the aviary the main entrance to the zoo was placed next to the aviary on the west, not on axis with Montrose as the Hare & Hare plan shows. Other deviations from the plan occurred as construction proceeded.

Hans Nagel had become the first zookeeper in 1922 in charge of forty animals, including a lion and several other animals purchased from a circus; initially they were all housed in a fenced section at the back of the Hermann Park in the area that Hare & Hare transformed into the Zoological Gardens.[11] Born in Germany and trained at the Hagenbeck Animal Company there, Nagel was a showman and brought a good deal of early publicity to Hermann Park. He trained his animals to perform in a circus setting and held shows on Sunday afternoons to the delight of both children and adults in a specially-built performance cage. He invited local journalists and photographers to document these performances as well as any other gathering at the zoo, focusing attention on Hermann Park and the needs of the zoo. In 1988 the Museum of Natural Science donated a large group of scrapbooks, correspondence, and clippings collected by Nagel to the Houston Metropolitan Research Center. Nagel's photographs and documents provide a detailed look at the zoo and its animals during the 1920s and 1930s.[12] It is clear from Nagel's photographs that he allowed zoo patrons to hold, pet, and even ride the animals in the early days. He also apparently lent out the elephants and camels for publicity campaigns of local businesses. By 1925 Nagel had acquired three hundred birds, one hundred reptiles, and four hundred other animals, including the Asian elephants Nellie and Hans (Nagel named for himself), and the zoo had expanded to fill thirty fenced acres.[13]

Nagel's flamboyance and fearlessness are evident in many stories that survive him. In November 1926 Nagel gave a zoo tour to park executives in Houston for a national convention. When the visitors entered the large enclosure of Houston's famous Bengal tiger, El Tex, he attacked North Dakotan Bert Wilson. Wilson had a trained white rat in his pocket whose tricks he planned to show off later that evening at a dinner party. Nagel drew his German Luger pistol and shot El Tex, killing the tiger and saving Wilson's life. Wilson's wounds required thirty-nine stitches, and El Tex was stuffed.[14] In another episode that captured national attention Nagel killed Black Diamond, who at nine tons was believed to be the

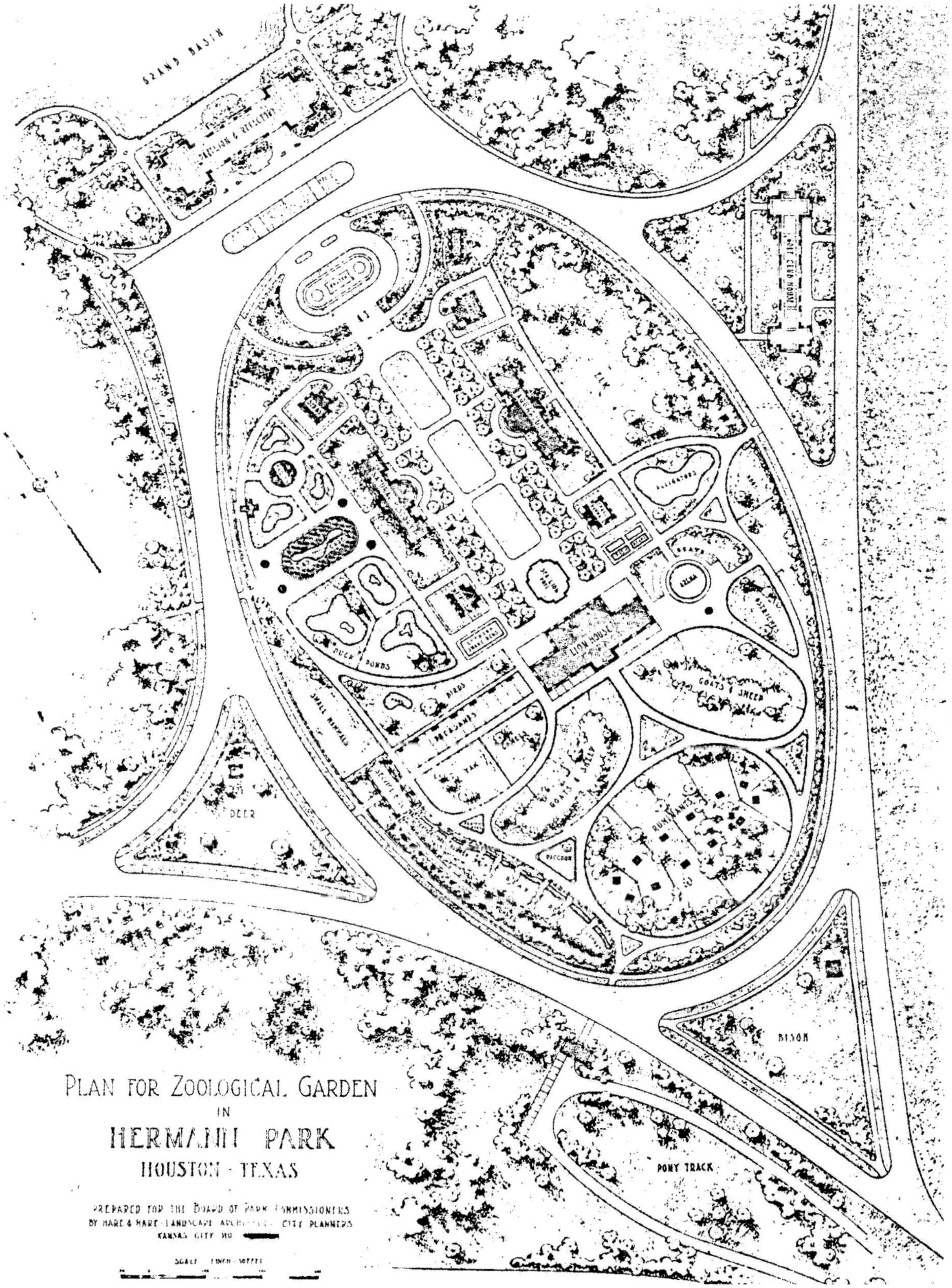

"Plan for Zoological Gardens" (Hare & Hare, 1924). This ink on linen drawing was generally followed as the zoo was constructed. Courtesy Houston Metropolitan Research Center, Houston Public Library (RGD 26).

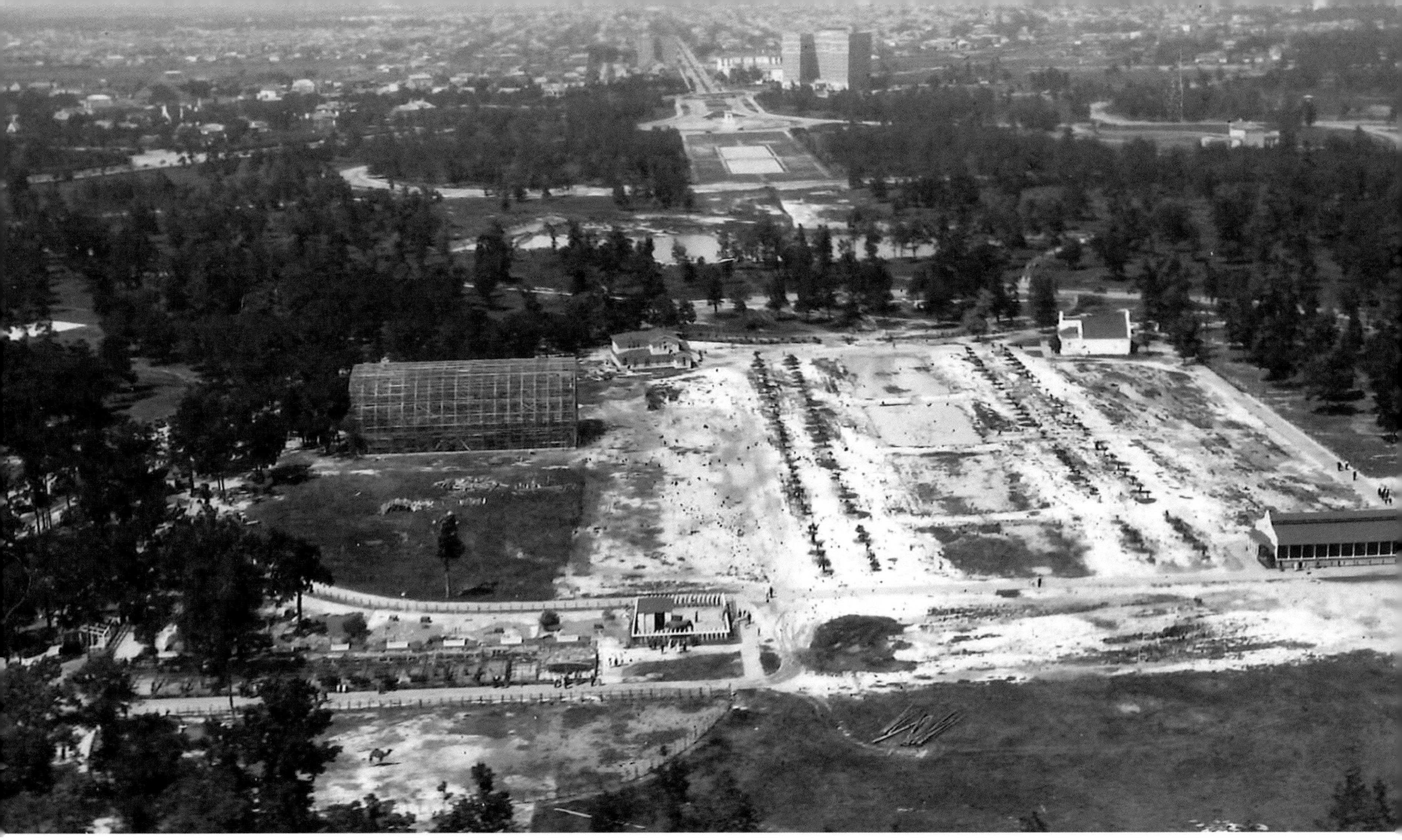

Zoological Gardens aerial view looking north, 1926, shows the great Aviary at center left, the first three zoo buildings, and the elephant enclosure at the four corners of the layout. Excavation for the three reflection pools is under way, and the double rows of live oak trees have been planted on either side of the pools to create a strong central axis. Courtesy State Historical Society of Missouri, Kansas City Research Center.

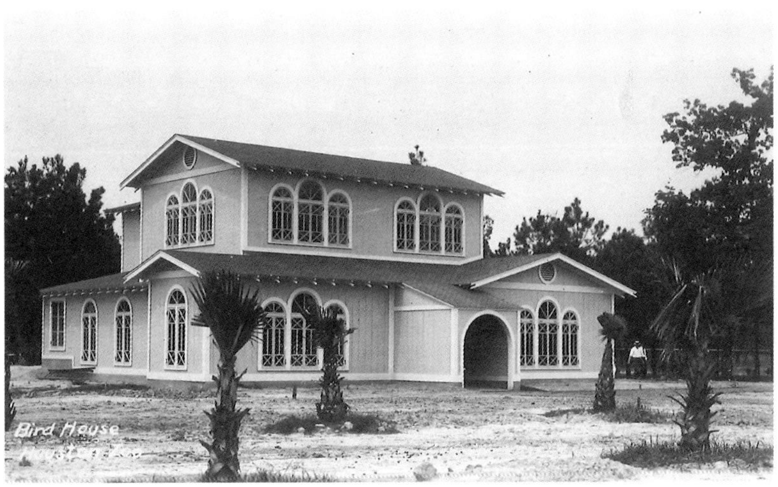

Bird House, c. 1925. The architect of this fanciful building is unknown. It stood in the northwest corner of the initial zoo layout where the Pelican Café, just inside the zoo's main entrance, is located today. Courtesy State Historical Society of Missouri, Kansas City Research Center.

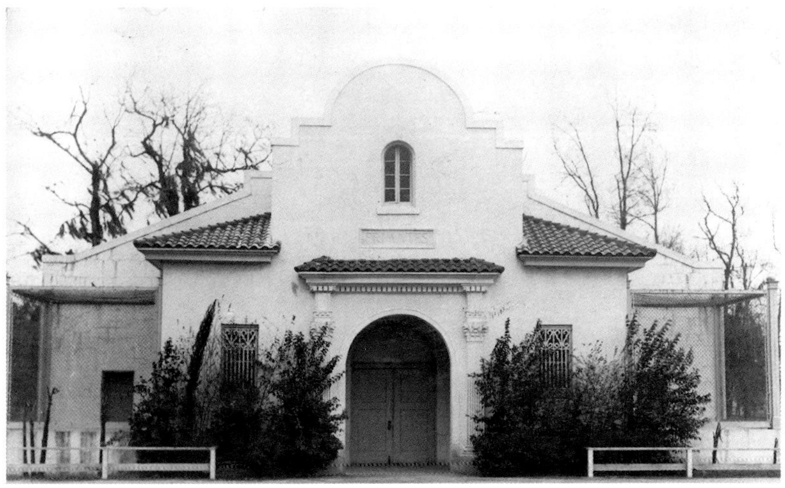

The Primate House, c. 1925, constructed with Spanish-style references emblematic of early structures in Hermann Park, stood at the northeast corner of the zoo approximately where the zoo gift shop is today. Courtesy Houston Metropolitan Research Center, Houston Public Library (332-226).

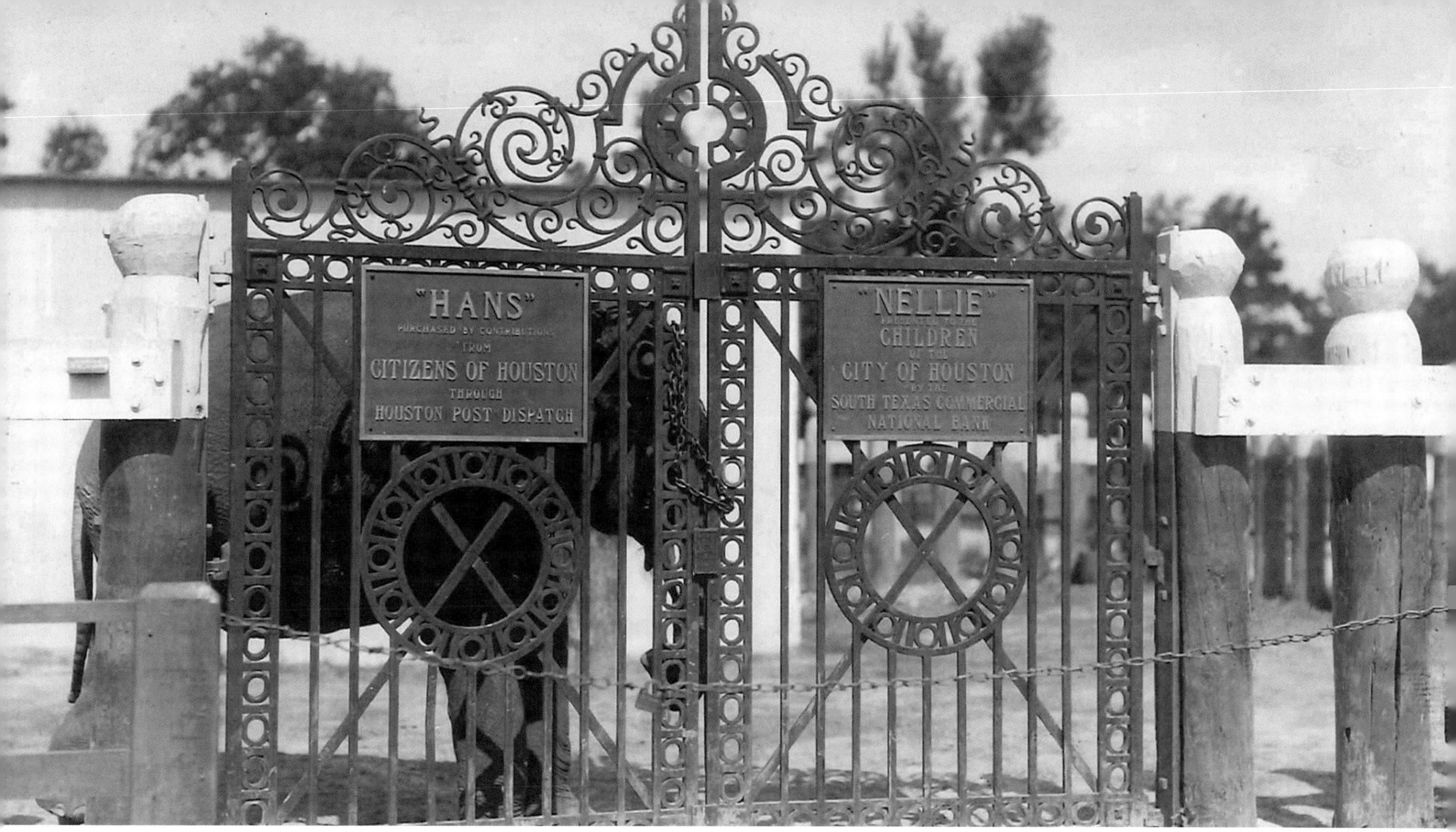

The elaborate gates of the elephant enclosure, c. 1925, which housed Nellie and Hans (named by the zookeeper for himself), the zoo's first elephants, which were purchased from a circus. This area today contains walkways and huge trees near the Cypress Circle Café. Courtesy State Historical Society of Missouri, Kansas City Research Center.

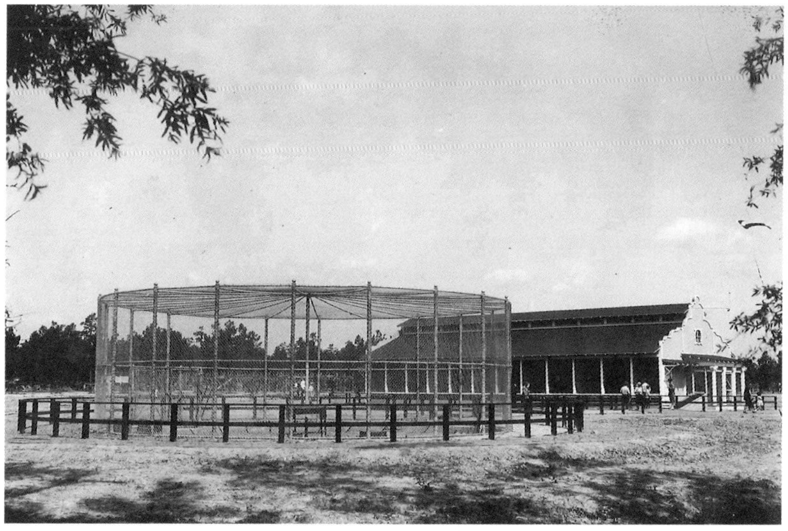

Zoo Performance Cage, c. 1930, where Hans Nagel held circus-like shows. A small animal house, located behind the cage, was the third original zoo building, which, like the other original buildings, has been demolished. This area is now the Wortham World of Primates. Courtesy State Historical Society of Missouri, Kansas City Research Center.

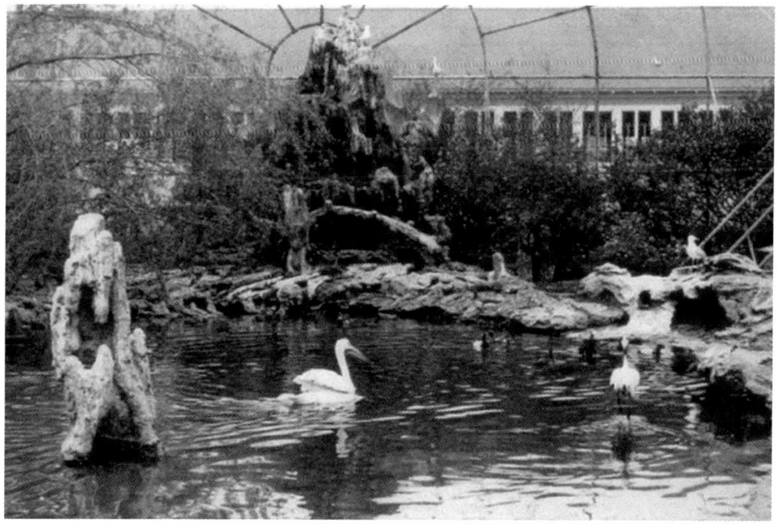

The Aviary, 1933, was a main attraction and landmark of the early zoo. The structure was destroyed in 1961, but the ponds and National Register designated simulated wood sculptures by Dionicio Rodriguez (c. 1891–1955) remain as part of the flamingo habitat. The large sculpture in the center inspired the painting by O. L. Davidson. Source: *Houston Chronicle*, April 1933.

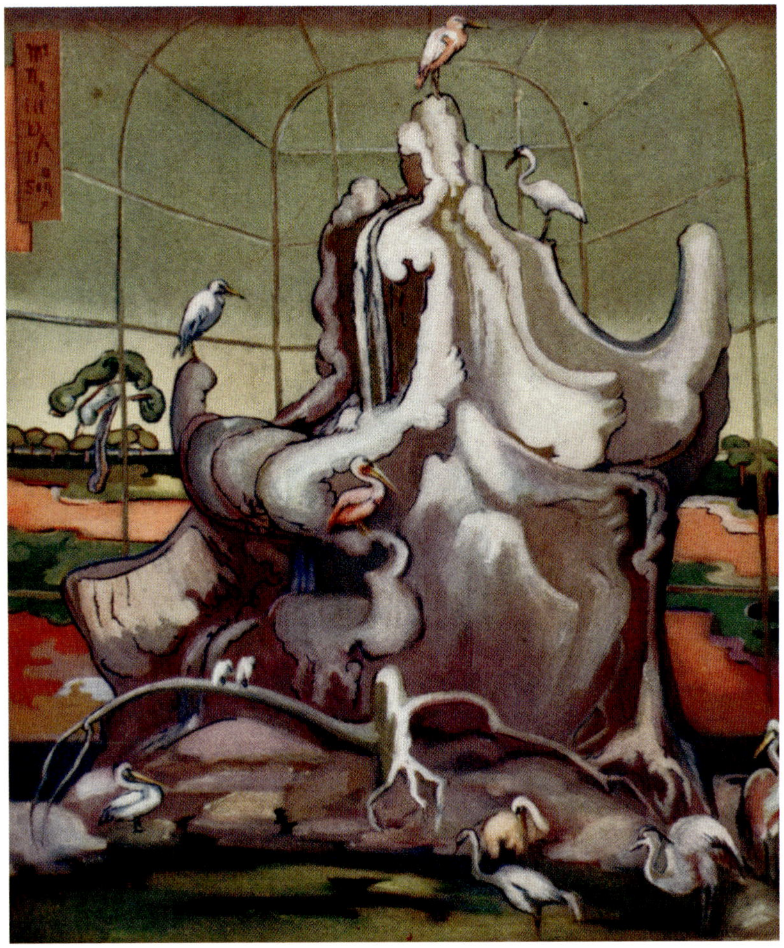

The Bird Haunt, c. 1928, by Houston artist Ola McNeil Davidson (1884–1976) was inspired by the largest Rodriquez *faux bois* sculpture in the Aviary. Source: *Civics for Houston* 1:6, 1928 (cover). Courtesy Houston Metropolitan Research Center, Houston Public Library.

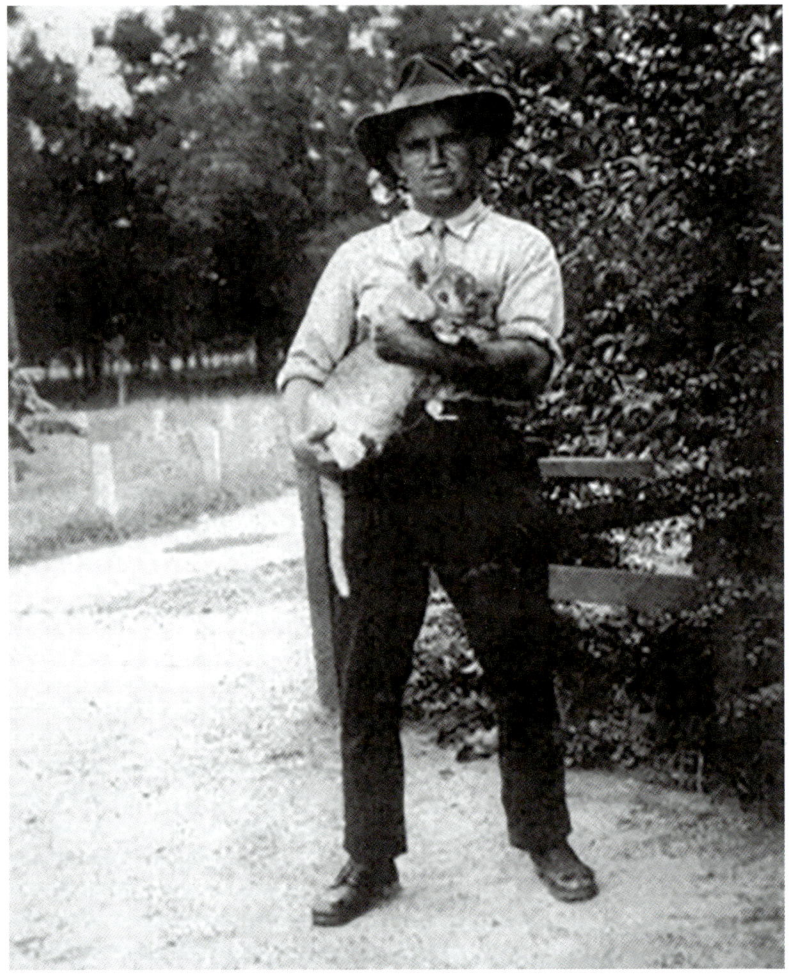

Hans Nagel (?–1941), Houston's first zookeeper, holding a lion cub, c. 1930. Nagel, who was trained in a circus, was quite a personality and attracted a good deal of attention for the park through his antics. Courtesy Houston Zoo–Sloan Collection.

largest Indian elephant in captivity. Owned by the Al Barnes Circus, the elephant went on a rampage and killed Eva Donohoo, who stepped out of the crowd watching the circus parade in Corsicana, Texas. She was not his first victim.[15] When the decision to put him down was made, Hans Nagel and four other sharpshooters were called in. After over 150 shots, Nagel was credited with the one that finally killed him. Black Diamond's mounted head became a fixture in the Houston Museum of Natural History until the 1970s, and Nagel retained one of his feet, which was used as a pedestal for a bust of Nagel created by Adrian R. Hines.[16]

Nagel's Luger, which he always wore in a holster by his side, and his aggressive personality finally got him killed. On the evening of November 17, 1941, Nagel was confronted by police officer Harold M. Warren when he, Warren, noticed someone (Nagel) in the woods behind a tree watching some teenagers who sat talking in a car on a dirt road that lead from Outer Belt Road to Brays Bayou near the golf course in Hermann Park. Warren had worked patrolling the park for three years and had full authority to question suspicious activity there. When Warren asked Nagel what he was doing, he was told to mind his own business. Warren got out of his police car and suggested that they go down to the station to see whose business it was to police the park. When Warren reached for Nagel's arm to handcuff him, Nagel pulled back and attempted to draw his gun. The witnesses corroborated Warren's statement that he fired on Nagel in self-defense. The celebrated Hermann Park personality was shot six times and lay dead in the dirt dressed in his usual costume of a tan safari suit and pith helmet.[17]

But before his death, Hans Nagel was instrumental in building a zoo for Houston. In 1927 a one-story building for the Museum of Natural History opened. An aerial view of the zoo shows the museum in front of the elephant enclosure and the extent of development in the early

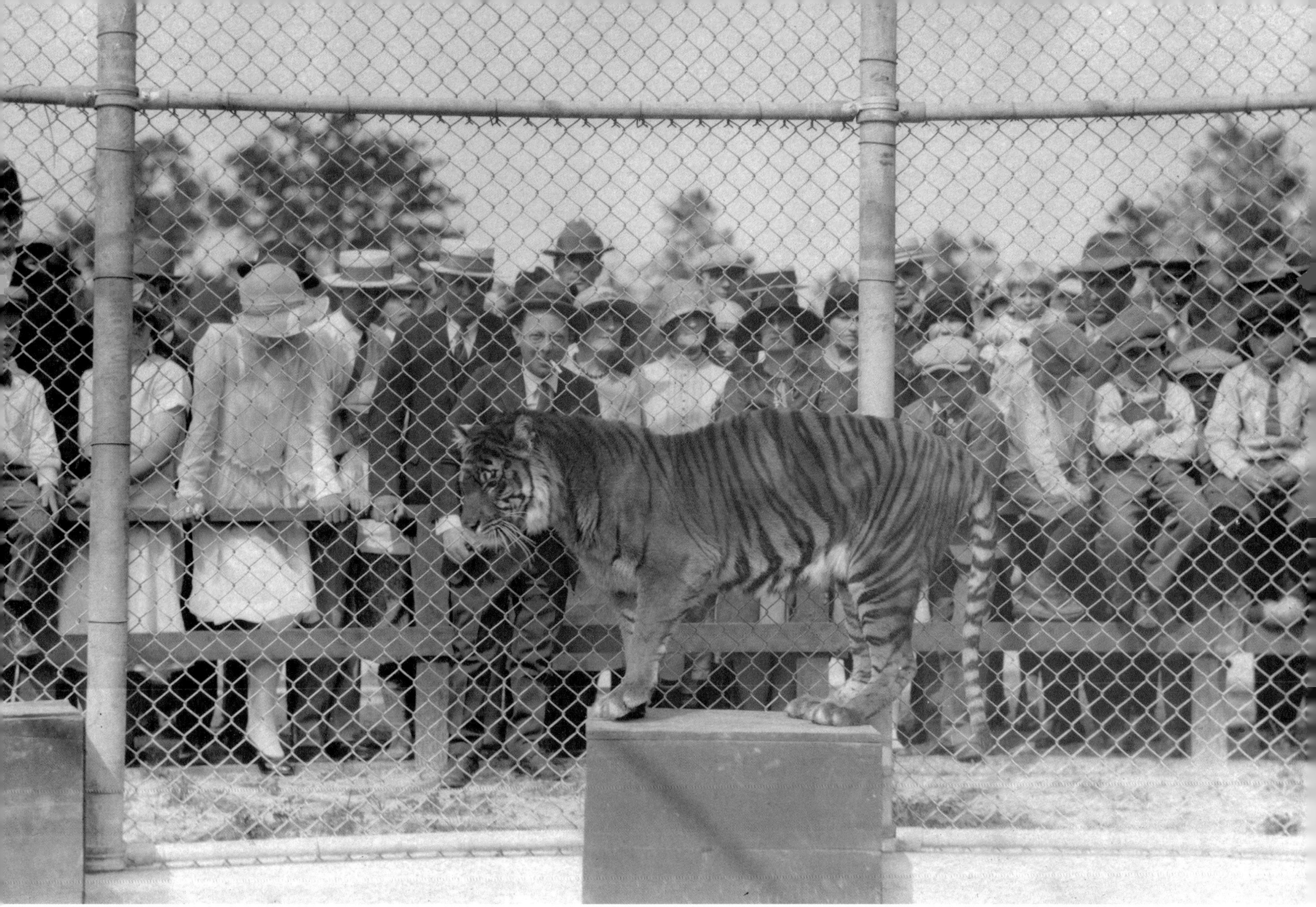

Crowds gathered outside of the show cage to watch one of Hans Nagel's Sunday circus performances featuring, in this instance, the zoo's tiger, c. 1930. Courtesy Houston Metropolitan Research Center, Houston Public Library (332-90).

1930s. Zoo buildings were constructed as the city could fund them. Small exhibitions were erected on either side of the central allée and three reflection pools. By 1938 a lion house, an elephant house, a deer and buffalo house, and the prominent sea lion pool at the entrance to the zoo were in place.

In 1942 a rather complete description of the Houston Zoological Gardens was published in the American Guide Series guidebook, *Houston, A History and Guide*, which indicates that considerable development had taken place.[18] This account describes the property as being shaded by evergreen, camphor, live oak, and Chinese tallow trees and notes that the entrance was across from the huge aviary from which the "zoo is bisected by a central panel, bordered with palms and camphor trees" running the width of the oval. Double avenues for pedestrians, named Pelican Lane and Flamingo Walk (the pedestrian concourse under the live oak allées), "traverse the panel and give access to a system of radiating paths." This description goes on to enumerate the various enclosures, buildings, and cages that go around the periphery of the oval. The list of habitats differs from the animal sections outlined on the Hare & Hare plan. Housed were owls, squirrels, birds, boas, a python, monkeys, elk, deer, lions, tigers, leopards, jaguars, wolves, hyenas, raccoons, badgers, donkeys, elephants, a chimpanzee, and even a "hinny"—the zoo-bred offspring of a Shetland stallion and a donkey. Peacocks, storks, geese, pheasants, and many native birds wandered the paths, and a "nationally-known" collection of albino animals was a popular feature of the Houston Zoo at this time.

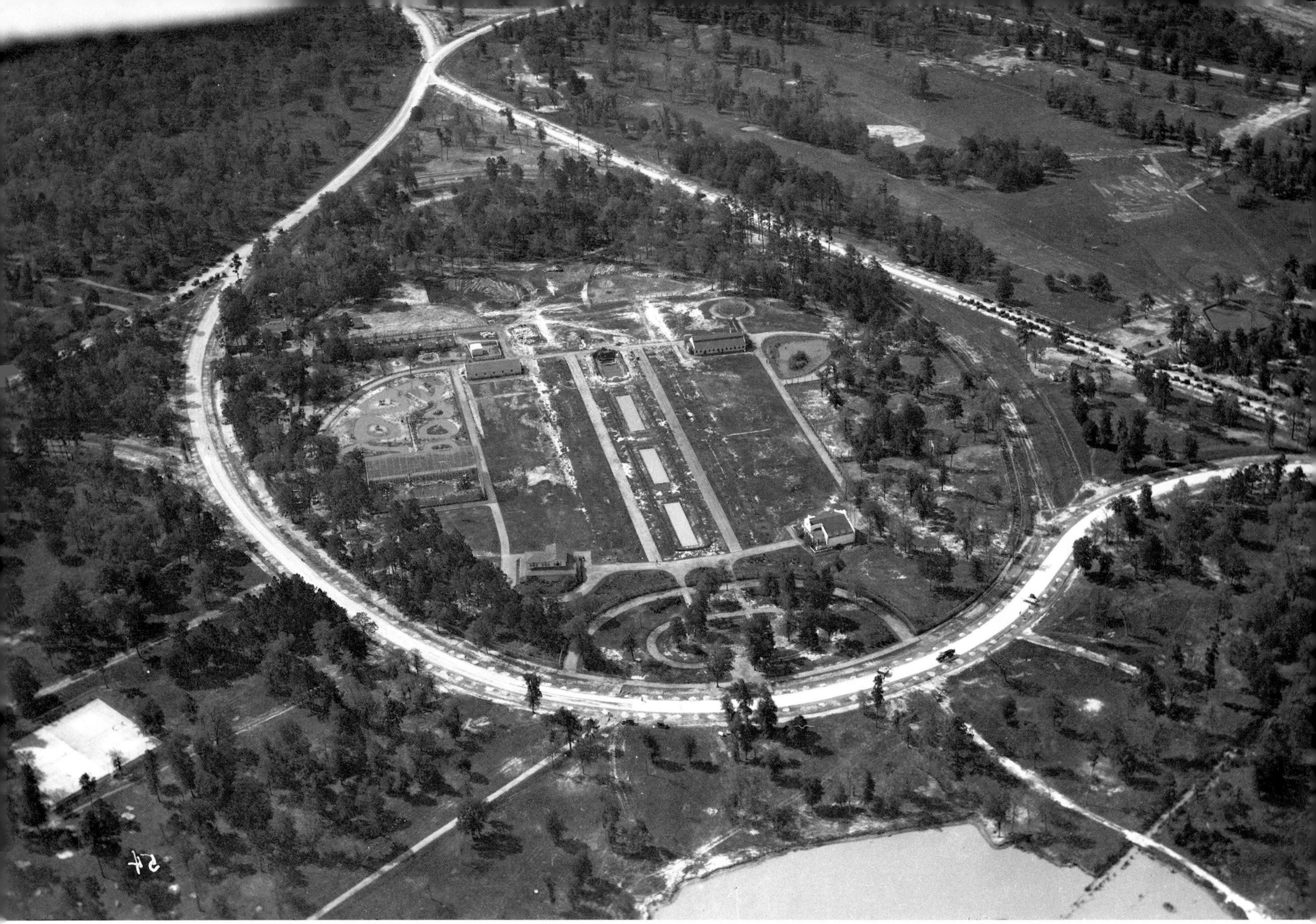

Zoological Gardens aerial view, c. 1933, showing development of the zoo grounds, including the new Museum of Natural Science completed in 1929 and opened in 1930 (in front of the elephant enclosure at lower left). Courtesy Houston Metropolitan Research Center, Houston Public Library (334-765).

The Annual Report of the Parks and Recreation Department in 1944 noted that a new entrance (where the current entrance is) to the "Hermann Park Zoo" was opened in 1943, and extensive improvements were made to the buildings and grounds. It also reported that tile drainage had been installed and lighting improvements had been made.[19] But these improvements did little but delay the inevitable. By 1947 space for the over nine hundred specimens had run out, and facilities had depreciated to the extent that Mayor Holcombe called for a study to explore where a new, improved zoo should be built. Three locations were proposed, including the existing site in Hermann Park and a new site in Memorial Park. The study concluded, as did Herbert Hare and Mayor Holcombe, that the zoo should remain in Hermann Park but be expanded to forty-three acres.

A new zoo plan was prepared by Hare & Hare that, for the first time, included parking (for seven hundred cars) to either side of the new main entrance.[20] Improvements were projected to take several years and cost between $2 and $3 million dollars.[21] The first of the new buildings was the monkey house, which was sited at the terminus of the central axis of the zoo. It was designed by Irving R. Klein & Associates (1949, demolished c. 1997).[22] Klein went on to design several new buildings, notably the reptile and amphibian building (1960) and central concessions building at Duck Lake (1950, renovated 2007).

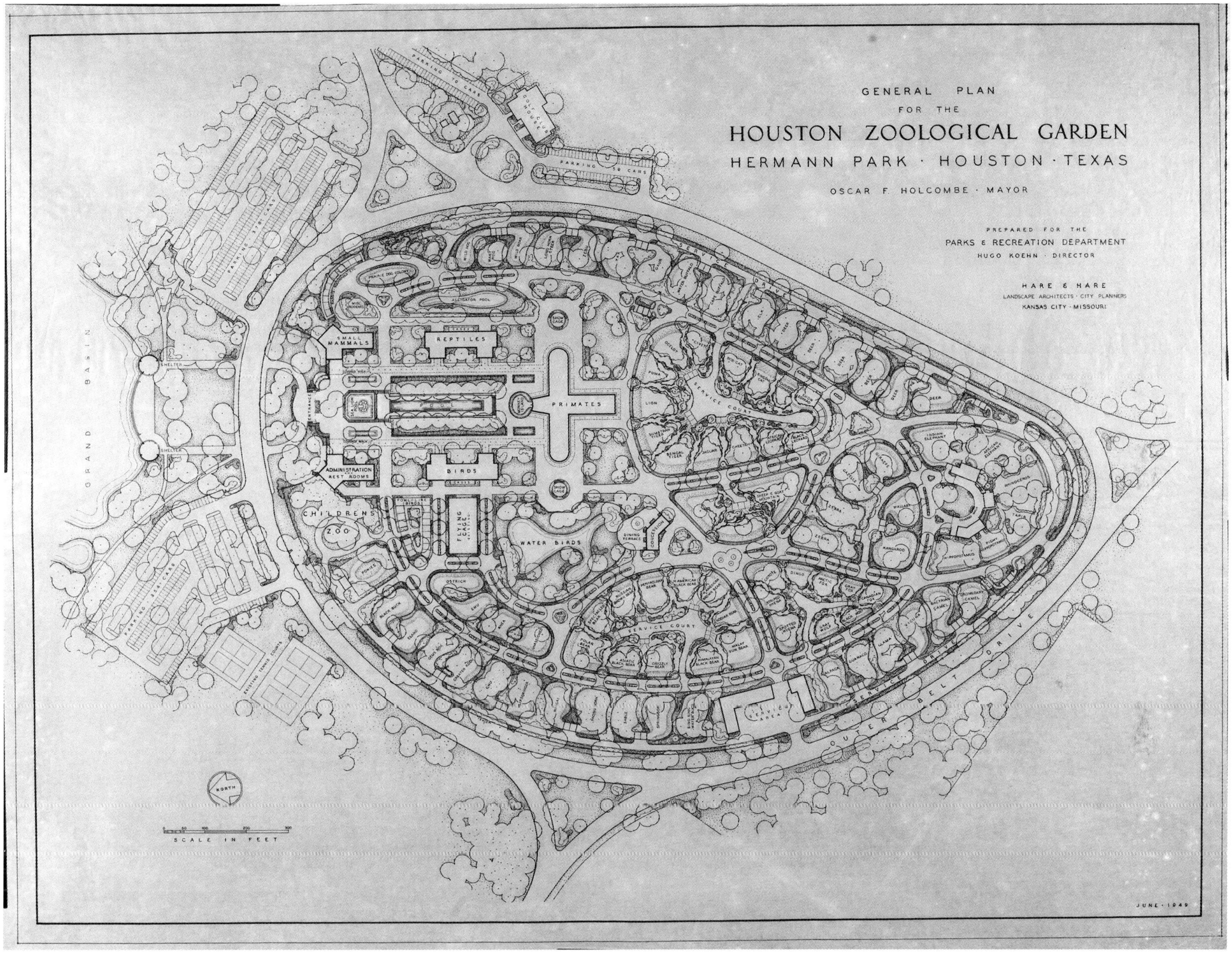

Houston Zoological Gardens Plan (1948, Hare & Hare). This new plan was created after a study that considered moving the zoo out of Hermann Park concluded that it should remain but be enlarged. Courtesy Houston Metropolitan Research Center, Houston Public Library (RGD 26).

Sam Houston Equestrian Statue

While plans and improvements for the zoo were under way, a significant addition occurred at the other end of Hermann Park. The Sam Houston Equestrian Monument, installed near the entrance to the park, is one of the most recognizable images of Hermann Park and one of Houston's most treasured icons. As early as 1917 the *Houston Chronicle* called for Houstonians to raise the money to erect a monument for the city's most famous hero and statesman, the man for whom the city was named.[23] The Women's City Club took up the challenge, raising most of the money to commission a statue and organizing a competition to choose the sculptor. They collected $40,000 in private donations, the State of Texas allocated $25,000, and the City of Houston donated $10,000 to reach the $75,000 needed for fabrication.[24] In 2012 dollars the cost would be almost one million dollars.

The competition was advertised in national magazines, calling on sculptors to submit drawings or models. Then an exhibition of entries was held in the Humble Building for three evenings in September 1923. A committee of prominent Houstonians judged the competition and

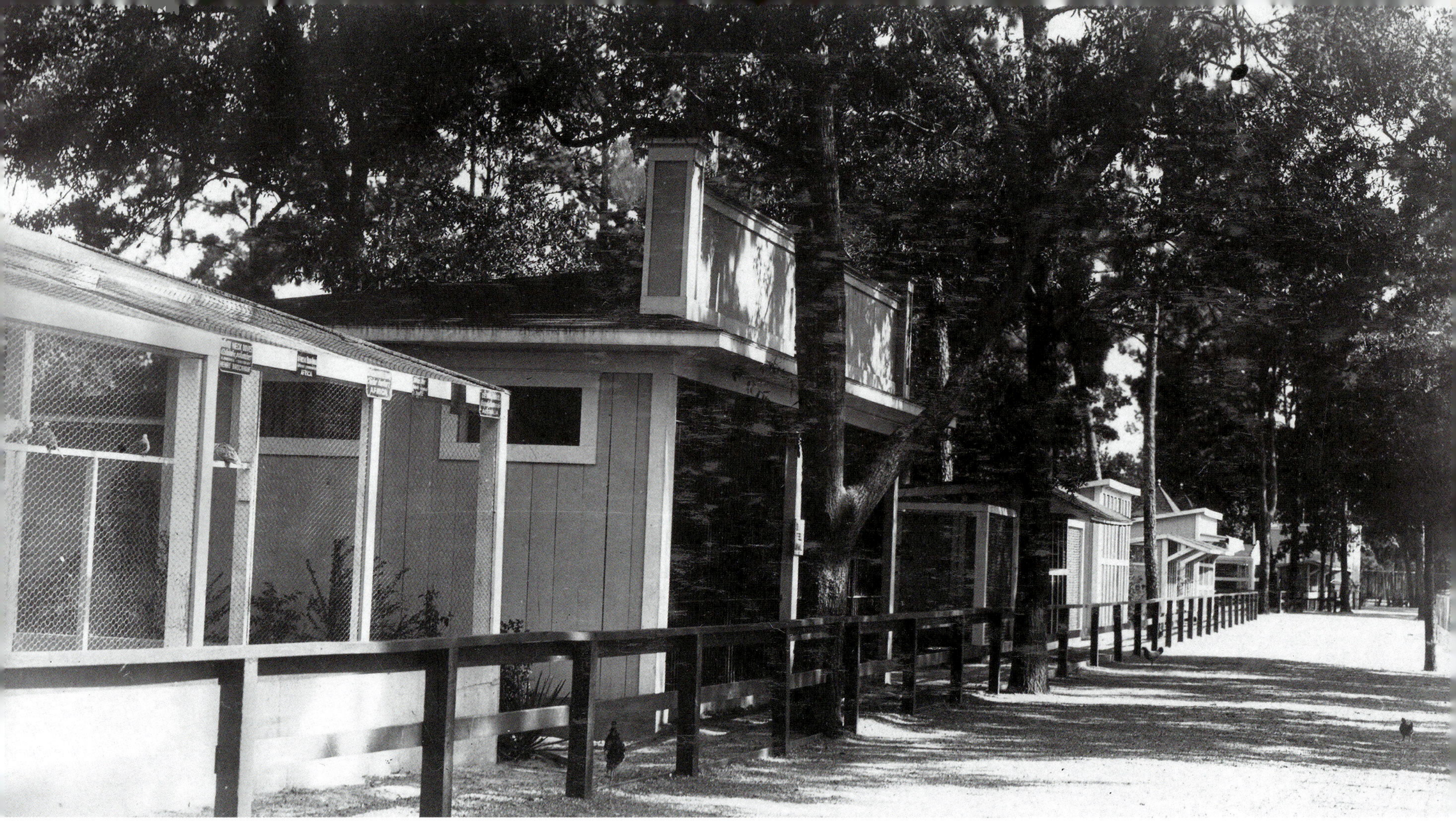

Zoological Gardens' animal cages along the concourse, c. 1940. Courtesy Houston Metropolitan Research Center, Houston Public Library (332-264).

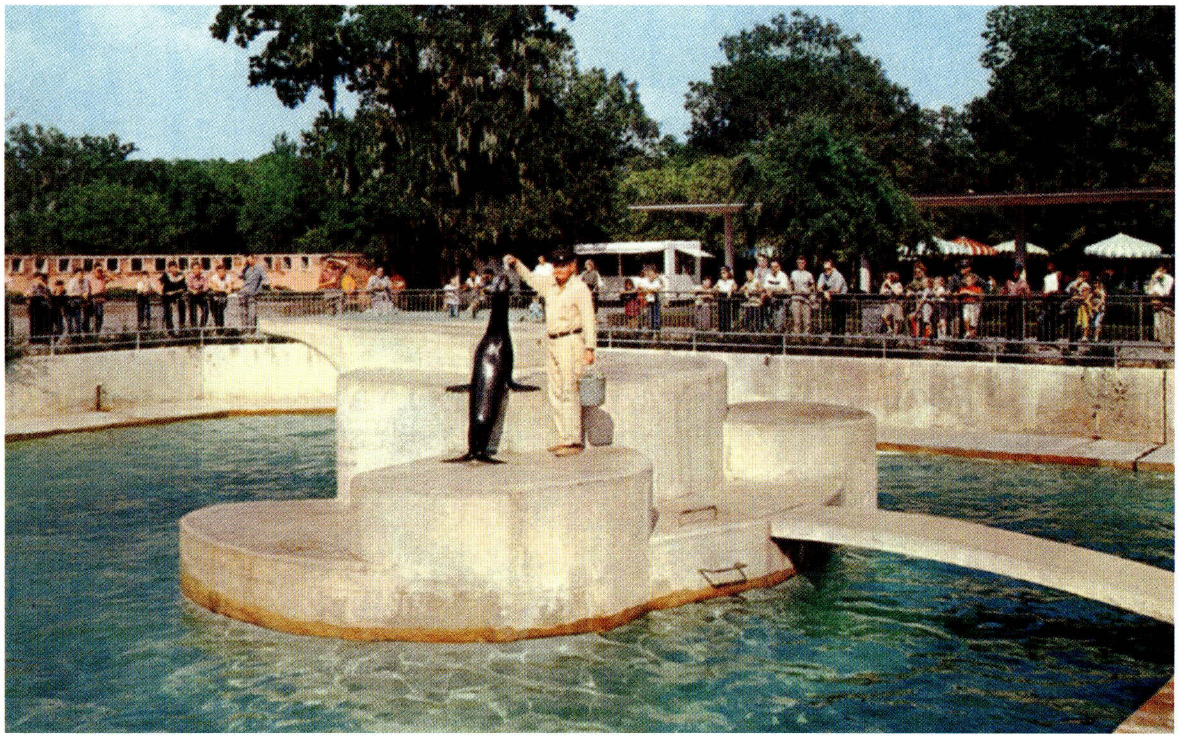

The Sea Lion Pool, 1950s, once provided a popular show at the entrance to the zoo. Courtesy private collection.

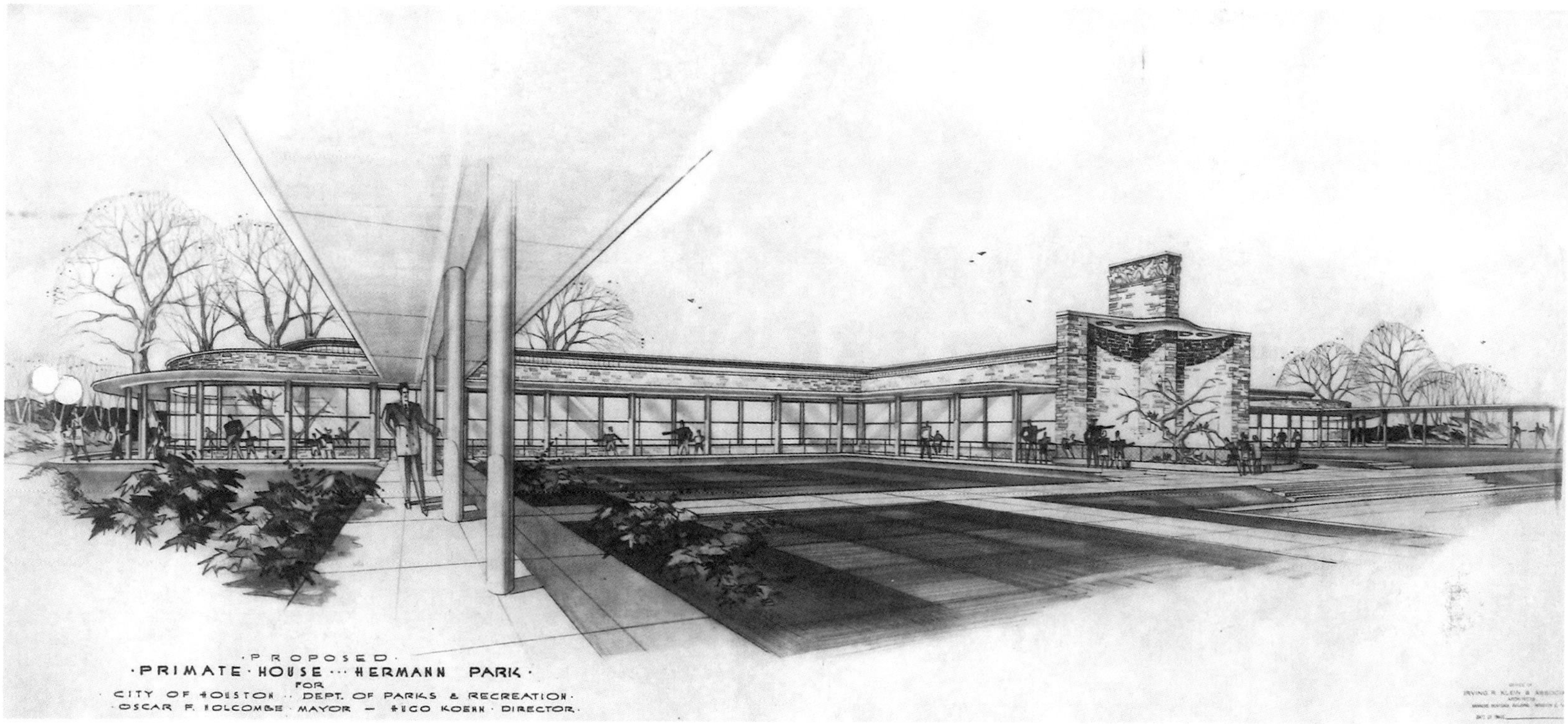

Primate House, familiarly known as the Monkey House (1949, Irving Klein). This modernistic structure was demolished in the late 1990s. Courtesy State Historical Society of Missouri, Kansas City Research Center.

awarded the commission to Enrico Filberto Cerracchio (1880–1956).[25] Cerracchio's proposal was based on a painting by Stephen Seymour Thomas (1868–1956) that had been commissioned for the Texas Building at the 1893 World's Colombian Exposition in Chicago.[26] Cerracchio had already established his reputation as a master sculptor. He was born in Naples, Italy, and studied at the Accademia di Belle Arti in Naples under the renowned sculptor Raffaele Belliazzi (1835–1917). Cerracchio immigrated to the United States in 1900 and moved to Houston that year after receiving medical advice that Texas would be helpful for his asthma. His studio was on the fourth floor of the Scanlan Building in Houston.[27] Cerracchio worked in both bronze and marble and became increasingly well known for his work throughout the United States. He eventually moved to New York, where he died in 1956.[28]

Mrs. John Miles (Lucille) Stewart went to New York to accept the statue in the name of the committee and to host a reception that was attended by over four hundred people. She wrote, "I saw both men and women with tears in their eyes."[29] Gen. Sam Houston (1793–1863), first president of the Republic of Texas and subsequently a US senator and state governor, embodied the myth of Texas. Three of his children were still alive in 1925, as were elderly Texans who remembered him. The forty-foot-high statue was placed in the monument circle at the entrance to Hermann Park, where Kessler in 1916 envisioned a monumental statue. The Sam Houston Monument was unveiled by Houston's great-granddaughter and dedicated in a speech by John Henry Kirby on August 16, 1925.[30]

The bronze sculpture depicts Houston sitting atop his striding horse, wearing nineteenth century military attire and a flowing cape. With his outstretched right arm, he points east toward the San Jacinto battleground where he defeated Santa Ana and the Mexican army in 1836, while his upper body and face are turned in the opposite direction as if giving orders. Motion and purpose are further indicated by the stance of Houston's horse with its front left and back right legs raised and detached from the base. The artist's signature (*E. Cerracchio SC 1924*) appears on the left, rear-vertical edge of the sculpture's base. The foundry mark (*Cast by Roman Bronze Works NY*) is on the right, rear-vertical edge.

The triumphal arch was fabricated by Frank Teich (1856–1939), a German-American sculptor who had supervised the stone carvers during construction of the state capitol in Austin (1885–1888).[31] Teich carved the Houston arch out of blocks of gray granite, which are centered on a matching granite pedestal surfaced with marble, creating a plaza under the arch. Steps descend from the plaza in both directions, which allow visitors to pass through the arch. "Sam Houston" is inscribed in relief on the pedestal's front and back surfaces. The names of

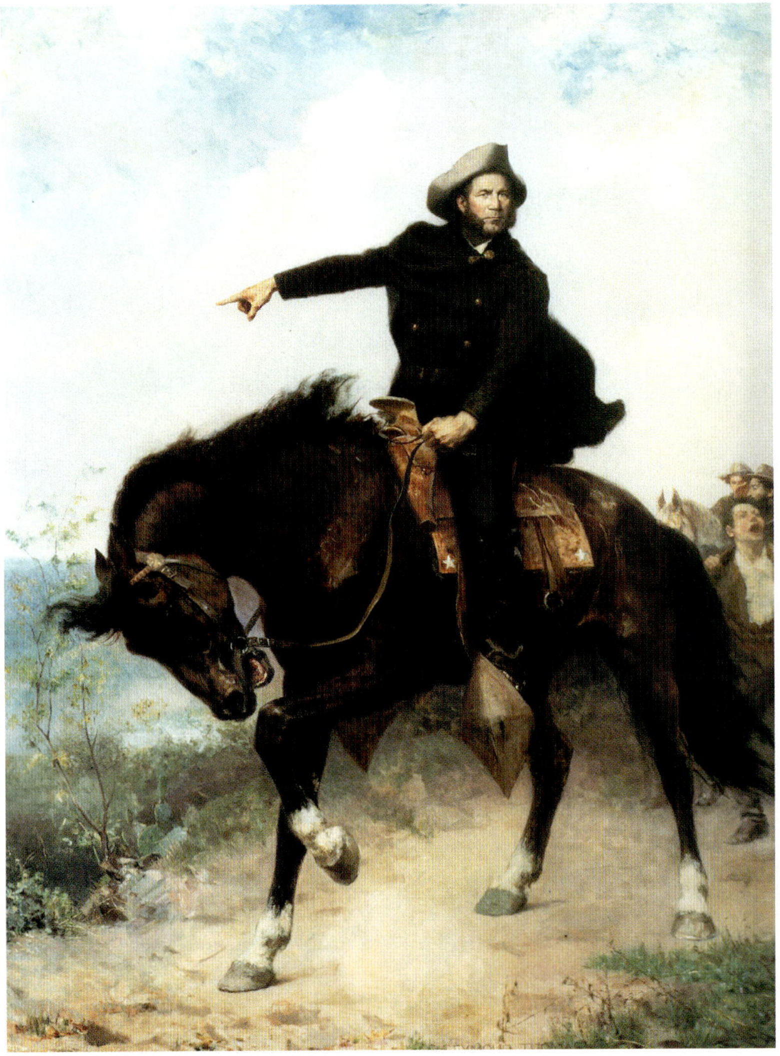

General Sam Houston at San Jacinto (1892, S. Seymour Thomas). This oil painting, commissioned for the Texas Building at the Chicago World's Fair in 1893, was the model for the Sam Houston Statue at the entrance to Hermann Park. Courtesy San Jacinto Museum of History.

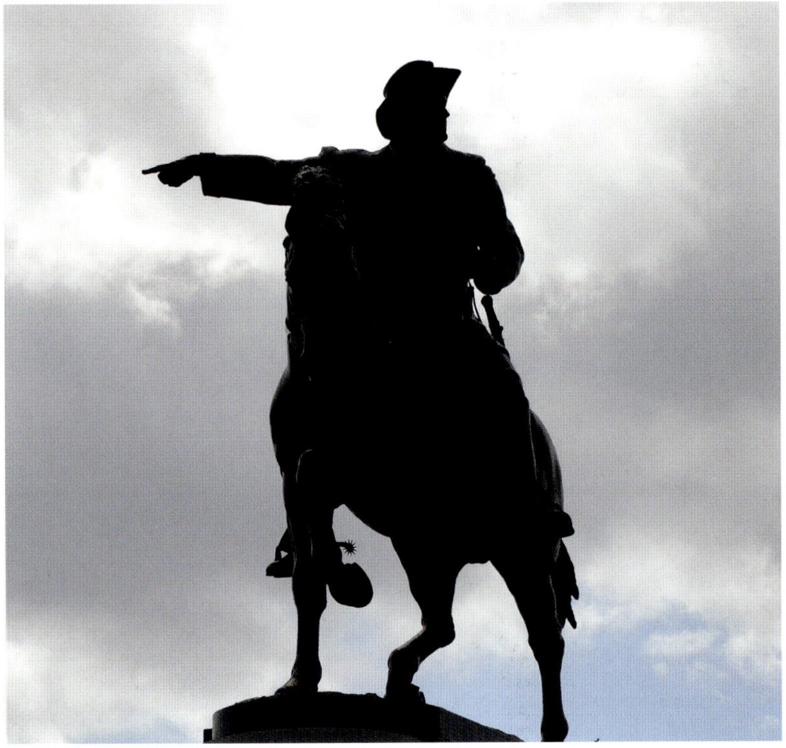

Sam Houston Equestrian Monument (1924, Enrico Cerracchio) is one of Houston's iconic landmarks. Photograph by B. S. Bradley.

the stone company (*Teich Monument Works*) and artist (*Enrico Cerracchio Sculptor*) are inscribed on the stair banister's left and right vertical edges. Architect Joseph W. Northrop Jr. designed the base.

Grand Basin

In Hermann Park, 1925 was a busy year, and construction in both the public and private sectors presaged a boom that lasted until the early 1930s, when the Great Depression slowed the local economy. During this period Houston experienced the construction of a number of imposing churches and schools as well as houses and commercial buildings that have become, like the Sam Houston Monument, Houston icons: notably the Niels Esperson Building (1927), Bayou Bend (1928), and the Gulf Building (1929). During this heightened period of activity, the two wings flanking the Museum of Fine Arts were completed in 1926.

In Hermann Park, between the Houston Zoo and the Sam Houston Monument, the Reflecting Pool was filled, and excavation for the Grand Basin was begun in 1925. However, the 13-acre lake called for in the Kessler Plan was reduced in size to just over 6 acres. The configuration of Hare & Hare's lake roughly conformed to that of Kessler, but the reduced scale narrowed Kessler's two large coves and curving canal to attenuated appendages. Fortunately, the width dimension was retained, leaving intact the vista from the entry sequence across the lake. Hare & Hare proposed to locate a new Museum of Natural Science at the terminus of this axis on the far side of the Grand Basin, where Kessler had drawn a structured pavilion. Even in its reduced size, the lake, as it was familiarly known, was a popular place for boating and fishing from a small pier.

Botanical Garden

The last major project in Hermann Park before 1930 was the design and installation of a Botanical Garden to the east of the entrance to the park where the Museum of Natural Science is today. The combined annual meeting of the American Institute of Park Executives (of which Clarence Brock was a director), the American Park Society, and the Society

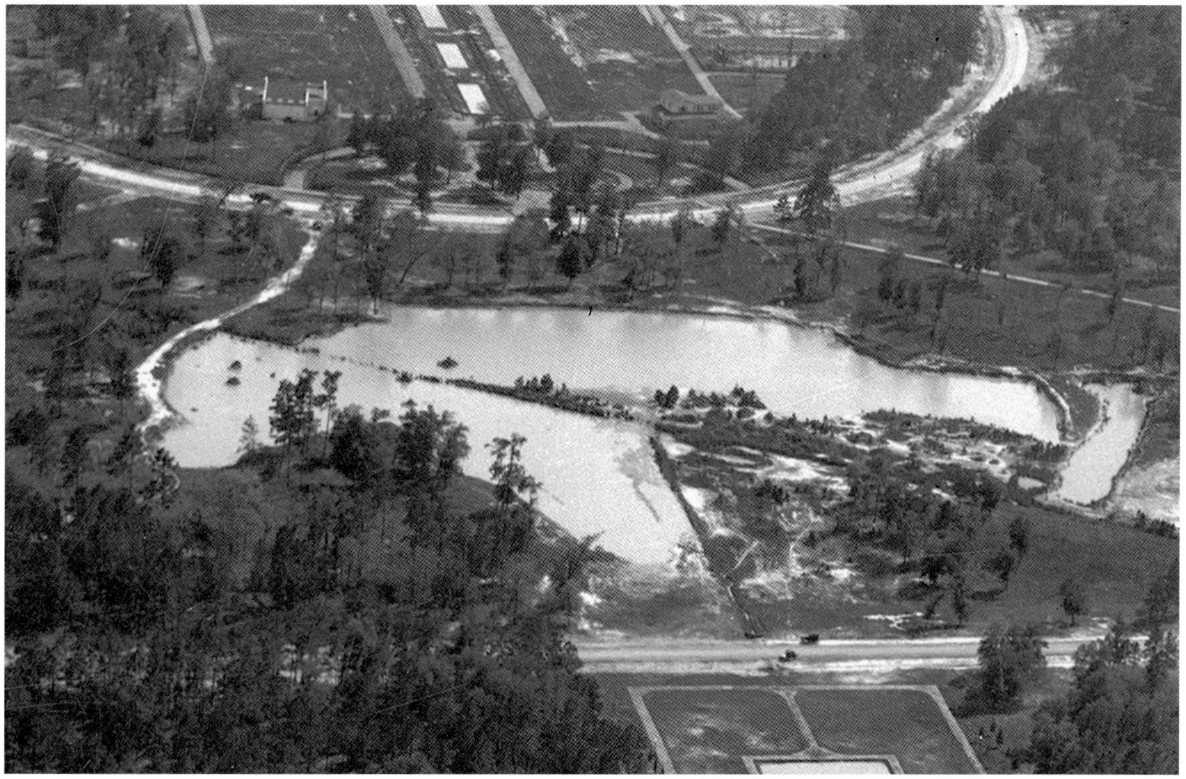

Grand Basin aerial view, 1928, looking south toward the zoo. Hermann Park's lake was developed at one-half the size envisioned by George Kessler's original plans. Courtesy Houston Metropolitan Research Center, Houston Public Library (334-764).

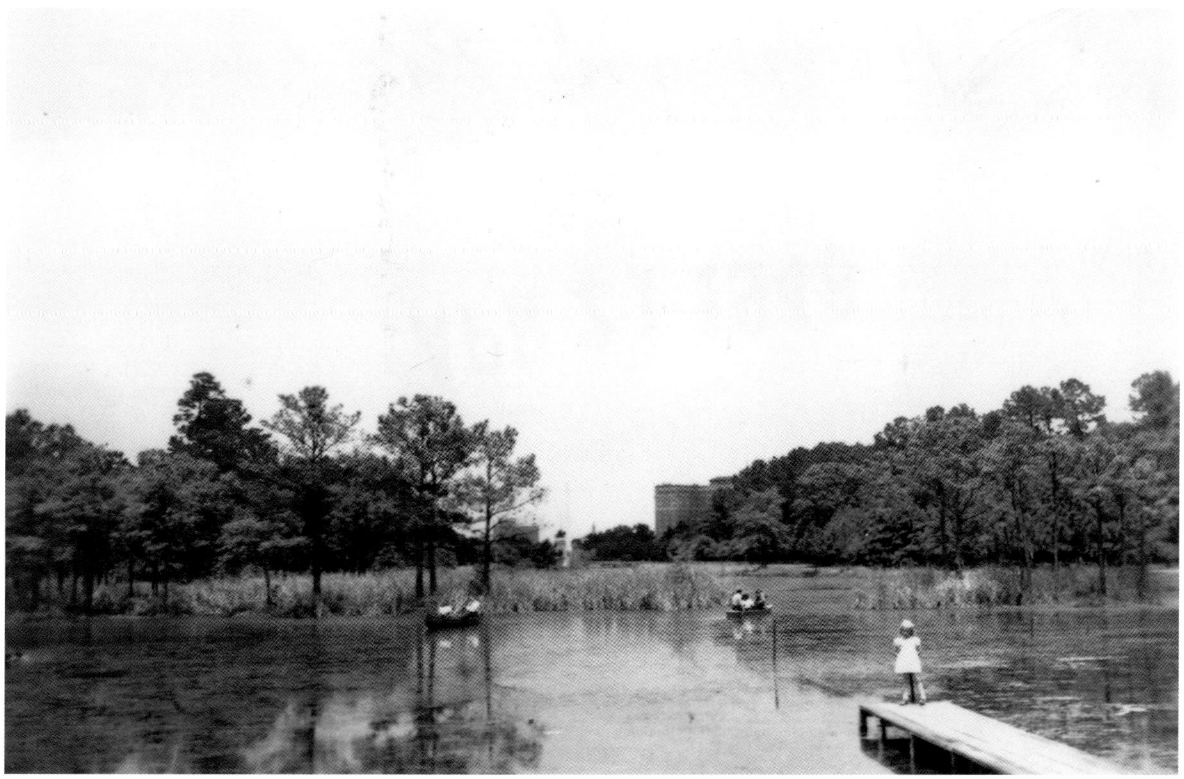

Grand Basin with boaters and fishing pier, c. 1930. Courtesy Houston Metropolitan Research Center, Houston Public Library (156-430).

of Zoological Gardens was held in Houston in 1926. This meeting provided the impetus for the establishment of the Botanical Garden. The *Houston Chronicle* published a long description of the proposed garden in January 1926. In an interview Brock noted that Texas "has a greater variety of wild flowers than any other site in the United States, and the semi-tropical climate of Houston is adapted to thousands of plants now grown in all parts of the world."[32] The 14-acre garden was to feature a large glass conservatory and small lakes. Members of the Garden Club of Houston, established in 1924, cooperated with the parks department to make the Botanical Garden a reality. Beyond providing a place for Houstonians to enjoy various flowering species, Brock emphasized the educational value: "It would be practical. . . . Each specimen of plant would be labeled with its Latin name so that naturalists and students in all parts of the world could come here and identify and study the garden."[33] Most of the plants were to come from the Biltmore Gardens nursery in North Carolina. Brock concluded by saying that the Hermann Park Botanical Garden would be "the first of its kind in the South."[34]

Implementation of the garden plan was slow—new plants were introduced as the Parks Department's budget allowed, and those already installed needed time to mature. A Hare & Hare drawing of the Botanical Garden, dated June 10, 1929, shows the central, formal section of the garden and indicates that development of this area of Hermann Park was an ongoing project. Instead of the planned glass conservatory, a garden center was eventually constructed in the 1940s.

By 1929 Hermann Park had begun to look like a real urban park, and Houston was growing into a significant American city. From a population of 44,633 in 1900, the 1920 census counted 138,276, then almost 300,000 in 1930, boosting Houston for the first time to the largest city in Texas and making it, after New Orleans, the second-largest city in the South. Another indication that Houston was booming in the 1920s was the number and value of building permits. In 1921 permits were issued for $10,398,295, in 1922 they totaled $13,390,469, and in 1923 the total value was over $19,000,000.[35] In the five years prior to the stock market crash in 1929, Houston experienced one of its greatest periods of development. Building permits climbed from $22,594,564 in 1924 to more than $40 million in 1929; bank clearings from $1,560,707,890 to more than two billion dollars; water connections from 25,559 to more than 50,000; telephone connections from 43,157 to almost 70,000; and electric light connections from less than 50,000 to almost 85,000.[36] The progressive Oscar F. Holcombe was mayor throughout the 1920s (1921–1929).

This economic and physical growth also brought problems, and in

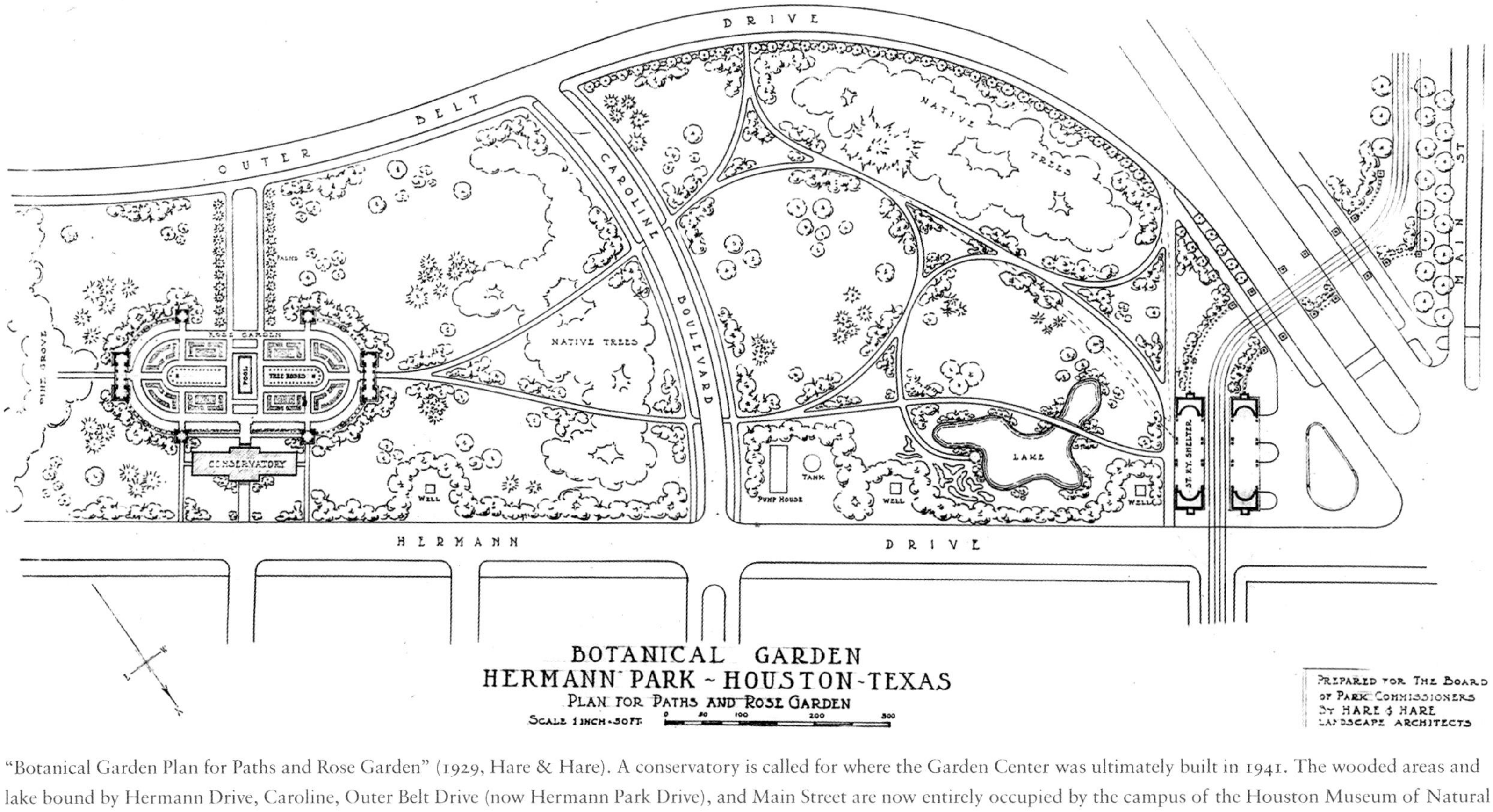

"Botanical Garden Plan for Paths and Rose Garden" (1929, Hare & Hare). A conservatory is called for where the Garden Center was ultimately built in 1941. The wooded areas and lake bound by Hermann Drive, Caroline, Outer Belt Drive (now Hermann Park Drive), and Main Street are now entirely occupied by the campus of the Houston Museum of Natural Science. Courtesy Houston Metropolitan Research Center, Houston Public Library (RGD 26).

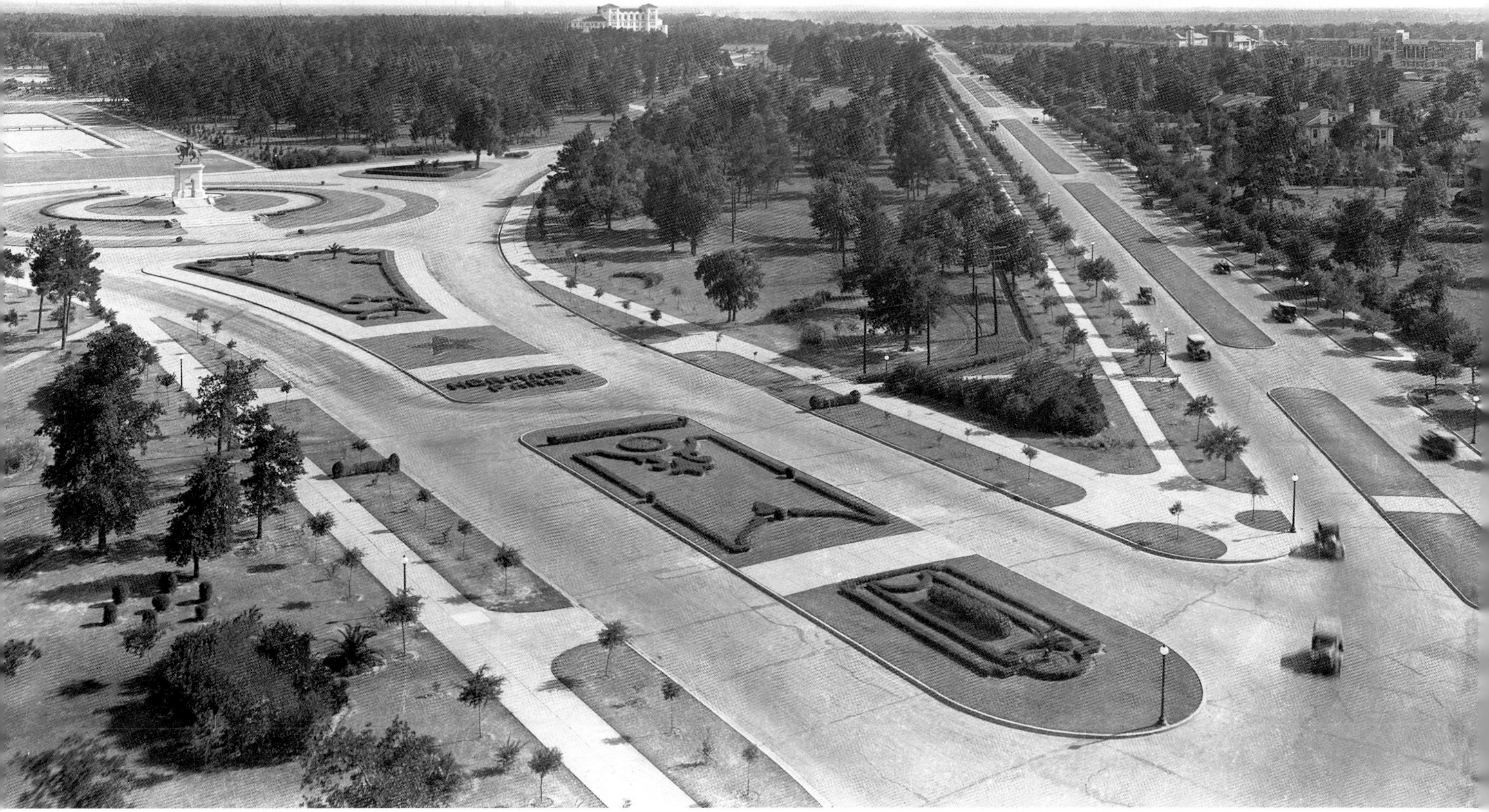

Grand Entrance aerial view, c. 1927, as it appeared after the Sam Houston Monument was placed in the monument circle. Today, this area is restored as the Grand Gateway to Hermann Park. Courtesy Houston Metropolitan Research Center, Houston Public Library (334-826).

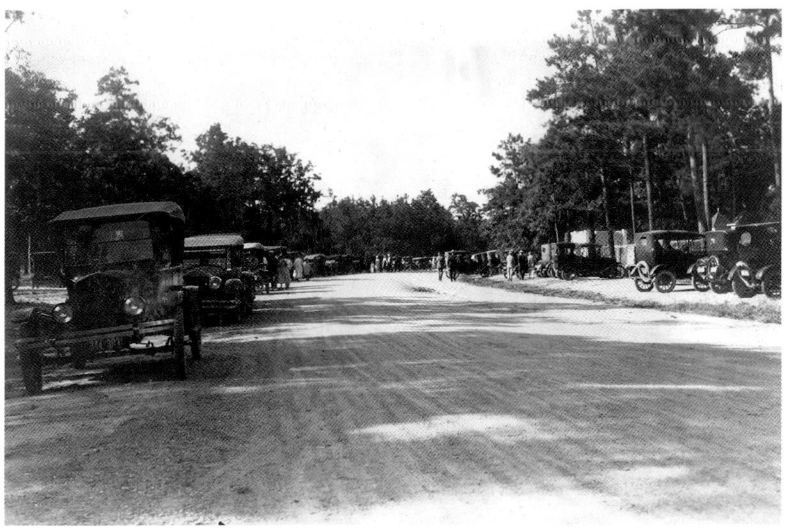

Traffic and parking were problems as early as the 1920s. No designated parking lots were in the park and cars were left anywhere and everywhere. Courtesy Houston Metropolitan Research Center, Houston Public Library (332-200).

Hermann Park these were particularly manifested by the traffic caused by the rise in automobile ownership in Houston. The leisurely pleasure drives through the park anticipated by Kessler were replaced with reckless drivers and speeding cars. As a result the streets around the park and carriage drives within it were paved with shell in 1928, and later that year the wide, landscaped esplanades on Main Street north of the Sunken Garden were taken out to accommodate this increased traffic. That year buses were substituted for electric streetcars on the South End line; pulling up of the tracks was a plus for the city and the park.[37]

Hare & Hare Plan

Although Hare & Hare had been involved in the planning and landscaping of Hermann Park since 1923, they had focused on specific areas of the park. It was not until 1930 that the firm produced a new general plan for Hermann Park that both recorded improvements up to that date and proposed new ones. They were careful in the title block to note that the plan was "Based on Original Plan by George E. Kessler, St. Louis,

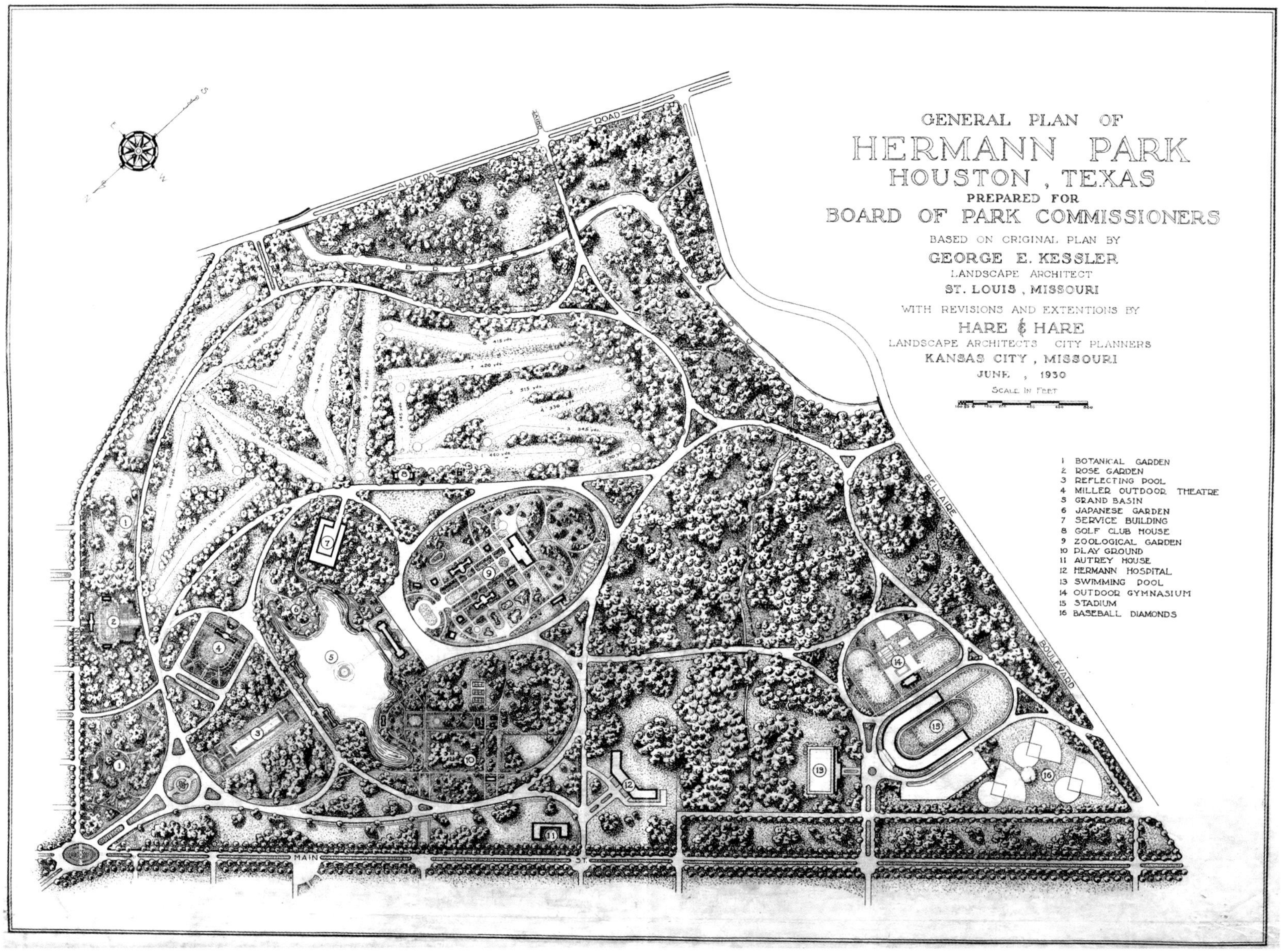

A new General Plan for Hermann Park (1930, Hare & Hare) was firmly based on Kessler's original plan. Courtesy Houston Metropolitan Research Center, Houston Public Library (RGD 26).

Missouri, with Revisions and Extensions by Hare & Hare, Landscape, Architects [and] City Planners, Kansas City, Missouri June, 1930." Hare & Hare were as faithful to Kessler's plan as was possible. The entry sequence was basically unchanged; the main roads within the park had been established by Kessler and built before Hare & Hare were in the picture. Miller Theatre had been pushed slightly to the northeast with a different orientation, not on axis with the reflection pool as Kessler had placed it. This situation elongated the oval sector that contained these two elements. Hare & Hare's 1930 plan shows additional secondary drives and paths. The golf course took up much more land; Kessler had confined the course to one outlying oval to the east of the central lobes. The Hare & Hare Plan showed a slight rechanneling of Brays Bayou with the tightest curves straightened out.

Hare & Hare's plan focused on sixteen specific parts of the park. The Rose Garden (2), the Reflecting Pool (3), Miller Outdoor Theatre (4), the Grand Basin (5), the Zoo (9), and the Playground (10) all exist today in the approximate locations shown by Herbert Hare. The Golf Club House (8) indicated on this plan was the 1922 structure, but its replacement was built in the same location. The large Service Building (7) was a maintenance facility demolished around 1990 when a new

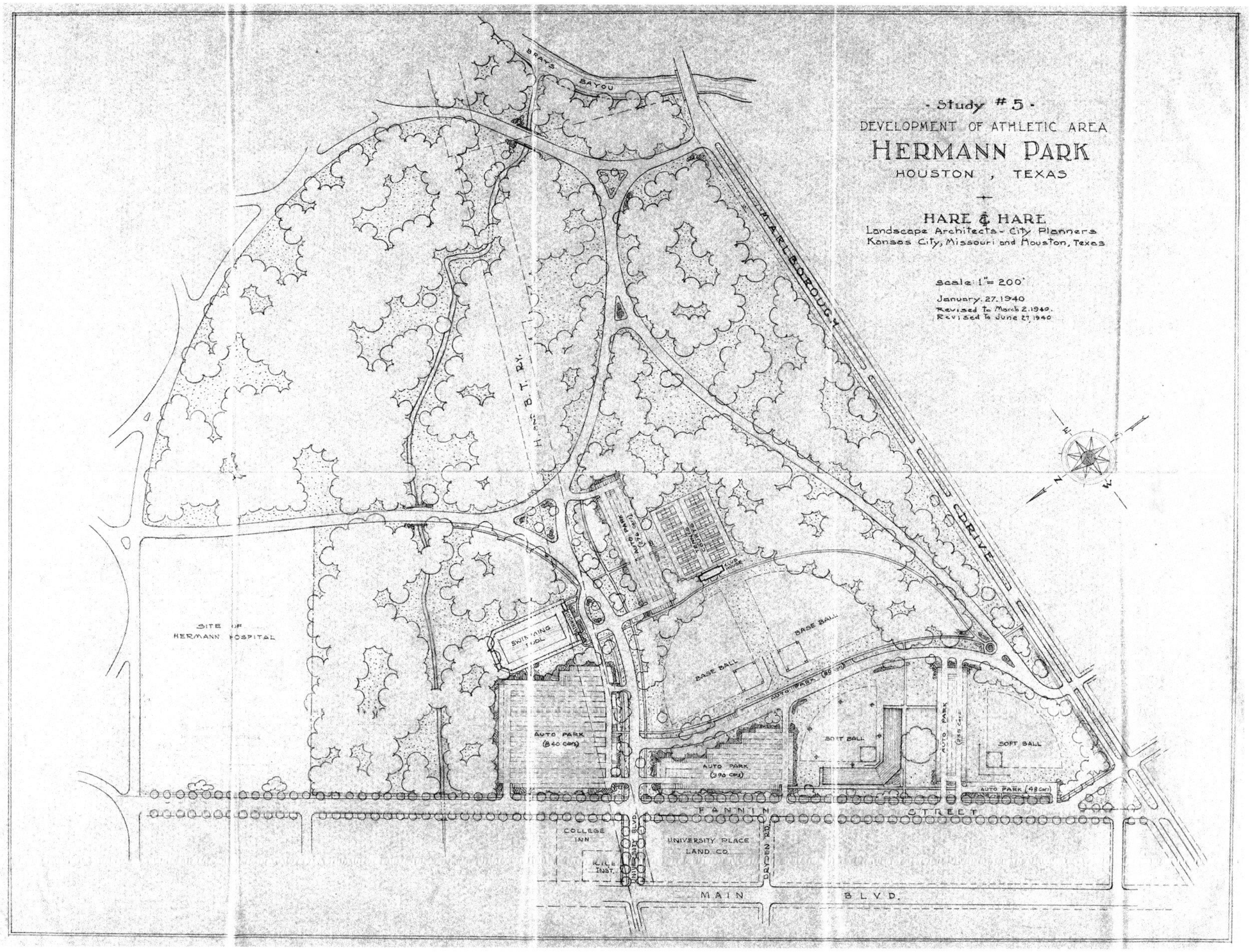

Plan for development of athletic area (1940, Hare & Hare) that was to have been built behind Hermann Hospital on parkland that was shortly sold off for the Texas Medical Center, eliminating the space for such an area in the park. Courtesy Houston Metropolitan Research Center, Houston Public Library (RGD 26).

maintenance building on Almeda Road was built. That area was paved over to become part of the large central parking lot next to the zoo and Lake Plaza.

One of the focal points of this plan was the Japanese Garden (6) to the left of the Grand Basin, surrounded by two coves of the Grand Basin. Because Japanese immigrants were not allowed to own land in California, where most of them lived in the 1920s, some took up gardening as a profession.[38] Japanese gardens, laid out and maintained by Japanese gardeners, became popular on large West Coast estates and in public parks in the 1920s and 1930s. Kessler's Overton Park in Memphis (1901) included a Japanese Garden, which was subsequently destroyed, as were many others, in the wake of World War II.[39]

Remarkable on the Hare & Hare Plan was the disposition of the land south of Hermann Hospital. It showed a large wooded sector and, in the triangle close to the intersection of Main and Bellaire boulevards, extensive athletic fields and facilities.

The first de-accessioning of park property had already occurred by the time the 1930 Hare & Hare Plan was created. Autry House (11) is indicated by a schematic L-shaped building indicating the footprint of Autry House and the Edward Albert Palmer Memorial Chapel. In 1919

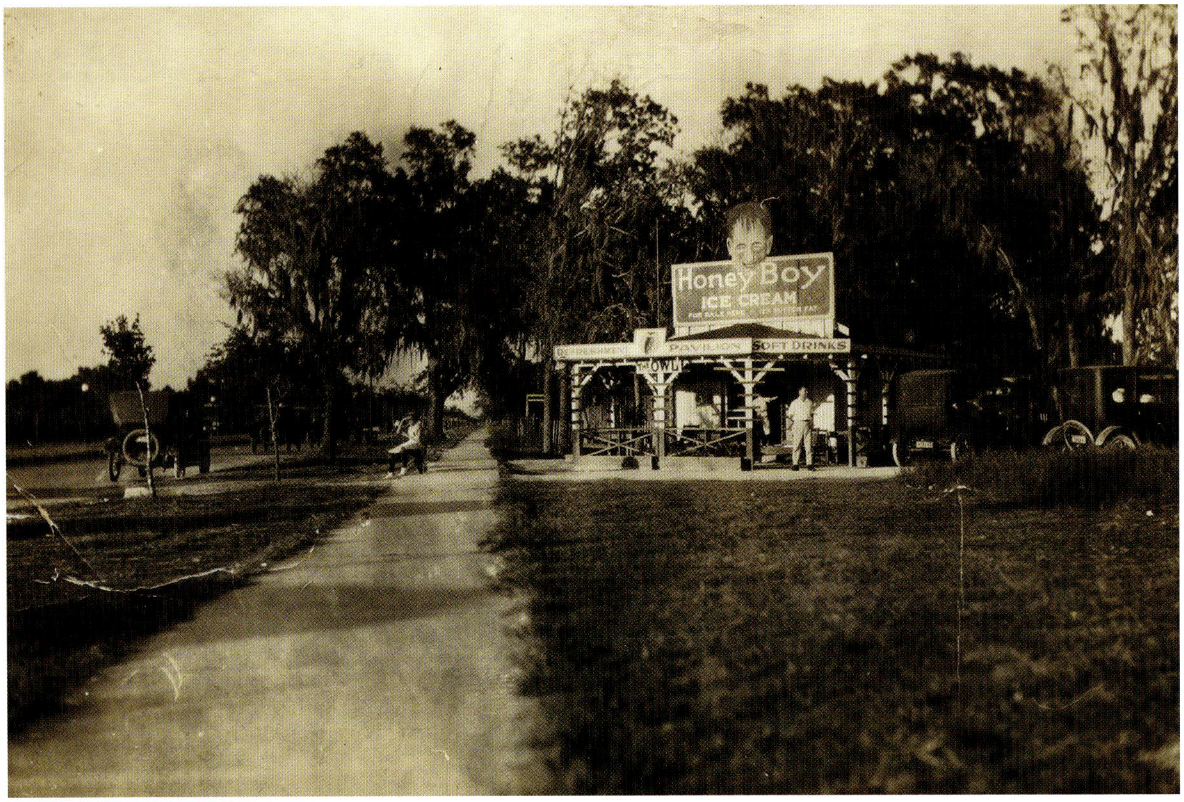

The Owl, at the edge of Hermann Park on Main Street across from the Rice Institute, was a refreshment pavilion enjoyed by Rice students. This photograph, looking north, shows an advertising sign and the newly planted row of small live oak trees stretching up Main Street, c. 1918. Courtesy Woodson Research Center, Fondren Library, Rice University.

the Episcopal Diocese of Texas bought property from the estate of the property owners, then traded it for a 250-square-foot site in Hermann Park, where Autry House is now located, for a "Rice student community house for study and recreation."[40] Before Autry House and Palmer Chapel were built on this site, The Owl, a popular food stand that catered to Rice students, occupied the property. When this establishment opened is unclear, but a 1919 photograph provides a good view of its site along Main Street, including a stand of mature trees, some of which may have been cut down for construction of Autry House and Palmer.

In early 1921 Allie Kinsloe Autry contributed $50,000 for Autry House, a memorial to her late husband, James Lockhart Autry, who had died the previous year. Cram & Ferguson, with William Ward Watkin, designed Autry House in a picturesque Mediterranean style with white stucco walls and red tile roofs to harmonize with the architecture of the Rice Institute. The cornerstone was laid on June 5, 1921, and construction was completed in the fall. In 1927 Daphne Palmer Neville agreed to provide $100,000 to the diocese for a student chapel to be built next door as a memorial to her brother, Edward Albert Palmer. Palmer Memorial Chapel (now Palmer Memorial Episcopal Church), designed by William Ward Watkin, was built on the remainder of the Autry House site and dedicated on March 27, 1927. Although these two structures were built on former park property, they were conscientious and responsible additions to the City Beautiful precinct along Main Boulevard.

Hermann Hospital and the Texas Medical Center

Before Palmer Chapel was planned, Hermann Hospital was completed in 1925 on what at the time was the middle of Hermann Park. George Hermann left most of his estate for the establishment of a charity hospital, and his will stipulated that the hospital be built on property he owned on the west side of downtown. However, after several delays the hospital was built across from Hermann Park on land owned by the Hermann Hospital Estate. In 1923 through their Varner Realty Company, Mike, Will, and Ima Hogg purchased 133 1/2 acres south of the hospital, which they sold at cost to the city a year later for expansion of Hermann Park.[41] The 1930 Hare & Hare Plan clearly intended the Hogg tract, as it was known, for athletic facilities in the park.

A little over two years after establishing his foundation, the Houstonian Monroe Dunaway Anderson (1873–1939) died on August 6, 1939. Anderson left the bulk of his estate, as George Hermann had done, to a foundation for the establishment of a hospital. Also like Hermann, Anderson had amassed a large fortune and never married. He was partner and treasurer of Anderson Clayton & Company, a Houston firm that Anderson and William L. Clayton built into the world's largest cotton merchandizing firm.[42] In 1941 the Texas state legislature voted to grant the University of Texas $500,000 to create a cancer research hospital. The M. D. Anderson Foundation proposed to match the state's appropriation and supply the necessary land, provided the hospital was

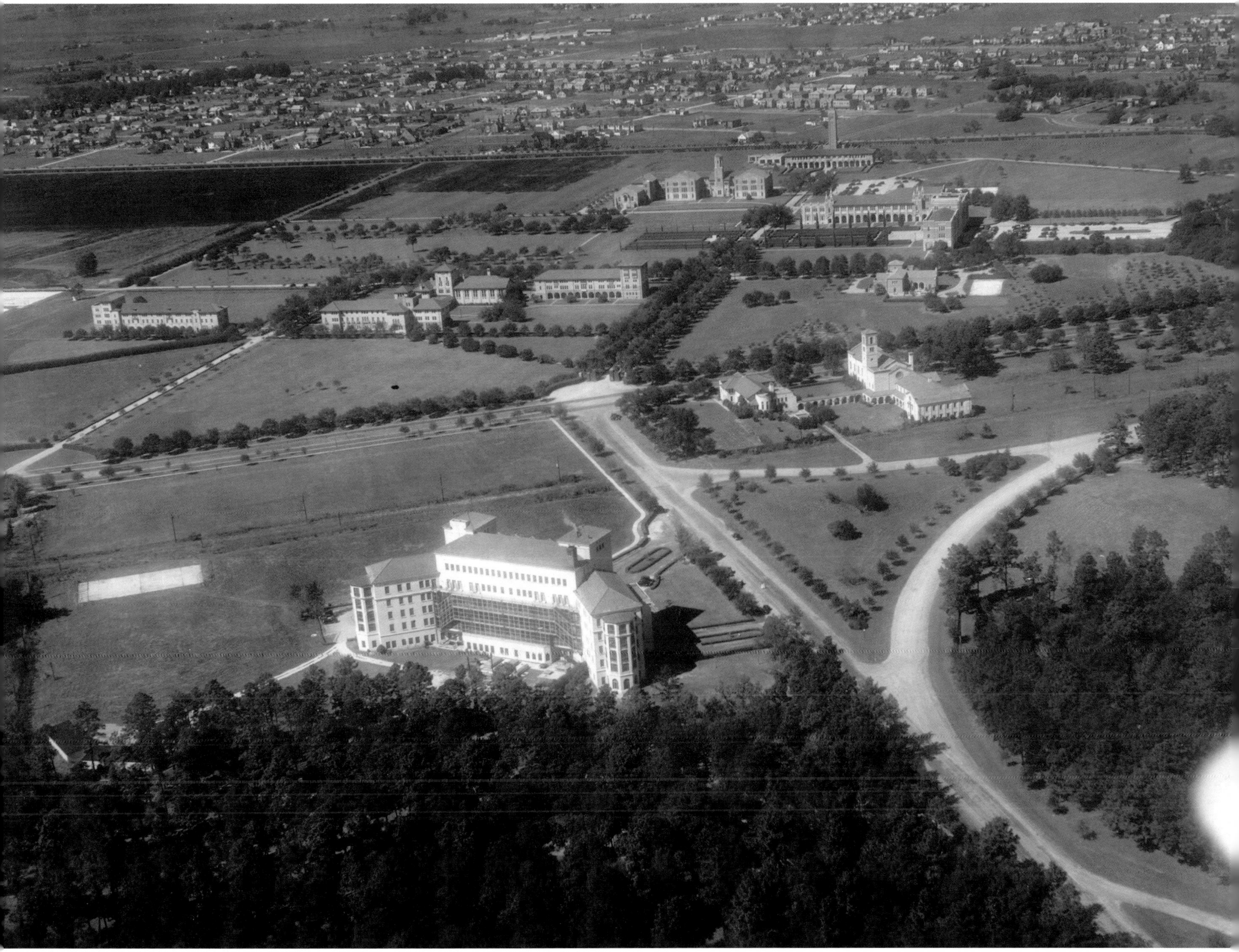

This 1933 aerial photograph shows Hermann Hospital's rear elevation in the foreground, Autry House and Palmer Memorial Chapel in the center with the Rice Institute campus beyond, and, in the far distance, the extent of residential development in the area at this time (Southampton, Broadacres, Shadyside, and others). Source: 11th Photo sec AC TX National Guard. Courtesy Woodson Research Center, Fondren Library, Rice University.

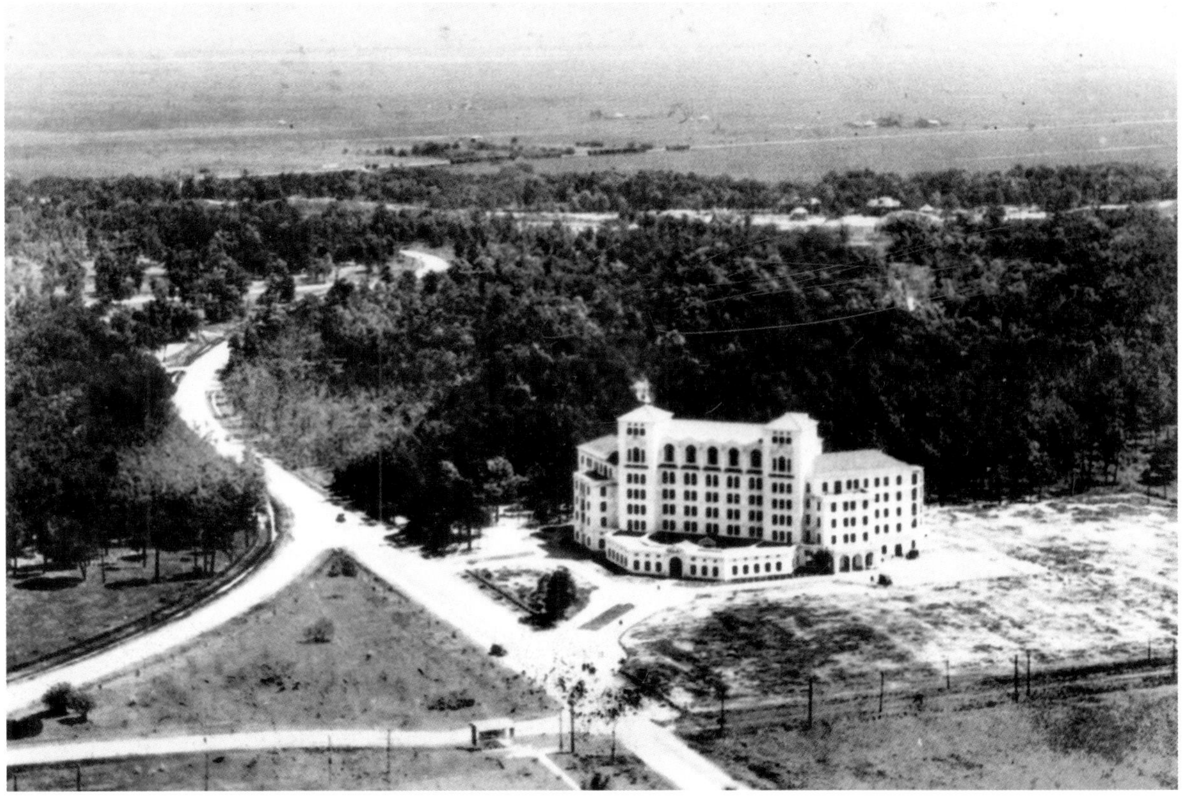

Hermann Hospital, 1926, before landscaping. This photograph shows the dense forest in what is now the Texas Medical Center behind the hospital as well as the wooded strips along Brays Bayou that give way to the prairie beyond. Courtesy John P. McGovern Historical Collections and Research Center, Houston Academy of Medicine, Texas Medical Center Library.

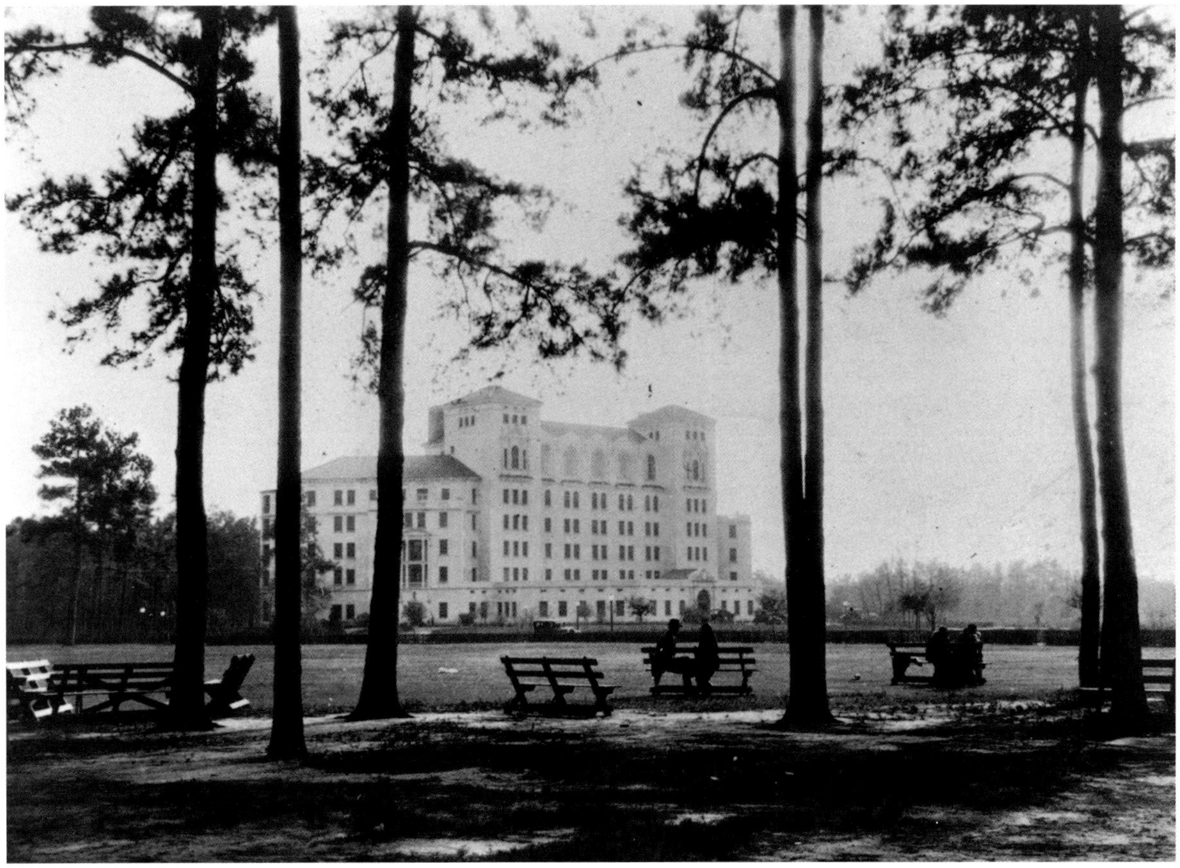

Hermann Hospital, c. 1930, seen from the sylvan grounds of Hermann Park. Courtesy John P. McGovern Historical Collections and Research Center, Houston Academy of Medicine, Texas Medical Center Library.

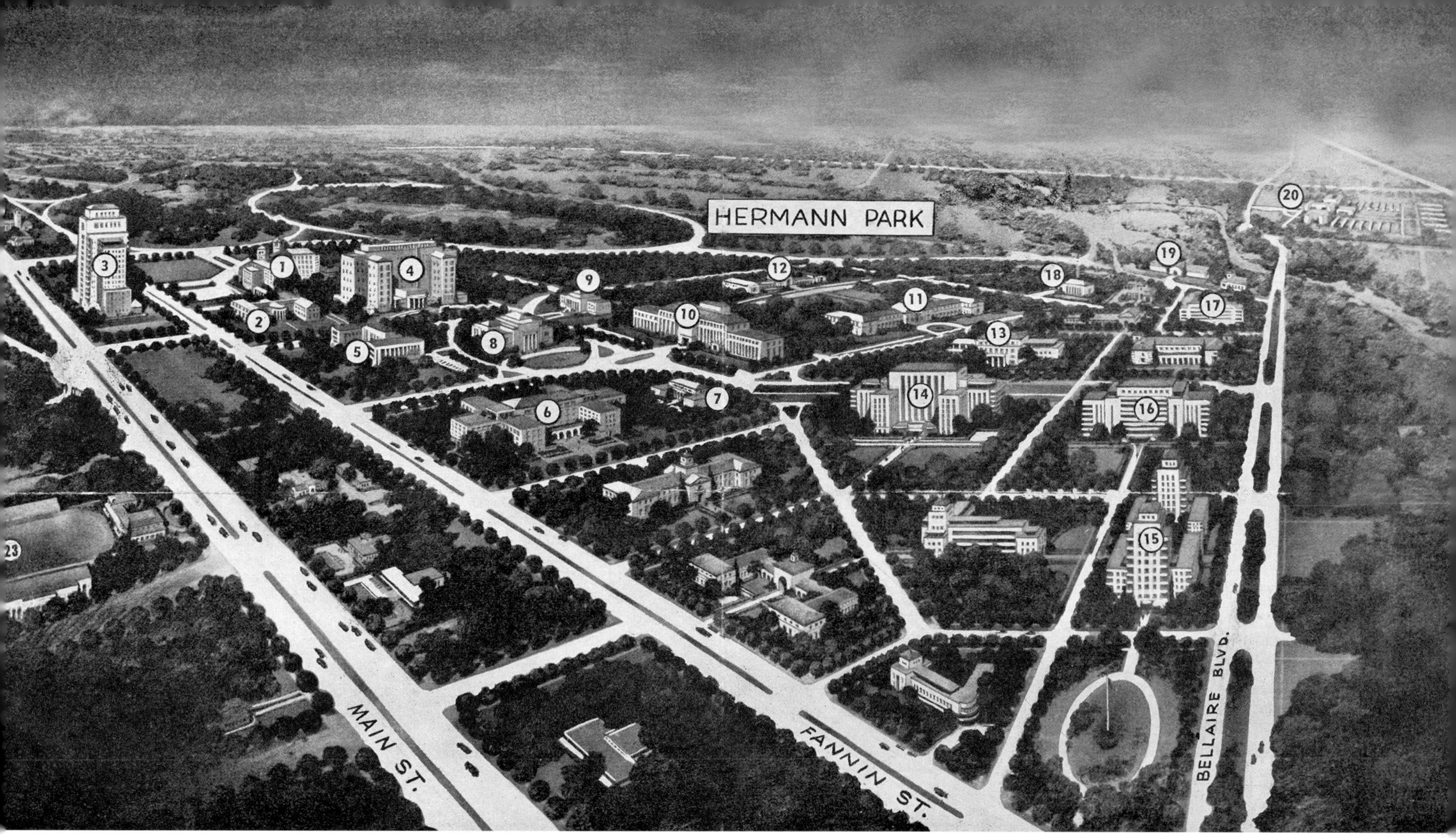

Texas Medical Center future projection (1946, Kenneth Franzheim). This drawing was created to show that medical center institutions could be built in park-like settings that would be a compatible extension of Hermann Park. No. 22 marks Palmer and Autry House; No. 1 is Hermann Hospital; No. 3 is the proposed Hermann Professional Building, and No. 10 is Baylor College of Medicine. Other buildings are speculative. Source: *Houston*, August, 1946. Courtesy Houston Metropolitan Research Center, Houston Public Library.

located in Houston. In 1942 the offer was accepted, and the projected institution was named M. D. Anderson Hospital for Cancer Research. The following year the M. D. Anderson Foundation offered Baylor University College of Medicine, then located in Dallas, $1 million dollars for construction of a facility and $100,000 a year for the next ten years if Baylor would come to Houston. The Houston Chamber of Commerce added $500,000 to that bid. The offer was accepted.

After promising to provide sites for the M. D. Anderson Cancer Center and Baylor, the M. D. Anderson Foundation trustees—the lawyers W. B. Bates and John H. Freeman and the banker H. M. Wilkins—decided that the Hogg tract in Hermann Park next to Hermann Hospital would be an ideal location. Despite opposition from the Parks Department and Mayor C. A. Pickett (1941–1943), Pickett's successor, Mayor Otis Massey (1943–1947), supported the proposal. In December 1943 a citywide referendum on the matter was held in which only 951 votes were cast. The result was approval for the city to sell the Hogg tract to the M. D. Anderson Foundation for $400,000.[43] One of the reasons this sale was approved and went forward was, as a plat by H. A. Kipp and a perspective rendering by Kenneth Franzheim illustrated, each new medical-related building was to be in the center of a large, landscaped island, creating a park setting, suggesting that these "healthful" institutions would be set in a logical extension of Hermann Park.[44] Ground was broken in 1945 for the Roy and Lillie Cullen Building of Baylor College of Medicine, beginning the development of the Texas Medical Center, which has seen continual construction and expansion ever since. Today, TMC is the largest medical center in the world, with forty-nine health-related institutions.

The Great Depression

The Great Depression effectively brought an end to the Houston boom on the 1920s and slowed the pace of development in Hermann Park. However, several additions were managed in the park. The most significant was a handsome new Golf Clubhouse constructed in 1933 on the site of the old clubhouse, which was demolished to make way for the new building. Architect Alfred E. Nutter (1874–1967) designed the building in a Spanish Colonial revival style that harmonized with the buildings in this City Beautiful precinct—the Rice Institute, Hermann Hospital, and Autry House—as well as the initial zoo buildings. Nutter was born in Boston but grew up and was educated in England. He immigrated to Ottawa, Canada, in 1920, where he practiced until moving to Houston in 1929. Although he never achieved widespread fame, he is remembered for the imaginative Spanish Colonial revival buildings he designed in the early 1930s in several Houston parks.[45] In Hermann Park Nutter also designed a pavilion and comfort station near today's playground area, with the same architectural attributes of white stucco and red barrel-tile roofs. The clubhouse was restored in the 2000s and currently is the temporary headquarters of the Hermann Park Conservancy.

The year 1936 marked the one-hundredth anniversary of the founding of Houston and the independence of Texas from Mexico. Hermann Park was the center of several commemorative activities that year. The San Jacinto Centennial Association, with a budget of almost $97,500, was formed to organize events celebrating this anniversary. Local business leaders and descendants of Houston pioneers headed up the Centennial Association, and, according to the bylaws, "any white person of good character and repute is eligible to active membership."[46] Major events occurred on Texas Independence Day, March 2, a weeklong celebration from April 13–21 to commemorate the Battle of San Jacinto, and four days in August to commemorate the founding of Houston.

On March 2, 1936, the Pioneer Memorial Log House in Hermann Park, erected by the San Jacinto Chapter of the Daughters of the Republic of Texas, was dedicated. In the fall of 1934, Mrs. George (Sarah Groce) Berlet, who had proposed the construction of an authentic log cabin, drew a rough sketch that became the basis for the design of the house by the Houston architect, Harry Weaver. More than 250 pine logs were cut, peeled, and saddle-notched for construction, and stones and bricks from old houses were used to build the foundation, chimney, and fireplace. In 1950 the Log House was moved a short distance across Cambridge Drive in front of Ben Taub Hospital to accommodate the expansion of the zoo.[47]

In April 1936 a concert was held at Miller Memorial Theatre with a grand fireworks display, and on August 30 another fireworks display in Hermann Park accompanied the dedication of the 50-foot-high pink granite Pioneer Memorial Obelisk erected in Hermann Park by San Jacinto Centennial Association "in honor of the pioneer men and women of Houston."[48] Obelisks, an ancient Egyptian form, had long been a popular shape for public monuments in the United States. And after "Cleopatra's Needle," a 68-foot-high ancient Egyptian obelisk, was given to New York City by the government of Egypt and installed in Central Park in 1881, such features became an aspiration of large public parks in the United States.[49] The Pioneer Memorial Obelisk in Hermann Park was completed three years before the celebrated San Jacinto Monument east of Houston, which commemorates Texas independence from Mexico.

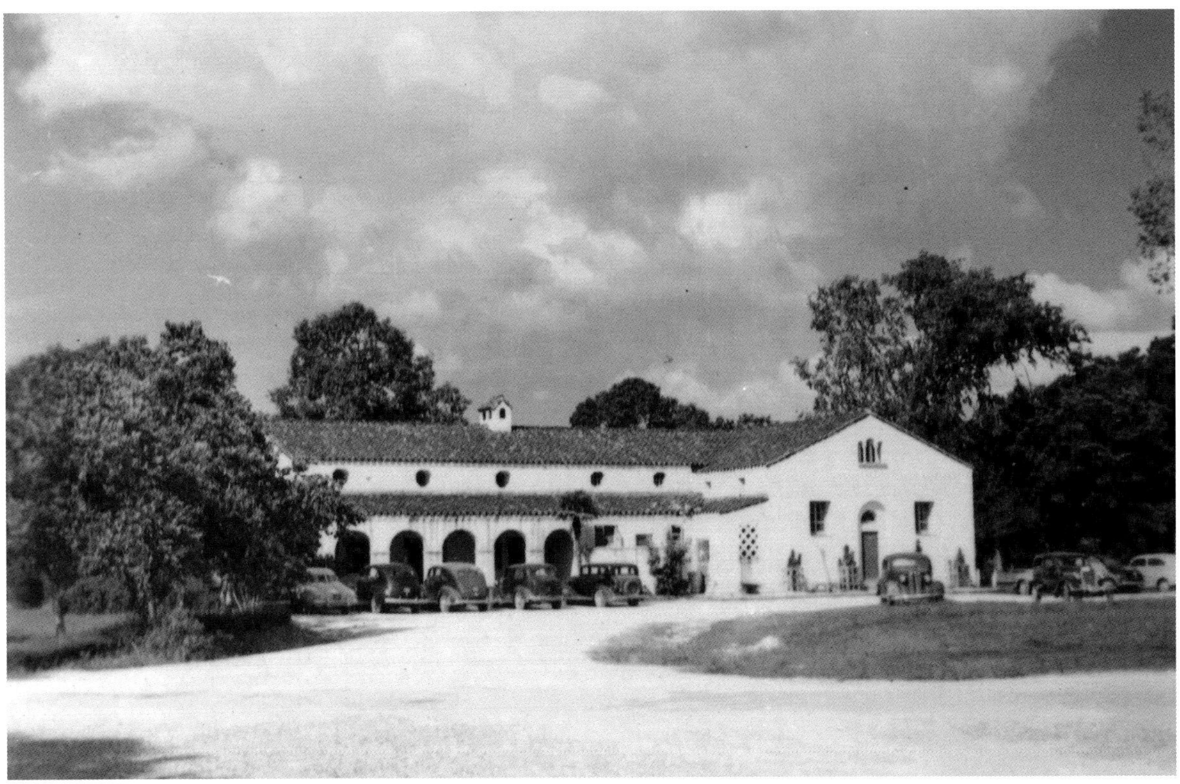

Hermann Park Golf Clubhouse (1933, Alfred E. Nutter) was built on the site of the first clubhouse in a Spanish style. The arched loggia looks onto the golf course, c. 1940. Courtesy Houston Metropolitan Research Center, Houston Public Library (156-276).

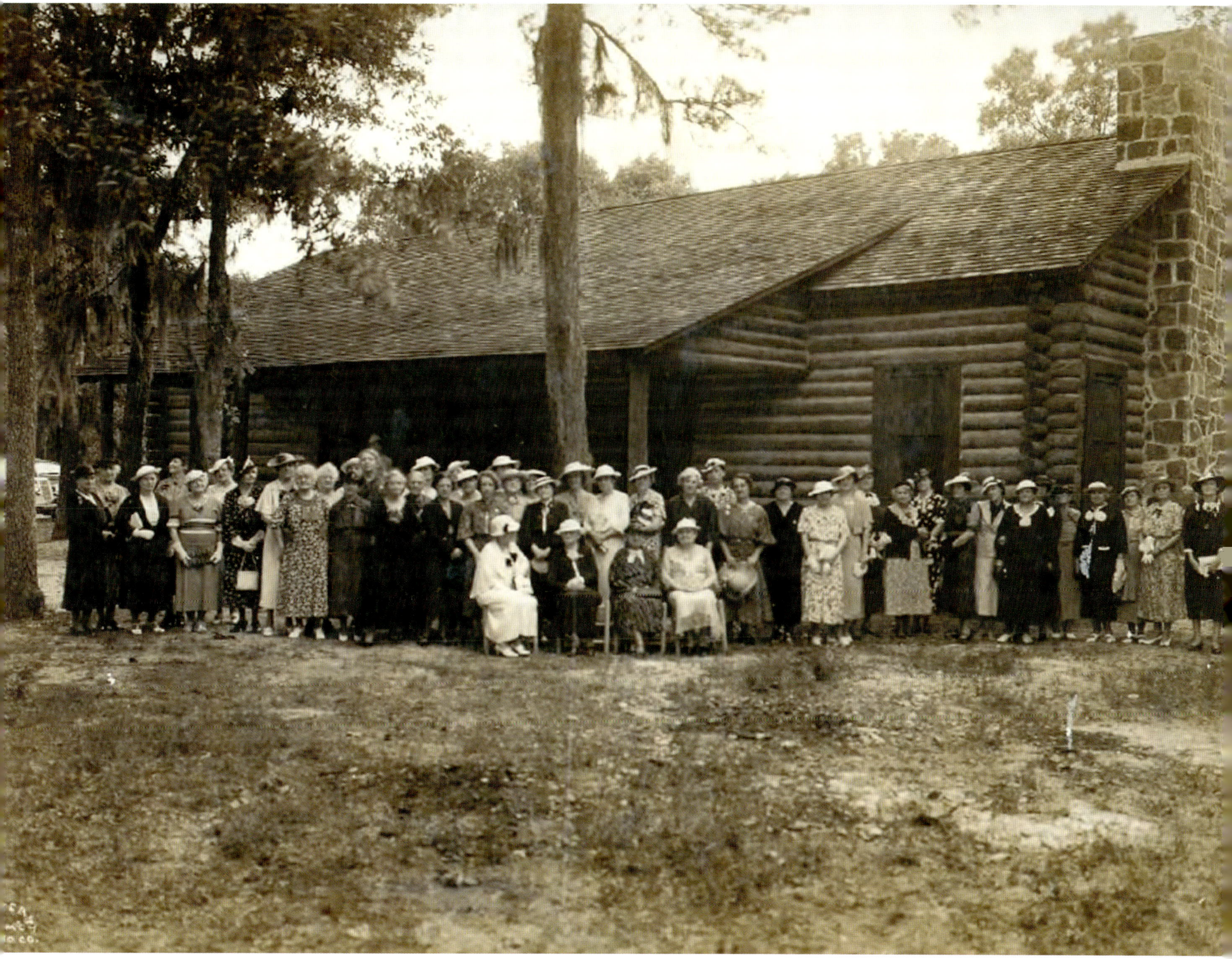

Pioneer Memorial Log House at its dedication, 1936, celebrating the centennial of Houston with members of the San Jacinto Chapter of the Daughters of the Republic of Texas, who donated the authentically built cabin for meetings and receptions in the park. Courtesy San Jacinto Chapter, Daughters of the Republic of Texas.

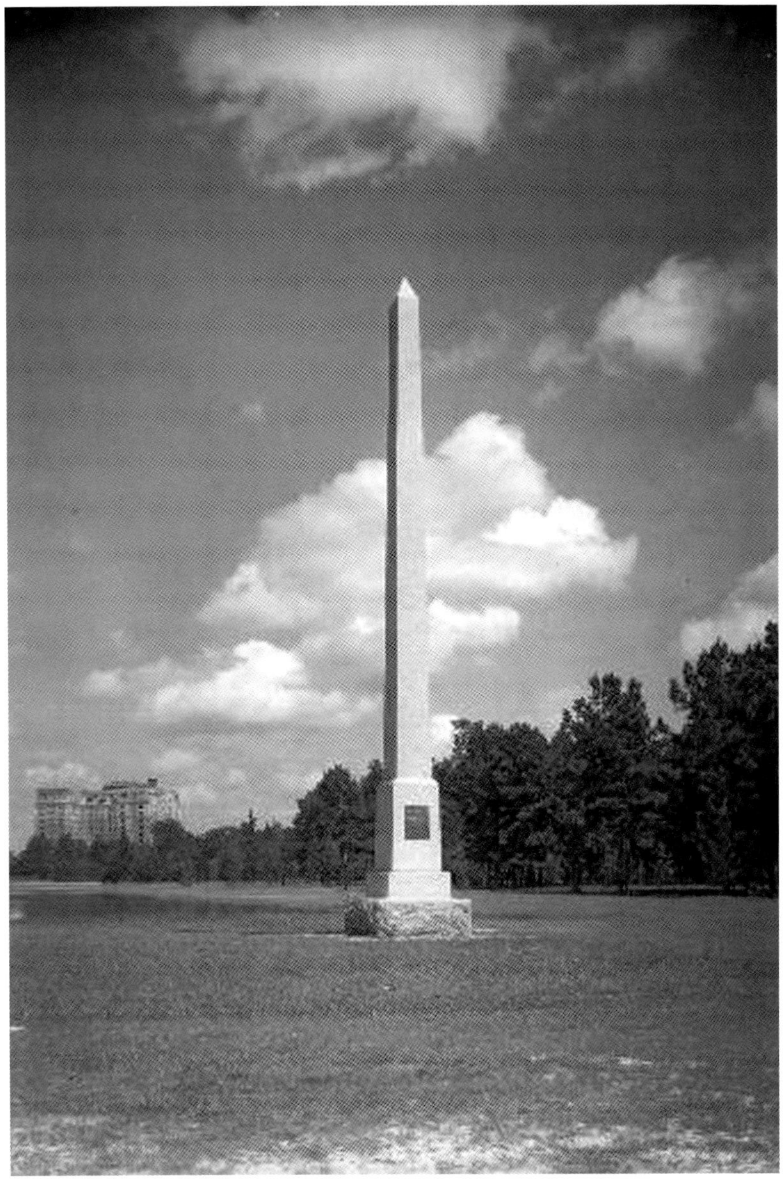

Pioneer Memorial obelisk, 1936, Frank Teich, sculptor, at the time of its installation at the far end of the reflection pool. The Sam Houston Monument and Warwick Hotel can be seen in the background. The plaque reads: "Pioneer Memorial in honor of the pioneer men and women of Houston erected by the San Jacinto Centennial Association, dedicated August 30, 1936, the one hundredth anniversary of the founding of the City of Houston." Photograph by Bob Bailey Studios. Courtesy Briscoe Center for American History University of Texas–Austin (e_bb_4367).

Also during the 1930s, North and South MacGregor Ways were built to join Hermann and MacGregor Parks thanks to the generosity of Peggy Stevens MacGregor, widow of real estate developer Henry F. MacGregor (1855–1923). In 1926 Mrs. MacGregor had donated 108 wooded acres on Brays Bayou 2 1/2 miles east of Hermann Park to the city for a park to be built in memory of her husband. She also gave $150,000 to finance acquisition of land on both banks of the bayou to link what became MacGregor Park and Hermann Park with landscaped drives.[50]

Hare & Hare remained active in Houston until 1962, two years after Herbert Hare's death. The firm was sold in 1979 and continues today under the name of Ochsner Hare & Hare.[51] According to Ralph Ellifrit, who came to Houston to work for Hare & Hare in 1939, Herbert Hare was primarily the client contact and overall planner. Sid Hare died in 1938 but had not been involved in the Houston projects because he was not a landscape planner. However, before his son joined the practice, Sid Hare had laid out Bellaire Farms for W. W. Baldwin in 1907 and 1908. The nurseryman Edward Teas, who settled in Bellaire, and the senior Hare were good friends and shared an interest in botany. When Ellifrit joined the firm, it consisted of Herbert Hare, Ralph Reinhart, and Donald Bush (c. 1912–1979). Reinhart was more of a planner and was responsible for Houston subdivisions planned by Hare & Hare, such as Braeswood and Garden Oaks.[52] Ellifrit recalled that Bush, a Fellow of the American Society of Landscape Architects, did most of the design work on the parks in Houston. Bush's name or initials are on a number of drawings in the Hare & Hare Collection at the Houston Metropolitan Research Center.

As consultants to the Board of Park Commissioners and to the City Planning Commission, the firm basically had charge of the city's entire park planning from 1923 to 1960. Ellifrit, in fact, stated: "Mr. Brock, the park superintendent, thought a great deal of Mr. Hare and didn't let any development occur without this guidance."[53] Among the major projects Hare & Hare had its hand in, besides Hermann Park, were Memorial Park, Hermann Square, Allen Parkway and Memorial Drive, the University of Houston, and many small park projects such as MacGregor Park. Hare & Hare were chiefly responsible for Houston's municipal park system inside of Loop 610 as it exists today.

The last section of Hermann Park for which Hare & Hare created a detailed landscape plan was the Garden Center (now Centennial Garden) area. The Houston Federation of Garden Clubs, organized in 1936, received permission from the city the following year to build a Garden Center in Hermann Park.[54] Plans for the center were under way in 1938 when Hare & Hare produced a site plan. William Ward Watkin designed a $20,000 Garden Center building to be constructed with part of the city's grant from the Federal Public Works Administration park improvement program, which allocated $9,000 for this project.[55] The federation committed to raise the rest of the funds for construction. However, this turned out to be a difficult task, and it was not until 1941 that construction began with reduced budget, evident in the simplification of the design as it was built, most obviously in the elimination of the grand arched windows.[56]

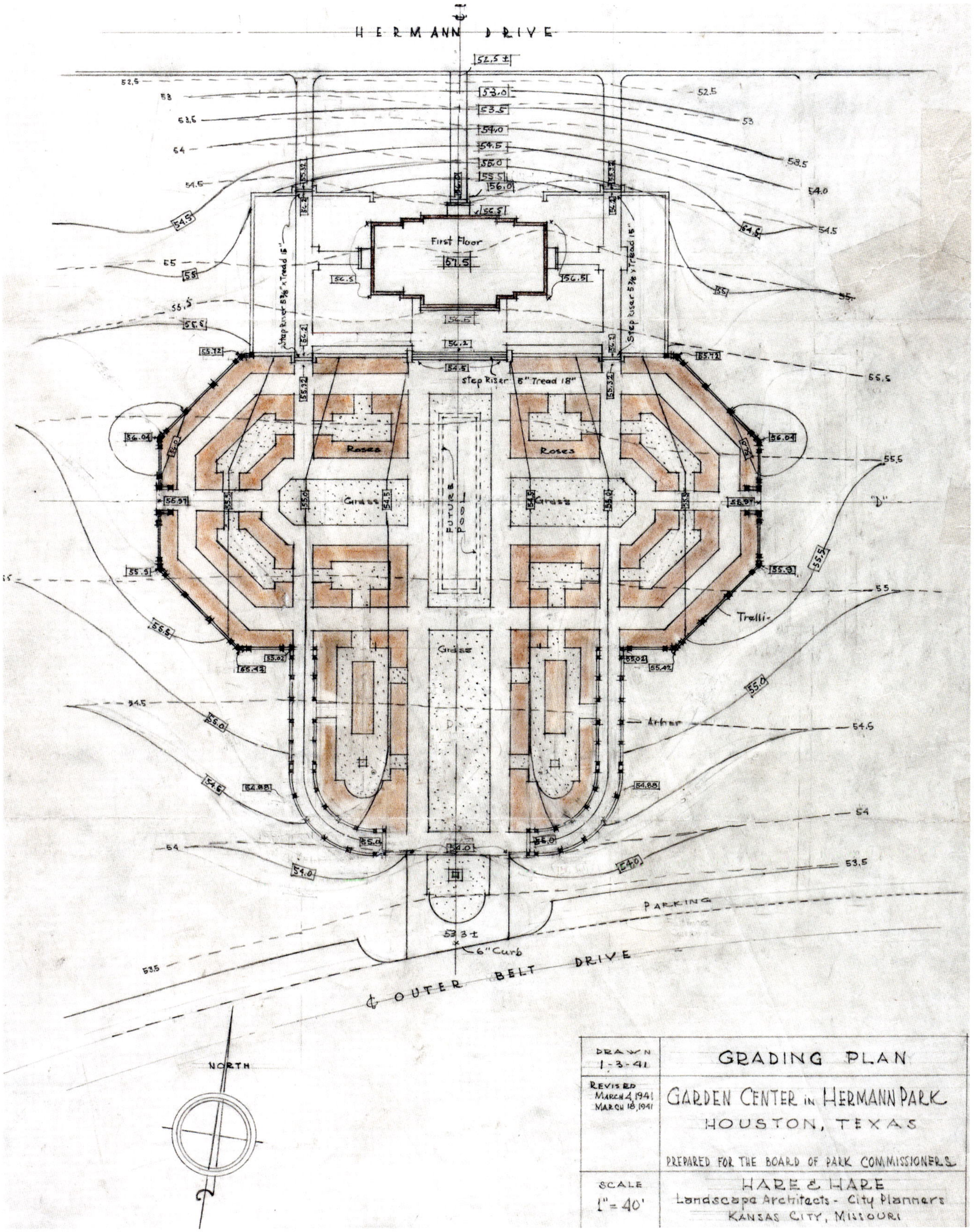

Garden Center Grading Plan (1941, Hare & Hare) shows the Garden Center building and formal gardens, which were never fully realized. Courtesy Houston Metropolitan Research Center, Houston Public Library (RGD 26).

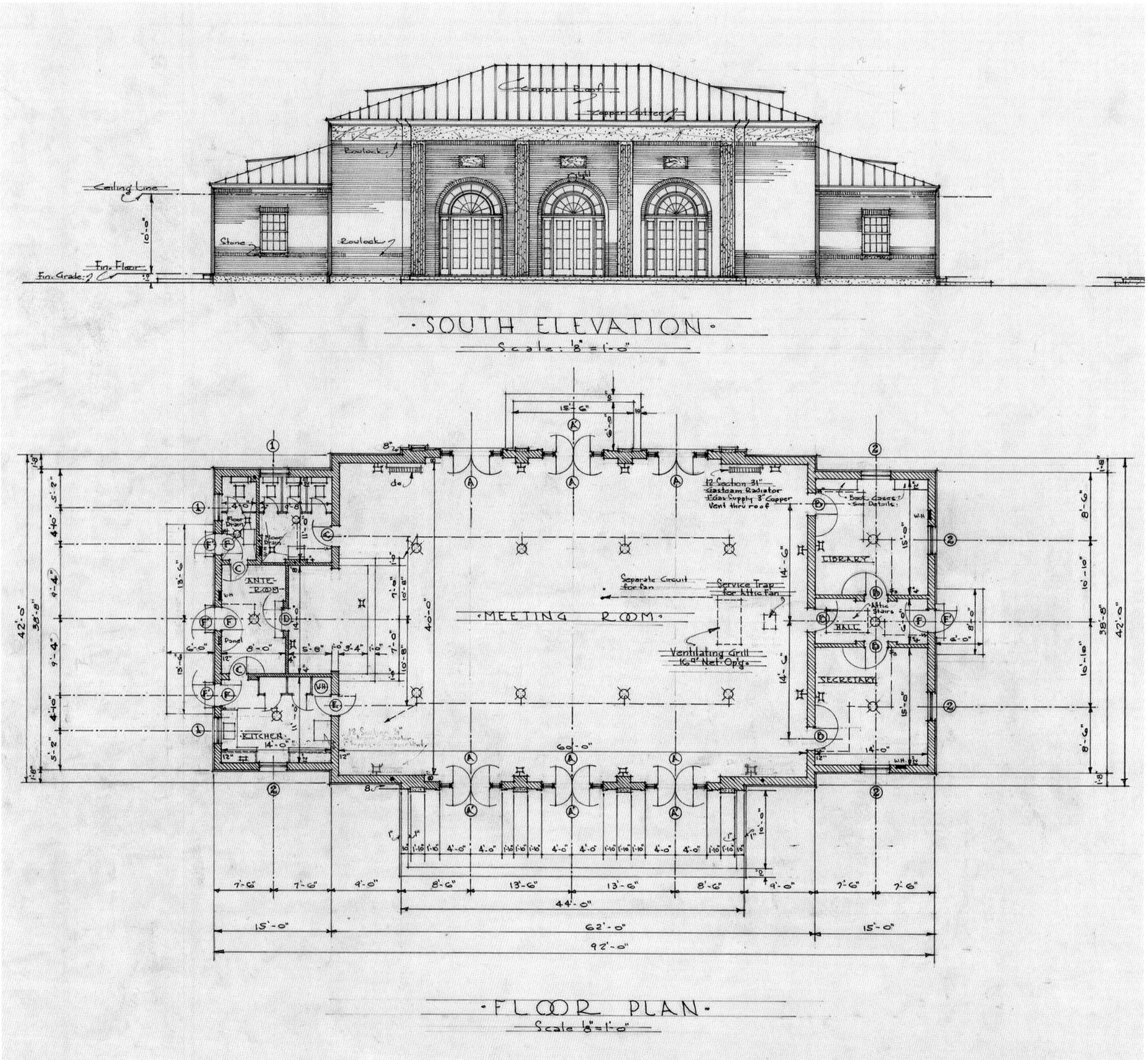

Garden Center elevation and floor plan (1940, William Ward Watkin). The plan was significantly altered before construction: the gracious round-arched windows were eliminated, as was the copper roof and other details. Courtesy Houston Metropolitan Research Center, Houston Public Library (RG-18-703).

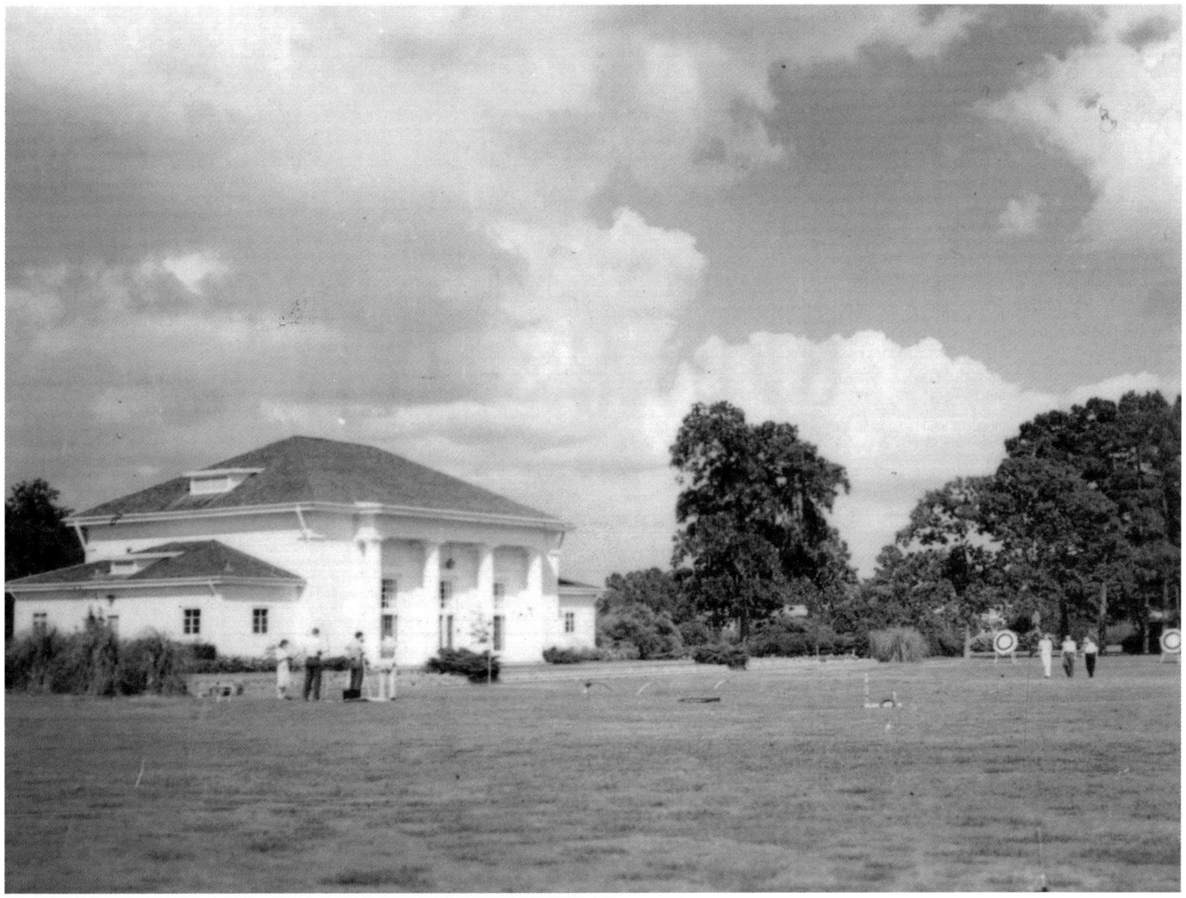

Garden Center as built, c. 1949. The main façades of the building, facing Hermann Drive and into Hermann Park, were identical. This photograph shows visitors playing croquet and archery targets in the area planned for formal gardens. The Garden Center is a meeting place for over twenty Houston area garden clubs. Courtesy Houston Metropolitan Research Center, Houston Public Library (156-27).

Originally, entrance to the one-story, 92-feet by 42-feet building was on Hermann Drive, although the north and south elevations were essentially the same. An open house and formal dedication were held on January 27, 1942. The federation turned over the Garden Center's maintenance to the city in 1958. In the early 1960s, Wilson, Morris, Crain & Anderson remodeled and expanded the building, adding two wings for classrooms, and reversed the entrance to face into Hermann Park.[57] As part of the Garden Center project, Hare & Hare created a new development plan in 1940 for the area around Miller Theatre that included revised theater seating and three large parking lots with some landscape improvements (screen trees) around them.[58] This plan is significant because it introduced large surface parking lots into the center of the park for the first time.

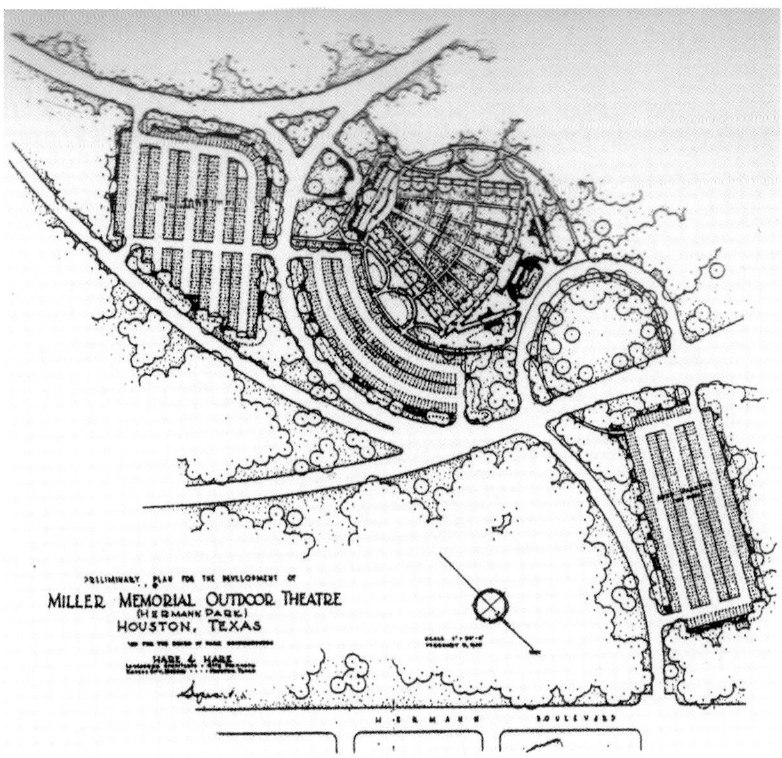

Miller Theatre Redevelopment Plan (1940, Hare & Hare) proposed the first designated parking areas in Hermann Park. Courtesy Houston Metropolitan Research Center, Houston Public Library (RGD 26).

CHAPTER FIVE

No Plan

1952–1961

A series of confidential reports on the condition of Houston's parks prepared for J. Robert Neal, a Houston banker and chairman of the Houston Board of Park Commissioners from 1938 to 1940, concluded that Houston's park system was inadequate. Miller Theatre in Hermann Park was described as being in "deplorable" condition. In the summer of 1938, Neal confronted the city council and asked for an increase in the park budget. When that was denied, along with a proposal to assign golf fees from Memorial and Hermann parks to the Parks Department, Neal proposed closing the zoo and selling all the animals. In a compromise, the city council agreed to give over the golf fees for park maintenance.[1]

Indicating the low priority assigned to parks that occurred during the Depression, a number of proposals were made to encroach on Hermann Park for nonpark uses. These included a request by the Houston Conservatory of Music for 3 or 4 acres on Main near Palmer Chapel and 50 acres for a public school stadium on Almeda. Oscar Holcombe, mayor again in 1940, created a City Planning Department and hired Hare & Hare's representative in Houston, Ralph S. Ellifrit (1909–1999), as director. Ellifrit and Hare & Hare successfully opposed plans to take over major sections of the park by other entities.

Even after World War II, as the economy of Houston gained strength, it was not until the mid-1950s that any serious attention was paid to Hermann Park. In 1951 Mayor Holcombe, who had been an advocate for Hermann Park, made it clear that he was in favor of postponing development of parks already owned by the city, including or especially Hermann Park, in favor of expanding Houston's park system by using city resources to purchase new parkland.[2] One exception was concern for overcrowding of the zoo. As previously discussed, an expansion and major changes were made, and the new Houston Zoo opened in 1950.

Museum of Natural Science

The zoo expansion in 1950 coincided with the continuing need for a larger building for the Museum of Natural Science, which some wanted relocated outside of the zoo property. The museum's initial building was constructed in 1929 and opened in 1930, allowing exhibits already owned by the Houston Museum and Scientific Society, as it had been known since 1909, to be moved from temporary locations in the Houston Public Library (now Julia Ideson Building) and the City Auditorium to the new museum building in 1930.[3] As early as 1943, C. C. "Pat" Fleming (1909–1996), the Houston landscape architect and director of the Parks Department from 1943 to 1945,[4] had called for an expanded zoo and a new building for the museum. Fleming proposed a ten-year improvement program for Hermann Park that was to include a lake for boat rides, a children's zoo, a tropical garden in the zoo, and parking for four hundred cars. He noted that there was a dwindling stock of animals at the zoo.[5] At the same time, the number of exhibits at the Museum of Natural Science was increasing not only with donations, but also from zoo animals that died and were stuffed or otherwise preserved as specimens for the museum.[6] From its beginning the museum had a symbiotic relationship with both the zoo and Hermann Park. Museum staff used the park as a laboratory, taking schoolchildren on field trips to study plants and animals. In 1943 an extensive inventory of plants in the park was compiled by the museum.

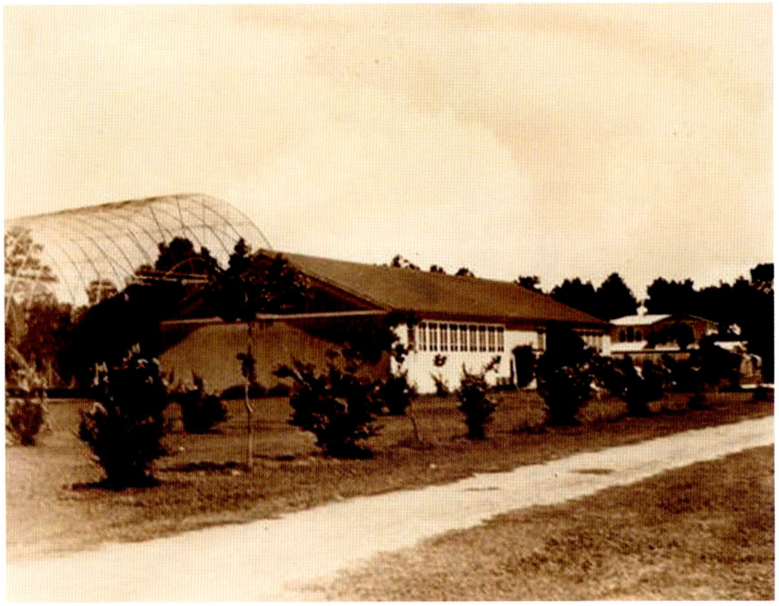

The Museum of Natural Science, 1929, was first located in this small building on the grounds of the zoo. Courtesy Houston Metropolitan Research Center, Houston Public Library.

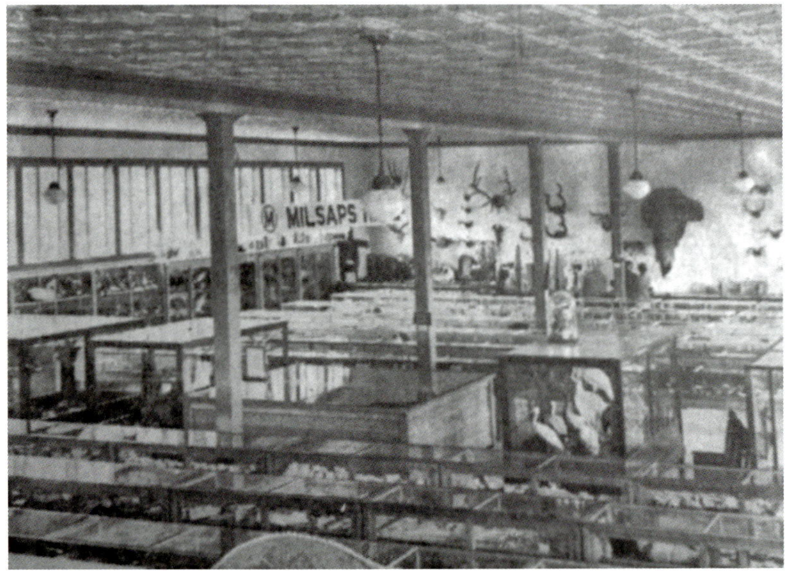

Museum of Natural Science, interior, 1937, shows cases of natural specimens and the head of "Black Diamond," a circus elephant killed by Hans Nagel in 1929 after it trampled a bystander in Corsicana. Courtesy Houston Metropolitan Research Center, Houston Public Library.

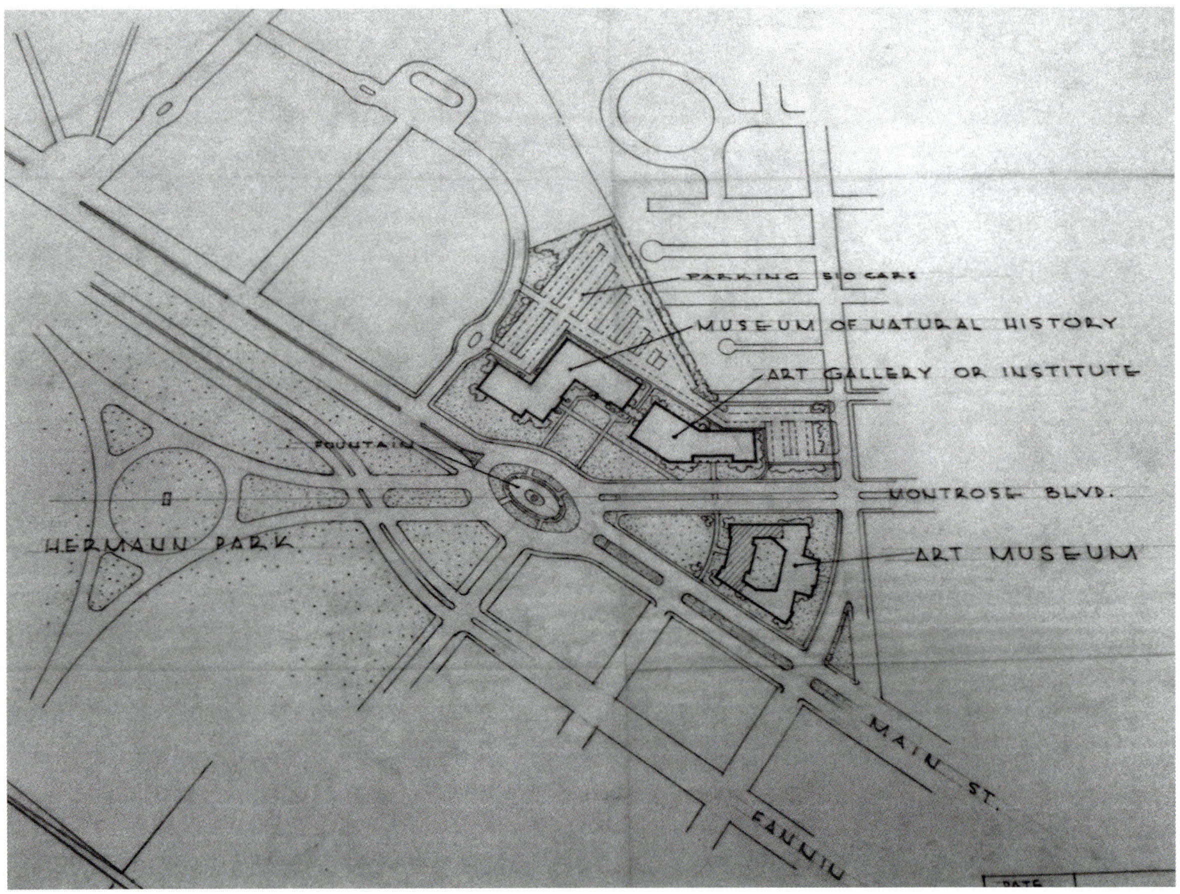

Proposal for development of a new Natural Science Museum and art institute in Shadyside (1948, Hare & Hare). Courtesy Houston Metropolitan Research Center, Houston Public Library (RGD 26).

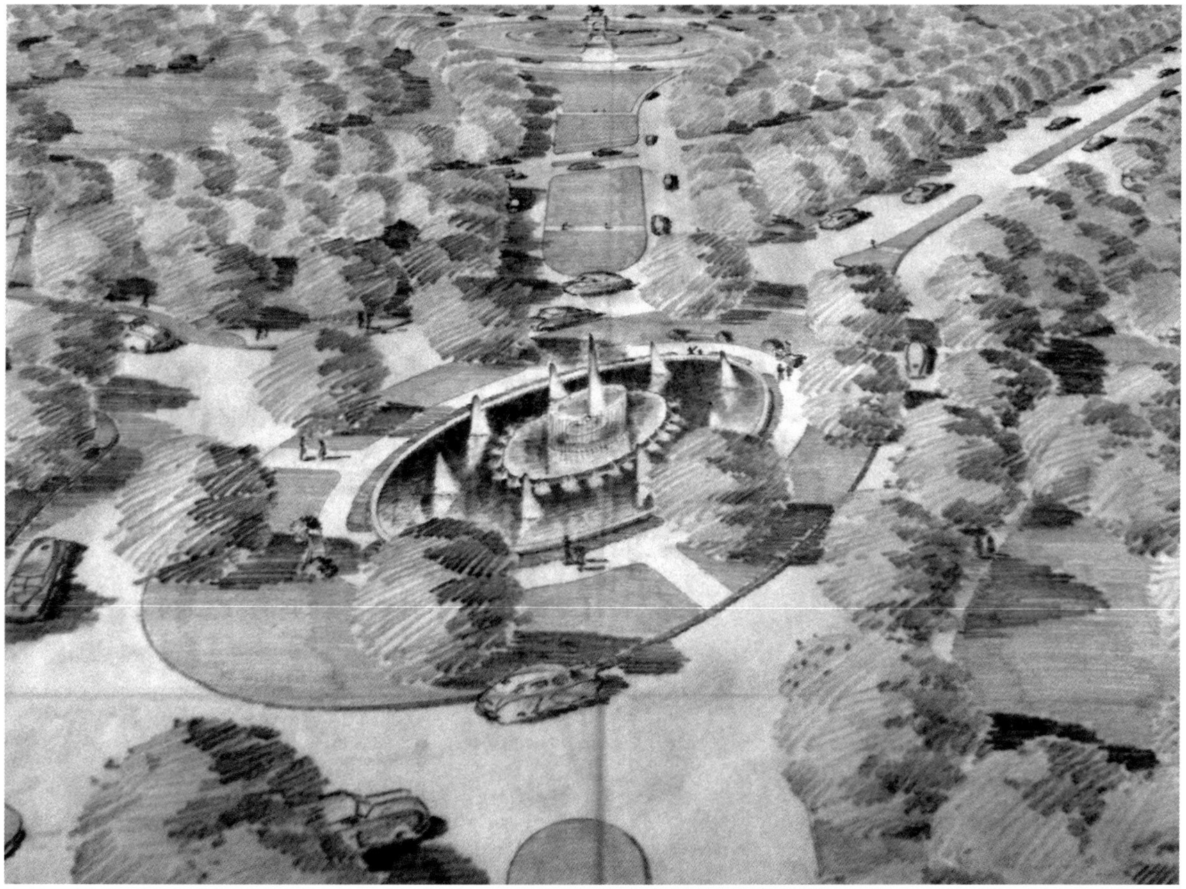

Proposal for fountain in the Sunken Garden (1948, Hare & Hare). Realizing that the Sunken Garden had become a traffic hazard, Herbert Hare proposed to replace it with a fountain sixteen years before this idea was realized when John and Mary Elizabeth Mecom, owners of the Warwick Hotel, presented the Mecom Fountain to the city. Courtesy Houston Metropolitan Research Center, Houston Public Library (RGD 26).

Along with zoo expansion plans in 1948, Hare & Hare devised a plan to locate a new Museum of Natural Science on the site of the Cullinan House in Shadyside, which had recently been acquired by former Texas governor William P. Hobby and his wife, Oveta Culp Hobby.[7] The Hare & Hare drawing was titled "Cultural Center," and, in addition to the Natural Science Museum, it diagrammed another building for an institute or art gallery and included parking spaces for 510 cars. This site for the museum was an intelligent solution; however, Mrs. Hobby's opposition ended this approach, a particular pity because the Hobby family ultimately demolished the whole Cullinan estate, and the land lay empty for several decades. The same year, 1948, Hare & Hare addressed the problem of traffic at the intersection of Main and Montrose and proposed that a fountain replace the Sunken Garden. This idea was also rejected until 1962, when the independent oilman John W. Mecom bought the adjacent Hotel Warwick (1924–1926, Brickey and Brickey, architects, C. D. Hill & Co., consulting architect, Don Hall, general contractor).[8] To enhance the front of the hotel, Mecom and his wife, Mary Elizabeth, presented the Mecom Fountain as a gift to the city in 1964. The fountain was designed by architect Eugene Werlin and cost $200,000.[9]

After Hare & Hare's plan to locate a new science museum building in Shadyside was suppressed, architect Hermon Lloyd proposed a design concept locating the new museum on the Grand Basin (current site of the aquarium), where George Kessler might have put it: on axis with the entrance sequence of the Sam Houston Statue, Reflection Pool, and Pioneer Monument.[10] This long, low building had a colossal columned portico facing the lake and a wide entrance flanked by two projecting wings to the zoo side. For five consecutive years, from 1948 to 1952, the Houston City Council rejected issuing a one million dollar bond issue for a Houston Museum of Natural Science, citing other projects as more pressing.[11] The frustration of the Parks Department and Hermann Park supporters as well as public opinion during these years is evident by the number of newspaper articles that constantly cited overcrowding of the museum and the need for a new home.[12] In 1957 Dr. T. E. Pulley, a University of Houston professor of biology, was appointed the new director of the museum, and he seemed to be able to turn circumstances around.[13] By February 1958, funds were becoming available, and Pulley unveiled a plan to take the museum out of Hermann Park altogether. A new $1,000,000 proposal by Staub, Rather & Howze was published early

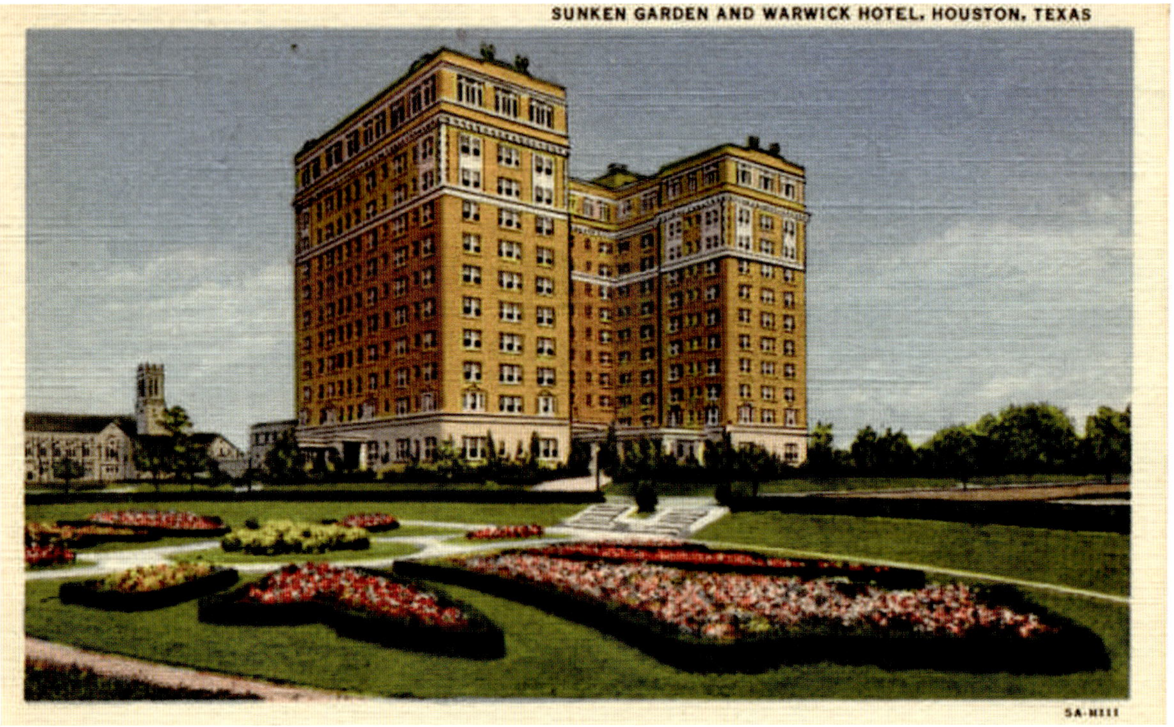

Warwick Hotel with Sunken Garden, c. 1950s. Courtesy Houston Metropolitan Research Center, Houston Public Library (178-615).

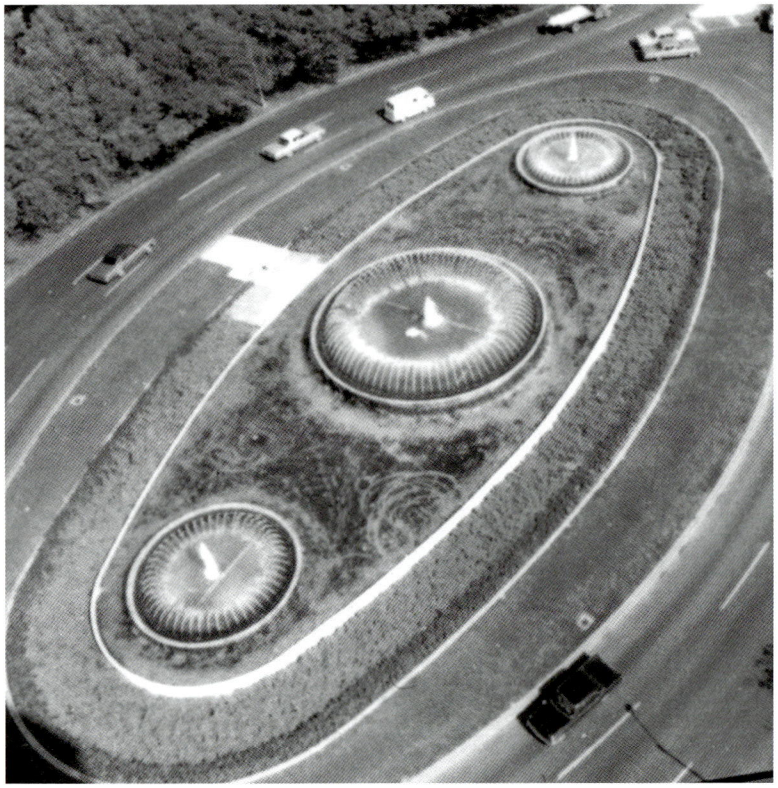

Mecom Fountain, 1964, as it appeared without landscaping when first constructed. The traffic ellipse around the fountain occurs at the merger of Main Street, Montrose Boulevard, and Hermann Drive. Courtesy Houston Metropolitan Research Center, Houston Public Library.

in 1958 for the Natural Science Museum to be located on a 22-acre site in Memorial Park.

Everyone seemed happy, but there were a number of restrictions placed by Will Hogg on the Memorial Park property, and the *Houston Post* noted that, before construction could begin, the city's legal department would have to approve this use in Memorial Park.[14] The Memorial Park site was not approved.

Finally, the museum's board of trustees received permission in 1959 to build a new facility at the north end of Hermann Park on a site across from the Warwick Hotel, where the Botanical Gardens were located. This decision to put the new museum in Hermann Park went forward despite the fact that park advocates again opposed the encroachment of new buildings on parkland. Fund-raising for construction began immediately, but it was 1963 before ground was broken for the first component of what has become a large complex of buildings. In 1964 the first increment, the Burke Baker Planetarium, opened along with a small area of exhibition space. By 1968 funds had been secured to construct a lateral wing, which opened in 1969 and was able to house most of the museum's collections. George Pierce–Abel B. Pierce and Staub, Rather & Howze were the architects for the initial buildings of the museum. In the 1980s another capital campaign provided the funds for a 40,000-square-foot wing designed by Hoover & Furr. The Wortham IMAX Theater was added in 1989 along with the Cullen Grand Entry Hall. At that time the museum took responsibility for landscaping its grounds, and installed the memorial sundial, fountain, and garden to

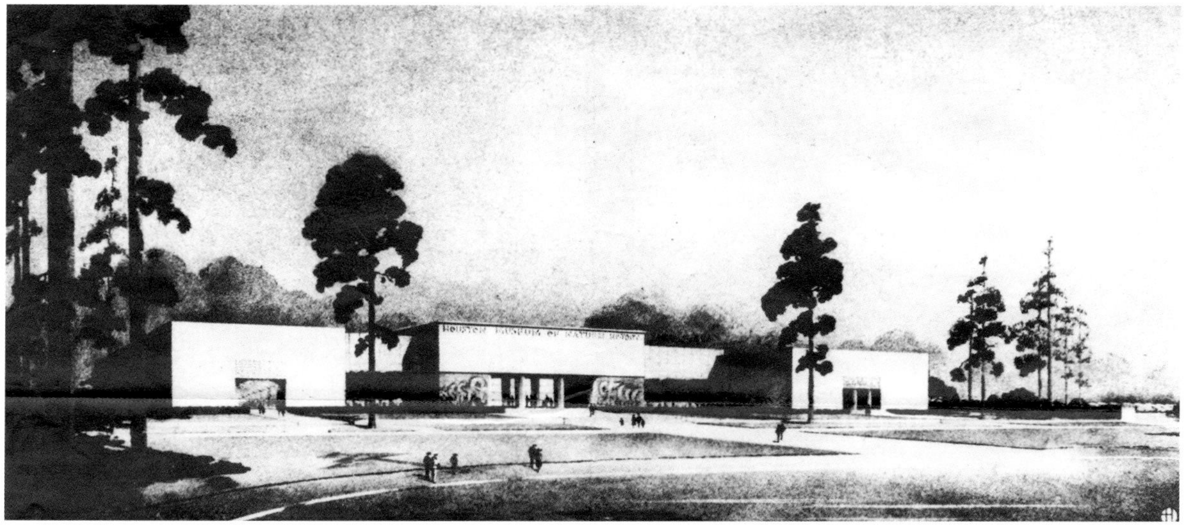

Museum of Natural Science proposal (c. 1957, Hermon Lloyd) rear elevation facing away from the Grand Basin toward the park interior and zoo. The Kipp Aquarium now occupies this site. Courtesy Houston Metropolitan Research Center, Houston Public Library (RGD 26).

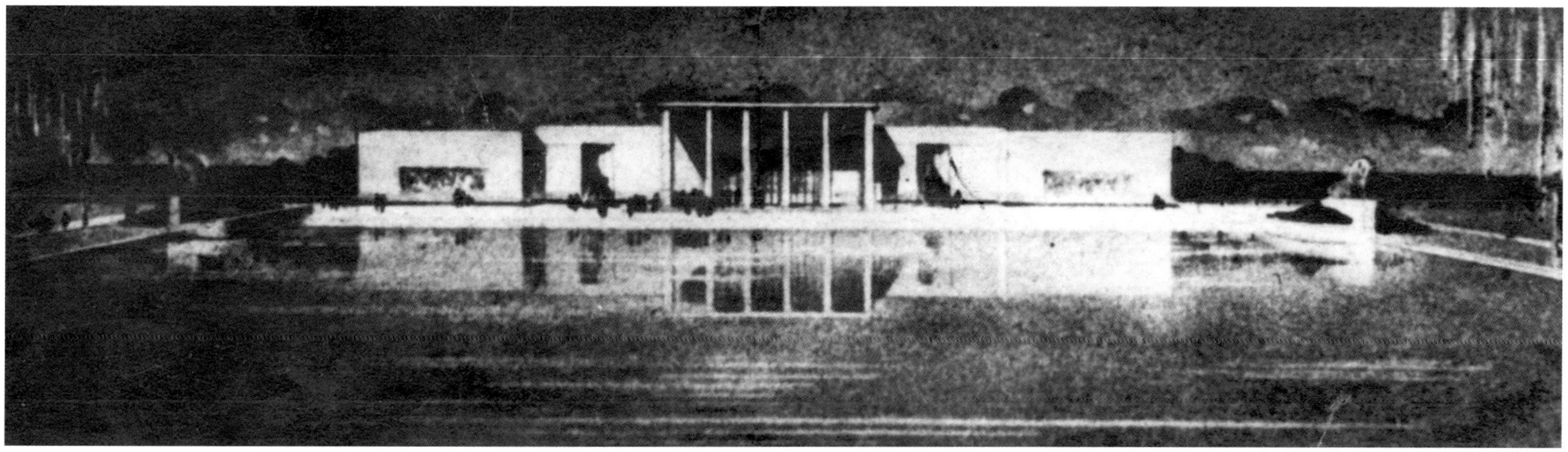

Museum of Natural Science proposal (c. 1957, Hermon Lloyd) front elevation facing the Grand Basin. Courtesy Houston Metropolitan Research Center, Houston Public Library (RGD 26).

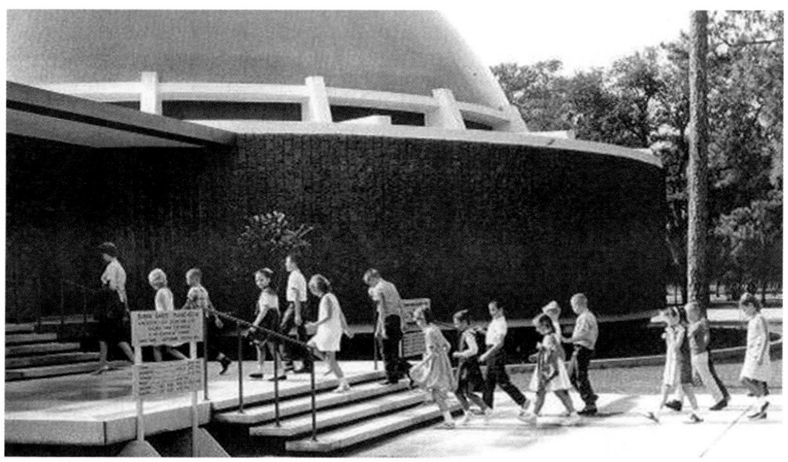

Burke Baker Planetarium (1964, George Pierce-Abel B. Pierce and Staub, Rather & Howze) was the first element of the new Houston Museum of Natural Science. Courtesy Houston Metropolitan Research Center, Houston Public Library.

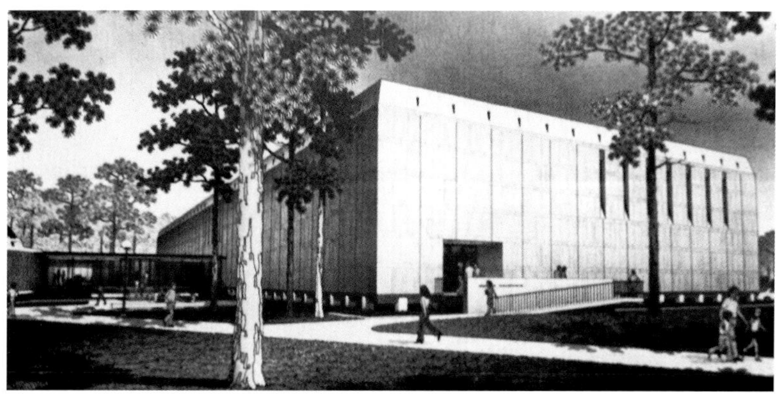

Houston Museum of Natural Science (1969, George Pierce–Abel B. Pierce and Staub, Rather & Howze). This original building is now almost obscured by additions. Courtesy Houston Metropolitan Research Center, Houston Public Library.

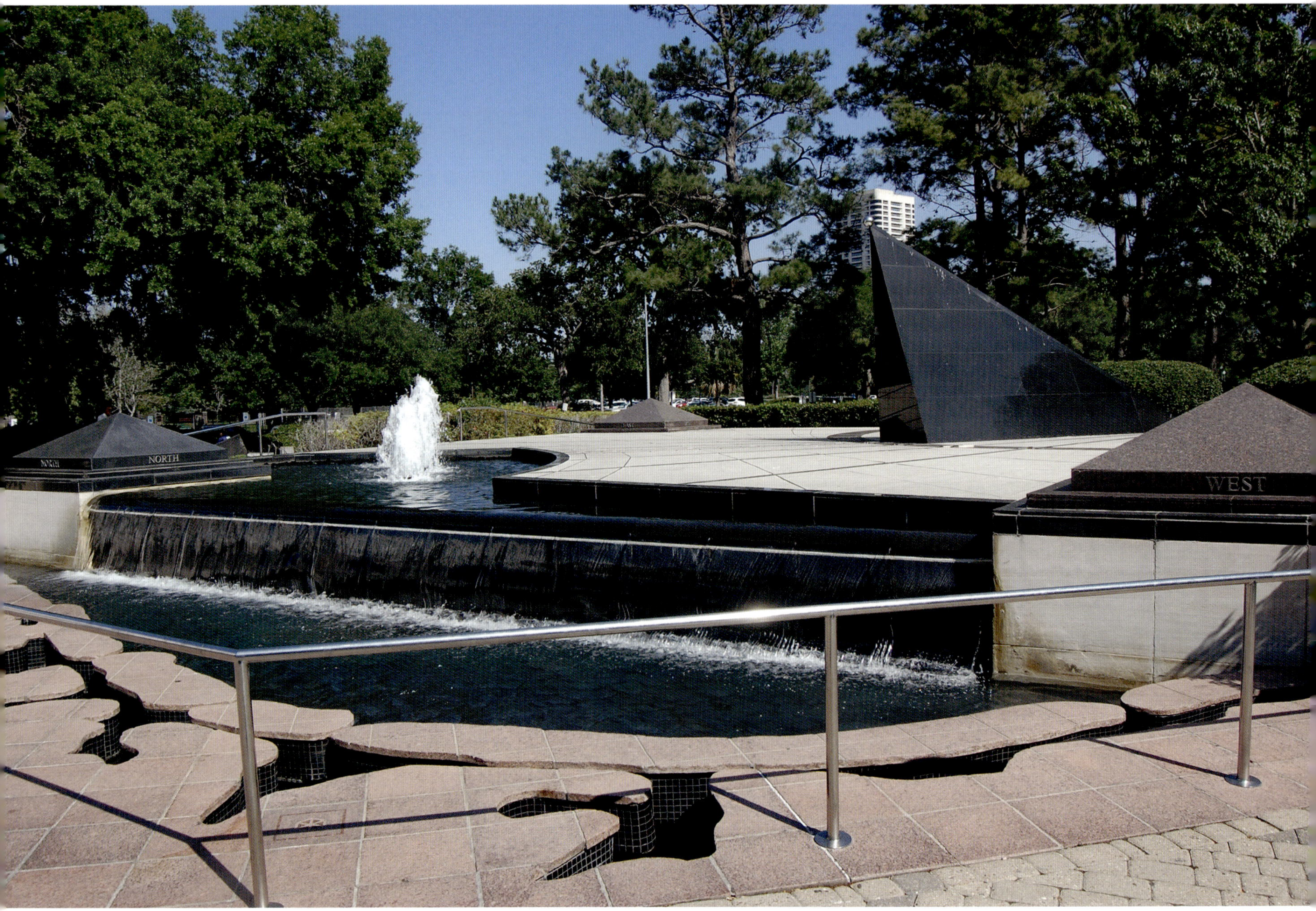

Memorial Sundial (1990) at the main entrance to the Houston Museum of Natural Science, 2012. Photograph by B. S. Bradley.

create a grand entrance plaza to the museum's main entrance, completed in 1990.

Racial Integration of Hermann Park

African American Houstonians lived under the US Supreme Court decision of *Plessy v. Ferguson* (1896), which upheld the constitutionality of state laws requiring racial segregation in public facilities under the "separate but equal" doctrine. This decision was not reversed until the Civil Rights Act in 1964. However, civil rights for African Americans in the South had become a serious issue before legislation ended legal segregation.

Many African American men in the South learned to play golf as caddies at private country clubs, where it had been a tradition that caddies were allowed to play on Mondays when the clubs were closed. In the Northeast and in large cities such as Chicago, upper- and middle-class African Americans formed country clubs and nurtured the careers of

African American professional golfers. The United States Colored Golf Association, now known as the United Golfers Association (UGA), was formed in 1925 because black men were barred from the Professional Golfers Association (PGA) and its tournaments until the exclusionary "Caucasian clause" was finally removed in 1961.[15] In a recent study of golf in the African American community, Sanjeev Baidyaroy noted: "While scholars are aware of the socioeconomic differences between northern and southern blacks during this period, not much attention has been given to the fact that northern blacks more regularly enjoyed UGA events and regular access to courses, while southern blacks were fighting time and again for either equal use or separate Jim Crow facilities that had been lacking for generations."[16]

The earliest lawsuits filed by black golfers were in Louisville, Kentucky (August 1947), Baltimore (January 1948), Miami (1949), and Houston (January 1950). Baltimore's Board of Recreation and Parks evaded a ruling in favor of the defendants by instituting separate playing time for blacks and whites. In Miami blacks were limited to one day a week, and a court decision upheld this regulation on the grounds that their involvement was hurting business to the point where the club would have to shut down.[17] Even with the minor victories, still nowhere did blacks and whites play together or share locker rooms and snack bars.[18]

Hermann Park's Municipal Golf Course brought Houston onto the national stage when five African American golfers brought suit in 1950, challenging the segregation of Houston's municipal golf courses. *Beal v. Holcombe* was filed in the Fifth Circuit of the US District Court in Houston on July 14, 1950. The five plaintiffs purchased the necessary tickets to play on the Hermann Park course, but they were denied access. Chief Judge Thomas Kennerly revealed in his written opinion that the City of Houston had twenty-one parks, seventeen for the use of white people and four for black citizens (Emancipation, Finnegan, Independence Heights, and Clinton; however, the latter two were under construction and not in use at the time of the lawsuit). Memorial Park, Glenbrook Park, and Hermann Park had golf courses for the exclusive use of white players. One witness testified that there were approximately five hundred Negroes in Houston who desired to play golf. Further, Judge Kennerly cited *Plessy v. Ferguson* in stating, "It has long been established that the States may provide for the separation of the negro race and the white race in certain public places and public institutions."[19] In his conclusion that the parks furnished to whites and negroes were substantially equal in their overall facilities, the judge stated, "I do not think the failure to provide golf courses in parks used by negroes is, either as matter of law or fact, a discrimination against negroes."[20]

In 1951 the US Court of Appeals for the Fifth Circuit reversed that decision, but it permitted the city "a reasonable opportunity to promptly prepare and put into effect regulations for the use of municipal golf facilities, which, while preserving segregation, will be in full and fair accord with its principle."[21] Over the next three years Houston officials debated whether to set aside one course for black golfers or allow them to play on all the courses on certain days. In 1952 the mayor sought a review by the US Supreme Court, but on May 24, 1954, the Supreme Court denied his petition in a ruling that came one week after the *Brown v. Board of Education* decision. This action left segregation of Houston's parks in place as long as equality of access was afforded. The next day the City Attorney, Will Sears, advised the mayor that continued litigation was useless and that the city's golf courses should be integrated.

On June 2, 1954, the Houston City Council, on its own accord, lifted all bans on African American players at its three municipal courses, effectively allowing free access to all of the city's parks and recreation facilities.[22] Because Hermann Park was near traditionally black neighborhoods and its course was preferred, it was the first of the city's golf courses to host large numbers of black players. Longtime Hermann Park advocate Marvin Taylor remembers the day well. On June 3 all the African American players in town, it seemed, showed up to tee off at 8:00 a.m. Taylor recalls that there were seven or eight paddy wagons parked at the clubhouse ready to take the players off to jail. But phone calls were made, there were no incidents, and the men enjoyed the rest of the day playing legally on what had been the day before a whites-only golf course.[23] This desegregation extended not only to all municipal parks in Houston but also to clubhouses, cafes, restrooms, showers, and lockers. With this action, the Hermann Park Golf Course became one of the first in the nation to achieve true desegregation.

During the 1950s and 1960s, there was little else in which Hermann Park could take pride. Both lack of adequate maintenance and bad decisions were made from the point of view of those who wanted to retain a natural, open space full of lawns, forests, recreation areas, and gardens. In addition to losing parkland to the Texas Medical Center, the expansion of the zoo, and construction of the Museum of Natural Science, Brays Bayou was stripped of all vegetation, its channel was rectified, and it was lined with concrete by the Harris County Flood Control District and the Army Corps of Engineers. This was, at the time, a standard flood-control solution.[24]

A small, but happier, addition was the zoo train, inaugurated in 1954. Harry Calvert copied the idea from the San Antonio Zoo and petitioned the city council for a train concession in Hermann Park. The first train was a truck tractor with two "coaches" that carried thirty people each. It ran not on tracks, but on rubber tires and toured the zoo at 2 miles per hour.[25] The train was an instant success, and by 1958 tracks had been laid for the "Hermann Park Special," which toured the park, not just the zoo. Louis Slusky (1910–1997) of Park Concession Inc., who also owned the cyclone ride at Playland Park, was concessioner for the min-

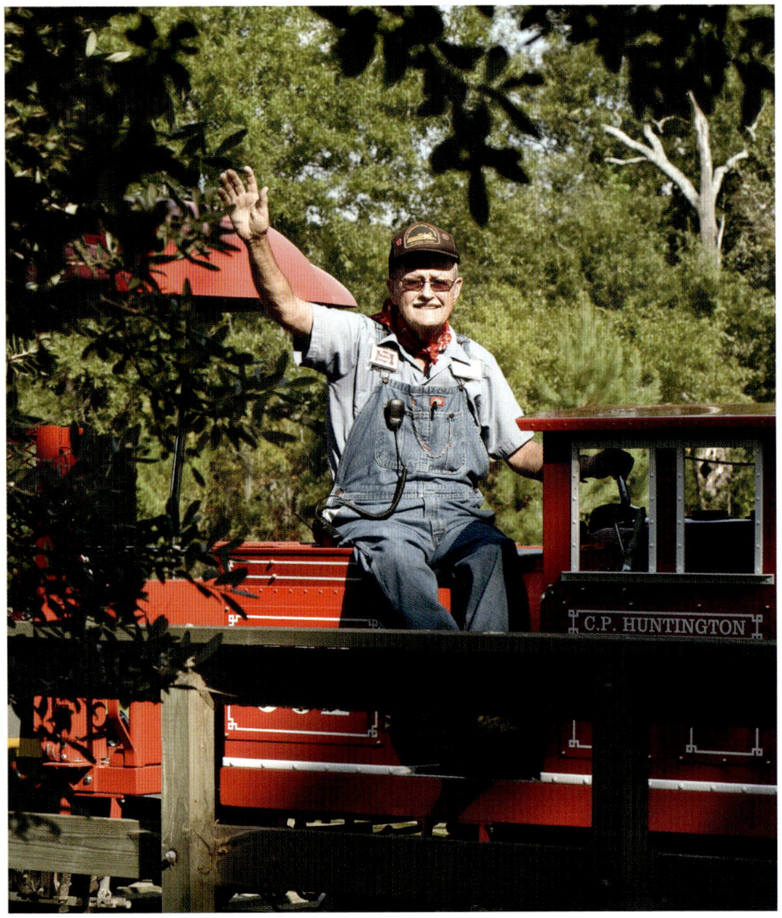

Big John Glaze, engineer of the beloved Hermann Park Railroad for many years. Photograph, 2009. Courtesy Hermann Park Conservancy.

iature train for many years. The Slusky trains ran on a 2-mile track with a 35-horsepower locomotive. In 2008 the Hermann Park Conservancy took over the operation of the train and funded a $4 million upgrade with new trains, new tracks, and three new train stops. "Big John" Glaze was the train engineer for forty years until he retired in 2009, after inaugurating the new train and Kinder Station.[26]

Miller Outdoor Theatre

In 1966 a much larger project was proposed that received overwhelming support from Houstonians: a new Miller Outdoor Theatre. Architect Eugene Werlin presented his unusual plan to the mayor and city council in March.[27] The city financed construction through a bond issue that was approved in the fall, and ground was broken in 1967. The opening performance was a summer Houston Symphony concert on September 1, 1968, attended by an audience of fifteen thousand people. Werlin's dramatic canopy structure is composed of three triangular folded plates of Cor-ten steel that span 95 feet between support points to preserve sight lines throughout the structure.[28] Eugene Werlin and Associates won several awards for Miller Theatre: the American Iron and Steel Institute's Biannual Award (1969), the American Institute of Steel Construction's Award of Excellence, and the James E. Lincoln Arc Welding Foundation Award. The new theatre has a 64' x 41' stage, fifty-four line sets for hanging lights, curtains, and scenery, an orchestra pit that can be raised and lowered, dressing rooms, offices, and a 110-ton air conditioning system that cools the performance area (stage). The expanded theatre grounds are located on approximately 7.5 acres of Hermann Park where a dramatically sloping, manmade hill provides

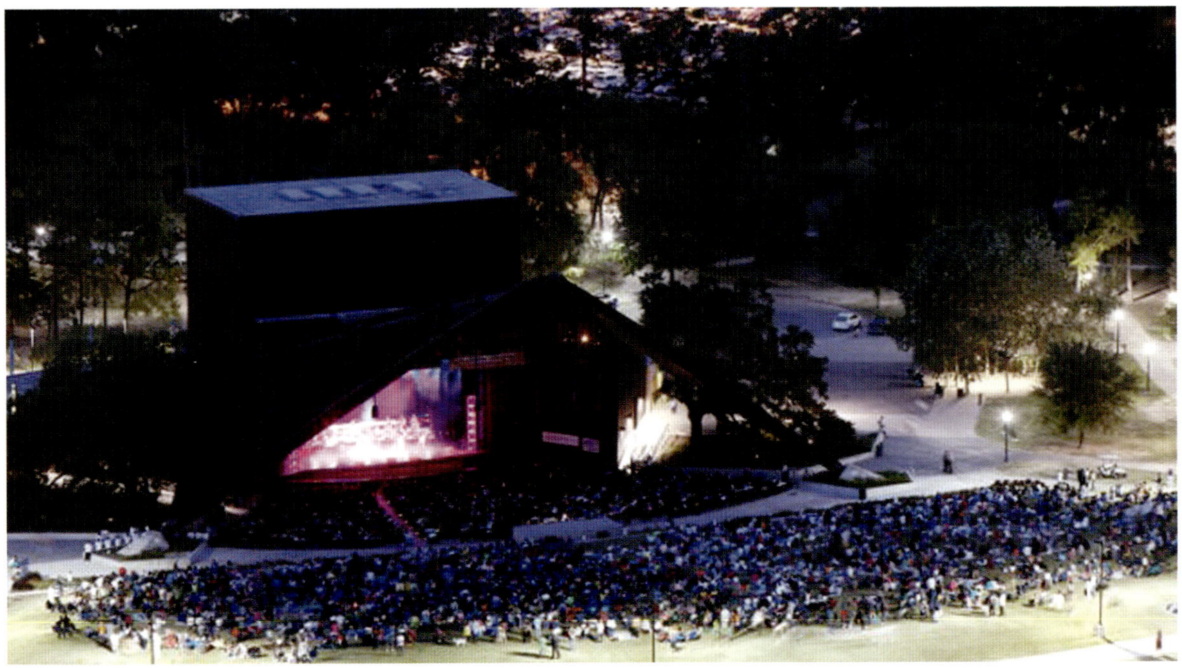

Miller Outdoor Theatre, evening concert, c. 1998. Courtesy Miller Outdoor Theatre.

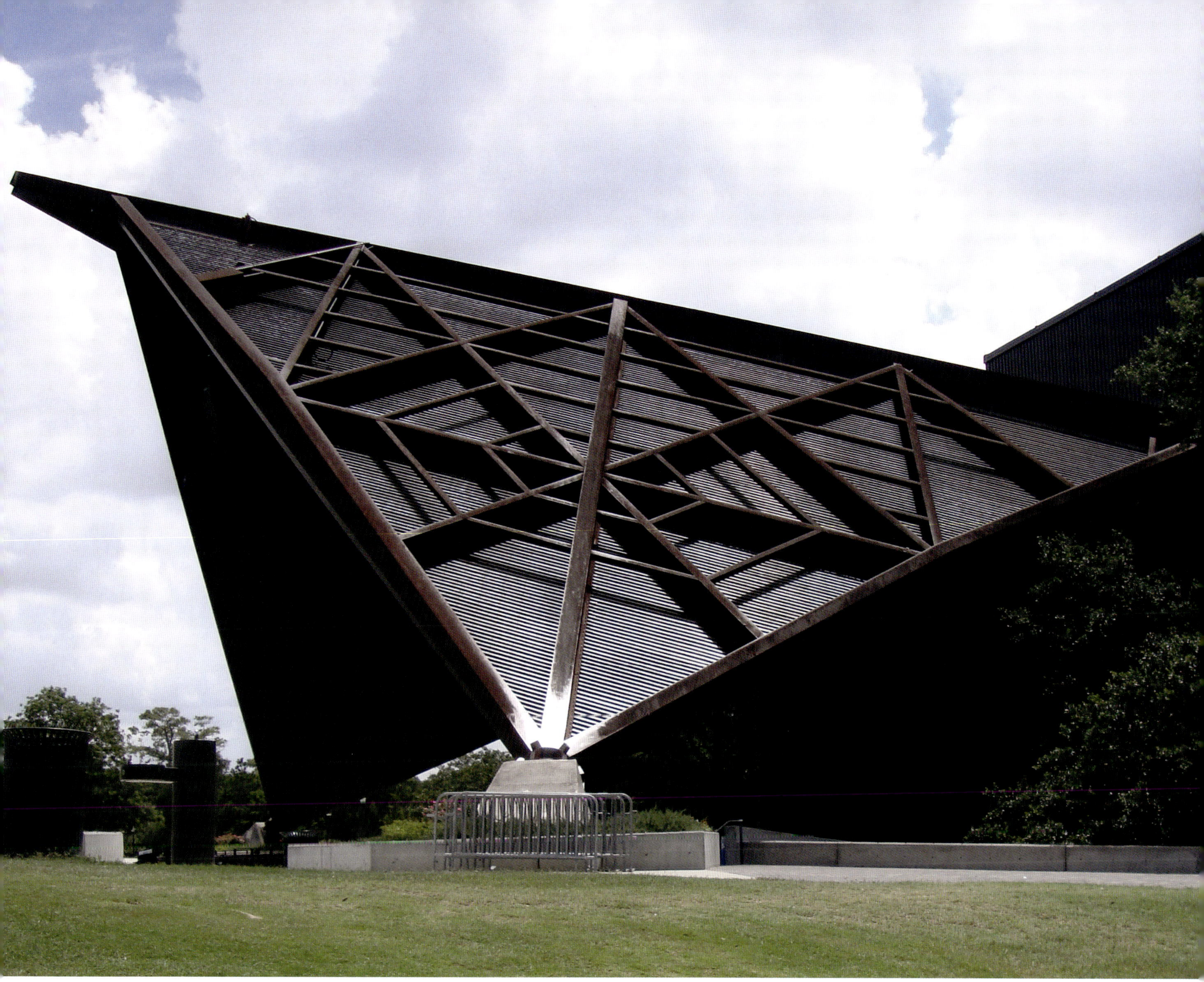

Miller Outdoor Theatre (1969, Eugene Werlin) features a prominent Cor-ten steel roof canopy. Courtesy Miller Outdoor Theatre.

good sightlines in an amphitheater configuration for those enjoying a performance on blankets under the stars. And almost all day, any day, one can find children rolling down the back of the berm with screams of delight. When Houston has a rare snowfall, this is a premier sledding site. When the original Miller Theatre was demolished for the new theatre, the columns were incorporated into the Mecom-Rockwell Colonnade, built on Hermann Drive between Fannin and San Jacinto in 1968 and 1969.[29]

CHAPTER SIX

Other Plans

1962–1989

Serious environmental damage will occur in Hermann Park unless several major problems are solved.

—LAN/Cummins Master Plan, 1972

After Herbert Hare's death in 1962, most activity in Hermann Park was limited to specific institutions: the Hermann Park Zoo, Miller Outdoor Theatre, and the Museum of Natural Science. Routine park maintenance continued but was not sufficient to keep the park and its greenery in good shape. Despite the straightening and concrete channeling of Brays Bayou, drainage in the park was not improved. The City of Houston was not unmindful of the needs in Hermann Park. In 1970 W. G. Scheibe, Parks and Recreation director, proposed to double the size of the zoo and fence its entire perimeter. He wanted a new golf clubhouse, authorization for a new road through the park, new parking lots, and expanded picnicking facilities. The city council turned down Scheibe's request because there were no cost estimates attached to his proposal. However, they did approve hiring a consultant to come up with a new master plan for Hermann Park. Mayor Louie Welch, revealing his views on Hermann Park, said that he thought it was unfair to the majority of park users that one-half of the park was given over to three or four thousand golfers.[1] Welch did not actually propose eliminating the golf course, but he intimated that this could be a solution to overuse in other park areas.

LAN/Cummins Plan

Two engineering firms, Lockwood Andrews and Newnam Inc. (LAN) and James A. Cummins Inc., along with the park and recreational planning firm McFadzean, Everly and Assoc. of Winnetka, Illinois, were retained by the City of Houston to conduct studies, compile statistics, and draw up a master plan based on a prioritized list of improvements. The Hermann Park Advisory Council was appointed by the mayor to work with the consultants. This included representatives from ten agencies and institutions: the Houston Zoological Society, the Municipal Arts Commission, the Miller Theatre Advisory Council, the Garden Center Advisory Board, the Houston Museum of Natural Science, the Texas Medical Center, Rice University, the Children's Museum, and the City of Houston's Traffic and Transportation and Parks and Recreation departments. The fledgling Children's Museum was included because it planned to locate a toy museum in Hermann Park.[2]

The 1972 master plan correctly concluded: "serious environmental damage will occur in Hermann Park unless several major problems are solved."[3] Park attendance in 1972 was estimated at three million people, and over three million cars drove through the park, with half of those vehicles stopping and parking in the park. Projections forecast over four-and-a-half million visitors by 1980 and more than six million by 1990. "It is apparent from the analysis that Hermann Park will not be able to function past 1980, even with the recommended improvements unless the demand is accommodated by other major urban parks."[4] Problems related to such heavy use were identified and ranked by priority: (1) parking, circulation, access, and egress; (2) drainage; (3) security and control; (4) park deterioration; (5) utilities; (6) inefficient park usage. These problems were addressed through recommendations that included a new circulation and parking system, relocating the Garden Center to Memorial Park, improving and expanding of the Museum of Natural Science, and installing a new water sculpture and pedestrian mall (to be achieved by filling in the reflection pool). Other suggestions included development of new playgrounds, construction of a toy museum, expanding picnic facilities, upgrading the zoo in Hermann Park and locating a second zoo at another site, building botanical islands in the lake, refurbishing the golf course and building a new clubhouse (and demolishing the 1933 clubhouse), and adding a new intrapark transit system. Of note were proposed athletic facilities across Brays Bayou on land now called Bayou Parkland. Tennis courts and playing fields were like those initially proposed for Hermann Park before the land on which they would have been built was sold for the Texas Medical Center. Further infrastructure improvements were recommended: new drainage facilities, improved water and sewer service, and expanded and improved lighting and electrical distribution systems. At the time, these proposed improvements were estimated to cost almost $15 million.[5]

One important consideration the 1972 master plan report pointed out was that no legal restrictions existed to prevent development of Hermann Park or the deaccessioning of its property other than George Hermann's nebulous stipulation that the land be used exclusively for park purposes. In a series of annotated maps and plans, LAN and Cummins outlined their proposals. The *Houston Post* reported in July 1972 on these recommendations, including construction of an aquarium on the lake shore in front of the zoo with funds from the bequest of Herbert Kipp. A toy museum was proposed for unused land southeast of North MacGregor Way that would be funded by the nonprofit Children's Museum Inc.[6] Director Scheibe said that the plan would cause clearing of some trees but that trees grow fast in Houston and could be replaced with trees at other locations.

After this master plan was formally accepted by the city council in 1973, funding, and therefore construction, was slow in coming. It was not until 1978 that $4.5 million was allocated for drainage improvements, new parking lots, and construction of a two-way, north-south street through the park.[7] During the next three years, 6 1/2 acres at the very center of the park were paved to provide for more parking. This

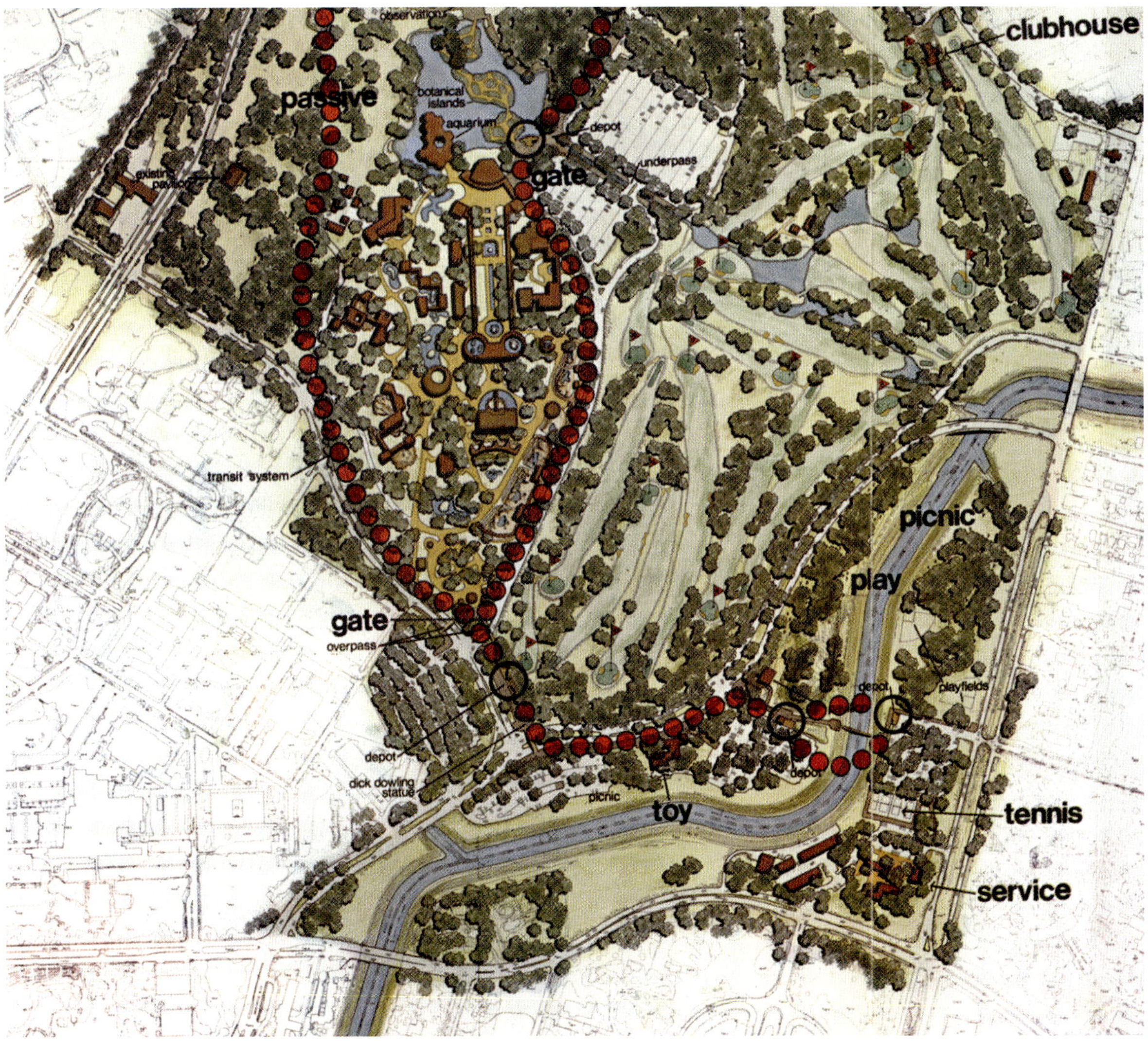

Hermann Park Master Plan (1972, LAN/Cummins). Few proposals from this plan were implemented because of lack of funding. The primary exception was construction of the aquarium. This plan also recommended moving the golf clubhouse to Almeda, which was done twenty-four years later. Courtesy Houston Metropolitan Research Center, Houston Public Library (T711.558).

more than doubled the number of spaces in the park to over 2,400. These were the only improvements recommended by the 1972 master plan that were implemented. Some of the carriage drives were closed to traffic, but proposed entry points were not added. "The result was to confine all circulation to a central, easily congested spine," concluded landscape architect Jane Anderson Curtis.[8]

Although the 1972 plan proposed solutions to obvious problems, the limited follow-through meant that the new road configuration and aquarium were not accompanied by other amenities that might have mitigated the unpleasant aspects of these changes. For example, the parking lots were not paved with the recommended Gobi mats that allow grass to grow through them and support a car's weight without damage to the turf, nor were replacement trees planted in the parking lots or elsewhere in the park, and the monorail for transporting visitors was not built. The 1972 master plan concentrated only on providing access to more and more cars and people—there is no mention of park preservation, much less restoration of its natural features. Stephen Fox wrote of the effect of the new parking lots and roadways: "Within the park, the historic infrastructure began to be eliminated in a piecemeal fashion."[9] Perhaps the most egregious mistake during this period was siting the Kipp Aquarium (1980–1982) astride the main axis. The drawings (and text) of the LAN/Cummins plan made no attempt to reinforce or even recognize the Kessler and Hare & Hare plans. This oversight led to building the aquarium with its broad, conical roof at the terminus of the most important structural aspect of the park, making this primary axis seem inconsequential.

Chinese Pavilion

In 1976 Houston's sister city, Taipei, gave a Chinese pavilion to the people of Houston as a sesquicentennial gift. It was constructed in Taiwan, then disassembled and shipped to Houston, where it was reassembled in Hermann Park at the center of a small meadow adjacent to Hermann Drive in 1978. The siting of the pavilion reinforced the fact that there was no organizational plan for Hermann Park's future.[10] Five years after the pavilion was placed in the park, the Houston Taipei Society proposed a 5-acre Chinese garden, designed by Fred Buxton, to surround the pavilion.[11] This plan, like so many others, died for lack of funding. However, the society did refurbish the pavilion in 1995.[12]

In the summer of 1978 a 2-mile "exer-trail" around the Hermann Park Golf Course opened.[13] This running path with five exercise stations was a welcome addition, given there were very few athletic facilities in the park. In fact, two inadequate clay tennis courts located east of the zoo and south of the Hermann Park Clubhouse along Hermann Park Drive were the only athletic facilities other than the golf course. Even though it is clear that George Hermann's intent was to include athletic fields and other sports facilities in the park, such facilities were never developed. Plans for such amenities were eclipsed when the Hogg tract, on which athletic fields and gyms were to be located, was sold to the Texas Medical Center.

In 1980 the Cravens Walkway was installed to address the isolated strip of land between Main Street and Fannin. New grass, sidewalks, and benches were placed in the shade of the graceful live oak allée along Main, making the area usable by pedestrians. Mary Cullinan Cravens, who grew up in Shadyside across from the park, donated the funds that allowed the City of Houston to complete this project. Mary Cravens and her sisters, Margaret Cullinan Wray and Nina Cullinan, were the daughters of J. S. Cullinan.

Another isolated addition occurred in 1981, when a statue of George H. Hermann was finally placed in the park. The artist, Lonnie Joe Edwards of Salado, Texas, was commissioned by the Hermann Hospital Estate in May 1979 to produce a standing figure of Hermann for the park. The 9-foot-tall cast bronze statue took two years to complete and was dedicated and unveiled May 16, 1981, at the corner of Fannin and Cambridge Street.[14] The statue depicts Hermann wearing a suit and tie, glancing toward his right. He is standing with his feet apart, arms at his side, holding a cowboy hat in his right hand.[15] The title *George Hermann USA* appears on the horizontal edge of the statue's base. The statue rests on a pink granite trapezoidal pedestal; on the face of each of the four sides is a legend with the titles "The Man," "His Gift," "His Concern," and "His Legacy." The first contains a brief biography, the second has descriptions of Hermann Park and Hermann Square, the third recounts details of Hermann's creation and endowment of Hermann Hospital, and finally a dedication to George Hermann.

In 1943 the Lions Club of Houston had commissioned Enrico Cerracchio, sculptor of the Sam Houston Equestrian Monument, to create a bronze statue of Hermann for the park. Cerracchio made a life-size, plaster cast of Hermann seated, legs crossed, looking down at an open book in his lap, but, once again because of a lack of funds, the monument was never cast. Cerracchio's painted maquette was located in City Hall until it was restored and moved to the Department of Parks and Recreation headquarters in the Gragg Building in 2009.[16] Cerracchio's "George Hermann" is more refined and captures Hermann's character and personality more effectively than the Edwards statue installed in the park.

Charles Moore Plan

Although Hermann Park was not totally neglected during the 1970s and 1980s, as Fox observed, "good intentions were often accompanied by a lack of judgment and discrimination."[17] One exception might have been a plan instigated by Drexel Turner and the Rice School of Architecture that was never realized because of lack of public support, and thus lack of funding. The Moore plan evolved after Turner, aware

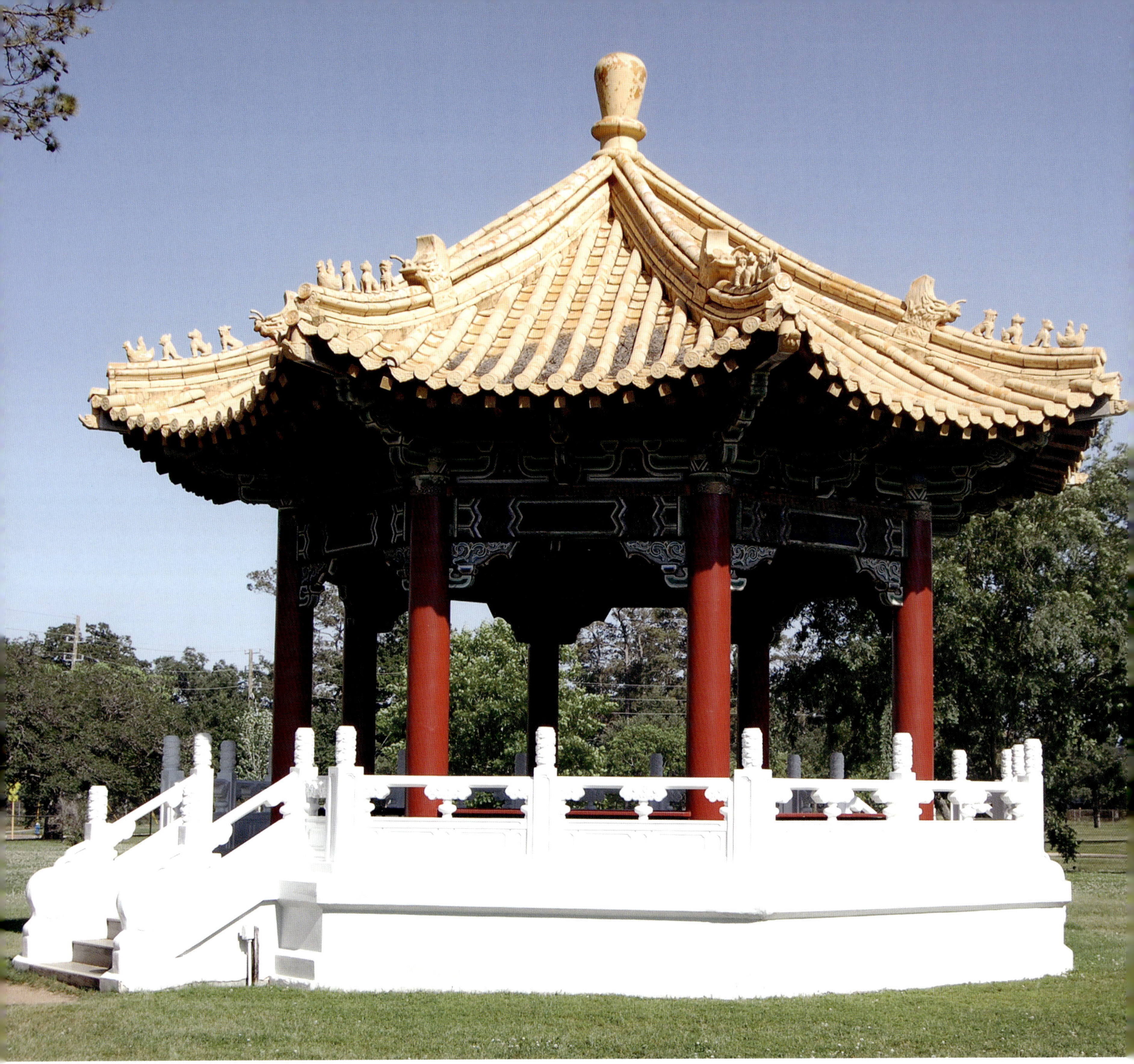

Chinese Pavilion, given to the City of Houston by its sister city, Taipei, was constructed in Hermann Park in 1978 in a meadow behind the Garden Center, where a proposed Chinese garden surrounding it was never built, 2012. Photograph by B. S. Bradley.

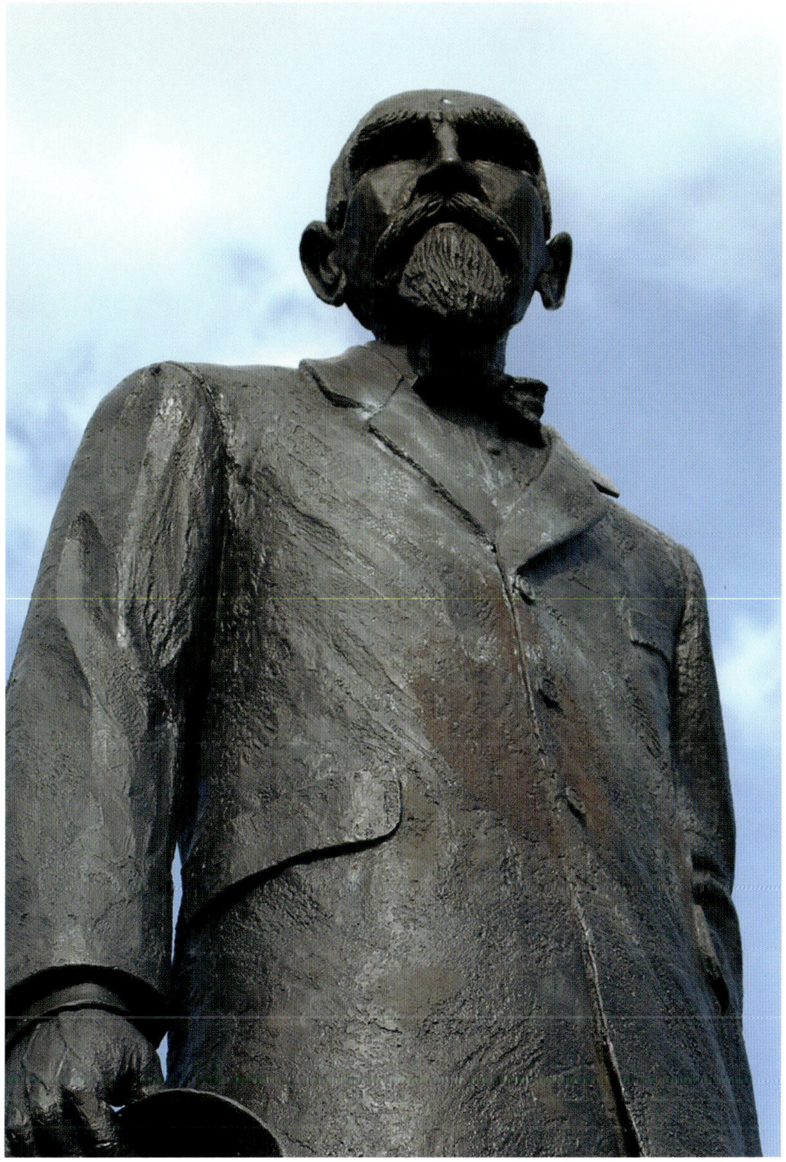

George Hermann Statue (1981, Lonnie Joe Edwards). This sculpture is located in the southwest corner of the park across from Hermann Hospital. Photograph courtesy Hermann Park Conservancy.

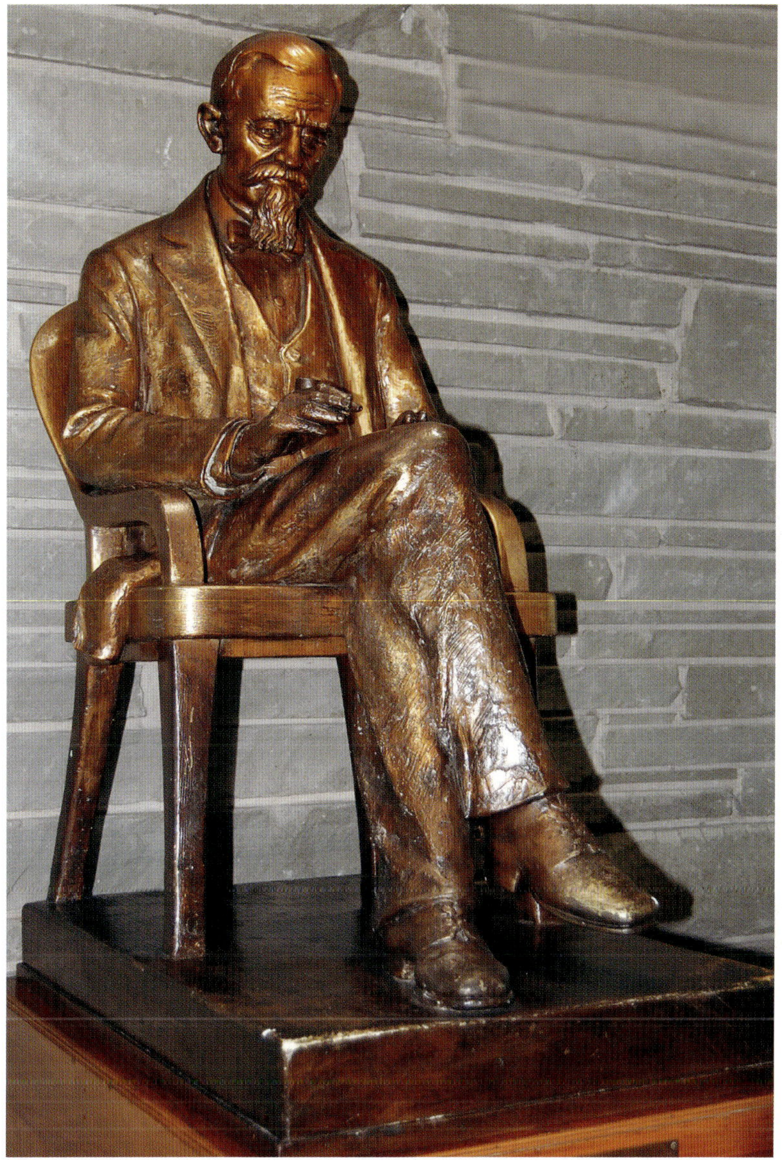

George Henry Hermann (1943, Enrico Cerracchio). This life-size plaster maquette for a proposed bronze statue that was never cast now resides in the lobby of the Houston Parks and Recreation Building, 2999 South Wayside Drive. Photograph by B. S. Bradley.

that plans for zoo expansion and refurbishment were afoot, suggested that the renowned Los Angeles architect Charles W. Moore (1925–1993) be commissioned to design an elephant-themed entrance to the zoo.[18] This idea was inspired by the Art Deco elephant towers (Bakewell and Weihe, architects, with Donald Macky, sculptor) at the 1939 Golden Gate International Exposition on Treasure Island in San Francisco Bay.[19] Moore had used these towers as a precedent for his elephant-centered entry in *Buildings for Best Products*, a 1979 exhibition at the Museum of Modern Art in New York.[20] In 1980 Turner urged the Municipal Art Commission to retain Moore to adapt his elephants for the Hermann Park Zoo. This idea was stillborn when the aquarium replaced the old entrance piers and gates to the zoo, leaving little room for any sort of new entrance. But Turner persisted.

Isabel Brown Wilson, chairman, and Nancy Crow Allen, a member of the Municipal Arts Commission, aware of a greater need than just a more attractive entrance to the zoo, listened to Turner and, with the Parks and Recreation Department, commissioned Moore and his associate Barton Phelps through their nonprofit firm, Urban Innovations Group at the University of California in Los Angeles, to produce designs for upgrading not only the park entrance and lake, but Miller Theatre

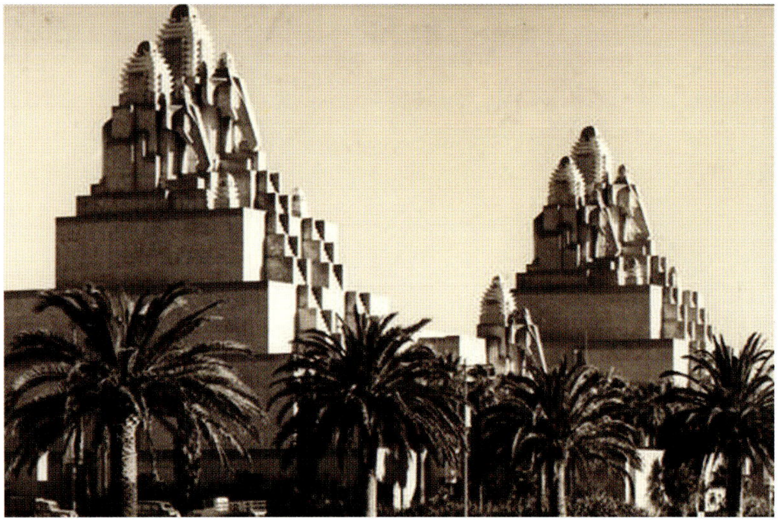

Elephant Towers at the Golden Gate International Exposition in San Francisco, 1932. These art deco forms were Charles Moore's inspiration for his 1982 proposal for Miller Theatre and the Reflection Pool in Hermann Park. Courtesy private collection.

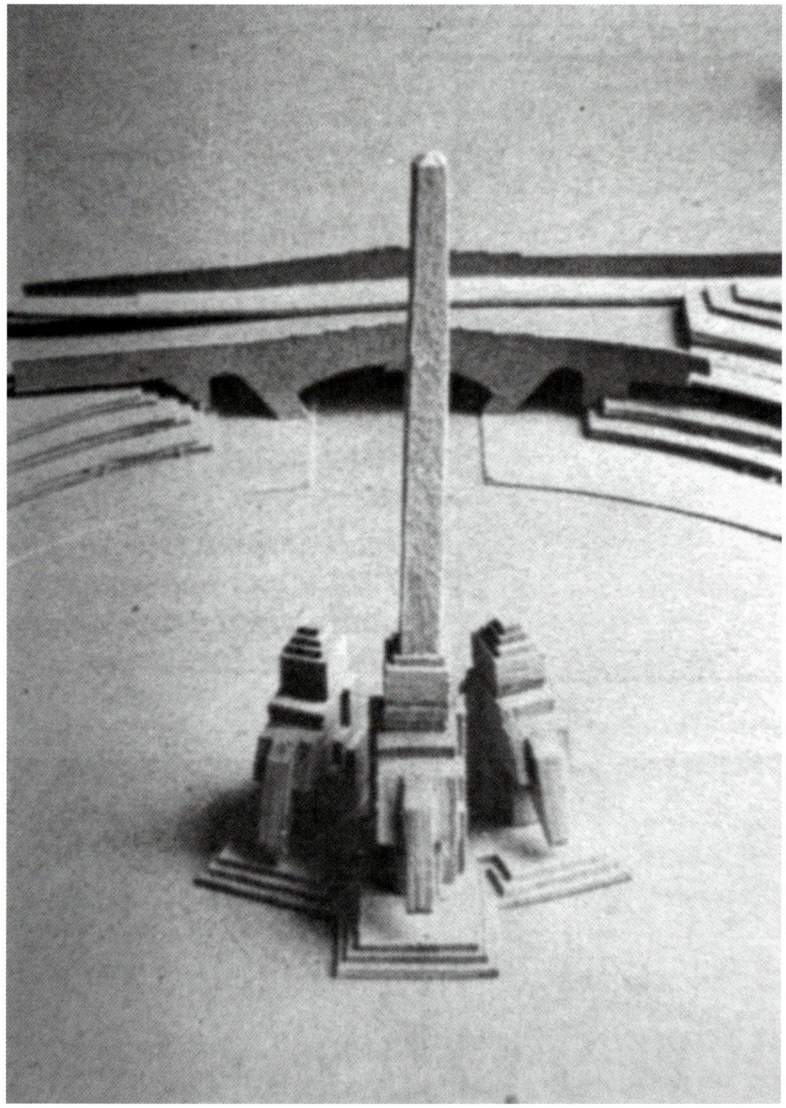

Elephant Obelisk proposal (1982, Charles Moore). Courtesy Houston Metropolitan Research Center, Houston Public Library (0456).

as well. Turner wrote, "Kessler's plan was only partially realized, and today the northwest quadrant remains a conspicuously underdeveloped scenic and recreational resource."[21] This was the first time since 1916 that consideration was given to the nurture and development of what Turner called the "window to the city" and the force behind the rejuvenation of the park at the turn of the twenty-first century.

The 1982 Moore Plan was resolutely based on the tenets of the then-popular post-modernism, of which Charles Moore was one of the most noted practitioners. Post-modern architecture evolved in reaction to the formalism and starkness of the modernism, influenced by the celebrated Viennese architect Adolf Loos's (1870–1933) 1908 essay called "Ornament and Crime."[22] In post-modern architecture classical motifs (such as columns and pediments) as well as other historical precedents were reused in witty, unconventional, and nonstructural ways to create new forms often appended to modern structures. The purpose was to enliven modern buildings, which, during the ascendancy of post-modernism, were seen as monotonous. In the United States Robert Venturi inspired the post-modern movement first in his book *Complexity and Contradiction in Architecture* (1966) and later in *Learning from Las Vegas* (1977), two influential works about post-modern architecture. Charles Moore, a celebrated educator and writer as well as architect, is known as the architect of perhaps the most notable post-modern project in the United States, the Piazza d'Italia (1978) in New Orleans.

Charles Moore's plan for Hermann Park, as recommended by Turner, raised the Pioneer Memorial Obelisk on a high pedestal closely guarded by a trio of post-modern stainless steel elephants inspired by Gian Lorenzo Bernini's (1598–1680) *Elephant Obelisk* (1667) in the Piazza della Minerva in Rome.[23] The Hermann Park entry sequence was to be redesigned with a new giant triple-arch base for the Sam Houston Equestrian Statue, a trapezoidal reflection pool that spilled into a secondary water feature with five diminishing pavilions on each side, creating a false perspective converging on Moore's Elephant Obelisk fountain surrounded by a circular basin. An arched bridge connected this basin to an enlarged lake. The *Houston Chronicle's* art critic, Ann Holmes, wrote that these "small belvederes" with choice views and restful seats, like the elephants, refer to India. She continued, "The stylized structure for the edge of the lake near the zoo takes its inspiration from the south colonnade of the viceroy's palace in imperial Delhi,

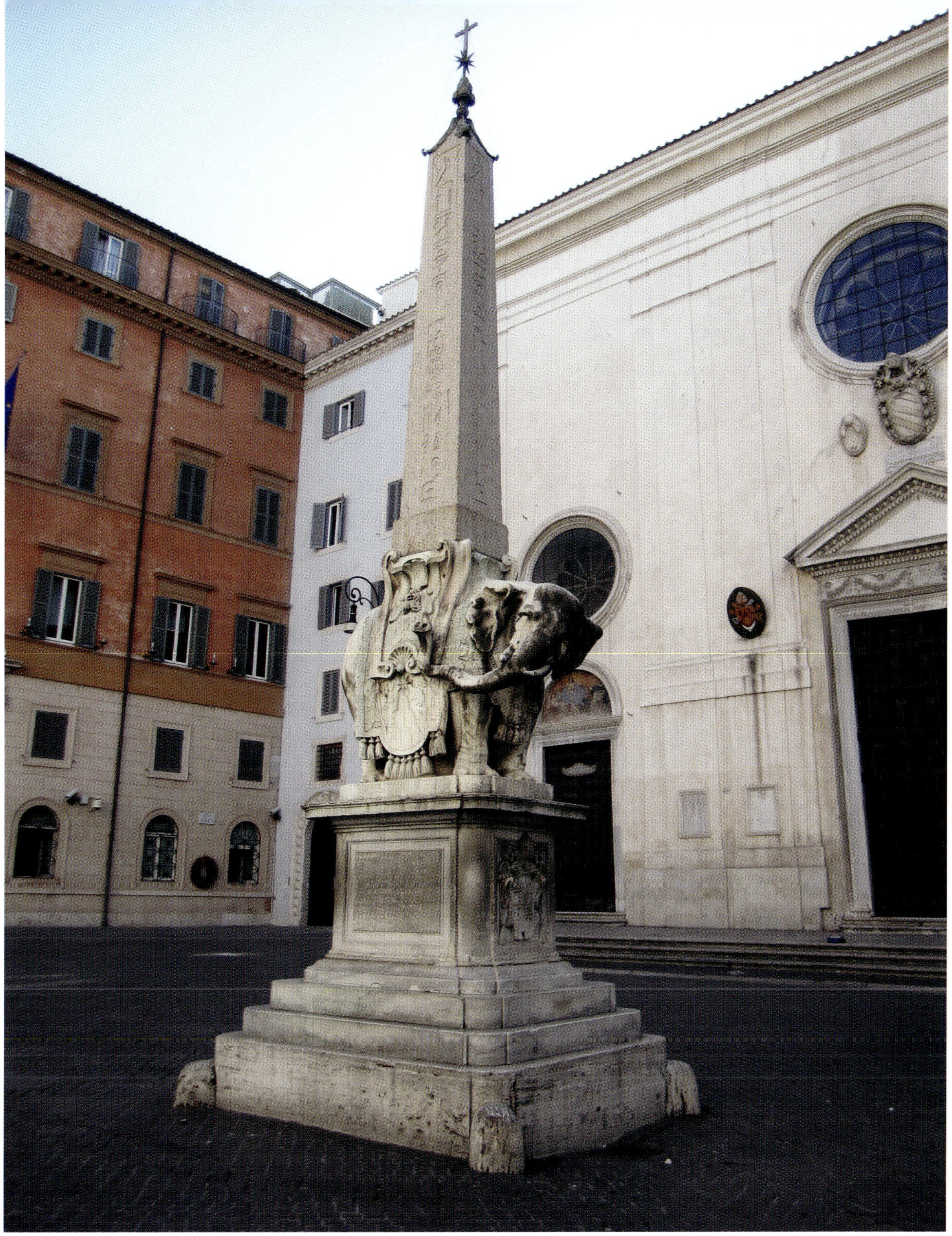

Elephant and Obelisk, Piazza della Minerva, Rome, Italy (1667, Giovanni Lorenzo Bernini). Bernini would have been familiar with *Hypnerotomachia Poliphili* (*Poliphilo's Strife of Love in a Dream*), published in Venice in 1499 by Francesco Colonna. This work was renowned for its detailed woodcuts, including one of an elephant and obelisk that resembles Bernini's work. Courtesy private collection.

designed by famed English architect Sir Edwin Lutyens."[24] There was also a Lutyens precedent for the arched Sam Houston Monument pedestal—*Monument to the Missing of the Battle of the Somme*, Thiepval, France, 1932.[25] The Grand Basin was to have been enlarged from 6 to 20 acres and made more accessible and enjoyable with pavilions and watercraft. The richness of these plans and their historical associations would have brought to the park a depth of meaning and sophistication that it lacked.

Because Miller Theatre's self-oxidizing steel roof plate was corroding and the audience area suffered from inferior sightlines and acoustics, Moore proposed a new superstructure over the stage and permanent seats. Sidewalls were created in "stylized silhouette townscape patterns (the profile of the Indian howdah or elephant chair) with three doorways on each sidewall."[26] Other perimeter walls were constructed around the Miller Theatre grounds, which would improve acoustics and control access so entry fees could be charged for

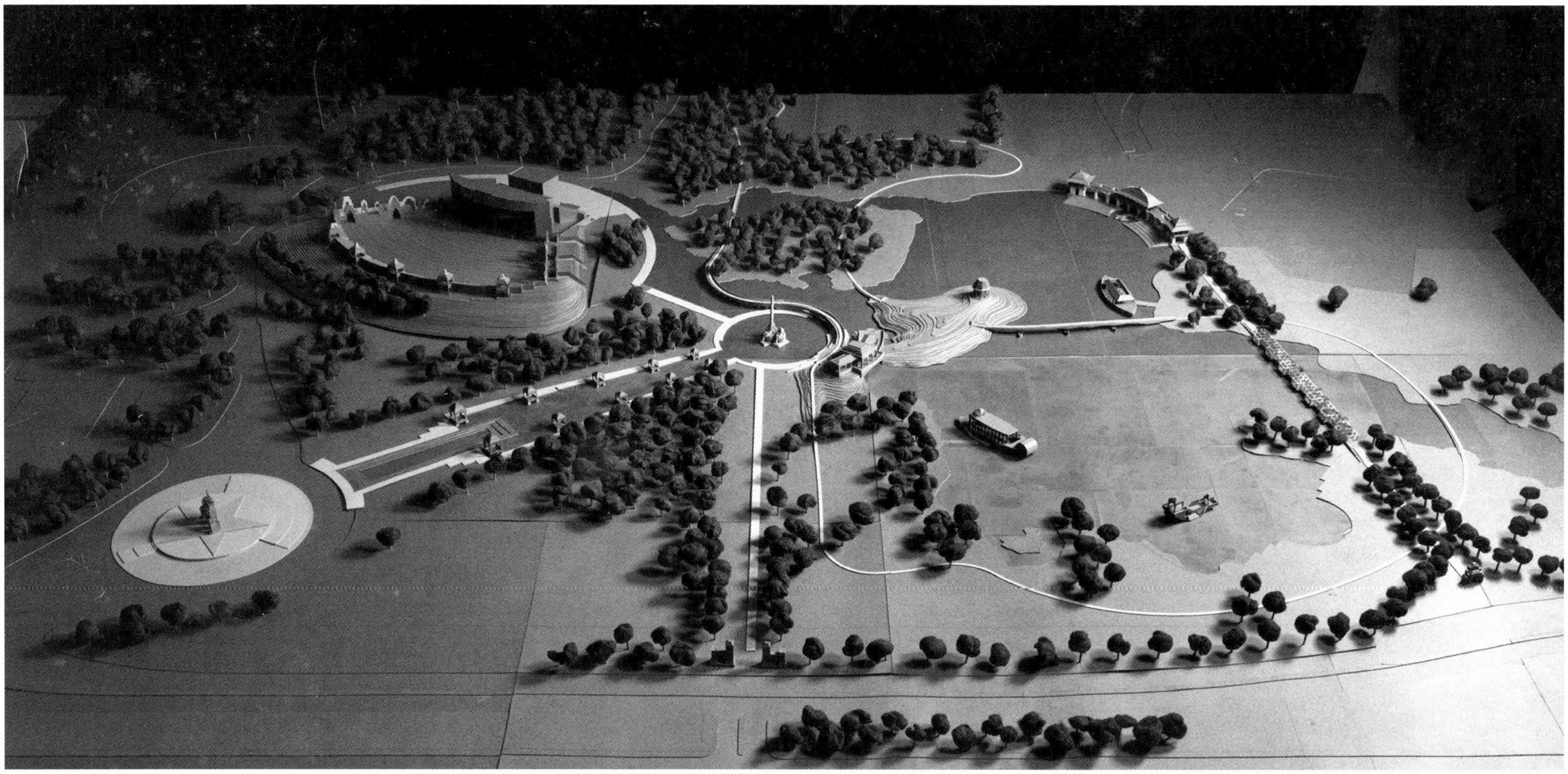

Model of Hermann Park proposal (1982, Charles Moore). Courtesy Houston Metropolitan Research Center, Houston Public Library (0456).

some events. This was done also to control the crowds that, at a peak of 35,000 for one event, had become unmanageable. Moore's plan would limit attendance at 12,000. There was no doubt that the plan addressed some serious problems with cleverness and style, but its level of whimsy was too much for some people, as was its $10 million price tag.[27]

Even though no aspect of the Moore Plan was implemented, it focused attention on a crucial area of the park that had been neglected, and raised issues that took another decade to address. Candace Rylander, executive director of the nonprofit South Main Center, in discussing this plan and the needs of the park in general, recommended a governing organization for Hermann Park like the Central Park Conservancy in New York. The lake needed to be expanded and managed for recreational use. A café or park restaurant needed to be built. And most important for future planning in the park, Moore and Phelps recognized the significance of Kessler's central axis. Turner, quoting John Kenneth Galbraith, concluded an article in *Cite: The Architecture and Design Review of Houston* by saying: "Hermann Park and its environs typify in microcosm the condition of civic art in Houston today: public squalor in the midst of private affluence."[28]

End of the Decade

In 1989 Hermann Park found itself a depository for haphazard projects, lacking sufficient maintenance, and with less than one-quarter of the park—fewer than 100 acres—devoted to general use. Approximately 100 acres were effectively severed from the park by roads (Fannin, Cambridge, and North and South MacGregor ways); 125 acres were devoted to the eighteen-hole golf course; the zoo occupied 45 acres; Miller Outdoor Theatre over 10 acres; the Museum of Natural Science, 5 acres; and finally, an astounding amount of parkland, 30 acres, was dedicated to parking lots.[29] Paul Hester's photographic essay published in *Cite* in 1983 showed a dismal state of affairs in the park. An accompanying legend read: "As Paul Hester's photographs reveal, the popularity of Hermann Park has not insured its careful maintenance or determined public conservation. Instead, official carelessness, expedience and uncontrolled development of various zones within the park continue to erode the qualities of this unique Houston place."[30]

PART II

Now

CHAPTER SEVEN

Community Action

There must be a message of healing and new strength of unity as well as high quality execution in the design [for Hermann Park].[1]

—William J. Johnson, 1992

The first organized group of Houstonians to take an active interest in Hermann Park was incorporated in 1987 as the Hermann Park Joggers, Runners, and Walkers, a nonprofit organization founded by Marvin Taylor for the purpose of maintaining and enhancing a running trail in Hermann Park along an old carriage drive.[2] Taylor grew up in Longview in East Texas, where he credits his experience as a Boy Scout and later as a Scoutmaster for instilling in him a sense of civic activism that has sustained his thirty-plus years of involvement with Hermann Park. After serving in the Navy, Taylor graduated from Prairie View A&M University in 1955 intending to become a teacher, however, he discovered he did not like teaching. Instead he moved to Houston and began a thirty-year career with the US Postal Service. Taylor, a high-school athlete, began running on the deck of his aircraft carrier for exercise when he was in the Navy during the Korean War.

When Marvin Taylor moved to Houston in the late 1950s, jogging was not popular. He ran in his Third Ward neighborhood but looked for more remote trails because, he says, people thought it was weird to be running on the streets. At first he cut his way through dense underbrush, clearing short trails along Brays Bayou and in MacGregor Park. But he soon discovered the old, overgrown carriage trail in Hermann Park. "I took my sickle and started clearing a trail over there."[3] Before long others who had taken up jogging joined him, and in 1978 the Parks and Recreation Department placed exercise stations along the picturesque trail overhung with giant live oaks that Taylor had begun clearing a few years before.[4] Taylor heard that attorney Larry Nettles was working on a jogging trail in Memorial Park. He contacted Nettles, who advised Taylor to form a nonprofit corporation so the Hermann Park runners could raise money to supplement what the city could do to improve the trail. With the support of Nettles and novelist Olive Hershey, one of Taylor's first running mates, Taylor began gathering signatures and writing letters to politicians, churches, neighbors, and anyone else he could think of asking for donations. In a series of meetings with Don Olson, then director of the Parks and Recreation Department, Taylor learned that the city would fund improvements to the trail, but it would not light it. The Houston Lighting and Power Company agreed to light the perimeter, but private funds were necessary to light the trail inside the park. In 1990, after years of telephone calls and several petitions, Taylor's efforts resulted in the city-funded construction of the trail with a crushed granite surface.[5]

It took another two years, but by late 1992 the trail had lights. Grants from the Jacob and Terese Hershey Foundation and Houston Endowment Inc. (supported by Olive Hershey and Ann Hamilton, respectively), many individual donations, and a gift of twenty-four acorn lamps along the 1/2-mile section next to the golf course by Burr Engineers Inc., in commemoration of their twentieth anniversary, made lighting the trail possible.[6] Fifty-two streetlights were installed along the carriage trail, North MacGregor, and Golf Course Drive. For a donation of $500 or more, a benefactor was honored with a plaque in front of a lamppost. One, inscribed "The Taylor Brothers," was given by Marvin Taylor in honor of three of his grandsons. When the 2.1-mile trail was named the Marvin Taylor Trail in 2003, Allan Turner wrote in the *Houston Chronicle*: "And in the 1980s, he [Taylor] began to cobble community sentiment into a potent force to urge rehabilitation of Hermann Park's trails."[7] This kind of "community sentiment" from a variety of other

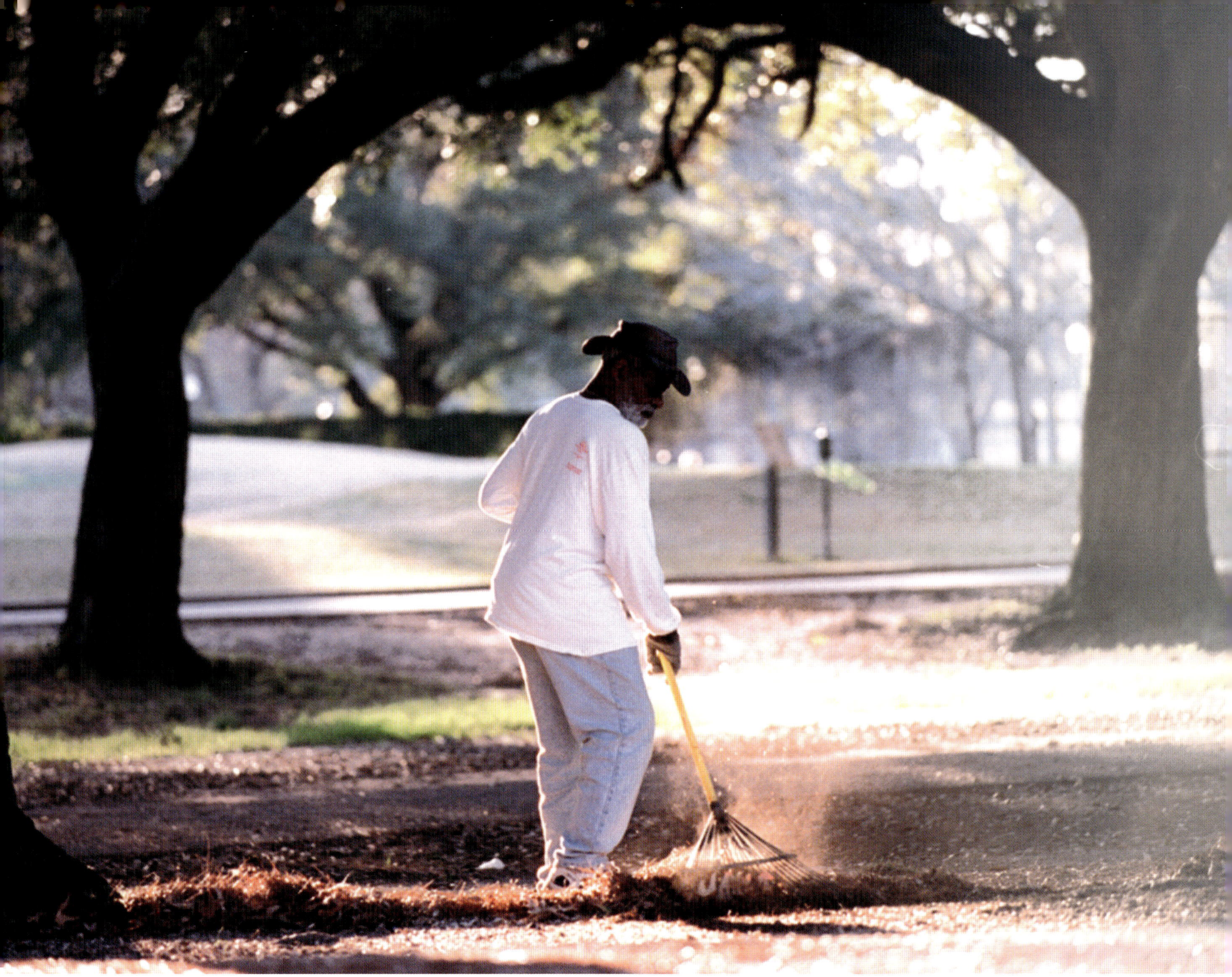

Marvin Taylor raking the Marvin Taylor Trail he initiated along one of the disused Hermann Park carriage drives in the early 1970s for the Hermann Park Runners, Joggers, and Walkers, one of the forerunners of the Hermann Park Conservancy, c. 2008. Photograph by Jay Baker, FAIA. Courtesy Hermann Park Conservancy.

groups as well has helped renew Hermann Park and make it into the celebrated place it is today.

In 1990 several residents of the Warwick Towers condominiums (1983, Golemon & Rolfe, architects) whose balconies overlooked Hermann Park, approached the Parks and Recreation Department and asked permission to plant grass around the Mecom Rockwell Fountain Colonnade. When this fountain was installed in 1968 as a way to save the columns of the old Miller Theatre, no landscaping had been provided. The triangular site gradually became a parking lot where cars pulled up right to the colonnade, creating an unsightly, often muddy rim around the circular colonnade. The Warwick Towers group, calling themselves the Neighbors of Hermann Park, raised more money than expected, allowing the scope of the grass project to grow much larger. With the approval of Don Olson, they hired architect Guy Hagstette, who designed a small plaza with radiating walkways and trees around the perimeter, and landscape architect

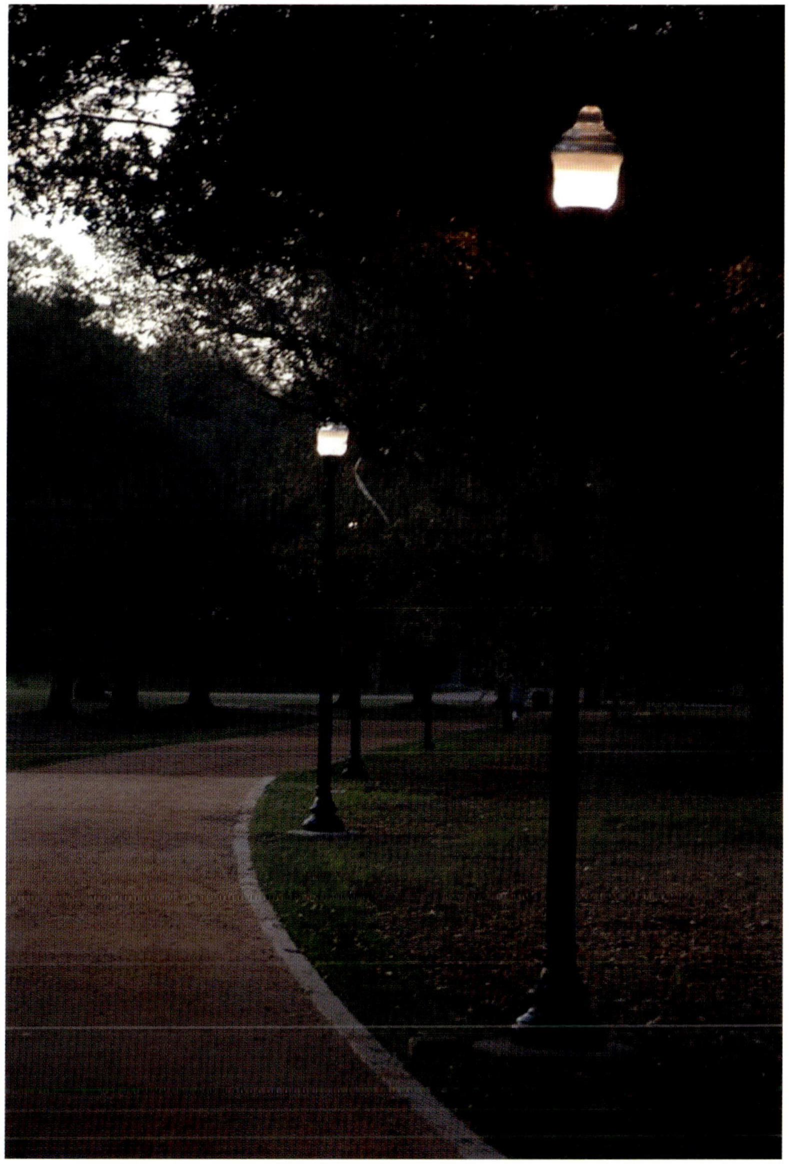

Acorn lights installed along the Marvin Taylor Trail in 1992. Courtesy Hermann Park Conservancy.

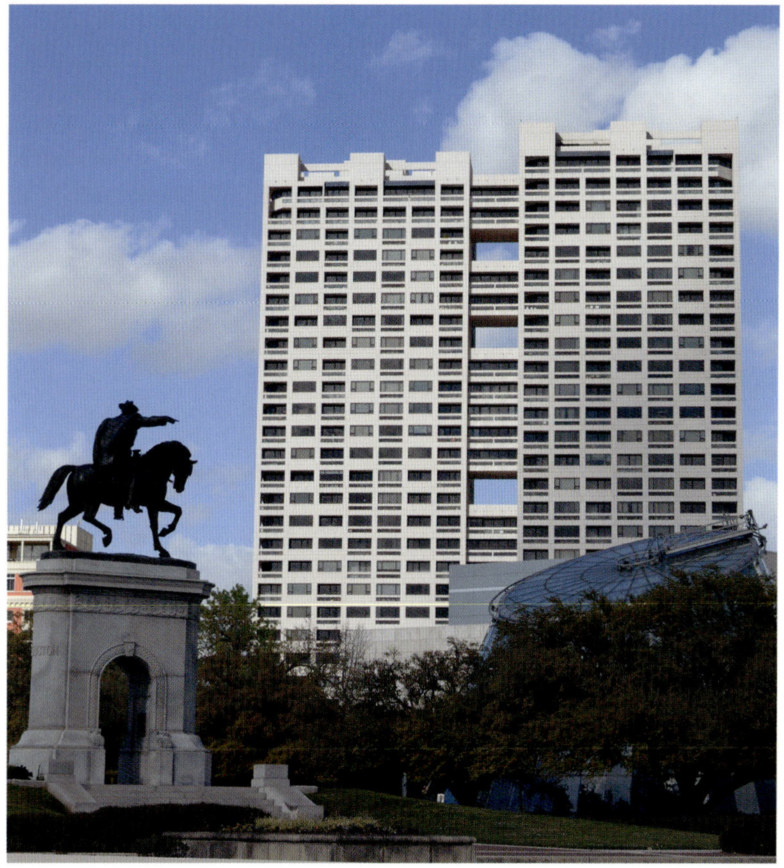

Warwick Towers, 1111 Hermann Drive (1983, Golemon & Rolfe) from Hermann Park, 2013. Photograph by B. S. Bradley.

Lauren Griffith, who took charge of the plantings. Mayor Bob Lanier and his wife, park advocate Elyse Lanier, attended the opening of this new park project, completed in time for the G7 Economic Summit, hosted by President George H. W. Bush in Houston in July 1990. The trees along Hermann Drive in the Mecom-Rockwell triangle were planted to commemorate the summit, as a bronze plaque on the site attests. The residents of the Warwick Towers had accomplished their mission.[8]

Meanwhile, several neighbors who lived west of the park were involved in the nonprofit Trees for Houston. Two lawyers, Bill Coats and Carroll Shaddock, wanted to expand their program of planting live oak trees along city streets into Hermann Park. In 1991 they organized the Friends of Hermann Park with the initial purpose of reforesting the park. Three groups, then, were working on separate projects in the park: the Hermann Park Joggers, Runners, and Walkers; the Neighbors of Hermann Park; and the Friends of Hermann Park.

Then O. Jack Mitchell died suddenly on February 18, 1992, and the catalyst to renew Hermann Park in a serious and comprehensive way began. Mitchell was an architect, urban designer, and a professor of architecture at Rice University from 1966 to 1990, serving as dean of the Rice School of Architecture for eighteen years.[9] Mitchell's colleagues and friends were determined to do something significant to honor his memory. Gathering at his home on the afternoon of his death, they considered the question, "What can we do?" The answer seemed obvious to everyone: "Something about Hermann Park." For more than a decade, Mitchell had advised the Houston Parks and Recreation Department on various park projects, but, as his friends knew, he was most passionate about Hermann Park. Mitchell began visiting the park with his two young sons shortly after coming to Rice in 1966 and, from then on, promoted his view that the park was one of Houston's most important civic

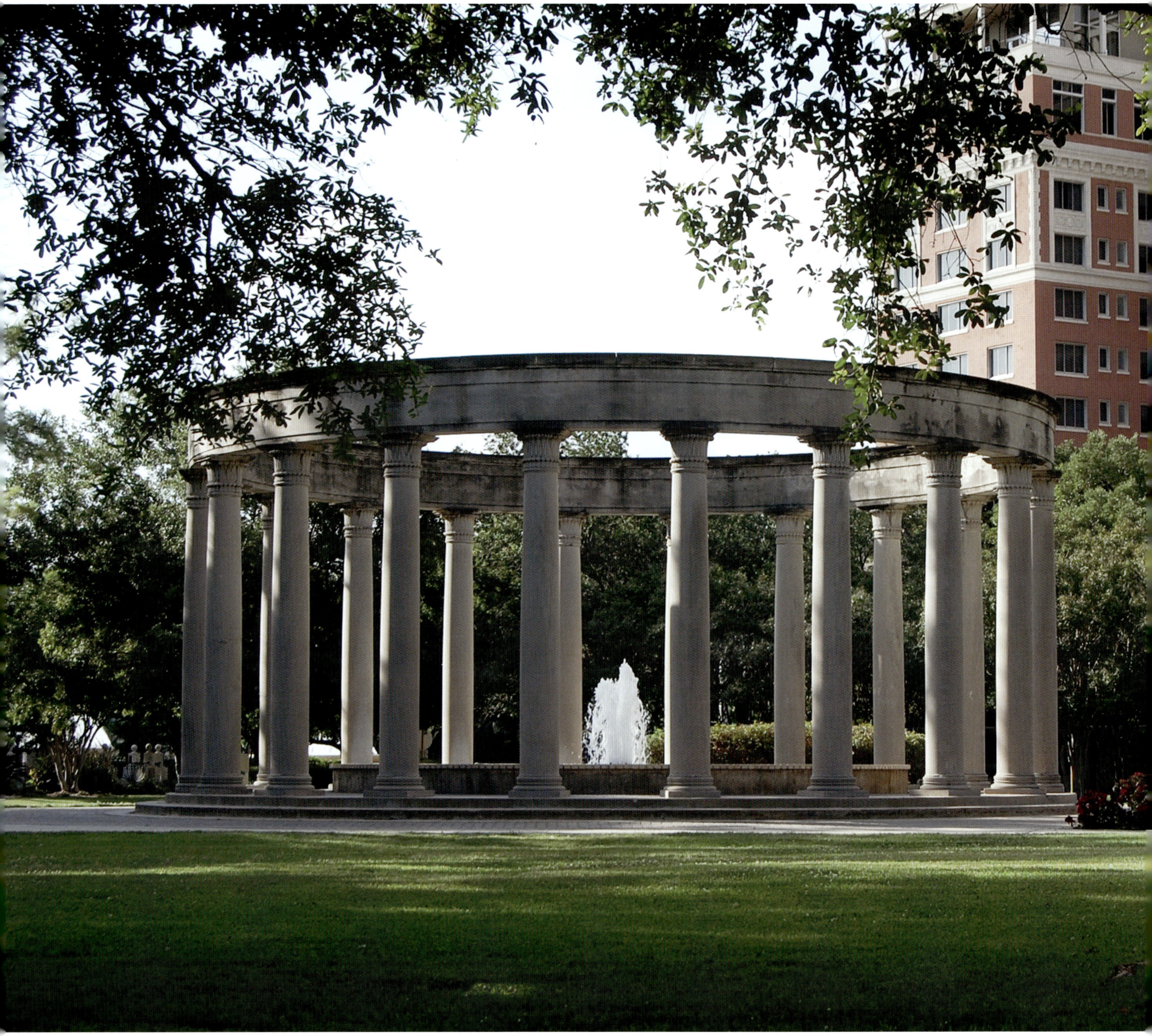

Mecom Rockwell Colonnade and Fountain, 2012. Photograph by B. S. Bradley.

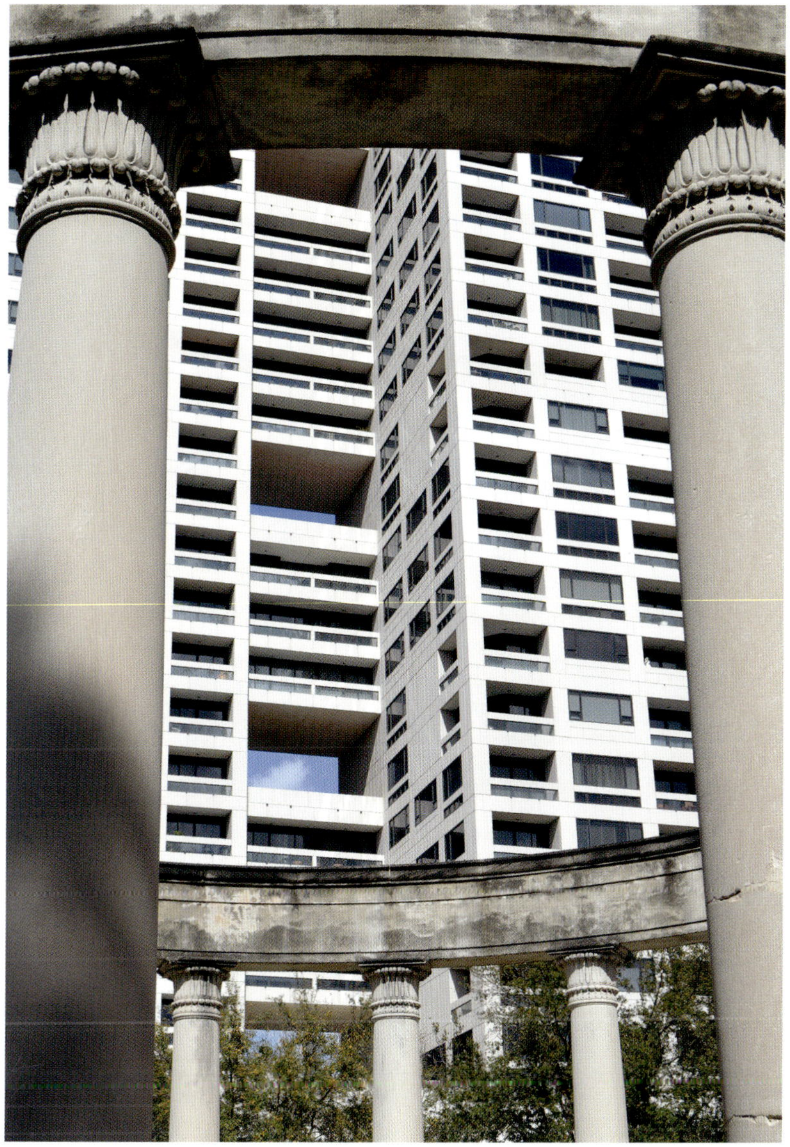

Warwick Towers from the Mecom Rockwell Colonnade and Fountain, 2013. Photograph by B. S. Bradley.

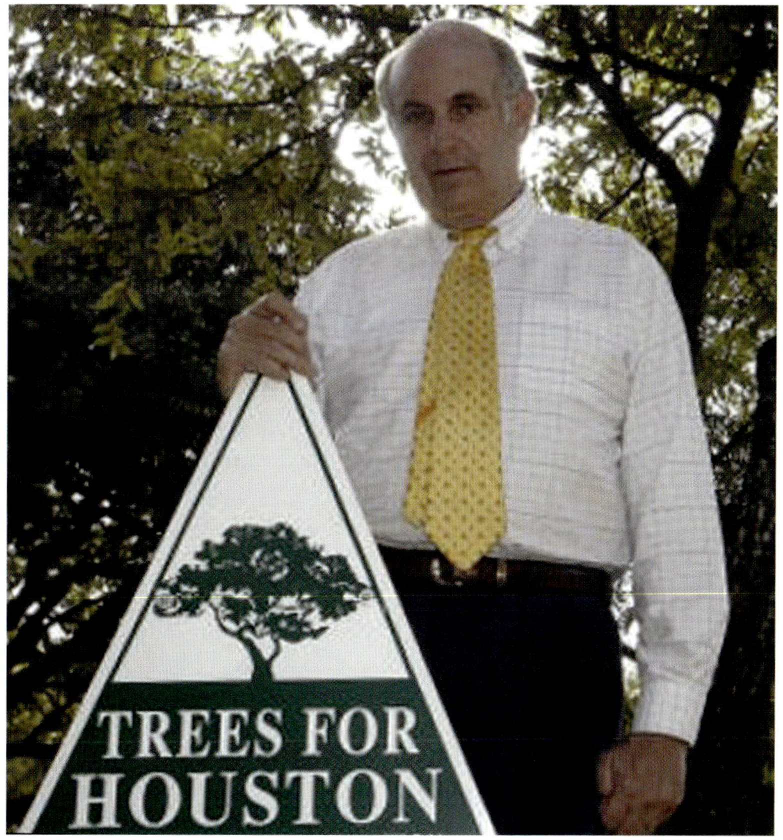

William M. Coats, Jr. (1940–2010) was a tireless advocate for Hermann Park and a founder of Trees for Houston and the Hermann Park Conservancy. The Bill Coats Bike Bridge in Hermann Park is named for him. Source: *Houston Chronicle*, May 30, 2010. Photograph by Kim Christensen. Courtesy Hermann Park Conservancy.

spaces.[10] Shortly before his death Mitchell wrote an article for *Texas Architect* that became a posthumous challenge:

> The fit between streets, places, parks, and institutions should have collective meaning. These elements become the public infrastructure and ultimately the symbol of our collective, communal lives. The making of a quality public realm in our cities is the most lasting act we design professionals can do.[11]

Architect Jay Baker, a friend and former student of Mitchell's and then-president of the Rice Design Alliance (RDA), set up a series of informal meetings to determine a course of action. RDA had sponsored other architectural competitions and that seemed to be a fruitful avenue to pursue. With the support of RDA's executive director, Linda Sylvan, Baker and Barrie Scardino met with Don Olson, director of the Parks and Recreation Department, to ask if the RDA could manage a competition for a new master plan for Hermann Park. Olson, while sympathetic, felt the scope was too broad and suggested that the competition concentrate instead on the Reflection Pool, an eroding eyesore at the center of the park. Native Houstonian and landscape advocate Susan Booth Keeton recalled that Jack Mitchell had recently drawn a sketch of the park's central axis, which he called "the heart of the park." Within a month of Mitchell's death, a group of committed park advocates was meeting weekly to organize the competition. The competition committee consisted of the chairs (Baker and Scardino), Natalye Appel (representing the American Institute of Architects, Houston Chapter), John Casbarian (Rice School of Architecture), Sanford Criner (Rice Design Alliance), Rick Dewees (Parks and Recreation Department), Bill Coats and Marley Lott (Friends of Hermann Park), Carolyn Mitchell (Jack Mitchell's widow), and Martin Reiner

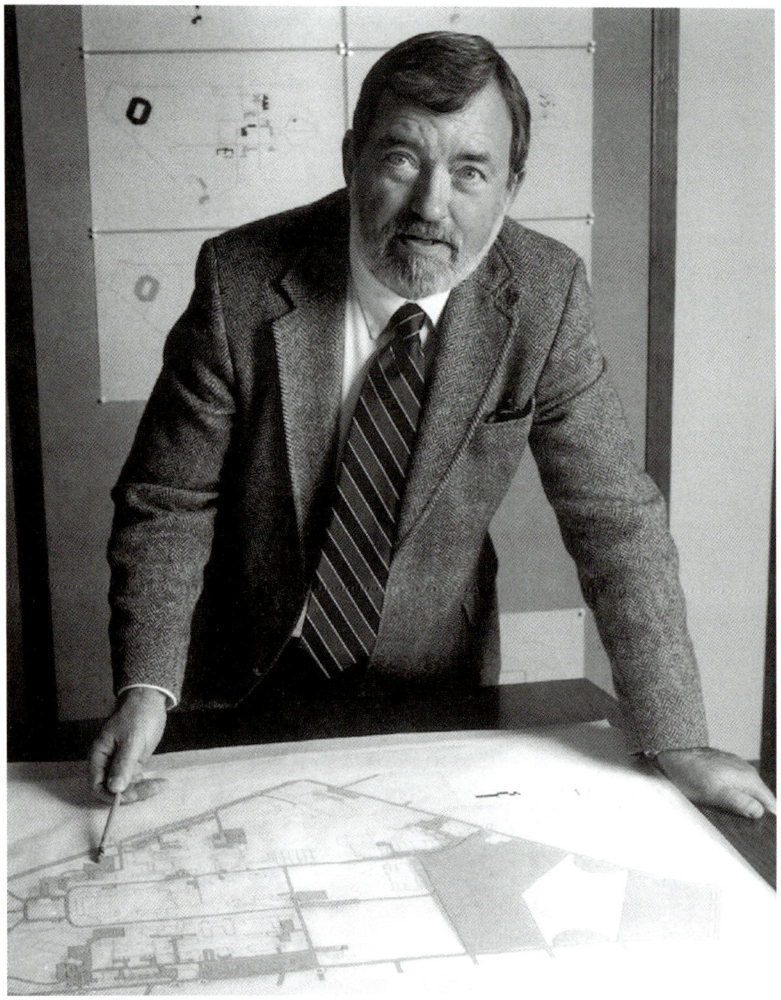

O. Jack Mitchell (1932–1992) was dean of the Rice School of Architecture and, as an architect and planner, was concerned with Houston parks, particularly Hermann Park. His death prompted the Heart of the Park competition, which set in motion the Hermann Park Conservancy and the Olin Master Plan that renewed the park. Photograph by Tommy LaVergne. Courtesy Rice Design Alliance.

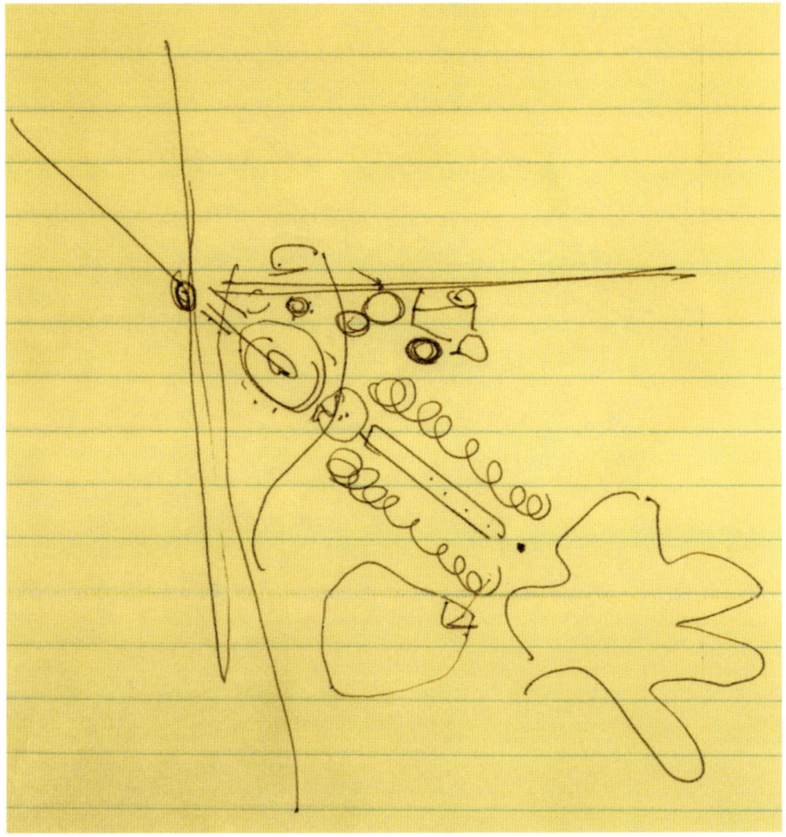

Heart of the Park sketch by Jack Mitchell, 1992, drawn just before his death. Illustrates his concern for the area of Hermann Park that most needed refurbishment. Courtesy Hermann Park Conservancy.

(South Main Center). This group organized the competition in only seven months.

Hermann Park's varied devotees were, of course, not the first private group to come together for the good of a community, but twenty years ago it was still a radical concept that private citizens would help finance improvements in a public park. An article in the *Houston Post* noted: "Hermann Park has long been an embarrassment to the city. Located in the midst of Houston's cultural and economic center, the 407-acre park is distinguished by a muddy, ill-tended reflection pool leading from a grand statue of Sam Houston to a large, ugly concrete lake bordered by thick metal handrails."[12]

The competition was an international, one-stage, open design competition. Each team was required to have at least one member who was

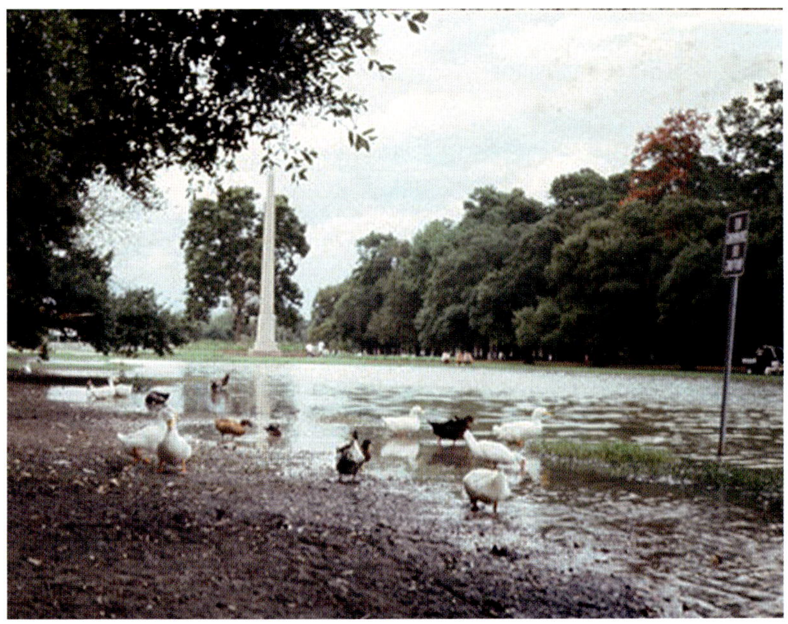

The Reflection Pool, 1992, before the Heart of the Park competition. Photograph by Anne Mendelsohn. Courtesy Hermann Park Conservancy.

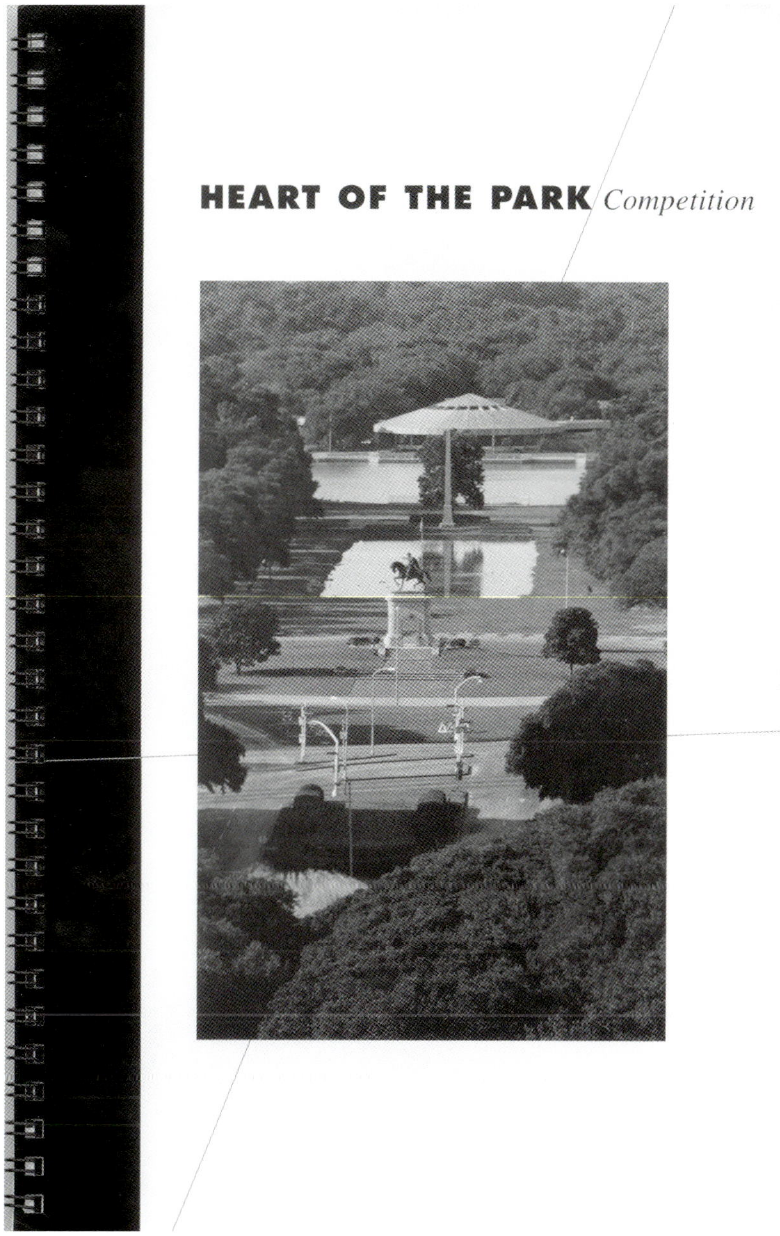

Heart of the Park Competition cover, 1992. Courtesy Rice Design Alliance.

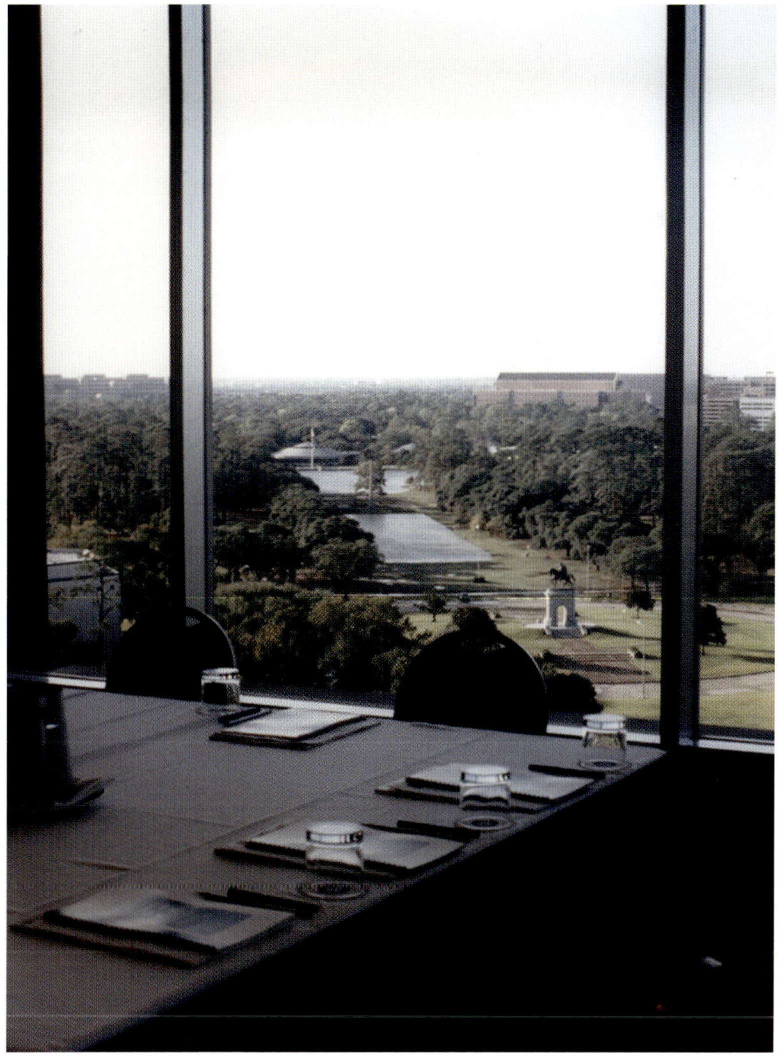

Heart of the Park jury room on the top floor of the Warwick Hotel overlooking Hermann Park, November 12–13, 1992. Courtesy Rice Design Alliance.

a licensed architect or landscape architect. Announcements were mailed in July 1992, and registration opened in August with an October 1, 1992, deadline. The competition book presented a brief history of the park, a description of the site, and seven design objectives: to design an urban park space that (1) brings people to Hermann Park, (2) is based on the historic Kessler Plan, (3) unites the Sam Houston Monument and the Grand Basin, (4) serves as a model for future development in Hermann Park, (5) has a specific identity both day and night, (6) introduces the play of sun, shade, and water, and (7) captures the imagination of Houstonians and invites varied use. The program asked for competitors to design a place that unified and anchored different components of the park and enhanced and strengthened the main axis while providing a place to commemorate Houston, to relax, to experience the natural setting, and, most important, to bring new life and meaning to Hermann Park. The budget was set at $4 million, which was to include building costs as well as support systems, professional fees, infrastructure, and maintenance.[13]

A surprising 117 entries were received from twenty-three states, Puerto Rico, and Italy. A distinguished jury of national stature met at the top of the Warwick Hotel overlooking the competition site the second week of November for two days to consider the entries, which required three presentation boards each. Mark Alan Hewitt, AIA (associate professor of architecture at the New Jersey Institute of Technology, Newark, New Jersey), served as the professional advisor and

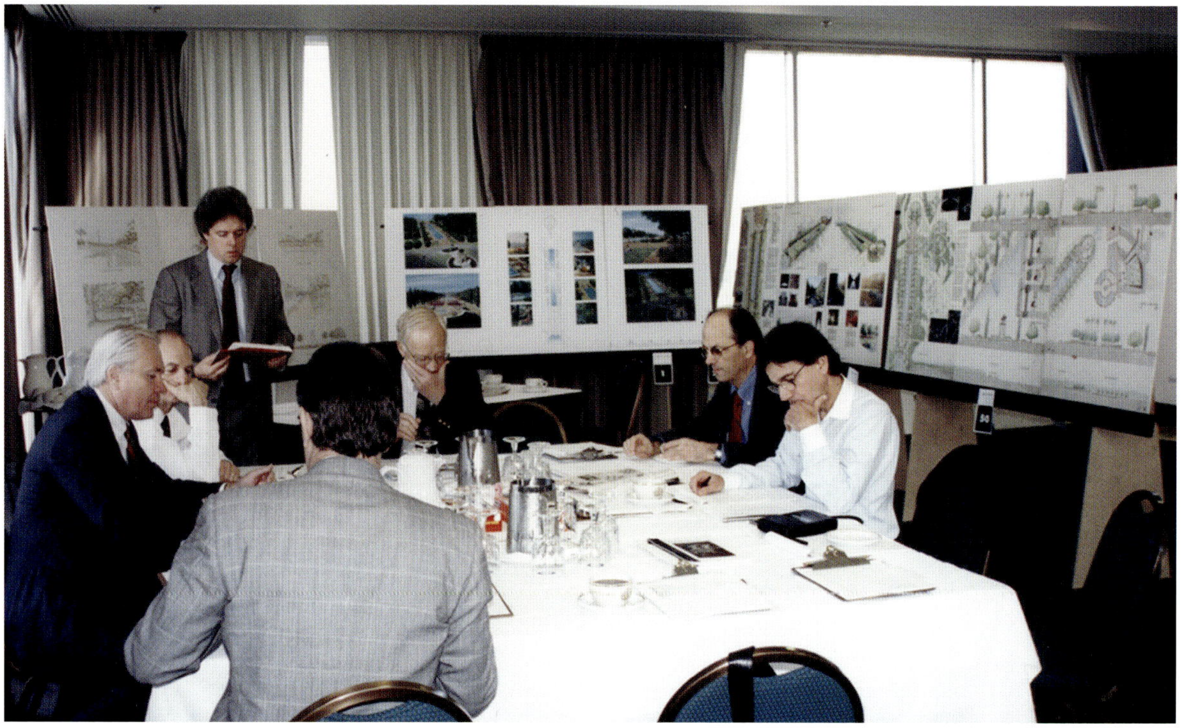

Heart of the Park jury deliberations, November 12–13, 1992. Courtesy Rice Design Alliance.

moderator of the jury. Jurors were Robert Campbell, FAIA (architecture critic, *Boston Globe*); William J. Johnson, FASLA (William Johnson and Associates Inc., Ann Arbor, Michigan); Peter G. Rowe (dean, Harvard University Graduate School of Design); Adele Naude Santos (dean, University of California, San Diego, School of Architecture); Anne Whiston Spirn (professor and chairman, University of Pennsylvania Graduate School of Fine Arts, Department of Landscape Architecture); and, from Houston, Raymond Brochstein, FAIA (president, Brochsteins Inc.); John Hansen (South Main Center Association, John Hansen Investment Builder); Susan Keeton (Friends of Hermann Park); Donald G. Olson, ASLA (director, City of Houston Parks and Recreation Department); and John Casbarian, FAIA (Rice School of Architecture), who served as jury chairman.

After the jury toured the park, it began deliberations, and by the end of the day, nine schemes were selected for further consideration the next day. Discussion centered on the goals of the competition as a vehicle for restoring dignity to the park. William Johnson noted, "You don't have to have a complex scheme to have richness," and he articulated what became a consensus shared by the jurors: "There must be a message of healing and new strength of unity as well as high quality execution in the design we choose."[14]

The winners of the competition were announced at the Rice Design Alliance's Heart of the Park Gala held in the Warwick Hotel on November 13, 1992. First place and a $15,000 prize went to Melton Henry/Maurice Robison Architects Inc.; Peter Brown Architect/Planners; Scott Slaney, landscape architect; and Steve Harding, graphic designer, all of Houston. The jury praised this solution for the strong connectivity and its discrete side gardens, including one in memory of Jack Mitchell. Second place, with a $7,500 prize, went to Jon Emerson of Baton Rouge, Louisiana, and Houston professionals James Burnett, Dale Busfield, Jack Hanna, and Heather Heimarck. This entry was appreciated for its series of fountains and the well-made end to the lake. The jury felt this, like the first-place winner, could be built and would be a good runner-up if for some reason their first choice could not be realized. Third place winner, with a $5,000 prize, was the team of SLA/Studio Land of Houston and Lake/Flato of San Antonio. This entry was recognized for its choice of land over water—creating a great lawn with a fountain at either end. Fourth place and $2,500 went to a team from Kansas State University: Stephanie Rolley, Amy Ackerman, Alton Barnes, Eric Hornig, Jason Jones, and Craig Rhodes.[15] These designers were cited for their subtle recognition of seasonal variations in the water level and character of the reflecting pool. The jury observed that this scheme showed a great sensitivity to environmental issues.[16]

The Heart of the Park Competition was a success in itself, but it did not a new park make. Raising $75,000 for prizes and competition expenses was one thing, but raising $4 million to rebuild the Heart of the Park was quite another. What this competition symbolized, however, was a historical turning point. Enough publicity and thoughtful consideration had been generated around the competition to make a forceful

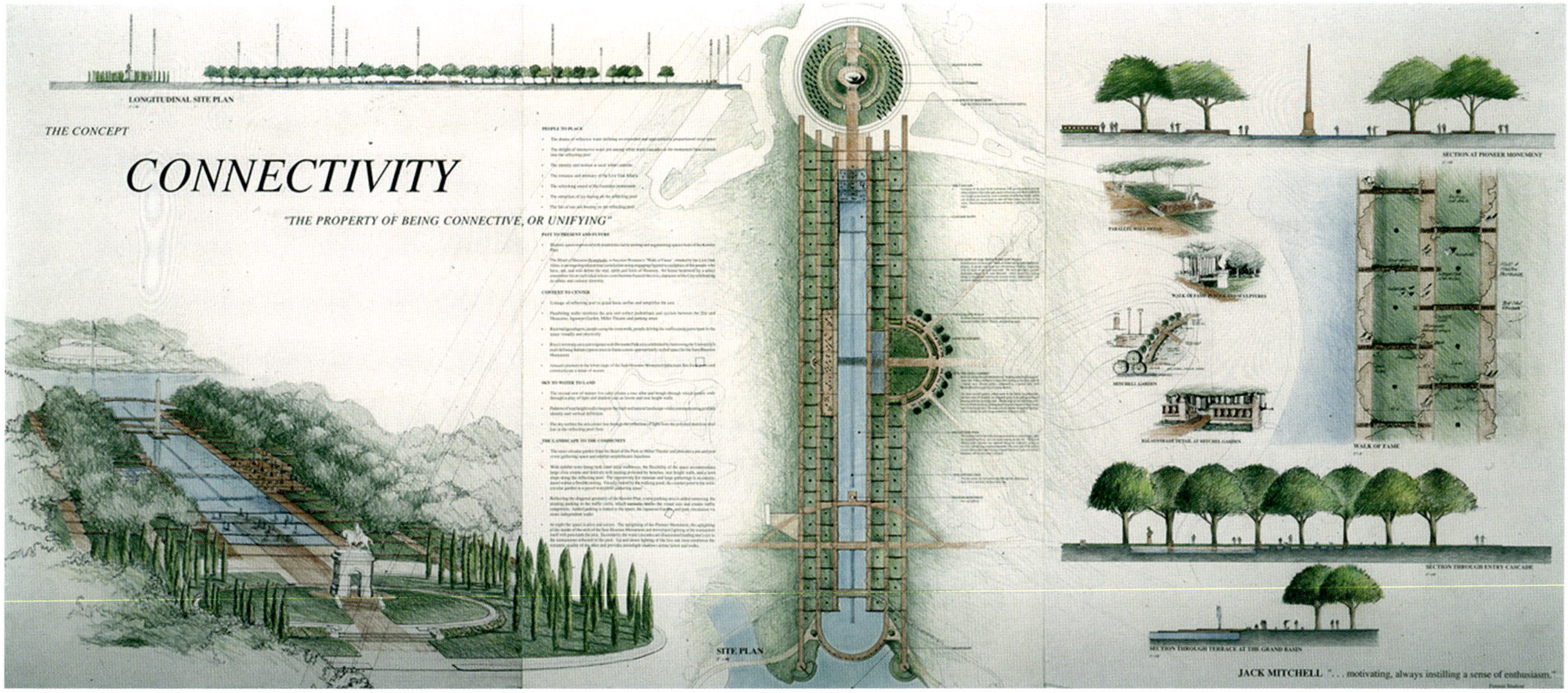

First place winner, Heart of the Park Competition, 1992: Melton Henry/Maurice Robison Architects Inc., Peter Brown Architect/Planners, Scott Slaney, and Steve Harding. Courtesy Rice Design Alliance.

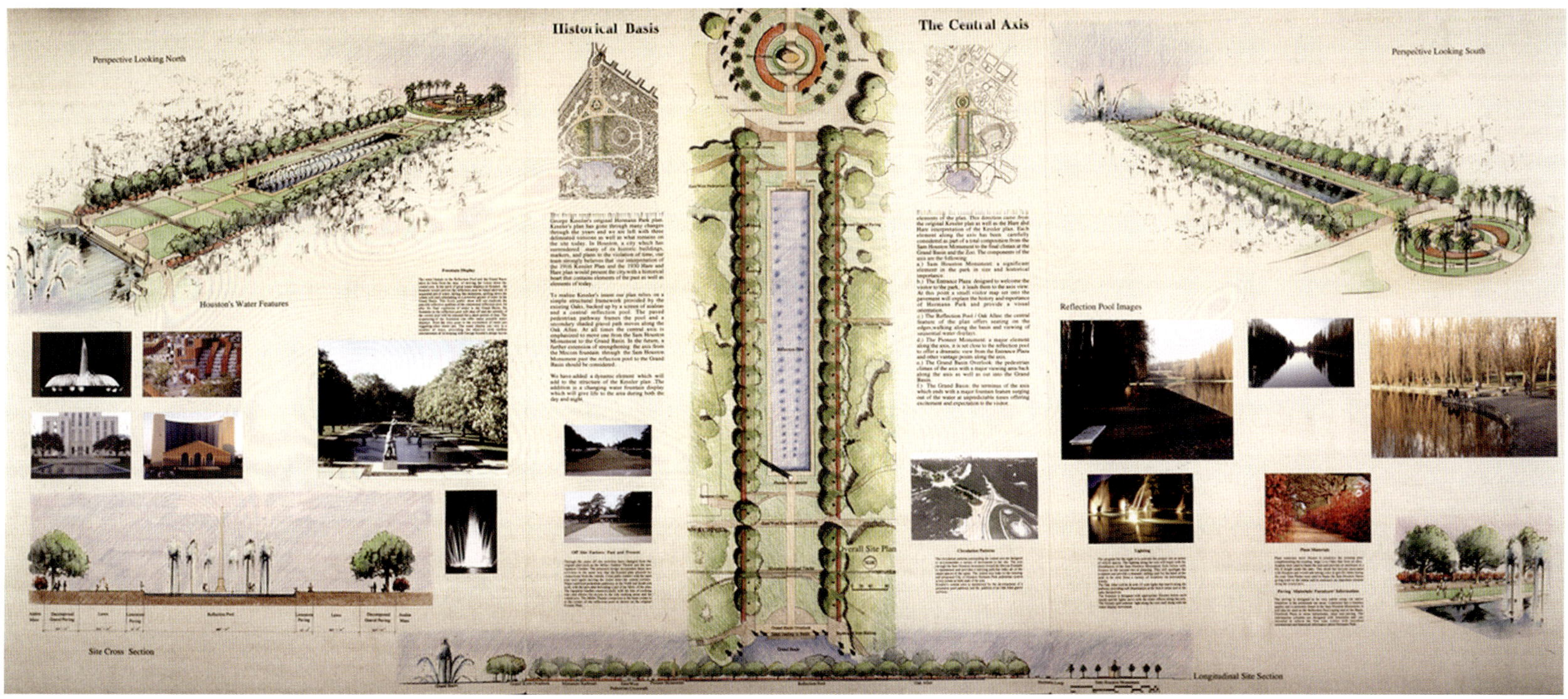

Second place winner, Heart of the Park Competition, 1992: Jon Emerson, James Burnett, Dale Busfield, Jack Hanna, and Heather Heimarck. Courtesy Rice Design Alliance.

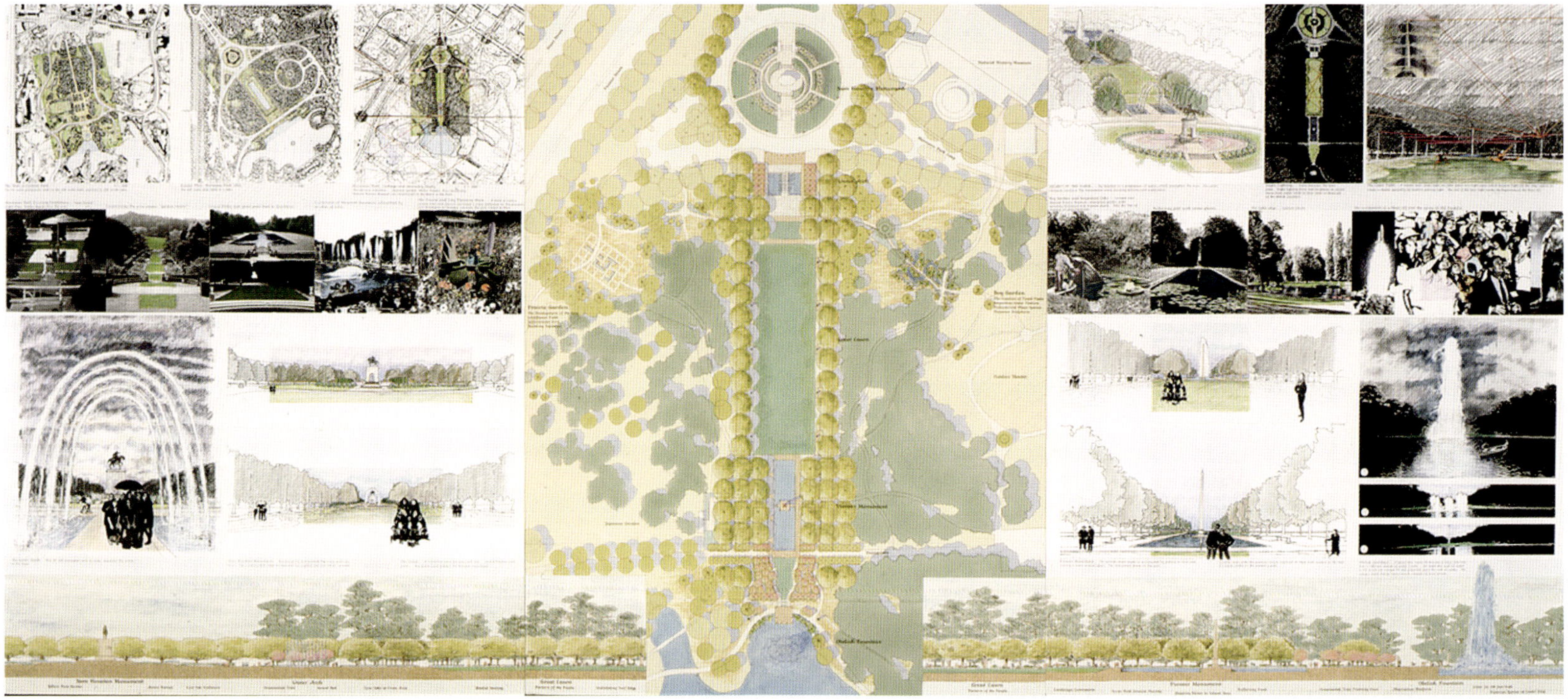

Third place winner, Heart of the Park Competition, 1992: SLA/Studio Land and Lake/Flato. Courtesy Rice Design Alliance.

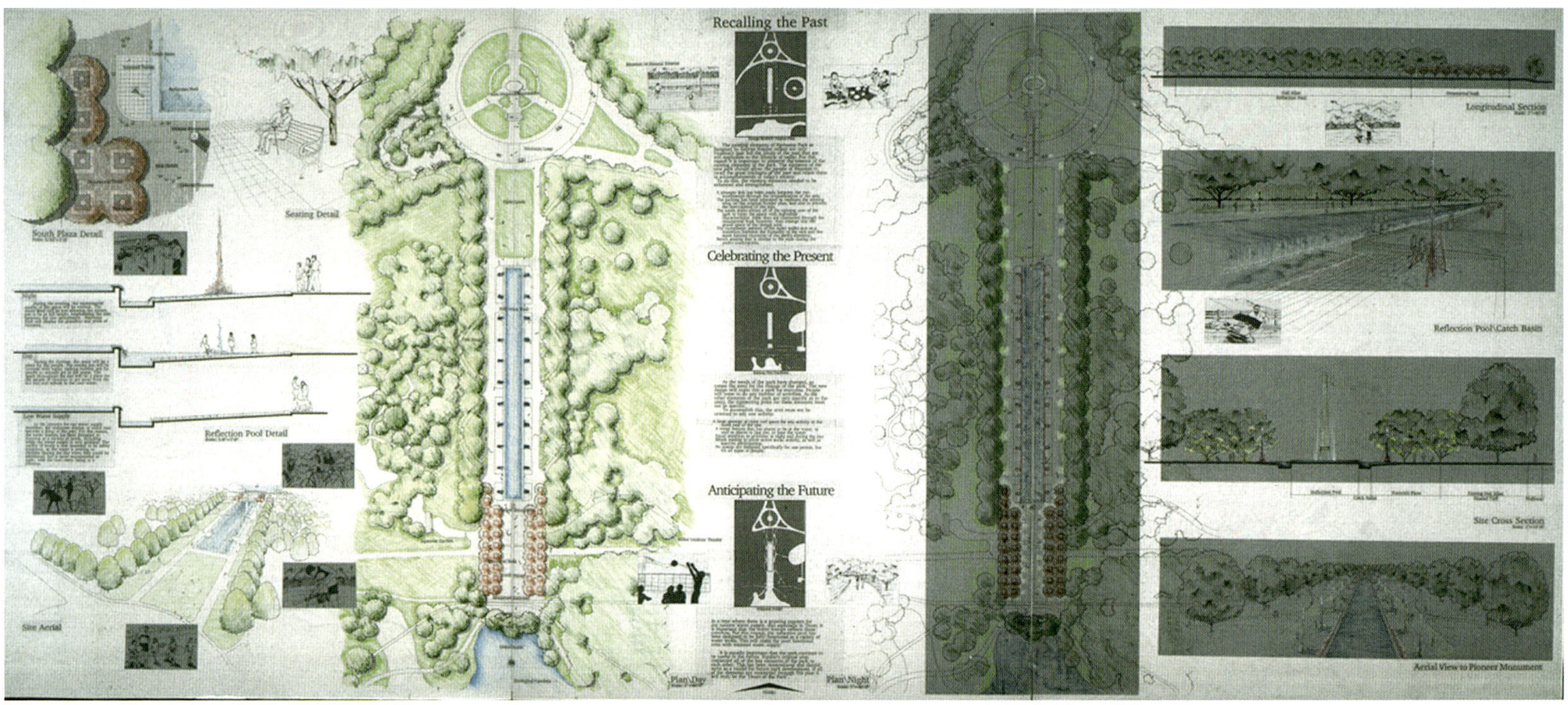

Fourth place winner, Heart of the Park Competition, 1992: Stephanie Rolley, Amy Ackerman, Alton Barnes, Eric Hornig, Jason Jones, and Craig Rhodes. Courtesy Rice Design Alliance.

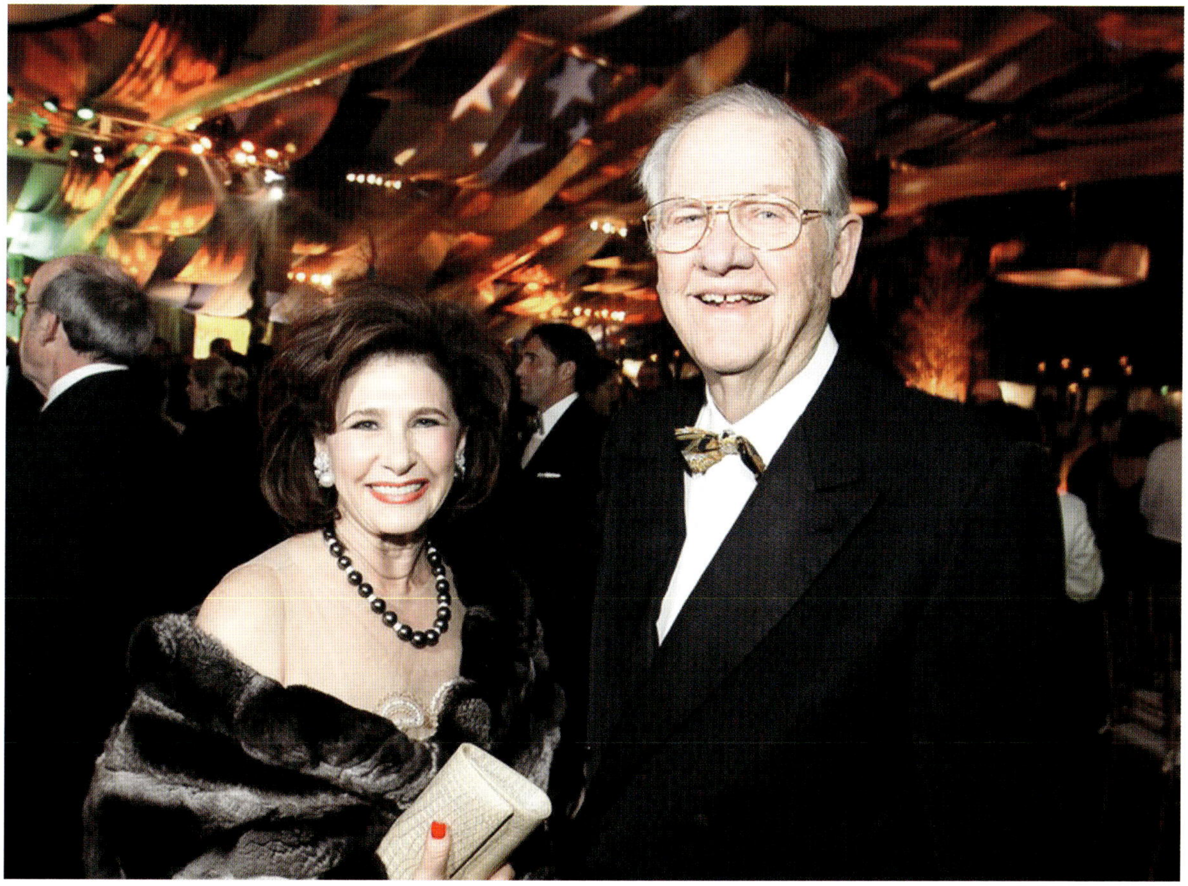

Bob and Elyse Lanier, c. 1995. Bob Lanier was mayor of Houston 1992–1998; both Mayor and Mrs. Lanier were great advocates for and supporters of Hermann Park. Courtesy Hermann Park Conservancy.

impression on the minds and hearts of those who had the power to make things happen in Houston. Bob Lanier, who knew how to get things done and had an affinity for parks and landscapes, was elected mayor in 1992. His wife, Elyse, poured her considerable energy and influence into Houston's public spaces during her husband's six-year administration and became an advocate for Hermann Park. Like the progressive mayors that preceded him—Baldwin Rice (1896–1898, 1904–1913), Ben Campbell (1913–1917), and Oscar Holcombe (1921–1929, 1933–1936, 1931–1941, 1956–1957)—Lanier backed the initiatives of what became the Hermann Park Conservancy. He appointed William R. Smith II as the new director of the Parks and Recreation Department, and Mayor Lanier and Smith soon affirmed the idea of generating a master plan for Hermann Park before any new capital projects were initiated, including the Heart of the Park.

This local energy coincided with a renewed national interest in parks that provided the intellectual support and gravitas that Houstonians needed to finance and rebuild Hermann Park. Rick Dewees, assistant director of Park Administration for the Parks and Recreation Department in charge of Hermann Park, recalls that American urban parks were decaying in the 1970s and 1980s.[17] Many inner city parks had been laid out at the end of the nineteenth century or the beginning of the twentieth century and were essentially in the same state. Dewees attended national meetings in the 1990s and early 2000s with other park administrators whose parks shared the same problems of decay, drainage, parking, vandalism, lighting, and safety. As a result of this concern for urban parks, the Lila Wallace–Reader's Digest Fund launched a national initiative in 1994 to increase the quality and quantity of urban parks by granting over $16 million for park restoration. The City Parks Alliance, formally established in 2000, was an outgrowth of the conferences of park administrators and the Lila Wallace–Reader's Digest Fund's Urban Parks Initiative.[18] The focus of the City Parks Alliance in the twenty-first century has become public–private partnerships.[19] As improvements went forward in Hermann Park, it benefitted both financially and strategically from the Lila Wallace–Reader's Digest Fund and the City Parks Alliance.

A second outcome of the Heart of the Park Competition was a clarification of interests and responsibilities in Hermann Park. Several different groups wanted to make improvements in the park, but consensus and a focused purpose had to be established before the city was willing to commit any new resources to Hermann Park.

CHAPTER EIGHT

Hermann Park Conservancy

The Hermann Park Conservancy is a citizens' organization dedicated to the stewardship and improvement of Hermann Park—today and for generations to come.[1]

—Mission Statement, Hermann Park Conservancy, 2004

Rick Dewees, Hermann Park administrator for the City of Houston Parks and Recreation Department, was aware that three groups were working separately for improvements in the park. When the Rice Design Alliance entered the picture with its proposal for the Heart of the Park Competition, it was time to introduce these groups to each other. The Neighbors and Friends agreed to join together as one group, called the Friends of Hermann Park, with Patricia Nelson, organizer of the Neighbors of Hermann Park, as the first president. The Articles of Incorporation were signed in 1992. Developer John Hansen (who had served on the competition jury) donated an office for the Friends of Hermann Park, and Susan Keeton volunteered as the first part-time executive director. It was in this capacity that Keeton met with Jack Mitchell concerning rejuvenation of the Sam Houston Monument–Reflection Pool axis. Within the next year the Joggers, Runners, and Walkers also merged with the Friends of Hermann Park and Marvin Taylor joined the board of the new organization. The group immediately tripled in size and threw its weight behind the RDA competition. However, once the competition was over, the Friends' board of directors realized that the lack of a professional staff with the organizational ability to raise funds and build the Heart of the Park project was a serious problem.

Mary Anne Piacentini, with a Master's degree in city and regional planning from the Harvard University Graduate School of Design and experience in the management of nonprofit organizations, was hired as the first full-time, professional director in 1993. Piacentini began to build the organization, and it was with her leadership and guidance that the Friends of Hermann Park board of directors understood that, before anything else was built in the park, a master plan was needed. Although the Friends were committed to building the Heart of the Park's winning scheme, they decided to integrate it with a comprehensive plan of improvement for the park. In addition, because the winning scheme was over budget, the design needed refinement.

While facilitating the Friends' coherence into a functioning organization, Piacentini submitted grant applications, generated publicity, expanded membership, and began to formulate an institutional identity.[2] Her major commitment was ensuring that a master plan for the park was commissioned. She wasted no time in getting the City Parks and Recreation Department to approve the commissioning of such a plan and gathering credentials of park planners qualified to take on this project. The field was narrowed to three finalists. By the summer of 1993, the Philadelphia landscape architect Laurie Olin, of Hanna/Olin Ltd., was selected. As the Friends of Hermann Park confronted political and financial issues, Olin's team went to work. The master plan was funded with grants from the Brown Foundation, ExxonMobil, the Ray C. Fish Foundation, Houston Endowment Inc., the Samuels Foundation, the Rockwell Fund, Continental Airlines, and the Wortham Foundation. With the support of Mayor Lanier and the Parks Department, the master plan began to take shape (see chapter 9 for more information).

The executive director and key board members of the Friends of Hermann Park collaborated to obtain significant grants. Board member Marley Lott emphasizes that it was a grant from the Lila Wallace–Reader's Digest Fund in 1996 that gave Hermann Park the credibility it needed to facilitate fund-raising in Houston. She recalls that when grant

FRIENDS OF HERMANN PARK

Friends of Hermann Park logo, 1992. Courtesy Minor Design.

officers from the Wallace–Reader's Digest Fund visited Houston to look at the proposed project in Hermann Park, Mayor Lanier personally met with them (he was the only mayor to do so) and urged that Houston be among the large cities to receive grants from its $16 million initiative to revitalize urban parks in the United States.[3] With the mayor's support, Hermann Park received a $1.5 million grant from the Lila Wallace–Reader's Digest Fund, an accomplishment that made it easier for the Friends of Hermann Park to approach local and state foundations for project funding.

In 2004 the board voted to change the name of the organization to the Hermann Park Conservancy, which more accurately reflected its mission and goals as well as indicating its expanded constituency. During the 1990s and 2000s the organization continued to grow, increasing its scope from project development to funding management and educational programs, the "conservation" work that the change in name acknowledged. In 1993 Mayor Lanier appointed Bill Smith director of the Houston Parks and Recreation Department. Piacentini worked with Smith through the master planning process, assuring that the conservancy and the city operated in tandem. Subsequent park directors Oliver B. Spellman, Jr. (1998–2002), Roksan Okan-Vick (2003), and Joe Turner (2004–), have supported the effective public–private partnership between the City of Houston and the Hermann Park Conservancy. Rick Dewees, the landscape architect who has been a staff member of the Parks Department since 1989, has been an essential constant. He has worked closely with successive boards and staff members for twenty-five years and effectively facilitated communication between the conservancy and the city.

In 1998 Patricia Winn succeeded Mary Ann Piacentini as executive director of the Hermann Park Conservancy. The following year Roksan Okan-Vick came to the job of executive director after her outstanding performance as Piacentini's project director. Okan-Vick demonstrated exceptional skill in managing pressures that the growing organization encountered. The conservancy matured under her leadership, and she

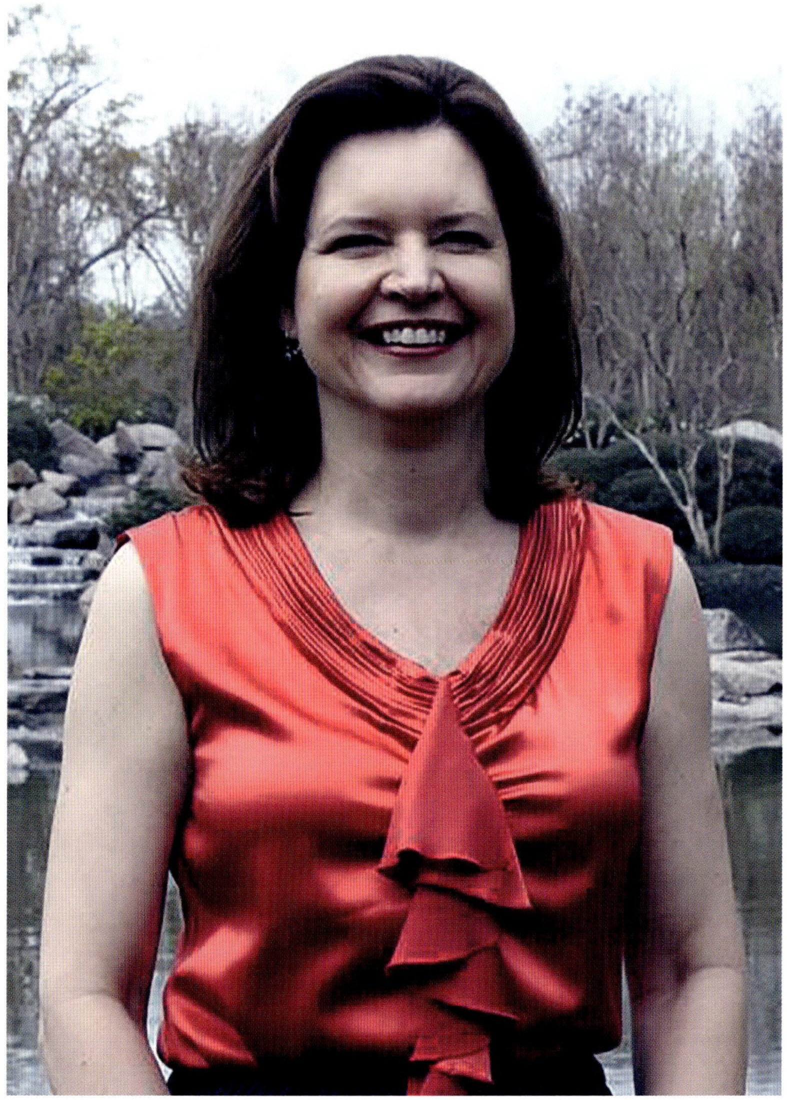

Doreen Stoller, Executive Director Hermann Park Conservancy, , 2013. Courtesy Hermann Park Conservancy.

was responsible for seeing that the Olin master plan became a reality. A ten-year strategic plan, "Action 2000," was implemented in 2000 to guide the conservancy as it launched a phased approach in constructing both major and minor projects recommended in the master plan. The conservancy lost Okan-Vick in 2002 when Mayor Lee P. Brown appointed her director of the Parks and Recreation Department. She went from that position to become executive director of the Houston Parks Board, a powerful and effective nonprofit group that supports park projects throughout the city, including some in Hermann Park.

When Okan-Vick left the conservancy, the board engaged Doreen Stoller as its executive director in 2003. Stoller's education and experi-

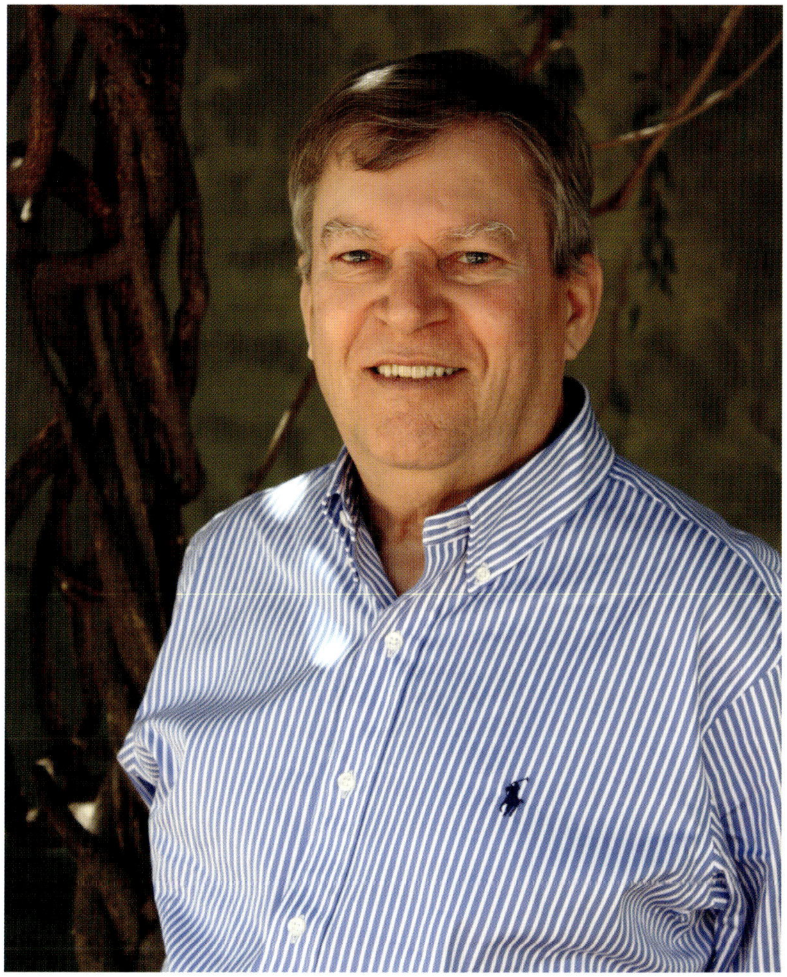

Rick Dewees, Hermann Park Administrator, Houston Parks and Recreation Department, 2013. Courtesy Hermann Park Conservancy.

ence, a Yale undergraduate degree, a Master's in art history from NYU, and an MBA from Rice, positioned her to guide the Hermann Park Conservancy in the twenty-first century. In ten years Stoller has solidified the conservancy's financial stability; net assets have increased from $5 million in 2003 to over $25.4 million in 2013. Stoller has also laid the foundation for substantial individual gifts, as well as strengthening the conservancy's relationships with the public sector. Since 1992 nearly one-half of the over $100 million invested in Hermann Park's renewal has come from the City of Houston, the Harris County Flood Control District, and the federal government.

Stoller's abilities, as well as her consistency and longevity, have proven to be strong assets to the conservancy, steadying what has become a huge vessel plowing through both calm and stormy seas. She has reorganized and enlarged the conservancy staff to thirteen full-time people including an accounting manager, conservation director, maintenance coordinator, project manager, manager of volunteer programs, director of development, director of visitor services, visitor services assistant, community development coordinator, and marketing manager. In addition, up to twenty-five part-time staff work outside in the park on the miniature train and pedal boats and provide supplemental park maintenance. Driven by their dedication to the park, the conservancy staff has augmented the hard work of the Parks Department team with their own extraordinary level of commitment. Together, they have created a vibrant, friendly, and fun destination for many families.

Maintenance and Operations

The conservancy sponsored a twelve-month study on park maintenance that concluded in March 2002. Personnel from all levels of the Parks Department were involved as well as conservancy staff and an advisory committee of community leaders. The goal of the study was to identify ways in which the conservancy could supplement the daily work of city maintenance crews. The final report, "Safeguarding Our Legacy: A Plan to Manage Maintenance and Operations in Hermann Park," called for the reorganization of park maintenance. According to this study, an annual gap of 20,000 hours existed in the amount of time the Parks and Recreation Department could dedicate to Hermann Park and the amount of time necessary to keep it property maintained. This report became a model for other urban parks in the United States.[4] The consulting firms Ukeles Associates Inc. and ETM Associates, LLC of Brooklyn and New York, who had completed similar studies of Central Park and Prospect Park, conducted the analysis.

The seventy-page report summarized maintenance operations in Hermann Park from a number of different perspectives. It investigated park use in various areas throughout the year to determine the impact that visitors have on the fabric of the park. It estimated the numbers of staff-hours needed, both seasonally and year-round, to keep the park in optimal shape. Three types of maintenance activities were identified: (1) cleaning work necessary for appearance and sanitary conditions; (2) horticulture, preservation, and repair of natural assets; and (3) operations related to facilities and equipment in the park. A matrix of all maintenance activities was created as a tool for classifying operations and a system for managing the work. One of the most useful recommendations divided the park into twelve geographic zones with dedicated teams responsible for maintenance and operations in each zone.[5]

The final report established detailed recommendations for park maintenance standards in thirteen areas. For example: "Turf: Grass height maintained according to species and variety of grass. Mowed at least once every five to seven working days. Aeration performed as required, not less than once a year. Reseeding or sodding as needed. Weed control should be practiced so that no more than one percent of the surface has weeds present."[6] Another outcome of this study was a reconfirmation of acreage in individual sections of the park:

Hermann Park Acreage[7]	
Bayou Parkland	60.0
Brays Bayou	29.5
Centennial Gardens	18.2
Golf Course	111.2
Heart of the Park	31.7
Houston Zoo	56.0
Japanese Garden	5.9
Judson Robinson Center	2.7
Marvin Taylor Jogging Trail	10.2
Miller Outdoor Theatre	5.7
Museum of Natural Science	31.9
Parking and Historic Clubhouse	17.7
Pavilion, Carruth Playground	13.1
Picnic Area	9.3
Roadways	15.3
SW perimeter	31.1
Wooded picnic area	12.9
Total acreage	**445.0**

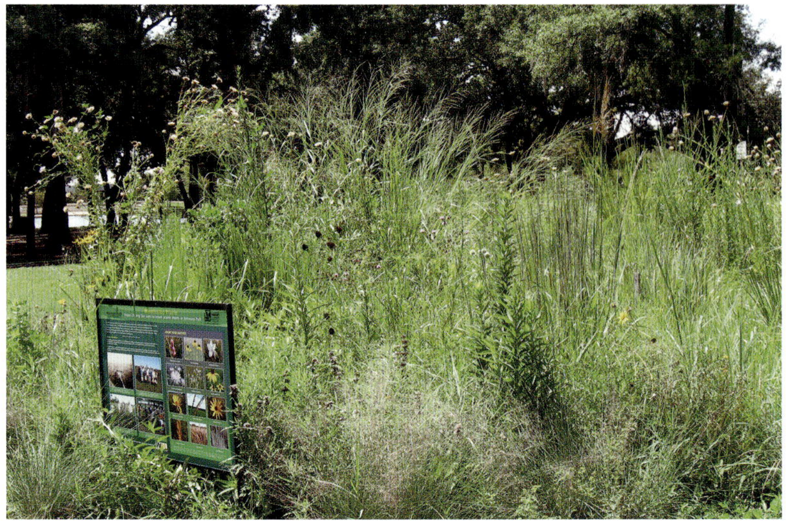

Whistle Stop Prairie, Project Blazing Star, a partnership project with the Coastal Prairie Partnership and Texas Master Naturalists to return three areas of Hermann Park to native prairie habitats with coastal grasses that once covered much of this area, 2012. Courtesy Hermann Park Conservancy.

Reforestation

An important part of maintaining Hermann Park involves reforestation. The master plan called for the planting of thousands of new trees, and old trees, lost each year through natural occurrences, need to be replaced. In addition the park lost over three hundred trees during Hurricane Ike in 2008, and many more died during the drought in the summer of 2011. This devastating drought caused the loss of 10 percent of the trees in Houston area,[8] but Hermann Park lost only 5 percent thanks to hand-watering by staff and volunteers. Both adults and children turned out with buckets and, with water from the lake, kept most of the park alive. Many kids "adopted" a tree and kept their tree alive by coming to the park every day during the summer of 2011 to water it, talk to it, and even hug it.

One thousand trees were planted in 2009 alone: 221 in the new Lake Plaza, 125 around the Hermann Park Railroad maintenance shed/tunnel, and the rest throughout the park. The conservancy updated the Hermann Park tree inventory in 2010, counting almost 8,000 trees (see appendix 4).

Conservation

In 2009 the conservancy joined with the Coastal Prairie Partnership and Texas Master Naturalists for Project Blazing Star, a multiyear effort to restore three small but highly visible areas in Hermann Park to native prairie. Historically sprawling vibrant grasslands known as the Coastal Prairie covered much of Houston, including parts of Hermann Park. Tall grasses, towering up to 8 feet in the fall, dominated this landscape. With the growth and development of Houston, native prairies were built over. Consequently these tallgrass prairies are now listed as an endangered ecosystem.[9] The goal of Project Blazing Star is to replace nonnative, weedy grasses at targeted sites with a diverse assortment of colorful, native, warm-season grasses and wildflowers to create a better habitat for birds, butterflies, rabbits, and other park wildlife while augmenting the aesthetic qualities of existing grasslands. Another benefit of this project is that it will help raise awareness of prairie conservation among those who visit the park.

Volunteers

One of the great assets of the conservancy has been its ability to organize volunteers to supplement its staff and the city's gardeners and maintenance crews. The conservancy welcomes families, individuals, and corporate, nonprofit, and student groups to participate in volunteer activities in the park. Volunteers find healthful activity and camaraderie while keeping Hermann Park clean and beautiful. They pull weeds, prune plants, mulch plant beds, clean picnic tables and benches, plant and water new trees, clean and repair trails, pick up trash, and much more. A full-time, professional volunteer program manager organizes volunteer efforts and training programs. All volunteers receive instruction in how to perform an activity and information about the environmental aspects and relationship to their community that the ac-

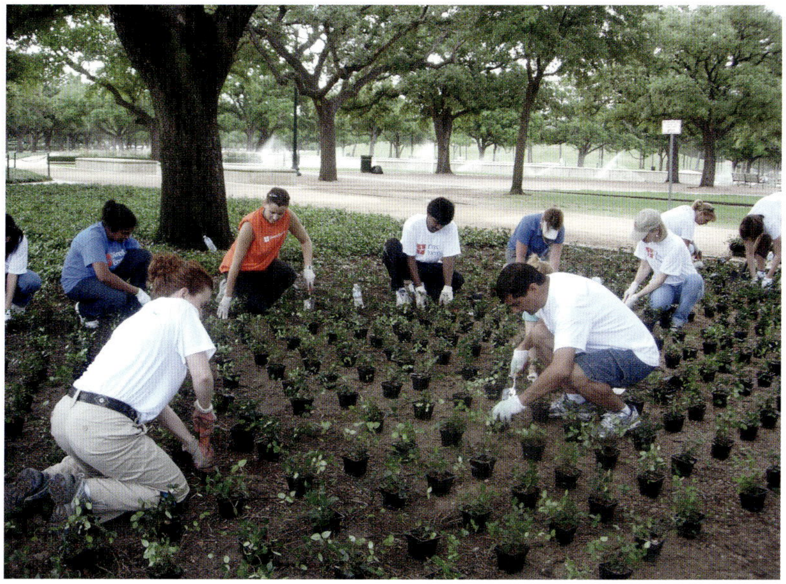

Volunteers planting in Lake Plaza, 2012. Courtesy Hermann Park Conservancy.

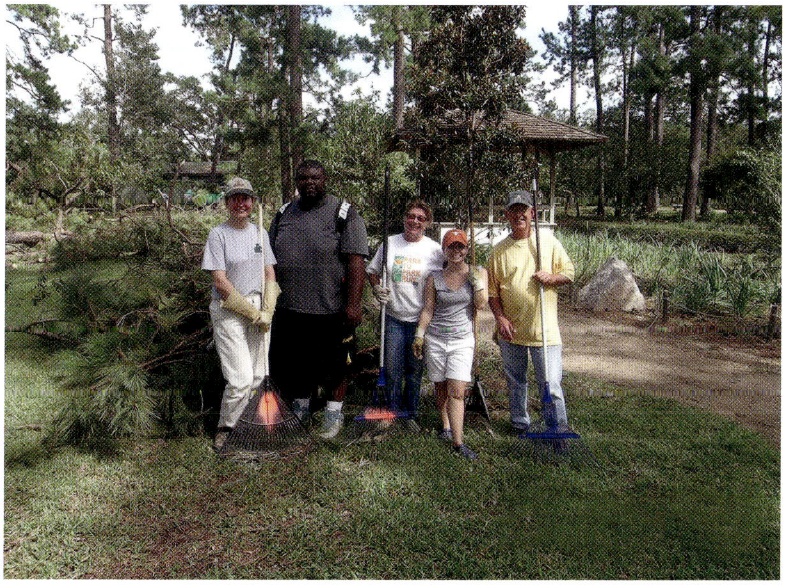

Hermann Park Conservancy staff cleans up after Hurricane Ike, 2008. Courtesy Hermann Park Conservancy.

tivity offers. Volunteers also help in the office with clerical tasks, such as preparing mailings, organizing archives, answering the phone, and filing. In 2011, over 3,900 volunteers dedicated their time to the park, contributing over 23,000 hours, more than the 20,000 hours the 2002 maintenance study found were necessary to maintain the park properly.

Volunteers have also turned out in times of crisis, as during the 2011 drought. The most notable effort, though, was in 2008 following Hurricane Ike, which passed over the park with winds up to 110 miles per hour. This was the worst hurricane to strike Houston in twenty-five years. For one to three weeks following the September 13 storm, power remained out over much of the city, and offices and businesses remained closed. The downtown area was off limits for a week, and fallen trees blocked most streets. With nothing else to do, neighbors came by the dozens to help clear Hermann Park. Ready to help where they were needed, they brought work gloves, hand tools, and rakes. Doreen Stoller remembers that parts of the park looked like it had snowed green. Leaf debris up to a foot deep in some places covered the ground, and trees were down everywhere.

Special Events

The Hermann Park Conservancy also counts on volunteer support at its fund-raising events throughout the year. Annual events that raise hundreds of thousands of dollars each year include the Evening in the Park gala, Hats in the Park luncheon, and Run in the Park. At Evening in the Park, held each spring with an attendance of roughly five hundred people, the conservancy honors individuals or institutions that have been stalwart supporters of Hermann Park. In addition, the conservancy has sponsored golf tournaments, a fall festival at the Bayou Parkland pavilion, and family adventure days. Activities and programs change over time according to park needs, program management, and needs of the community.

To inspire a new generation of Hermann Park supporters, the conservancy formed Urban Green in 2004, a membership and event group of young professionals between the ages of twenty-one and forty dedicated to supporting the mission of the conservancy. Urban Green hosts fund-raising events that draw three to four hundred young people dedicated to the protecting the environment.

To introduce even younger Houstonians to the park, the conservancy organizes an annual Student Performance Series in Lake Plaza through its Visitors Services department. Hundreds of talented youngsters from elementary, middle, and high schools throughout the Houston area provide free band and orchestra performances, jazz, vocals, dance, cheerleading, puppetry, and theater productions. In its first year (2010), twenty-eight schools participated. This continuing program schedules as many student performances as possible throughout the year.

Another popular event has been Holiday Lights in Hermann Park. This month-long festival began in November 2002 and became a holiday tradition for thousands of Houston families, and it opened the park to nighttime activities around McGovern Lake and along the Reflection Pool. Holiday Lights, free to the public throughout December, was generously underwritten by H-E-B for five years, with considerable support from the Houston Parks and Recreation for security and equipment. A local company, Eventions, came up with the idea and provided logistics, from electricians to entertainment. Dramatic light installations at dif-

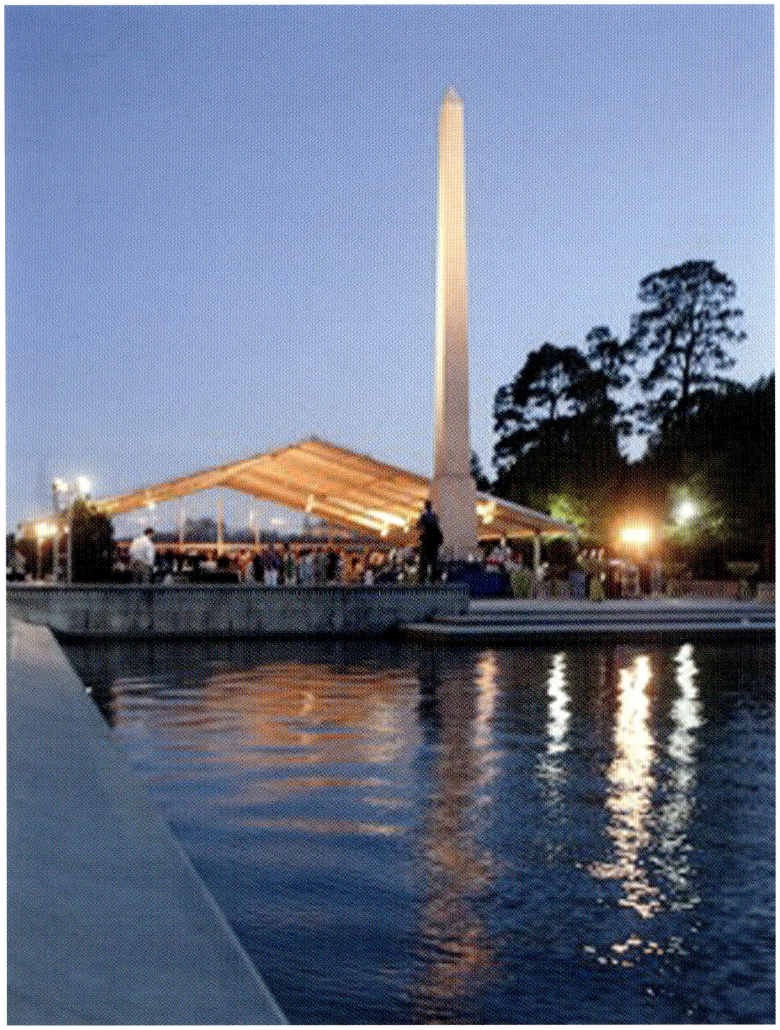

Evening in the Park, 2011. Photograph by Michelle Watson, Catch Light Group. Courtesy Hermann Park Conservancy.

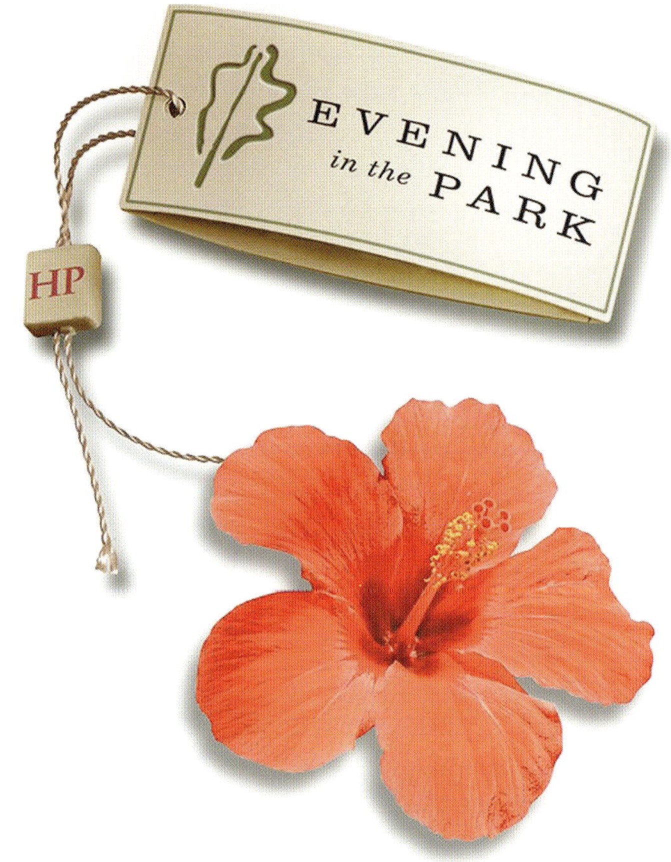

Evening in the Park logo (2010, TPRB Advertising). Courtesy Hermann Park Conservancy.

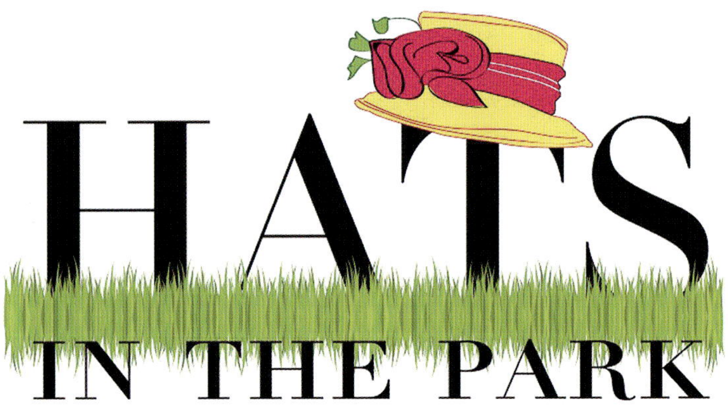

Hats in the Park logo (2011, PH Design). Courtesy Hermann Park Conservancy.

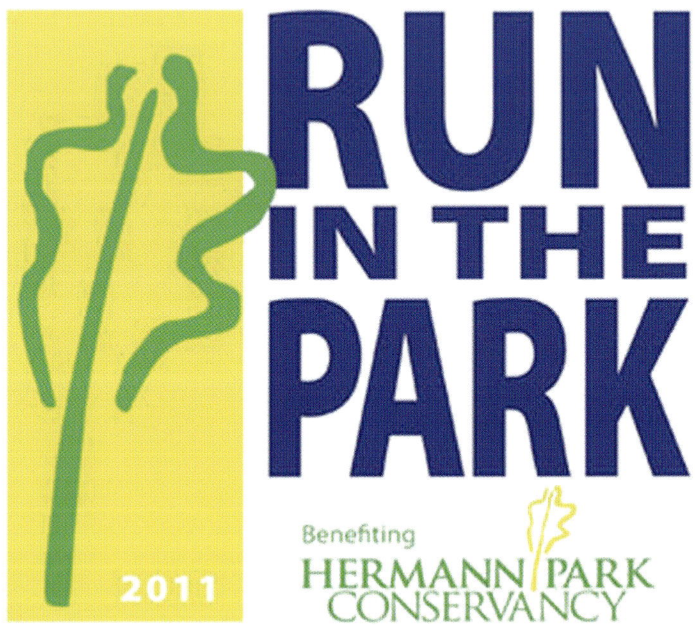

Run in the Park logo (2011, W. J. Ford & Associates). Courtesy Hermann Park Conservancy.

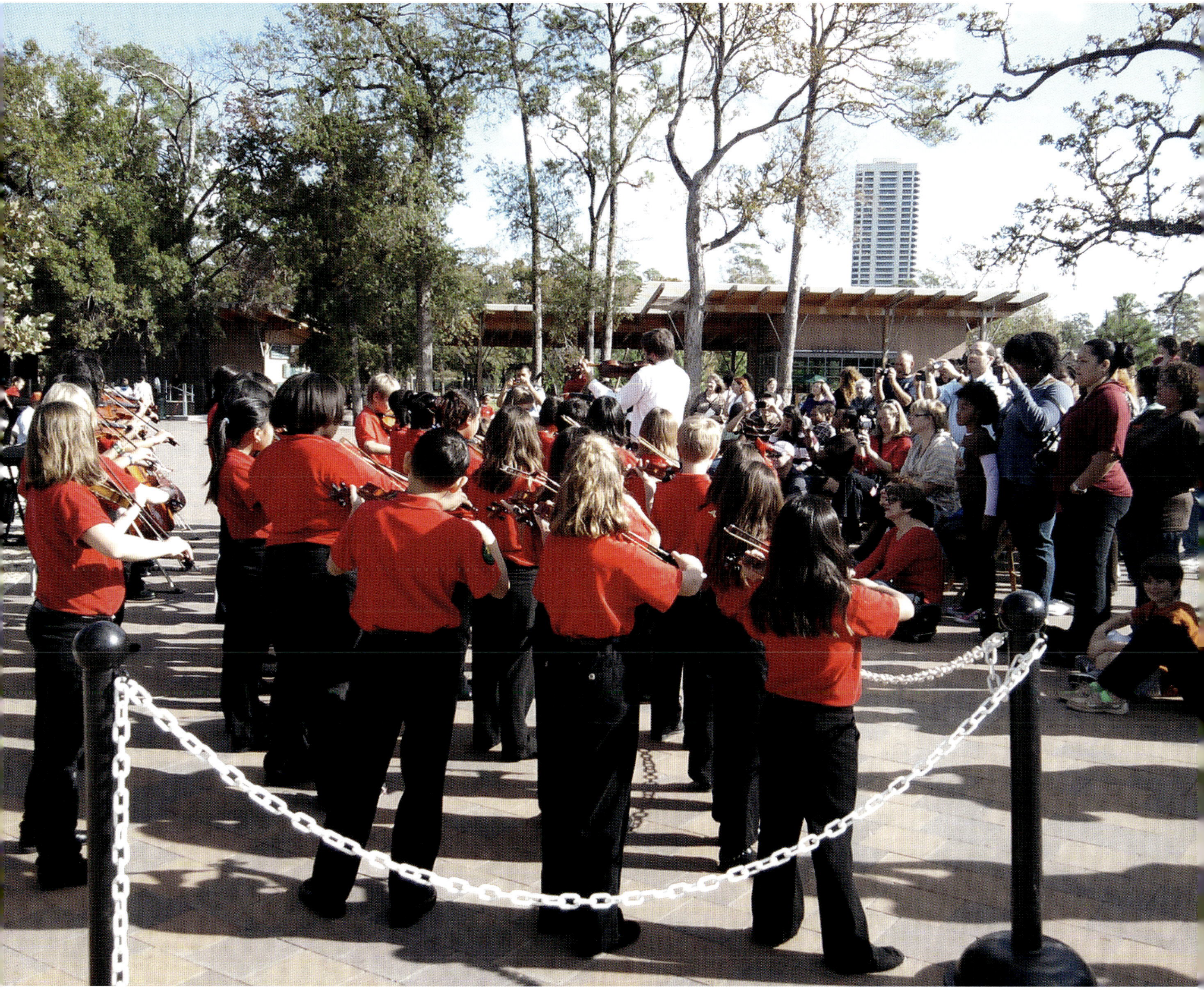

Parker Elementary School students performing in Lake Plaza, 2012. Courtesy Hermann Park Conservancy.

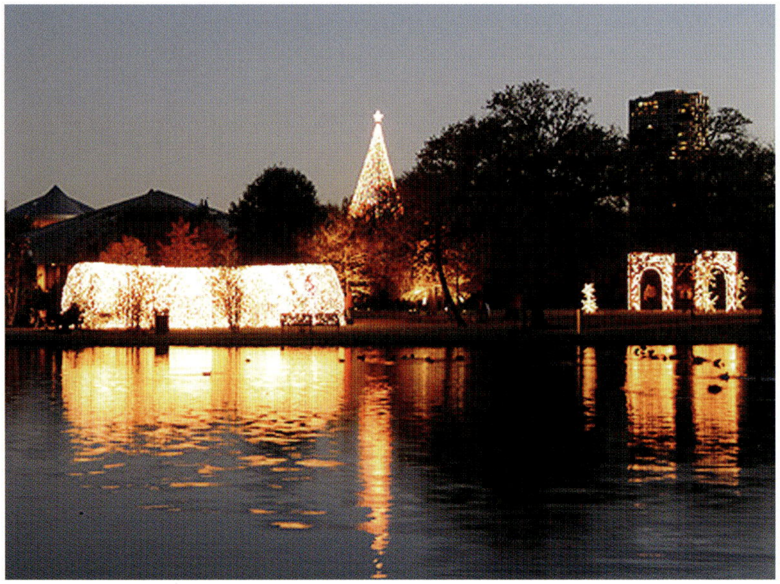

Holiday Lights at McGovern Lake, c. 2004. Courtesy Hermann Park Conservancy.

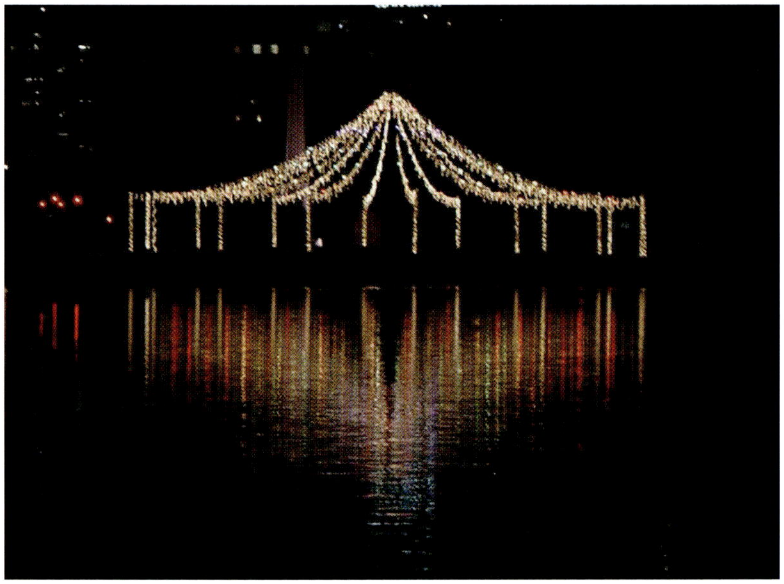

Holiday Lights, tent of lights, c. 2005. Courtesy Hermann Park Conservancy.

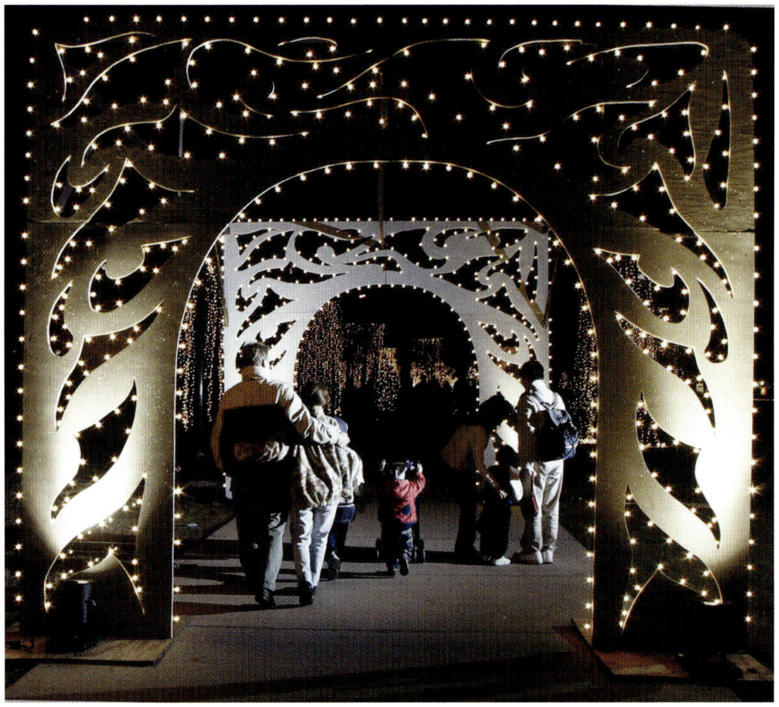

Holiday Lights, tunnel of lights, c. 2005. Photograph by John Everett. Courtesy Hermann Park Conservancy.

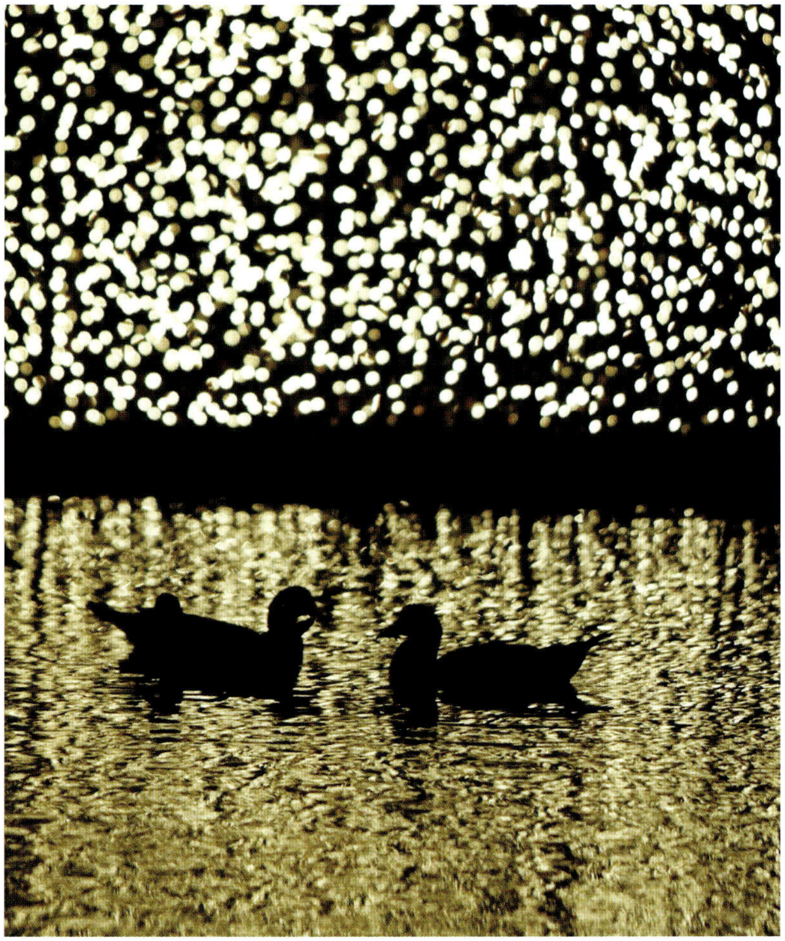

Holiday Lights, c. 2005. Photograph by John Everett. Courtesy Hermann Park Conservancy.

ferent times included traditional lighting of trees along the Reflection Pool allées, a giant, "Air Star" globe, a series of light-covered woodcut arches, and a dazzling walk-through tunnel of lights. Holiday Lights was suspended during Houston's economic downturn in 2008.

Fund-Raising

While the goal of all of these events is fund-raising for Hermann Park, they generate fun and goodwill for the park as well. Every year new supporters are found when people who have not seen the park (or have not seen it recently) are invited by friends and associates to participate in some aspect of park activity. In addition to a general endowment fund, the conservancy has established several special funds and other opportunities for giving that improve the conservancy's ability to maintain and improve Hermann Park. In 2004 a Tree Conservancy Fund, a Habitat Conservancy Fund, and a Garden Conservancy Fund were put in place to ensure long-term support for these aspects of the park. The George Hermann Society was established in 2006 to recognize donors who have provided for the future of Hermann Park through bequests or life income gifts to the Hermann Park Conservancy. Since 1992 the Hermann Park Conservancy has raised over $50 million dollars in private funds, which have not only been used for major capital projects and a variety of free programs for the community, but also leveraged for matching grants and governmental allocations.

Hermann Park Conservancy was founded to provide a nonprofit vehicle to raise private money for the improvement of a public institution, Hermann Park. In the early 1990s, there was still an expectation that local taxes would pay for everything associated with public property. The conservancy's success in changing that perception has been fundamental to the improvements that have occurred in Hermann Park over the last twenty years. The community—individuals, corporate supporters, and foundations—now understands that private investment is essential to having a top-quality park. The high interest and investment in Hermann Park today speak to a change in attitude and signify that a critical mass in Houston recognizes the importance of public parks.

Foundations and corporations give to Hermann Park because it is good for the community, but individuals give because the place touches them in a particular and special way. Generations of Houstonians have come to the park with their families and friends and left with memorable experiences. Today, grandparents bring their grandchildren to the park because they enjoy reliving times they spent in the park with their children, and they may remember certain places or activities (the picnics, the train) from their childhoods. Veteran board member Christopher L. Knapp holds dear his own memories of spending time in the park with cousins when visiting his grandparents, Genevieve and James Lykes, who lived nearby. "My grandparents had five children, so I had lots of cousins. After my grandfather died in 1943, my grandmother had parties and kids around all the time. And there were a lot of kids in the neighborhood. We all loved going over to play in the park."[10] Among Knapp's earliest memories of Hermann Park is looking up at the amazing tree canopy, which he still loves. He also recalls a "rocket ship" on the playground and the lion drinking fountain at the zoo.

Many members of Knapp's large extended family—Lykes, Knapps, Duncans, and Fondrens—have been generous to Hermann Park. Letitia Lykes, granddaughter of James and Genevieve, married David Knapp, who with his father, Alfred, was a cofounder of Fannin Bank, which was among early corporate advocates of aggressive tree planting in Houston. As an active member of the South Main Center Association, Fannin Bank was responsible for extending the majestic live oaks on the Main Street edge of Hermann Park from University Boulevard to Holcombe

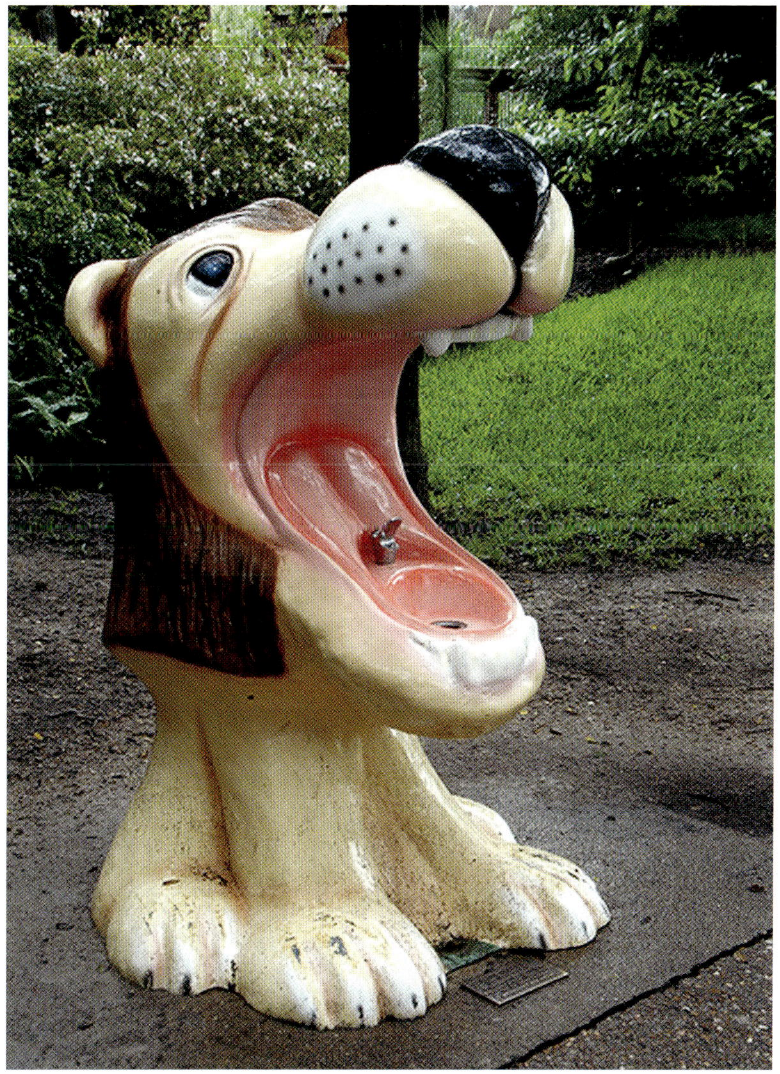

The Lion Drinking Fountain, a historic zoo icon for over fifty years, was recently refurbished. Courtesy Houston Zoo.

in the early 1970s. David Knapp's sister, Lynda, married David Underwood, longtime chairman of the Texas Medical Center board. The Underwoods and their Fondren cousins were founding supporters of Hermann Park Conservancy and have been integral to the restoration of Hermann Park, both individually and through grants made by the Fondren Foundation.

This extended family group has long set an example of what an important impact multigenerational families can have on civic improvement. Even though they have scattered across the United States, their affectionate memories of growing up in the park have tied them to this place. Knapp's aunt Genevieve Lykes Duncan (1914–2010), who lived her adult life in San Antonio, was a regular supporter of trees and habitats in Hermann Park and remembered the Garden Conservancy Fund in her will. Her daughter May Shelmire Duncan made the earliest gifts to the Habitat Conservancy Fund and supported volunteer programs. When she died in 2007, she left one million dollars, not for a project to be named in her memory, but for a maintenance endowment. Genevieve Lykes' other three children, Cameron, Genny, and Bowie, have funded a significant portion of the Grand Gateway project, and the Lower Garden section of the gateway will be named for Genevieve Lykes Duncan.[11] Many other multigenerational families continue to enjoy and support Hermann Park. Old houses are sold, and people move, but the park is a constant and always welcoming place.

Educational Programs

One of the benefits that the conservancy provides through its fund-raising activities is an array of educational opportunities. One of the first was Field Studies 101, instituted in 1997, in which educators were trained in techniques for teaching environmental science. These teacher workshops were followed by field trips for their students to the Bayou Parkland area, where the children participated in experiential learning by studying native plants, insects, and birds, while at the same time learning respect for the natural environment. Summer Adventures, taught by conservancy instructors, provided a more extended program with similar content. These programs were made possible by the Lila Wallace–Reader's Digest Fund grant.

The Conservation Posse summer program for teens began in 2008. In six weeks, fifteen Posse participants executed volunteer projects in the park, learned from weekly speakers about environmental issues, and took field trips to the Weather Museum and the Montgomery County Preserve. They also acquired practical skills, such as composting and urban gardening, and learned what it takes to maintain a 445-acre park. The ongoing Job Shadow Program, initiated in 2008 as an extension of the Conservation Posse program, was designed for students between ages fourteen and twenty-one to help them understand the importance of public land management. Participants shadow staff members in daily routines or on specific projects, working alongside an experienced employee who can answer questions and provide accurate and timely advice. This hands-on experience exposes students to a variety of career opportunities, from gardening to park management.

For adults, the conservancy held a Master Gardener program in 2005. Aspiring Master Gardeners attend thirteen weekly sessions, receive horticulture training, and learn specialty gardening skills. Texas Master Gardeners is a program designed to disseminate horticultural information throughout the state. To become a Texas Master Gardener, a participant needs a minimum of fifty hours of instruction conducted by the local county extension agent; then he or she is expected to share this knowledge by donating at least fifty hours of volunteer service to the community. Master Gardeners are certified in landscape design or as specialists in such fields as entomology, earth-kind landscaping, irrigation efficiency, plant propagation, greenhouse management, vegetable gardening, and rainwater harvesting.[12] Each student in the Hermann Park Master Gardener program contributed over sixty volunteer hours of maintenance in the park. This program was eventually moved to Bear Creek Park, where Harris County authorities needed volunteers.

Art in the Park

The permanent monuments, statues, and sculptures in Hermann Park are owned by the City of Houston and maintained by the Houston Arts Alliance. However, their placement and landscaping are the responsibility of the Hermann Park Conservancy in consultation with the Parks Department. The park's most iconic statue is the Sam Houston Equestrian Statue at the entrance to Hermann Park. Another historical monument, the Dick Dowling Statue, was the first public monument in Houston. It was unveiled on St. Patrick's Day, March 17, 1905, in front of the old City Hall in Market Square, where it stood until 1939 when it was moved to Sam Houston Park. After fifty-three years downtown, it was moved in 1958 to its current location at the east entrance to the Hermann Park. The Texan sculptor Frank Teich, whose firm carved the base for the Sam Houston Statue, fabricated the 8-foot-high, Italian marble statue and its 20-foot-high granite base.[13] Richard William Dowling (1838–1867) and his family escaped the Irish potato famine and settled in New Orleans, where four of his six siblings and parents died from yellow fever. Dowling moved to Houston in 1857, established several successful saloons, and then became a celebrated Civil War soldier, leading the victory at the Battle of Sabine Pass. The jovial redhead was much loved in Houston, and several Irish societies joined together to raise the money for a statue in Dowling's memory after he too died of yellow fever.[14]

A majestic welded-steel sculpture, *African Elephant* (1982), at the Zoo's West Entrance, is the work of Houston sculptor Robert Fowler (1931–2010). It is a 5-ton, life-sized figure comprised of strips of Cor-

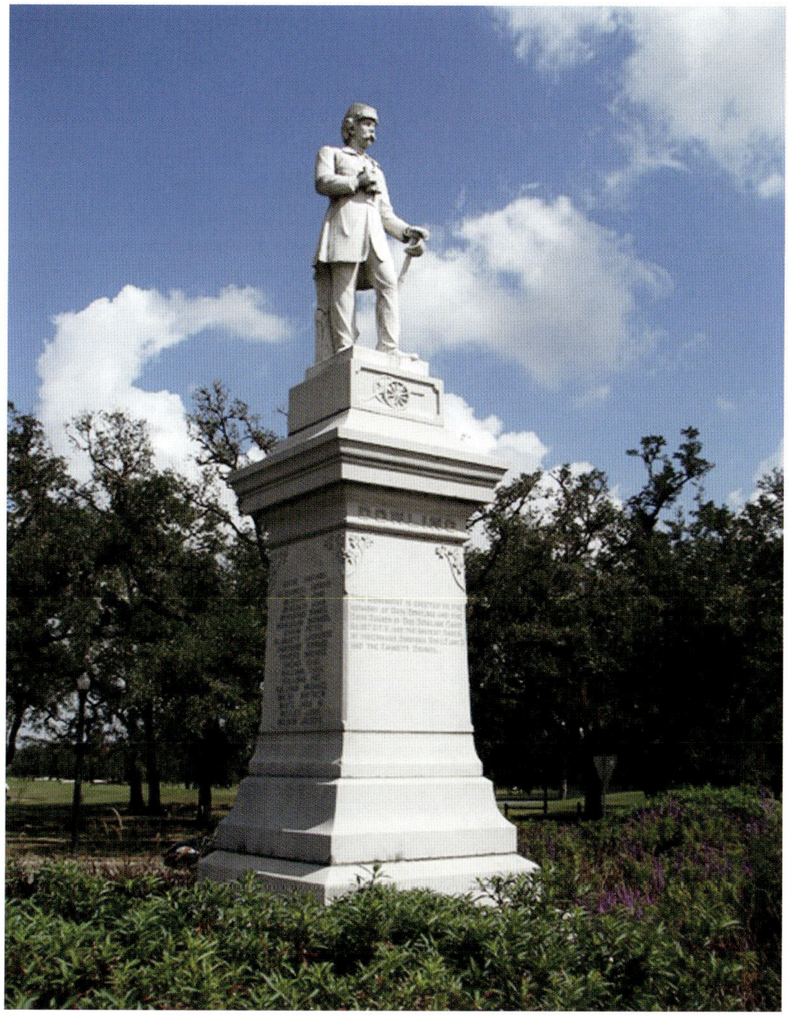

Dick Dowling Statue (1905, Frank Teich), originally in front of the old Houston City Hall, since 1958 it has been located at the east entrance to the park, 2012. Photograph by B. S. Bradley.

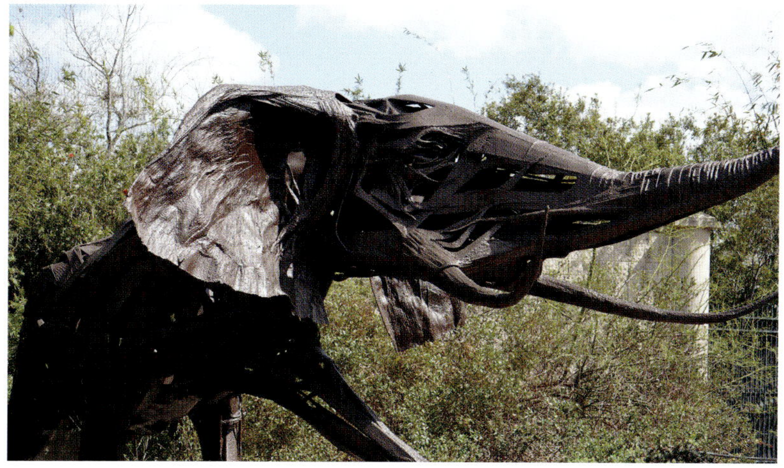

African Elephant (1982, Robert Fowler) was moved from the primary zoo entrance in 2000 to the west entrance on Cambridge Street, 2013. Photograph by B. S. Bradley.

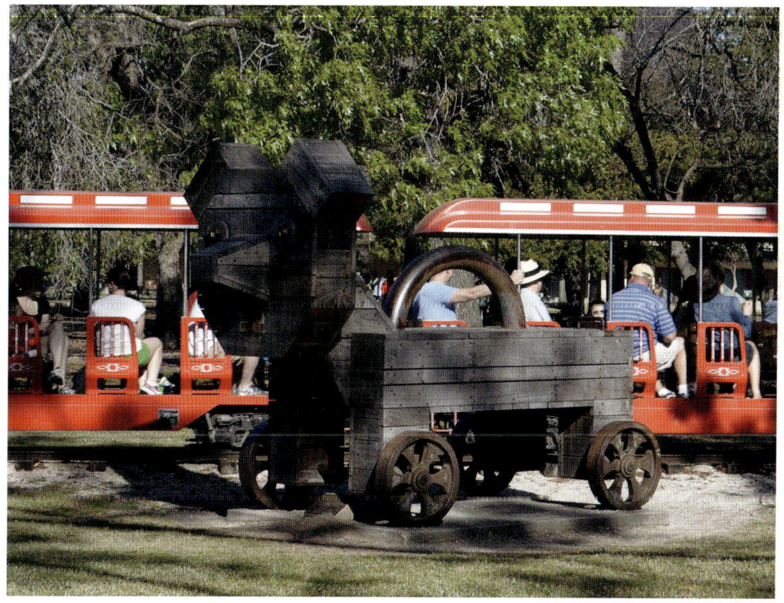

Portable Trojan Bear (1974, Jim Love) was first situated across Bissonnet from the Museum of Fine Arts, Houston, where the Cullen Sculpture Garden is now. In Hermann Park the sculpture faces Hermann Park Drive on the route of the Hermann Park Railroad, 2013. Photograph by B. S. Bradley.

ten steel and rods that are fused to give the elephant its form. The steel armature supports are exposed and act as anchoring points in the legs. *African Elephant*, donated by Isabell and Max Herzstein to the Houston Zoo in 1982, was originally located at its main entrance. It was restored and relocated in 2000.[15]

The pine and steel sculpture, *Portable Trojan Bear* (1974), was the first public commission for Houston artist Jim Love (1927–2005). The Cultural Affairs Committee of the Houston Chamber of Commerce commissioned the work, which was donated to the City of Houston by Cameron Iron Works. Today *Portable Trojan Bear* commands a prominent location on Hermann Park Drive, visible to children riding the miniature train. Originally installed at the corner of Montrose and Bissonnet, now the location of the Museum of Fine Art's Cullen Sculpture Garden, it was moved to Hermann Park in 1984. Miller Theatre, the Houston Zoo, the Museum of Natural Science, and the Centennial Gardens also contain works of public art.

Master planner Laurie Olin suggested that no additional permanent works of art be placed in the park. Instead, he recommended that the conservancy commission or host temporary exhibitions. The conservancy's art committee reviews proposals and makes recommendations to the Hermann Park Conservancy board. The first such temporary exhibition occurred with the placement of twenty art cows in the park as part of Cow Parade Houston from September to November 2001.

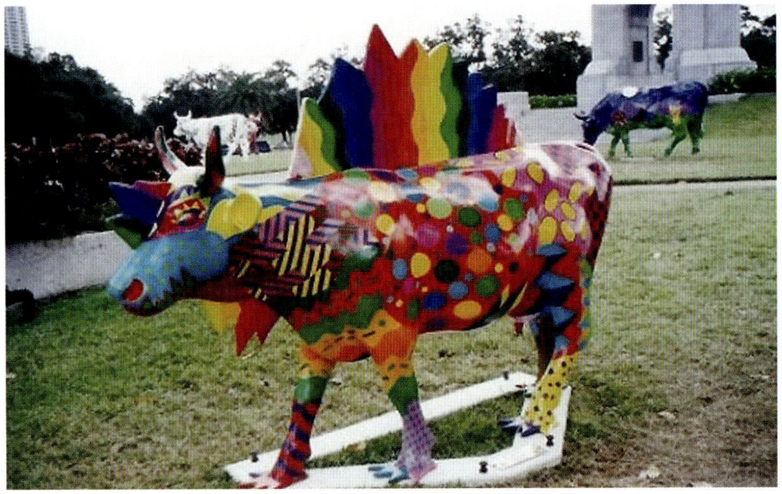

Cowasaurus-Camp for Allasaurus (2001, Donna Lane Vadala) was sponsored by Rhonda and Paul Gerson for placement in Hermann Park during the 2001 Houston Cow Parade when dozens of fiberglass cows were painted and decorated by local artists and placed throughout the city. Photograph by Peggy Woods.

There were 350 cows, produced by Swiss artist Pascal Knapp, decorated and placed throughout Houston. Following the close of the event in December 2001, Sotheby's conducted a live auction at the Wortham Center downtown for the benefit of Texas Children's Hospital.[16]

In 2010 Houston joined Paris, Hong Kong, and New York in hosting an exhibition by the French artist Bernar Venet (b. 1941). Venet's fifteen monumental, Cor-ten steel sculptures, some as high as 30 feet, were placed in eight locations throughout Hermann Park. This exhibition was mounted in association with the Texan French Alliance for the Arts, the City of Houston, Hermann Park Conservancy, the Consul General of France, Houston Parks and Recreation Department, AXA Art Insurance Corporation, and McClain Gallery. In an interview with the *Houston Chronicle*, Venet spoke of the special nature of outdoor sculptures. "When you go to a museum, you know why you go there—you want to see art," Venet said. In a park setting, "one day you are surprised to discover those things. They raise questions in the minds of people. . . . It really opens their mind, and they discover what art can be today."[17]

Another remarkable temporary exhibition in Hermann Park was managed by the Houston Arts Alliance. It featured the work of dissident Chinese artist Ai Weiwei, who served as artistic consultant for the Beijing National Stadium ("The Bird's Nest") constructed for the 2008 Summer Olympics. From Los Angeles and London, Weiwei's twelve bronze sculptures, titled *Circle of Animals/Zodiac Heads*, were installed at the edge of McGovern Lake from March to June 2012. Each weighing 800 pounds and standing roughly 10 feet high, Ai Weiwei's work is a re-creation, on an oversized scale, of the traditional zodiac sculptures that once adorned the fabled fountain at Yuanming Yuan outside Beijing. Erected in the eighteenth century, the original animal heads surrounding the fountain spouted water at two-hour intervals until 1860, when French and British troops raided the palace and looted the heads. To date, only seven of the legendary twelve heads have been recovered.

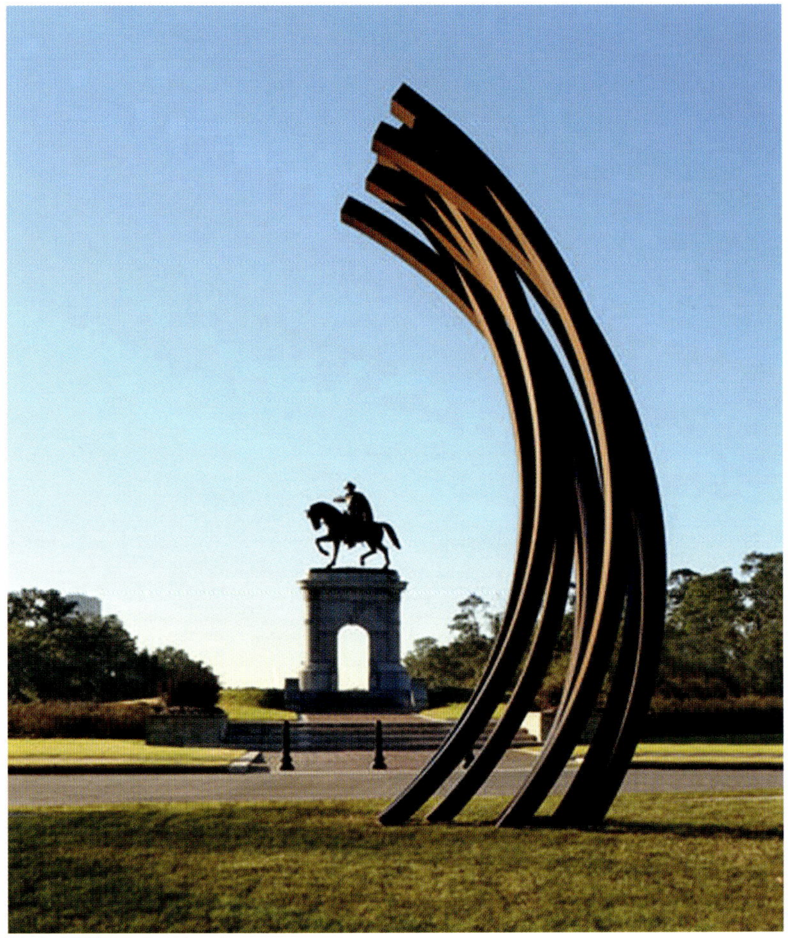

Vertical Art FC (2009, Bernar Venet), one of fifteen monumental steel sculptures by the internationally known French artist that were placed throughout Hermann Park during a temporary exhibition in 2010. Courtesy Hermann Park Conservancy.

The Houston exhibition was presented by the Hermann Park Conservancy with the City of Houston through the Houston Arts Alliance and the Houston Parks and Recreation Department, and AW Asia, a private organization and exhibition space located in the Chelsea art district in New York City.[18] The twelve heads—rat, rooster, ox, tiger, rabbit, dragon, snake, horse, ram, monkey, dog, and boar—were rendered with varying degrees of realism. Christopher Knight, art critic for the *Los Angeles Times*, described them as "sweet and silly," noting that many of them seem to be grinning at visitors, who pose for a steady stream of pictures at their own zodiac sign.[19] Both adults and children surrounded the sculptures throughout the exhibition's run in Hermann Park.

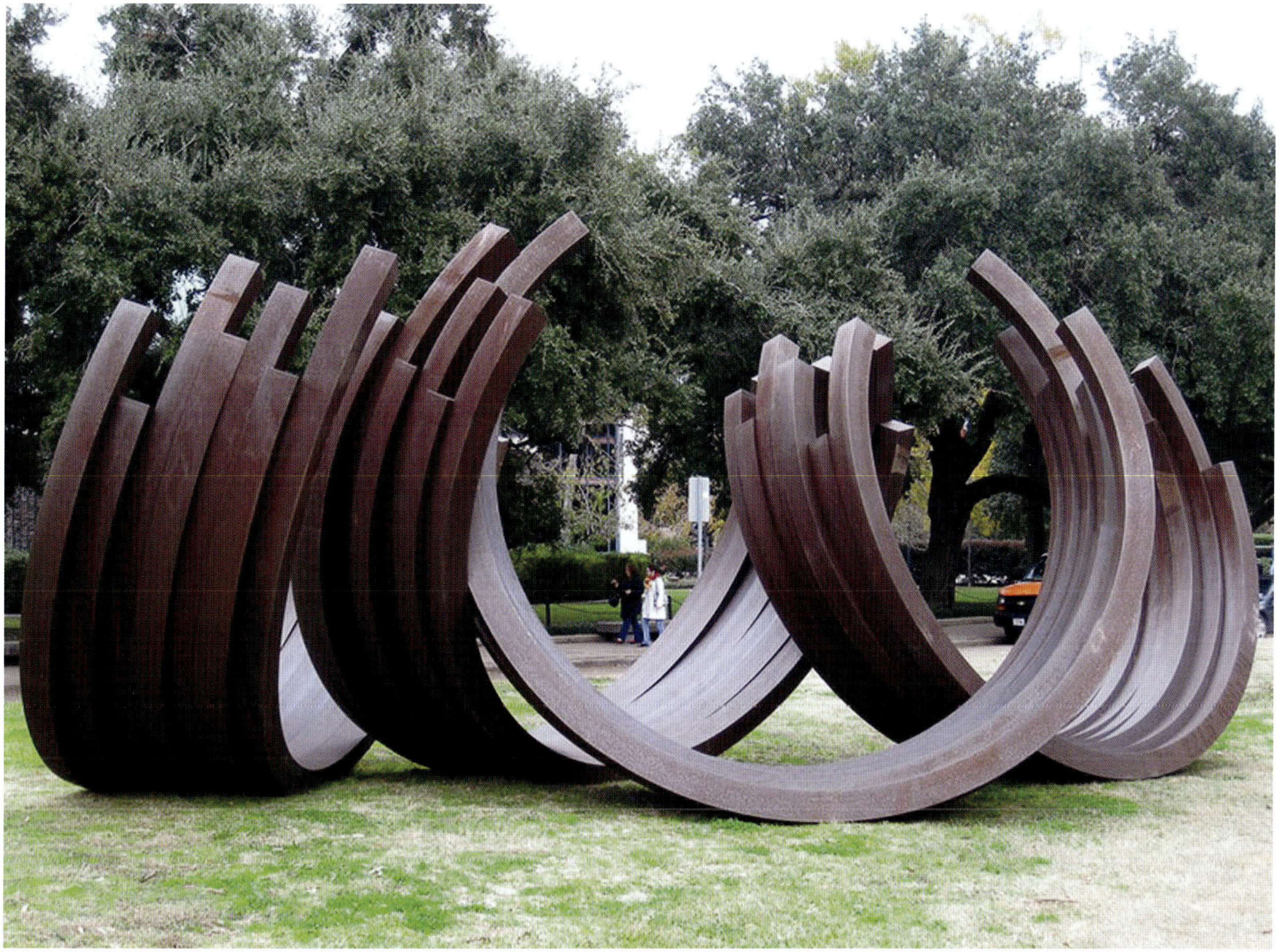

Leaning Arcs in Disorder (2009, Bernar Venet), one of fifteen monumental steel sculptures by the internationally known French artist that were placed throughout Hermann Park during a temporary exhibition in 2010. Courtesy Hermann Park Conservancy.

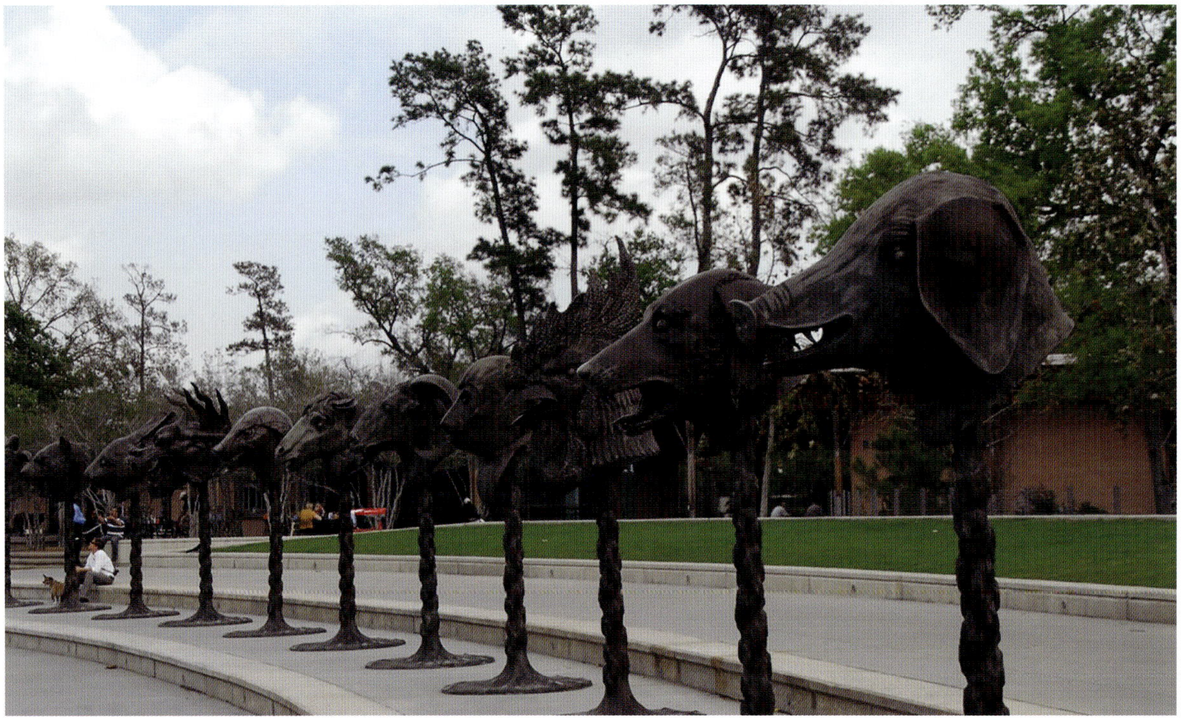

Circle of Animals/Zodiac Heads (2005, Ai Weiwei), twelve massive bronze sculptures in a popular temporary exhibition along McGovern Promenade overlooking McGovern Lake, 2012. Courtesy Hermann Park Conservancy.

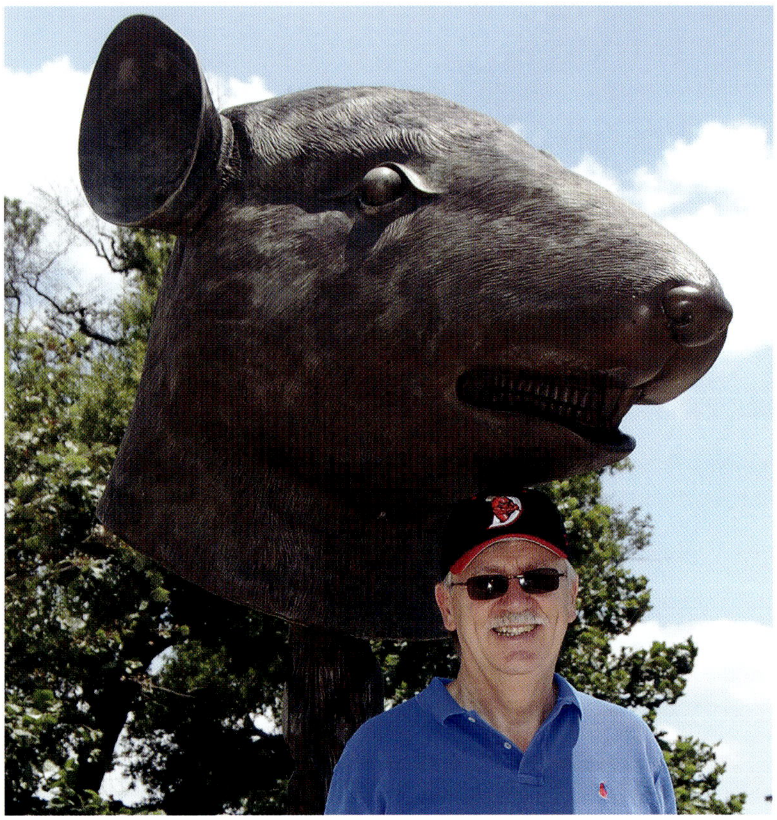

Head of the Rat (2005, Ai Weiwei). Hundreds of visitors posed throughout the exhibition with the zodiac head representing the year of their birth, 2012. Photograph by B. S. Bradley.

Visitor Services

The Hermann Park Conservancy has a park-wide concessions agreement with the City of Houston that allows the Visitors Services department of the Conservancy to manage programs that bring in revenue to support the conservancy's maintenance programs, while providing amusing activities and a wider variety of food and beverages. The agreement covers all areas of the park not served by park institutions—Houston Zoo, Hermann Park Golf Course, Miller Theatre, and the Museum of Natural Science. Members of the Visitors Services team are most evident around Lake Plaza, where they greet visitors and make sure that operations are running safely and efficiently. Kinder Station and the Hermann Park Railroad, the gift shop, and the pedal boats concessions are all operated by the conservancy. The railroad sells nearly 400,000 tickets per year and generates over $1 million in revenue. Pedal boat rides exceed 20,000 per year for an annual income of over $200,000. In addition, both the train and pedal boats can be rented out for private parties.

Awards

The Hermann Park Conservancy has gained national recognition for its efforts to improve, restore, and maintain Hermann Park. These awards are important to those who have donated, volunteered, and worked to improve the park because they recognize the excellence and high standards with which the conservancy conducts its projects and programming. In 2001 the conservancy received state and local awards from the Texas Recreation and Parks Society and Keep Houston Beautiful. The conservancy received its most prestigious national award in 2005: the Stewardship Excellence Award from the Cultural Landscape Foundation and the General Award of Excellence from the American Society of Landscape Architects for the Heart of the Park restoration. Preservation Houston recognized preservation and restoration work in the park with its Good Brick Award in 2006.

Other awards include the Community Improvement Award from the Museum District Business Alliance (2008); the Parks and Natural Areas Award of the Houston-Galveston Area Council for the Mary Gibbs and Jesse H. Jones Greenway (2009); the Mayor's Proud Partner Award, Keep Houston Beautiful, for Lake Plaza and the Hermann Park Railroad (2009); the Leadership in Action Award from Leadership Houston for Lake Plaza and the Hermann Park Railroad (2009); the Parks and Natural Areas Award from the Houston-Galveston Area Council for Conservation Posse teen summer program (2010); the Parks and Natural Areas Certificate of Recognition from the Houston-Galveston Area Council for Project Blazing Star (2010); a Merit Award from the Texas Chapter of the American Society of Landscape Architects for Lake Plaza (2010); the Development of Distinction Award from the Urban Land Institute, Houston for Lake Plaza (2010); and a Certificate of Recognition, Mayor's Proud Partners Award, Keep Houston Beautiful for the Lake Picnic Area renovation (2011).

The Hermann Park Conservancy's board of directors is composed of Houstonians from all walks of life. These volunteers are the backbone of the organization. Almost two hundred individuals have served on the board since 1992. Some, such as Jay Baker, Sadie Gwin Blackburn, Sanford Criner, Susan Keeton, Marley Lott, Jackie Mazow, Marvin Taylor, and Keith Wade, have remained on the board or in continued service on the advisory board since the beginning of Friends of Hermann Park (see appendix 6). Another long-term board member, Jane Curtis, notes that the continuity from such longtime service has been critical to keeping the conservancy focused on restoring the park and in avoiding what she calls "mission creep."[20]

The 1995 master plan for Hermann Park makes clear in its conclusion that in order to create the physical and psychological changes needed for the renewal of the park, a strong and committed nonprofit organization had to demonstrate singular dedication to the park. Such a group was the one thing that US cities that have been successful in rebuilding their parks have had in common. The Hermann Park Conservancy has proved its mettle. Throughout the rebuilding process, the conservancy has served and continues to serve as the armature and organizing structure from which planning, funding, construction, maintenance, and operation have germinated and grown. The successful relationships the conservancy has forged with the City of Houston and other institutions in the park, as well as dozens of other agencies and Hermann Park stakeholders, promises a long and happy life for this Houston treasure.

CHAPTER NINE

The Olin Plan

Its goals are to preserve, protect, and nurture what is special and worthy, to mend what is broken or has begun to unravel, and to remove or relocate what has come to harm the park or impede public access.[1]

—Laurie Olin, 1995

Laurie Olin presented Hermann Park's new master plan on March 17, 1994, after eight months of research, field study, and meetings. Olin and his associates analyzed an immense compilation of data about the park and the region—reports, maps, traffic counts, and site information. They also met with representatives of institutions, agencies, community organizations, municipal and county officials, and park users seeking insight, consensus, and support. Response from numerous groups informed the direction of the park plan. Olin's curiosity about history led him to an extensive study of the history of Hermann Park. This in turn led to a plan firmly and obviously based on the initial Kessler Plan and its subsequent revisions by Hare & Hare. Jane Anderson Curtis, a recent graduate of the University of Virginia's landscape architecture program and new employee of Hanna/Olin, was sent to Houston in 1994 with the Hanna/Olin team to conduct a detailed analysis of park conditions. Drawings, maps, and sketches were prepared in Olin's Philadelphia offices. The extensive groundwork, planning, and local responses led to the publication in 1995 of *Renewing Hermann Park: A Comprehensive Master Plan*.[2]

In the plan's preface, "A New Leaf," Mayor Bob Lanier, Parks Director William R. Smith II, conservancy chairman William M. "Bill" Coats, and executive director Mary Anne Piacentini wrote that the plan "will enhance and preserve the best of the park, restore areas that are old and worn-out, and develop under-utilized areas to provide new recreational opportunities for park visitors."[3] In the first section of the report, "A Vision for Hermann Park," Olin wrote that the plan seeks a park that is "both greener and bluer . . . a sanctuary with more shade, more lawn, and more water . . . a magical place alive with wonder and mystery,"[4] a vision projected in his watercolor drawings. In summarizing his concepts, Olin emphasized that the renewed park should serve as a catalyst and model for changing the landscape of Houston. "The vision for Hermann Park aligns with [the effort to promote the quality of life in Houston to a higher standard], driven by a desire for equity and justice, for beauty, and for delight both in the place and in each other's company. These should be the joys of urban life, this is the role for the urban park."[5]

Olin began his first presentation by showing a series of sketches that illustrated then-current uses of parkland and highlighted what little land was left over. Of the 445 acres in the park, only 90 provided contiguous, usable open space. His early studies looked at the amount of water in the park and how the lake could be enlarged and connected to Brays Bayou along natural gullies, existing but generally covered over and ignored. Other studies focused on parking and transportation. Too much of the interior of the park was taken up with parking lots, an appalling 30 acres. Olin outlined master planning principles and related them to what was needed in Hermann Park. The highest priority was access. Congested vehicular circulation and intrusive parking made it obvious that extensive spatial reorganization was needed.

The second principle was restoration. Many elements of the park that are integral to its history had been overused and neglected. The live oak allées, for example, needed to be revived, enhanced, and nurtured. One goal of the Hermann Park Conservancy was readily understood by the Olin team: the new master plan needed to recapture the character of the original park plans, "where the intention was to provide the public

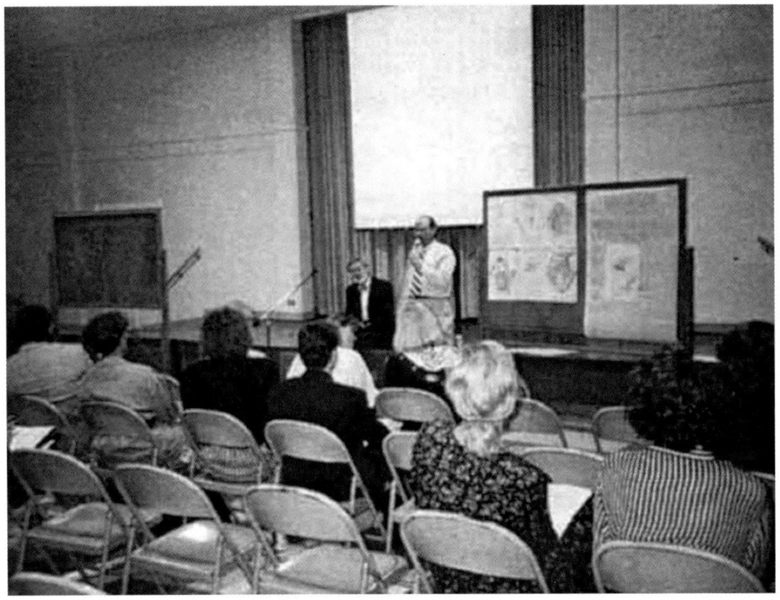

First community meeting held by Laurie Olin for public input on a new master plan for Hermann Park, 1994. Courtesy Olin Partnership.

with a green sanctuary in which to meet, play, relax, and enjoy fresh air and natural beauty."[6]

Life in the park was the third concern. "The separation of activities within a diverse landscape is a key consideration . . . to ensure that the park feels open and free to urban dwellers who seek an expanse of space and greenery."[7] Security, adequate services, renovation of old facilities, and building new ones all needed to be addressed. Finally, a plan for stewardship of Hermann Park would be necessary to assure that this special place retained a central civic purpose within the city of Houston.

Olin's assessment of the condition of Hermann Park in 1995 was dismal:

> Around the Reflection Pool, the hill at Miller Theatre, and in the adjacent picnic groves, Hermann Park has been loved to death. The ground is beaten down by foot traffic, the grass struggles to stay green through the hot summers, and the trash barrels overflow. Soils rich in clay have been compacted by overuse, exacerbating the existing drainage problems. Large areas in the picnic groves on the golf course, and around the Reflection Pool are routinely flooded and unusable, drying later to baked mud. Shallow pools of standing water provide ample habitat for Texas-sized mosquitos.[8]

But, like washing the face of a dirty child, the chances for improvement in Hermann Park were good. The master plan was not only full of insight, but it was also realistic. Olin warned, "The existence of a master plan at any scale is no guarantee that short-term solutions can be avoided or that natural systems can be restored. Its success requires

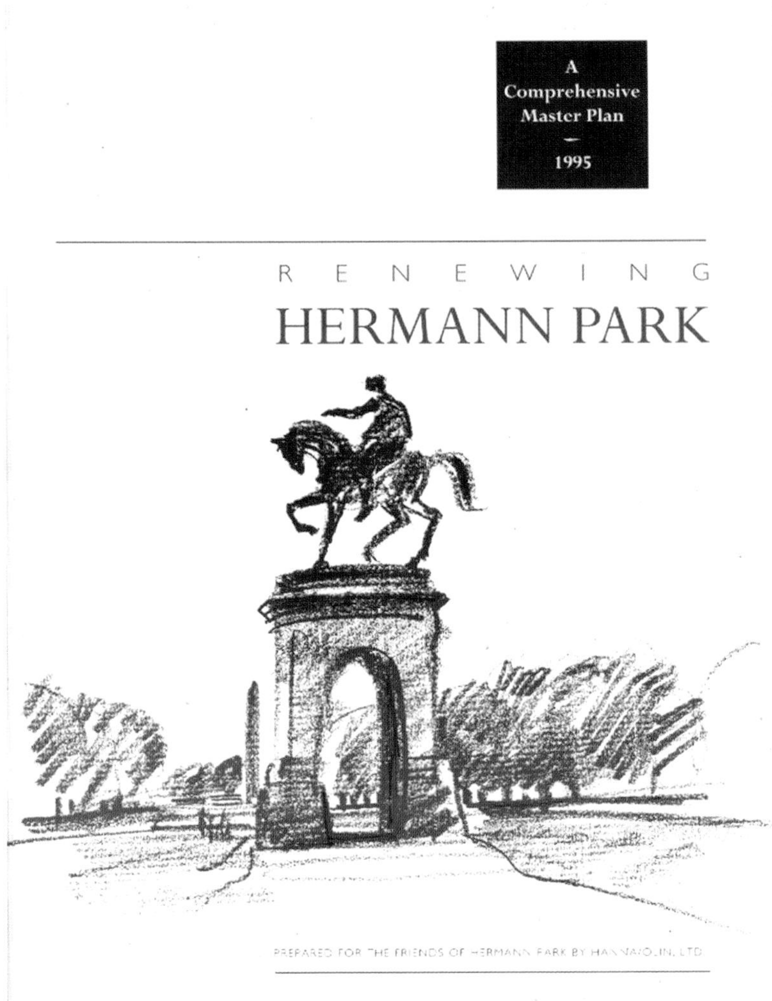

Renewing Hermann Park: A Comprehensive Master Plan cover, 1995. Courtesy Hermann Park Conservancy.

vision, cooperation, flexibility, and continual commitment to examine each small detail in light of the whole."[9]

In a second series of comparative images, Olin showed how much of the park's tree canopy had been lost. A canopy drawing by Hare & Hare in 1930, when compared to the canopy in 1995, showed a dramatic loss of trees. Olin's plan for reforestation did not mimic Hare & Hare's plan. For one thing, there was less land (notably the lost Hogg Tract, where the Texas Medical Center was built), and new road and path configurations as well as more buildings (the Museum of Natural Science in the northwest corner and the expanded zoo at the center), which left less land for reforestation. Yet, comparing the 1995 state of affairs with the master plan proposal showed that substantial improvement was possible.

A more focused problem was the minimal use of parkland near Brays Bayou. No facilities of any kind or convenient connections to the rest

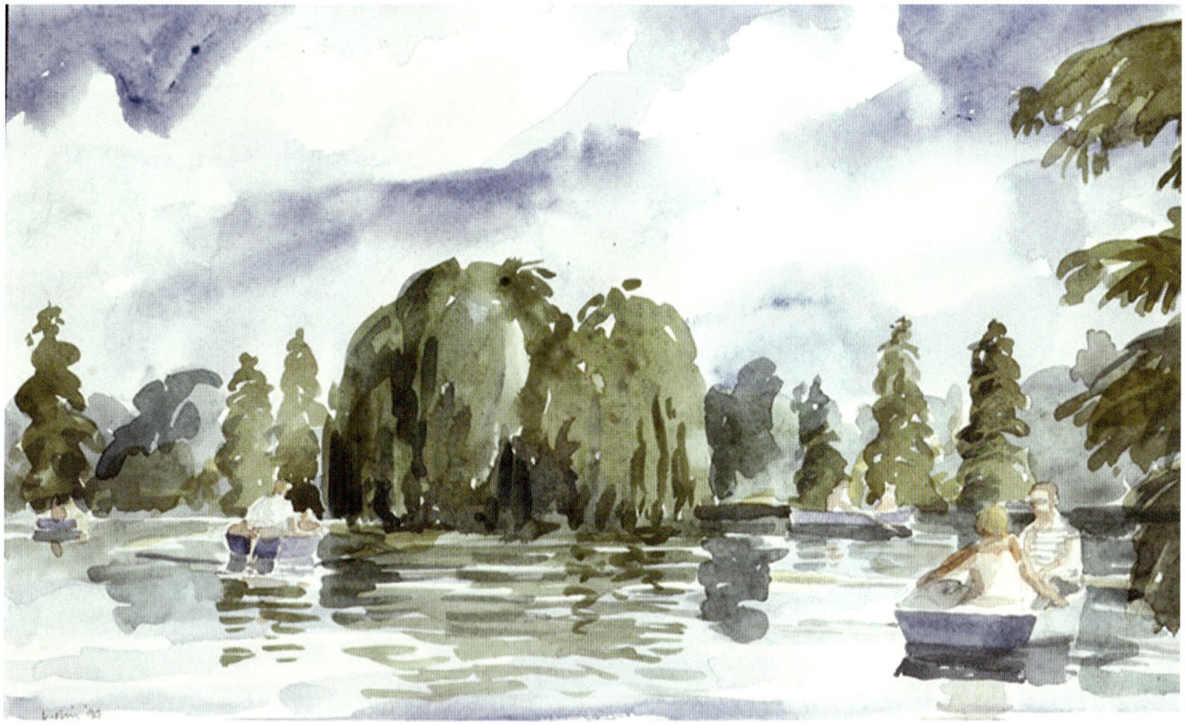

"Lake in Hermann Park," watercolor by Laurie Olin, 1993. Courtesy Olin Partnership.

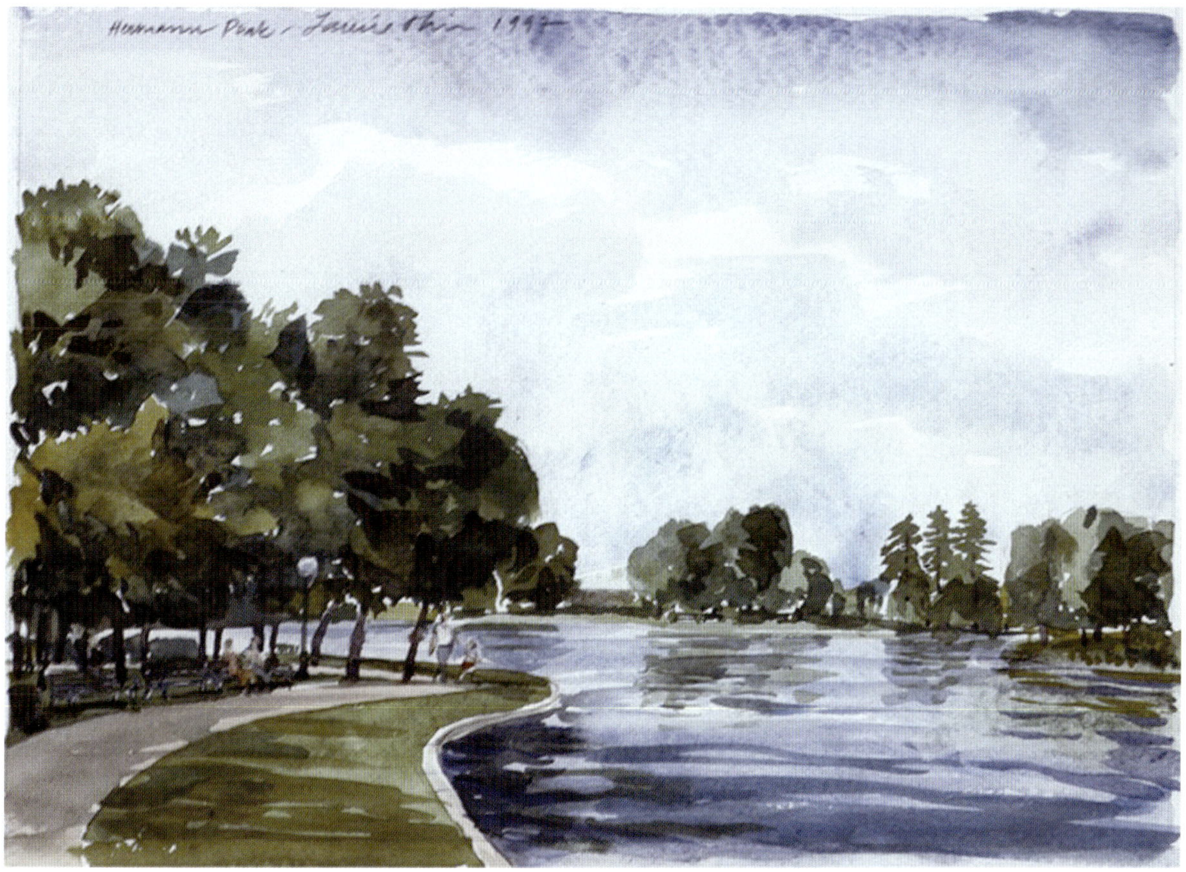

"Hermann Park Lakeside," watercolor by Laurie Olin, 1993. Courtesy Olin Partnership.

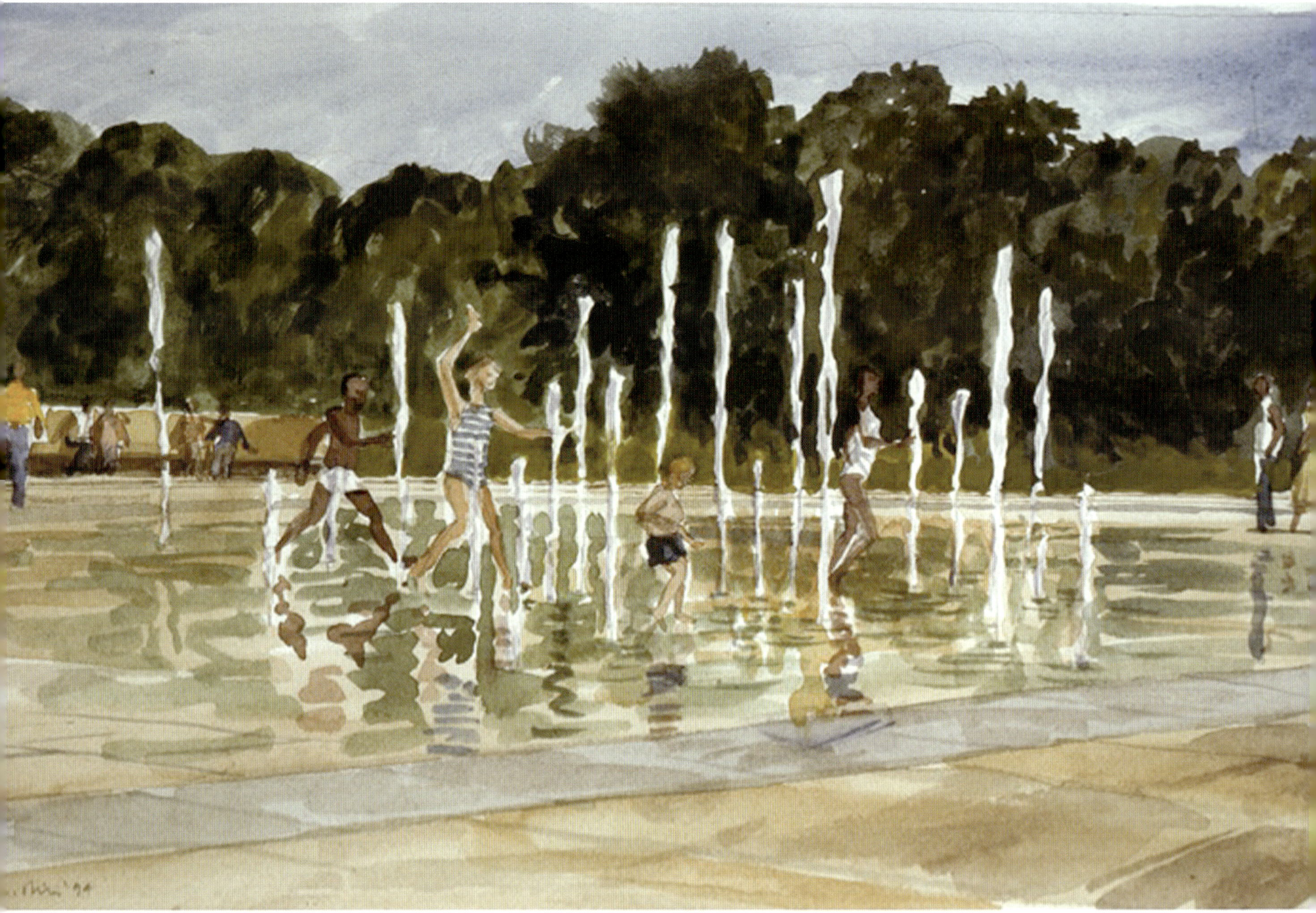

“Plaza Fountains,” watercolor by Laurie Olin, 1993. Courtesy Olin Partnership.

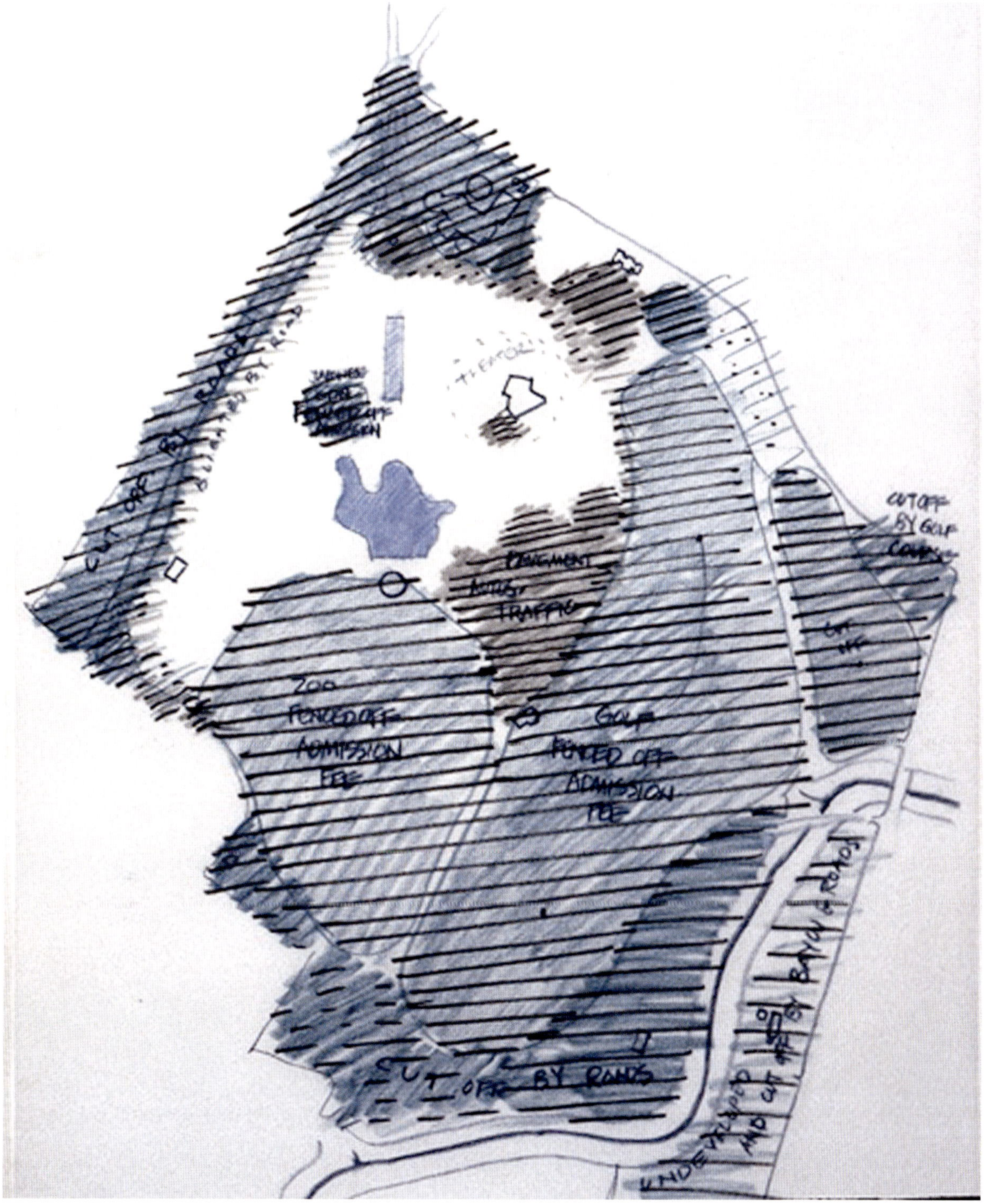

Usage study, Hermann Park, pencil sketch by Laurie Olin, 1994. Areas in blue identify land in use for roads and parking lots, institutions, the Japanese Garden, buildings, and the golf course. Courtesy Olin Partnership.

Laurie Olin Interview with Barrie Bradley Philadelphia, PA, April 11, 2012

In considering Hermann Park's recent history, it seems that, after Hare & Hare, architects and engineers took over what planning there was in the park. How did that happen?

In the decade leading up to World War II, landscape architecture as a profession began to dry up. All that was left after the Depression began was work in the civic and public spheres, largely on parks and with the WPA [Works Progress Administration]. Then the war stopped everything. The University of Pennsylvania even closed its Department of Landscape Architecture until Ian McHarg came in after the war. From 1946 until the 1960s, there was a tremendous amount of work—highways, suburbs, and housing projects—but that was taken over by engineers and architects. The change came as the profession unexpectedly began to reclaim its role with commercial work, [such as] shopping centers—Old Orchard Shopping Center, Chicago (1956) and North Park Center, Dallas (1965) by Lawrence Halprin & Associates, for example, whose first prominent civic work was the 1962 Seattle World's Fair.

What precipitated this change?

Just before the publication of *Silent Spring* [1962, Rachel Carson], concern for the environment began with a few people, mostly out of Harvard's Graduate School of Design, who were interested in cities and planning. Bob Zion, Larry Halprin, Ian McHarg, and Hideo Sasaki became early voices advocating trees in cities, fountains, plazas, small parks, and environmental use of the land. If there was a moment, it was Halprin's urban design and fountain plazas in Portland (1968–1970). The city as a landscape idea grew, and my generation became fascinated with systems and infrastructure.

What happened?

The 1960s and 1970s happened! Everything—sex, the war, civil rights—was about politics. As landscape architects began to look at the new idea of "landscape urbanism," they began to understand that the job of a landscape architect is very political. The question is always: "Who suffers, and who gains?" Our job is to try to be fair and democratic and ecologically responsible. Once the landscape architecture profession realized that it existed in the public realm, the social agenda changed for them; it became a socioecological dilemma. The job of a landscape architect is one of negotiating among all the interested parties to move society in a direction that is both fair and responsible. You have to listen to everyone, even if you can't meet all the needs. In Hermann Park we spent months and months with various stakeholders—citizens, vendors, park users, politicians, donors, institutions, environmentalists, neighbors, and anyone else who wanted to lend an opinion. We created complicated spreadsheets organizing hundreds of bits of information that informed many choices we made for the final master plan. I might add without buy-in from Mayor Lanier and his administration, we wouldn't have gotten to square one. Those initial meetings with the city administration and members of the parks department were crucial.

(*continued*)

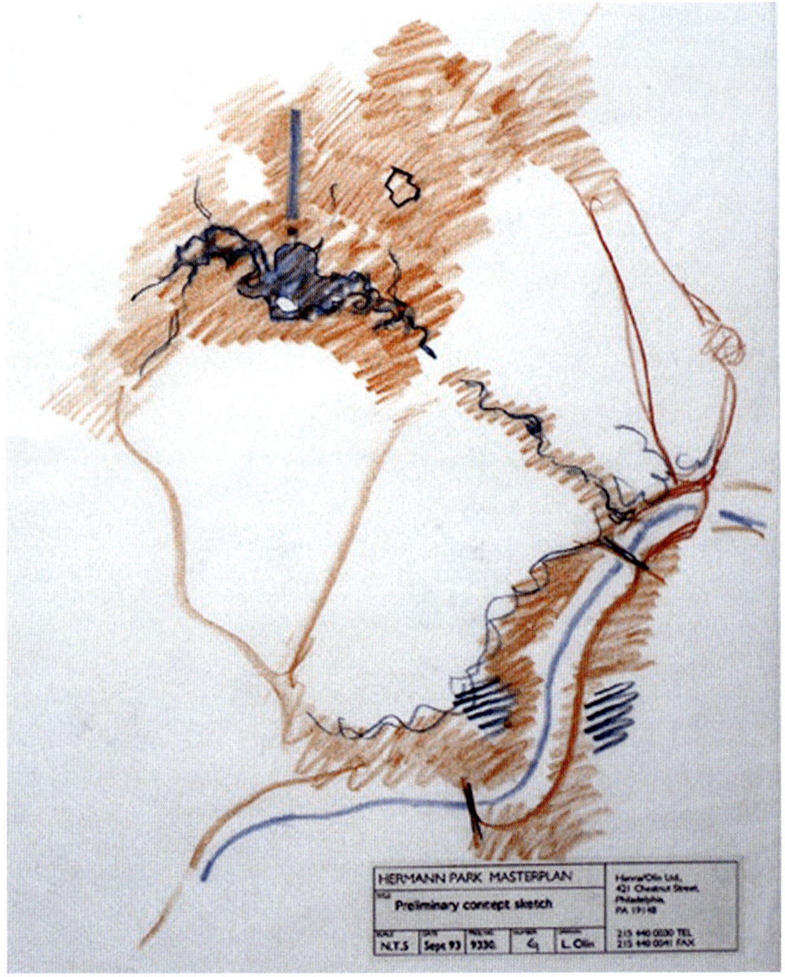

Preliminary concept for reclamation of underused areas and water enhancement, pencil drawing, Laurie Olin, 1994. Areas in orange indicate areas to be redeveloped; blue indicates current and new wet areas. Courtesy Olin Partnership.

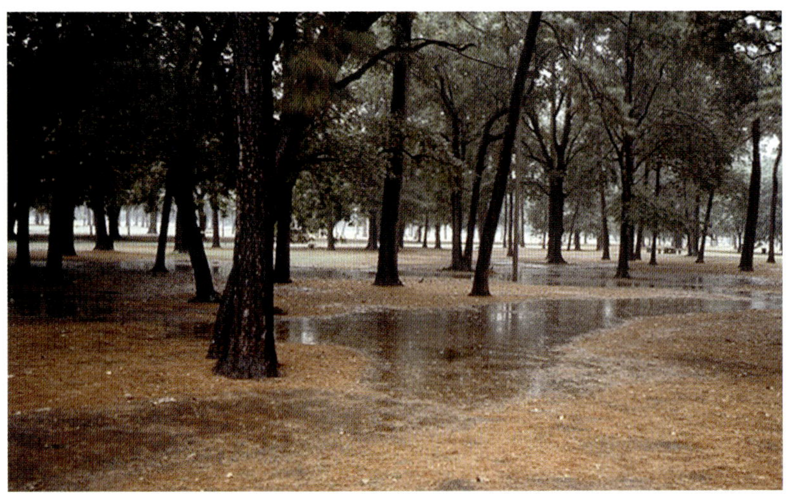

Standing water was a severe problem in several Hermann Park areas, 1993. Photograph by Laurie Olin. Courtesy Olin Partnership.

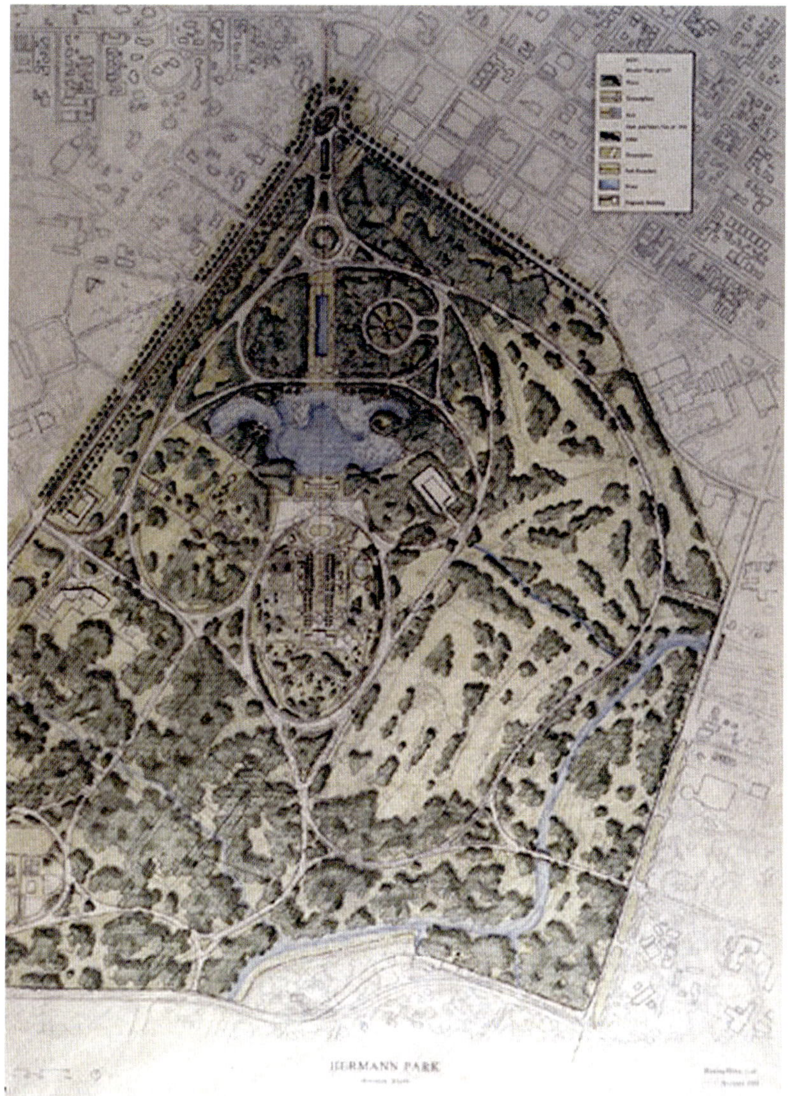

Tree canopy in Hermann Park, 1930s. Hanna/Olin. Courtesy Olin Partnership.

of the park were available. The bayou, a once verdant area, had been rechanneled and concreted in the 1950s, creating a barren landscape. Realizing that it would be a long time before the concrete channel might be removed, Olin proposed improving the Bayou Parkland, the southeast corner of the park, by planting trees to screen maintenance structures, redirecting traffic, introducing additional water features in the form of small ponds, and providing trails that wandered into the park's center to make this area more accessible and desirable.

Perhaps the most difficult but crucial challenge the master plan tackled was the reorganization of parking and circulation to create better access from all sides of the park as well as more green space within the park. By showing existing and proposed parking solutions side by side, Olin demonstrated how parking areas could be redistributed, retaining

Laurie Olin Interview *(continued)*

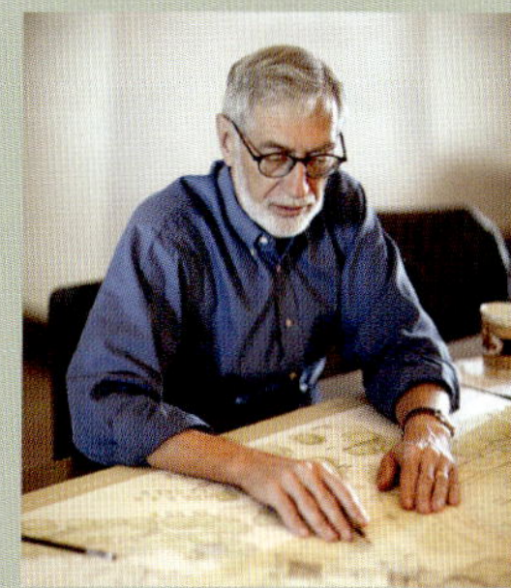

Laurie Olin, Olin Partnership, Philadelphia, Pennsylvania, c. 1996. Photograph by David Schmoll. Courtesy Hermann Park Conservancy.

Frederick Law Olmsted deplored the addition of monuments and other fixtures to Central Park, which he called "incidents." How do you feel about public art in public parks?
I love art in all forms. But parks have become an attraction for everyone's things. Americans still see parks as empty places and don't value a park for itself. However, our parks, including Hermann Park, are already program rich. People have pet projects, and they are looking for a place to put them. Whether it is art, vendors, highways, or anything else, it is simply parasitism. Other people want to capitalize on your hard work and success by stealing your space. I feel like it's the same thing as someone trying to put their stuff in my living room.

So you agree with Olmsted?
Absolutely. The answer is temporary exhibitions. Betsy Barlow Rogers created a policy against adding anything permanent to Central Park at the beginning of the Central Park Conservancy. You should do that in Hermann Park.

What about commissioned pieces? The Bean was a home run for Millennium Park in Chicago.
That and other successes like it—which are very rare—are just dumb luck. You commission a great artist, but you may not get his or her best work. The site might be wrong. A lot can change between the commission and the art, between the idea and the reality. In most cases it is not worth the chance.

When you look at an aerial view of Hermann Park, you see very clearly how much of the park is taken up with the golf course. Many have questioned keeping it in the park when so comparatively few people use that space. What do you think?
I have two reasons for believing that the golf course should remain in Hermann Park. The first is to be a land bank for the future. We don't know today what the needs of the community for a public park may be in fifty or a hundred years. We need to preserve every square inch of open space we can. The second is romantic and emotional—and perhaps the most important. This was the first golf course in the United States where black and white people played on the same course at the same time. This wonderful social history should not just be a plaque somewhere in the park. The Hermann Park Golf Course should be a living reminder where young people can experience an emotional connection to their pioneering grandfathers (and probably grandmothers) who found in this park a place where they could be part of the whole community—not just the black community. This is what a public park should be: a place where everyone can come together in a healthy, recreational space.

(continued)

Laurie Olin Interview (*continued*)

Speaking of recreational space, the perceived wishes of George Hermann and original designs for the park provided for a number of athletic fields, tennis courts, gyms, and so forth. Hermann Park once had tennis courts, but, other than the golf course, it has no other athletic facilities. Should it?

There is no room in Hermann Park for athletic facilities. Plus the City of Houston has made a great effort to provide swimming pools, basketball courts, and these types of facilities throughout the city in neighborhood parks where they should be. These other parks, including Memorial Park, provide for such active recreation. Hermann Park is a place of passive recreation where trails, walks, the lake, even the museum and zoo, are recreational spaces.

Do you have any theoretical basis for your work? What underlying philosophy drives you?

Natural systems follow biophysiographic imperatives. To make a project life-enhancing and matter beyond itself, a landscape architect needs to understand what is still germane today, what uses and activities are important to the clients/users. They also need to differentiate what is eternal and what is of the moment. One of the central issues is how to make the old new again, and that was our challenge in Hermann Park. In the 1960s J. B. Jackson wrote in an essay called "The Sociological Obsession," and I paraphrase here: "Every American is entitled to an environment that is biologically wholesome, socially just, and spiritually rewarding." Firmness, commodity, and delight.

What are the current trends in landscaping public places? What are students passionate about today?

Adaptive reuse. Recycling the environment. Incorporating natural systems. The High Line (2009–2011) in New York is a great example. There a place that was used up, dangerous, ugly, and forlorn has become a destination where the "wildscape" of native plants and wildflowers that grew there after the trains were discontinued was kept and enhanced. The High Line demonstrates how we can have nature and lots of people in the same place. People love it. Another imperative today is water. People don't realize that a sufficient water supply is the major issue facing the world today. We need to understand hydrological systems, nurture them, and provide water features everywhere we can.

When you talk about parks incorporating natural systems, what do you mean by "natural"?

In a lecture at Columbia about 1968, Buckminster Fuller said, "The opposite of natural is impossible." Nature is what is. Natural disasters should be called human disasters. They aren't a disaster for nature; they are just nature acting up on a particularly bad day. The disaster is for us. Nature isn't for us or against us. We are part of it.

Most of the projects recommended in your 1995 master plan for Hermann Park have been completed or are in progress. One exception was your plan for breaking up the huge parking lot at the center of the park and dispersing parking

(*continued*)

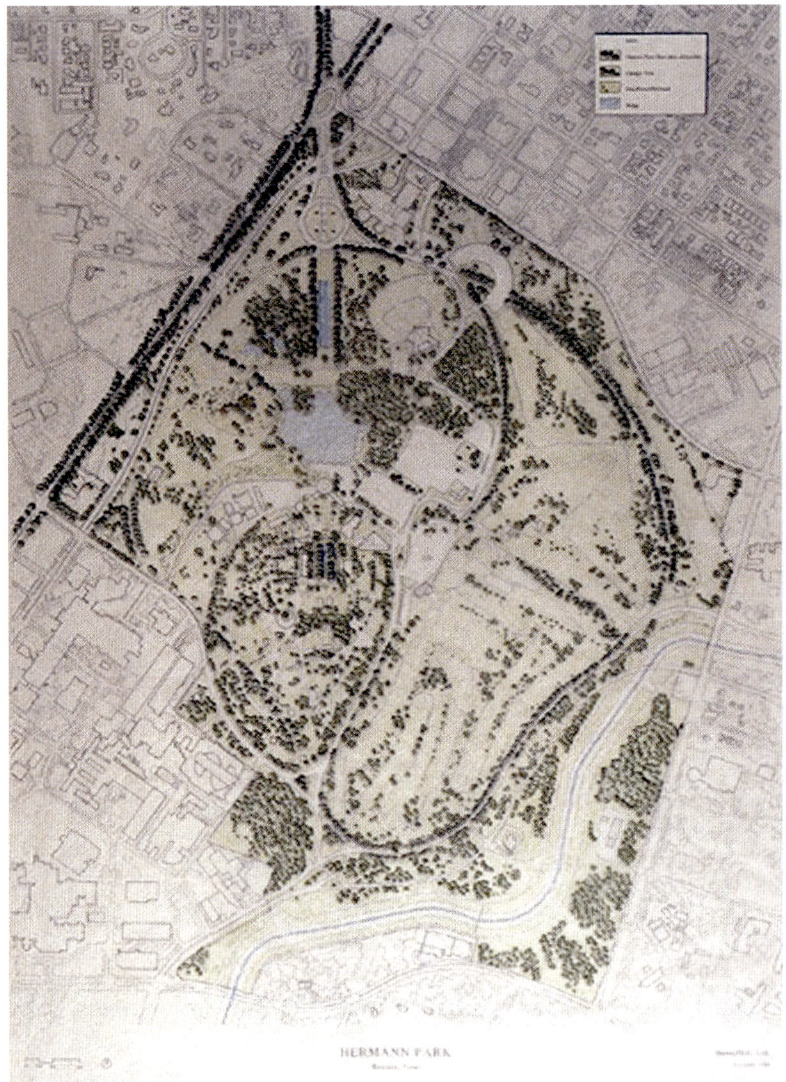

Tree canopy in Hermann Park, 1994. Hanna/Olin. Courtesy Olin Partnership.

the same number of parking spaces. A close-up of the zoo parking lot at the center of the park shows the happiest solution. Most parking in this area would be moved and the asphalt pavement converted into a green lawn. When this alternative seemed to be possible only in the long run, Olin showed how the current parking configuration in this area could be made more appealing with the introduction of a green swath and pathway down the center and numerous trees dividing the parking lot into discreet sectors. The parking area at the Garden Center, which also serves Miller Outdoor Theatre, could be improved with tree screening.

The 1995 Hermann Park master plan concluded with an enumeration of ten major projects that would have, the report asserted, the most dramatic effect in unifying and transforming Hermann Park.[10] Achieving these objectives was initially seen as a ten-year project. And as fund-

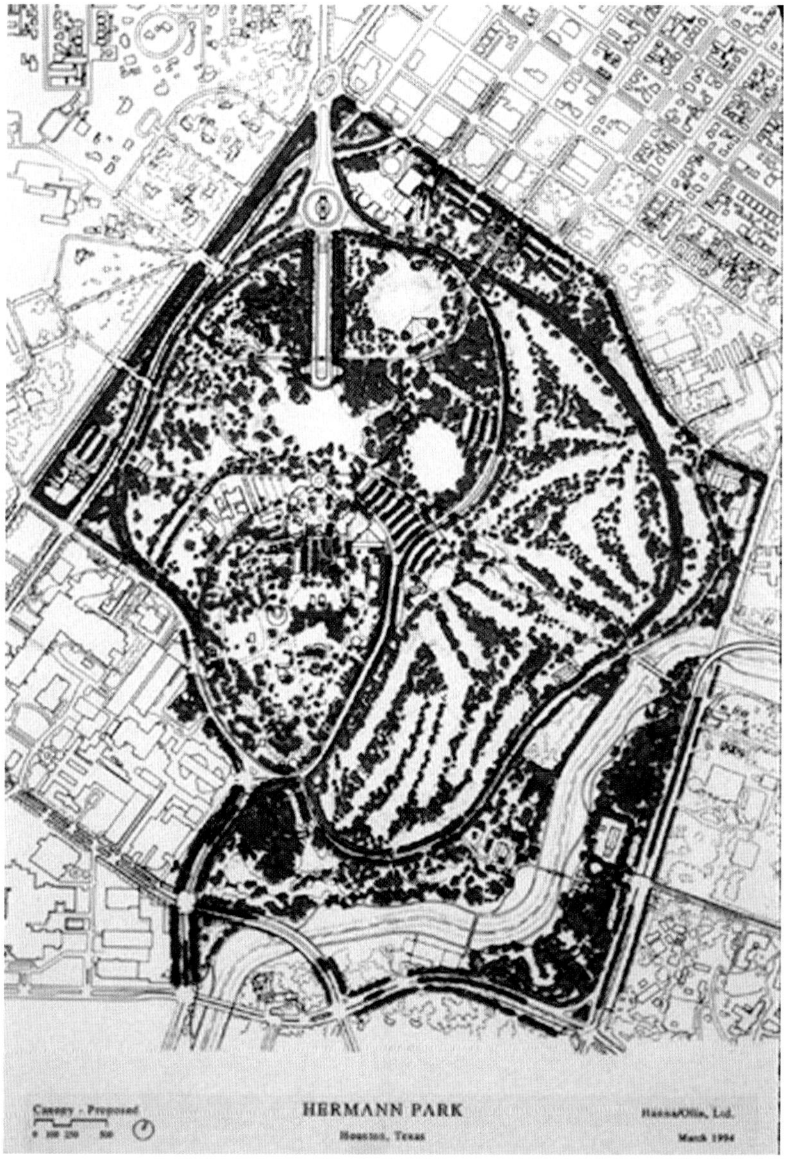

Proposed tree canopy, 1995. Hanna/Olin. Courtesy Olin Partnership.

raising and construction took place from 1995 until what turned out to be 2009, Laurie Olin remained involved, making design decisions and revisions.

The Reflection Pool

Rehabilitation of the Heart of the Park including the Reflection Pool was the most important initial step. The areas adjacent to the central entry axis had been defined, and within the context of the master plan final designs for the Heart of the Park area could begin. Scott Slaney and the SWA Group, with Peter Brown Civic Design, began producing working drawings based on their winning entry in the Heart of the Park competition. Laurie Olin's plan and drawing of this area along

Laurie Olin Interview *(continued)*

spaces to the periphery. This would give the park a Great Lawn like the Sheep's Meadow in Central Park. How do you feel about this shortcoming?
This is the one significant defeat we encountered in Hermann Park. We had hours and hours of meetings and finally came to an understanding with the zoo, but, so far, that has been ignored. We had many proposals that were all possible and financially feasible, including an underground garage, a multistory garage with a restaurant on top and views of the park, and so forth. Houstonians are wrongheaded in always expecting free parking right in front of their every destination. Why should private vehicles take up public space—and for free—in the park? Hermann Park is public land, and as much of it as possible should be for public use. And there is no payback for the park for providing all this free parking. Nothing!

Members and staff of the Hermann Park Conservancy who worked with you and your team feel that their relationship with you was special in many ways. You have left an impression of providing not just an extraordinary plan, but you have given them and the park an extraordinary amount of concern and attention. Can you comment from your perspective?
Not all jobs are created equal. Everyone knows that to produce a great plan, you need a good client. The Hermann Park people are wonderful. They were all new to me when I started, but I made good friends that I still enjoy seeing. At the beginning I knew this park was really important and the city was important, and somehow all this hit a nerve. There were so many problems—a dysfunctional budget, politics, a park that had been loved to death, and the project took a year longer than everyone (except me) thought it should—nevertheless, this was a special project. It is like falling in love, but you can have only one project at a time that you love like I love Hermann Park. Hermann Park is one of the great flagship parks in the US.

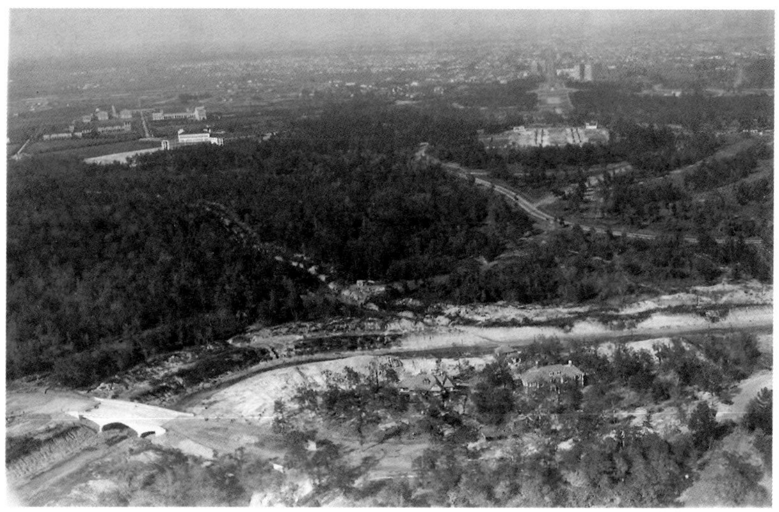

Brays Bayou, aerial view with Hermann Park in background. Note large houses in foreground, c. 1934. Courtesy Missouri Historical Society, Kansas City Research Center.

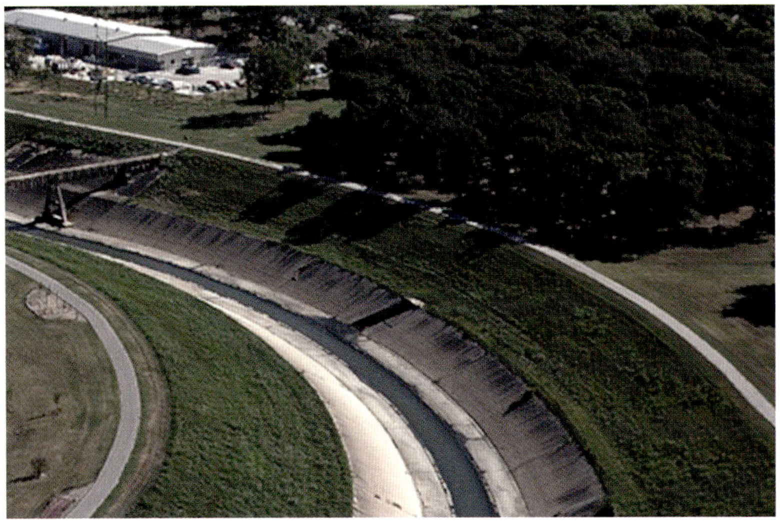

Brays Bayou with concrete channel concreted. Service buildings at the top left are on the approximate site of the houses in the 1930s photograph, 1993. Courtesy Olin Partnership.

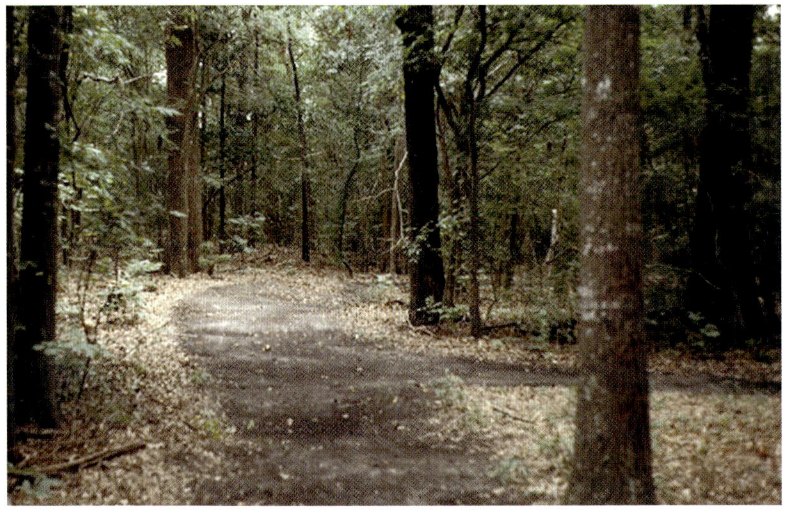

Bayou Parkland trail through natural woodlands preserved in Hermann Park. Few realize that an accessible forest exists in the inner city, 1995. Photograph by Laurie Olin. Courtesy Olin Partnership.

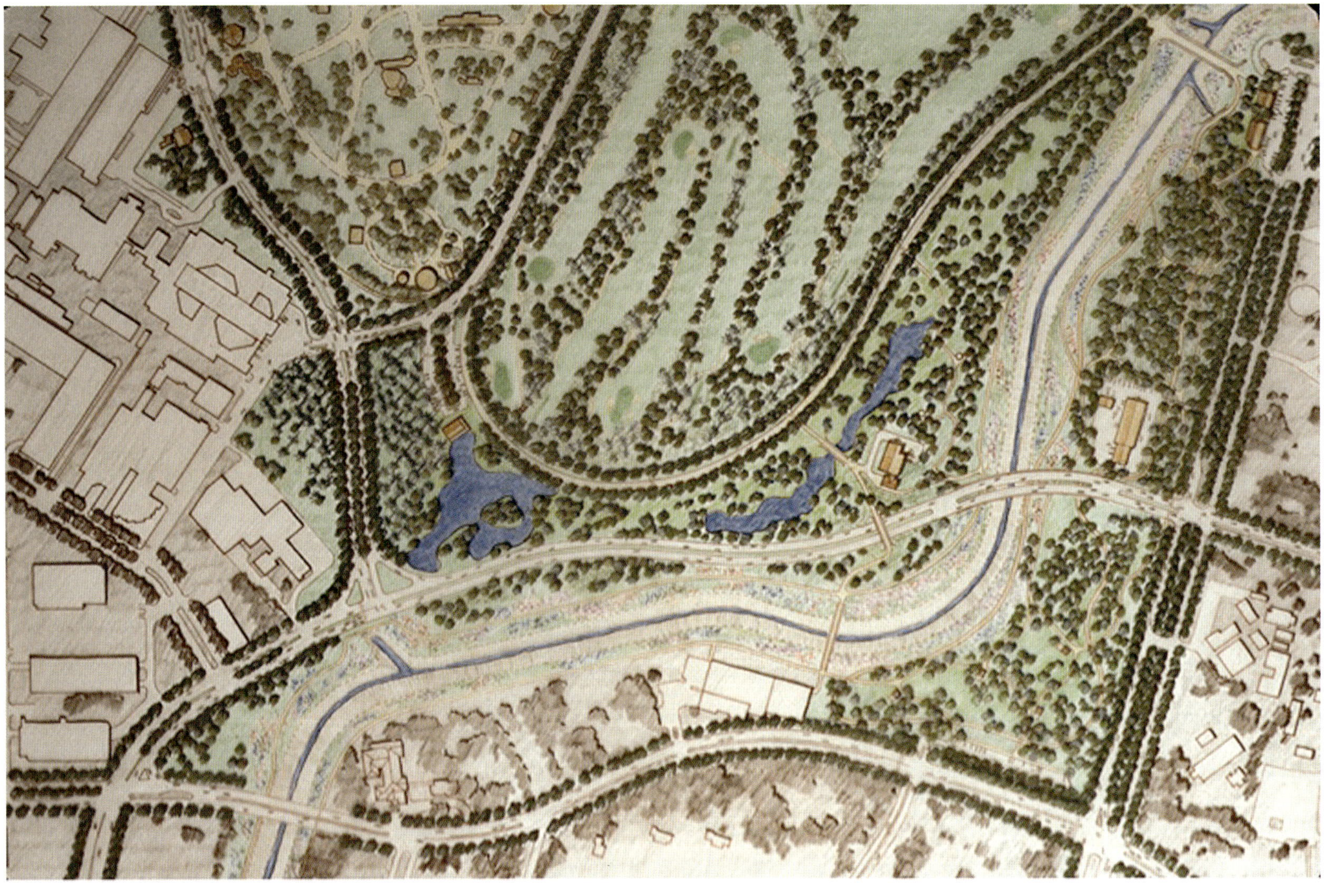

Bayou Parkland proposal for enhancement of Hermann Park sector adjacent to Brays Bayou, 1995. Hanna/Olin. Courtesy Olin Partnership.

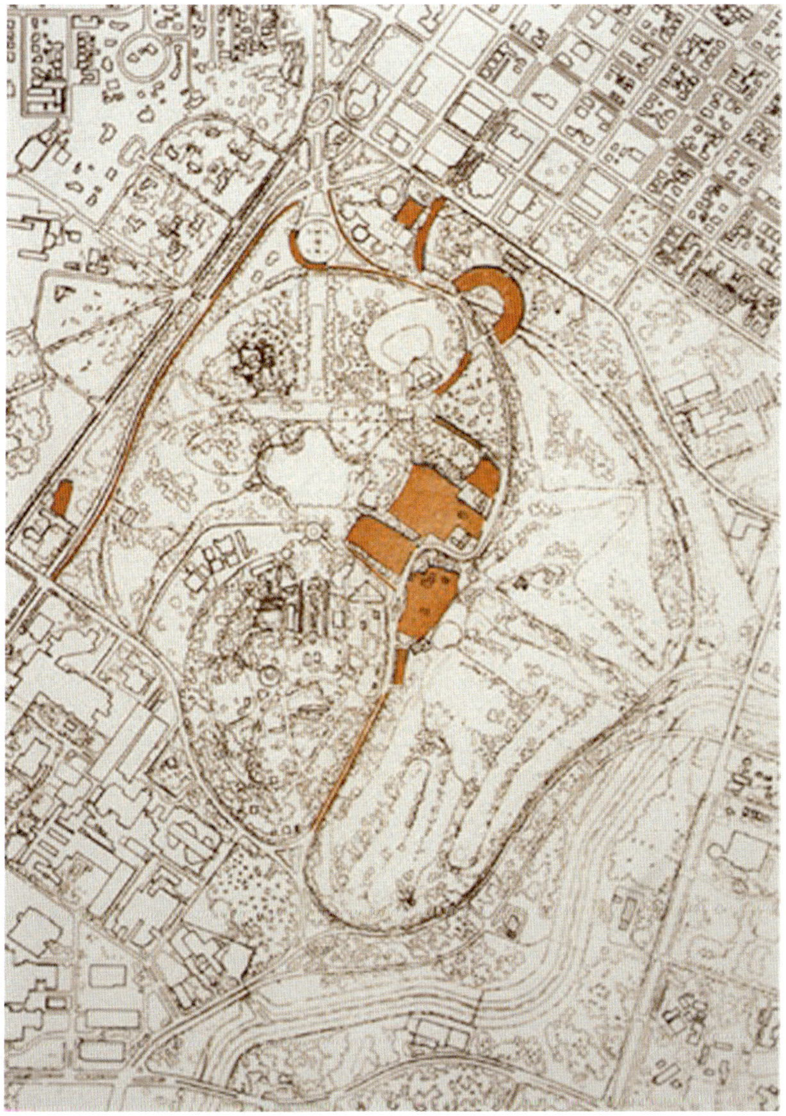

Existing parking areas in orange, 1994. Hanna/Olin. Courtesy Olin Partnership.

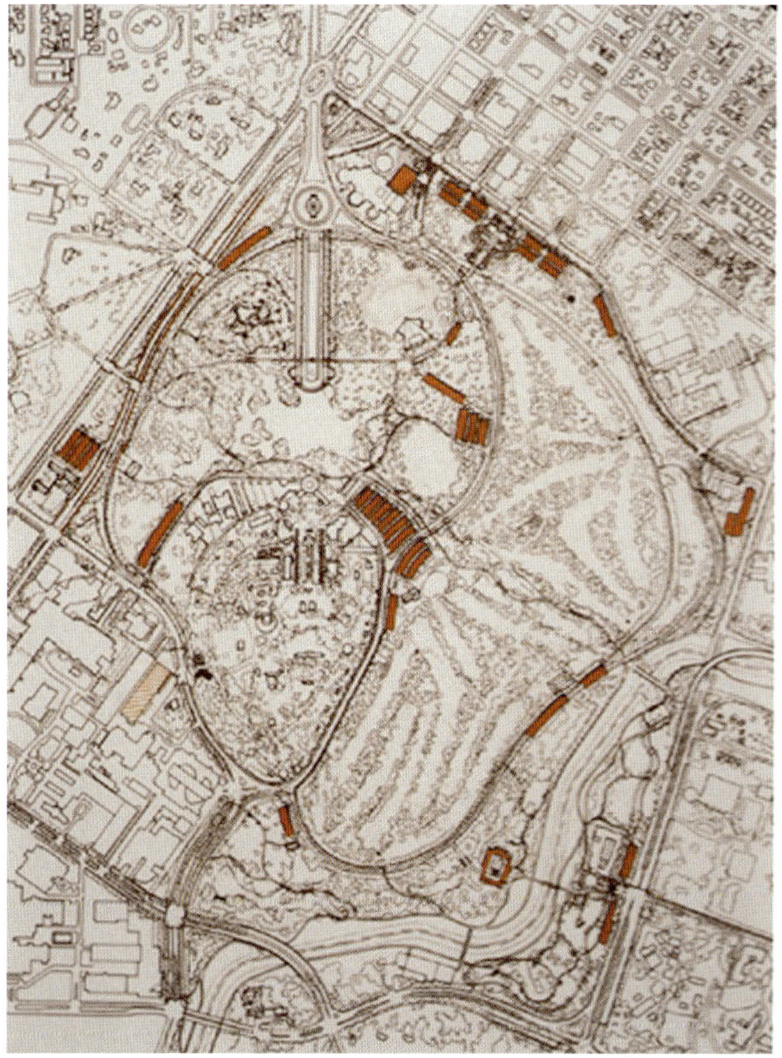

Proposed redistribution of parking lots, 1995. Hanna/Olin. Courtesy Olin Partnership.

the Reflection Pool reiterated the double rows of live oak trees flanking the extended pool. "The Reflection Pool and the rows of live oak are an enduring element of Houston's urban plan, providing a clear example of the connection between the city and the park."[11]

The Civic Plaza

Between the terminus of the Reflection Pool and the lake, Olin suggested a Civic Plaza and small lawn at the lakefront, with steps down to the water. The Pioneer Memorial Obelisk needed to be slightly relocated to become the central element of the plaza in alignment with the Sam Houston Monument. Olin suggested that this terrace could serve as a water feature with the introduction of water jets that sprouted from the pavement at irregular intervals. The plaza would be a gathering place at the end of the paths along the Reflection Pool, where special events and parties could take place.

The Grand Basin

The master plan envisioned extending the lake in several directions "with a sinuous edge richly articulated with a mixture of trees and grasses." The Grand Basin, as it was originally called, was one-half the size envisioned in Kessler's park plan, and its configuration was rather compact. New lake fingers would reach out in several directions to provide longer views across the water and create the illusion of an even grander lake. A larger body of water would also enhance the sunlight sparkling off its surface, shadows, and reflections of plantings along its borders. Olin's purpose was to bring the lake into disconnected areas

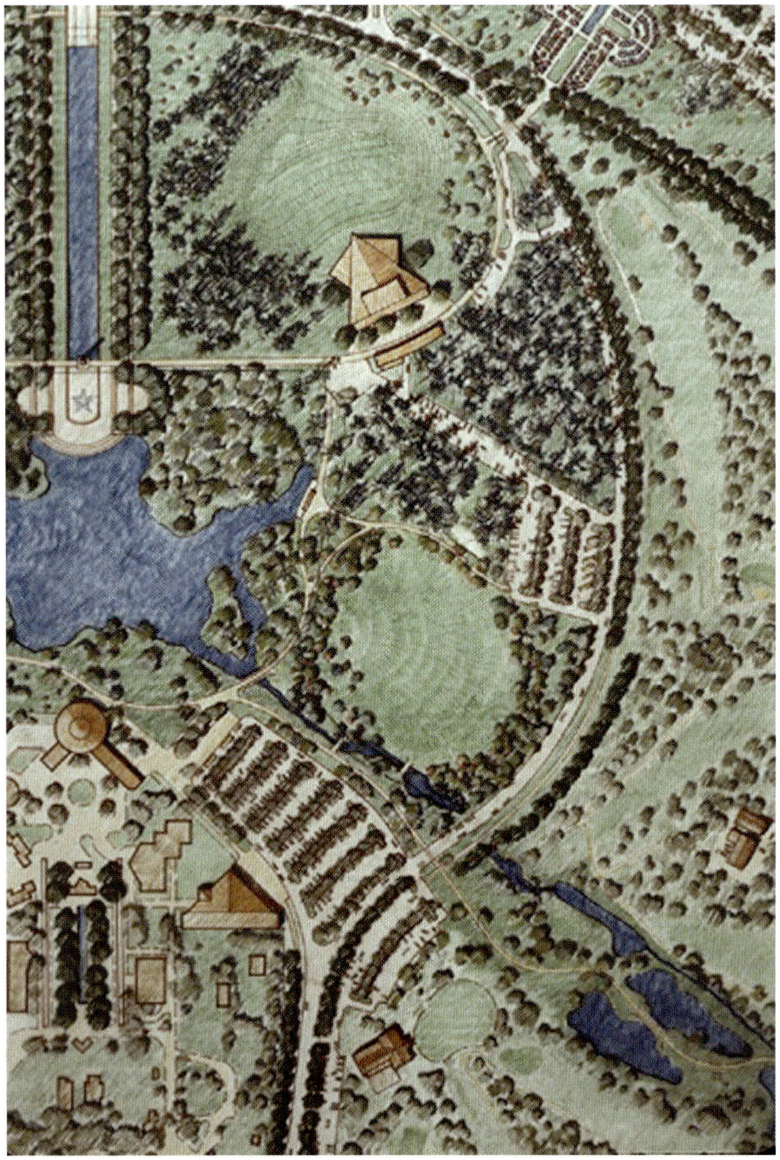

Zoo parking area proposal to break up large parking lots leaving space for a great lawns, 1995. Hanna/Olin. Courtesy Olin Partnership.

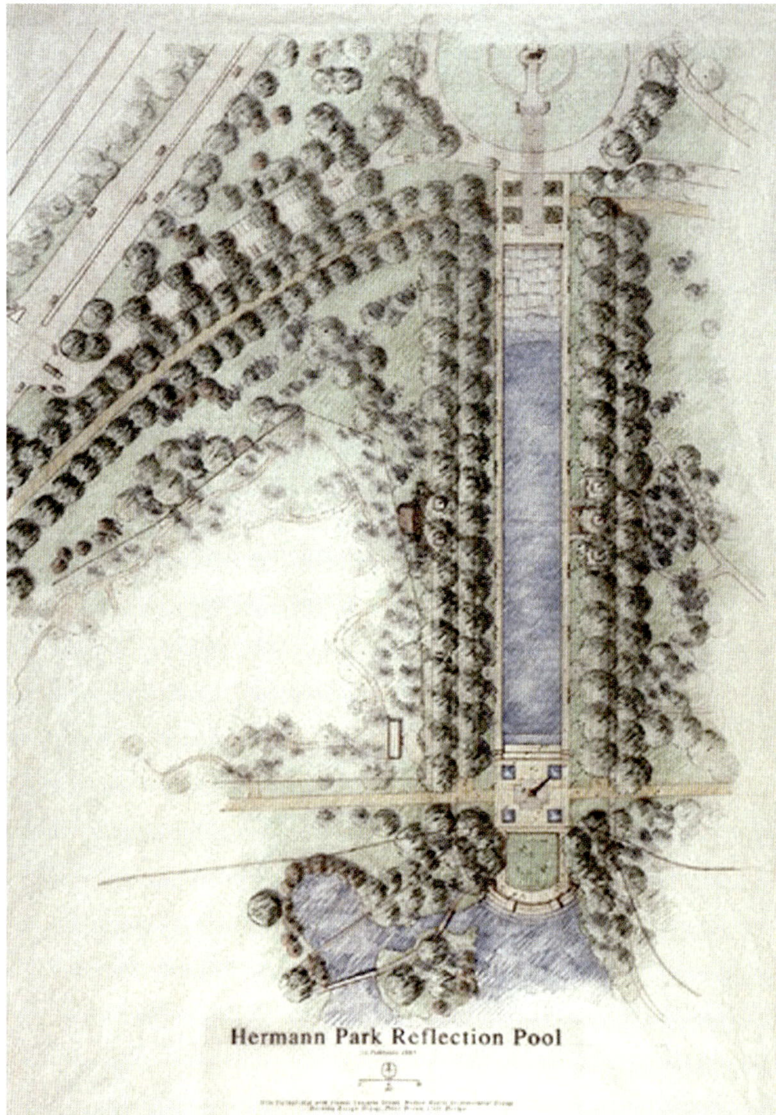

Heart of the Park Reflection Pool proposal that was essentially followed, 1994. Hanna/Olin. Courtesy Olin Partnership.

of the park. He suggested that one of these extensions could meet the children's playground on the west, and another could provide a mooring for paddle boats accessible from a new Lake Plaza that would front the lake and include a new train station.

Golf Course Greenway

"A final lake extension," the report explained, "will reach out in segments along the old drainage swale leading toward the bayou, to define a pedestrian trail by which visitors to Hermann Park can cross the Golf Course safely, and reach the southeastern quadrant of the park."[12] Olin's plan to build a safe pedestrian path across the golf course connecting the center of the park with other areas, including the Bayou Parkland south of Brays Bayou, increased access to underused areas of the park. Olin noted that the excavation of additional ponds and gullies along the golf course pedestrian trail would increase the irrigation capacity for the fairways and provide more wetland habitats for waterfowl.

Miller Theatre

"The Hill at Miller Theatre is one of Houston's most loved landmarks—a theater in its own right," this section of the master plan begins. Here children can't resist rolling down the grassy slope, families and couples

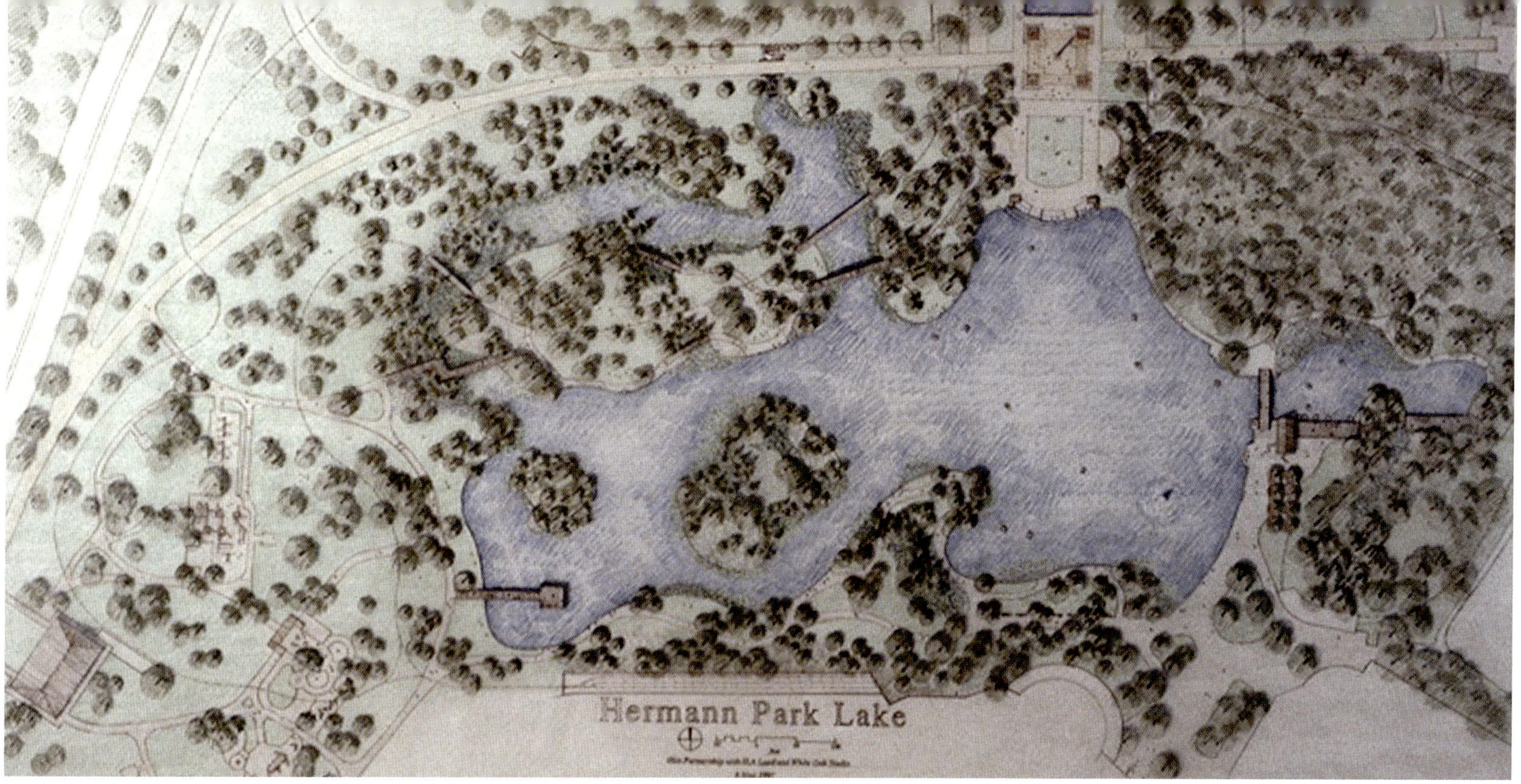

Lake expansion proposal that was implemented, 1995. Hanna/Olin. Courtesy Olin Partnership.

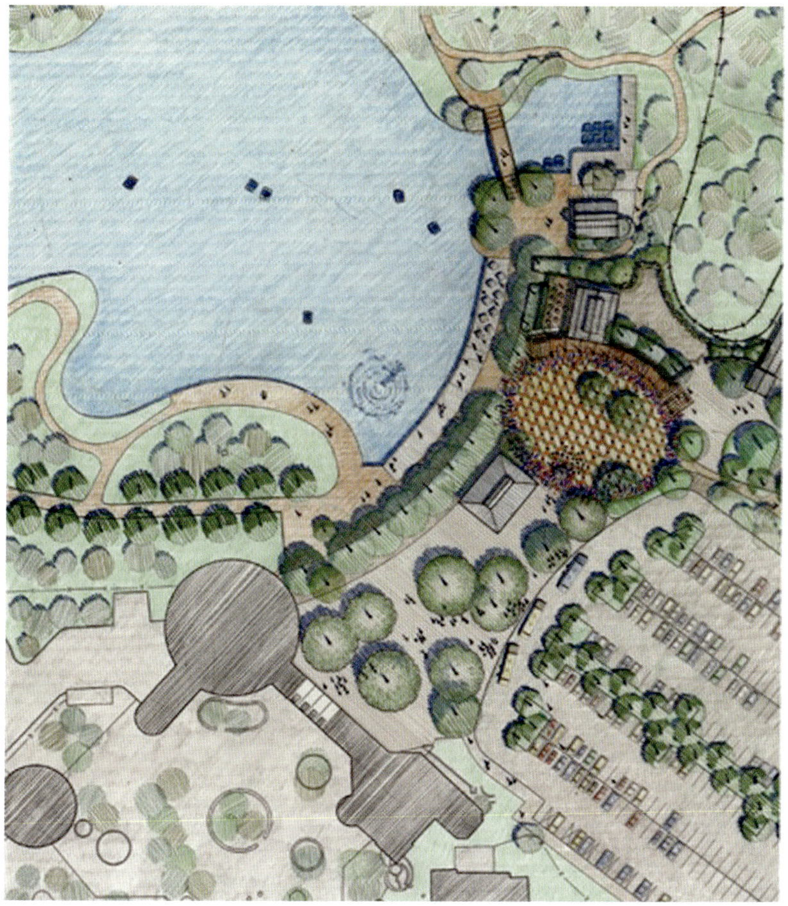

Lake plaza and zoo entrance proposal, 1995. The Lake Plaza as built is different in configuration than this master plan proposal, but similar in purpose and feeling. Hanna/Olin. Courtesy Olin Partnership.

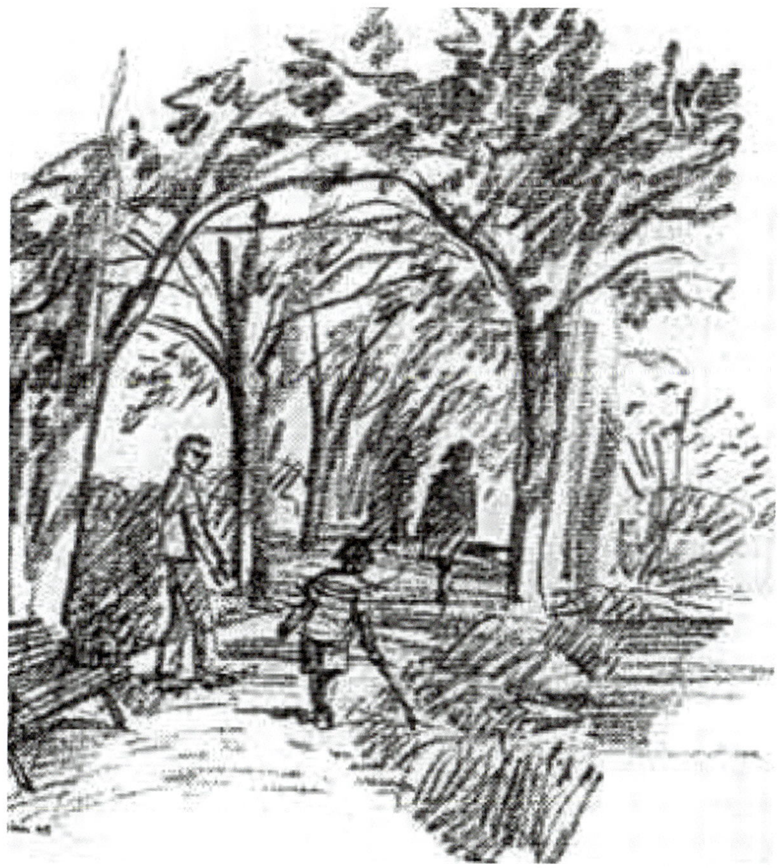

Golf Course Greenway, Laurie Olin sketch, 1994. Olin made numerous such concept sketches during the Master Plan design process. A greenway across the Golf Course was built. Courtesy Olin Partnership.

in love have picnics, teenagers play touch football, and there is plenty of people-watching. However, at the bottom of the hill, little landscaping protected the hard earth or enhanced the connection along Hermann Park Drive with the Science Museum and the Sam Houston Monument. The master plan proposed to use fill generated by the excavation of the expanded lake to reshape the hill and build a woodland amphitheater in a grove of pine trees on the backside of the hill, where impromptu performances, readings, and classes could take place.

The Great Lawn

One of the great joys of New York's Central Park is a wide-open, grassy space where dogs and children run free, grown-ups throw Frisbees, and bikini-clad beauties show off and sunbathe. Hermann Park has no such great lawn, but Olin's plan proposed one at the center of the park where a paved parking lot now sits. Such a great, green meadow, he points out, would provide a large area not only for gathering and open play, but also a grand area for special events. Acknowledging that some parking should be retained in that area, he suggested that shady groves should surround the lawn, screening the cars parked beyond it.

The Garden Center

The Houston Garden Center consists of a small building flanked by curved parterres of roses, a meadow to the east, and a large parking lot facing the interior of the park. Olin suggested that these elements be inverted. Parking should align with access from Hermann Drive and the gardens reconfigured to recall those proposed by Hare & Hare in the 1930s. He also suggested that new gardens might lead to an extension of the Marvin Taylor Trail along the live-oak sheltered path of an original carriage drive. A new crosswalk to Miller Theatre should be part of the reconfiguration of this area.

Café on the Green

The Spanish-style clubhouse designed by Alfred Nutter in 1933 was run-down and no longer adequate for golfers. Olin proposed that a new

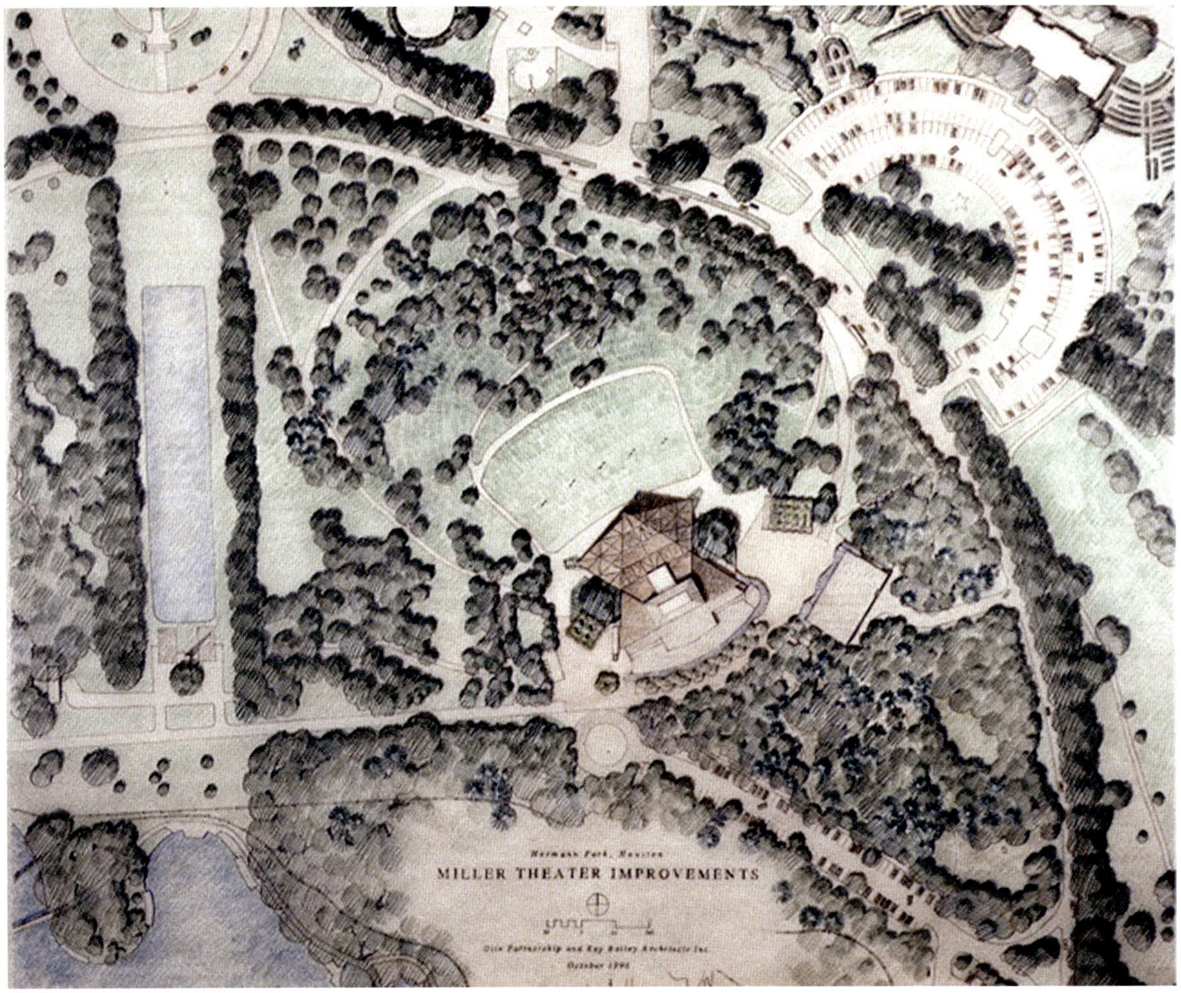

Miller Theatre area landscape and parking proposal, 1994. Hanna/Olin. Courtesy Olin Partnership.

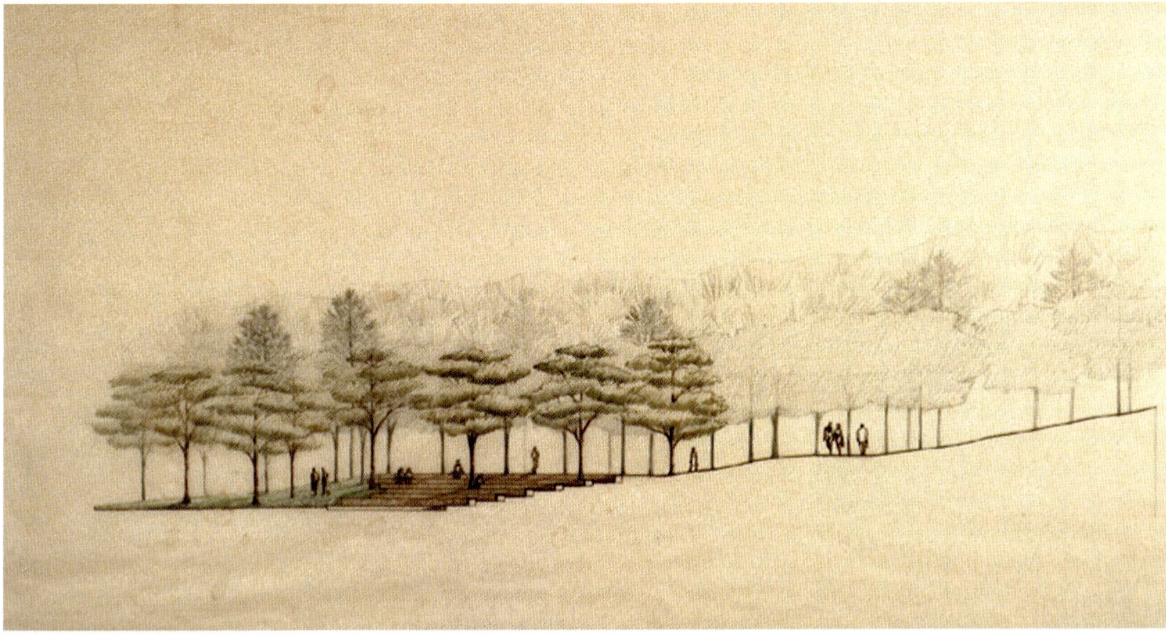

Woodland Amphitheater proposal on Miller Theatre grounds, drawing by Laurie Olin, 1995. Courtesy Olin Partnership.

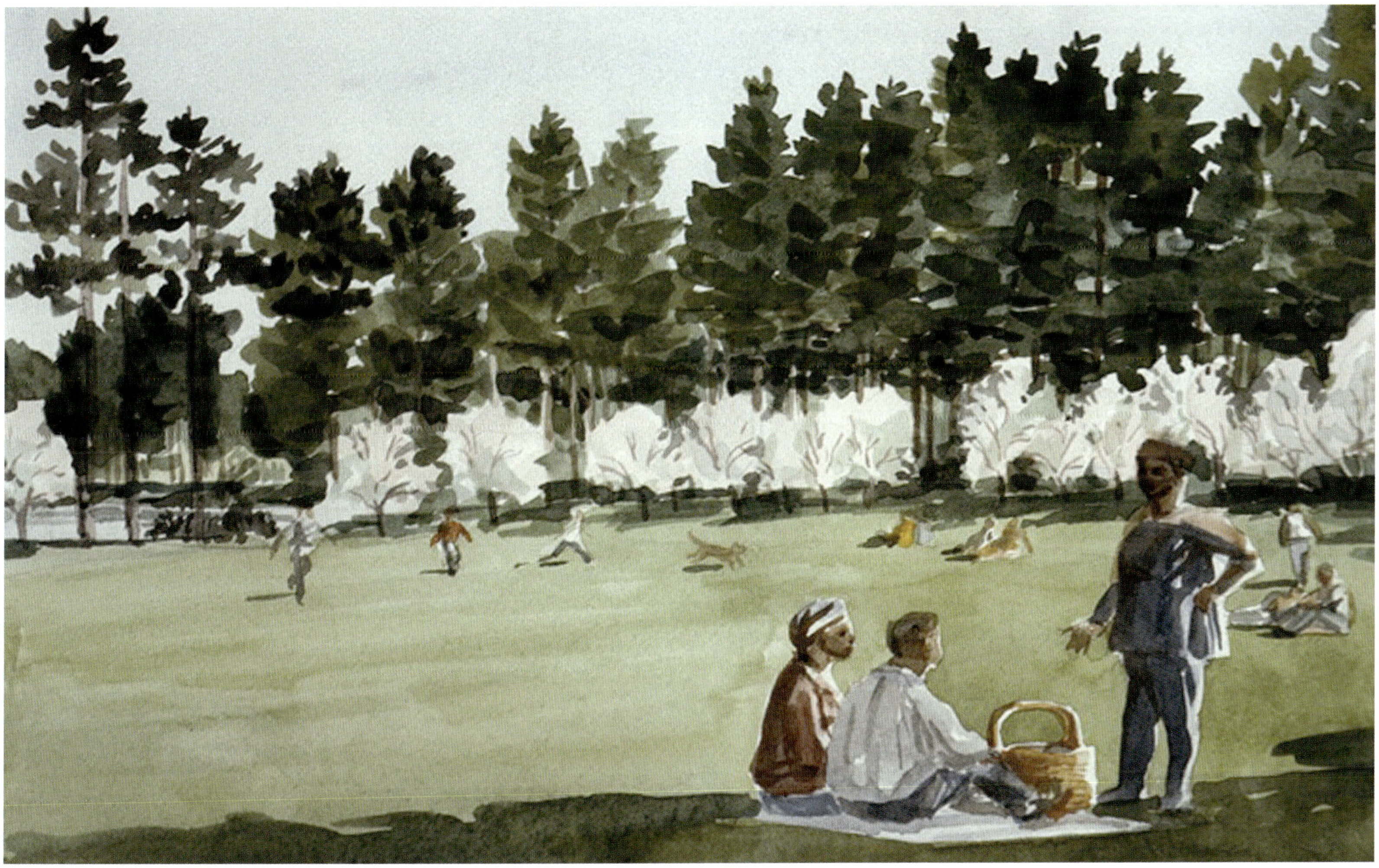

Great Lawn, watercolor by Laurie Olin, 1994. A great lawn in Hermann Park is yet impossible for lack of space. If and when parking lots are moved out of the park or built underground such a feature could become a reality. Courtesy Olin Partnership.

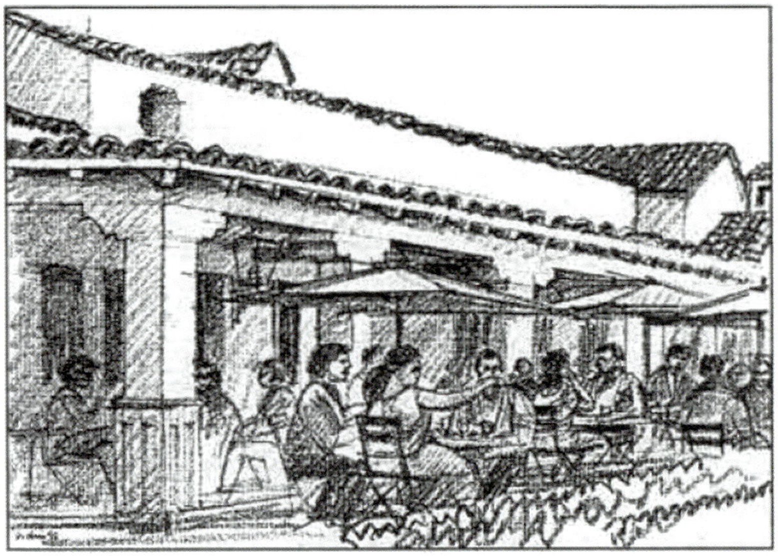

Café on the Green proposal for historic Hermann Park clubhouse, Laurie Olin sketch, 1994. Plans are under way to restore the 1933 clubhouse for use as an event venue. Courtesy Olin Partnership.

clubhouse be built off Almeda and the Nutter clubhouse restored and converted into a restaurant with views across the golf course and ponds.

Zoo West Entry

The Houston Zoo has continually reinvented itself since it opened in 1924, but overcrowding and difficult access from the park interior present problems. Olin suggested a new entrance off of Cambridge Drive accessible for the many school buses that bring children to the zoo on a regular basis and for those coming from the Texas Medical Center. A connection between the west zoo entrance and the children's playground would be a welcome addition to the park.

Bayou Parkland

Eighty acres of parkland along Brays Bayou was cut off by roads, traffic, the zoo, the golf course, and the bayou channel. Olin proposed an expanded series of trails and ponds that would attract park users to a more remote woodlands experience. Noting that this area lacked restroom facilities and parking, the master plan advocated building such

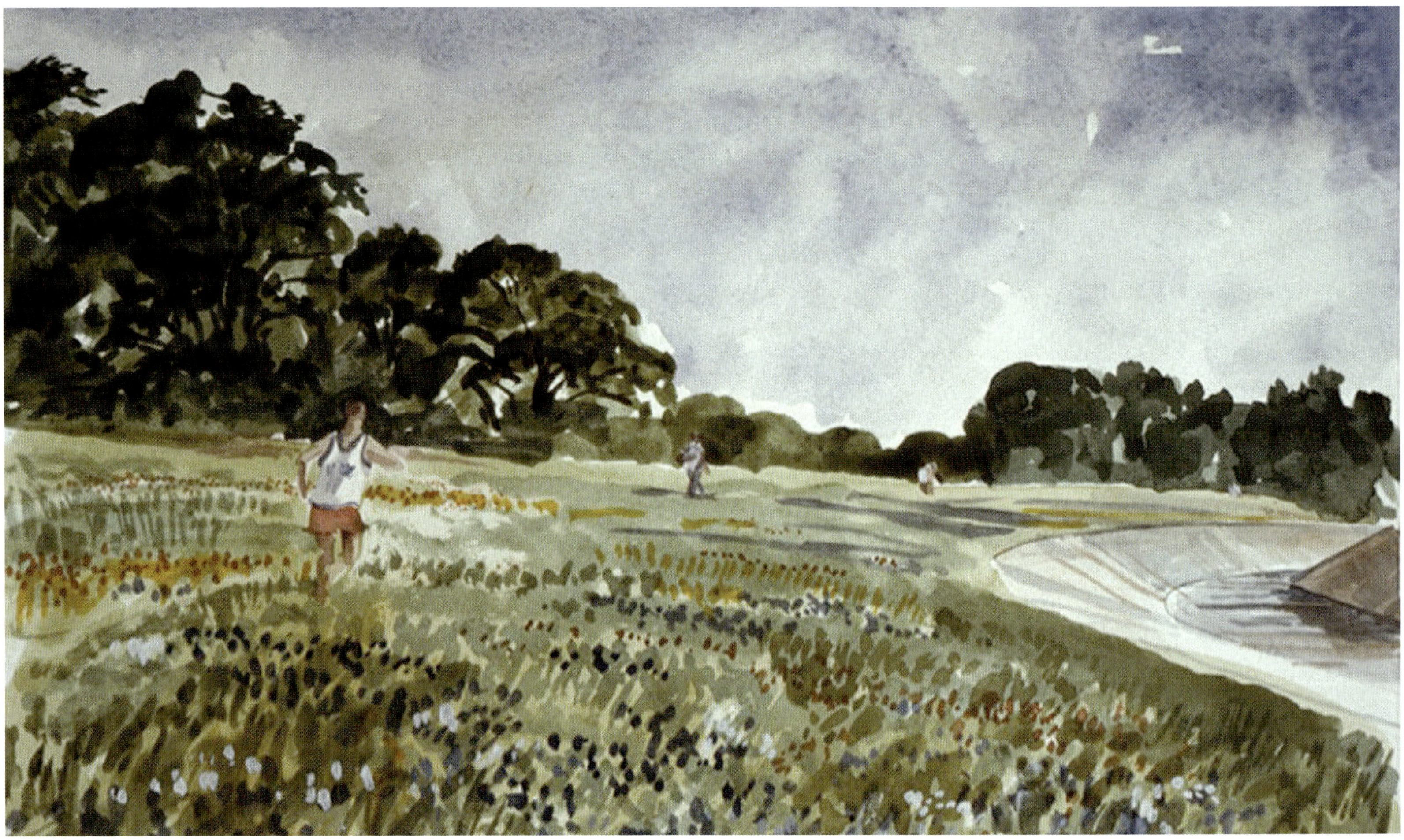

Brays Bayou Parkland, watercolor by Laurie Olin, 1994. Wildflowers, growing denser every year, bloom in spring along the bayou. Courtesy Olin Partnership.

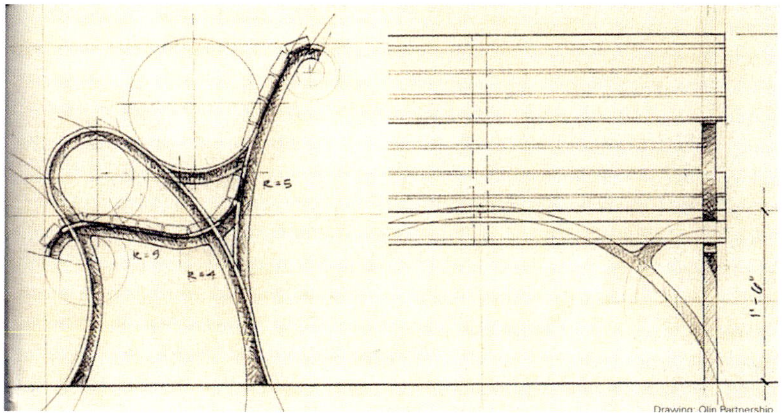

Laurie Olin designed these benches especially for use in Hermann Park, 1998. They have been manufactured and are in place throughout the park. Hanna/Olin. Courtesy Olin Partnership.

amenities, along with the construction of new trails and planting of wildflowers along the banks of the bayou.

In addition to the ten major projects, the report identified over seventy smaller projects in the park. Many would be easy to implement, such as better signage, new trashcans, and new plantings in certain areas. One addition was the manufacture and placement of new benches designed by Laurie Olin. The realization of this feature presaged the achievements that began with the Hermann Park master plan document.

The hard work and wisdom that produced this plan is evident almost twenty years later as Hermann Park approaches it centennial. The "Implementation" section of the plan warned that the proposed revitalization of Hermann Park would cost an enormous amount of money, require exceptional administrative management, and entail a good deal of patience. In discussing what other cities have done to rescue their public spaces, Olin emphasized that a strong public–private partnership and a dedicated full-time organization focused solely on the park's planning, rehabilitation, maintenance, and operation would be required. "Hermann Park is a city-wide resource, a social good that needs the support of the full community."[13] The 1995 master plan for Hermann Park concluded: "Our vision for Hermann Park in the next century is practical, achievable, and eminently desirable."[14]

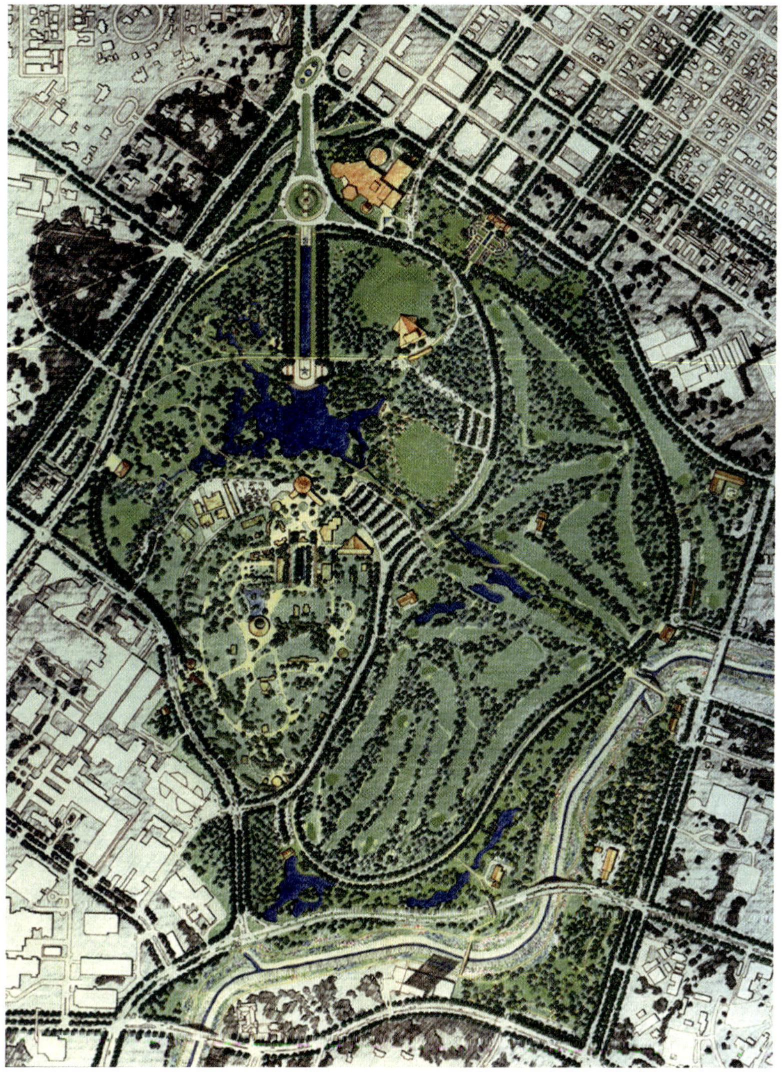

1995 Master Plan drawing for Hermann Park shows proposed projects throughout the park that have been essentially completed in 2014. Hanna/Olin. Courtesy Olin Partnership.

CHAPTER TEN

It Happens!

We were selling a dream.[1]

—Jane Anderson Curtis, 2012

Even before the Houston City Council accepted the Olin master plan in 1995,[2] several projects were in the works, including expansion of Miller Outdoor Theatre, the just completed Japanese Garden, and the Buddy Carruth Playground for All Children. Construction of major projects outlined in the master plan was phased over the next fifteen years, instead of the ten years hoped for by Olin. It is a great accomplishment that by 2014 eight of the ten major capital projects have been completed, along with smaller endeavors and some new ventures not foreseen in 1995. Houston did indeed come together, and funding for each project was achieved through special allocations of the Houston City Council and donations from institutional, corporate, and individual philanthropic sources. Hermann Park in 2014 is a stunning array of spaces and places that are unified by paths, sight lines, and attractive, helpful signs. Beginning at the Mecom Fountain and the entrance to Hermann Park, this chapter moves counter-clockwise through the renewed Hermann Park to emphasize both the individual character of special projects and places and the collective whole.

Grand Gateway

The historic entrance to Hermann Park is located at the convergence of Main Street and Montrose Boulevard on the axis of Montrose Boulevard. Anchored by two prominent Houston landmarks, the Mecom Fountain and the Sam Houston Monument, this axis lies at the physical and metaphorical cultural hub of Houston. The SWA Group of Houston designed the new gateway to Hermann Park. The renovations include an Upper Garden, Lower Garden, and Grand Gateway Promenade. Plant materials were selected to complement those at the Sam Houston Statue and Lindsey Plaza, joining the spatial sequence to make a grand entrance to the park.

An important part of the Grand Gateway project focuses on the live oak trees at the entrance to the park and along Main Street. Replacement of missing trees in existing oak allées adds shade for pedestrians and emphasizes this historically significant axis. Protecting these century-old trees, which have a significant environmental impact on the surrounding community, includes installation of drainage and irrigation throughout the area. These measures will safeguard the century-old trees and encourage the growth of a protective understory groundcover. Improvements will be made to entrance and exit ramps along the length of the gateway, making them accessible by the handicapped and safe for those using a variety of transportation modes. New lighting, benches, trashcans, and bike racks will encourage greater use of the gateway area.

The conservancy received a $3 million matching grant from the Texas Department of Transportation's Texas Transportation Enhancement Program for the renewal of this area in 2010. The conservancy then raised an additional $2 million needed to fund the project. Providing for future maintenance, such as seasonal annual plantings, a $1 million maintenance fund was incorporated into the project cost. The project completion date in the fall of 2013 was in time to welcome visitors to the park for a year of centennial celebrations in 2014.

Bloch Cancer Survivors Plaza and Mecom–Rockwell Fountain

Just east of the Mecom Fountain, to the left along the Grand Gateway, is the Richard and Annette Bloch Cancer Survivors Plaza (1983), designed

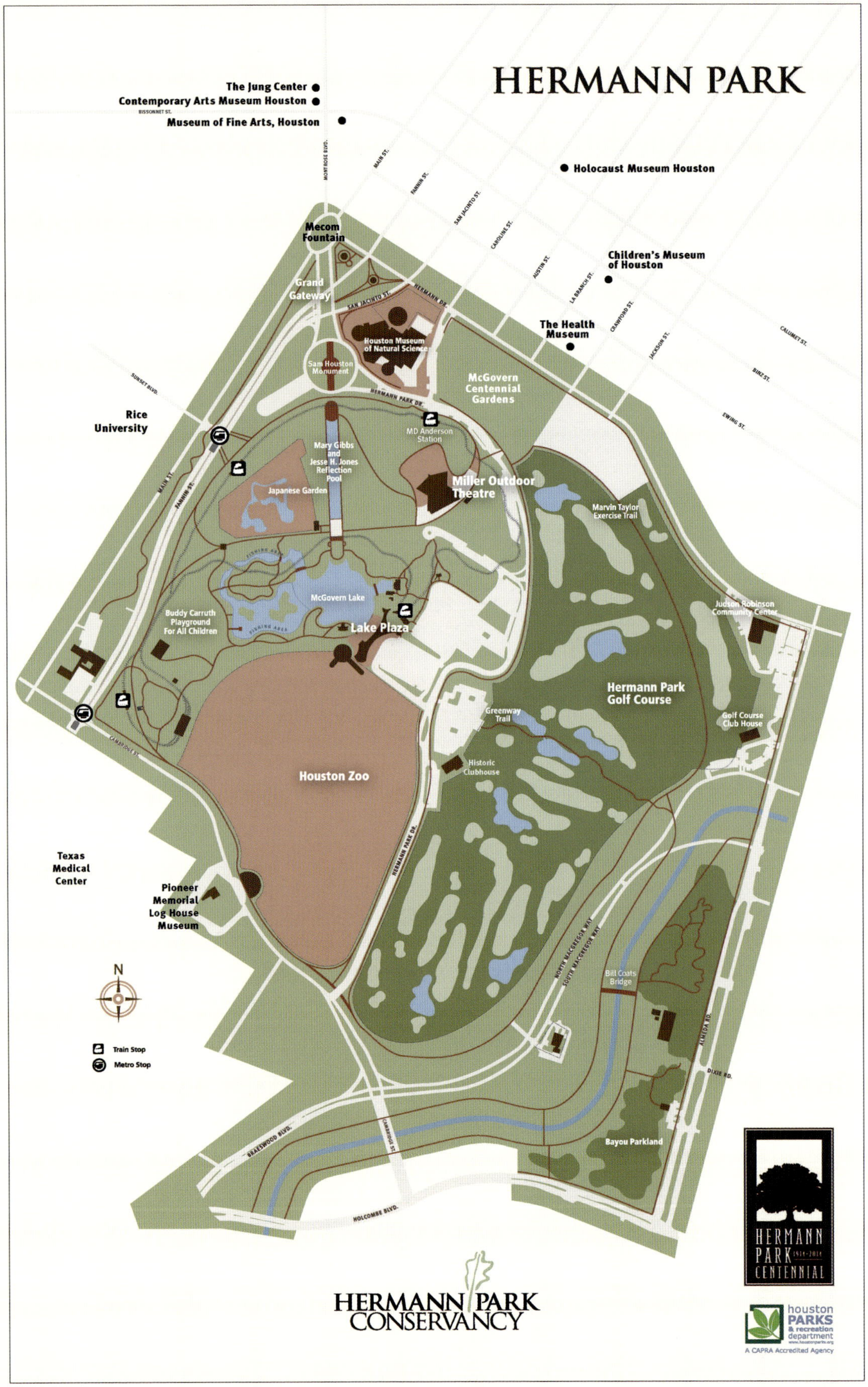

Map of Hermann Park, 2014. Courtesy Hermann Park Conservancy.

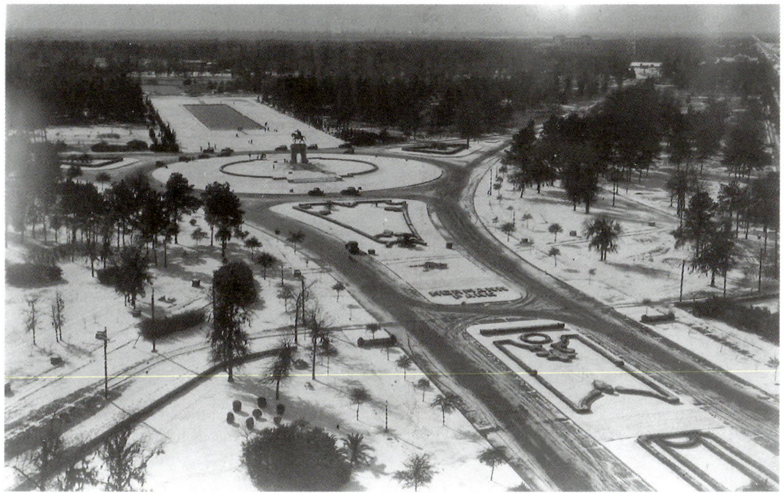

Hermann Park Grand Entrance in a rare Houston snowstorm, December 1929. Courtesy State Historical Society of Missouri, Research Center–Kansas City.

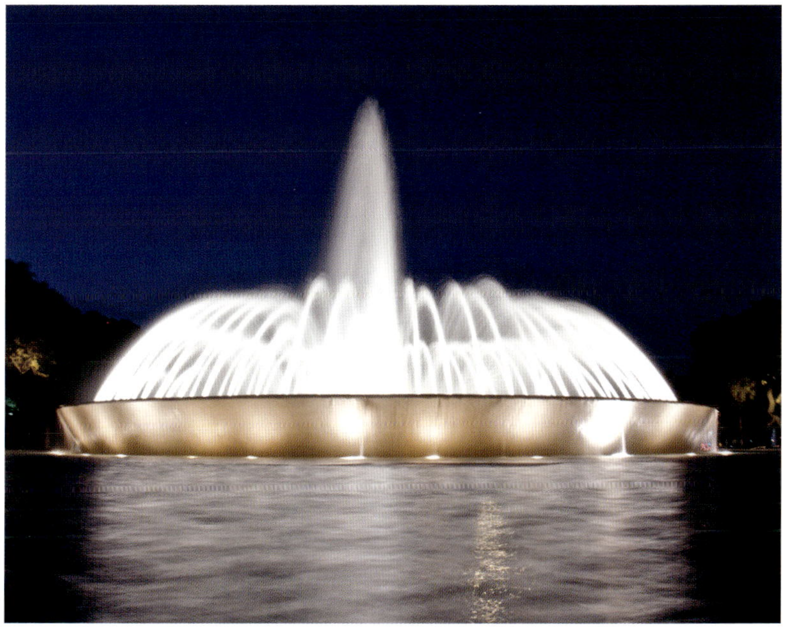

Mecom Fountain (1964, Eugene Werlin) is a three-fountain ensemble in the former Sunken Garden at the convergence of Montrose Boulevard and Main Street at the entrance to Hermann Park, 2008. Source: Wikimedia Commons.

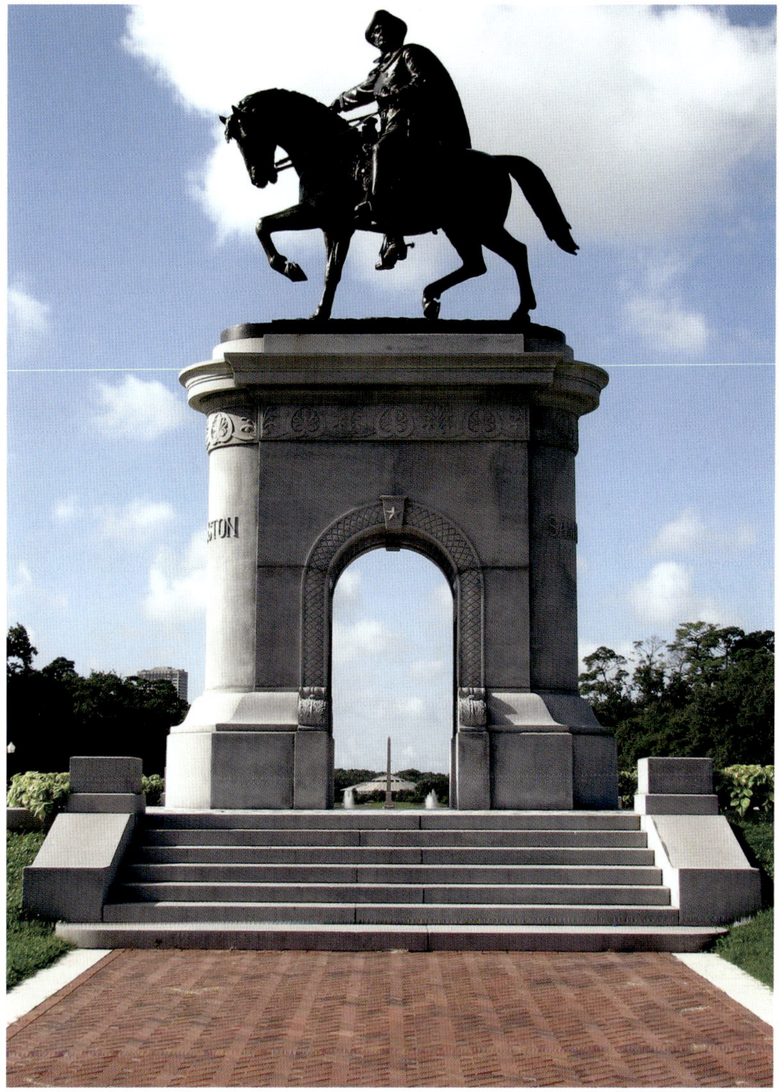

Sam Houston Equestrian Statue (1924, Enrico Cerracchio). Through the marble triumphal arch, designed and sculpted by Frank Teich (1856–1939), one appreciates Kessler's strong visual axis from Hermann Park's entrance across the Reflection Pool, Pioneer Monument, and McGovern Lake to the Kipp Aquarium in the far distance. Courtesy Hermann Park Conservancy.

by architect Milosav Cekic of MC/A Architects of Austin, Texas. The triangular site of Bloch Plaza features a fountain and gazebo, specialty paving, new trees and benches, and a bronze sculpture that is common to all Bloch Gardens. The gazebo's limestone pillars are rough at their bases and become more refined as they rise to capitals inlaid with ceramic medallions. The dome, fabricated by Jim Thomas of Thomas Studio & Foundry of Jonestown, Texas, is made of hundreds of stylized magnolia blossoms hot forged by Nick Brumbder of Ornamental Iron of Georgetown, Texas. After Richard Bloch, of H&R Block Tax Services, survived a terminal form of lung cancer, he and his wife, Annette, dedicated their lives to helping others discover the strength and hope necessary to fight cancer. From 1943 the Bloch Plaza site was a gardenesque area of Hermann Park with a small fountain that, in the 1990s, no longer functioned. When Bloch approached the city, wanting to fund a garden in Houston near the Texas Medical Center and MD Anderson Cancer Center, the Parks Department felt this site needed rejuvenation and would be appropriate. Director Don Olson and Park Administra-

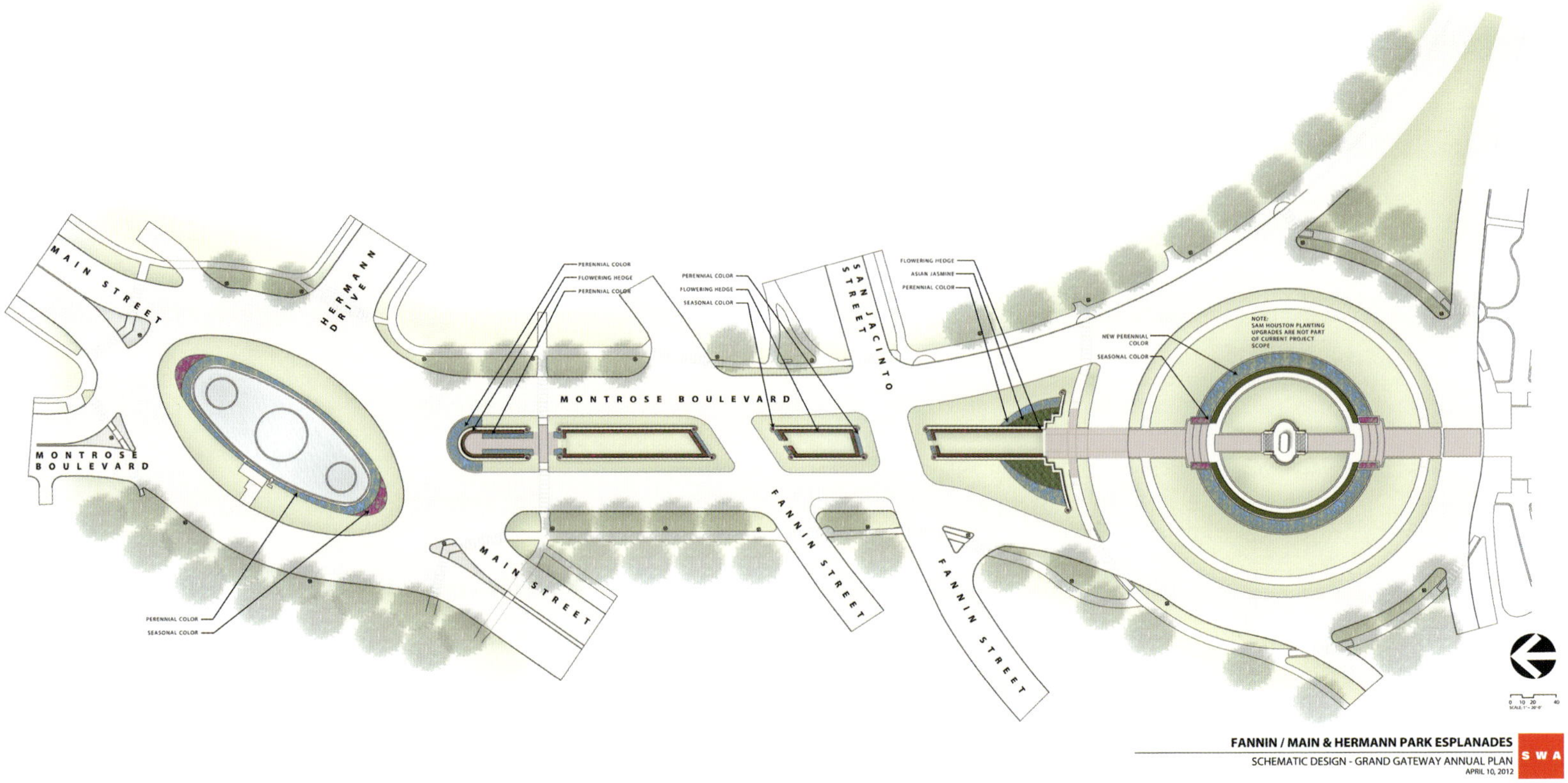

Grand Gateway plan (2012, SWA Group) will be completed in 2014 with extensive new landscaping and seasonal plantings between the Sam Houston Monument and Mecom Fountain, improved pedestrian walkways, lighting, benches, and bike racks. Courtesy Hermann Park Conservancy.

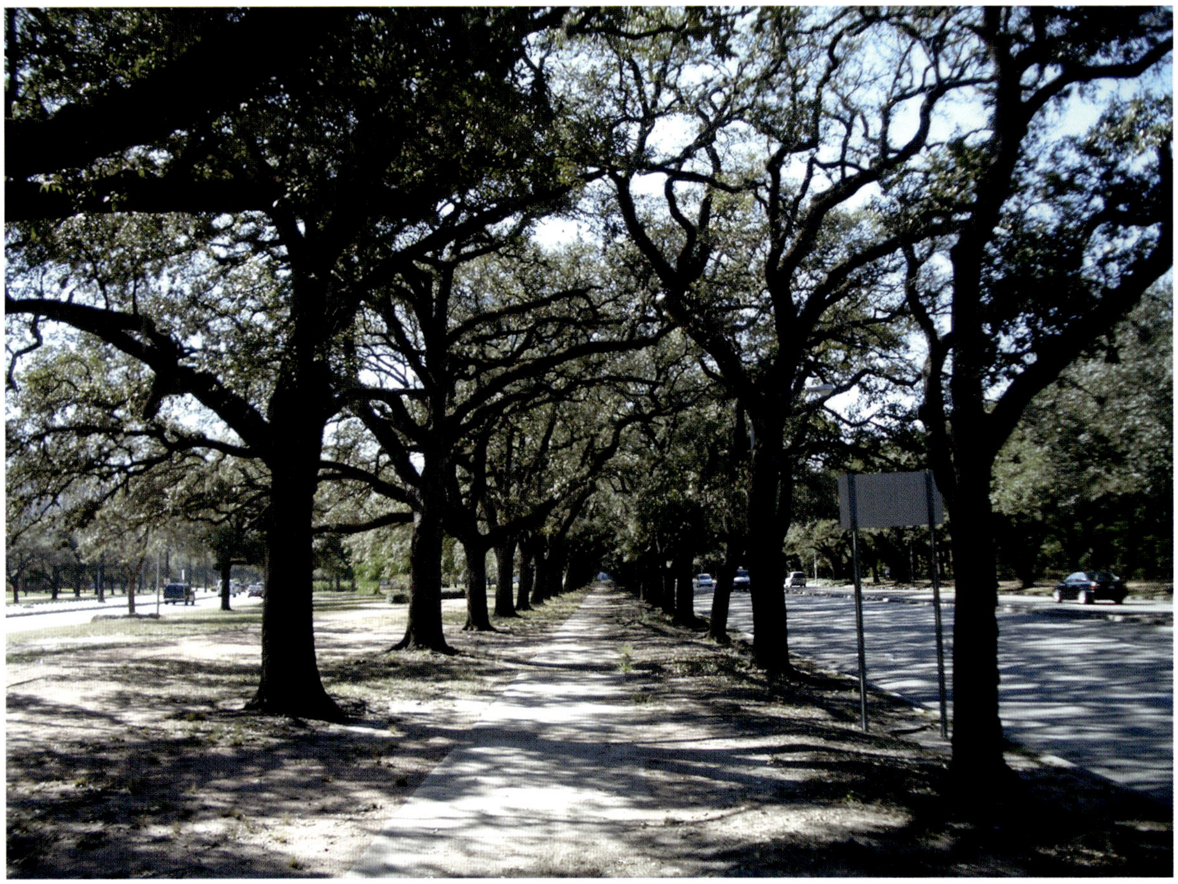

The Double allée of staggered live oak trees along the edge of Hermann Park on the east side of Main Street was proposed by George Kessler and planted c. 1916 after the passage of Houston's first parks bond issue in 1915. New drainage and irrigation to preserve these trees is part of the Grand Gateway project. Photograph by Laurie Olin. Courtesy Olin Partnership.

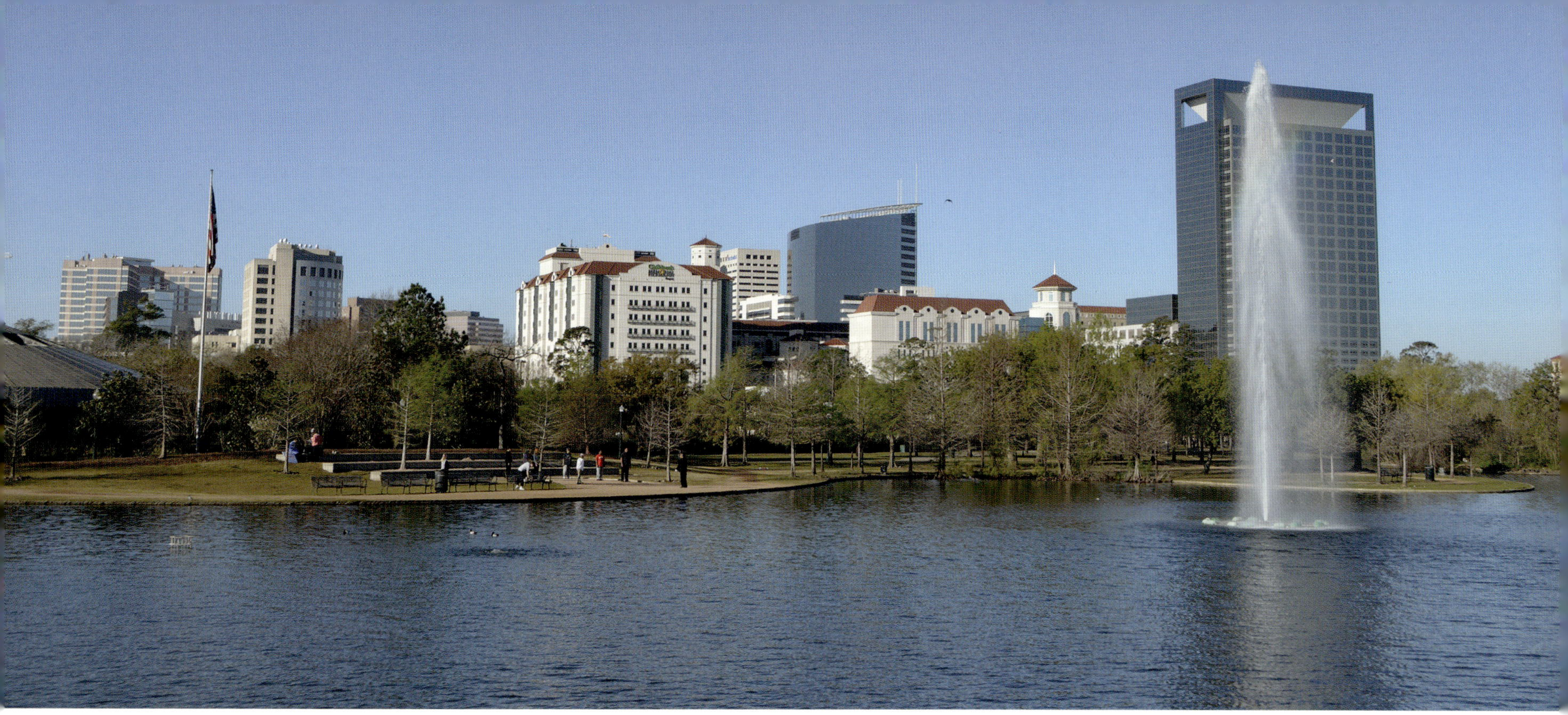

The Texas Medical Center as seen from McGovern Lake, 2013. Photograph by B. S. Bradley.

tor Rick Dewees worked with Bloch and his architect through several schemes before the final plan was approved.[3]

The Bloch Foundation has built twenty-four similar parks in the United States and Canada near cancer hospitals. Although each park is individualized, all have three common elements: fourteen bronze plaques display inspirational and instructional messages; the "Road to Recovery" section consists of seven plaques explaining what cancer is and basic actions to overcome the disease; and a sculpture of life-size bronze figures passing through a maze that represents cancer treatment. The maze sculptures, *Cancer, There's Hope*, were designed individually for each park by the Mexican sculptor, Victor Salmones (1937–1989).[4]

Just east of Bloch Plaza along Hermann Drive between Fannin and San Jacinto streets, another triangular site contains the Mecom–Rockwell Fountain and Colonnade, erected to preserve the columns from the original Miller Theatre and landscaped in 1991 by the Neighbors of Hermann Park. Today this area is well-maintained and is a favorite background for photographs of Houston brides and young girls celebrating their *quinceañeras*.

Houston Museum of Natural Science

The Houston Museum of Natural Science began an expansion program in 1994 with the 70-foot-high Cockrell Butterfly Center designed by Hoover & Furr. This structure, appended to the west end of the museum building, has become another landmark in Hermann Park. Its angular

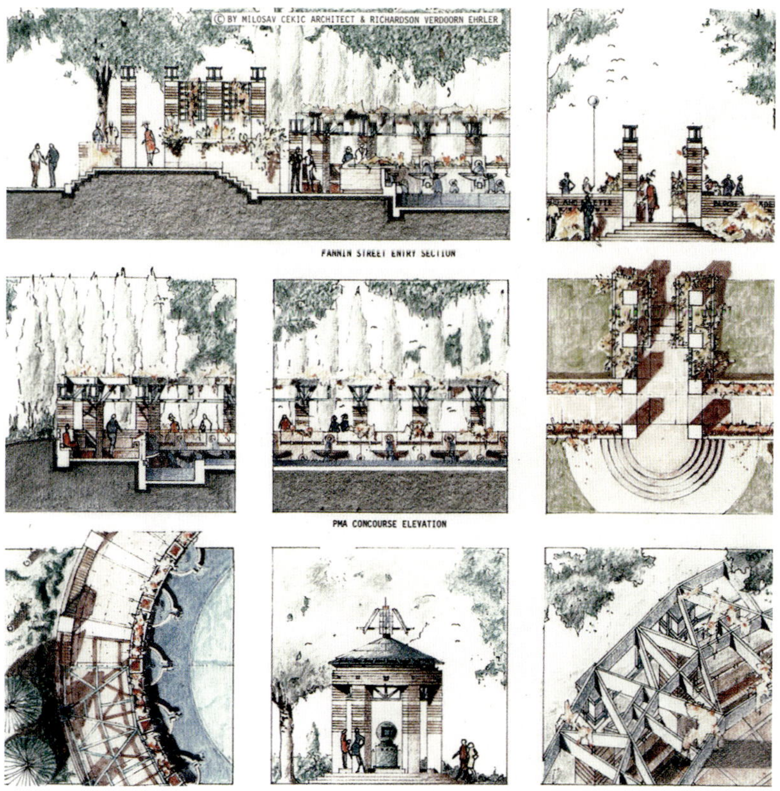

Richard and Annette Bloch Cancer Survivors Plaza (1983, Milosav Cekic Architects) drawings of early proposals. A revised design was constructed near the Hermann Park entrance in a small triangular plot that originally held a drinking fountain and minimal landscaping, 2009. Courtesy Houston Parks and Recreation Department.

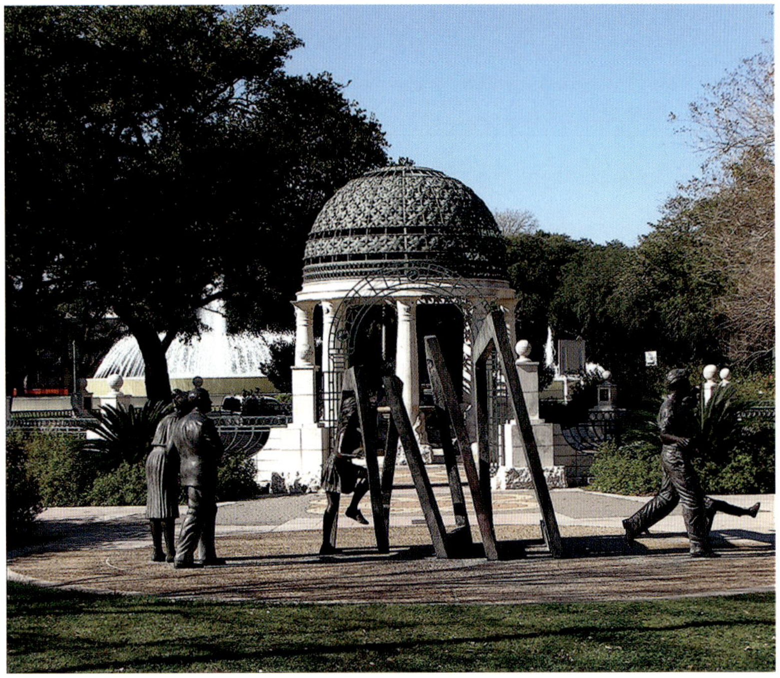

Bloch Plaza with *Cancer, There is Hope* (1984, Victor Salmones), a maze sculpture that symbolizes cancer treatment. Various versions by Salmones have been installed in twenty-four Bloch Plazas throughout the United States and Canada, 2012. Photograph by Andrew Rebman.

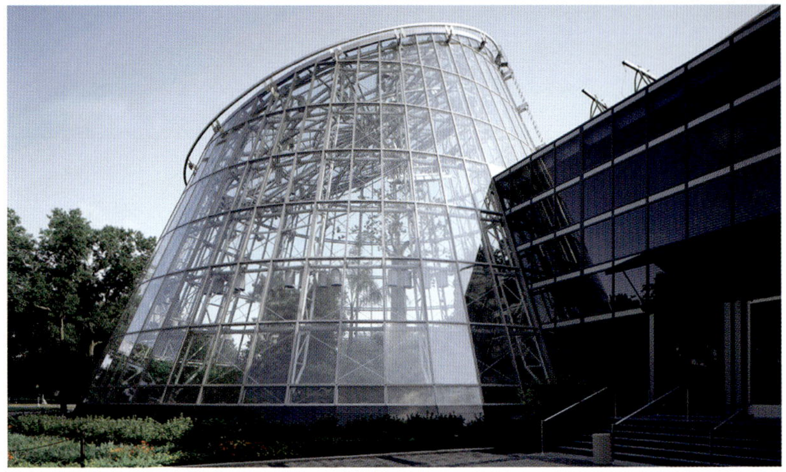

Cockrell Butterfly Center, Houston Museum of Natural Science (1994, Hoover & Furr) is another landmark that stands out in Hermann Park, 1996. Photograph by Jerry W. Courtney. Courtesy Façade Consultants Inc.

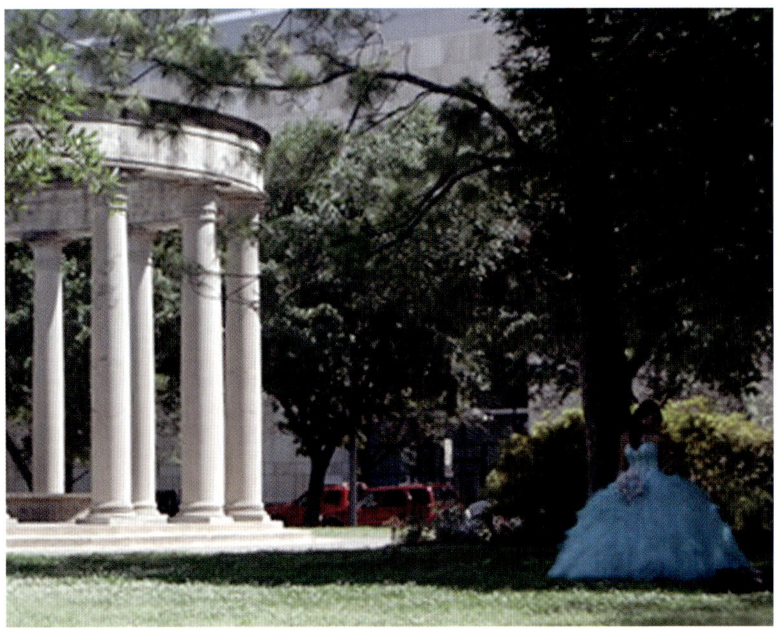

Mecom Rockwell Colonnade and Fountain, between Fannin and San Jacinto streets, was constructed in 1968 with the limestone columns from the original Miller Outdoor Theatre (1923). Landscaping of this area prompted the formation of Neighbors of Hermann Park in 1991, one of the forerunners of the Hermann Park Conservancy. This is a popular Houston photographic backdrop, especially for brides and girls celebrating their *Quinceañera*. Photograph by B. S. Bradley.

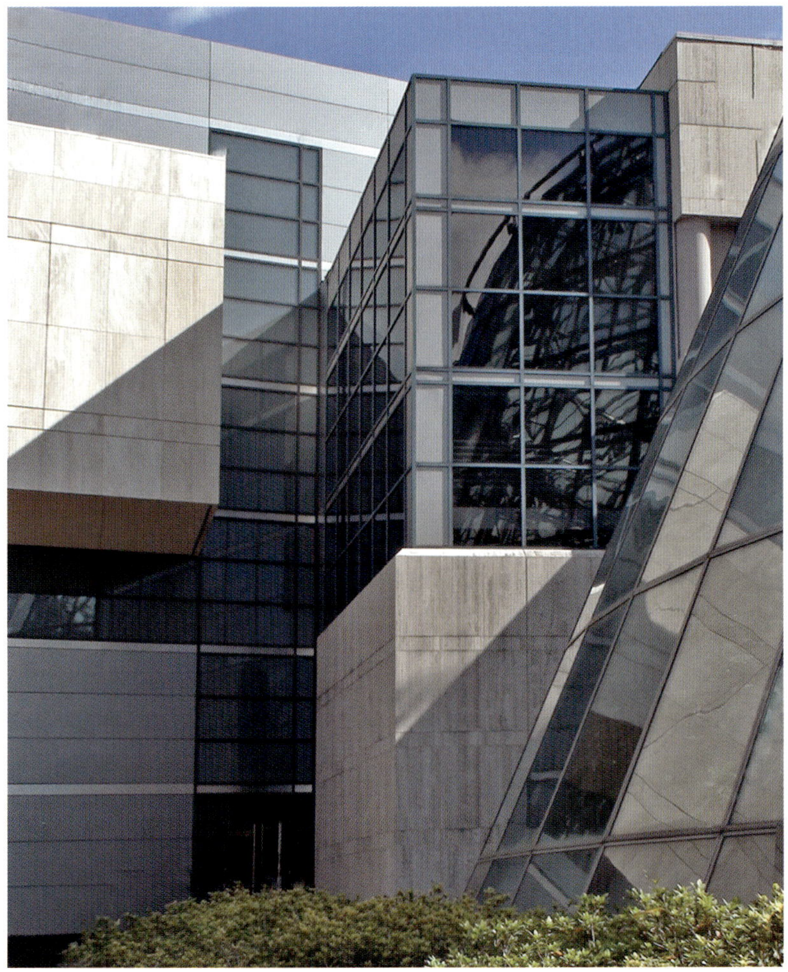

Dan L. Duncan Family Paleontology Wing, Houston Museum of Natural Science (2011, Gensler) at its conjunction with the Cockrell Butterfly Center, which is reflected in the corner windows of the Duncan Wing. The interior of this building is a vast space filled with imaginative exhibitions, including gigantic dinosaur skeletons, 2012. Photograph by Norman Hoover, FAIA. Courtesy Gensler.

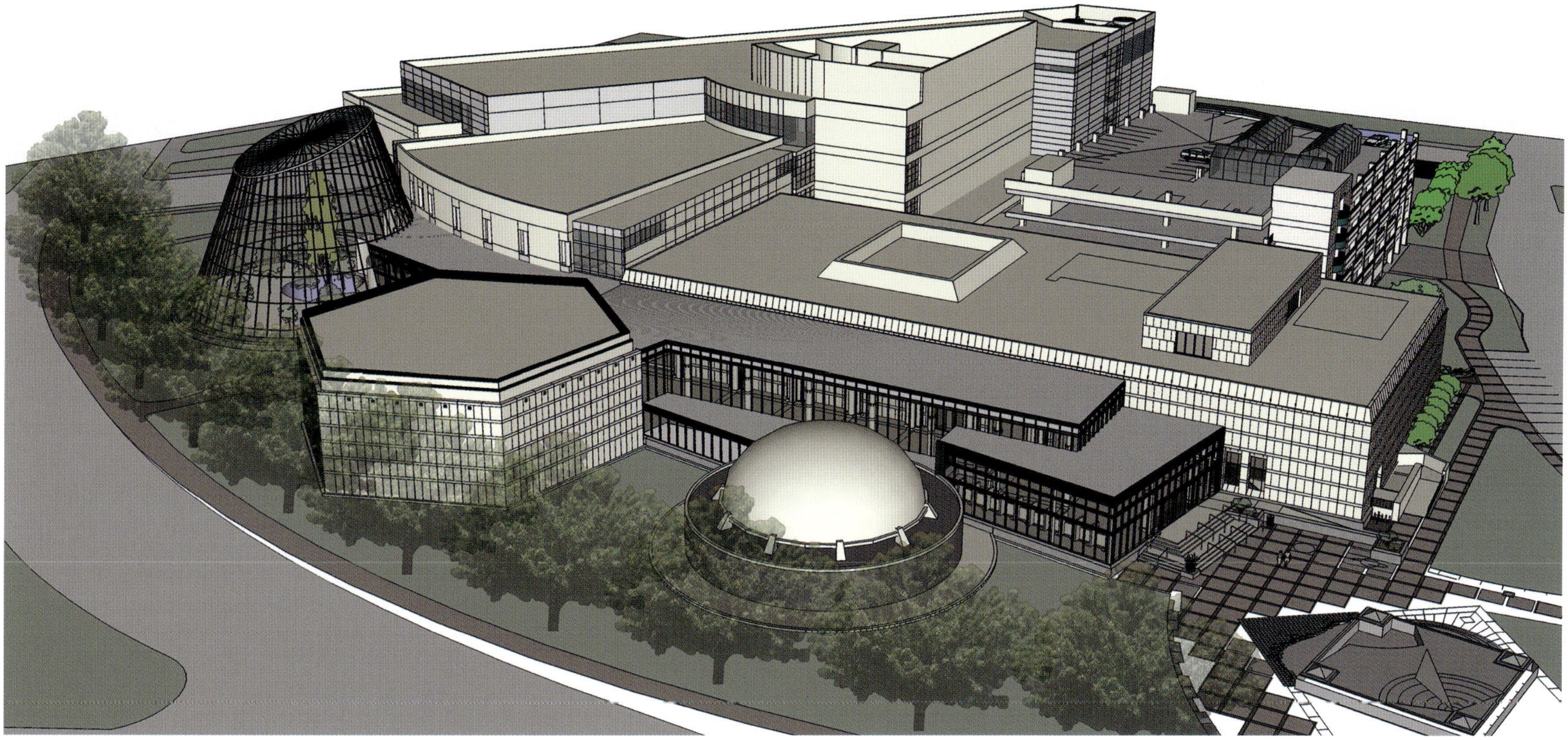

Houston Museum of Natural Science campus site plan shows all the components of the museum, 2011. Courtesy Gensler.

roof and giant ovoid glass terrarium fascinate as much from the exterior as the butterflies and plants do inside.[5]

The Houston Museum of Natural Science hosts over three million visitors every year, making it the most-visited non-Smithsonian museum in the United States. Construction has barely kept up with its expanding programs. Just north of the museum along Hermann Drive, the first parking garage in the park was constructed in 2000. The museum added the four-story, $85 million Dan L. Duncan Family Wing in 2012, containing the vast Paleontology Hall and 115,000 square feet of new exhibition and classroom space. The expansion doubled the number of classrooms for educational programs, doubled public exhibition space for temporary and permanent installations, and tripled the amount of collection storage space.[6] Designed by Gensler, the Duncan Wing replaced a city water tank at the intersection of Hermann Drive and San Jacinto behind the museum. The Houston Museum of Natural Science now fills the site bounded by Caroline, Hermann Park Drive, San Jacinto, and Hermann Drive.

Sara H. and John H. Lindsey Plaza

Traffic congestion around the Sam Houston Monument circle was alleviated by the construction of Lindsey Plaza and a new parking lot to the west of the traffic circle. Parking around the circle was eliminated, and new paving and landscaped gardens were installed. A distinctive part of Lindsey Plaza is the special paving that traverses the street and enters the park from the monument circle, proving a dramatic introduction to the Heart of the Park and a platform from which to enjoy the Reflection Pool.

Sara and John Lindsey began coming to the park together when they were fifteen years old. Mrs. Lindsey tells a story of winning a scavenger hunt when they were sixteen. They needed to find ten watermelon seeds, but it was December. They bundled up and came with flashlights to hunt under the picnic tables until they found the seeds—and they won because no one else thought to look in Hermann Park![7] The Lindseys' generosity is well known, especially in College Station, where they have been strong supporters of Texas A&M for many years. But it was not until Doreen Stoller took them on a treacherous golf-cart tour of the park in 2003 that they rediscovered Hermann Park. They had wanted to do something about the miniature train, not realizing at the time that it was operated by an outside concession. Instead they took on the responsibility for the last piece that allowed the completion of the Heart of the Park.

The new parking lot to the west of the Sam Houston Circle is landscaped with Laurie Olin's master plan concepts: providing overhanging trees and landscaping to minimize the impact of paved areas and provide shade.

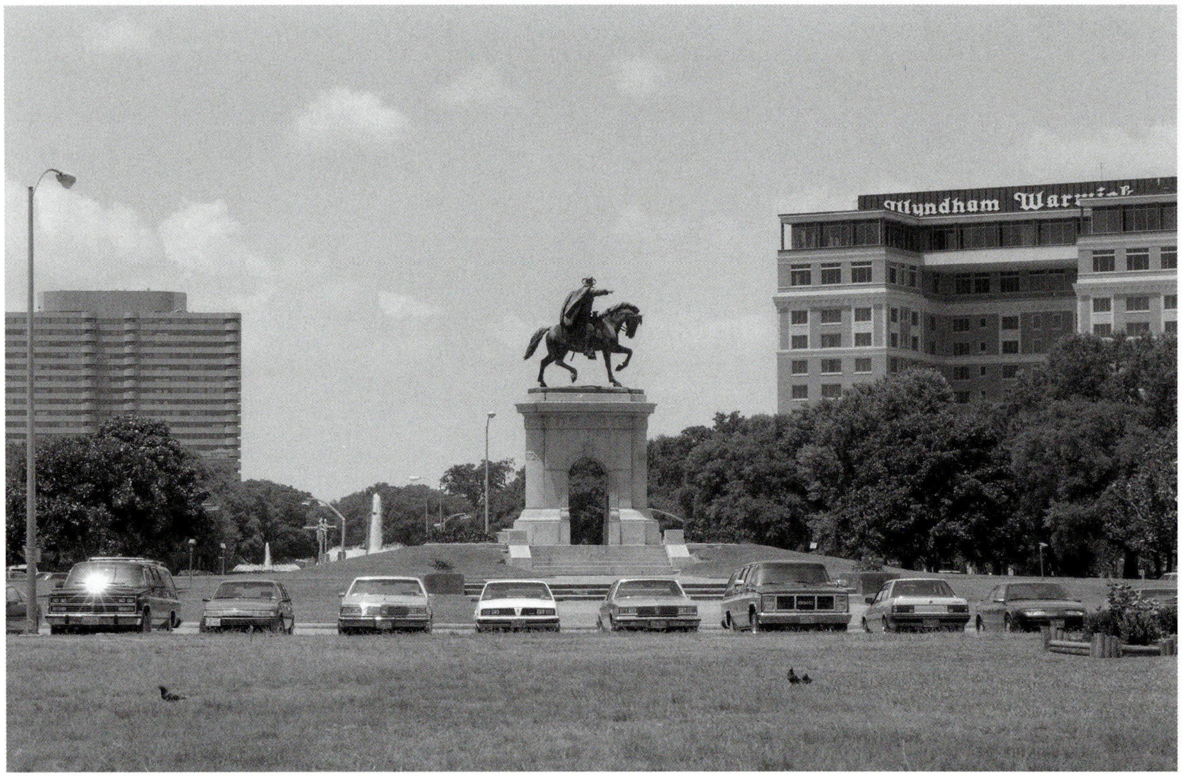

Sara H. and John H. Lindsey Plaza area when parking was allowed around the monument circle and landscaping was neglected, 1992. Photograph by Paul Hester.

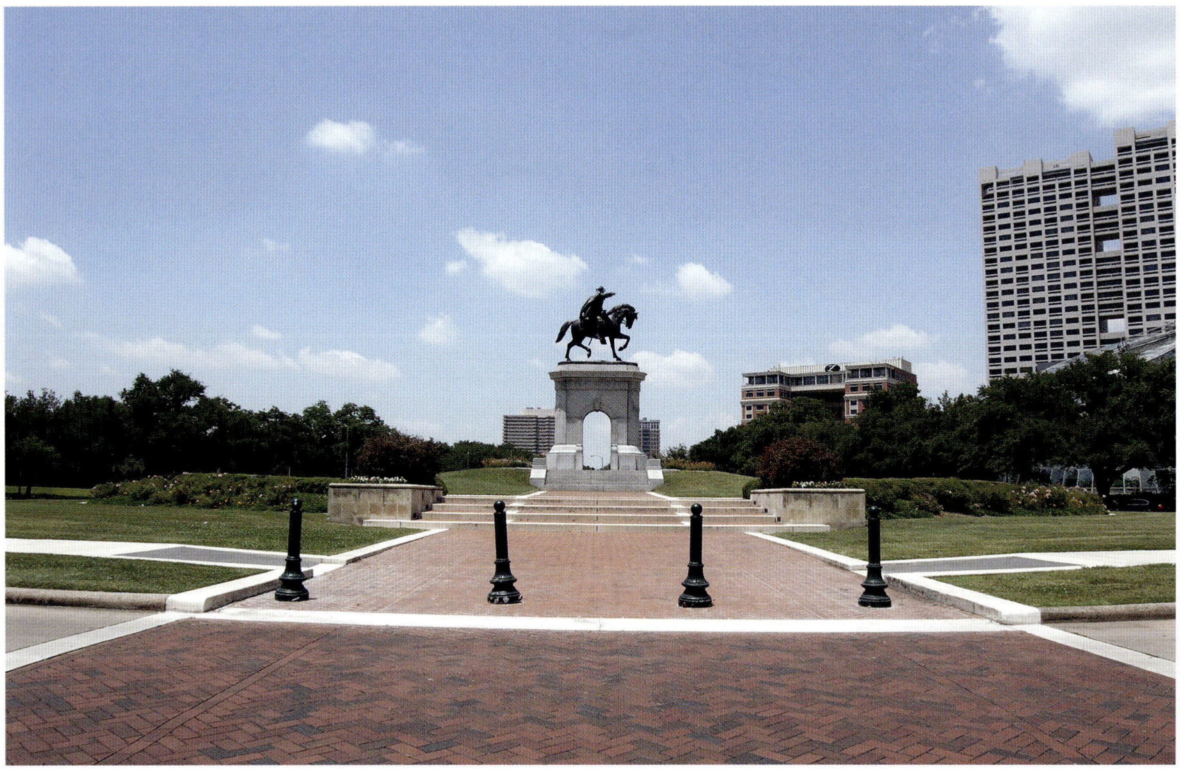

Lindsey Plaza, after parking was removed and new paving visually connected the Sam Houston Statue to the Heart of the Park, 2012. Photograph by B. S. Bradley.

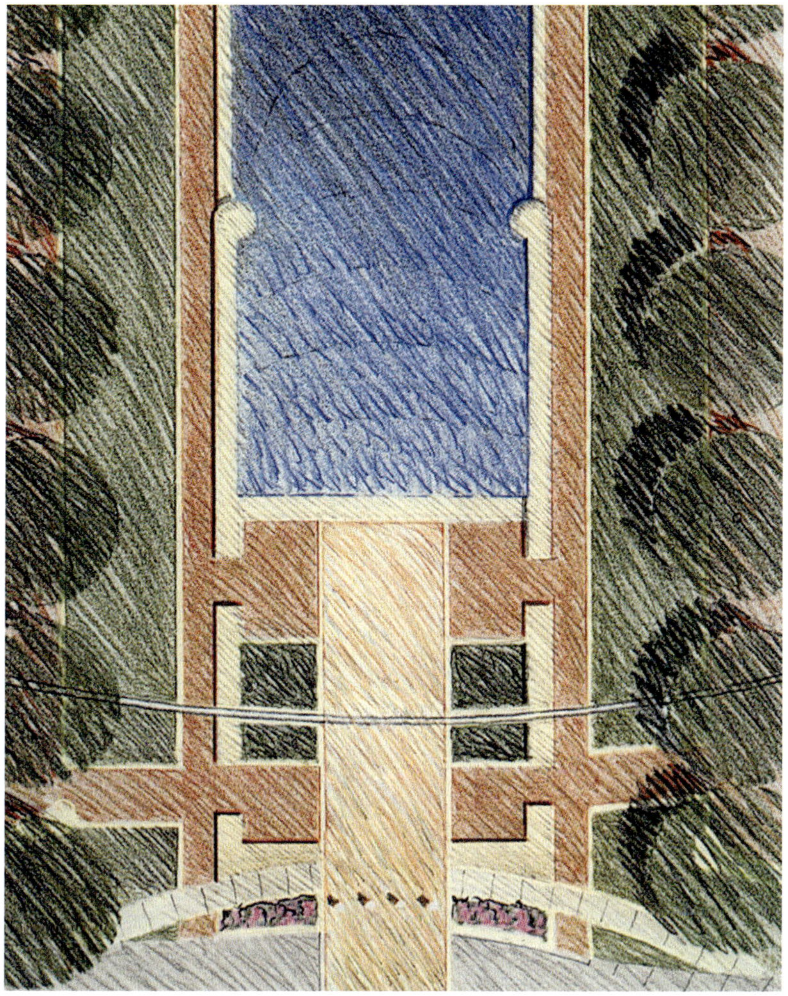

(*Left*) Lindsey Plaza plan showing connection to the Jones Reflection Pool, presentation drawing by Jay Baker, FAIA, c. 2002. Courtesy Hermann Park Conservancy.

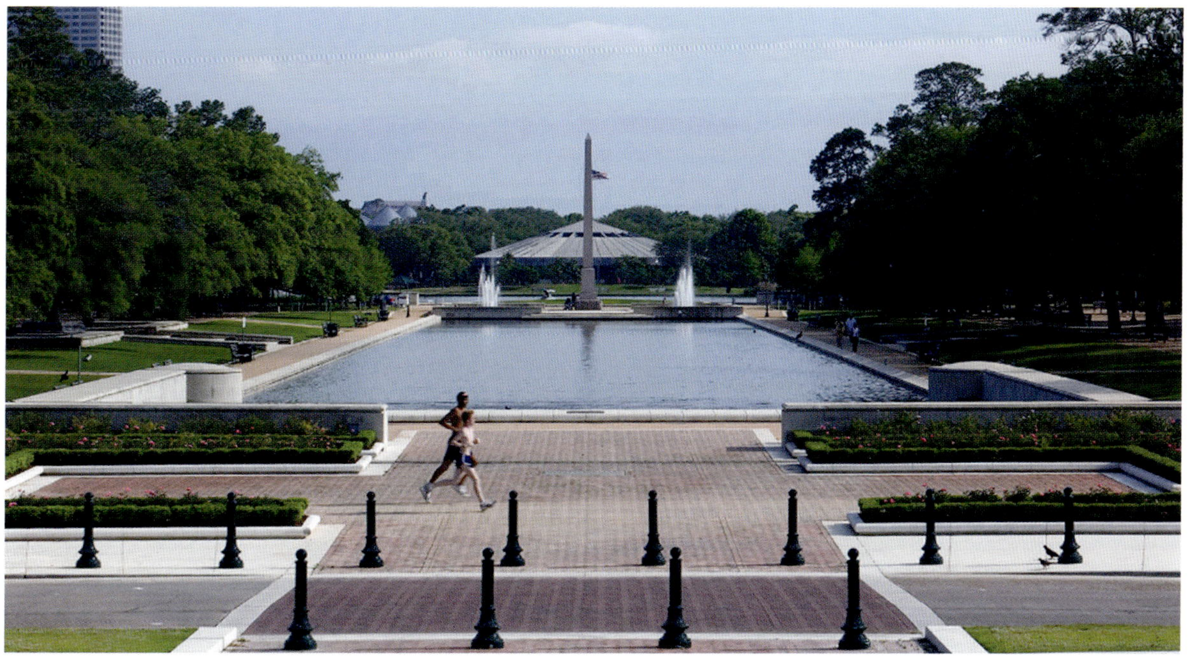

Lindsey Plaza (2004, SWA Group) facing the redesigned Jones Reflection Pool, showing the vista across McGovern Lake to the Kipp Aquarium, c. 2010. Courtesy Hermann Park Conservancy.

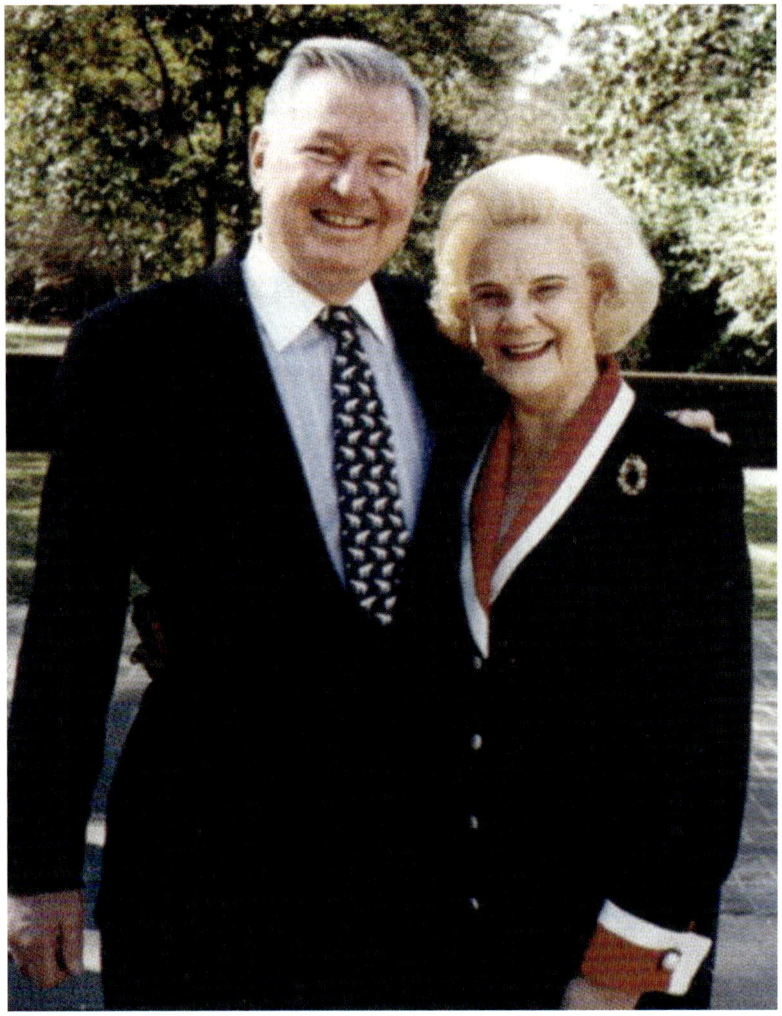

Sara H. and John H. Lindsey in Hermann Park, c. 2002. Courtesy Hermann Park Conservancy.

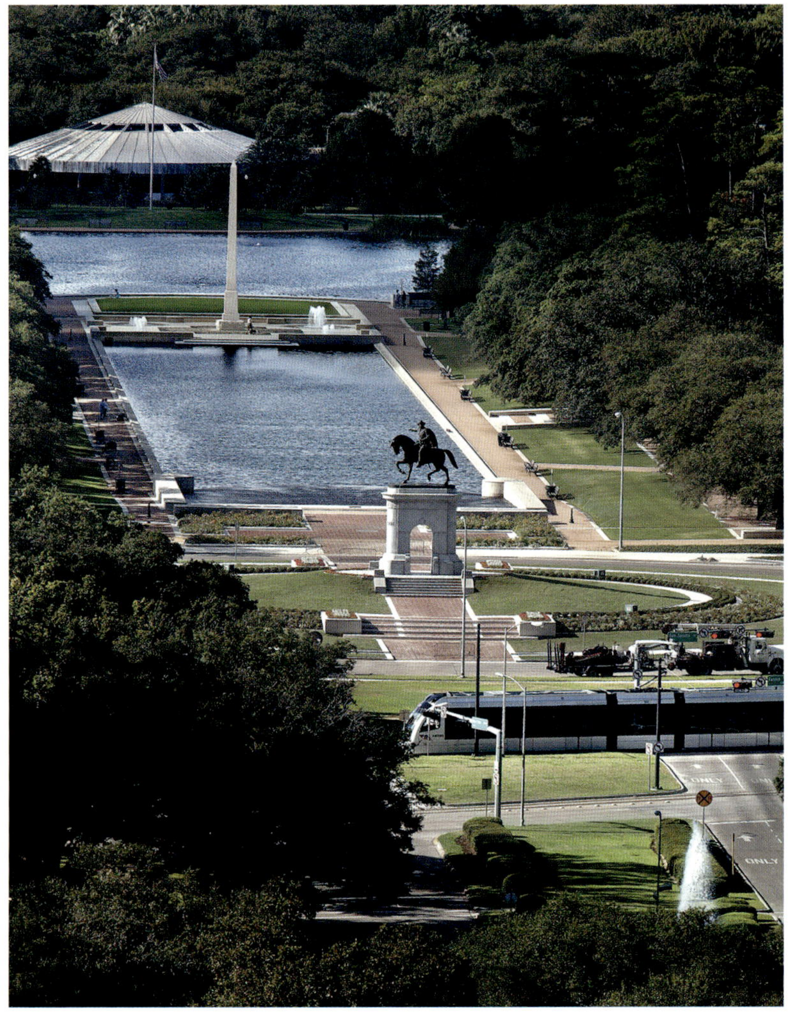

Heart of the Park aerial view, 2004. Photograph by David Schmoll. Courtesy Hermann Park Conservancy.

Mary Gibbs and Jesse H. Jones Reflection Pool

Many consider the Jones Reflection Pool, its paths, lawns, allées, and gardens, the *pièce de résistance* of the last twenty years in Hermann Park. Redesign of this area along the central axis of the park was the goal of the 1992 design competition. Although the Heart of the Park includes the Sam Houston Monument Circle, Lindsey Plaza, Arbor in the Pines, Mitchell Garden, and Smith Plaza, this centerpiece connects these segments and is easily accessible from most active areas of the park. The original budget of $4 million dollars was more than doubled to complete its construction. Fund-raising was a long process, and ground was not broken until July 19, 2001, once all the funds were in hand.

Historically the Reflection Pool was crisper and cleaner in the 1920s and 1930s, even though the paths were dirt and the edges were packed and cut. A footbridge that crossed over the pool at its center point was removed in 1929. By the last decades of the twentieth century the pool

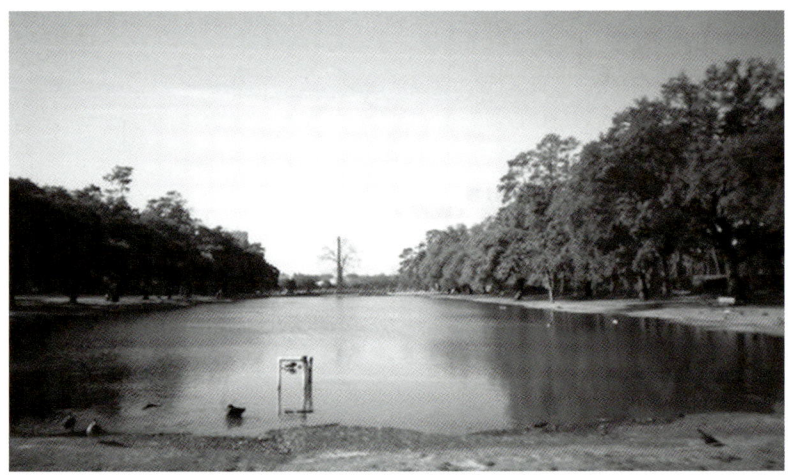

Reflection Pool before reconstruction, c. 1995. Photograph by Tom Fox, SWA Group. Courtesy Hermann Park Conservancy.

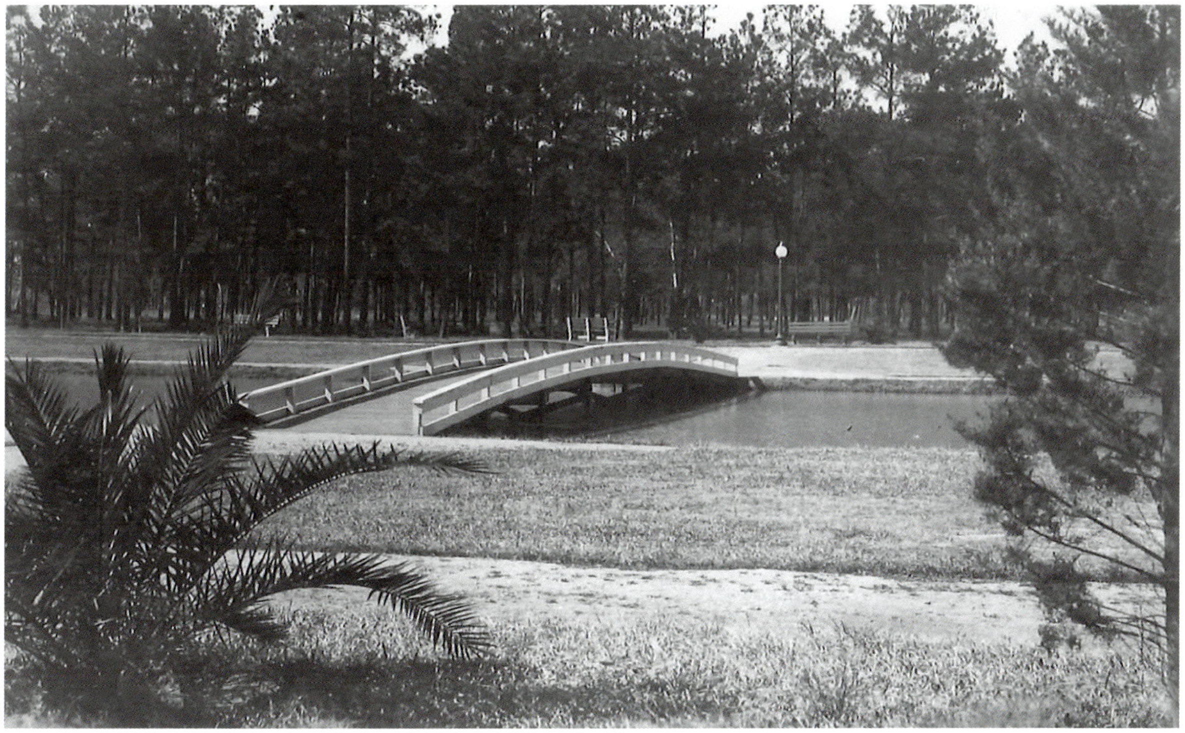

Bridge over Reflection Pool, c. 1926, when the packed edges of the pool held, and the area was maintained. Courtesy State Historical Society of Missouri, Research Center–Kansas City.

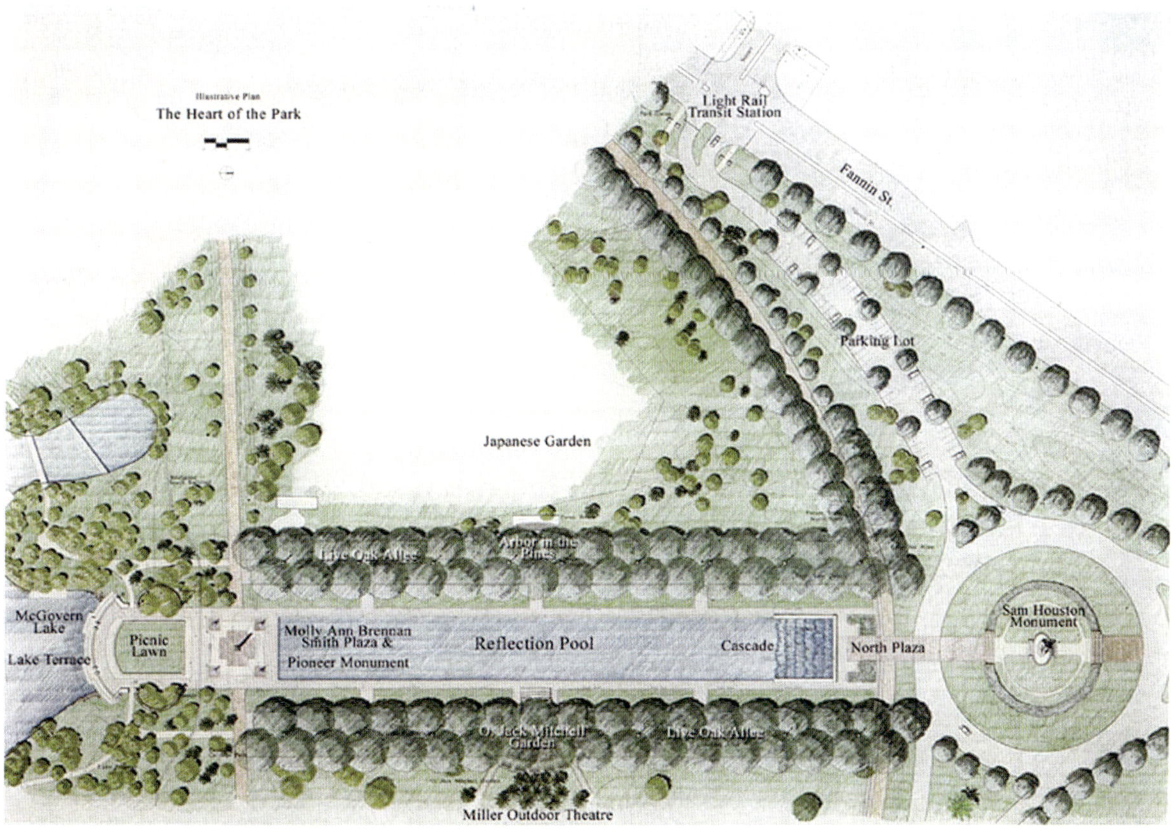

Final plan for the Heart of the Park (2000, SWA Group). Courtesy Hermann Park Conservancy.

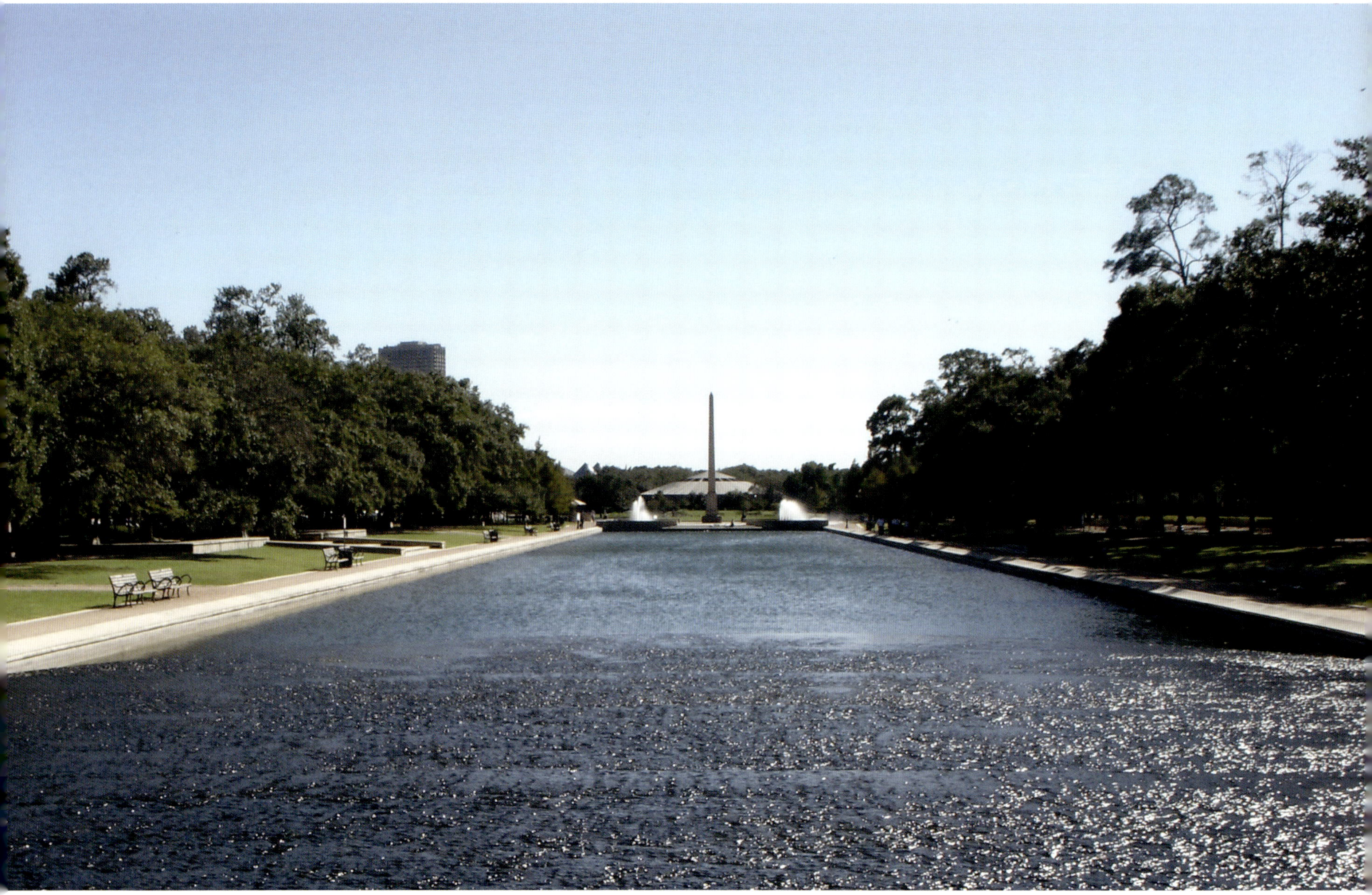

Mary Gibbs and Jesse H. Jones Reflection Pool after reconstruction that included lengthening and widening of the pool, from the top of the water cascade at the edge of Lindsey Plaza, c. 2004. Photograph by Laurie Olin. Courtesy Olin Partnership.

had deteriorated into a mud hole. The competition winner, The SWA Group, working with Laurie Olin as their consultant, modified their original proposal. The pool was edged with limestone and lengthened to 740 feet, again one-third as long as its original size, and widened to 80 feet. From the top of Lindsey Plaza, a whitewater cascade now rushes into the calm pool, over a black, highly reflective bottom.

Environmental issues were carefully considered. Although construction areas were closed off for safety reasons, care was taken not to disturb park inhabitants. A bio-filtration system was installed, avoiding the use of chemical treatments and excessive power consumption, to assure that the clear, reflective water would stay that way. At the bottom of the pool's clay-lined basin, perforated pipes draw water and debris through a gravel bed where organics are trapped and gradually decompose. To limit potential damage from water run-off, the pedestrian promenade and other nearby paths have been paved with porous, decomposed granite gravel.

During construction, preserving the existing live oak trees was of paramount concern. All excavations were done by hand to avoid damag-

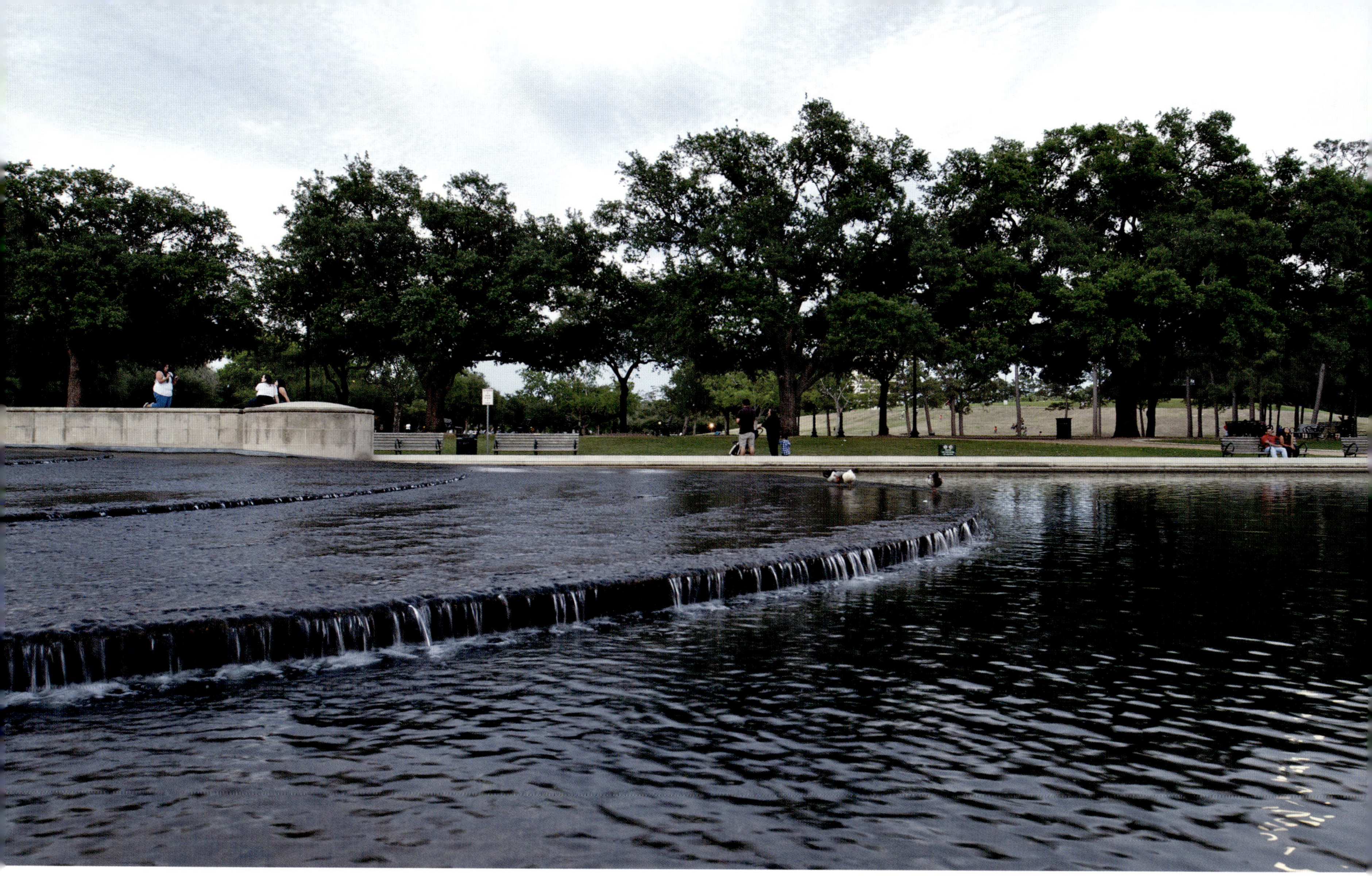

The rippling water cascade rushes down into the Jones Reflection Pool with the satisfying natural sound of rushing water, 2011. Photograph by Nash Baker Photography, courtesy Hermann Park Conservancy.

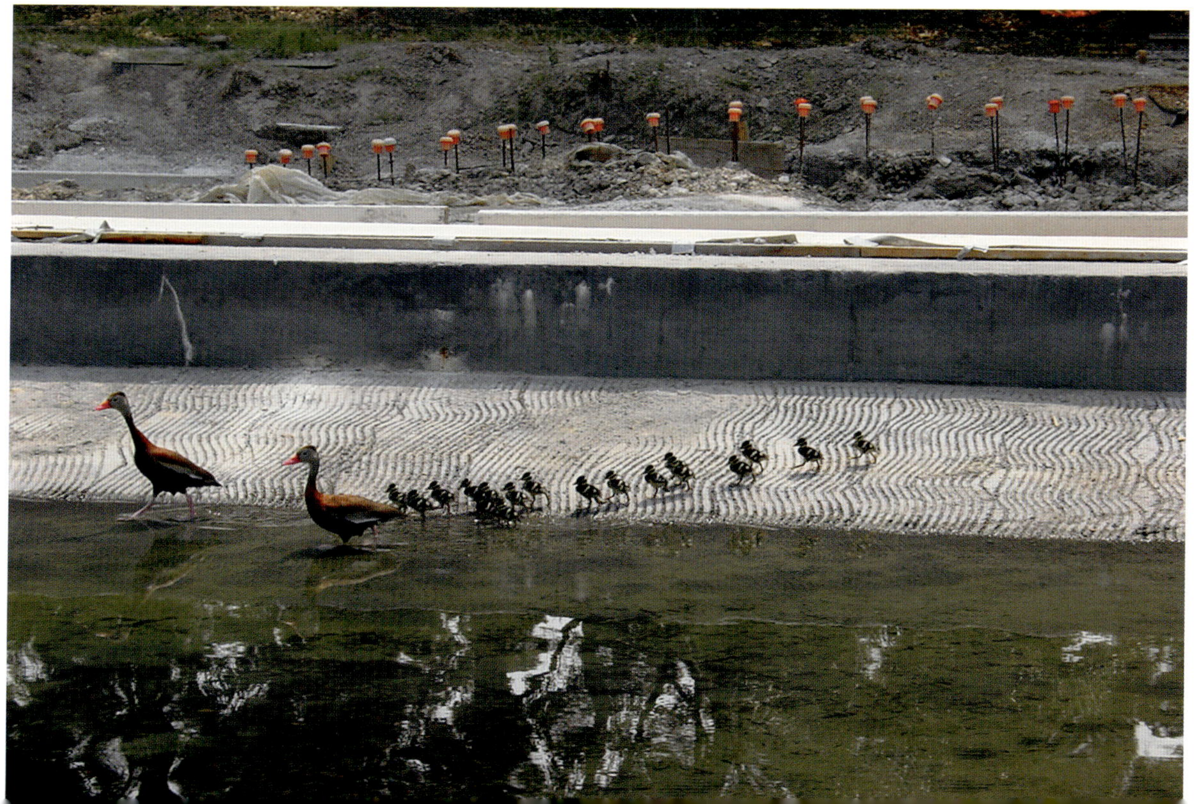

During construction of the Reflection Pool, a duck family crosses the area in line with the orange rebar caps, 2001. Photograph by Jay Baker, FAIA. Courtesy Hermann Park Conservancy.

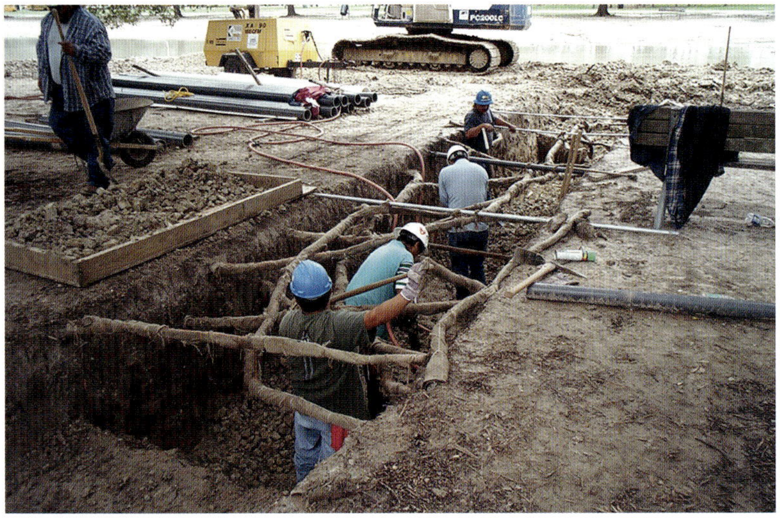

Live oak tree roots were carefully avoided and wrapped during excavation for the Jones Reflection Pool, 2001. Photograph by Jay Baker, FAIA. Courtesy Hermann Park Conservancy.

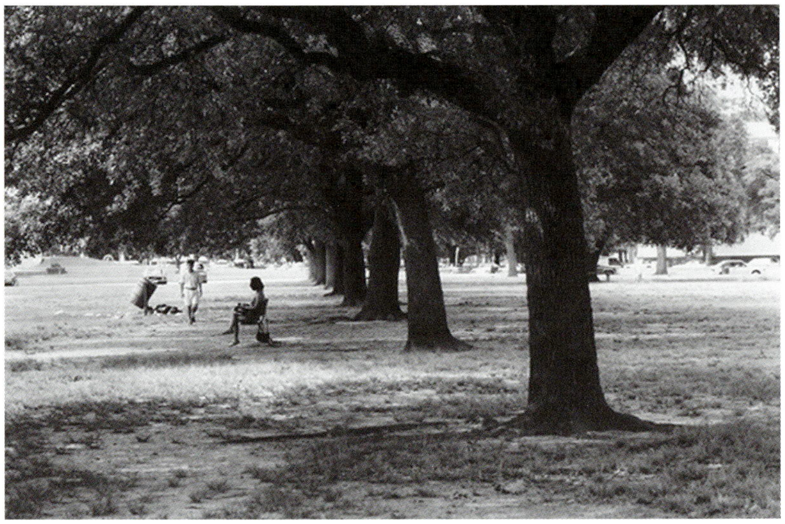

Allée of old live oak trees before renewal in the Heart of the Park, 1992. Photograph by Paul Hester.

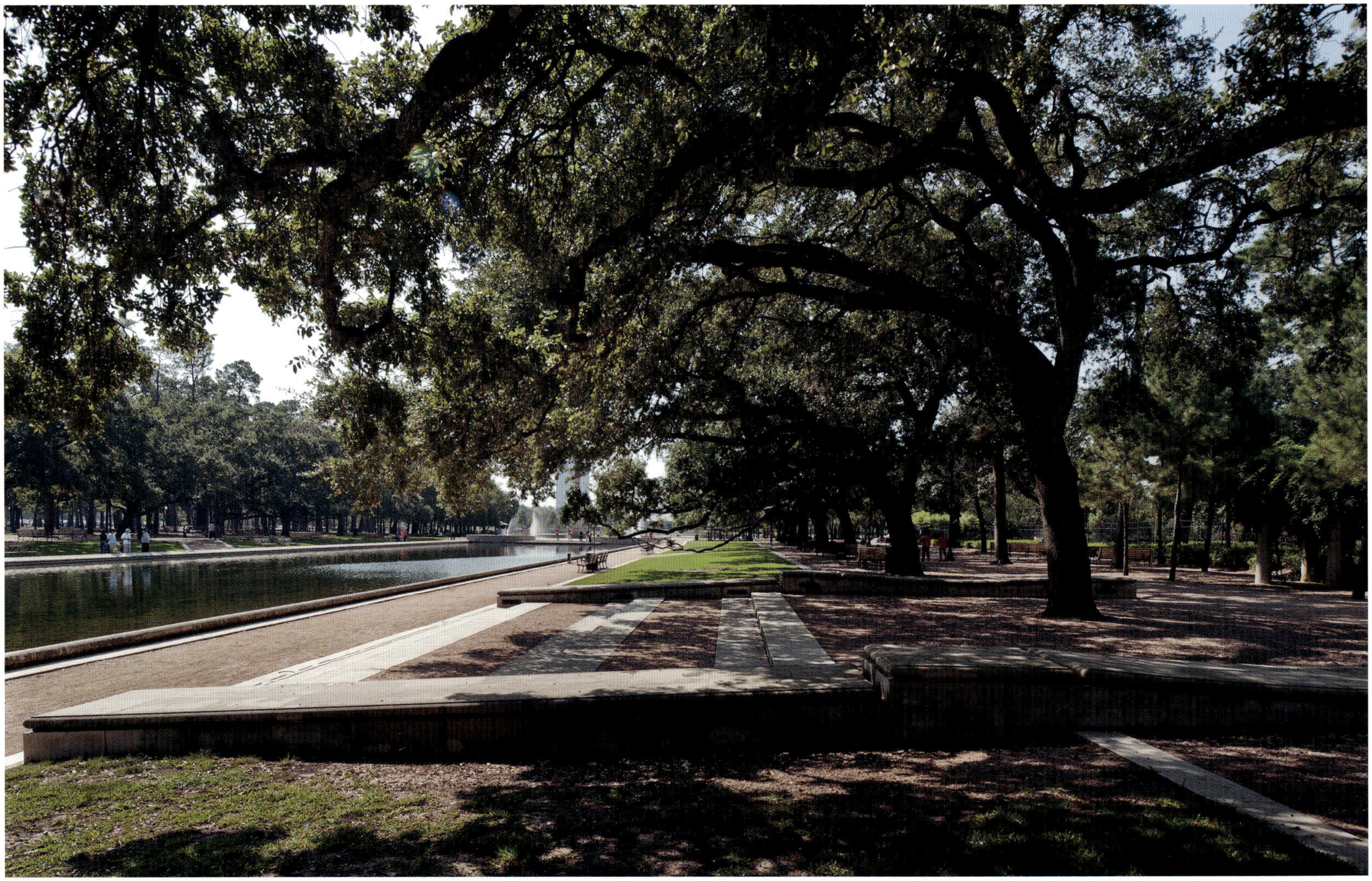

Live oak allée after the trees were conserved and the area was banked and landscaped to create a pedestrian promenade alongside the Jones Reflection Pool, 2011. Photograph by Nash Baker Photography. Courtesy Hermann Park Conservancy.

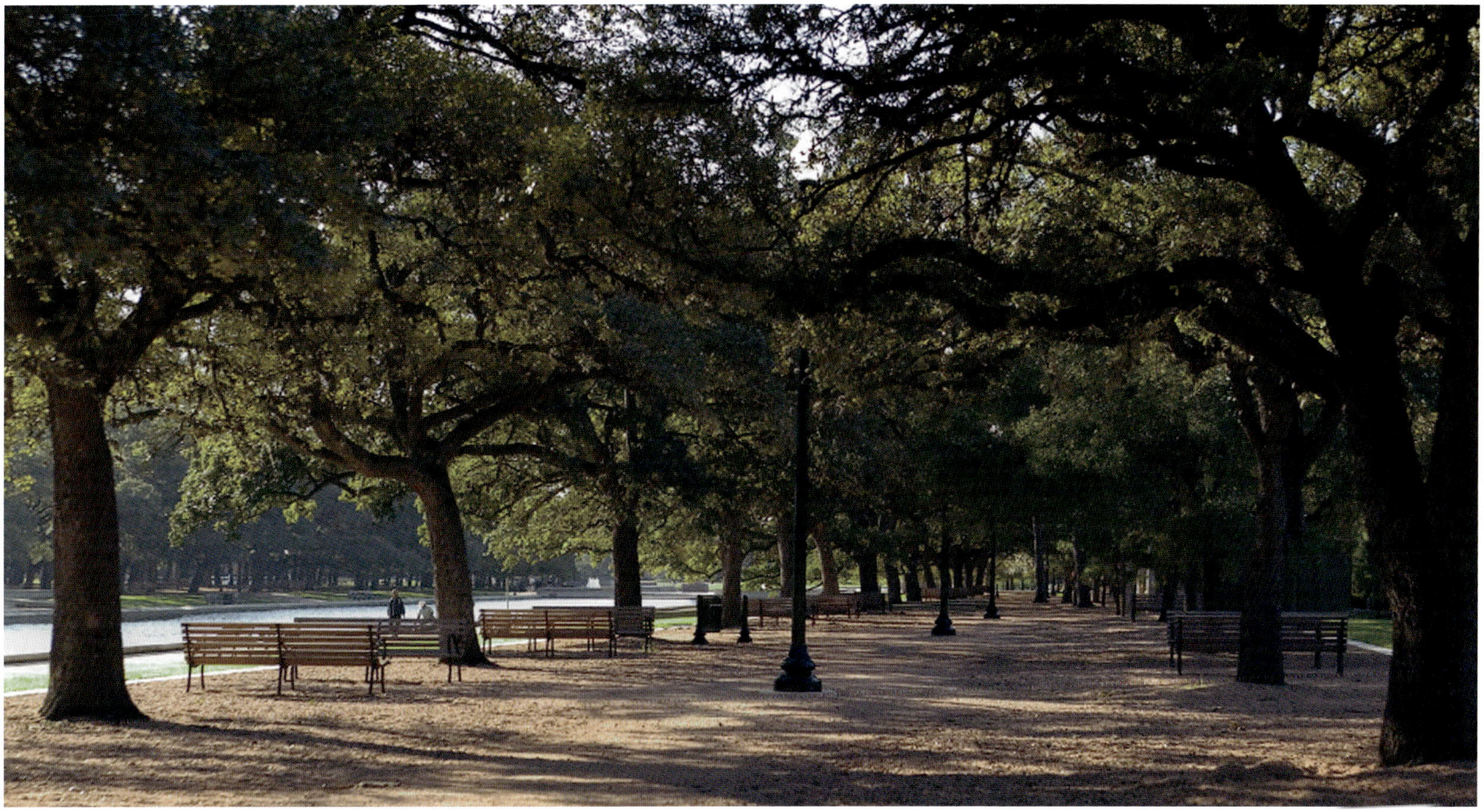

Double allée of live oak trees was filled (where trees had died) and extended with mature live oaks trees transplanted from elsewhere in Houston to create a wide shady path flanked by Hermann Park benches designed by Laurie Olin and lit by traditional acorn lamps like those in other areas of the park, c. 2008. Photograph by Tom Fox, SWA Group. Courtesy Hermann Park Conservancy.

ing sensitive roots, and, during installation of underground piping, the contractors wrapped each individual root with moisture-preserving insulation and watered them regularly. The then eighty-year-old live oaks along the pedestrian promenades were joined by a second row behind them on both sides of the Reflection Pool. Forty-four mature trees were transplanted from other sites around the city, where they would have been lost to development.

Arbor in the Pines

On the west side of the Jones Reflection Pool, midway along the west allée, the Arbor in the Pines, a wisteria-draped colonnade, was designed by W. O. Neuhaus & Associates for the purpose of disguising the large pump house that serves both the Reflection Pool and the McGovern Lake. The columns are finished in Venetian plaster—plaster mixed with marble dust and applied by hand in thin, multiple layers. Benches under the arbor offer quiet resting places, always in the shade.

O. Jack Mitchell Garden

Directly across Jones Reflection Pool from the Arbor in the Pines is the O. Jack Mitchell Garden, named for the dean of the Rice School of Architecture, whose sudden death inspired the Heart of the Park competition. The entrance to the Mitchell Garden, midway along the east allée, is through columned arbors at the north and south ends of the garden that match the colonnade in the Arbor of the Pines. This garden is a contemplative place where a central fountain spills water into a small pool. Azaleas frame the seating area that includes an Olin-designed Hermann Park bench encircling a large live oak tree.

Molly Ann Smith Plaza

Named in memory of a longtime Houstonian who loved bringing her grandchildren to Hermann Park, the Molly Ann Smith Plaza at the south end of the Jones Reflection Pool incorporates the Pioneer Memorial Obelisk and four spouting water fountains. Because of Mrs. Smith's affinity for the miniature train, her family wanted a memorial for her

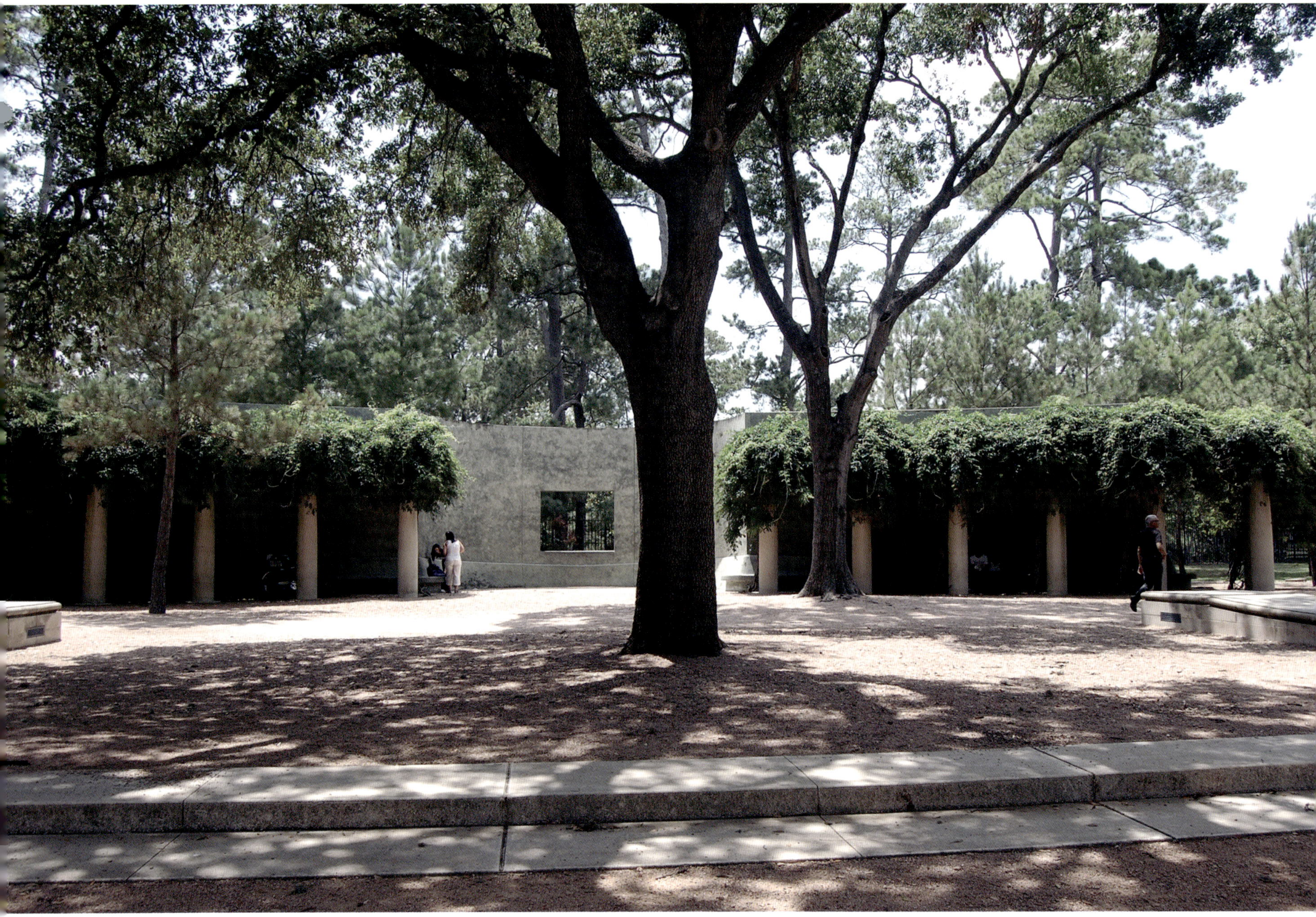

Arbor in the Pines, on the west side of the Jones Reflection Pool, is a wisteria draped colonnade designed by William O. Neuhaus & Associates to disguise the large pump house for McGovern Lake and the Jones Reflection Pool, 2011. Photograph by B. S. Bradley.

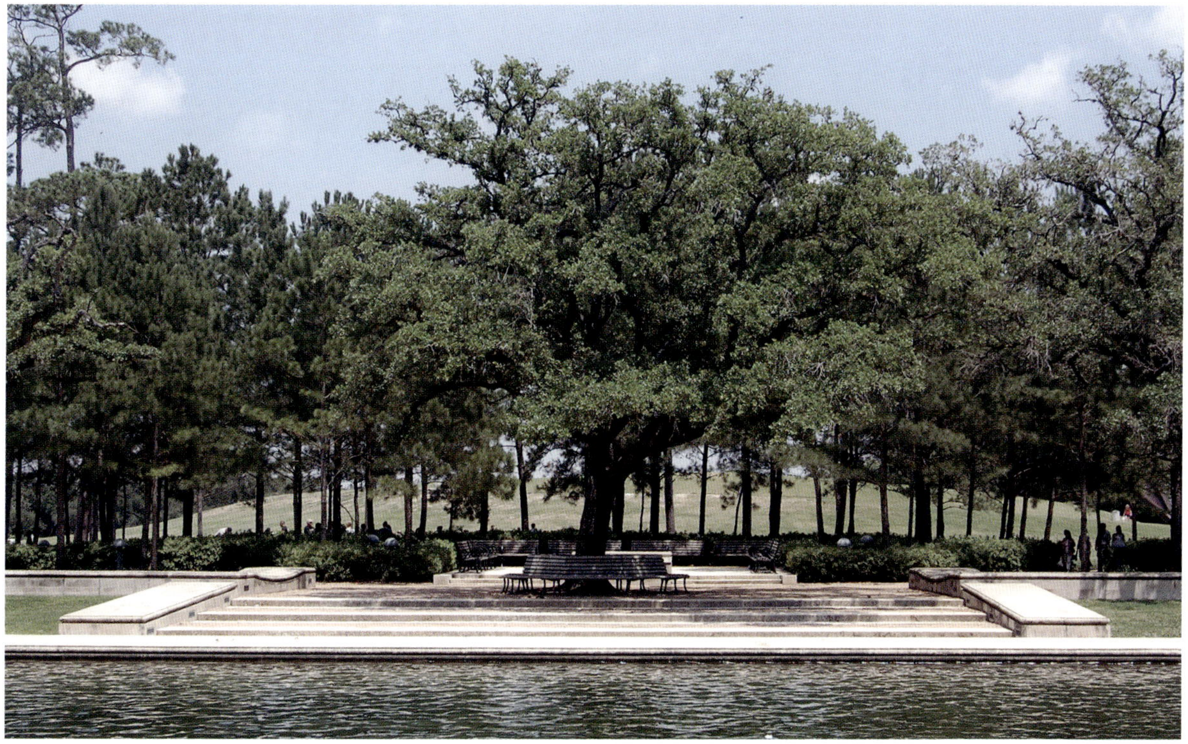

The O. Jack Mitchell Garden, across the Reflection Pool from Arbor in the Pines, is a contemplative place centered along the east allée of the Reflection Pond. The memorial garden is named for the former dean of the Rice School of Architecture, whose sudden death prompted the Heart of the Park competition, 2011. Photograph by B. S. Bradley.

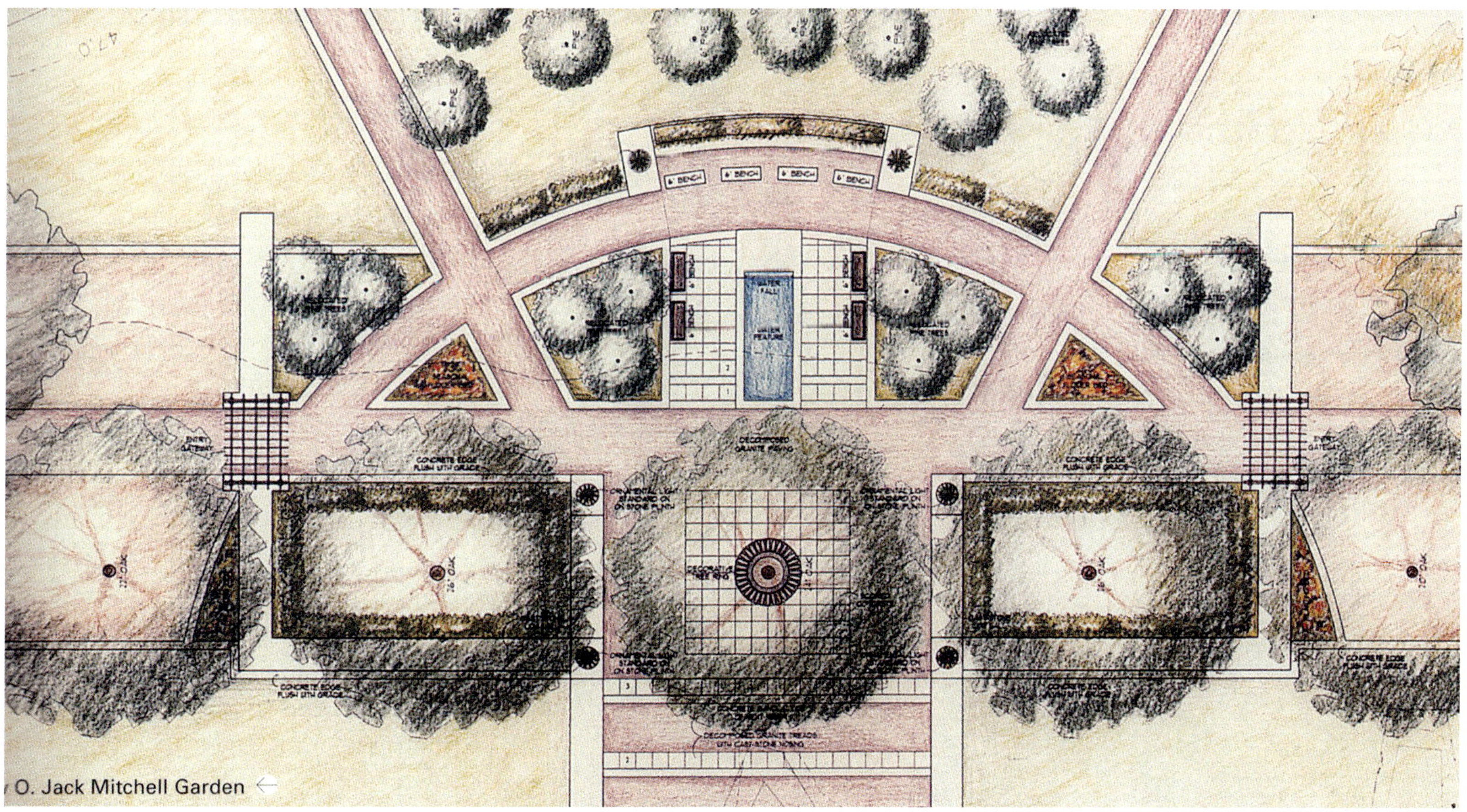

O. Jack Mitchell Garden plan (2004, SWA Group) features a dense tree canopy, azaleas, and space for annual color as well as a small fountain and plaza with walkways that connect this area to park spaces beyond the Heart of the Park, 2004. Courtesy Hermann Park Conservancy.

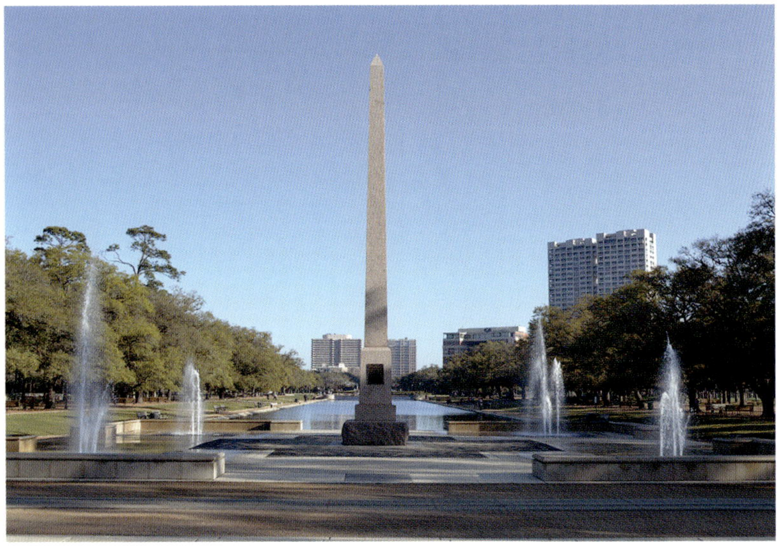

Molly Ann Smith Plaza, located on the north shore of McGovern Lake, offers picnicking on a raised lawn, shaded seating, and playful, interactive fountains. The Pioneer Memorial obelisk is located in the center of the plaza, 2013. Photograph by B. S. Bradley.

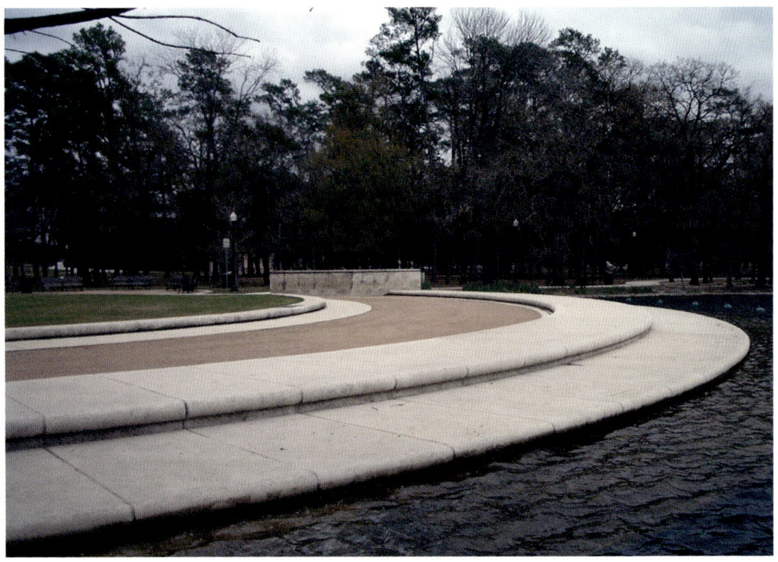

Wide, curving steps gently descend from Smith Plaza to the northern edge of McGovern Lake, c. 2004. Photograph by Laurie Olin. Courtesy Olin Partnership.

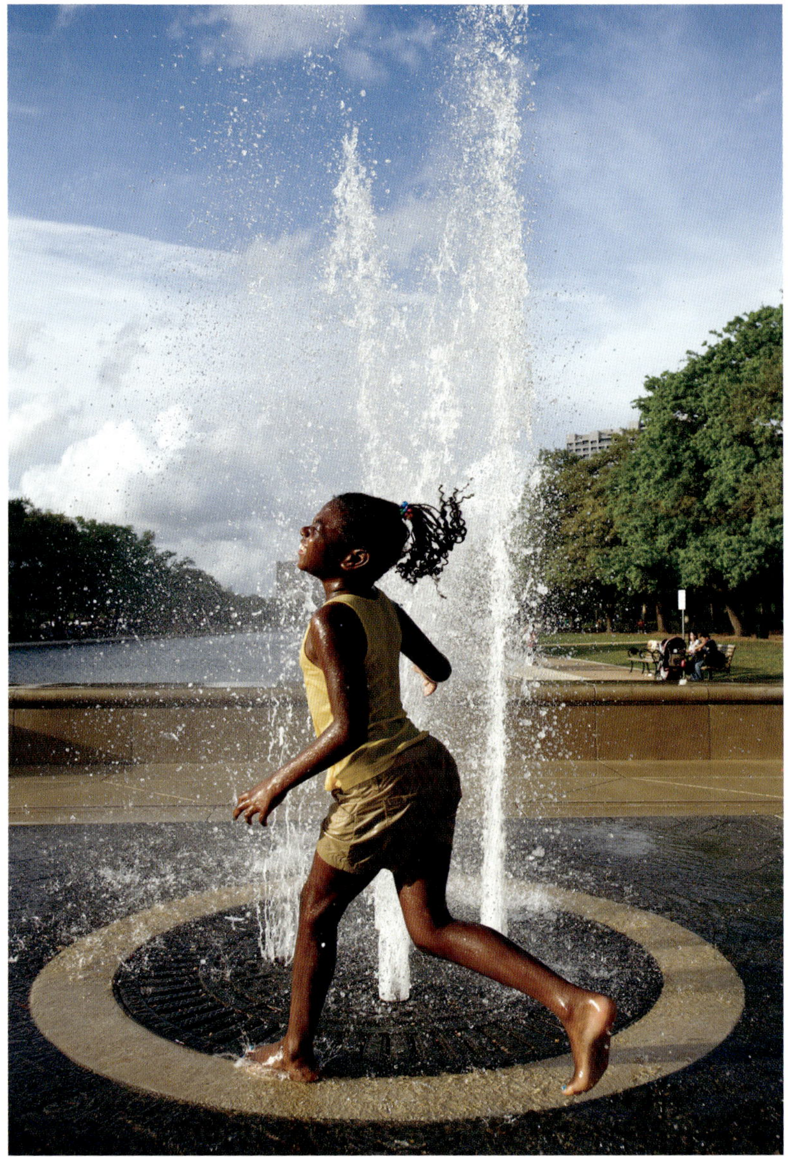

Girl playing in one of the four Smith Plaza fountains. The fountains spurt up intermittently and are a favorite with children, especially on hot summer days, 2011. Photograph by Nash Baker Photography. Courtesy Hermann Park Conservancy.

in Hermann Park connected with the train. Therefore the path of the train now traverses Smith Plaza in the midst of the fountain spouts. The granite dedication panel quotes Molly Ann Smith, "Just Have Fun!"

From Smith Plaza a series of wide, shallow limestone-lined steps descend to McGovern Lake. This plaza configuration, suggested by Olin in the 1995 master plan, is a joy for children playing in the fountains by day and for those attending evening events. Because Houston's weather is so mild, Smith Plaza welcomes activity most days of the year.

After twelve years of planning, raising $9.5 million, and carefully orchestrated construction, the Heart of the Park projects—Lindsey Plaza, Jones Reflection Pool, Arbor in the Pines, Mitchell Garden, and Molly Ann Smith Plaza—were dedicated in 2004. Ten years later the trees have matured, the grass seems greener, and the water bluer. The Heart of the Park has become a favorite place of Houstonians—a place of beauty in both day and night.

This project won a national award from the American Society of Landscape Architects, the 2005 General Award for Design Excellence. In its summation of the project, the society's jurors wrote: "Simplicity,

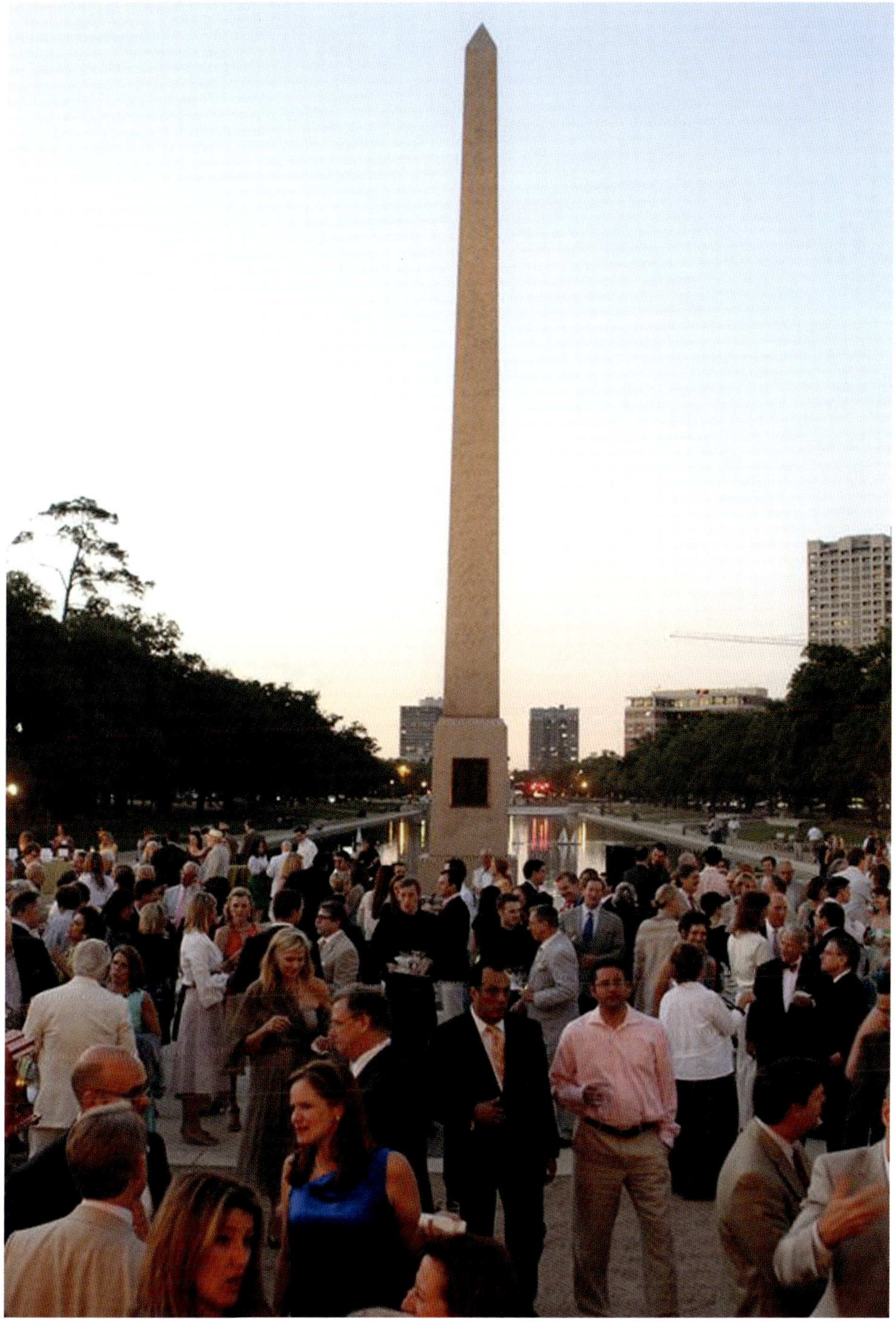

Molly Ann Smith Plaza filled with partygoers attending an Evening in the Park for the benefit of the Hermann Park Conservancy, 2012. Photograph by Pricilla Dickson. Courtesy Hermann Park Conservancy.

perhaps the most significant challenge in the design of any active park space, was attained through clarity of form, a refined materials palette, and by the distribution of activity throughout the space. . . . The Heart of the Park represents the best of civic mindedness and philanthropy for which Houston is acclaimed, and serves as a successful example of the value of great civic spaces."[8]

A local award for the project (Mayor's Proud Partners Award, Keep Houston Beautiful, in 2004) highlighted the partnership between the conservancy and the city that made this space possible: "The crown jewel of the revitalization of Hermann Park by the Hermann Park Conservancy is the Mary Gibbs and Jesse H. Jones Reflection Pool. The principal attraction to the park's grand entrance is a testament to what the collaboration of a dedicated citizenry and municipal involvement can achieve."[9]

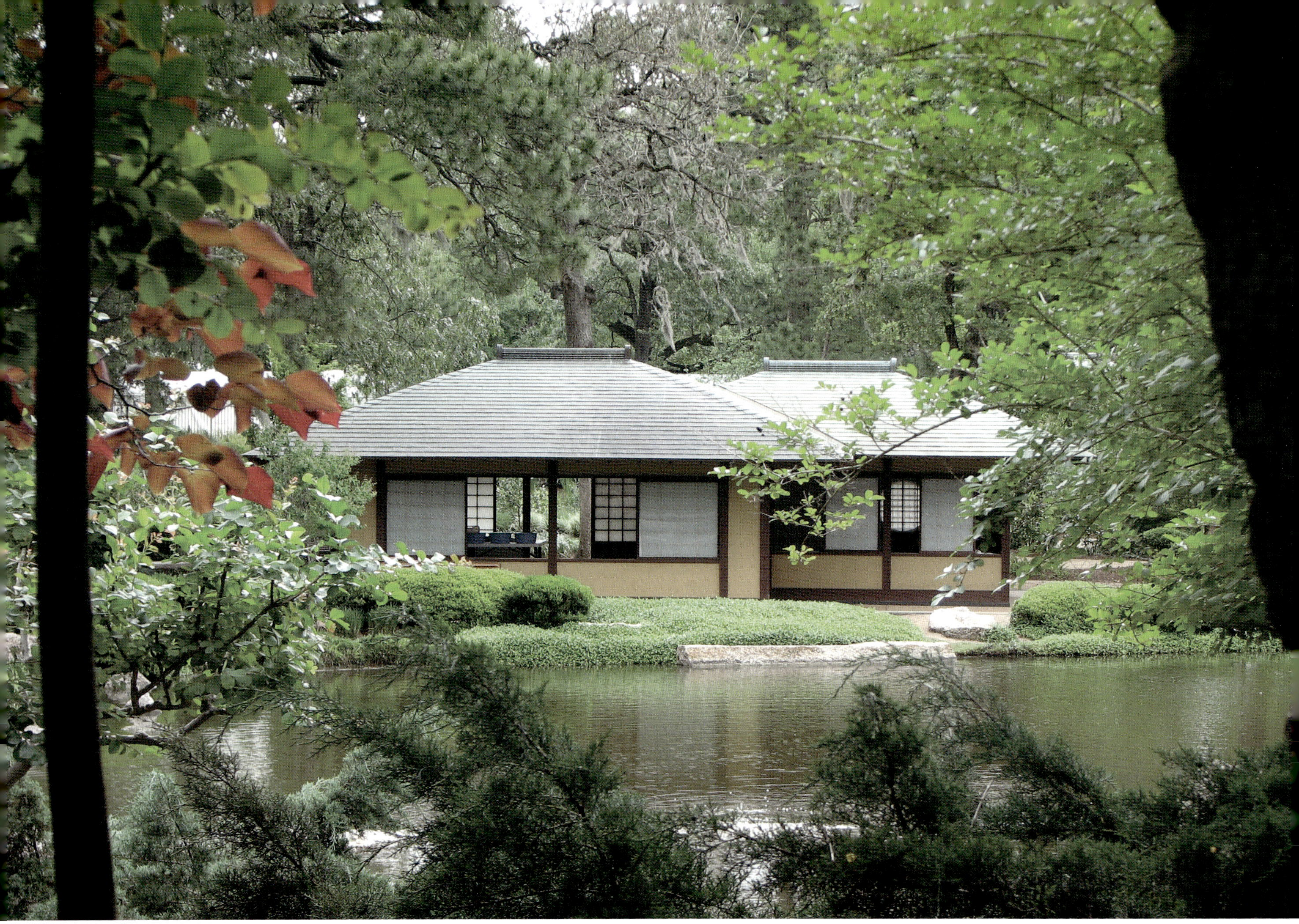

Japanese Garden Teahouse, constructed in Japan using traditional Japanese techniques and materials, dismantled and shipped to Houston, then reassembled in 1992, c. 2000. Photograph courtesy Hermann Park Conservancy.

Japanese Garden

In 1988 several Japanese businessmen began to explore the possibility of constructing a Japanese Garden in Houston.[10] The idea came to fruition the following year when Toshiki Kaifu, prime minister of Japan, visited Houston for the 1990 G7 Economic Summit. In a gesture of goodwill toward Houston, Kaifu arranged for the Commemorative Association of the World Expo Fund of Japan to donate a Japanese teahouse to the City of Houston. The teahouse was constructed in Japan using traditional Japanese materials, then shipped to Houston where Japanese artisans reassembled it without nails using traditional Japanese hand tools. The floor plan of the small teahouse follows the traditional design for tea ceremonies, which are performed here on special occasions.

Before the teahouse arrived, the Tokyo landscape architect Takeshi "Ken" Nakajima (1914–2000) was commissioned to design the Houston garden. Nakajima was responsible for significant Japanese gardens in Montreal, Cowra, Australia, and Moscow. Director Don Olson agreed to place the Houston Japanese Garden on a 5.5-acre tract in Hermann Park that was chosen by Nakajima.[11] "We must work with nature," Nakajima wrote of the Houston project, "to create a new space and sense of beauty. This is the essence of the Japanese garden."[12]

Ground was broken on March 26, 1991; the structural parts of the garden—lakes, streams, paths, and rocks—were completed before the teahouse arrived. Fourteen months later, with the teahouse and plantings installed, the Japanese Garden in Hermann Park was dedicated

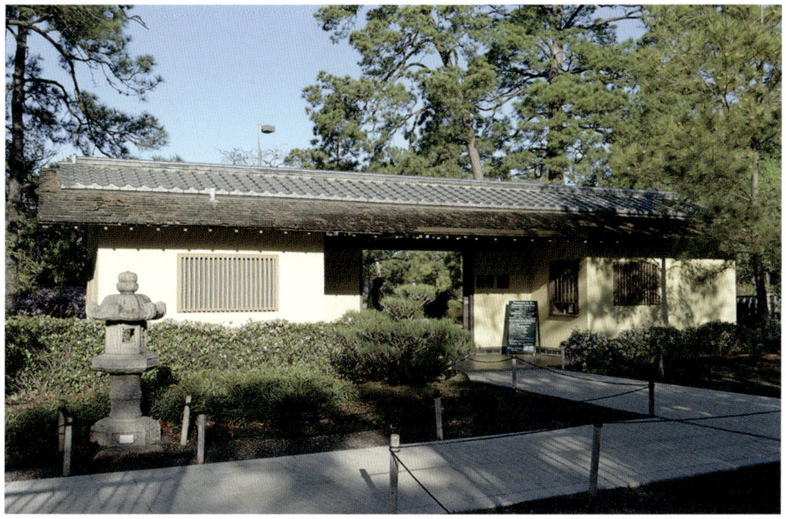

Japanese Garden Entrance pavilion, 2013. Photograph by B. S. Bradley.

on May 4, 1992. Rick Dewees was the project manager for the Parks Department, and Lauren Griffith was the local landscape architect who worked with Nakajima on selection of plant materials that would be appropriate for Houston's climate. John Roberts was the project manager for the Japanese Garden Inc., the donor group.[13]

Nakajima designed Houston's Japanese Garden in the *daimyo* style, named for the feudal Japanese warlord gardens built from the tenth through the late nineteenth centuries. The *daimyo* garden is an excursion garden laid out in winding paths that encourage the visitor to wander through and around a sequence of landscape elements at a leisurely pace. Pines, oaks, and shrubbery at the gate and small blue pebbles that recall blue moonstone create a Japanese aesthetic using local materials. One enters through a traditional gateway, flanked by rooms on each side of the entrance, that in Houston house a ticket booth and utility room on one side and restrooms on the other, a useful adaptation.

A stone lantern at the entrance is symbolically placed to light one's way through the garden. Such iconic lanterns are always present in Japanese gardens. There are three others in Houston's Japanese garden; two of them are *yukimi* lanterns, or "snow-viewing" lanterns, which are low to the ground with a broad cap. This type of lantern is usually placed at the edge of the water, as they are in this garden. The prominent *yukimi* across the pond from the teahouse was a gift from Houston's sister city, Chiba City, Japan. The second *yukimi* is near the garden gazebo. Other than lanterns, Japanese gardens usually have no other sculpture or monuments but focus on natural features in a series of carefully planned vistas, often with symbolic meaning.

To the right of the entry garden is a small wisteria arbor, blooming purple in the springtime, which provides a place to sit, meditate, and clear the mind before journeying through the garden or to a tea ceremony. Tea ceremony guests wind down a stone path, which the host moistens to appear damp with morning dew, to the tea garden gate. The teahouse itself is a simple and elegant structure with handmade details. When opened, the sliding rice paper screens of the teahouse reveal a pond into which a boisterous water cascade flows. In Japan garden rock formations would be of naturally shaped, weathered stones, but there are no natural stones in Houston. Instead Nakajima chose quarried pink granite from the Marble Falls area just northwest of Austin for the water cascade.[14] But he was pleased with the result: "The majestic appearance of the rock structure contributes to attaining an over-all balance in the garden."[15] To him, "The overwhelming force of the massive rocks seemed symbolic of Texas."[16]

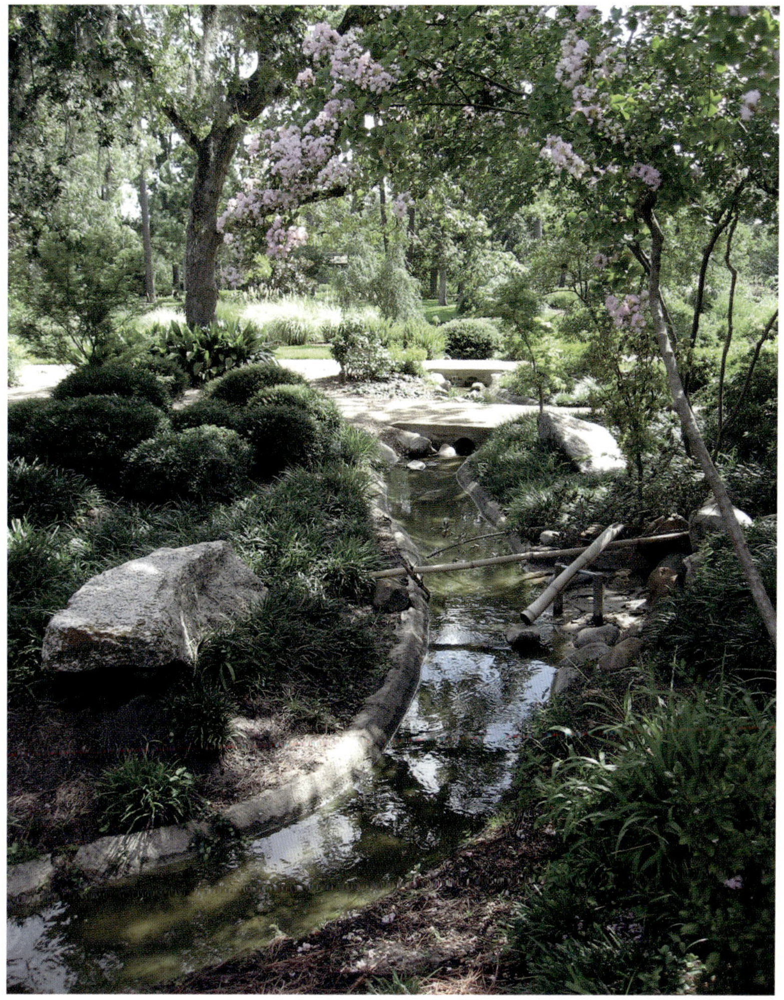

Winding paths and streams in the Japanese Garden provide quiet, intimate places to wander, c. 2011. Courtesy Hermann Park Conservancy

The hill beyond the cascade is landscaped with pink crepe myrtles that in winter display beautifully sculptural bare trunks and limbs. In spring the meandering paths wind among blooming crape myrtles, aza-

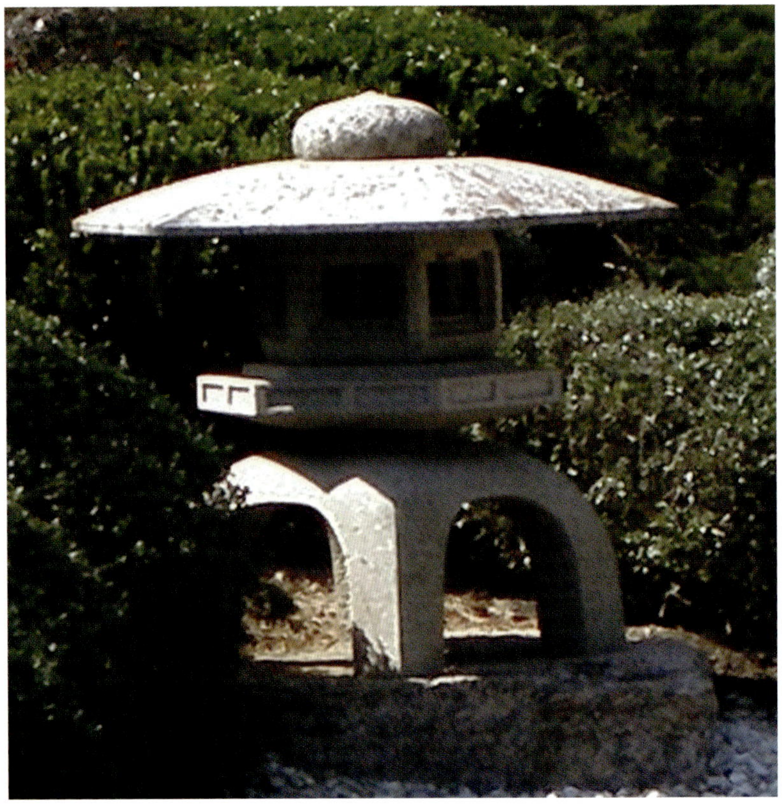

Yukimi Lantern, a gift from Chiba City, Japan (Houston's sister city), is placed at the edge of the pond across from the Teahouse, 2008. Courtesy Hermann Park Conservancy.

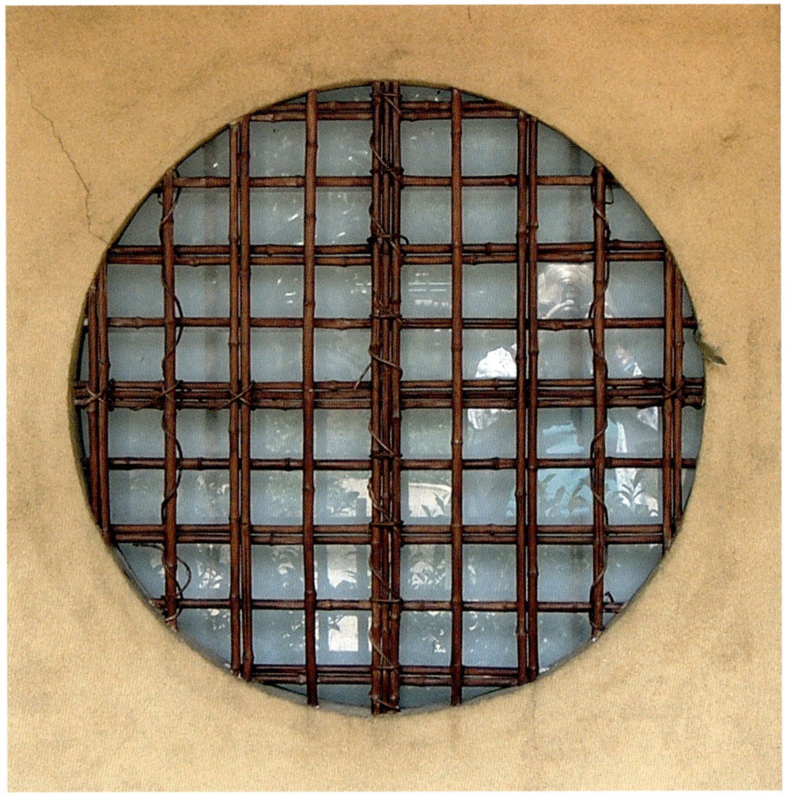

Teahouse window with hand-tied mullions, 2012. Photograph by B. S. Bradley.

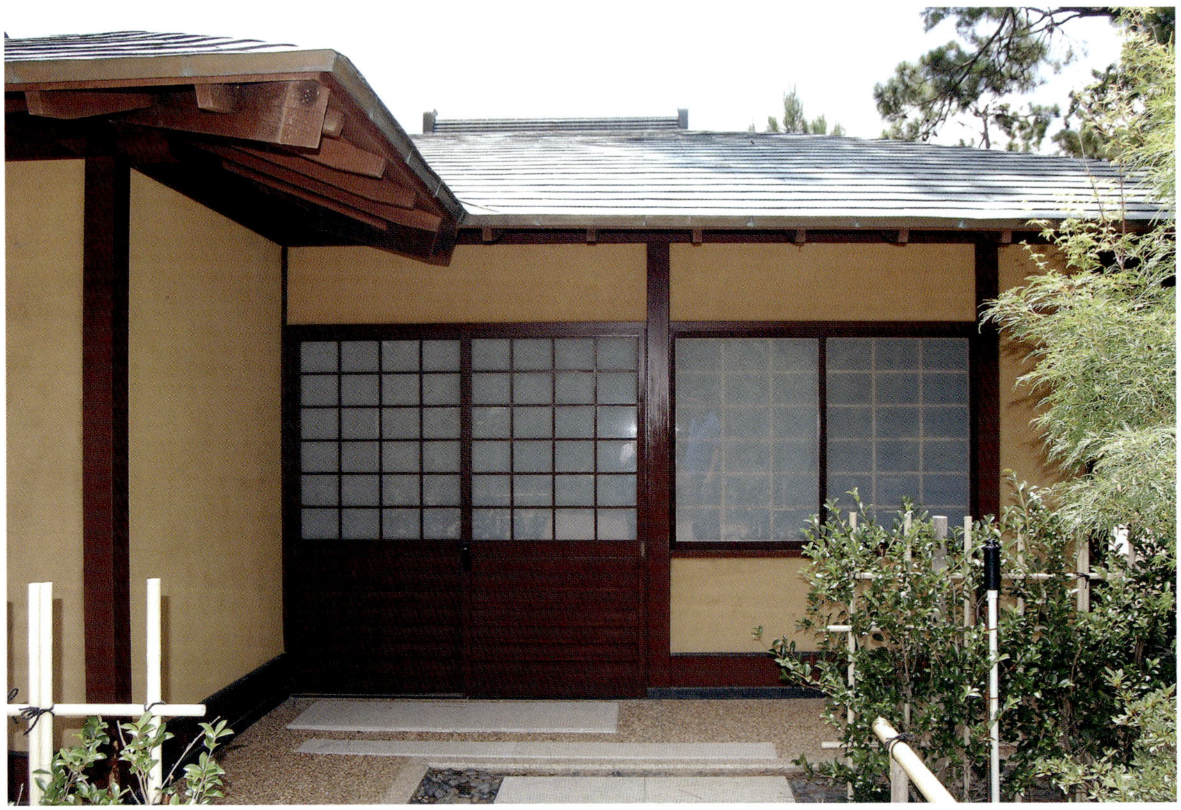

Traditional entrance to the Japanese Teahouse, with sliding rice paper screens, 2012. Photograph by B. S. Bradley.

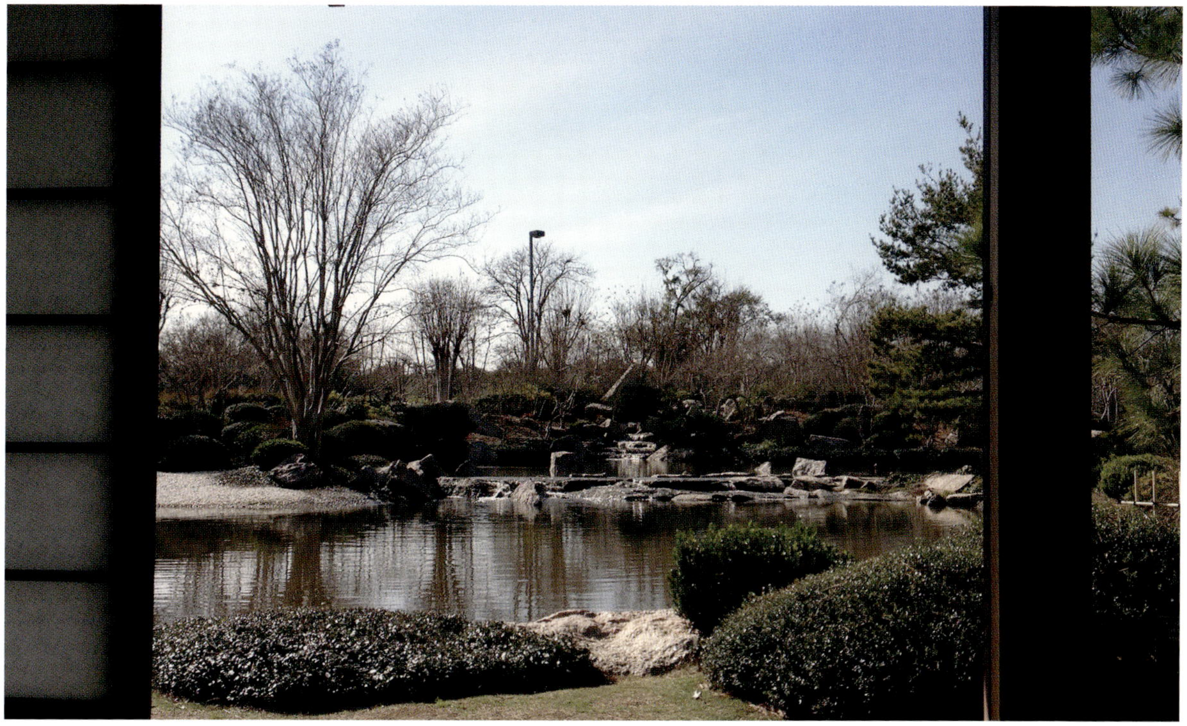

Pond and waterfall viewed from the open Teahouse window, 2012. Photograph by B. S. Bradley.

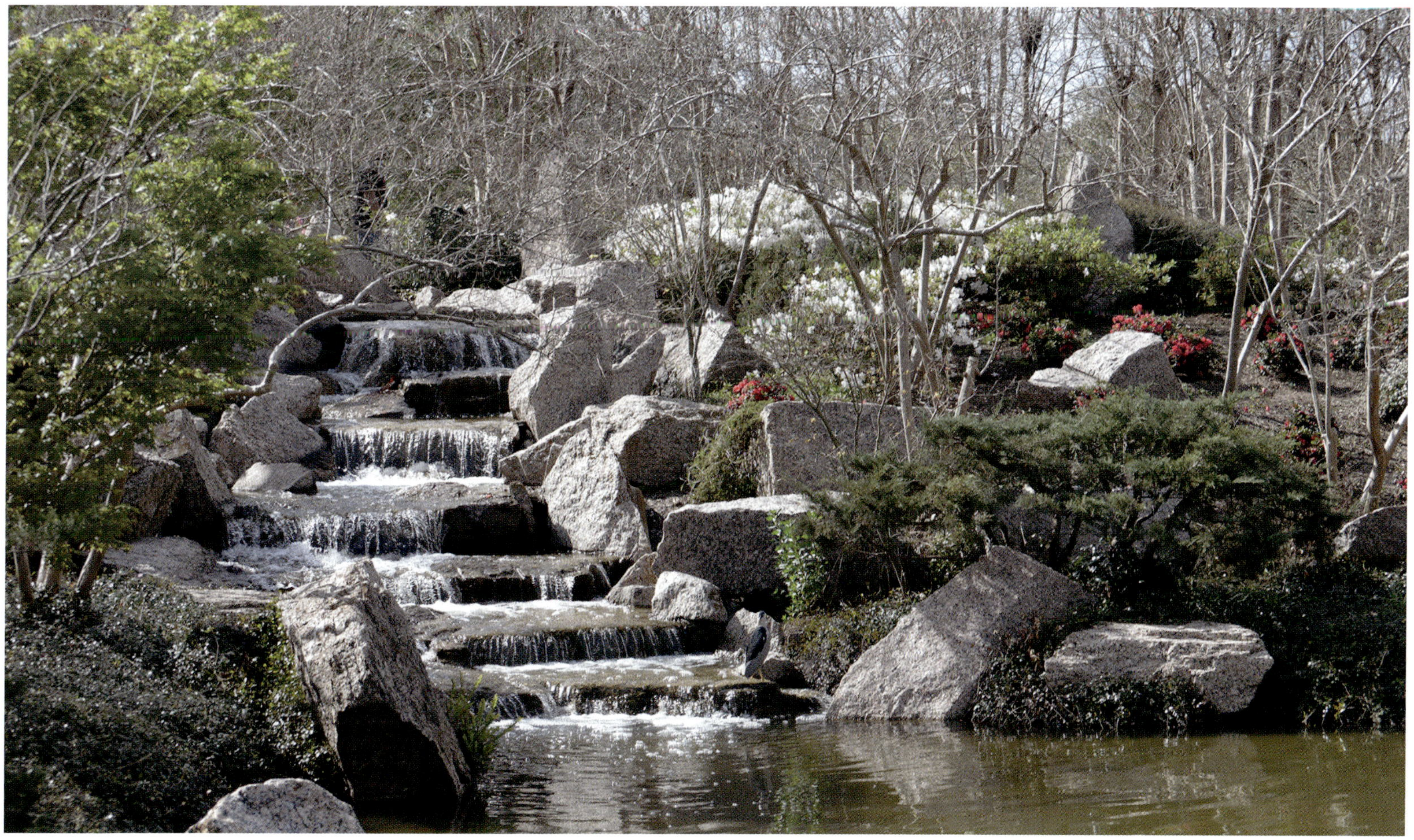

Water Cascade on the far side of the pond from the Teahouse is made of boulders hand chosen by the landscape architect Takeshi "Ken" Nakajima (1914–2000) from Marble Falls, Texas, 2013. Photograph by B. S. Bradley.

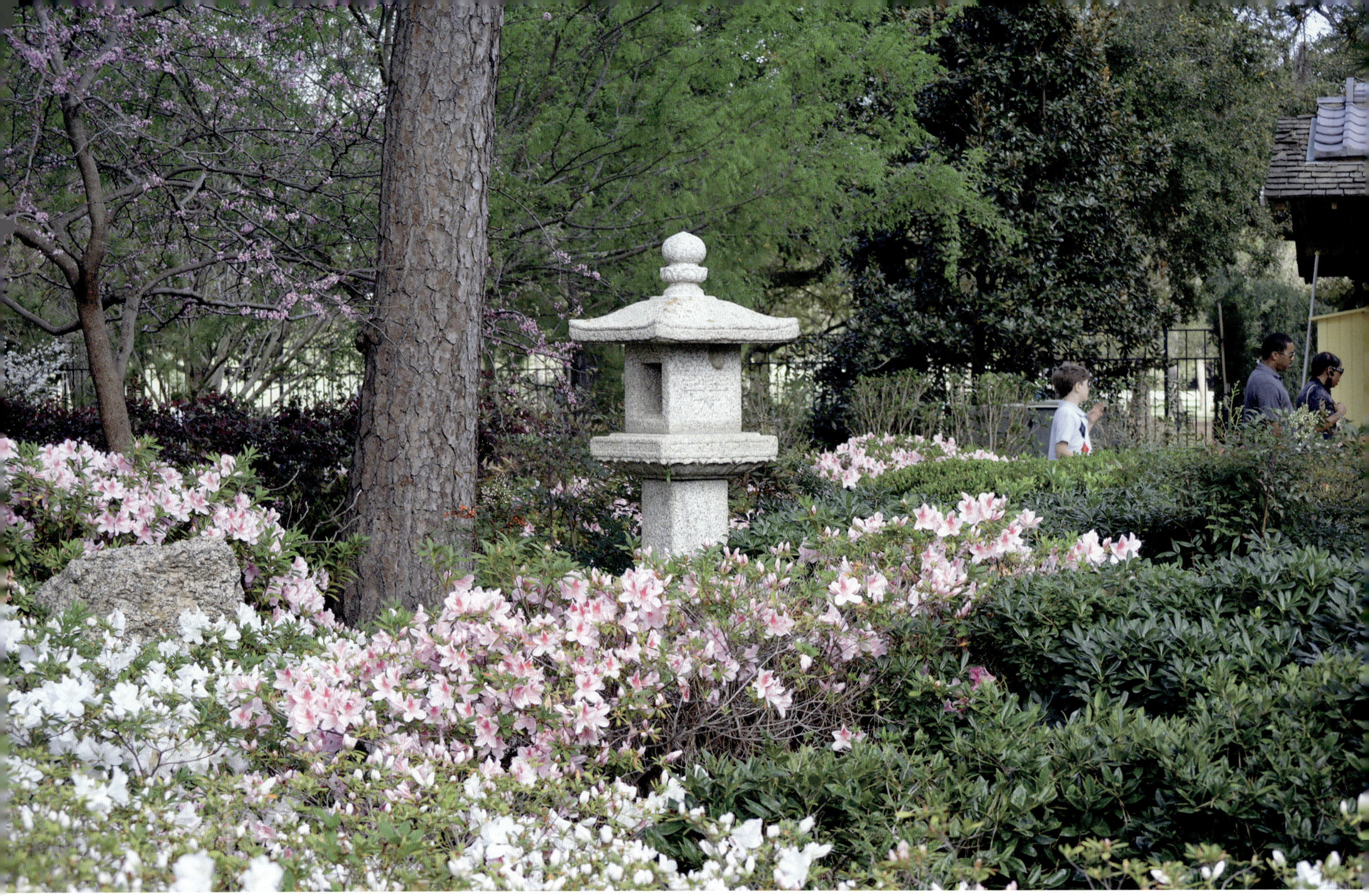

Azaleas and Redbud trees bloom in early March, filling the Japanese Garden with color. The *kasuga* lantern is one of two of this type in the Japanese garden, 2013. Photograph by B. S. Bradley.

leas, Japanese maples, redbuds, dogwoods, peach trees, and cherry trees across arched bridges and through an old pine grove. Nakajima was pleased that Houston's humid climate allowed many species common to gardens in Japan, especially azaleas and crape myrtles. In 1992 he listed the plants with which he "decorated" the garden: "240 crape myrtles, 50 Japanese Maples, 60 Dogwoods, 100 cherry trees, 50 flowering Brazilwoods, 30 Peach trees, 2,500 azaleas, 1,800 grasses (30 varieties), and 1,800 other trees and shrubs (121 varieties)."[17]

A gazebo at the edge of a stream is another contemplative place to rest. From this vantage point one can study the animals that grace the garden: birds, turtles, fish, and squirrels. Japanese gardens purposely provide a sanctuary for animals that, to the Japanese, are as important to the natural world as plants, trees, water, and rocks. While in the garden the senses of sound, sight, touch, and smell should all be engaged. One should journey through Houston's Japanese Garden slowly but attentively, looking up and down as well as straight ahead. The notion of sequence is important in Japanese garden design. Light and shadows across the landscaped paths add another layer of experience. Although Houston does not experience radical seasonal changes, the Japanese Garden does display different atmospheres during spring, summer, fall, and winter. In any season, and perhaps more than any other part of Hermann Park, the Japanese Garden provides a quiet refuge for restoration of the spirit and mind.

By 2006 the Japanese Garden had become Americanized. Houstonian Kunio Minami remembers that annuals like pansies and petunias were planted with little regard for the Japanese aesthetic with which the garden was designed. "It had lost the flavor of a genuine Japanese garden," Minami said.[18] Nakajima's successor, Terunobu Nakai, was hired in 2007 to oversee restoration of the garden. For the next six years until his death in 2012, Nakai made an annual visit to Houston with his

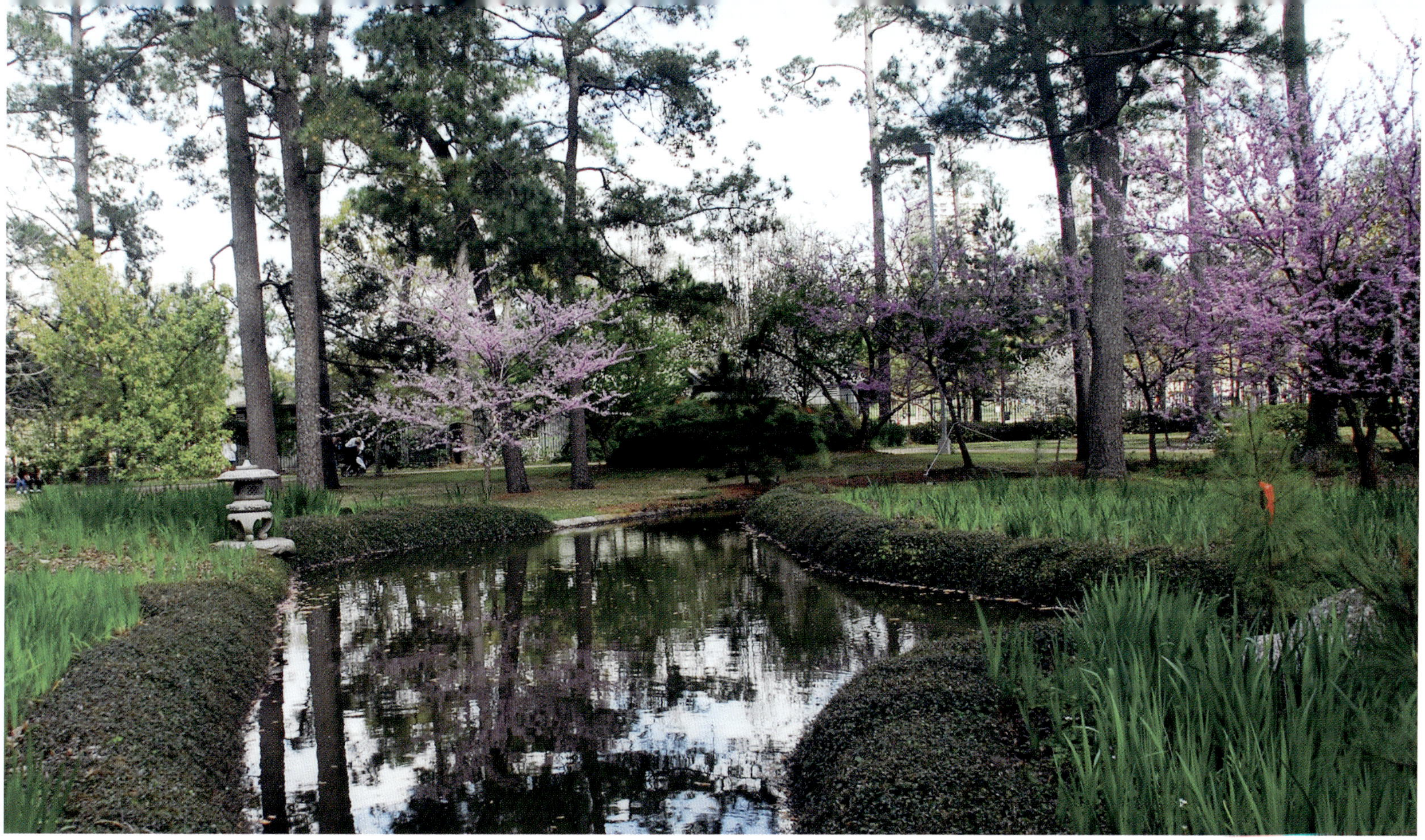

Redbud trees bloom throughout the Japanese Garden in late February and early March, c. 2011. Courtesy Hermann Park Conservancy.

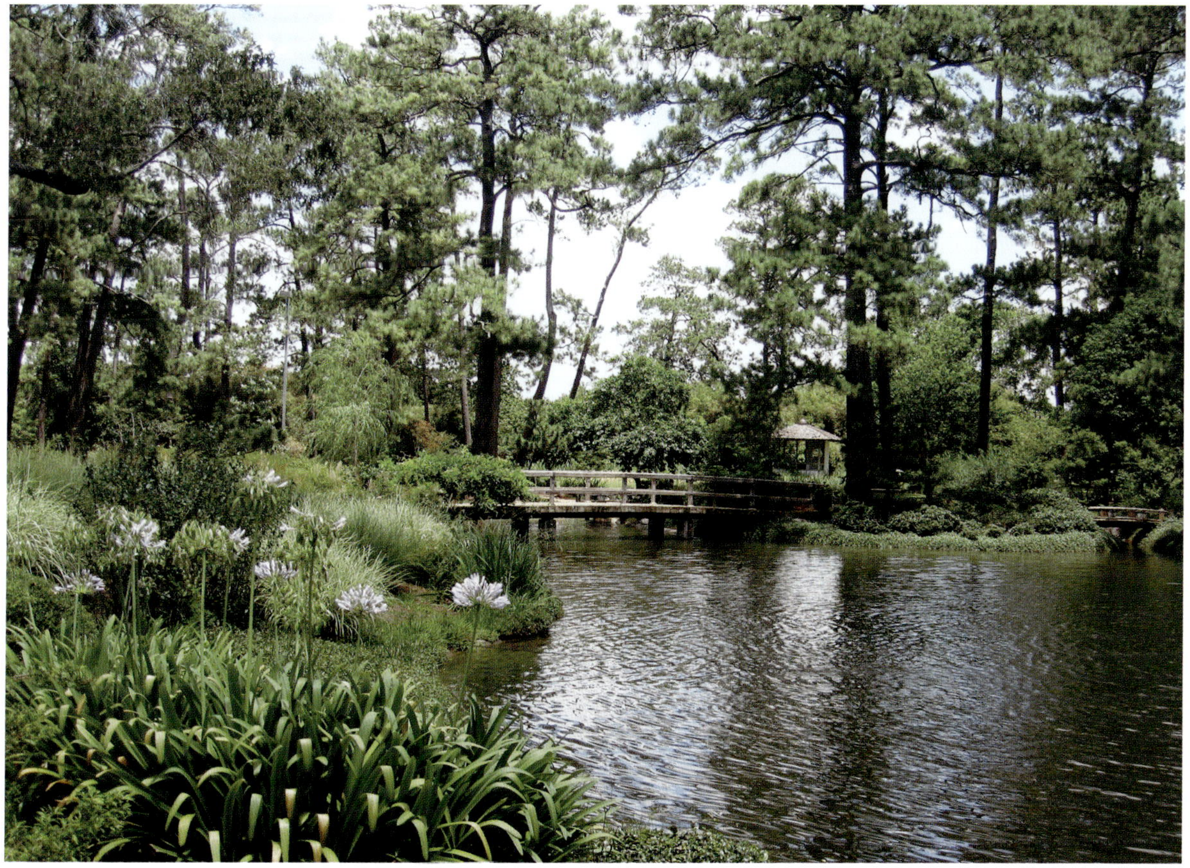

Japanese Garden Bridge with the gazebo in the background and blooming Agapanthus lilies in the foreground. Courtesy Hermann Park Conservancy.

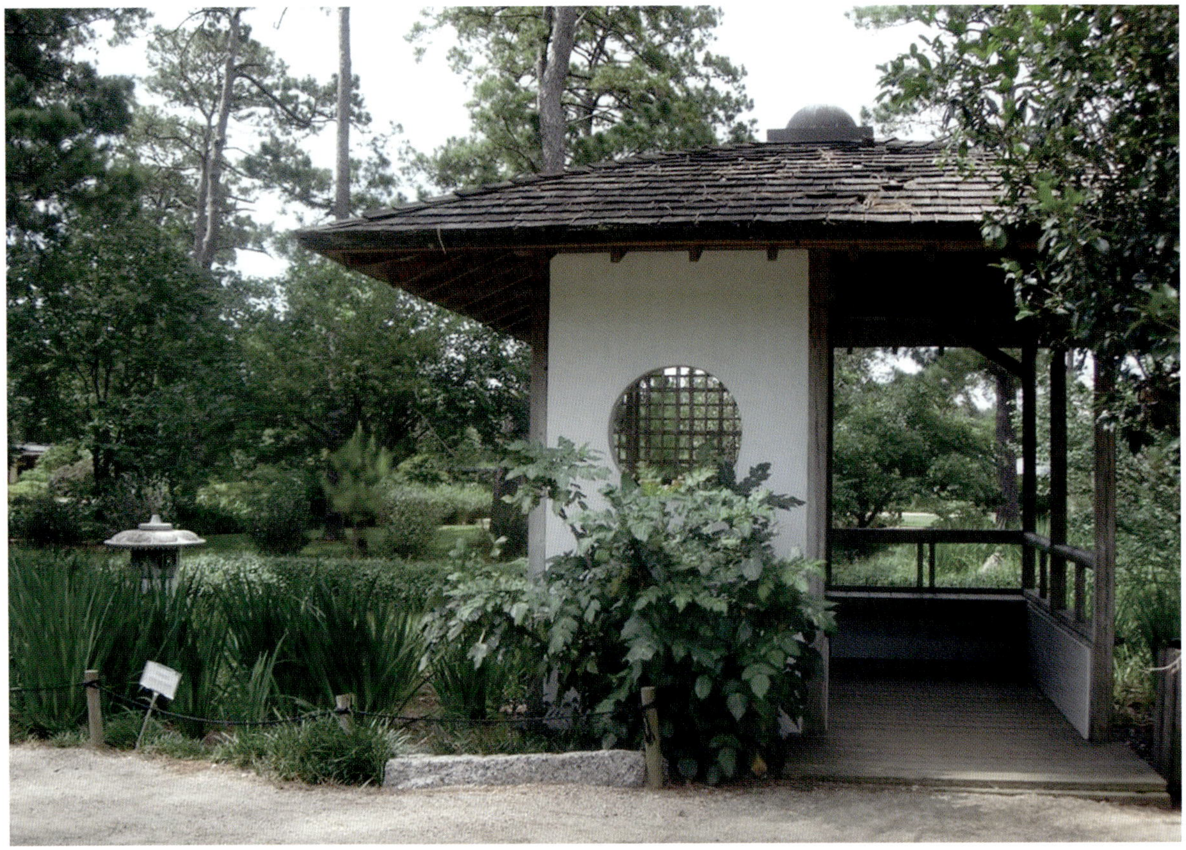

Japanese Garden Gazebo, 2012. Courtesy Hermann Park Conservancy.

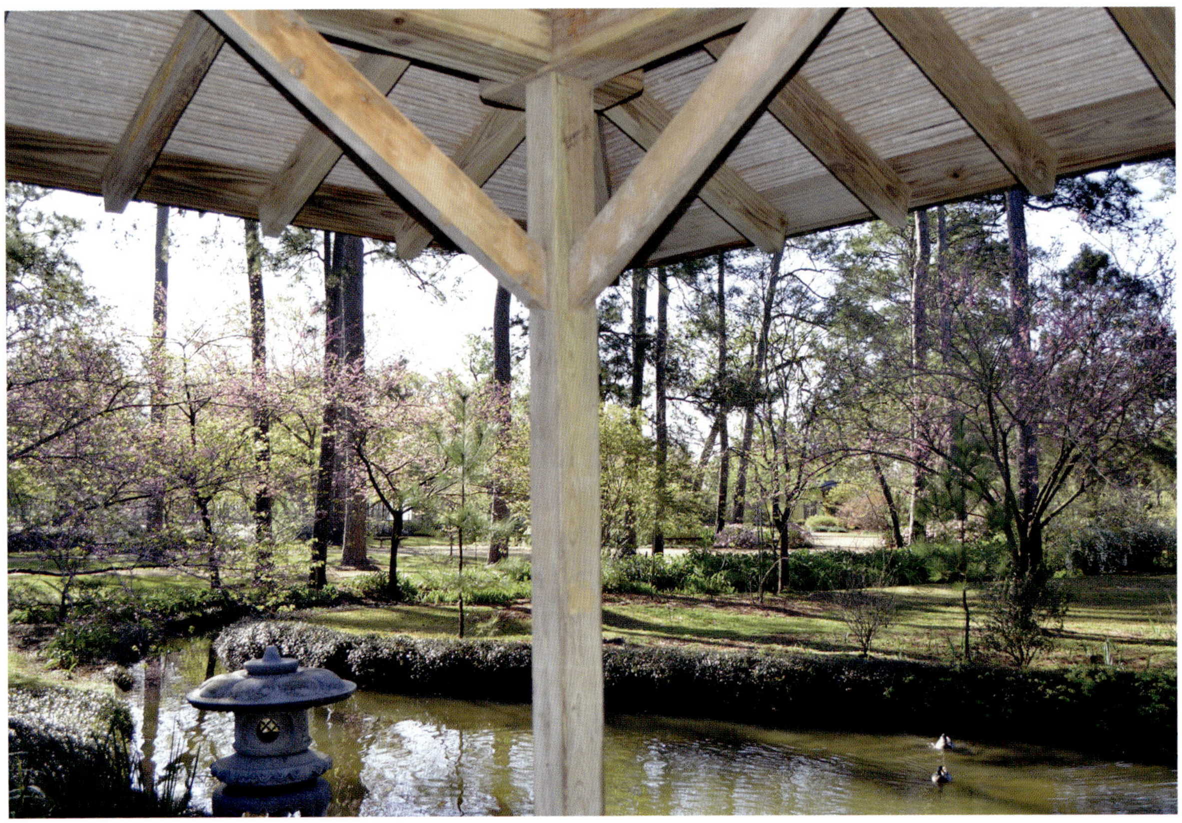

View of the Japanese Garden from the gazebo, 2011. Photograph by B. S. Bradley.

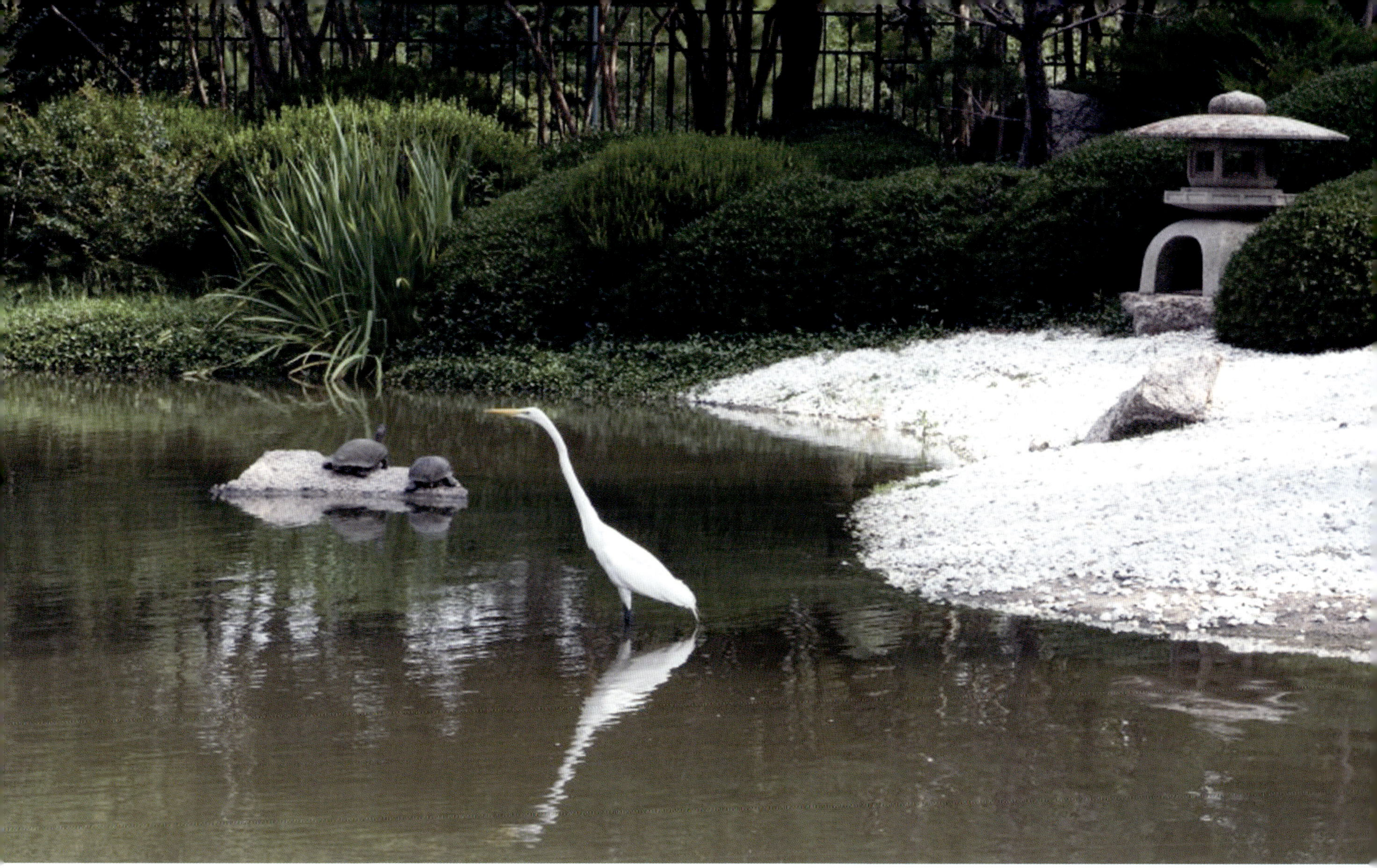

Great white egret and turtles climbing on a rock into the sun at the edge of the pond near the Chiba city lantern, 2010. All sorts of wildlife are protected and enjoyed in Hermann Park. Photograph by Chiani Ridley.

associate Aya Hashimoto and master Japanese gardeners Hiroshi Iwasaki and his son Taiki Iwasaki to teach as well as prune and improve the garden. The entrance gate area, wisteria trellis, bamboo fences, and tea garden were created by Nakai. New stepping stones are from local stone yards, but the white granite pavers around the teahouse are from China, the origin of most stone now used in gardens throughout the world.

From their first visit, Nakai, Hashimoto, and the Iwasakis have continued to train those who work in the garden in the art of *sukashi*, a Japanese pruning technique that takes into consideration the tree's foliage, character, and background. Nakai noted that flowers do not play a large part in Japanese gardens. Greens predominate, while rocks and other hardscape elements offer balance. Japanese gardens use flowering plants with solitary blooms, such as irises and lilies, because flower forms are more important than a mass of color. In Japan, he explained, gardens are for relaxing, revitalizing, and communing with nature.[19] Houston's Japanese Garden is about 90 percent organic. This environ-

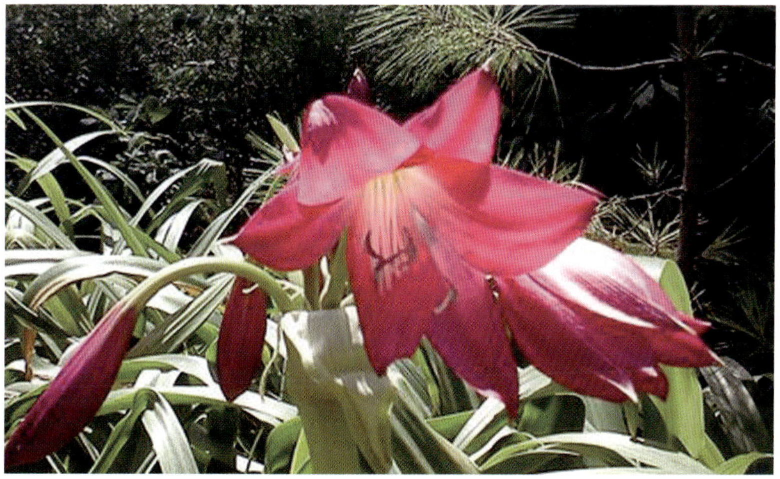

"Ellen Bosanquet" Crinum Lily blooms in the Japanese Garden in spring, 2012. This is an example of the single bloom type of flower found most often in Japanese gardens, where masses of annuals are never used. Courtesy Hermann Park Conservancy.

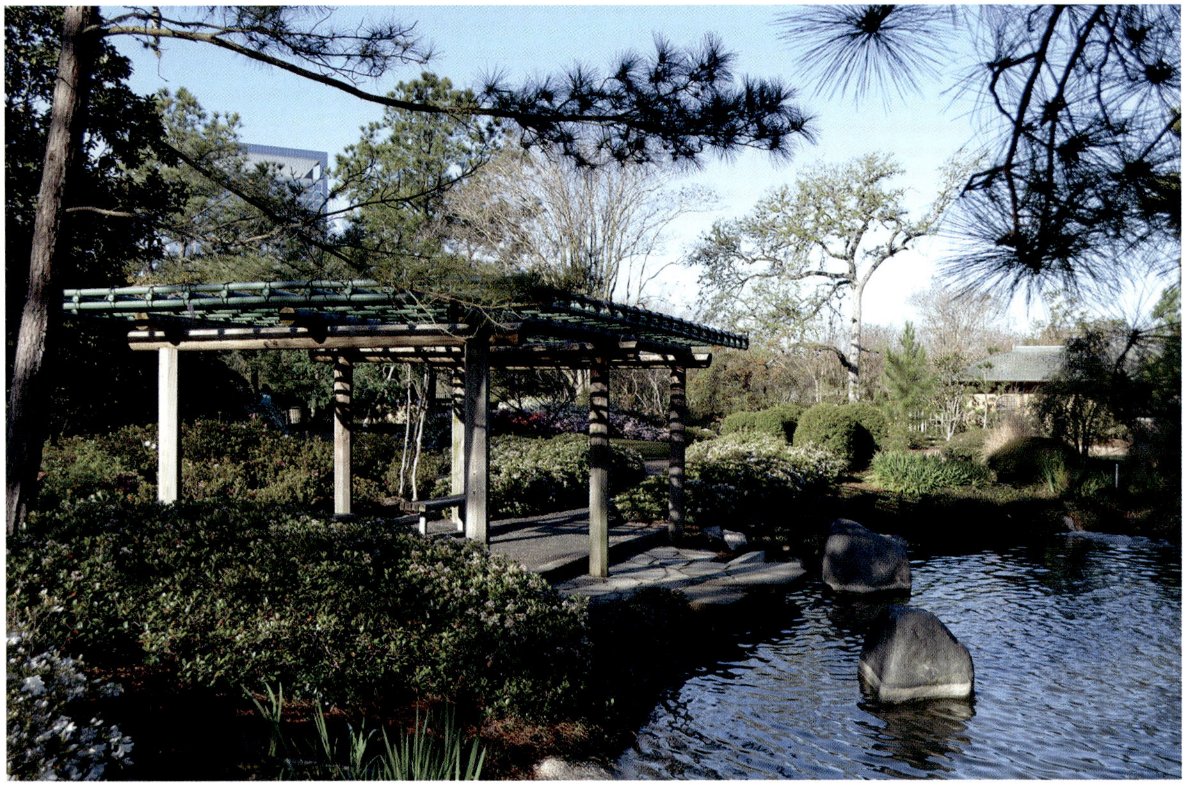

The wisteria pergola provides a place to view the lush landscape and calming water that make the Japanese Garden peaceful and green throughout the year, 2013. Photograph by B. S. Bradley.

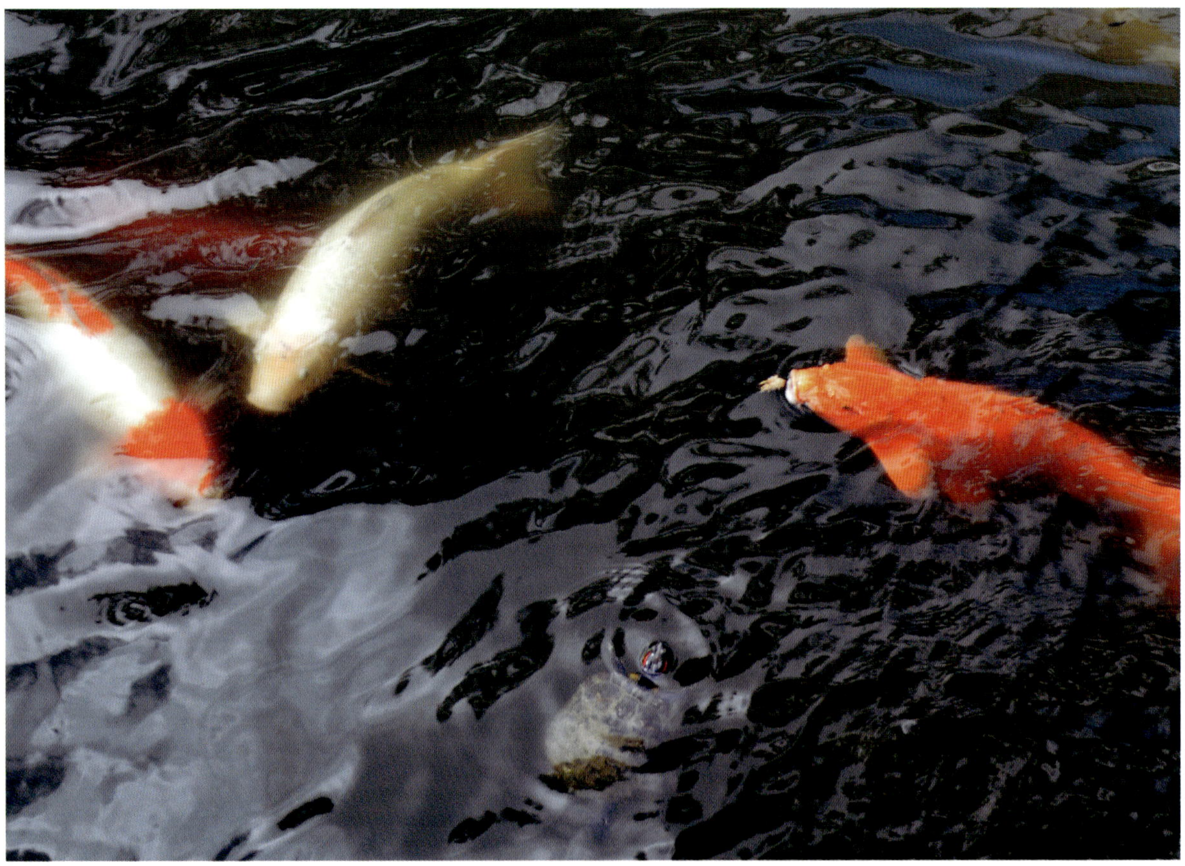

Large Koi (*nishikigoi*) swim with turtles in the Japanese Garden pond, 2013. Photograph by B. S. Bradley.

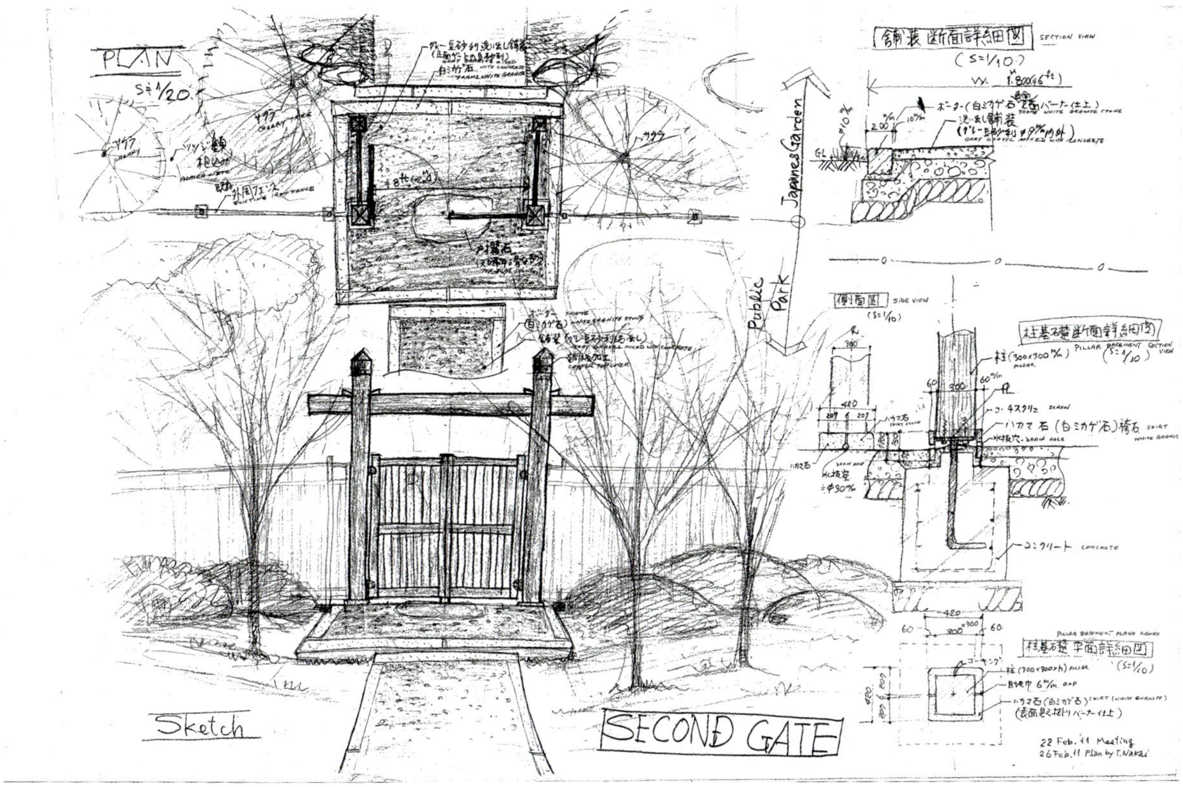

Drawing for a second gate to the Japanese Garden (2012, Terunobiu Nakai). Courtesy Hermann Park Conservancy.

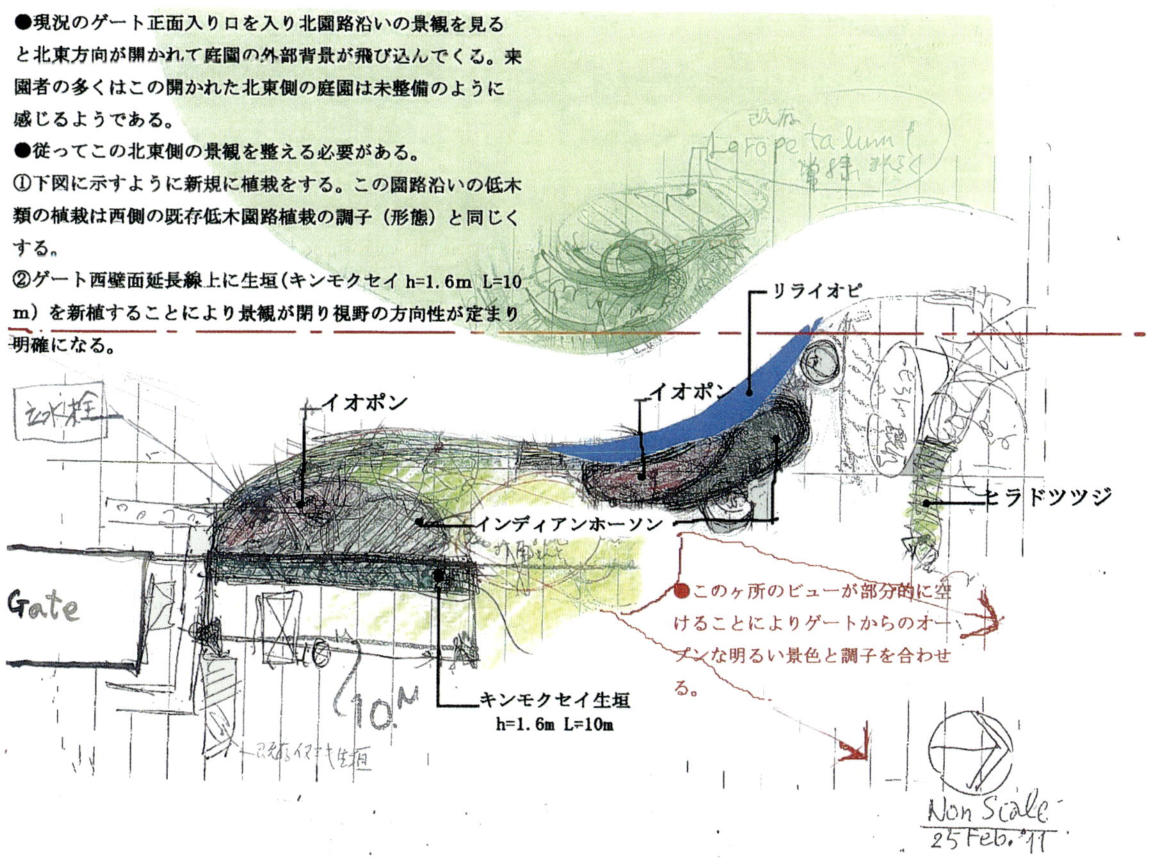

Drawing and specifications in Japanese for Japanese Garden (2012, Terunobiu Nakai). Courtesy Hermann Park Conservancy.

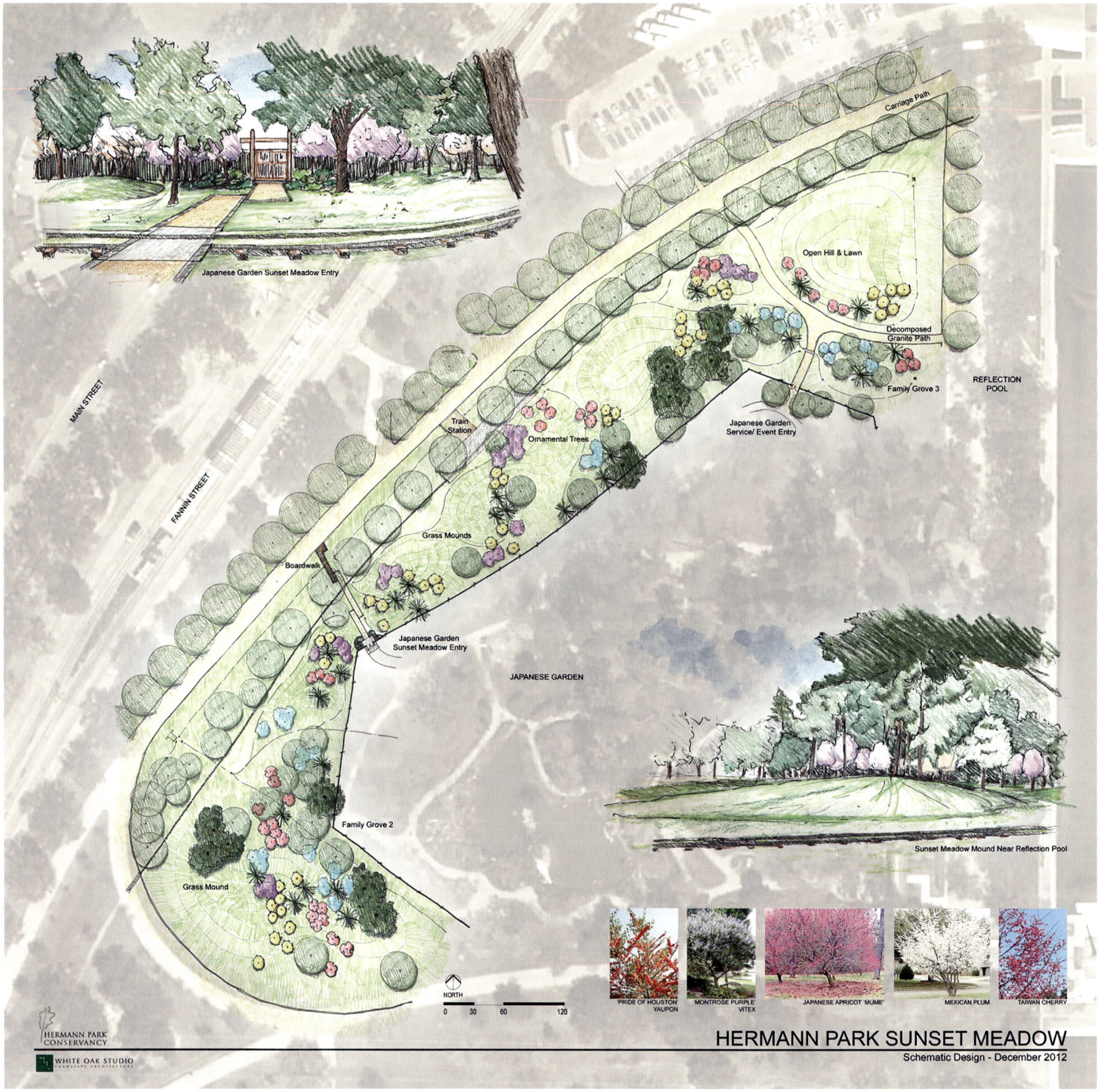

Sunset Meadow (2012, White Oak Studio) will be located outside of the northwestern edge of the Japanese Garden and will include a second gate to the Japanese Gardens envisioned by Nakai. Courtesy Hermann Park Conservancy.

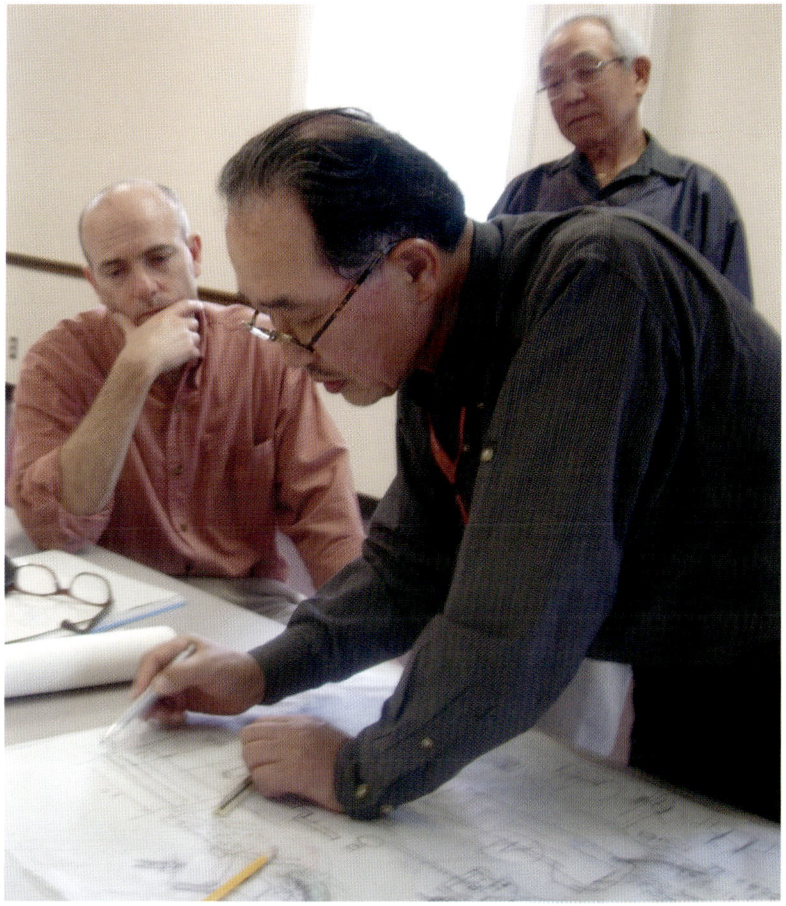

Terunobiu Nakai at work on Japanese Garden plans with Jim Patterson of White Oak Studio and Kunio Minami, 2011. Courtesy Hermann Park Conservancy.

mental responsibility is not only an outgrowth of traditional Japanese gardening, but also for protection of the beautiful Koi that live in the ponds.[20]

On his last visit in 2011, Nakai met with White Oak Studio landscape architect Jim Patterson, who has long been involved in fulfilling the park's master plan objectives, to discuss improvements to the Fannin Street side of the park and explore the possibility of installing a second pedestrian gate into the Japanese Garden. A design charrette took place during the visit, which resulted in renderings of the potential gate, trail access, landscaping around the entry, and repositioning of two service gates into the garden. The new entrance would accommodate those entering the park from the Rice University METRORail stop.[21] Aya Hashimoto, who has taken over Nakai's work here, focused her 2012 visit on planning for the new gate and landscaping along the outer perimeter of the garden.[22]

As beautiful and well-maintained as the Hermann Park Japanese Garden is, Kunio Minami laments that some children who come into the garden with their parents run off the paths, trample fragile plants, and are unaware that their loud, boisterous behavior is disturbing in this type of garden setting. "This garden is supposed to be a place of peace where you listen to the water and the birds and look at the beautiful flowers and trees."[23]

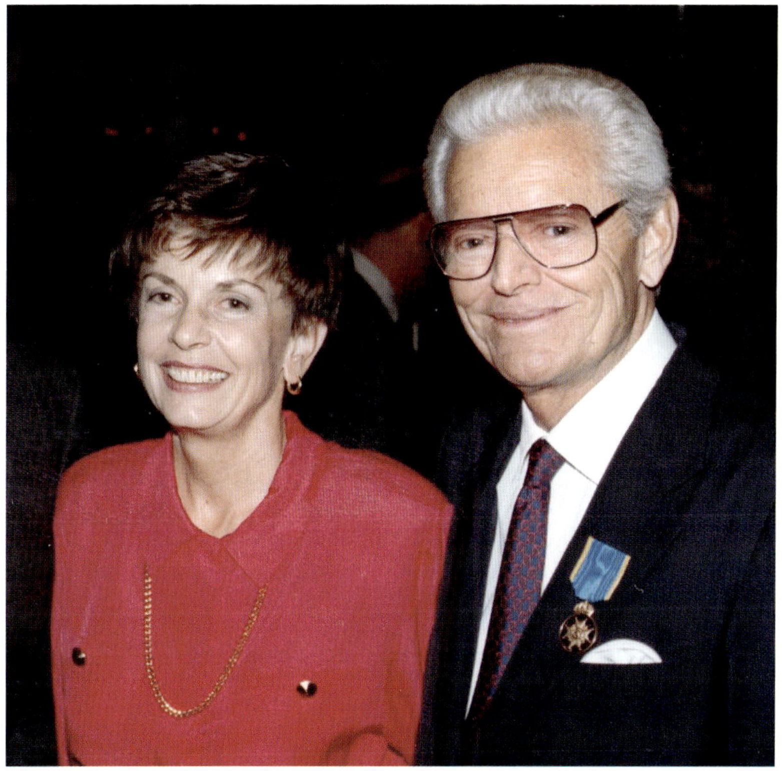

Dr. and Mrs. John P. McGovern, 1988. Courtesy Kathrine McGovern.

John P. McGovern Lake

The generosity of Kathrine and John McGovern made possible the expansion and conservation of Houston's only inner-city lake. Dr. and Mrs. McGovern's interest in Hermann Park began in the 1960s, when they played tennis on the clay courts that Kathrine McGovern remembers as being quite shabby. The nature-loving couple was drawn to the lake where geese chased them as they fed peanuts to the squirrels and looked for holes, visible from the lake edge, where bass laid their eggs. They would watch the holes day after day looking for the baby bass to hatch and swim away. When they decided to make a substantial gift to the Hermann Park Conservancy to enlarge and refurbish the lake, Dr. McGovern stipulated that areas in or around the lake had to be set aside for nesting and migratory birds where boats and people could not go.[24]

Kathrine McGovern is among the many birdwatchers who enjoy the birds of Hermann Park. One of her favorites is the yellow-crowned night heron, which she notes has returned to the area since the establishment of the bird habitats in McGovern Lake. The Houston Audubon

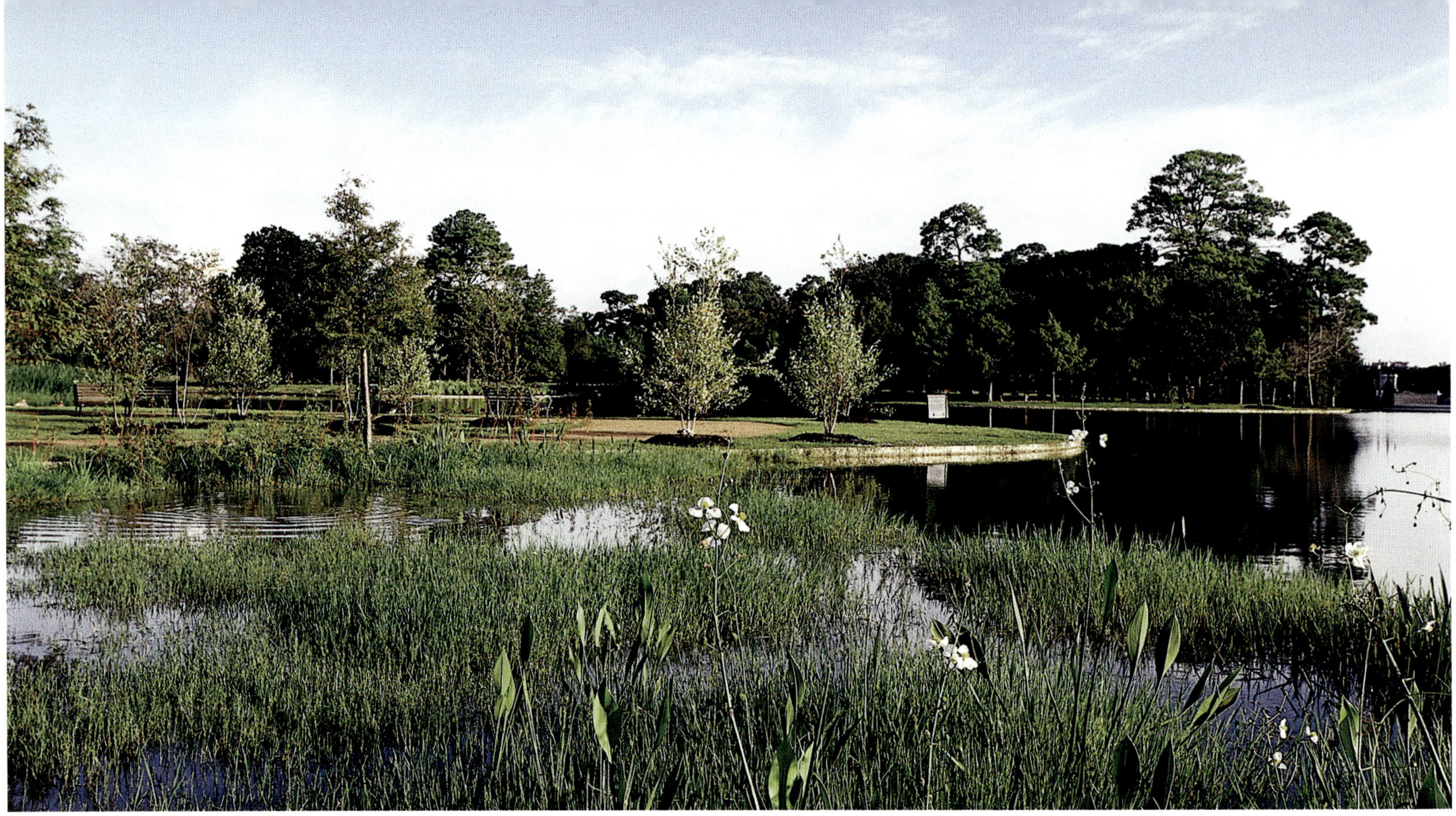

Wetland plantings including marshy grasses and lilies beautify the shores of McGovern Lake, c. 2010. Photograph by Joe Aker. Courtesy Hermann Park Conservancy.

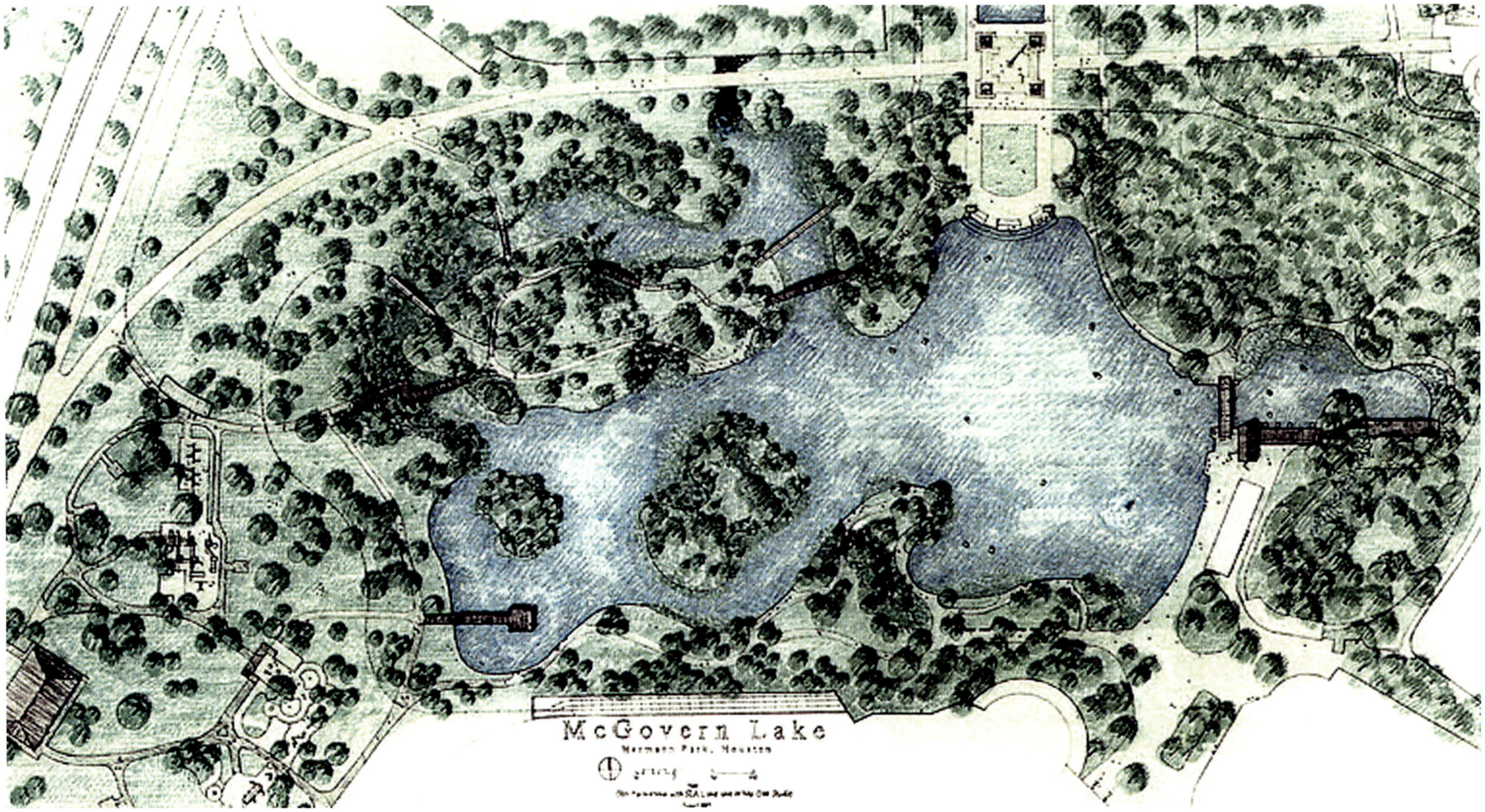

McGovern Lake rendering (2004, White Oak Studio) that shows the large and small islands established as sanctuaries for migrating birds. The lake, or Grand Basin as it was originally known, was doubled in size. Courtesy Hermann Park Conservancy.

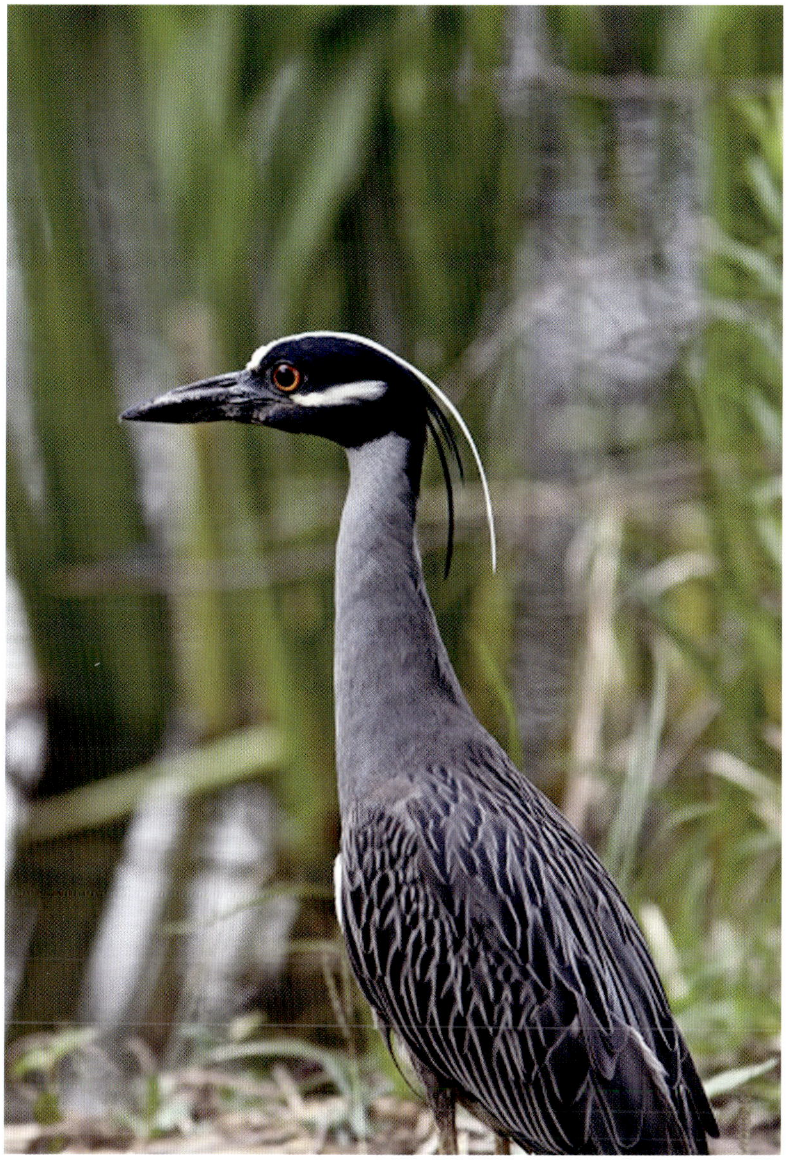

Yellow-crowned Night Heron in Hermann Park, 2012. The birds of Hermann Park have multiplied year by year as the park is reforested and bird habitats are established. Photograph by Ben Hulsey, Houston Audubon Society.

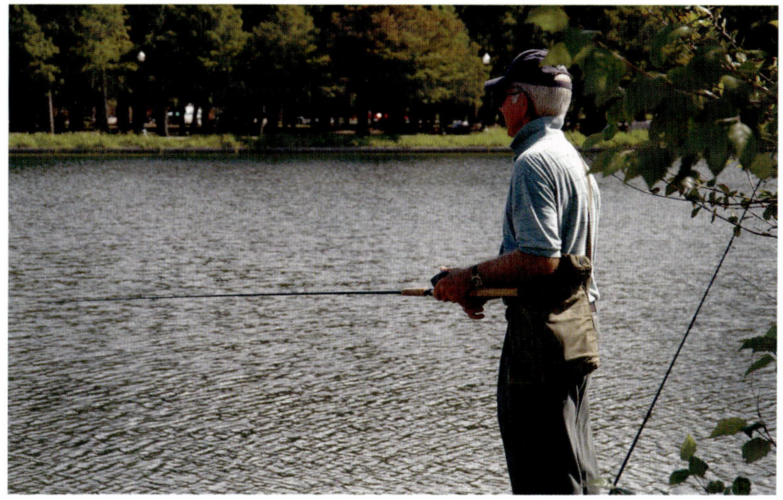

Fishing on McGovern Lake is a popular pastime, but it is limited to those under age twelve and over age sixty-five. Catch and release is strongly recommended and adhered to by most of those who fish in Hermann Park, 2005. Photograph by Kasey Marsh. Courtesy Hermann Park Conservancy.

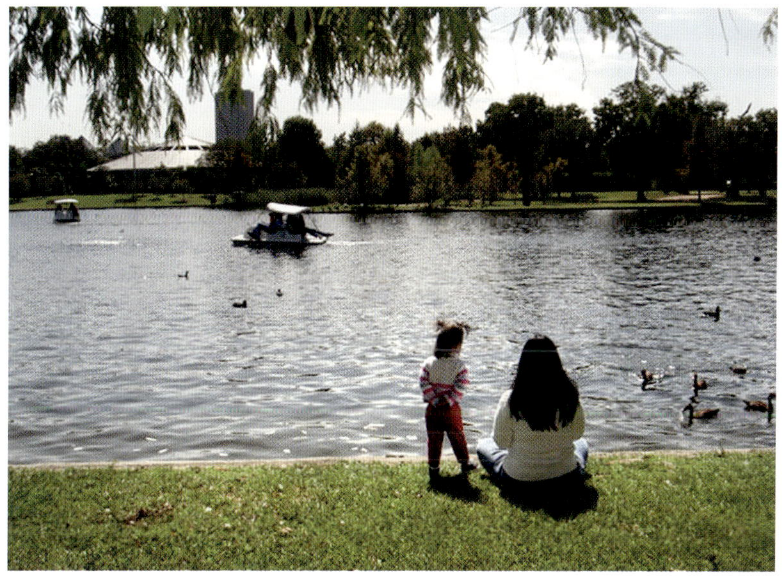

Mom and daughter feeding ducks on McGovern Lake, 2010. Courtesy Hermann Park Conservancy.

Society, whose volunteers compile monthly bird counts in Hermann Park, has identified ninety-nine different kinds of birds that have been seen in the park at one time or another in recent years. Their statistics for a seven-month period give a good overview of these park inhabitants (see appendix 5). Volunteers have also compiled a remarkable photographic archive of birds seen in the park.[25] Photographer Ben Hulsey notes, "Hermann Park is a good place to watch or photograph birds because you are more likely to find birds that are used to having people around and, as a result, are more cooperative subjects."[26] The birdcalls and birdsongs of avian life can be heard throughout the park, adding sound to the senses that are constantly and delightfully stimulated in Hermann Park.

When Laurie Olin gave form to the "new" lake during the master planning process, he made sure bird sanctuaries were included. The lake was enlarged to almost twice its size and an extensive portion of it was dedicated to wildlife habitat on three new islands with wetland plantings and native meadow grasses. White Oak Studio and SLA Studio Land prepared the final design and construction documents. The de-

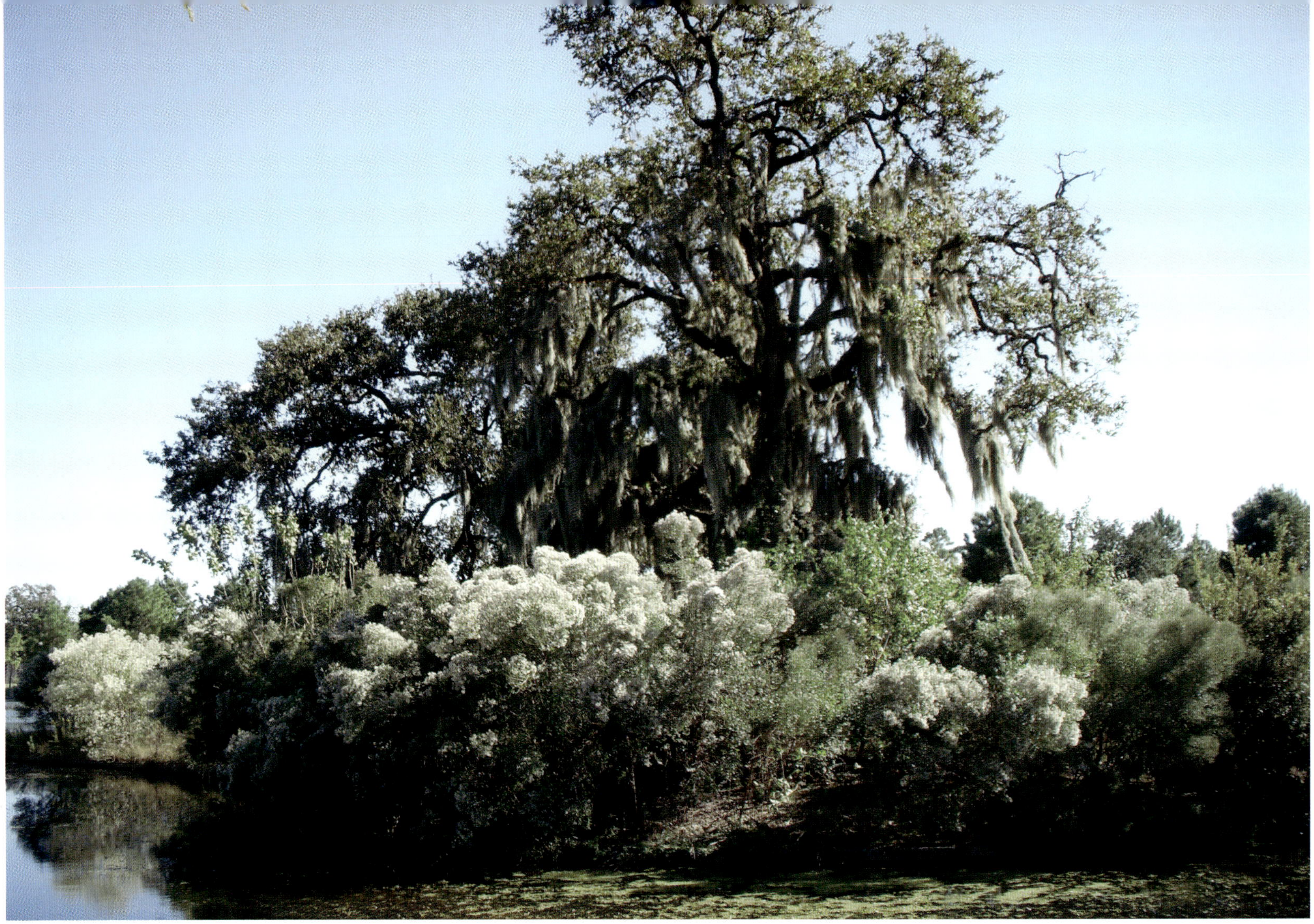

McGovern Lake's large island was established as a habitat for migratory birds. The graceful overhanging trees and plants soften the edge of the lake, 2010. Courtesy Hermann Park Conservancy.

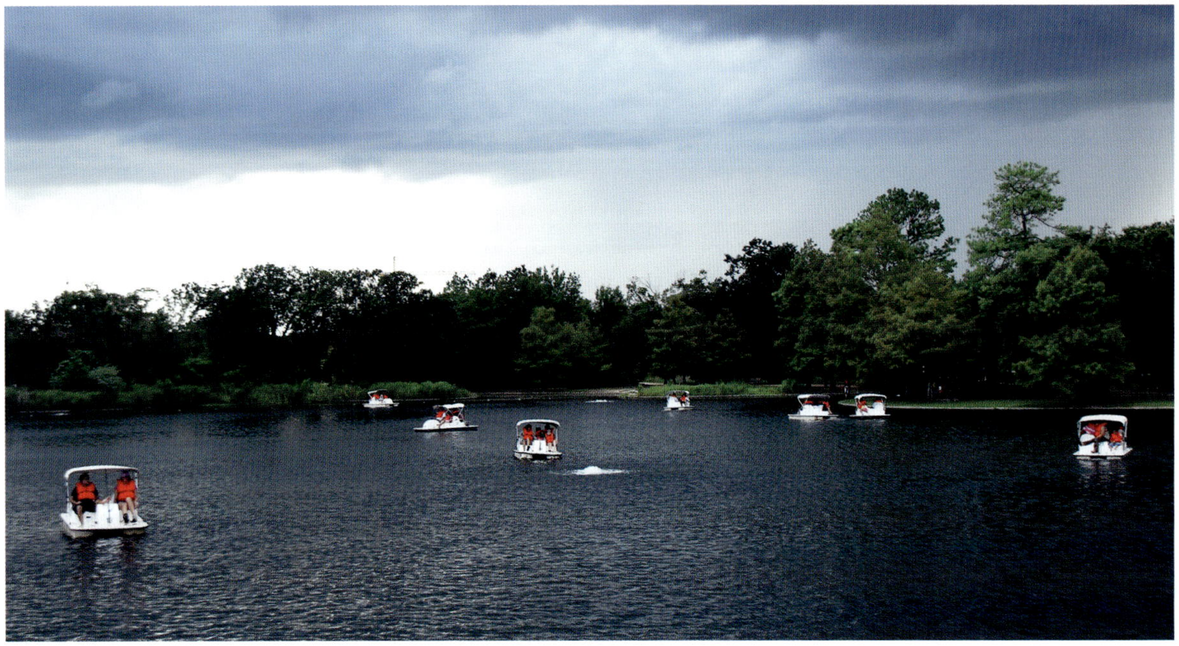

Pedal boats on McGovern Lake viewed from the Tiffany Bridge, 2012. Courtesy Hermann Park Conservancy.

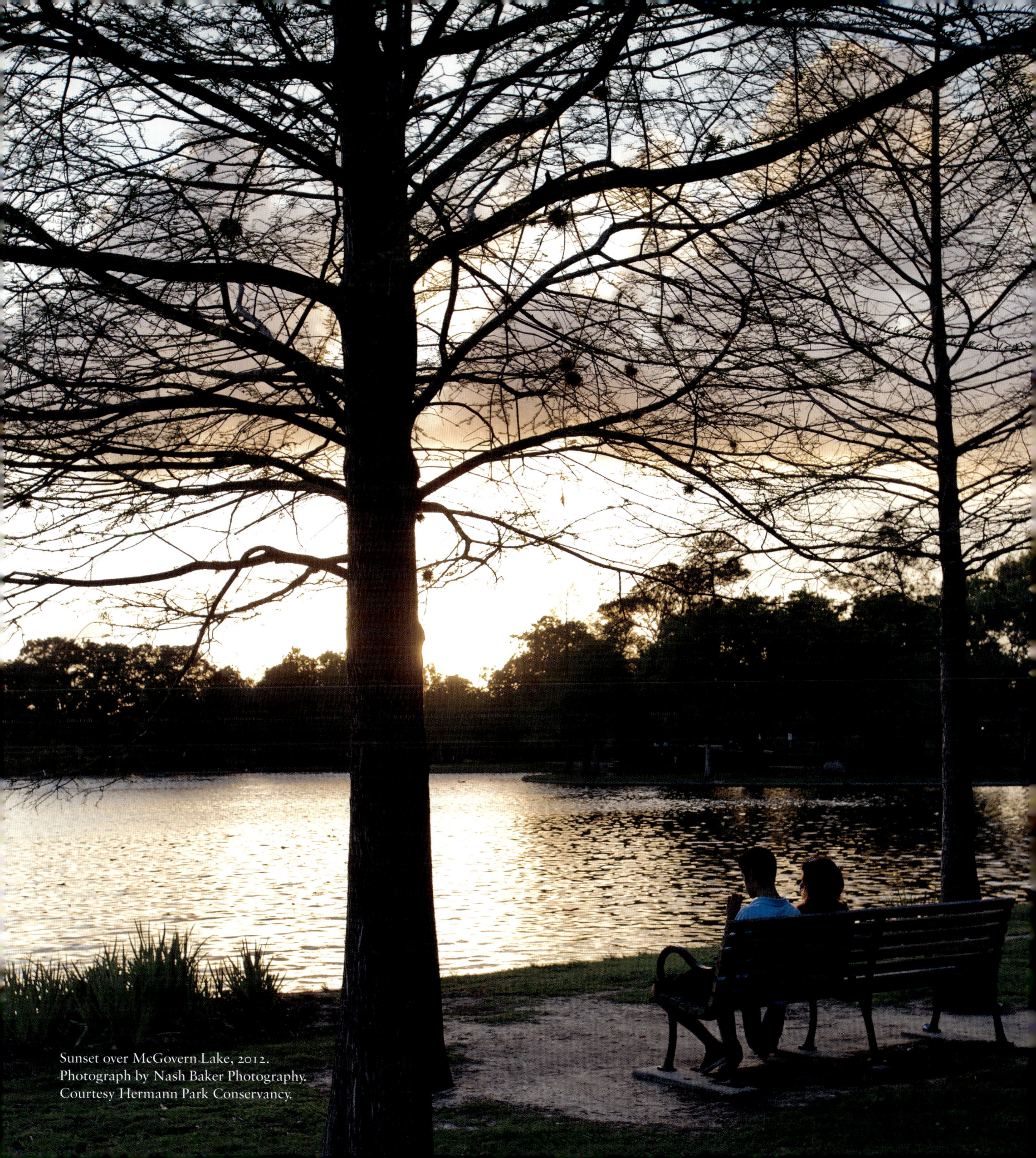

Sunset over McGovern Lake, 2012.
Photograph by Nash Baker Photography.
Courtesy Hermann Park Conservancy.

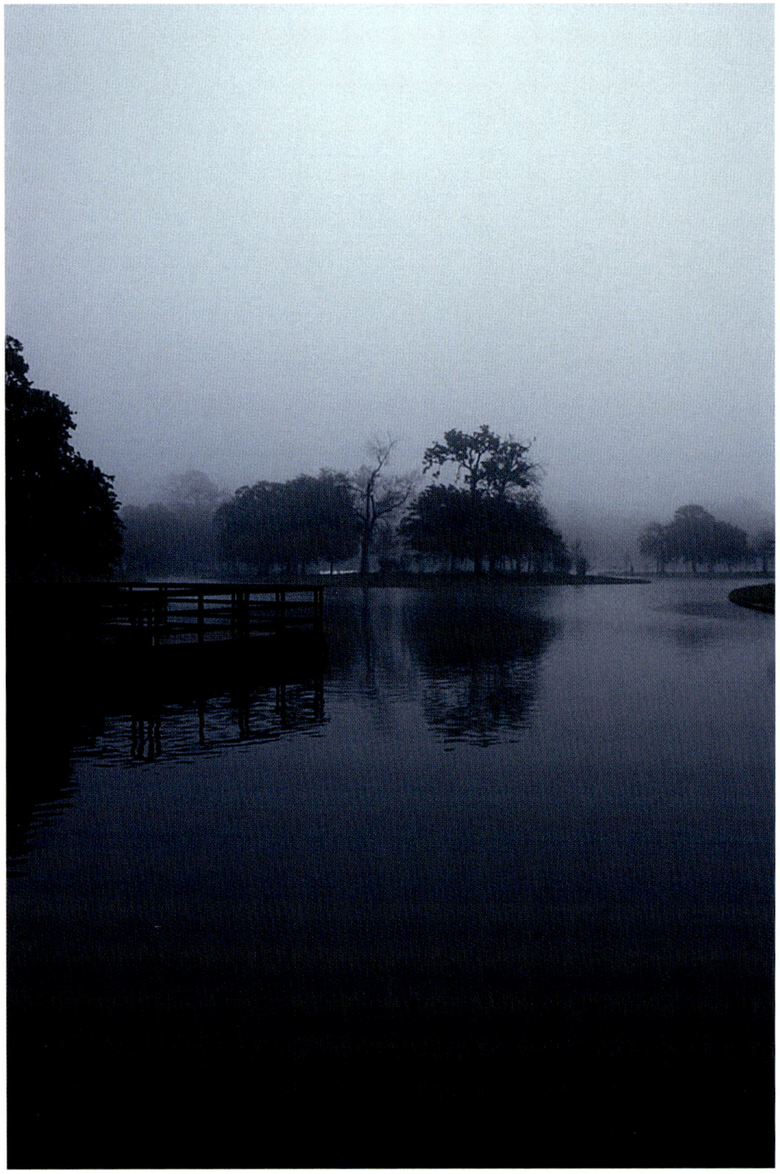

McGovern Lake in morning fog with Bob's Fishing Pier, 2008. Photograph by Jay Baker, FAIA. Courtesy Hermann Park Conservancy.

sign team consulted many experts to ensure that McGovern Lake would be environmentally responsible and safe: the Texas Parks and Wildlife Commission, the Harris County Flood Control District, childhood safety experts, lake maintenance experts, and environmental design professionals. Two key people involved were Jeff Henson, a biologist with Texas Parks and Wildlife Commission, and Joe Doggett, a fishing and outdoor expert and a writer for the *Houston Chronicle*.

After the Texas Parks and Wildlife Commission relocated all the fish, the lake was drained, and excavation began in August 1999. Filling the lake began in September 2000, and, by spring of 2001, the water was ready for restocking of the fish. Fat head minnows, blue gill, fingerling largemouth bass, and channel catfish were introduced one species at a time. A sophisticated aeration system was installed to maintain a healthy environment for fish and wildlife, while minimizing growth of undesirable vegetation. After the fish had a chance to acclimate, grow, and reproduce, Bob's Fishing Pier was opened in April 2002 for those under twelve and over sixty-five. Picnic tables and new paths from the pier that lead to the playground make this a prime area for grandparents to take grandchildren. The pier is named in memory of Bob Kaim, who was a prominent Houston businessman and managing principal of the Galleria.

All the borders of McGovern Lake have a trenched concrete edge that enhances safety for families with young children, who are tempted to wander too close when they feed the ducks. The concrete is softened and obscured by overhanging trees and plantings around the lake. The miniature train travels across the largest of the three bird islands to give its riders a chance to see a number of bird species that inhabit the island or pass through on migration. The two smaller islands are kept isolated. In addition to new plantings on the islands, new trees, shrubs, and native perennials were introduced on all sides of the lake.

McGovern Lake was opened to the public on April 21, 2001. The highlight of opening ceremony was an art boat parade in the tradition of Houston's famous Art Car Parade. Institutions in and around the park decorated fifteen pedal boats. The number of pedal boats, a popular attraction in Hermann Park, was increased, and, as part of the Lake Plaza project, new docks and facilities were built. McGovern Lake has been dubbed one of the most romantic places in Houston to take a date. In the fog, at dawn, or at dusk, the lake is particularly bucolic. Construction of McGovern Lake was accomplished in record time and within its $3.8 million budget. Completion of the lake was quickly followed by the groundbreaking of the Heart of the Park projects.

Lake Plaza

After completion of the Heart of the Park and McGovern Lake, it was time for the conservancy to tackle the lakefront between McGovern Lake and the entrance to the zoo. This $15 million, 8-acre project was the most program-rich and complicated one the conservancy had undertaken. The San Antonio architects Overland Partners teamed up with Jim Patterson of White Oak Studio to design the buildings, terraces, and plantings, with the Olin Partnership as planner and consultant. Construction began in January 2008 on a café, restrooms, the train station, and a boathouse and docks.

This was a large, bleak open area that led from the treeless parking lot to the zoo and lakefront. The goal of the Lake Plaza project was to update services and landscape the area in an environmentally responsible and beautiful way. Energy conservation was also a major factor in the design. Surveys told planners that this area needed rest-

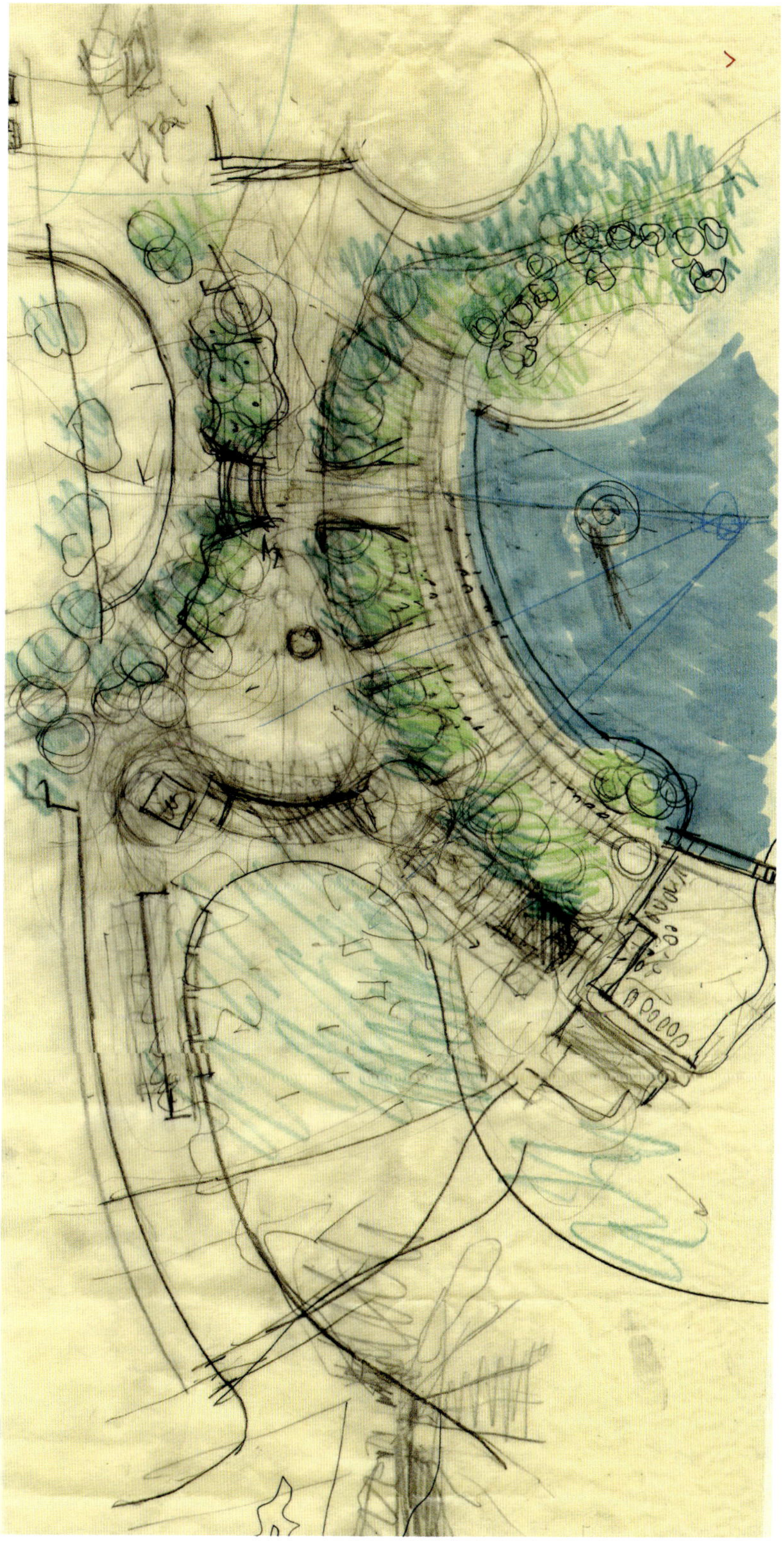

Conceptual design sketch for Lake Plaza (2008, Overland Partners). Courtesy Hermann Park Conservancy.

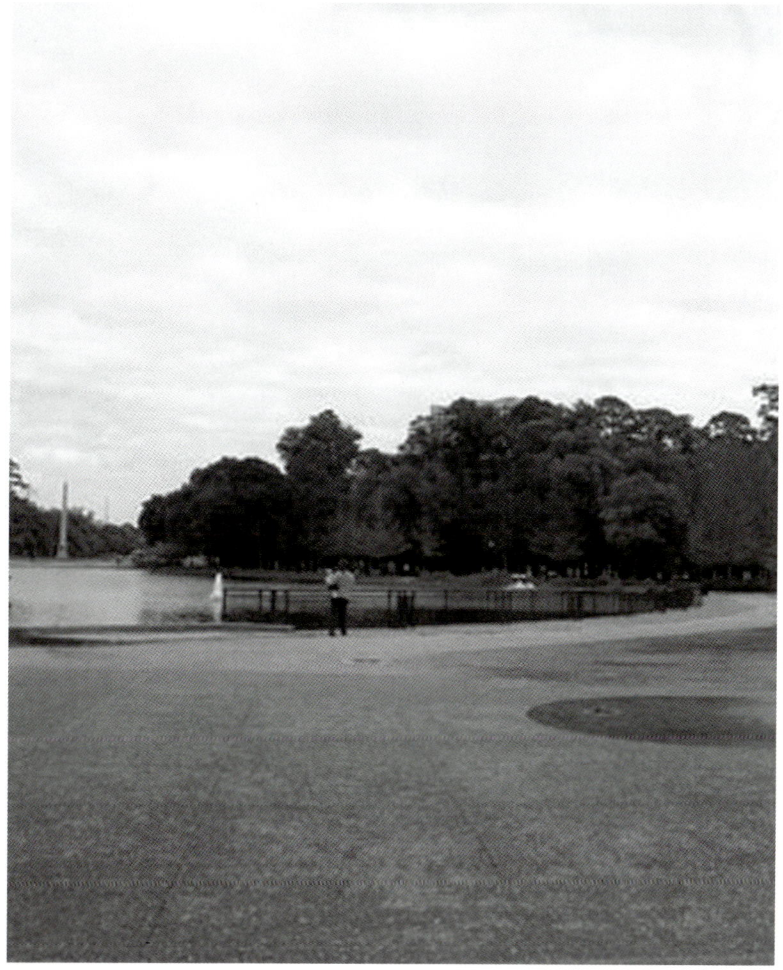

Lake Plaza area with barriers to lake access before reconstruction, c. 1995. Courtesy Hermann Park Conservancy.

room facilities and a café, which were incorporated between the train and pedal boat concessions. Kinder Station, the new railroad station, incorporated ticket sales and a gift shop. Brick paving, low concrete garden walls, and concrete coping echo in Lake Plaza the subtle, warm color and materials used in the Heart of the Park. Mature trees in this area were revived, and beds of blooming herbaceous plants accent the generous open walkways. Completed in record time, most of Lake Plaza opened in April 2009.

The Mary Gibbs and Jesse H. Jones Greenway

The Jones Greenway replaced a drainage ditch that ran through the main parking lot. Now runnels and rocky rills collect rainwater from Lake Plaza and channel it to flow underground into Brays Bayou along a natural gulley. Pollutants are filtered by plants in the greenway, which also serves as a detention basin by holding water during heavy rainstorms to reduce the chance of flooding along the bayou.

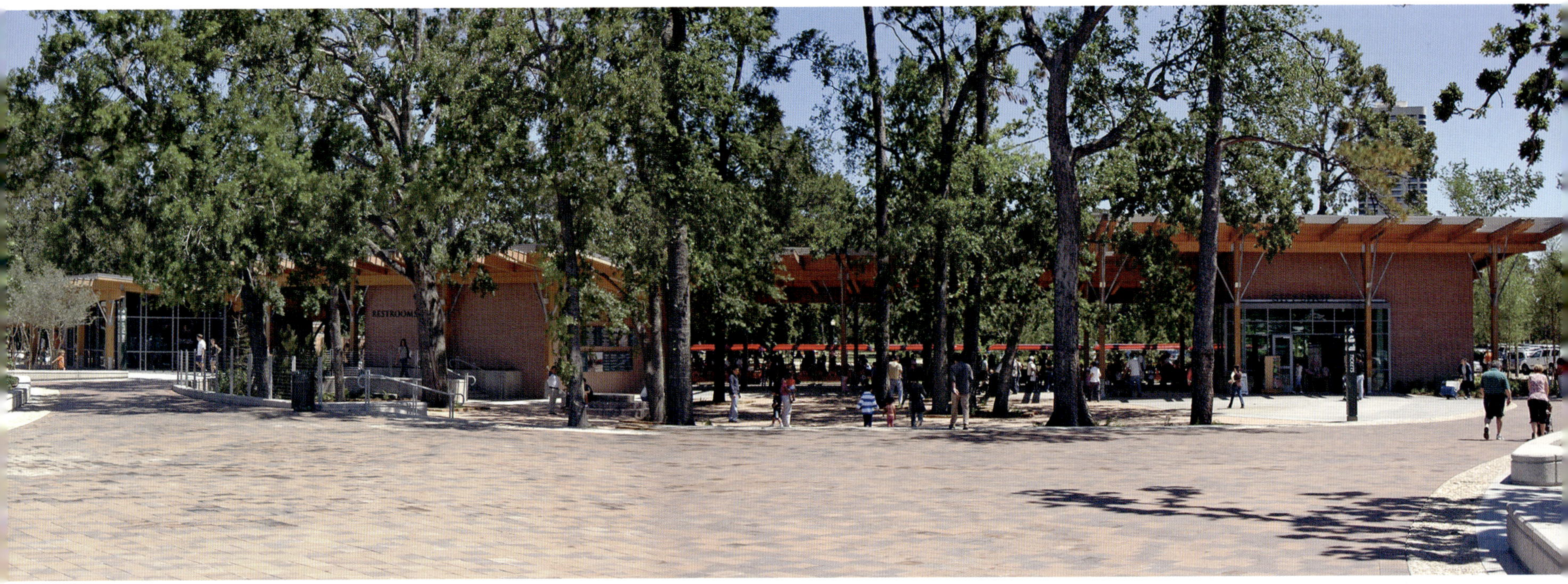

Lake Plaza (2010, Overland Partners with White Oak Studio) consists of five buildings, including Kinder Station and Conservancy Gift Shop (right), restrooms, café, and terrace (left), and the new Tiffany & Co. Foundation Bridge. The new red-topped train is in the station. Lake Plaza incorporates many sustainable strategies and was awarded LEED Gold certification. Photograph by Scott Adams. Courtesy Hermann Park Conservancy.

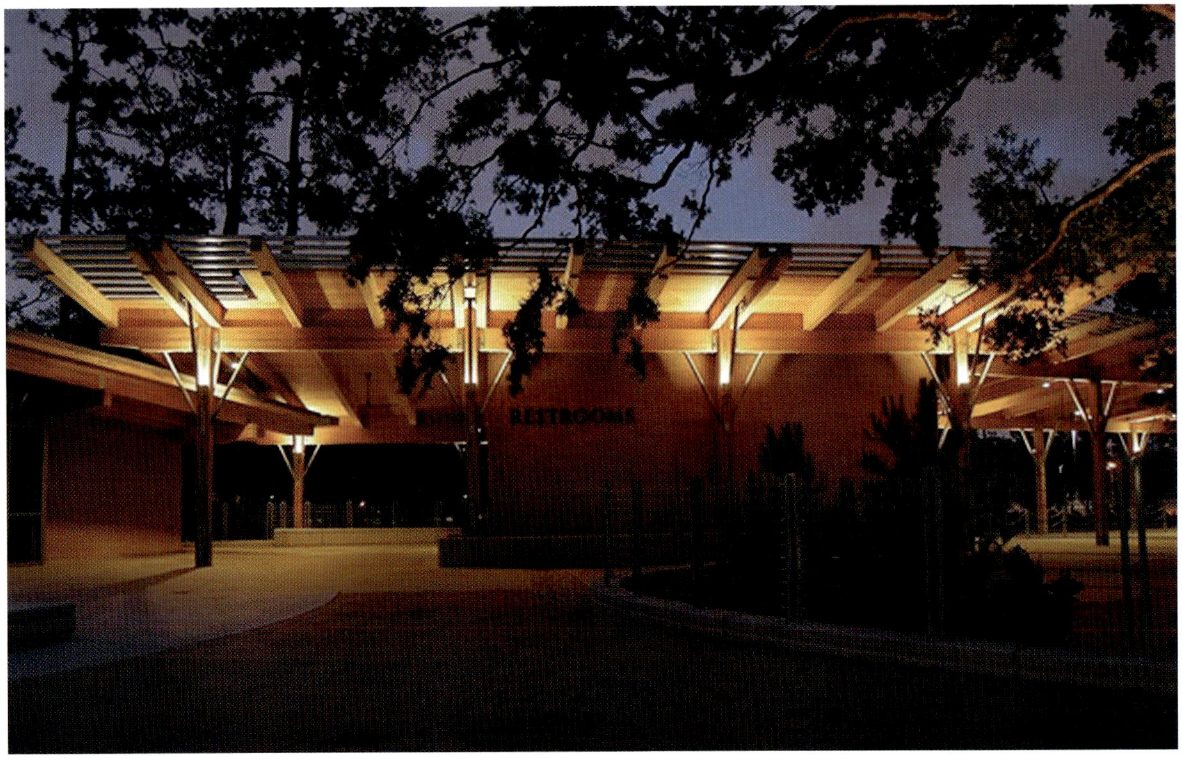

Lake Plaza buildings are lit at night, 2009. Photograph by Overland Partners. Courtesy Hermann Park Conservancy.

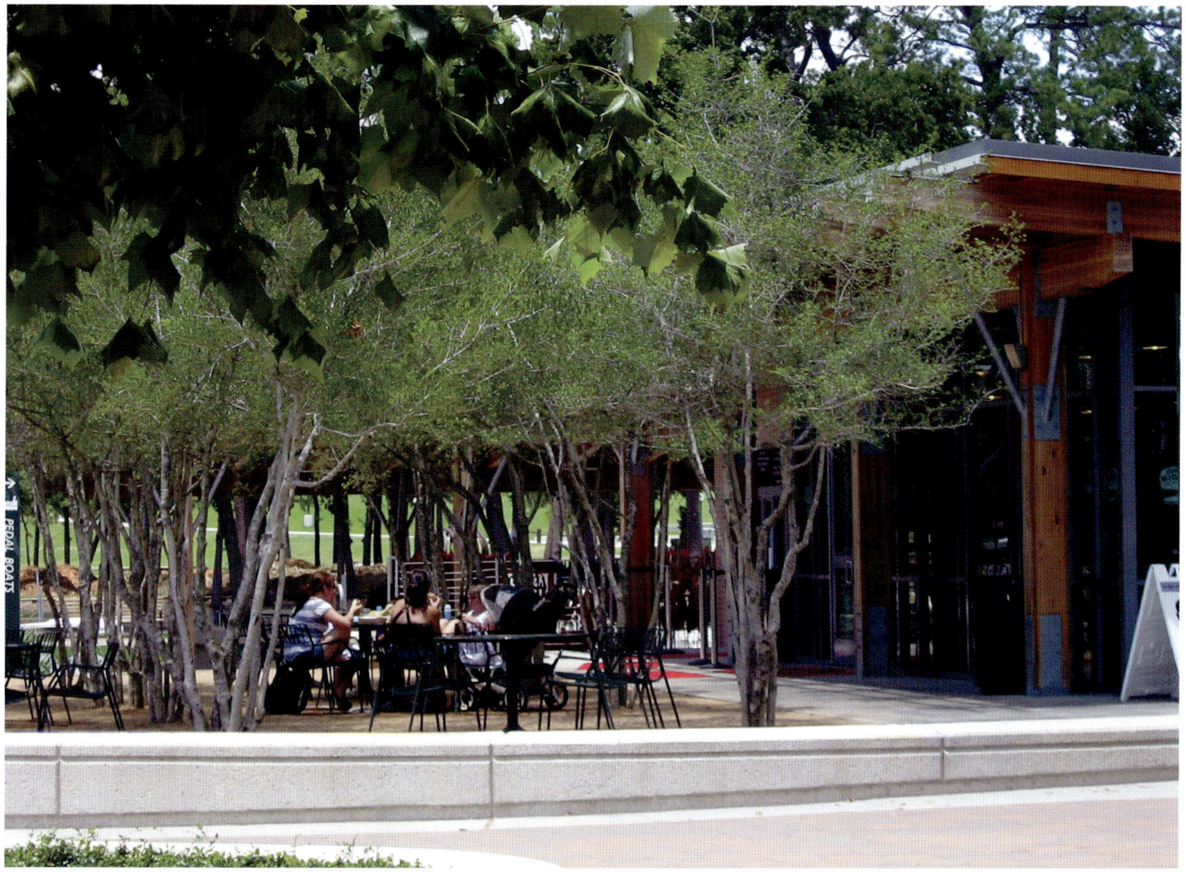

The small Lake Plaza Café provides most of its seating *al fresco* on the terrace, 2009. Photograph by Overland Partners. Courtesy Hermann Park Conservancy.

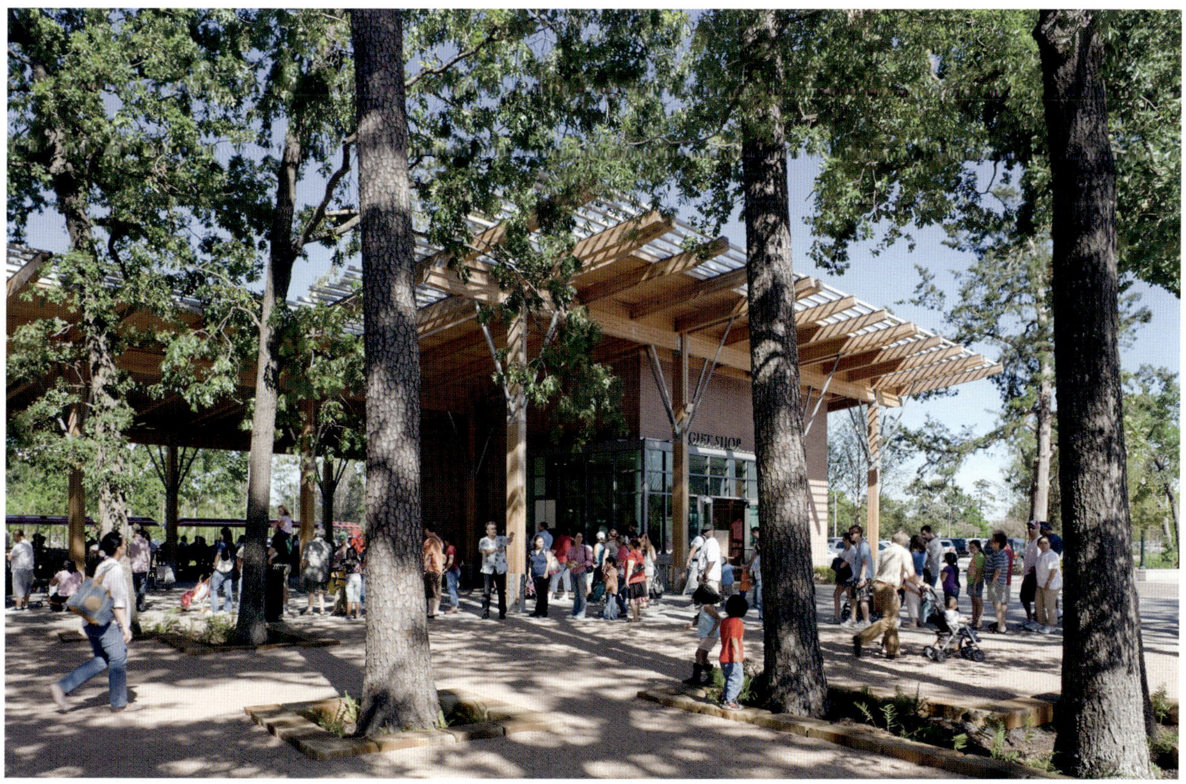

Kinder Station sells tickets for the McGovern Lake pedal boats and the Hermann Park Railroad, a Hermann Park institution that has been entertaining visitors for over fifty years. Train rides take visitors on a scenic 1.8-mile tour through the park, 2009. Photograph by Overland Partners. Courtesy Hermann Park Conservancy.

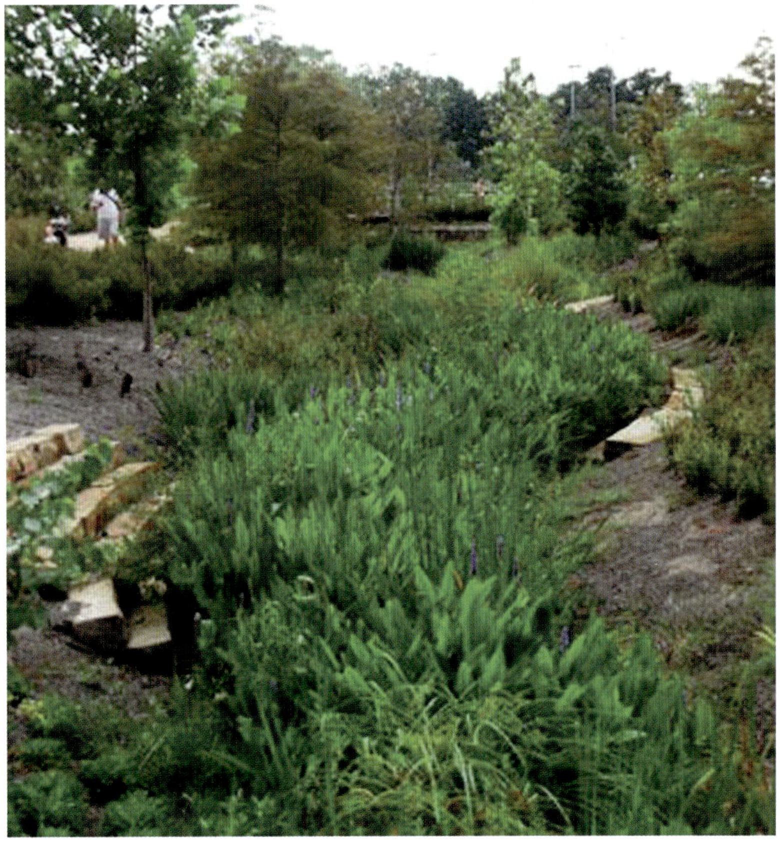

Mary Gibbs and Jesse H. Jones Greenway replaced an unsightly drainage ditch that ran along a natural gully through the zoo parking lot. Rainwater from Lake Plaza is now channeled through rocks and plants that filter pollutants and create an attractive swale, 2012. Courtesy Hermann Park Conservancy.

Tiffany & Co. Foundation Bridge

A crucial part of the Lake Plaza development was construction of a bridge to connect one part of the park to another—the Lake Plaza and Houston Zoo areas to the Heart of the Park and the Japanese Garden. The Tiffany & Co. Foundation provided a $1 million grant to build a handsome structure that accomplishes this connection, isolates the pedal boat cove, and provides elevated views of McGovern Lake. On March 24, 2009, city officials, park friends, and the president of the Tiffany & Co. Foundation, Fernanda Kellogg, were on hand to mark the opening of the bridge. The new bridge has been called Hermann Park's "clasp on the necklace," using a jewelry metaphor appropriate to both its name and function.[27]

Also accessible from the Tiffany Bridge, behind Miller Theatre, picnic areas to the northeast of the pedal boat facility have been restored. This area has contained picnic tables for a long time, but it was boggy during the rainy months and parched and unsightly in the hot summer. New tables, trash barrels, and, most ingeniously, a boardwalk through the trees have made this a pleasant destination in the park.

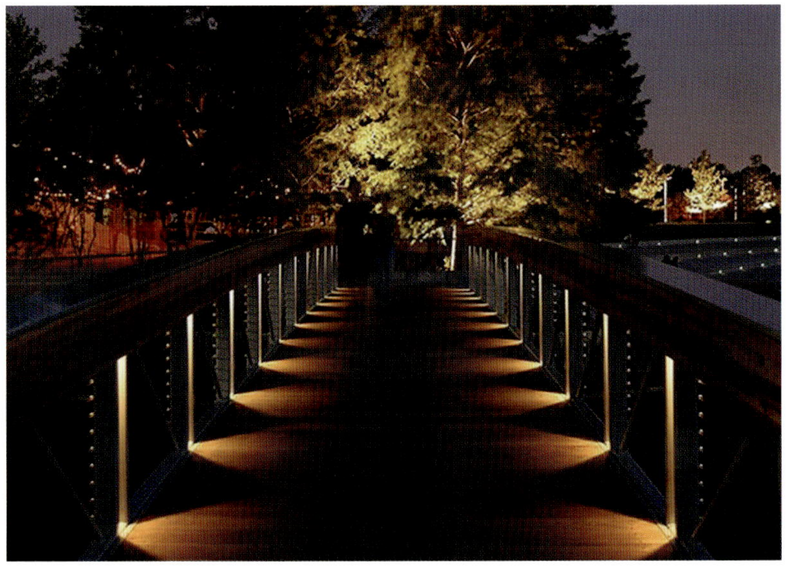

The arched Tiffany & Co. Foundation Bridge (2009, Overland Partners with White Oak Studio) provides access between the Heart of the Park and Lake Plaza. Photograph by Overland Partners. Courtesy Hermann Park Conservancy.

Hermann Park Railroad

One of the most popular activities in Hermann Park is the miniature railroad. For over fifty years, it has delighted little children, taking them around the park with a toot and whistle. Over the decades new engines and cars have replaced worn out ones, and the tracks have periodically been rerouted. With Lake Plaza finally came an adequate and attractive point of departure, Kinder Station. New rail cars are handicapped accessible, with one car at the front of each train with wheelchair ramps. Seats are larger for adult comfort. Modern controls and safety features also have been installed. The Kinder Station gift shop sells tickets along with engineer's hats and other train- and park-related souvenirs. As the train meanders through the park on its two-mile route, riders see varied aspects of the park and its plant and animal life. The train leaves the station and travels through the woods along the east and north edges of the Reflection Pool to the museum area at the foot of Miller Hill, goes past the Sam Houston Monument, and then moves along Fannin Street edge of the park to the playground and picnic shelter, through a "tunnel" at the maintenance barn, over the large island across McGovern Lake, across the Molly Ann Smith Plaza, around the new boathouse, and back to the station. Artist Trenton Doyle Hancock created the artwork inside the tunnel. New substations along the train route allow people to get on and off at the Buddy Carruth Playground for All Children and at the Museum of Natural Science as well two METRORail stops: the Hermann Park/Rice University stop at Sunset Boulevard and the Houston Zoo/Memorial Hermann stop at the corner of Cambridge and Fannin.

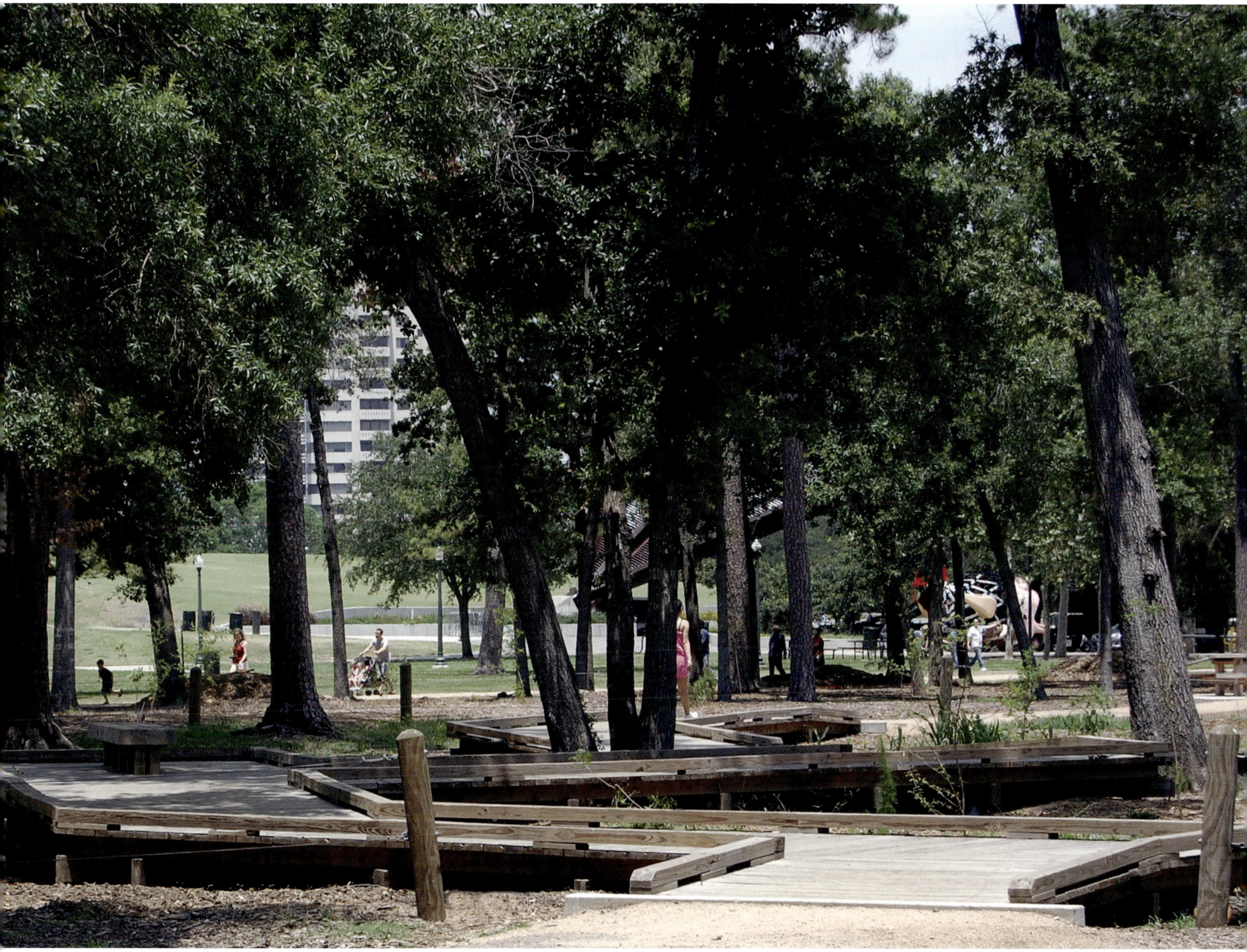

The once boggy picnic area between Lake Plaza, Miller Hill, and the Heart of the Park has been refitted with elevated wooden walkways over low-lying areas and new picnic tables, 2012. Photograph by B. S. Bradley.

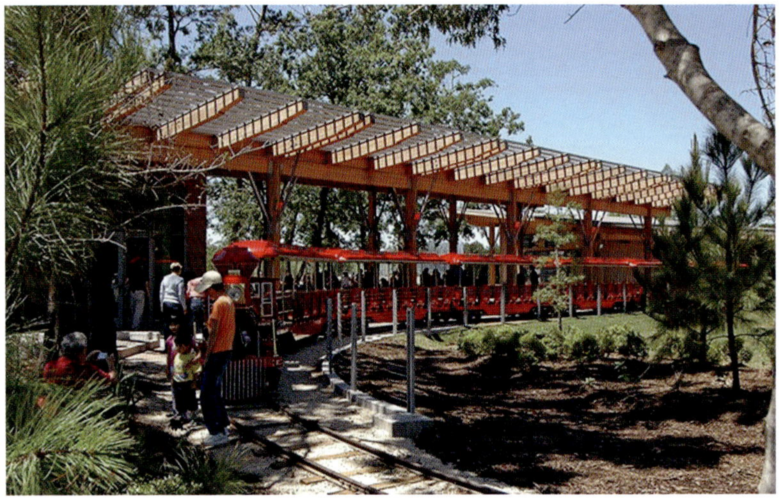

The new Hermann Park Railroad is a 24-gauge train with wheelchair access. Chance Morgan is the manufacturer of this scale replica of the famous nineteenth-century C. P. Huntington 4-2-4T steam locomotive, 2011. Courtesy Hermann Park Conservancy.

Buddy Carruth Playground for All Children

The $1.3 million, 8-acre Buddy Carruth Playground for All Children was planned and financed through the Houston Parks Board. Landscape architect Lauren Griffith & Associates completed designs in 1994 in accord with the master plan, and the playground opened in 1995. This playground was built for children of all abilities, and most of the equipment is handicap accessible. Just after its completion, this innovative play area was acclaimed "the finest public playground in the country" by Dr. Joe Frost of the University of Texas, a leading child development and playground safety expert. Its design allows physically challenged and able-bodied children to engage in side-by-side play.[28] In addition to specialized playground equipment, this, the major playground in Hermann Park, incorporates a water play area, the Sandy Reed Memorial Kugel Ball, shady seating areas, restroom facilities, and landscaping. The playground is named for philanthropist Allen H. "Buddy" Carruth, who was a partner of the Wortham Insurance Company (American General) and for many years chairman of the Houston Livestock Show

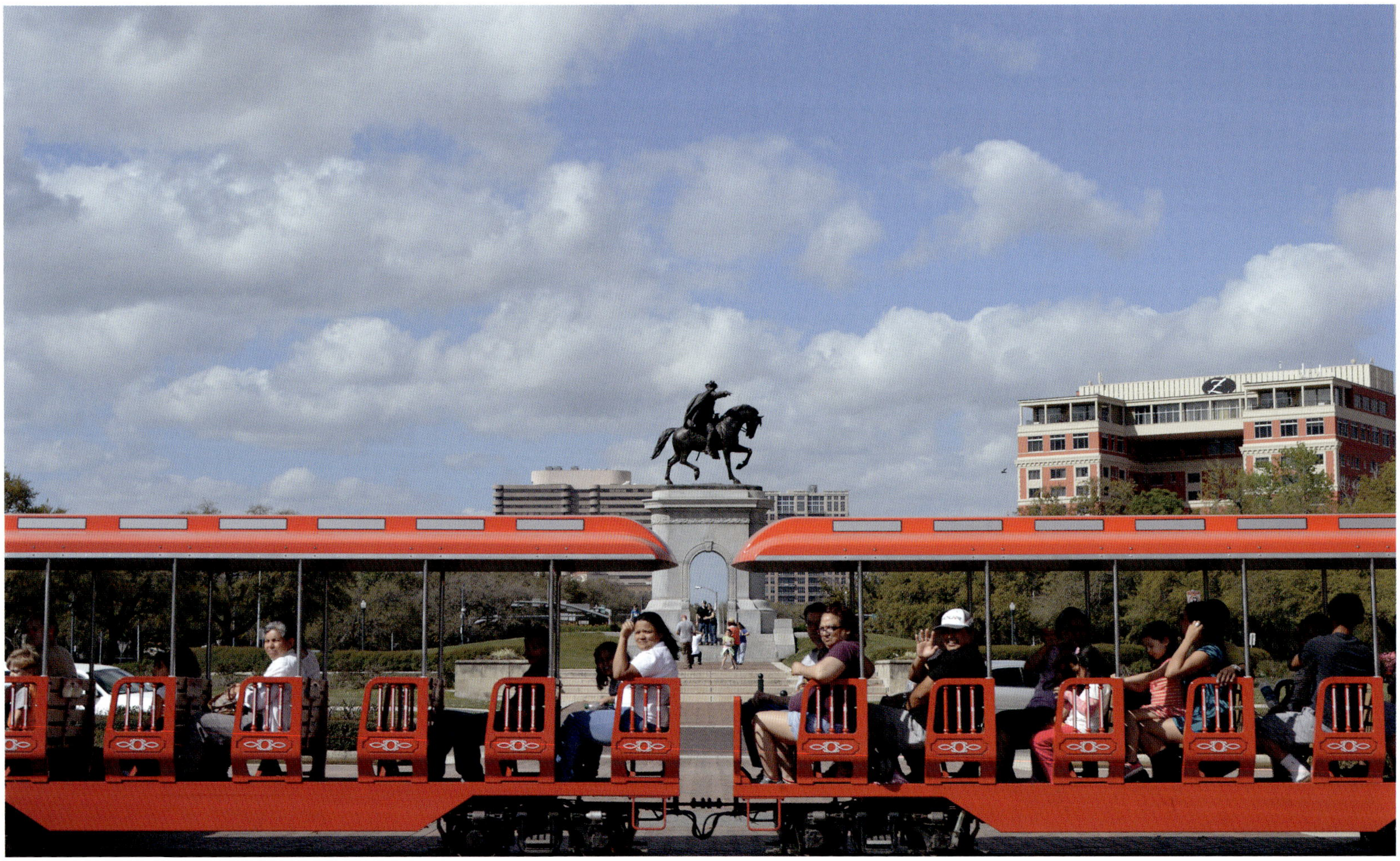

Red Train passing the Sam Houston Monument, 2013. Photograph by B. S. Bradley.

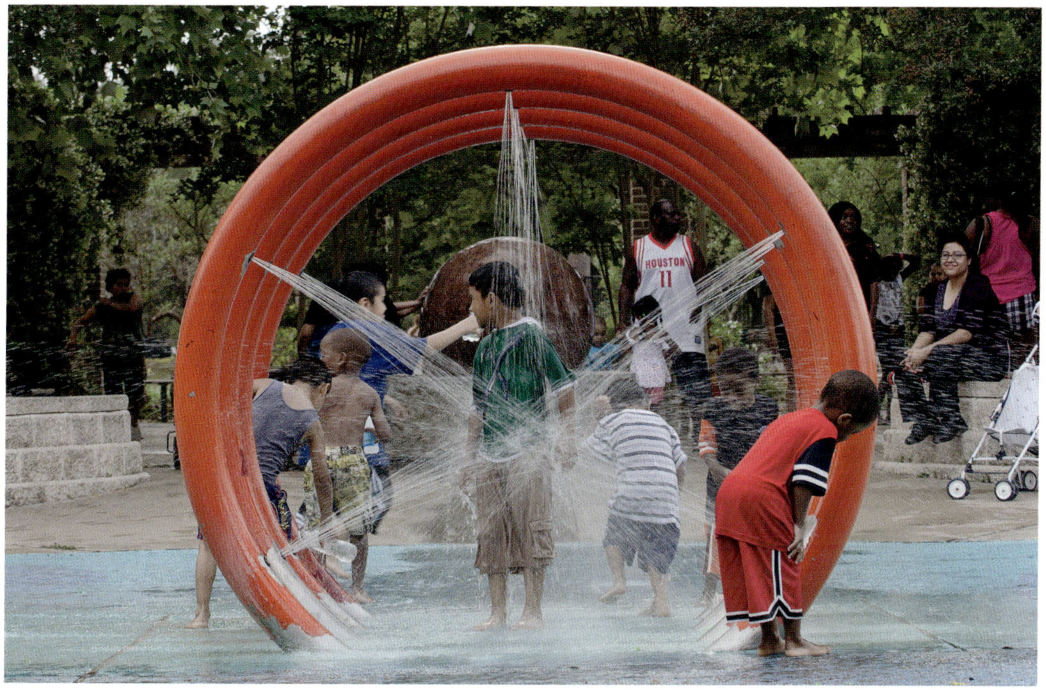

The interactive water play area in the Carruth Playground is a joyous element for children in the park, 2012. Photograph by Nash Baker Photography. Courtesy Hermann Park Conservancy.

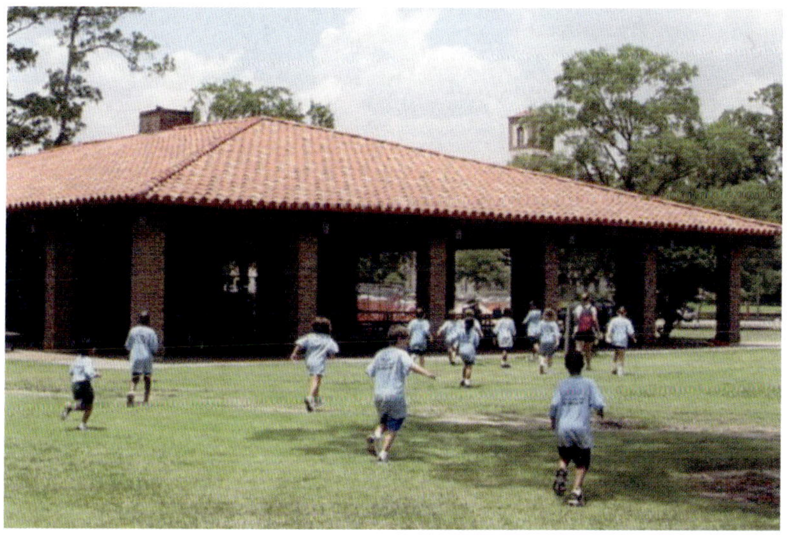

Fannin Picnic Shelter near the Carruth Playground, 2005. Photograph by Jay Baker, FAIA. Courtesy Hermann Park Conservancy.

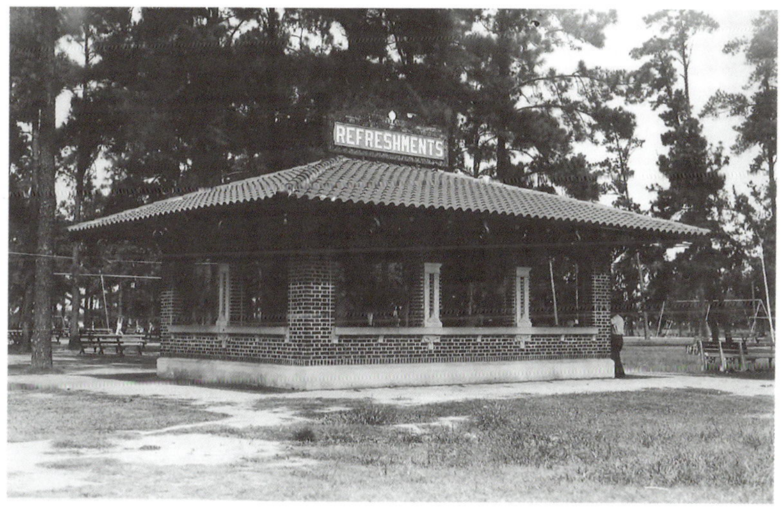

The Refreshment Stand that once stood in the playground area was architecturally similar, although more decorative, to the Fannin Picnic Shelter, c. 1950s. Courtesy State Historical Society of Missouri, Kansas City Research Center.

and Rodeo. His wife, Ethel G. Carruth, was a director of the Houston Zoo and through her generosity, the Ethel G. and Allen H. Carruth Natural Encounters Building at the zoo opened in 2005, a year after she died.

Next to the playground, the Fannin Picnic Pavilion, the oldest structure in Hermann Park, was restored in 2002 with a new roof, six new restrooms, and a park storage area. In 2005, in honor of the centennial of Rotary International, the Rotary Clubs of Houston funded the Rotary Club Picnic Grove adjacent to the Carruth Playground. Charles Tapley, FAIA, was the landscape architect for this project that provided new shade trees, a new path, picnic tables, and trash receptacles.

Houston Zoo

The Houston Zoo, like the Museum of Natural Science, is a private, nonprofit institution, Houston Zoo Inc., which is "dedicated to conserving endangered species, to providing engaging educational opportunities, and to creating stimulating exhibits that broaden the experiences of our guests and encourage their curiosity."[29] Houston Zoo Inc. was

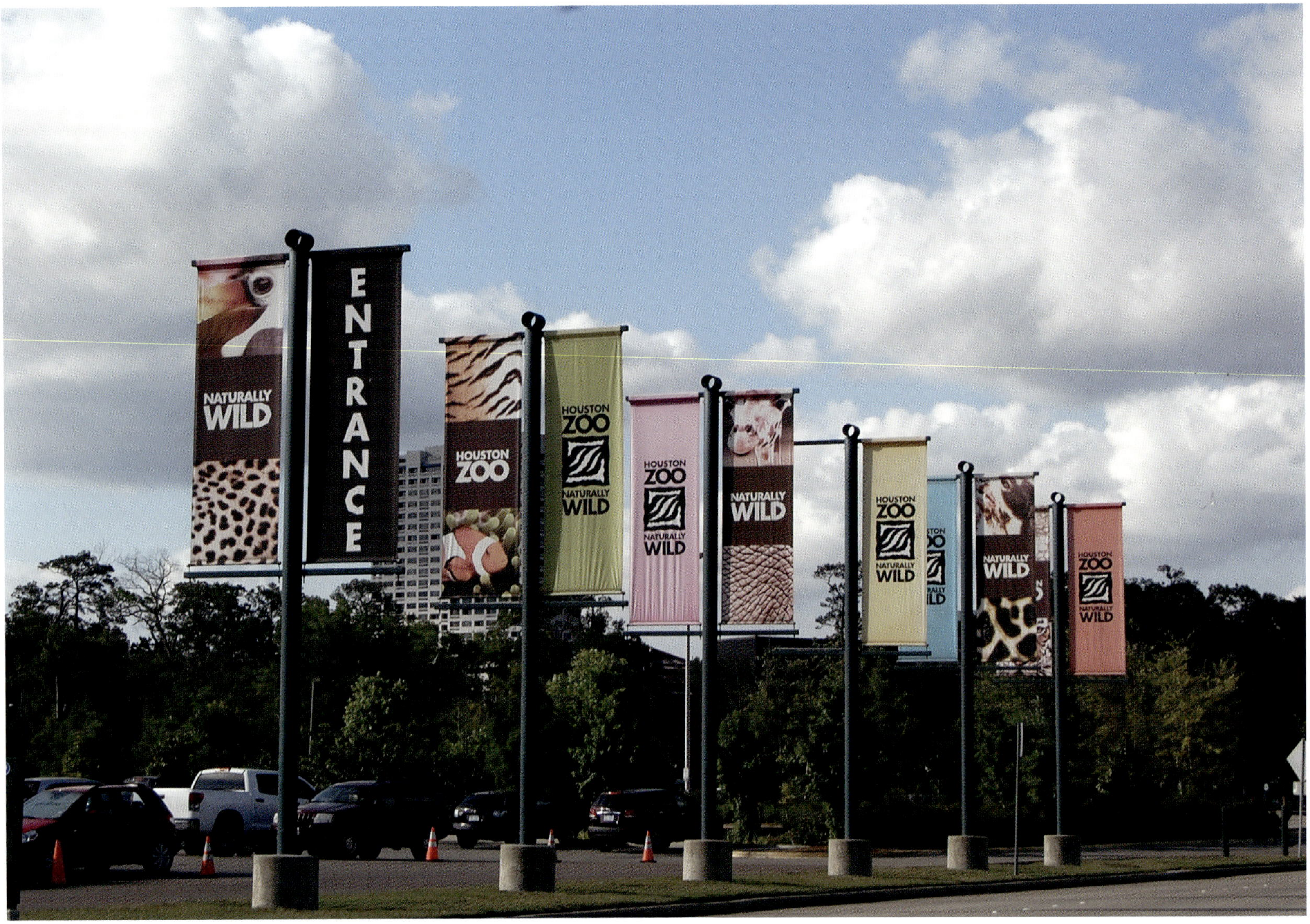

Colorful banners along Hermann Park Drive advertise zoo activities and help to obscure the huge zoo parking lot, 2012. Photograph by B. S. Bradley.

founded in 2002 and is managed by a president and Board of Trustees. In January 1989, the zoo began charging admission fees to supplement allocations from the City of Houston to pay the mounting cost of staff salaries, food for the animals, and maintenance of the grounds. The Zoological Society, an independent nonprofit organization associated with the zoo, raises funds for the zoo by operating the onsite food and gift concessions and by soliciting donations for special projects. Yet another partner organization, the Zoo Friends of Houston Inc., began sponsoring the alternating biannual Zoo Ball and family picnic to raise money for the purchase of new animals and new animal habitats.[30]

Nearly two million adults and children visit the zoo annually, and most of them enter from Lake Plaza. The historic center of the zoo retains its three reflection pools, designed by Hare & Hare in 1924 and constructed by 1926, with flanking live oak allées intended to replicate, on a much smaller scale, the Reflection Pool located on the entrance axis of Hermann Park. Although the pools and trees remain, the area surrounding them has been drastically altered with a new entrance and reconfiguration of the Sea Lion Pool. However, the lush landscaping, much of it dating from the 1930s to the 1950s and planned by Hare & Hare, remains. Habitats have been rebuilt and updated for better care of the animals and the best current zoo practices. A few original habitats remain, notably the home of the Mexican flamingos in what remains of the Aviary.

The Wildlife Carousel in the zoo is a favorite new destination in Hermann Park. It opened May 1, 2004, and contains sixty-four hand-carved wooden animals. Craftsmen from Carousel Works in Mansfield,

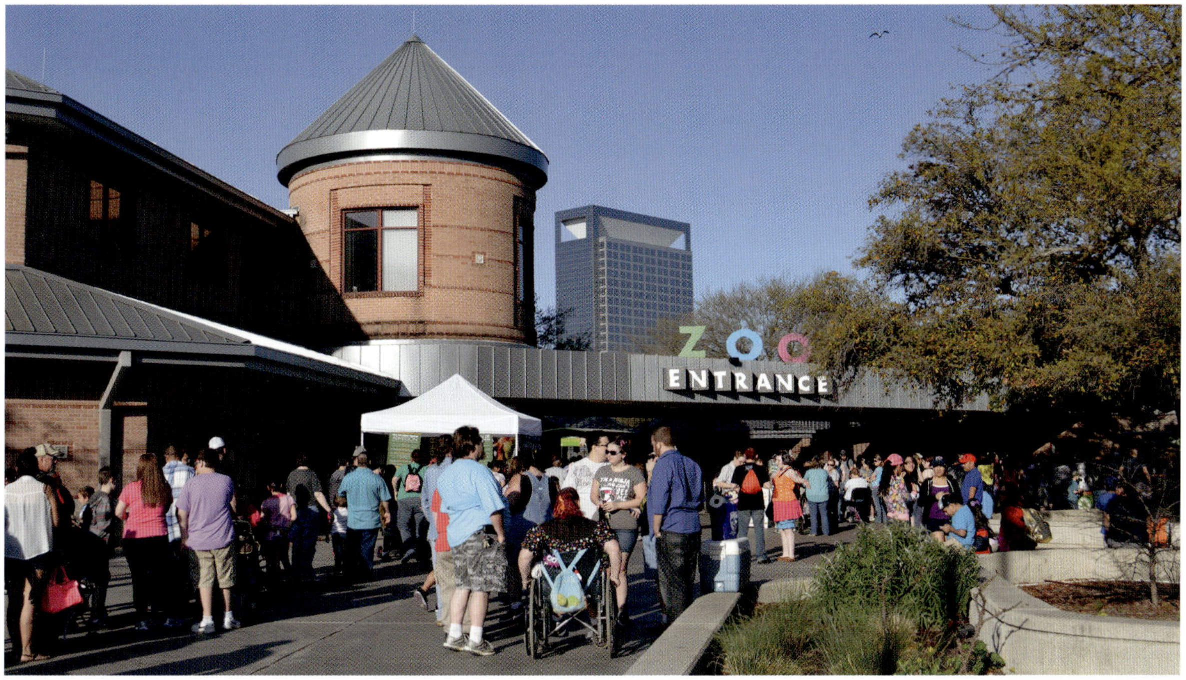

The entrance to the Houston Zoo from the Lake Plaza. The location of the entrance to the zoo has not been moved, but new ticket booths and bright signage help guide thousands of visitors each week. The turreted building on the left is a large gift shop with offices above. Photograph by B. S. Bradley.

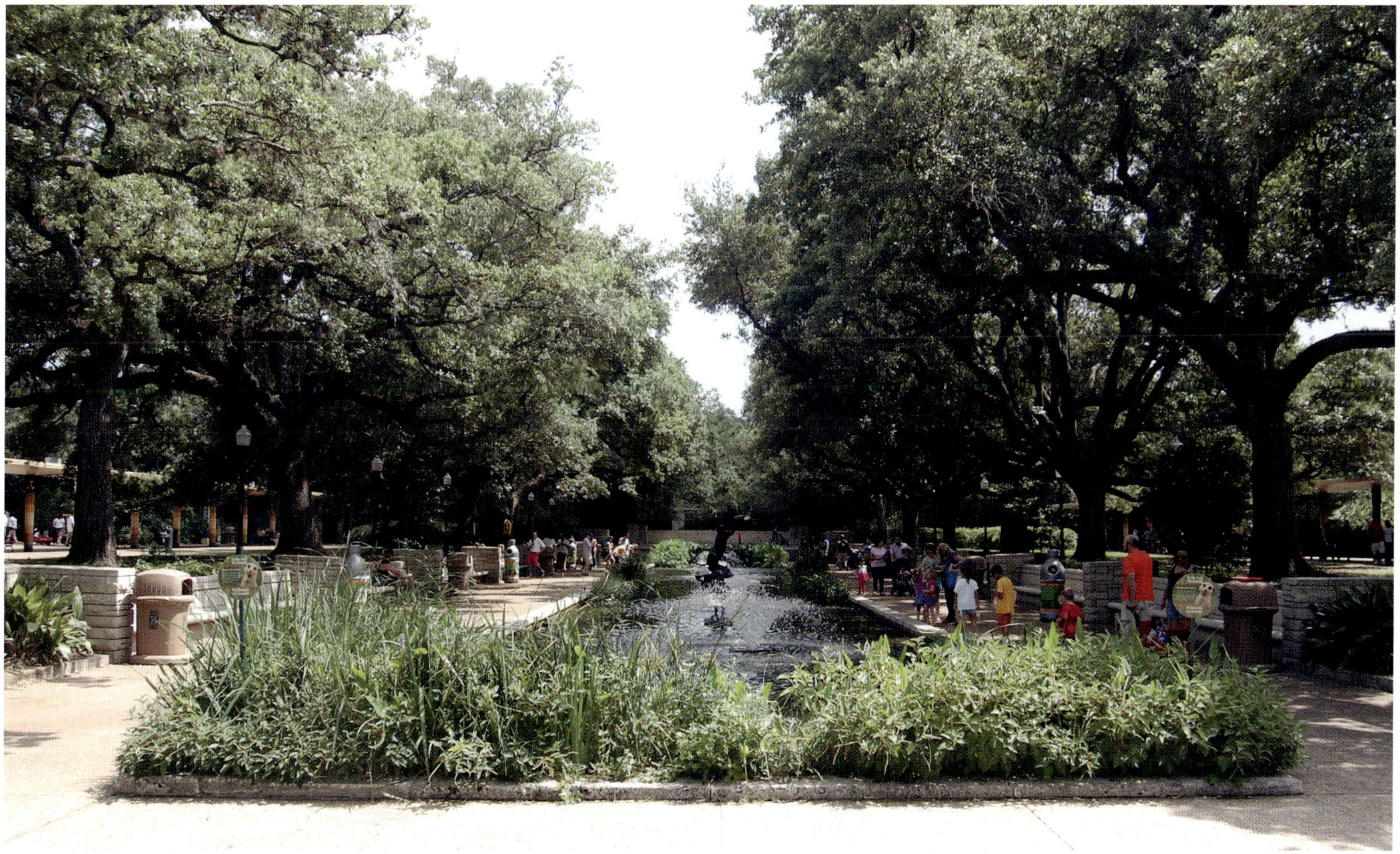

The historic center of the zoo has been maintained as Hare & Hare designed it in 1924, with live oak trees flanking a series of three reflection pools in a miniaturization of the Kessler plan for the Heart of the Park, 2012. Photograph by B. S. Bradley.

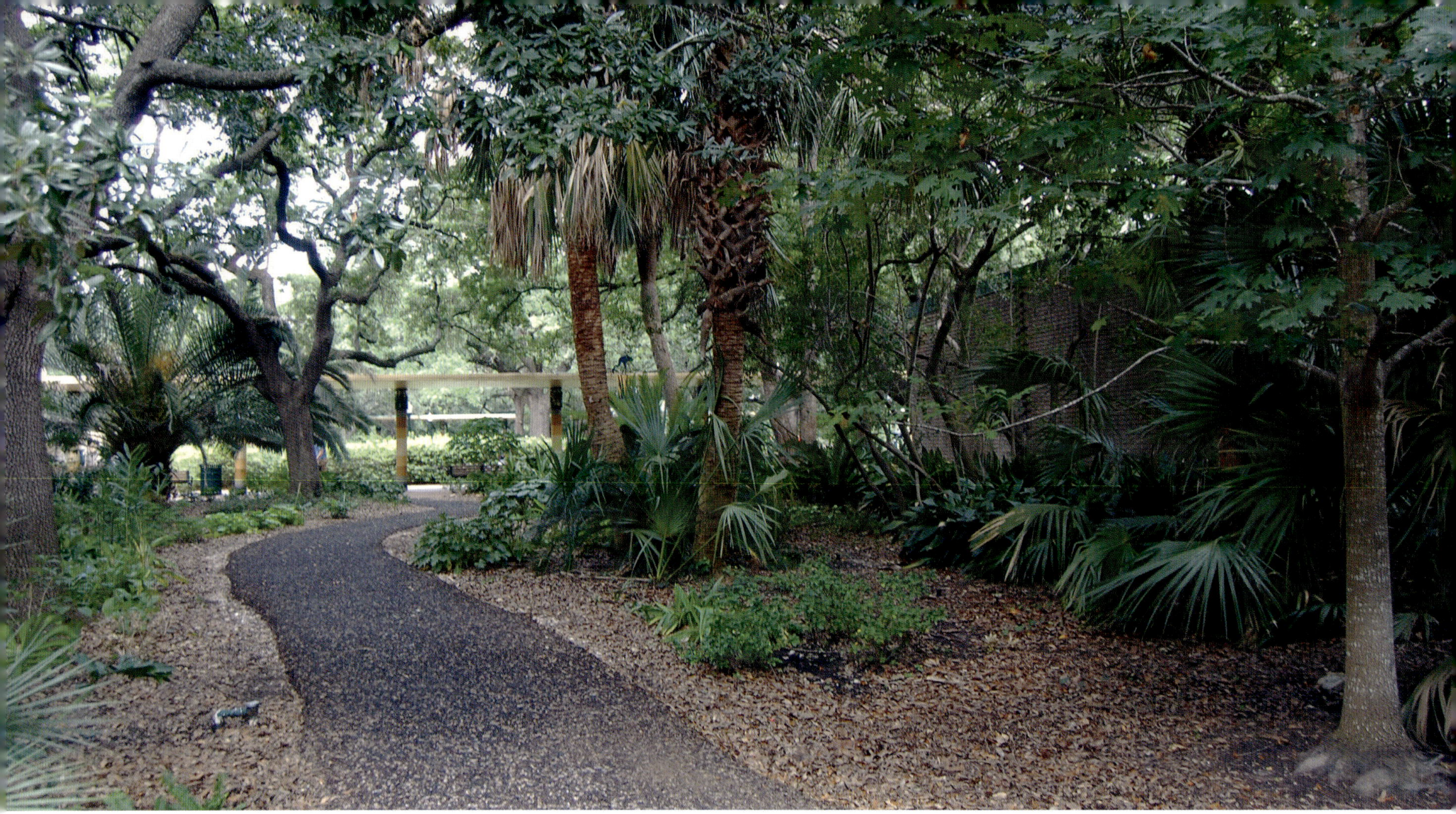

Although animal habitats at the zoo have been continuously updated and rebuilt for the safety and well-being of the animals, much of the original landscaping along pathways has been retained and nurtured, 2012. Photograph by B. S. Bradley.

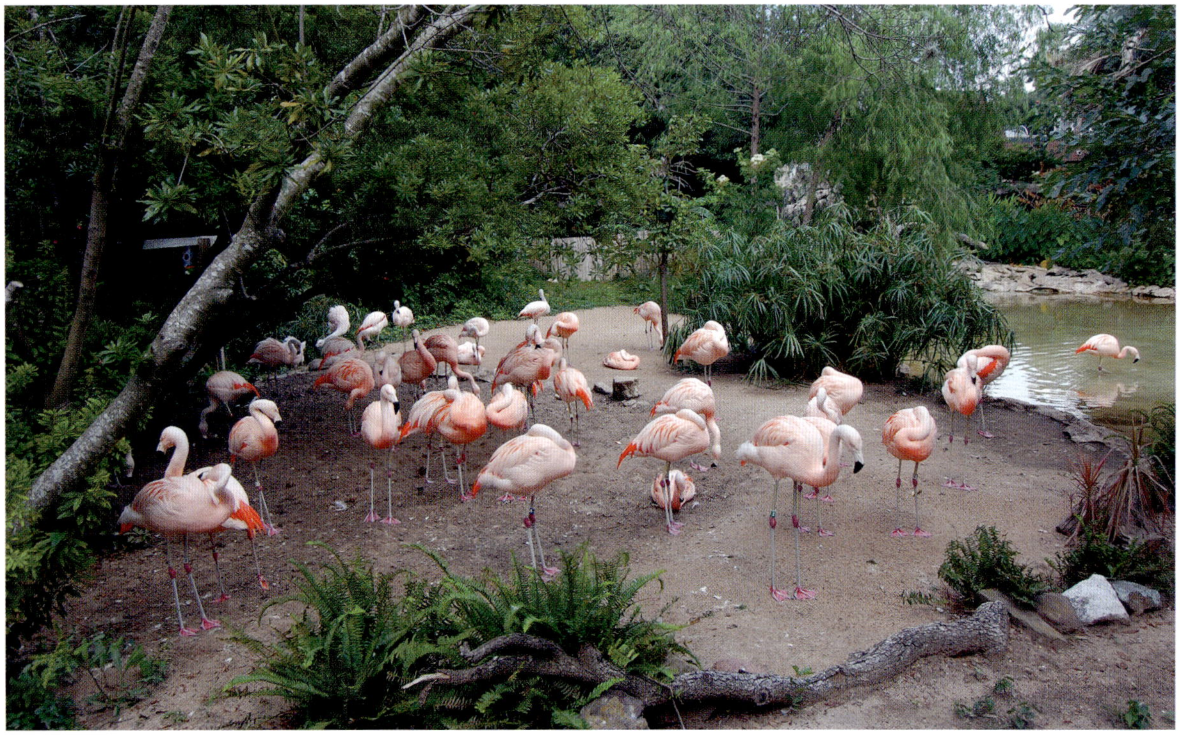

A flock of pink Mexican Flamingos now lives in the remains of the historic Aviary, 2012. Photograph by B. S. Bradley.

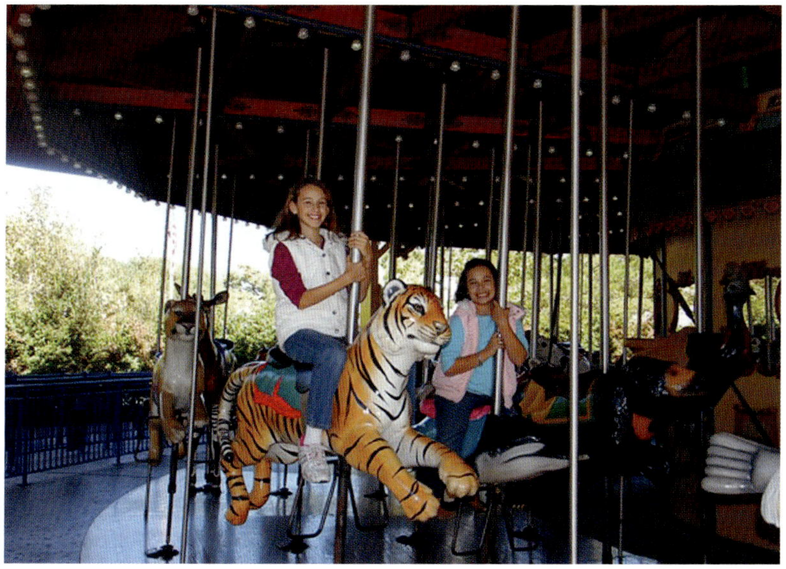

The Wildlife Carousel at the Houston Zoo (2004, Carousel Works) features sixty-four different hand-carved, painted, and lacquered wooden animals, 2009. Photograph by B. S. Bradley.

Ohio, created each figure out of sixty to eighty blocks of wood, painted them with vibrant Japan oil paint, then sealed them with eight coats of clear enamel with mildew-resistant additives. The carousel weighs approximately 36,500 pounds and is built on a "jumper" system that makes the animals go up and down. Very near the carousel is the popular McGovern Children's Zoo, which opened in 2000.

A number of historic sculptures are located within the zoo, including *The Great Adventure/Dolly's Ride*, 1994, by Ann Armstrong (bronze and composite stone); *Rolling Bear Cubs*, 1937, by William M. McVey (carved Indiana limestone); *Leap Frog*, 1976, by Victor Salmones (bronze); and *Brownie*, 1907, by Louis Amateis (bronze). New sculptures in the zoo include a bronze orangutan at the entrance to Wortham World of Primates, a rhino sculpture that looks as if it is crashing through the wall into the plaza next to the entrance to the Kipp Aquarium (one of the most popular photo sites in the zoo), and a life-size sitting giraffe at the African Forest.

In conformance with the master plan's recommendations to reduce traffic congestion on the park interior, the Hermann Park Conservancy constructed a west entrance to the zoo off Cambridge Street in 2000.

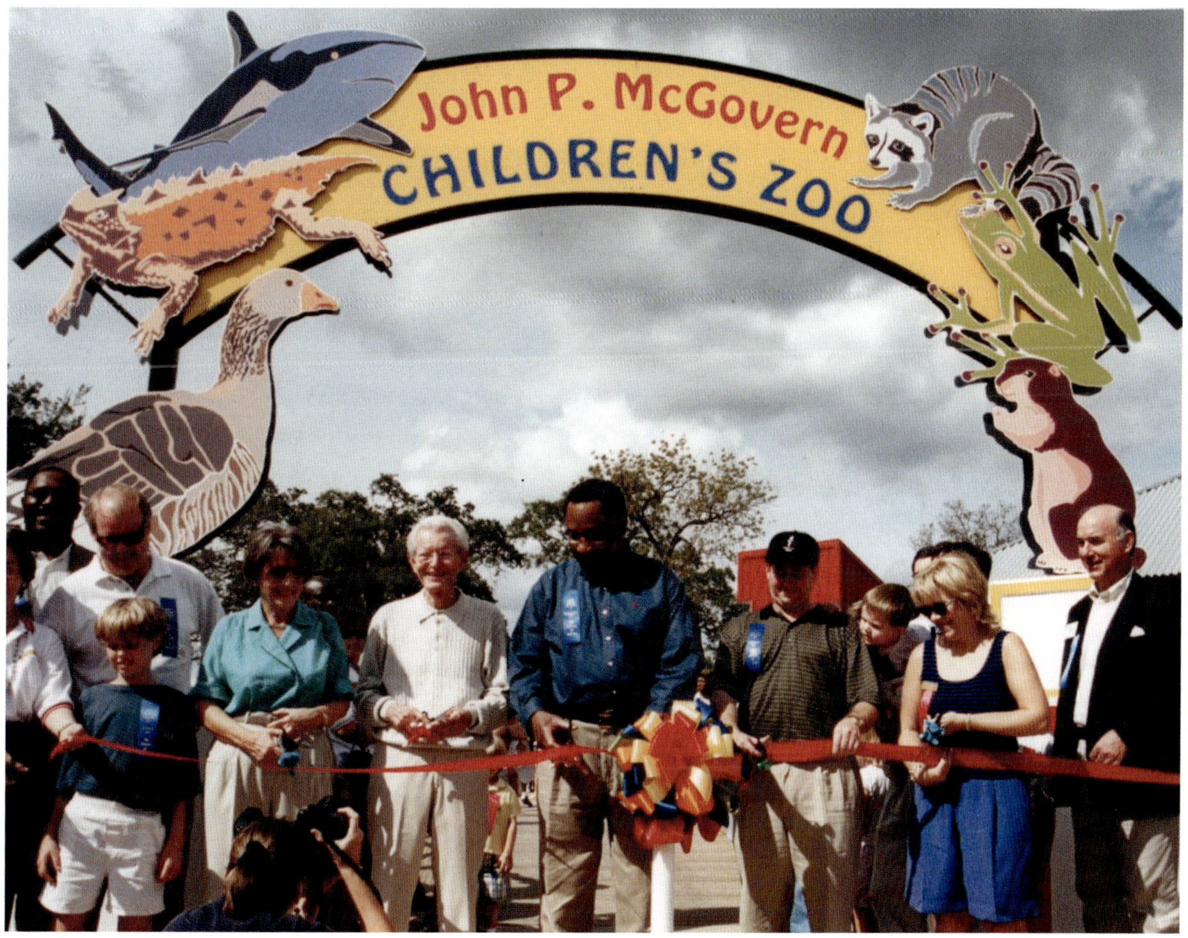

Opening ceremony of the John P. McGovern Children's Zoo. Kathrine and John McGovern are pictured left of center. This area contains a petting and feeding zoo as well as other activities for young children, including forty exhibits showcasing the six ecosystems of Texas: the city, Gulf Coast, desert, forest, prairie, and farm, 1998. Courtesy Kathrine McGovern.

This festive gateway has three ticket booths, a large landscaped semicircular plaza designed to accommodate school bus drop-offs, sixteen mature magnolia trees, and the life-size elephant sculpture by Robert Fowler. The zoo's west entrance also provides access to Hermann Park for pedestrians coming from the Texas Medical Center and for those who park in the Ben Taub and Texas Medical Center garages.

A strategic part of this project was the realignment of North MacGregor Way, combining it with South MacGregor Way and moving this important traffic artery closer to Brays Bayou. This increased green space, improved emergency access to the Medical Center from Texas State Highway 288, and provided more effective flood control on the south side of the park. North MacGregor, renamed Cambridge Street in 2009, was widened to allow for a continuous left-turn lane, and 254 200-gallon live oak trees were planted along the street, transforming it from a roadway into a parkway. In a separate project, North MacGregor's old roadbed, which had been built on one of Hermann Park's historic live oak-shaded carriage trails, was reclaimed for pedestrians. The picturesque path, which winds along the edge of the Hermann Park Golf Course, was widened up to 14 feet. This renewed old trail is one segment of a 2-mile trail system in the park that was rehabilitated thanks to the federal funding administered by the Texas Department of Transportation.

Pioneer Memorial Log House and Healing Garden

The Pioneer Memorial Log House, located on a 2-acre site across Cambridge Street from the zoo's west entrance, is owned and managed by the Daughters of the Republic of Texas as a museum and education center for Texas history. The Hermann Park Conservancy plans to install a healing garden next to the log house on an 11-acre undeveloped site, the Warnecke Tract, which is ideally located at the edge of the Texas Medical Center. The medical center is Hermann Park's largest neighbor, with millions of patients, visitors, volunteers, and employees who use and benefit from improvements to Hermann Park. The idea for a healing garden was born from the conservancy's and the Institute for Rehabilitation and Research's collective realization that Hermann Park was the optimal place to provide a special garden for patients and their families. This space will enhance the park's role as a place for rehabilitation and sanctuary as well as the conservancy's partnership with the Texas Medical Center.

Bayou Parkland

When the Hermann Park Conservancy began in 1992, this area of the park was a flood-prone dumping ground and tangled woods south of Brays Bayou. Realizing its potential, Laurie Olin stressed the need in his master plan to develop this section of the park. Work began gradually, with volunteers clearing the urban forest of invasive plants and debris ranging from old, dead trees to flat tires and hypodermic needles. The goal was to make room for the construction of a 2,000-square-foot pavilion, new picnic areas, forest pathways, boardwalks, and a hike and bike trail. With receipt of the Lila Wallace–Reader's Digest Fund grant in 1996, the conservancy was able to focus on the Bayou Parkland.

The Houston landscape architects Clark Condon Associates prepared a plan for Bayou Parkland in 1998 that provided for new plantings of grassy areas, shrubbery, and new trees. Construction of the pavilion, designed by the Olin Partnership with a large open "classroom" area, restrooms, drinking fountains, and a storage area, was complete in 2000, accompanied by the opening of boardwalks and safe trails. The banks of Brays Bayou are now glorious each spring with native blooming wildflowers.

Bill Coats Bike Bridge

Opened in 2012, this structure links bicycle and walking trails on both sides of Brays Bayou in the Bayou Parkland area of Hermann Park. The bike bridge was conceptualized by MC^2 Architects, completed by Barnhart Engineering, and constructed by SpawGlass. The $3.6 million arched bridge spans more than 290 feet across the bayou. Federal programs provided significant support, and the City of Houston participated by funding 20 percent of the total cost. To reach the bridge from the park, a pedestrian underpass takes walkers safely under North and South MacGregor.

Pedestrian Greenway Trail

The ribbon cutting for another accessibility/connectivity project in November 2006 opened the 1.4-mile, decomposed granite path that bisects the Hermann Park Golf Course along a natural ravine and offers Hermann Park visitors quick, beautiful, and safe access from Bayou Parkland area to the Heart of the Park. Along the greenway trail, lighting, footbridges, boardwalks, and several high, arced screens that protect hikers from errant golf balls have been installed. The diversity along this trail—sun and shade, grass and water, rocks and a variety of native plants and trees—make this an unusual part of the park.

Hermann Park Golf Course and Clubhouse

Houston-based BSL Golf Corporation, with the assistance of golf architect Carlton Gipson, was selected on October 15, 1997, to work in cooperation with the Hermann Park Conservancy and the Parks Department to restore the aging but historically significant Hermann Park Golf Course. A new course layout, extensive landscaping, a new irrigation system, a new driving range, and a new clubhouse were all part of the broad agenda to make the course more challenging and more beautiful. Construction began in July 1998 and was completed in eighteen months. The clubhouse was built on Almeda Road, alleviating

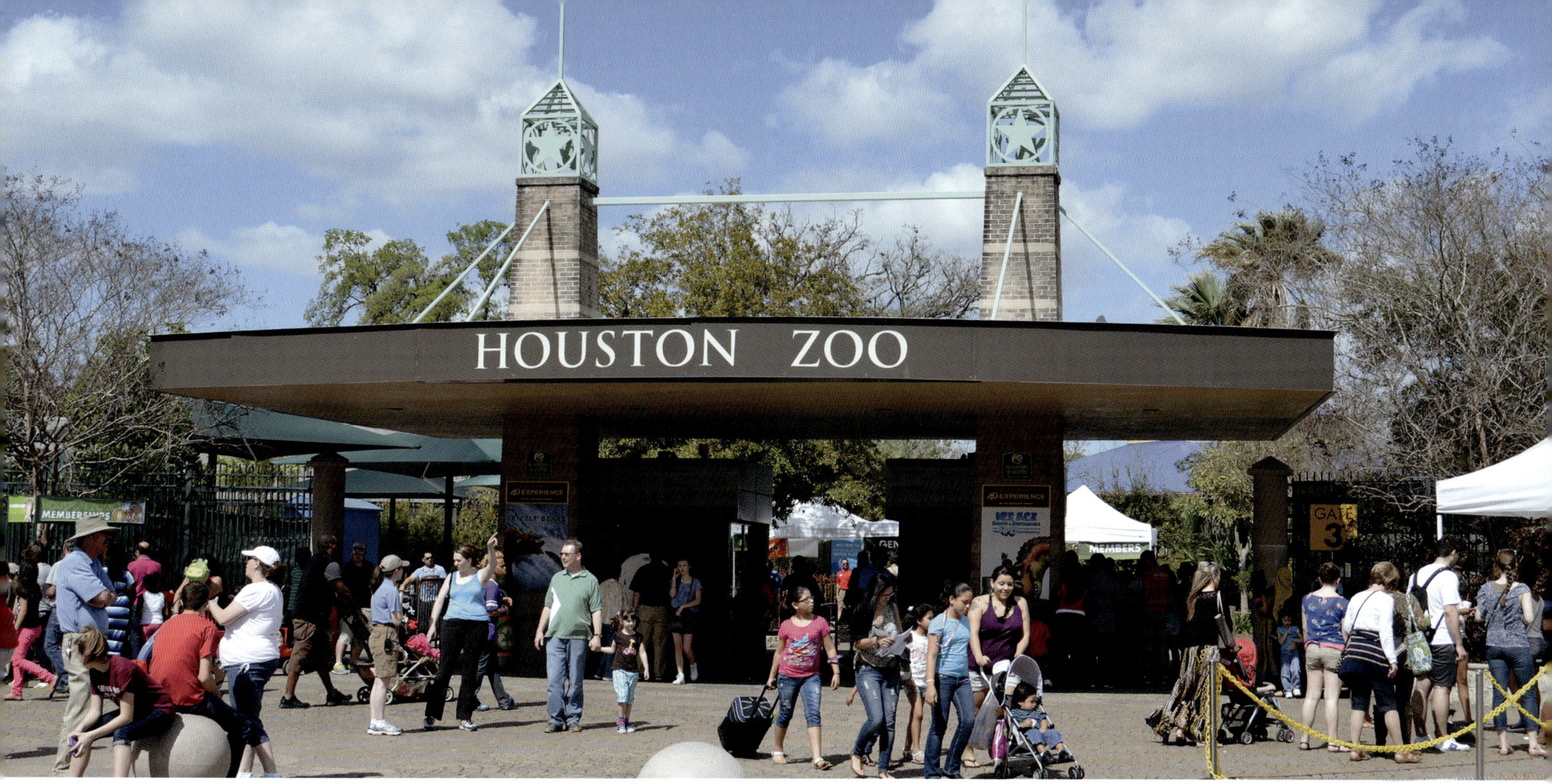

The West Entrance to the zoo from Cambridge Street across from the Texas Medical Center was created in 2000 to move school bus traffic from the center of the park and provide access to the park from Cambridge Street, 2013. Photograph by B. S. Bradley.

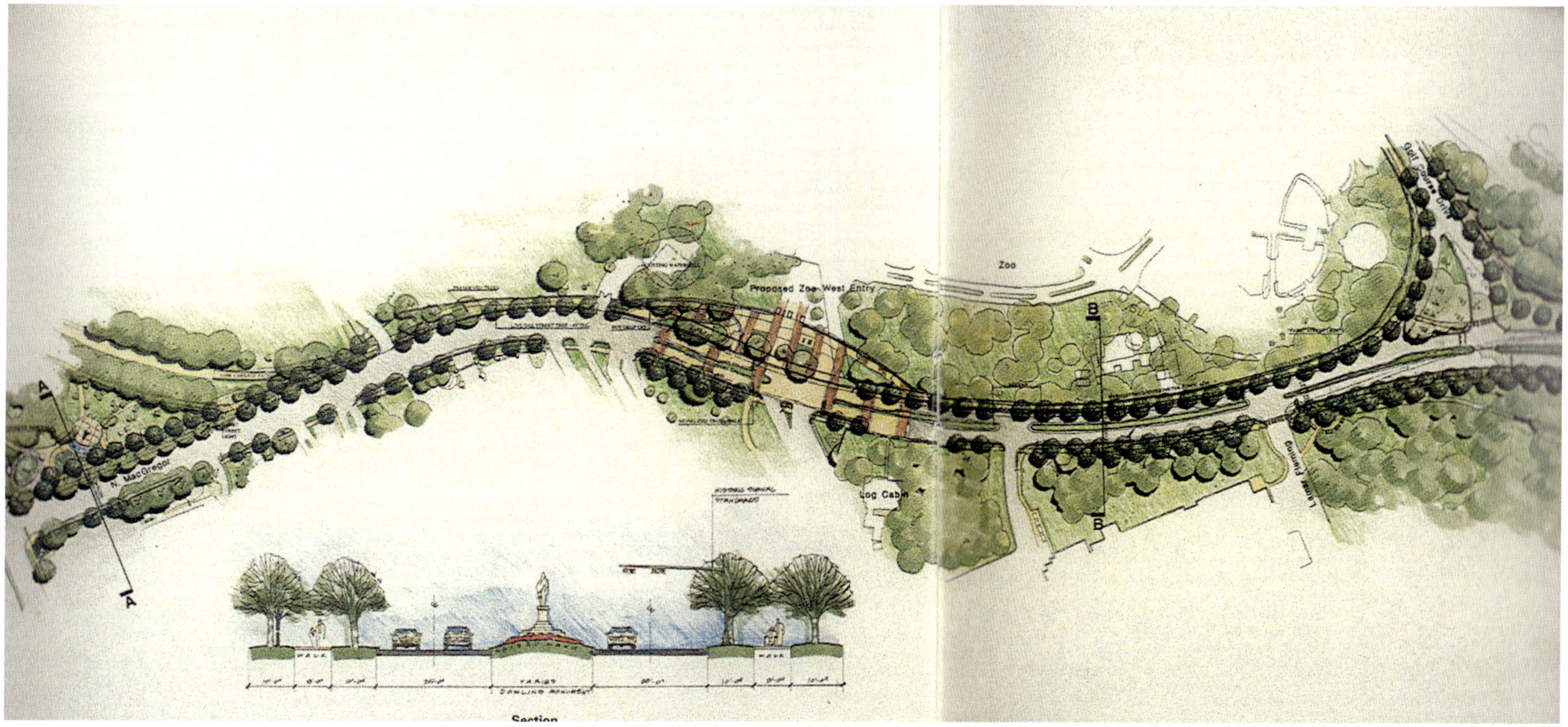

Proposal drawing (1998, SWA Group) of the realigned North MacGregor, now named Cambridge Street, and new landscaping along the right of way shows the zoo's west entrance and the Pioneer Memorial Log Cabin that was relocated to this site from the center of the park. The sectional drawing of the Dick Dowling Monument is of the esplanade on Cambridge between Braeswood Boulevard and Hermann Park Drive (shown on this drawing as Golf Course Drive). Courtesy Hermann Park Conservancy.

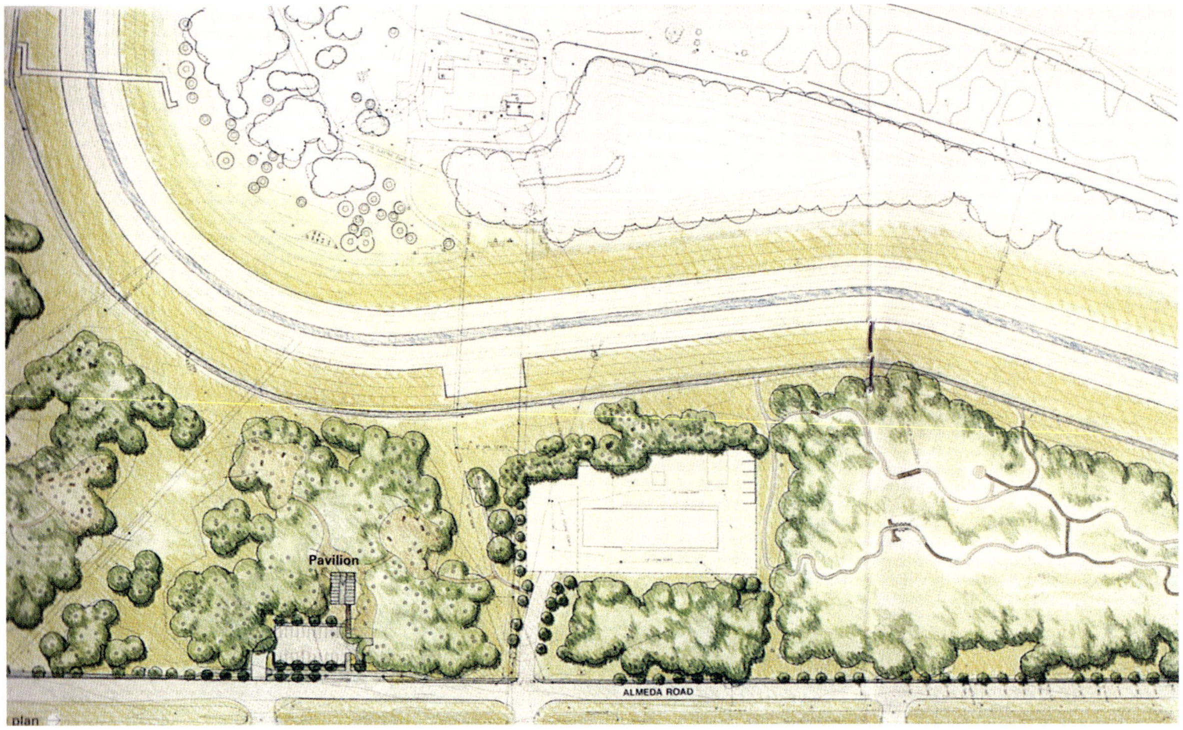

Bayou Parkland plan (1998, Clark Condon Assoc.) shows redevelopment of the 80-acre natural areas of Hermann Park that flank Brays Bayou. The section on the south side of the bayou includes an educational pavilion with a parking lot, picnic area, nature trails, and tree screening of the maintenance buildings. Courtesy Hermann Park Conservancy.

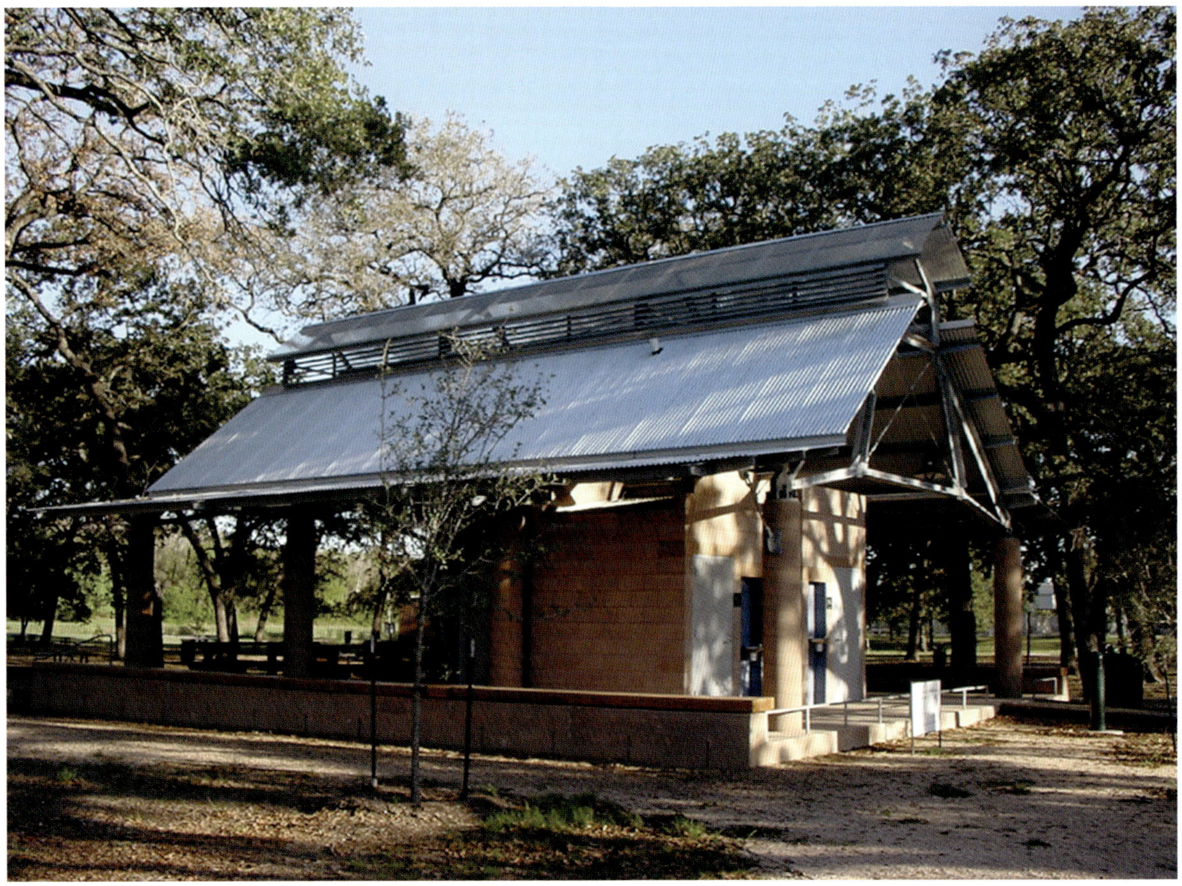

Bayou Parkland Pavilion (2000, MCCM Architects) provides an open-air classroom, restrooms, and storage areas, as well as a nearby parking lot for those exploring the wilderness in the city that Bayou Parkland provides. Clark Condon Associates was the landscape architect. Photograph by Jay Baker, FAIA. Courtesy Hermann Park Conservancy.

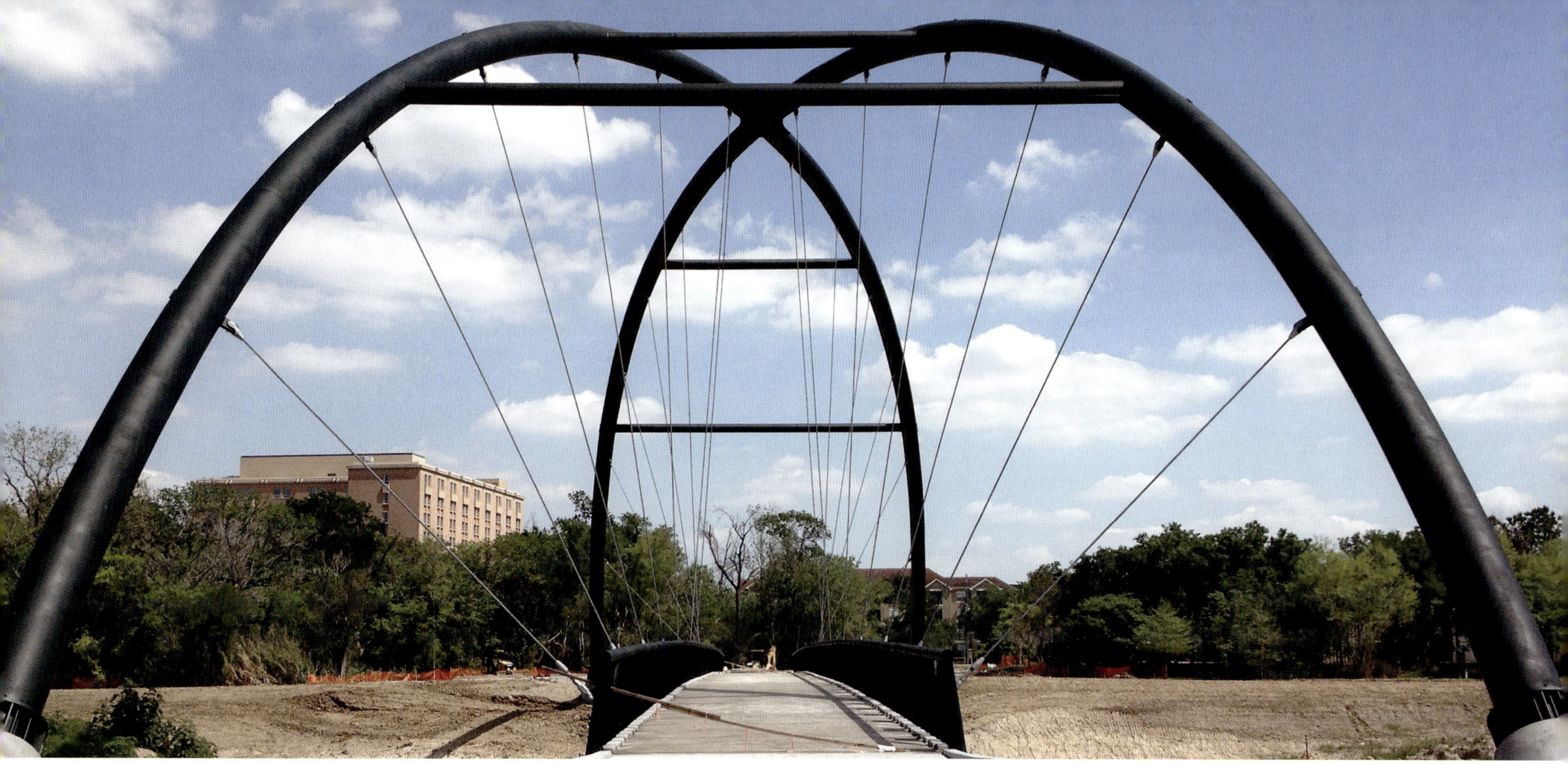

The Bill Coats Bike Bridge, a 290-foot suspension bridge over Brays Bayou with an associated pedestrian underpass, was dedicated November 16, 2012, in memory of a founder of the Hermann Park Conservancy, attorney William M. Coats. The bridge features soaring, intersecting tubular arches reminiscent of bicycle wheels. It connects to a Brays Bayou pathway that is part of the Harris County Flood Control's "Project Brays" that eventually will follow the stream from Barker's Reservoir to the Houston Ship Channel. The bridge allows park visitors to explore parkland on both sides of the bayou. Courtesy Hermann Park Conservancy.

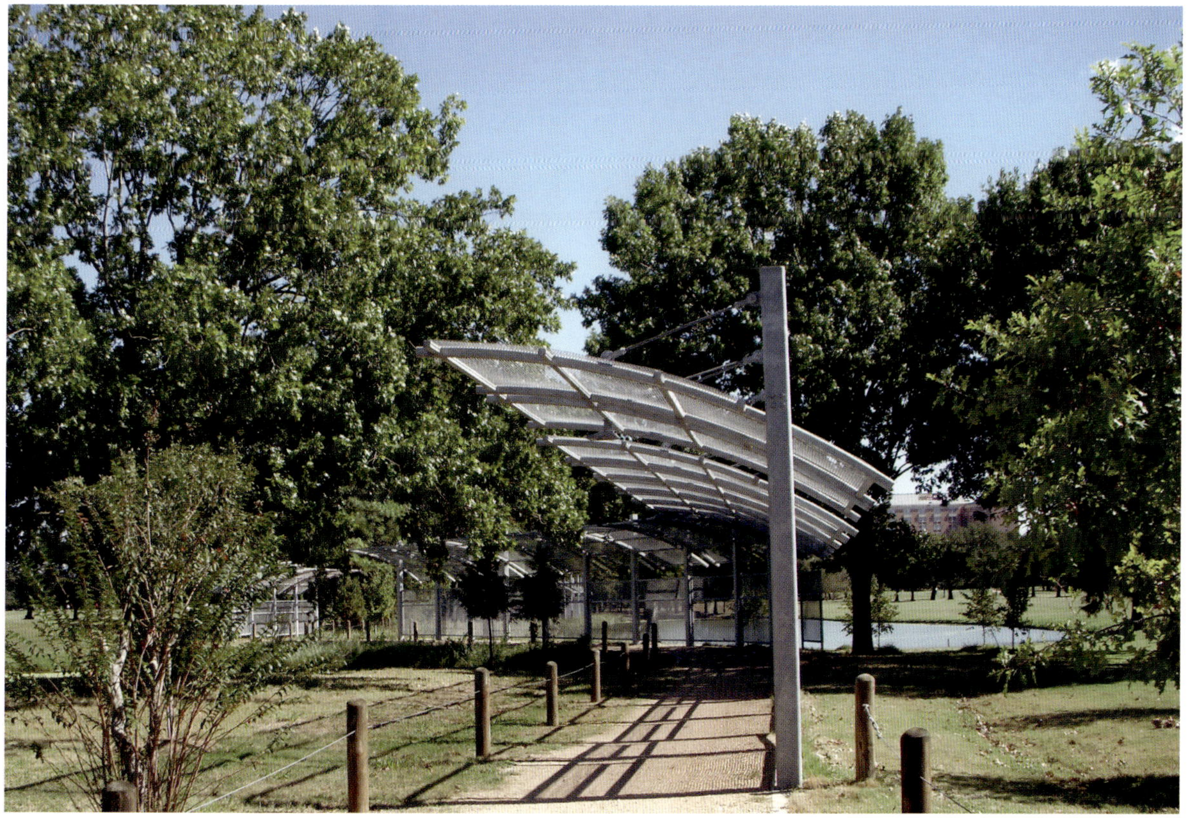

The Pedestrian Greenway, a quarter-mile-long crushed granite trail with curved overhead screens to protect from flying golf balls, opened in 2006. The trail allows a safe and interesting pathway across the golf course which, like the Coats Bridge, improved access to underused parts of Hermann Park and provided more direct pedestrian access to various park amenities, c. 2008. Photograph by Laurie Olin. Courtesy Olin Partnership.

traffic congestion in the center of the park. BSL, which solely funded the almost $4 million project, planned the clubhouse to provide golfers with a larger, more modern facility and ample, convenient parking. In 2000 a new halfway house, designed in stucco with a red tile roof to be compatible with the Mediterranean style of the historic clubhouse, was built on the course.

Historic Clubhouse

The Hermann Park Conservancy and the Hermann Park Administrator's office of the Parks and Recreation Department are now housed in the historic golf clubhouse (1933, Alfred E. Nutter). The building is a picturesque Spanish-style building with an open loggia facing the golf course. The interior is arranged around a central flagstone-floored common room with heavy iron chandeliers and a vaulted wood ceiling with dark-stained beams upheld with scrolled corbels. The conservancy put on a new roof in 2001 and rehabilitated the building in 2006, cleaning, patching, and painting inside and out. The ultimate use of this landmark building in Hermann Park is currently undetermined. Olin suggested a Café on the Green restaurant, and others would like to reserve the building for a special events venue.

Marvin Taylor Trail

Along an old carriage drive that winds around the golf course at the north end of the park, a wide, granite gravel running trail designed by Lauren Griffith Associates was improved though a Texas Department of Transportation $2 million grant in 2002. The running surface was replenished, and bike racks, lighting, benches, and water fountains were added along the 2-mile track. Existing exercise stations were also upgraded. Marvin Taylor, for whom this trail is named, organized the Hermann Park Joggers, Runners, and Walkers in 1986.

Judson Robinson, Jr. Community Center

A plot of land at the corner of Almeda Road and Hermann Drive was never part of Hermann Park. In 1951 the Jewish Community Center, which had been founded in 1933, built its first purpose-designed clubhouse on this site.[31] When a new Jewish Community Center was built on South Braeswood, this facility was acquired by the City of Houston for a public community center. The center was named for Judson Robinson, Jr., who in 1971 became Houston's first black city councilman since Reconstruction. The facility, adjacent to the Hermann Park Golf Course, provides a wide range of services and contains a full-service fitness center.

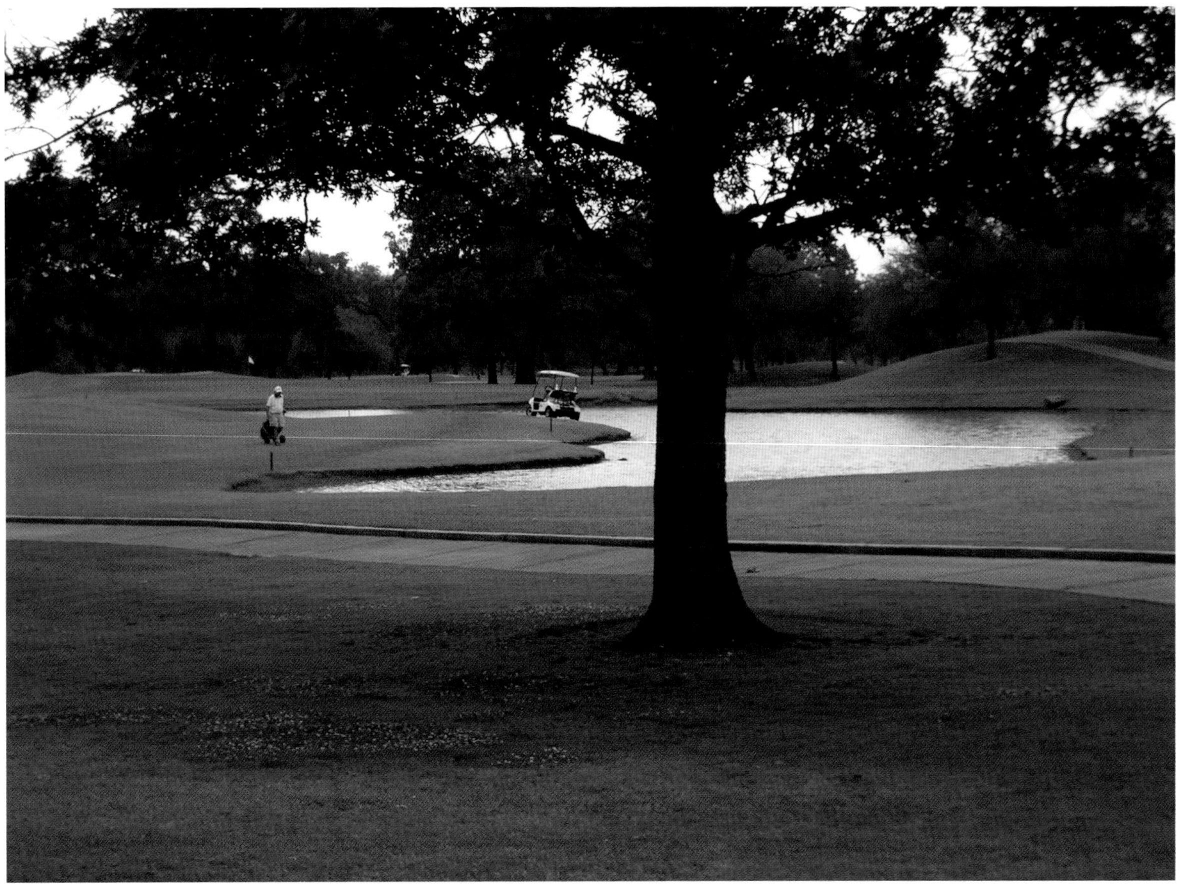

The 18-hole Hermann Park Golf Course, redesigned in 1997 by Carlton Gibson for Houston's BS Golf Corporation, is one of Houston's oldest and most popular municipal courses, 2005. Photograph by Laurie Olin. Courtesy Olin Partnership.

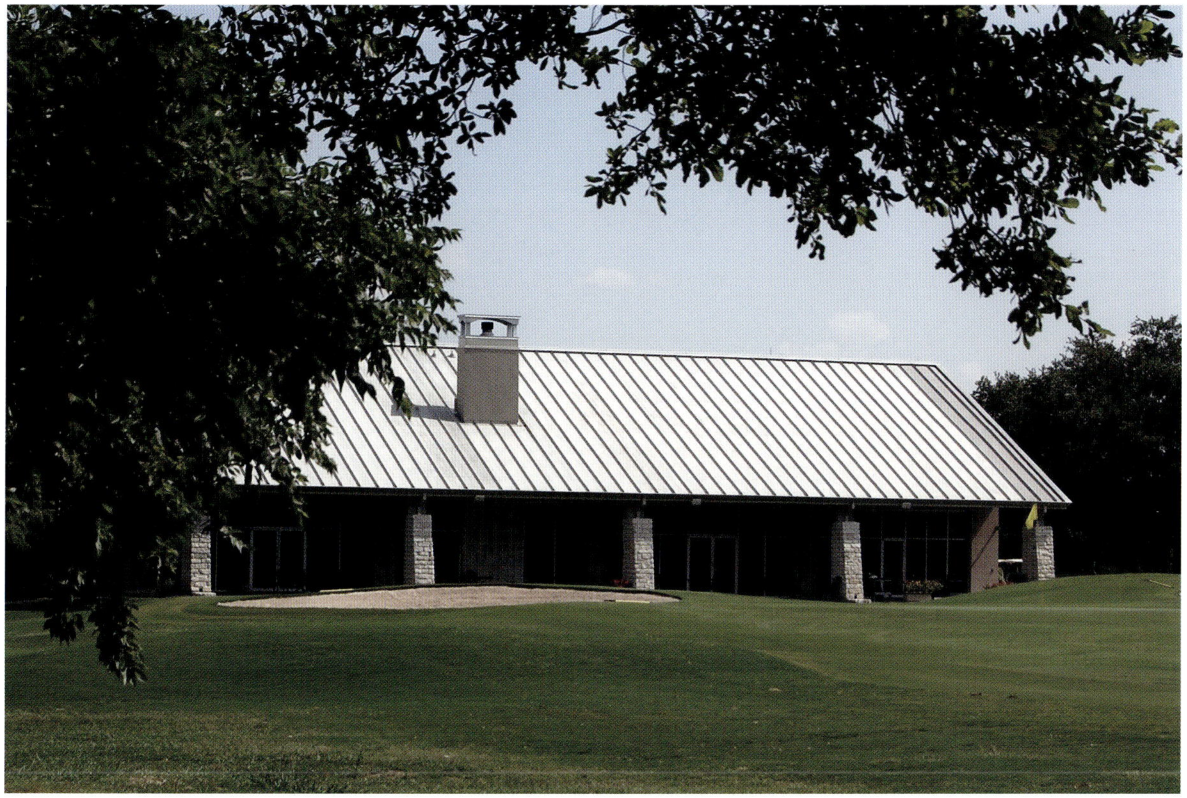

Hermann Park Clubhouse (1998, Leroy Hermes) 2155 North MacGregor, was built to accommodate a larger, more up-to-date facility for Hermann Park golfers. The new building off of Almeda Road also provides better access and more parking, removing golf course related traffic and parking from the center of the park, 2012. Photograph by B. S. Bradley.

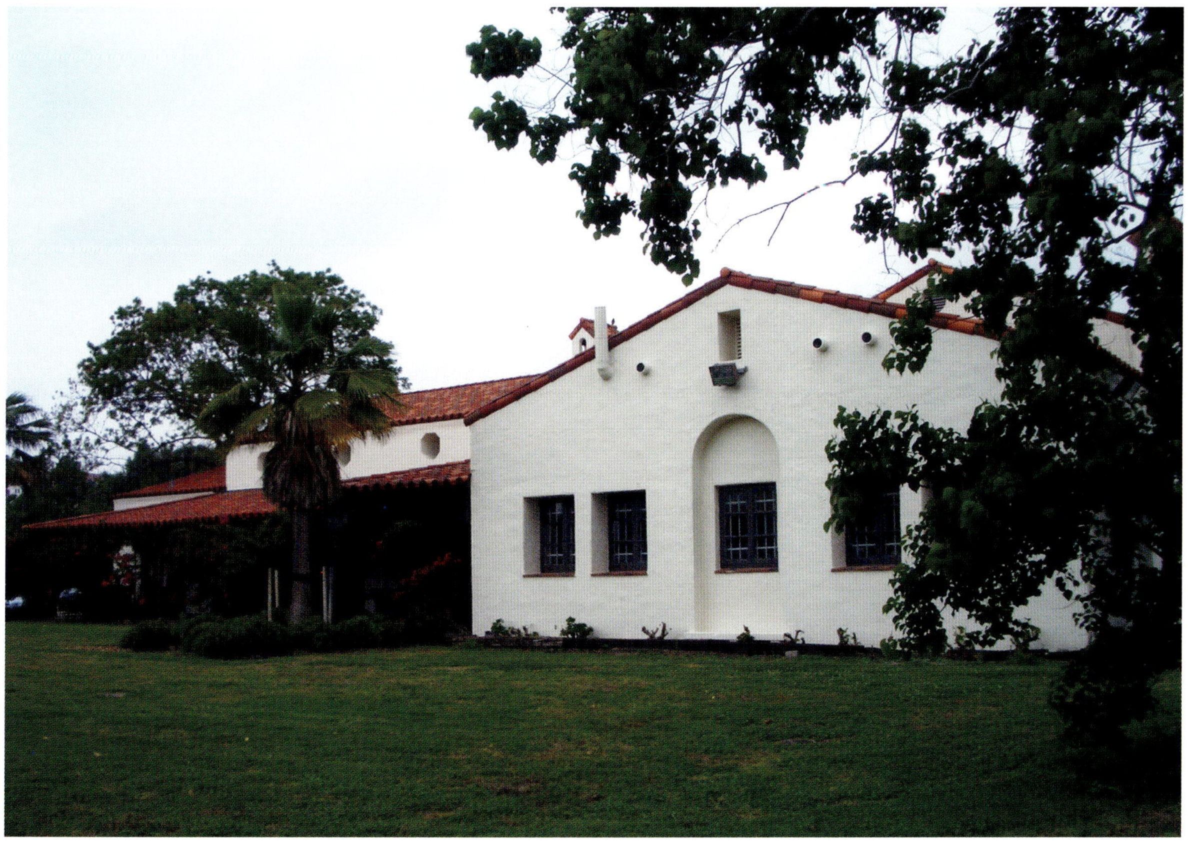

Hermann Park Historic Clubhouse, 6201 Hermann Park Drive (1933, Alfred E. Nutter) was designed in a Spanish style with stucco walls and a red barrel-tile roof. Currently housing the Hermann Park Conservancy and Houston Parks and Recreation offices, it will be restored for event use after those offices move to a new building adjacent to the Centennial Gardens parking lot, c. 2005. Photograph by Laurie Olin. Courtesy Olin Partnership.

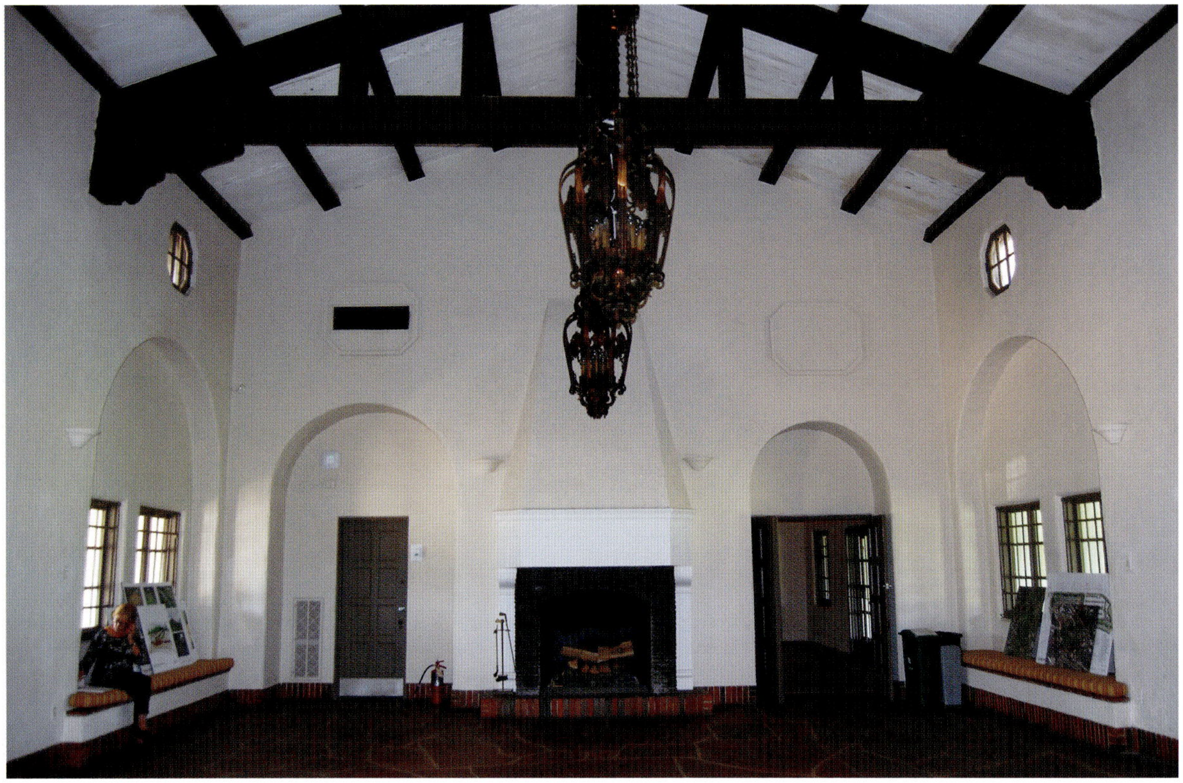

Historic Hermann Park Clubhouse, interior of the common room, once a lounging and dining area for golfers flanked by locker rooms, offices, and a pro shop, 2012. Photograph by B. S. Bradley.

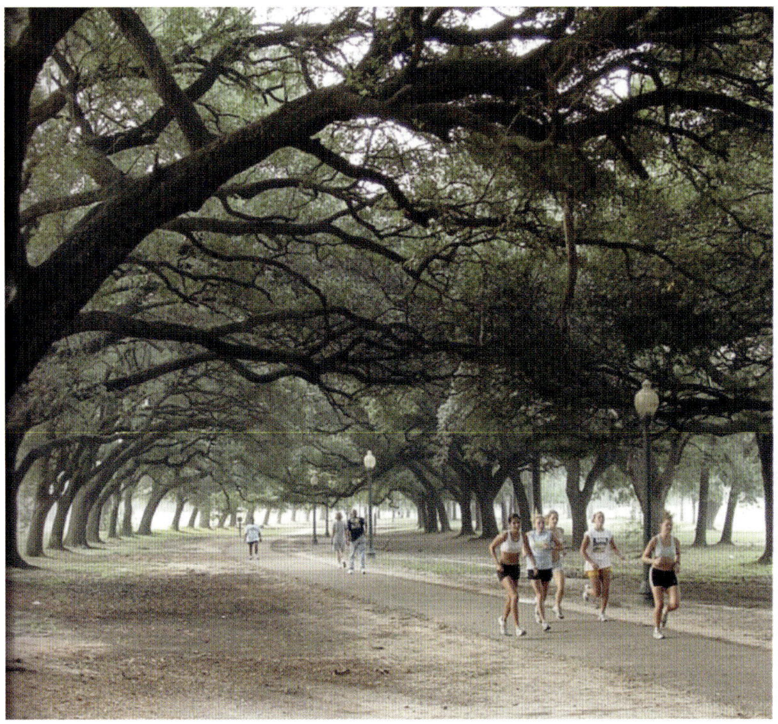

Marvin Taylor Exercise Trail is approximately 2 miles long and connects to the 3-mile trail around the perimenter of Rice University. The Hermann Park trail follows an old carriage drive lined with mature live oak trees planted about 1916, 2002. Photograph by Jay Baker, FAIA. Courtesy Hermann Park Conservancy.

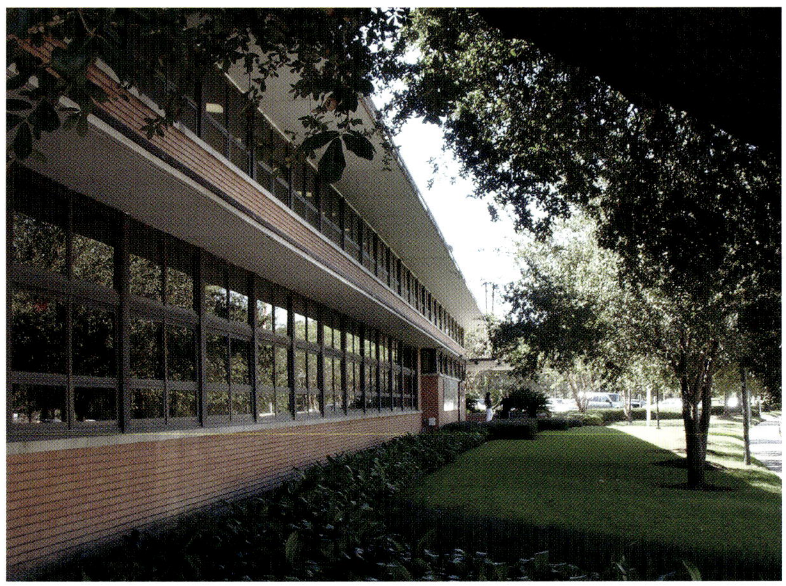

Judson W. Robinson, Jr., Community Center (1951, Lenard Gabert and W. Jackson Wisdom), 2020 Hermann Drive at Almeda Road, was constructed for the Jewish Community Center. It was later acquired by the City of Houston and renamed for Houston's first African American City Councilman. Photograph by Laurie Olin. Courtesy Olin Partnership.

Miller Outdoor Theatre

The first capital project undertaken by the Hermann Park Conservancy was to construct improvements to Miller Theatre. Ray Bailey Architects designed the building expansion for new restrooms (from seventeen to eighty-five toilets), a new ticket and staff offices, a storage and utility area, a new, larger food concession building, and a plaza. All systems within the building were upgraded. Landscaping was expanded and improved to include plazas and terraces, new outdoor lighting, staff parking, and service areas. In addition, the Cor-ten roof and siding were replaced. The conservancy and the City of Houston each paid about half of the $6 million construction budget. The improvements were complete for the opening of the 1998 Miller season on May 21.

Ten years later in 2008, additional improvements were carried out. A $1.2 million project was undertaken to increase accessibility for people with disabilities and to add lighting along the aisles. Stern and Bucek Architects designed a reconstructed walkway around the hill, decreasing the incline and making it wider to improve pedestrian flow, and relandscaped the general area. During the winter of 2008 to 2009, an additional $1 million in further improvements included regrading and raising the hill, new irrigation, new sod, and improved drainage. Seats under the canopy were replaced, and the concrete floor under the seats was given a new textured, colored surface. A permanent sound and lighting mix position booth was constructed at the back of the seating area, and, in the 2010 off-season, a $1.5 million sound system was installed. These changes improved the functioning and aesthetics of Miller Theatre, providing audiences with a first-class experience of performances under the dramatic Cor-ten steel shell, where there is seating for 1,705, with twenty wheelchair spaces.[32] The 80,000-square-foot sloping lawn now accommodates about 4,500 people. The theater building itself consists of a 64 by 41 foot stage; fifty-four line sets for hanging lights, curtains, and scenery; an orchestra pit, which can be raised and lowered; dressing rooms; offices; and a full complement of theatrical equipment. Miller Outdoor Theatre opened the 2010 season with a $1.5 million sound system, the latest upgrade in a sweeping set of $3.9 million in improvements since 2008. “The new speakers mean that everyone will be able to hear the performance more clearly throughout Miller, regardless of where you’re sitting,” said Dawn Ullrich, then director of the city’s Convention and Entertainment Facilities Department, which manages the city-owned theater in Hermann Park. “Miller is truly in the twenty-first century with this improvement, and we invite everyone to come hear for themselves. Both audience members and producers will notice.”[33]

The grounds of Miller Outdoor Theatre contain two sculptures of note. *Atropos Key* (1972), sited prominently atop Miller Hill, was donated to the city by Patricia S. Woodard. In Greek mythology At-

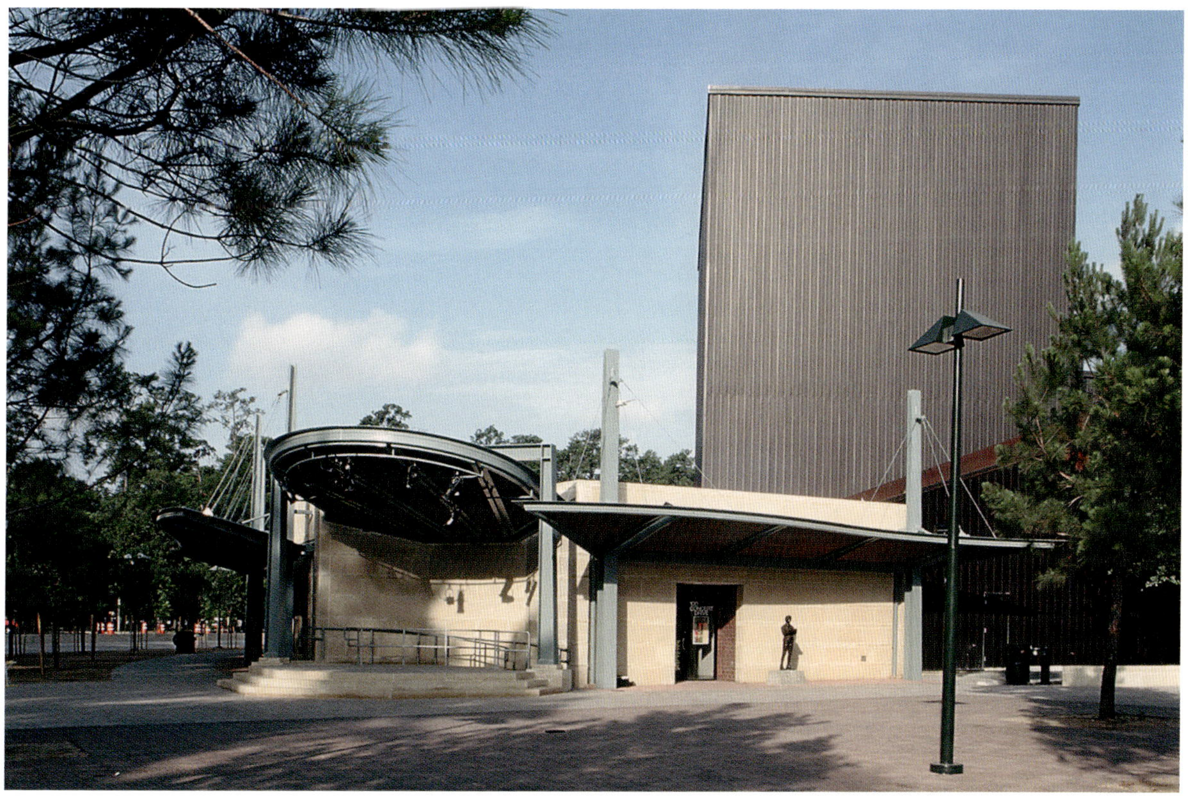

Miller Outdoor Theatre’s additions and renovations (1998, Bailey Architects) were the first capital project of the Hermann Park Conservancy and included new restrooms, concession building, and plaza along with offices and storage, 1998. Photograph by Richard Payne. Courtesy Bailey Architects.

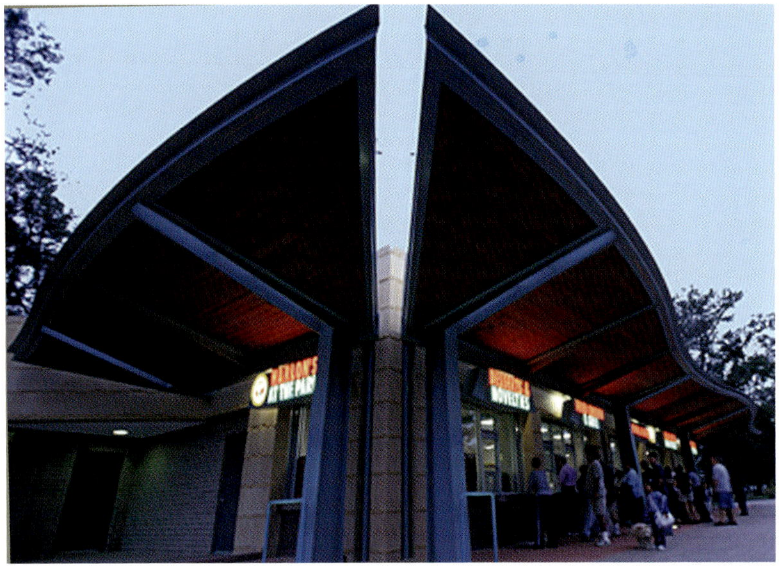

Miller Outdoor Theatre's concession stand (1998, Bailey Architects), c. 1999. Photograph by Jim Olive. Courtesy Miller Outdoor Theatre.

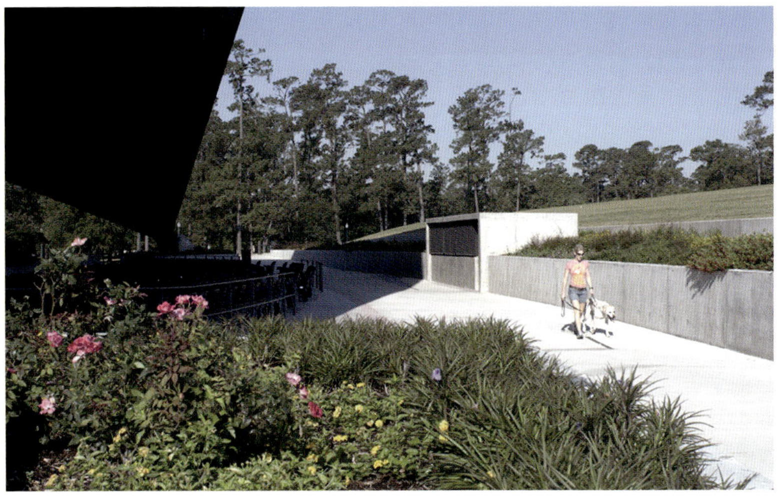

Miller Outdoor Theatre improvements (2008, Stern & Bucek Architects) included aisle lighting, handicap accessibility, and new walkways around the theater. The entire area was also relandscaped, 2009. Courtesy Stern and Buck Architects.

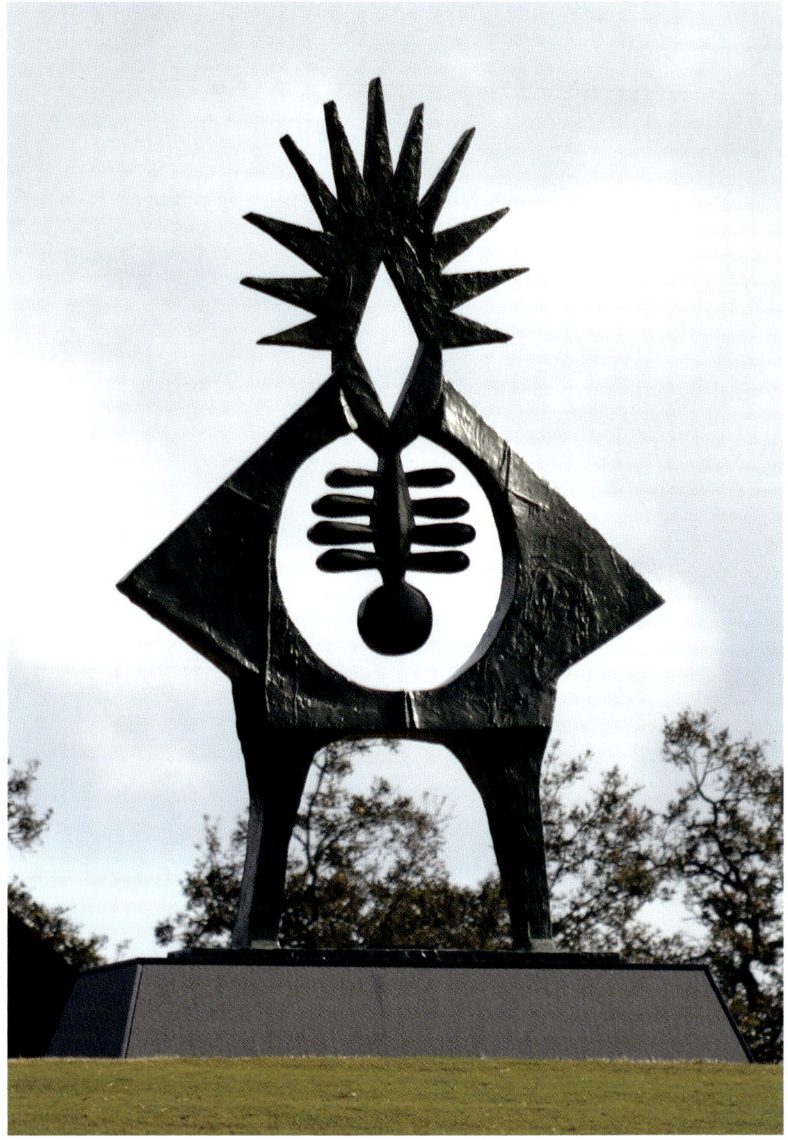

Atropos Key (1972, Hannah H. Stewart) is a cast bronze sculpture placed on a prominent site atop Miller Hill. Atropos, daughter of Zeus, was the oldest of the three goddesses of fate, or daughters of the night, who decided life and death. Atropos was the cutter of the thread of life and is often portrayed with a pair of scissors; Morta is her Roman equivalent, 2013. Photograph by B. S. Bradley.

ropos and her sisters, Clotho and Lachesis, were responsible for human destiny. The work of Hanna Stewart, *Atropos Key* is a polished, tool-surface cast bronze sculpture mounted on a trapezoidal concrete base faced with black slate. The second piece, *Oliver Twist* (1976), was dedicated as a "continuing plea to city fathers for support of free shows at the Miller Theatre." *Oliver* is the work of Houston sculptor Tracey Gutherie and was commissioned by Pamela Martens, a member of the Theater Under the Stars guild. The statue is life-size and portrays a young boy with an outstretched empty bowl with only a spoon in it. The sculpture, composed of cast bronze, sits on a concrete base outside the stage door.[34]

International Sculpture Garden

Hermann Park is the repository for various sculptural gifts from foreign governments to the City of Houston. As of 2013, twelve busts and statues of international heroes and leaders were in this collection.[35] One example is *Confucius* (2009, Willy Wang, artist), which was presented to the City of Houston from the People's Republic of China in com-

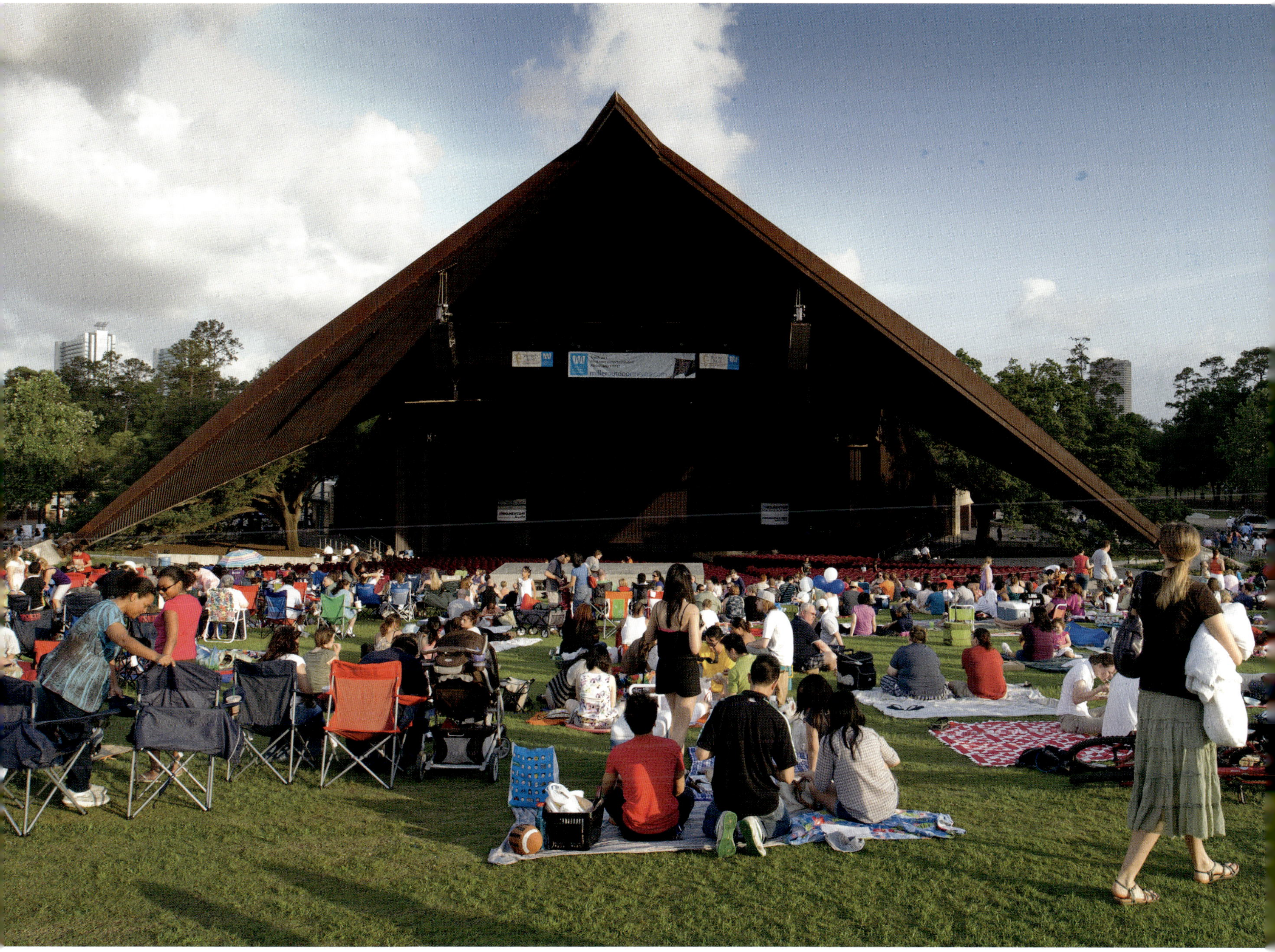

Open air concerts are held throughout the summer months at Miller Theatre. Patrons may obtain tickets to sit under the canopy, but most people arrive early and enjoy sitting on the hill with picnics, friends, and family, 2012. Photograph by Nash Baker Photography. Courtesy Hermann Park Conservancy.

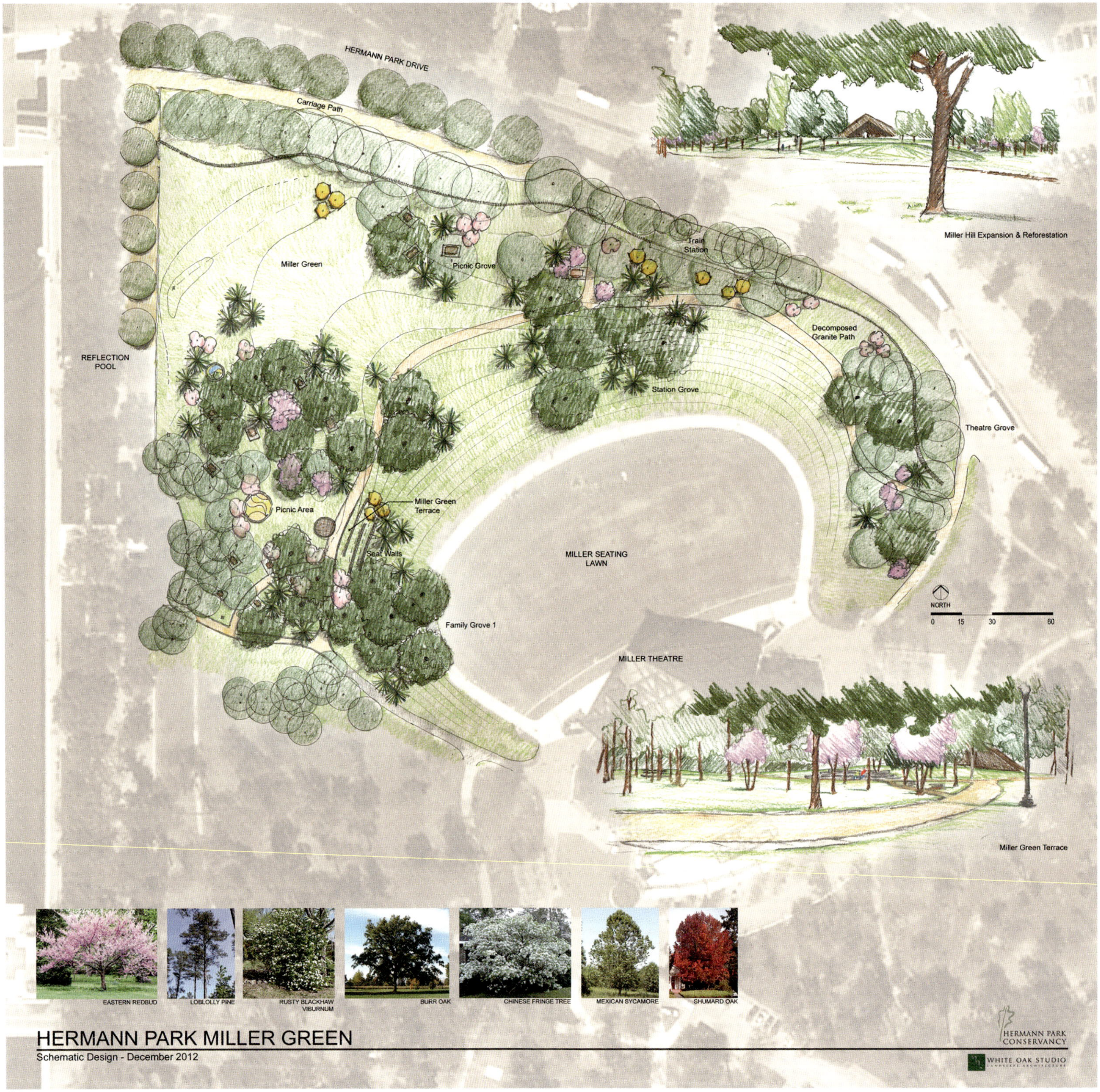

Miller Green (2012, White Oak Studio) is a relandscaped area northwest of Miller Hill that will include a small terraced area, a lawn, and new picnic grove, as suggested by the 1995 master plan. Courtesy Hermann Park Conservancy.

memoration of the thirtieth anniversary of the establishment of Sino–US diplomatic relations and the 2,560th anniversary of the birth of Confucius.[36] Once scattered throughout the Garden Center grounds, when the Centennial Gardens are completed in 2014, the statues will be aligned along a landscaped promenade leading into the gardens from the Caroline gate at the northwest corner of the garden, where they can be appreciated more fully.

Flores Garden Pavilion and McGovern Centennial Gardens

In 2014 ground will have been broken for the Centennial Gardens and new Garden Pavilion on a 15-acre site across the street from Miller Theatre. This area formerly contained a large parking lot along Hermann Park Drive, the 1941 Garden Center building, and a meadow along Hermann Drive where the Chinese Pavilion was placed, around which a planned garden was never built. The many varieties of roses that were on either side of the Garden Center will be incorporated in the new Centennial Gardens. While this area was a busy activity center, its configuration and condition created a barrier between the neighborhoods to the north and the rest of the park, including access to Miller Theatre and the Museum of Natural Science. The Garden Center grounds developed in a haphazard fashion, and this lack of planning resulted in an absence of cohesive design or substantial garden areas.

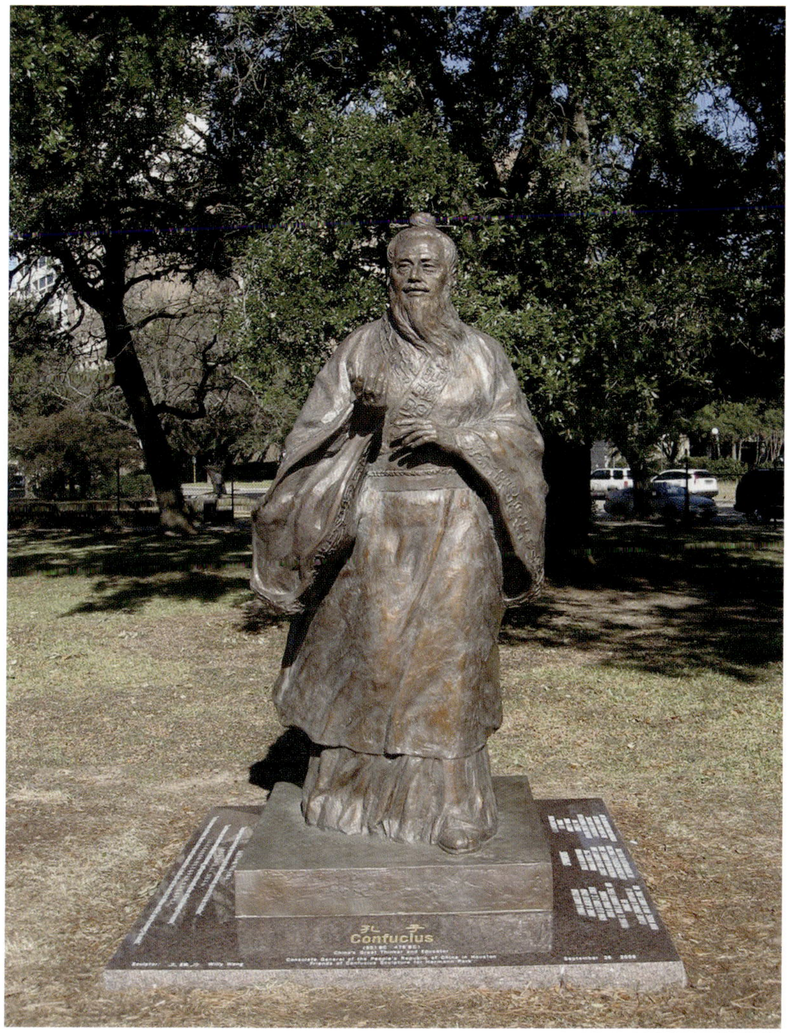

Confucius (2009, Willy Wang), is one of several busts or statues presented to the City of Houston by foreign governments and placed in the International Sculpture Garden in the Centennial Gardens of Hermann Park, 2013. Photograph by B. S. Bradley.

In 2012 the Chicago landscape architectural firm Hoerr Schaudt created a thoughtful master plan for the Centennial Gardens. The Wilkes-Barre, Pennsylvania, architect Peter Q. Bohlin, FAIA, who won the Gold Medal of the American Institute of Architects in 2010, was commissioned to design a new garden center/entry pavilion for the gardens. Bohlin Cywinski Jackson's elegant glass and stainless steel structure will pay homage to a glass conservatory planned by Hare & Hare but never built. The Centennial Gardens Pavilion will welcome visitors to the gardens and provide a venue for flower shows, meetings, and special garden club and community events.

Eight acres of the site will be entirely dedicated to gardens: a formal rose garden into which the old roses will be transplanted; an arid garden that will feature stone paths among cacti and succulents; an informal woodland garden with winding paths; a family garden for fruits and vegetables that will serve as an educational demonstration garden; a celebration garden that will be configured for events such as weddings; and a pine hill walk into which the Chinese Pavilion will be moved. Three pedestrian entrances to the garden will be from Hermann Drive at Caroline, from Hermann Park Drive across from Miller Theatre, and from the parking lot through a landscaped entrance promenade behind the new pavilion by Peter Bohlin. Access to the parking lot, studded with rows of trees, will be only from Hermann Drive at the north boundary of the park. The central, and most striking, features of the park will be a telescoping green lawn that will lead from the pavilion to a surprising 30-foot-high garden mount. There, on the west side of the lawn across from the pavilion, visitors will climb a winding path to the top to enjoy an entirely different prospect of the gardens and surrounding Hermann Park landscape. The Centennial Gardens will join the Japanese Garden in Hermann Park as a special destination. It will be a place where flowering plants follow the seasons and provide color and informal and formal beauty.

Hermann Park, in all of its 445 acres, is difficult to experience all at once, even from the air. It is always full of people there to visit different places for a variety of reasons: hundreds of children come on school buses to visit the Houston Museum of Natural Science or the Houston Zoo, retirees wander the gardens or sit in the shade; runners and walkers move along the Marvin Taylor Trail, patients and their families from

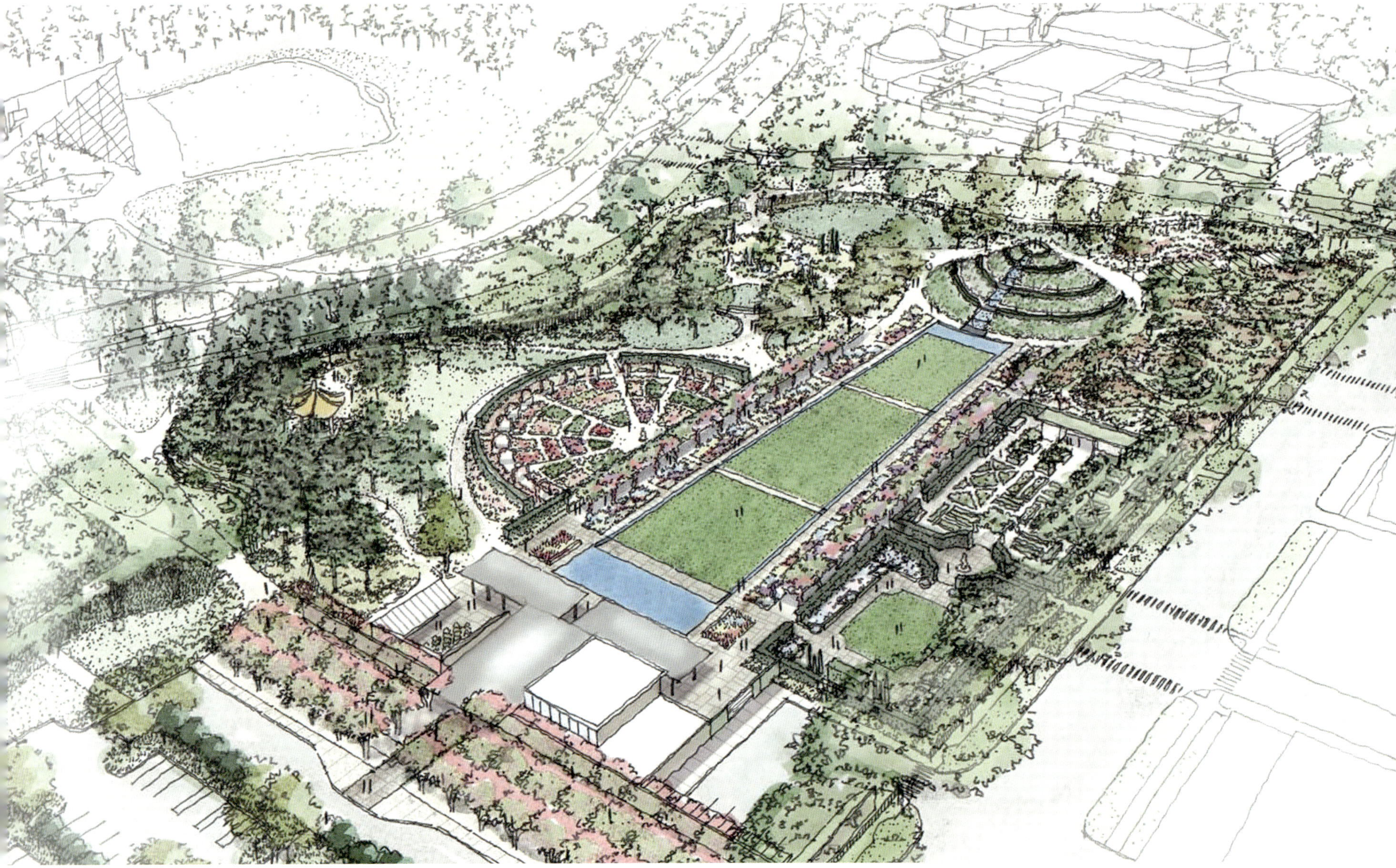

John P. and Kathrine G. McGovern Centennial Gardens Bird's-eye View (2012, Hoerr Schaudt with White Oak Studio) depicts elements planned for the new gardens: (from left to right) parking lot with access from Hermann Drive, a broad walkway through the landscaped International Sculpture Garden, the glass and steel entrance pavilion that gives way to a formal lawn, called the Centennial Green, reminiscent of the Reflection Pool in the Heart of the Park. The Green is bordered with perennial gardens and punctuated by shallow pools at either end; it narrows, creating a false perspective leading up to the 32-foot tall pyramidal Garden Mount ascended via a spiral pathway. A cascading waterfall will flow from the top of the Garden Mount to the pool at the far end of the Green. South of the Green the Chinese Pavilion will be resituated in a landscaped area under new loblolly and long-leaf pines. A formal Rose Garden will be a focal point, and paths beyond will wind through varied landscapes. North of the Green enfilade garden rooms include a hedge-enclosed Celebration Garden for special events, an interactive Family Garden with herbs, vegetables, and fruit trees, a woodland garden, and a new entrance gate at the corner of Caroline Street and Hermann Drive. Courtesy Hermann Park Conservancy.

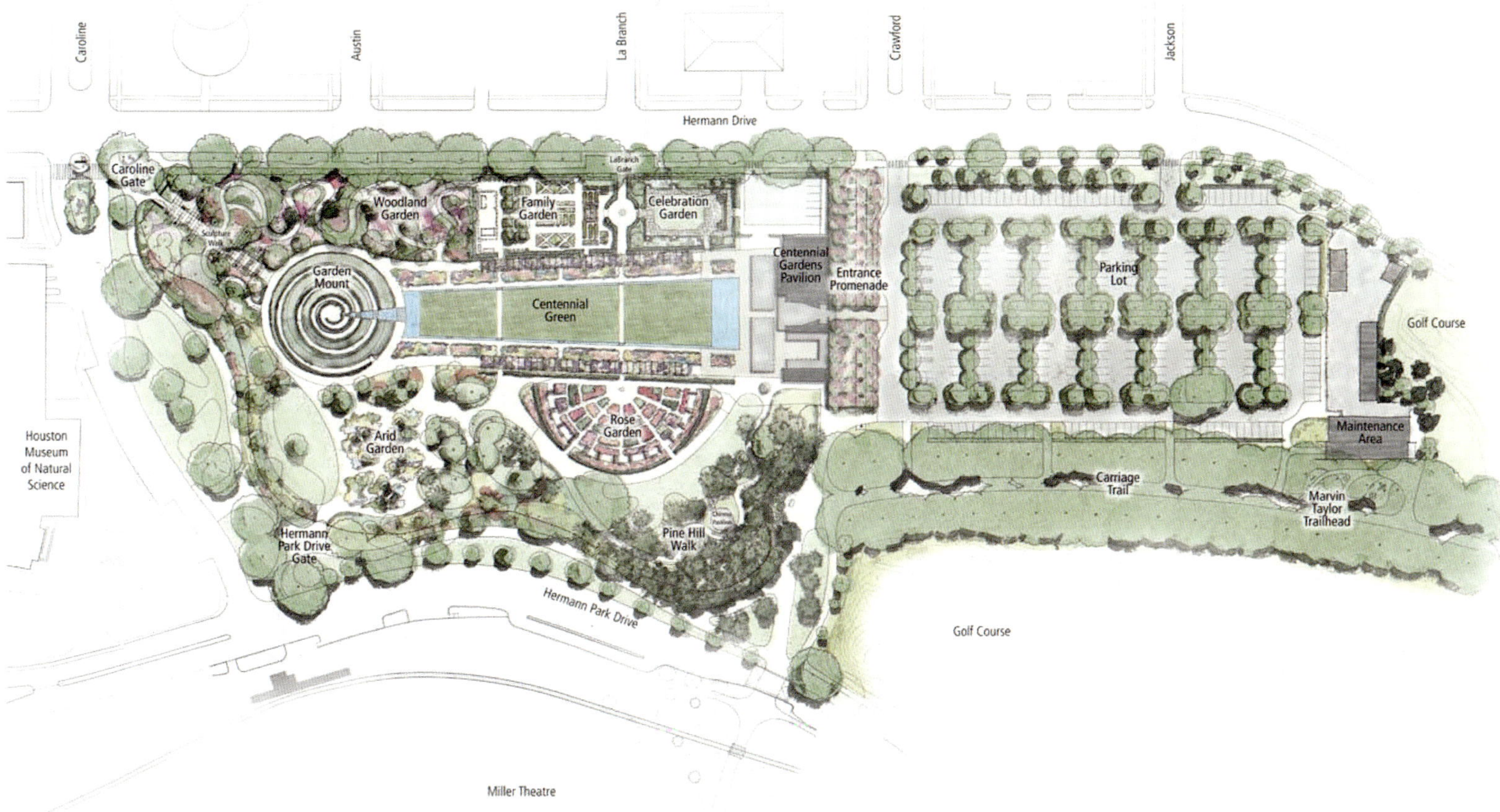

McGovern Centennial Gardens Site Plan (2012, Hoerr Schaudt with White Oak Studio). The Chicago landscape architecture firm Hoerr Schaudt developed this initial plan for the remaking of a 15-acre site at the north end of Hermann Park, where previously a large parking lot, meadow, and the 1941 Garden Center existed across from the Houston Museum of Natural Science. This plan will be fine-tuned as the garden configurations are developed and finalized. The landscape horticulturalist Dr. William C. Welch of Texas A&M University serves as a consultant on horticultural aspects of the Centennial Gardens. Courtesy Hermann Park Conservancy.

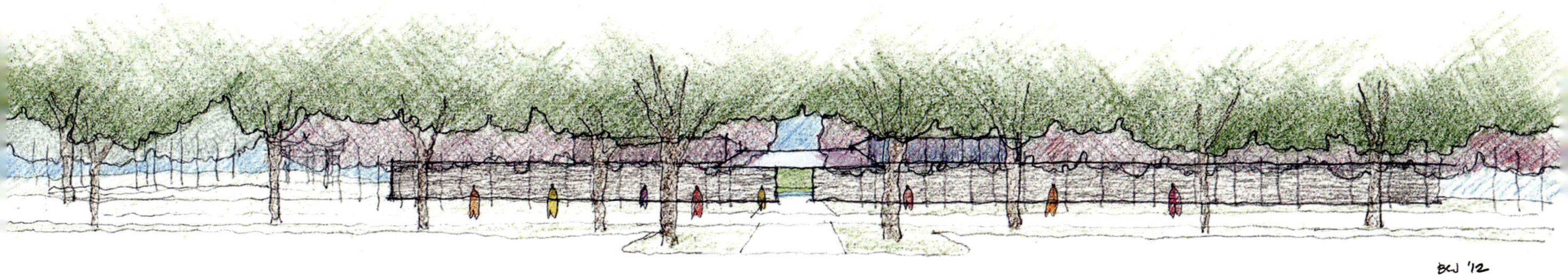

Entrance Promenade (2012, Bohlin Cywinski Jackson) looking west toward the interior of the Centennial Gardens from the parking lot. Courtesy Hermann Park Conservancy.

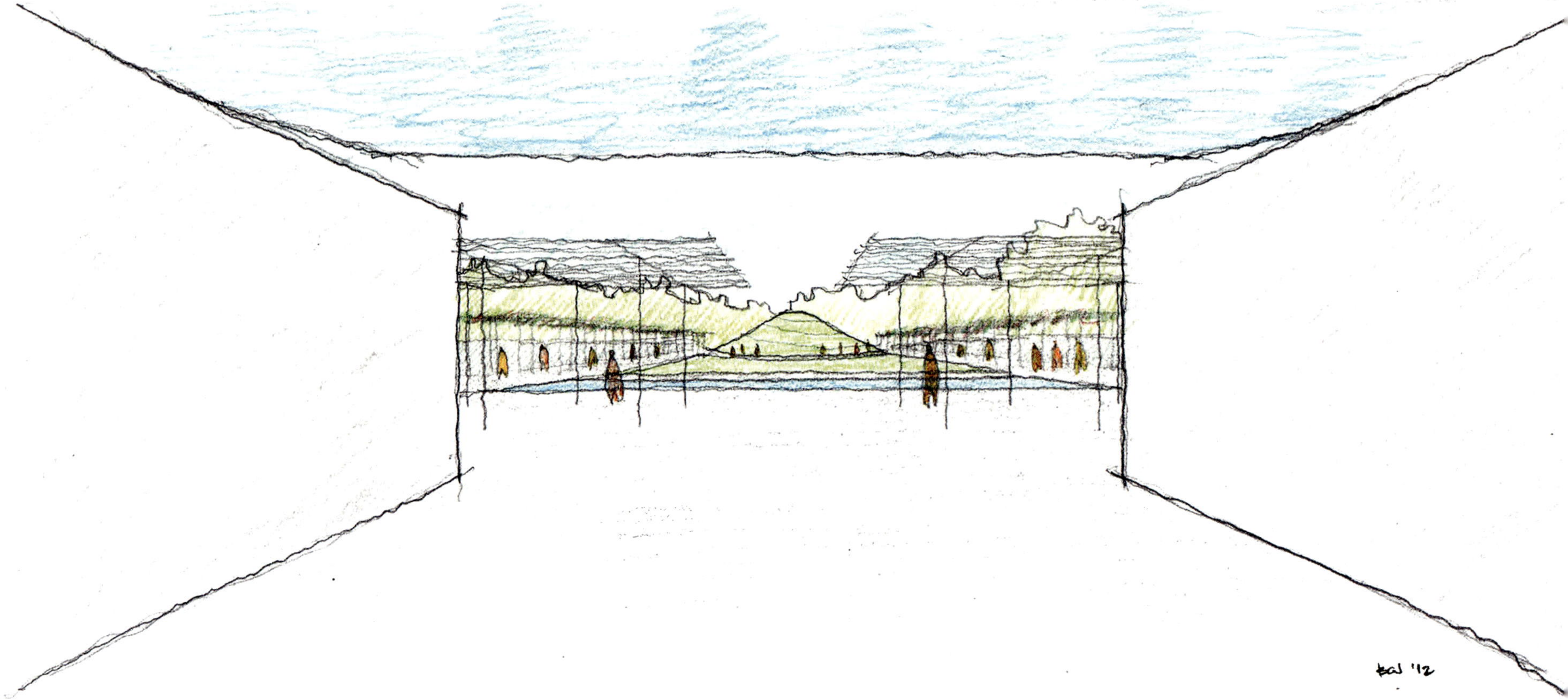

Walkway through the Cherie Flores Garden Pavilion into the gardens (2012, Bohlin Cywinski Jackson). Peter Bohlin, FAIA, is the architect for the Entry Pavilion designed to give the entrance to the gardens the feeling of a secret passageway that opens up to the surprise of the gardens on the other side. Courtesy Hermann Park Conservancy.

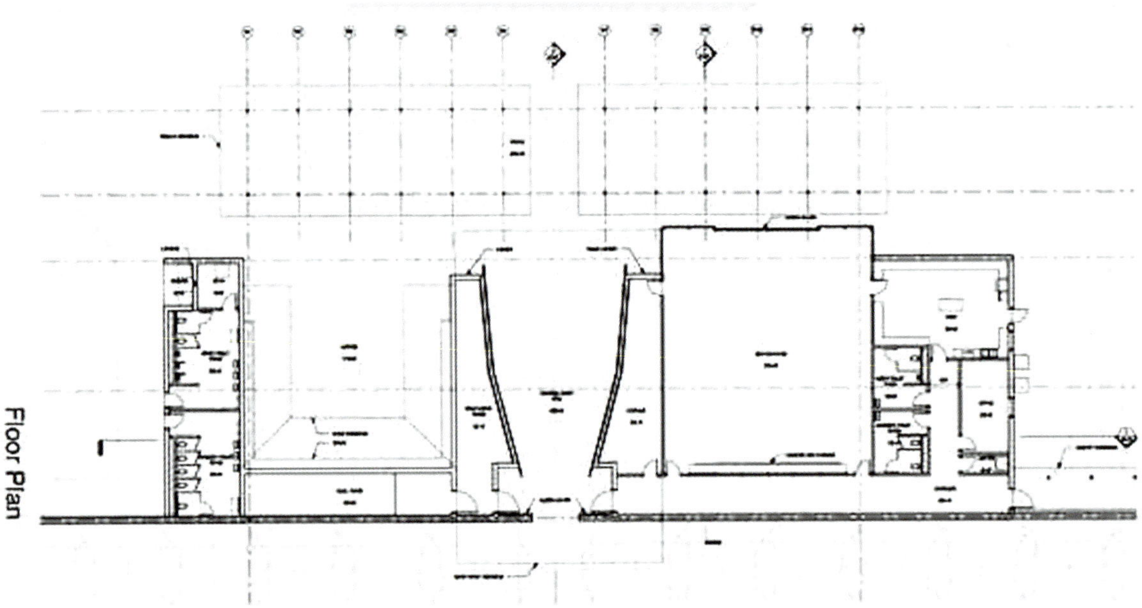

Floor Plan, Flores Garden Pavilion (2012, Bohlin Cywinski Jackson) shows that a kitchen, office, storage, and public restrooms are thoughtfully incorporated into the building without compromising its design intentions. Courtesy Hermann Park Conservancy.

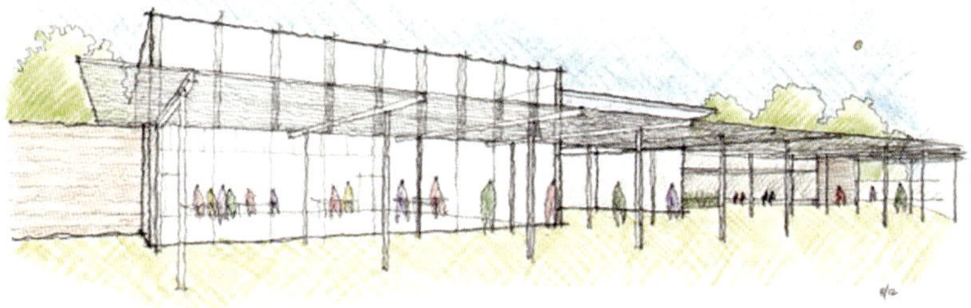

Cherie Flores Garden Pavilion Perspective (2012, Bohlin Cywinski Jackson). This jewel-like building contains on the north side (left) a large double-height glass box that looks onto the gardens and will be used for events, meetings, and flower shows. On the other side of the enclosed walkway, an open-air, roofed pavilion (that may someday be enclosed) will provide additional space. The design of this building is intended to take a backseat to the gardens and landscape yet provide an area from which the gardens can be appreciated. Courtesy Hermann Park Conservancy.

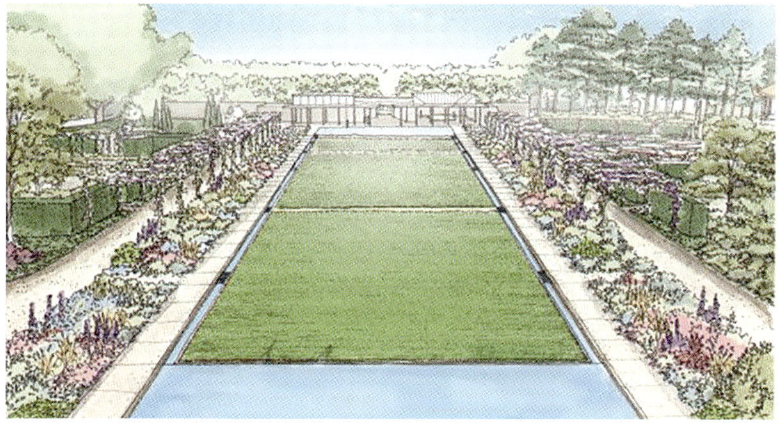

Centennial Green (2012, Hoerr Schaudt with White Oak Studio) looking east from the Garden Mount toward the Entry Pavilion showing perennial garden borders and wisteria pergolas. Courtesy Hermann Park Conservancy.

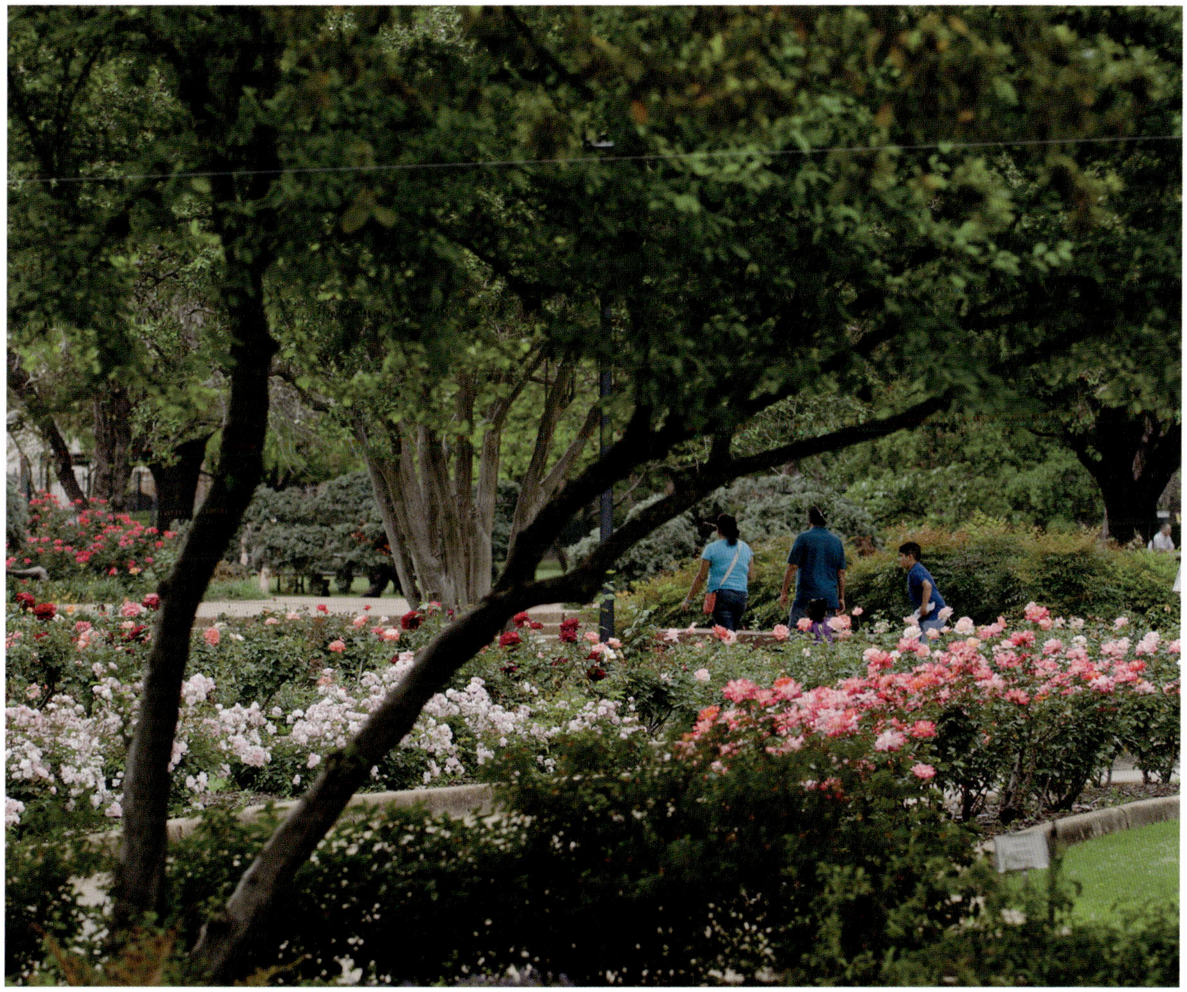

Rose beds will be reconfigured in the Centennial Gardens, 2012. Photograph by Nash Baker Photography. Courtesy Hermann Park Conservancy.

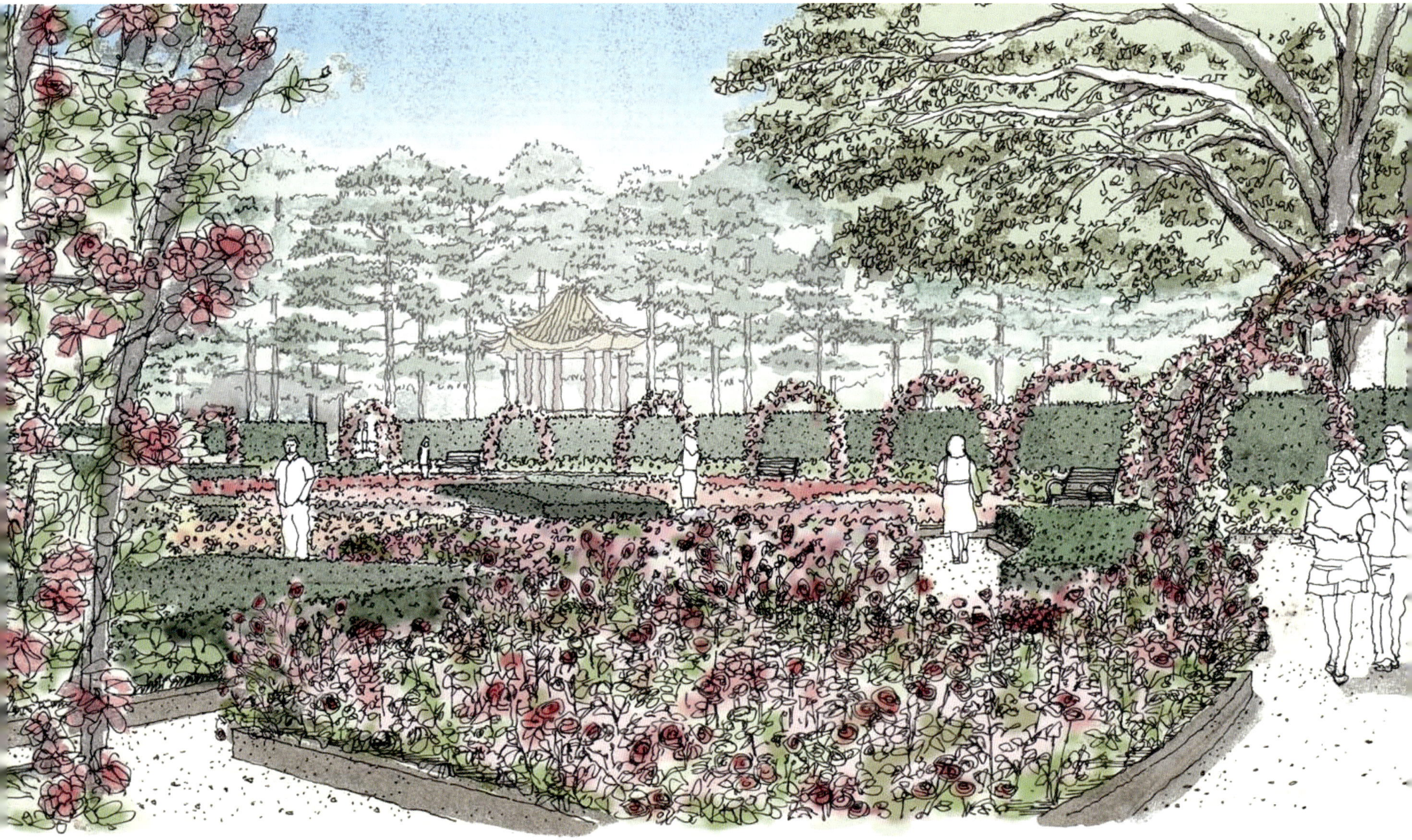

Centennial Rose Garden (2012, Hoerr Schaudt with White Oak Studio) with Chinese Pavilion among the pine trees in the background. Courtesy Hermann Park Conservancy.

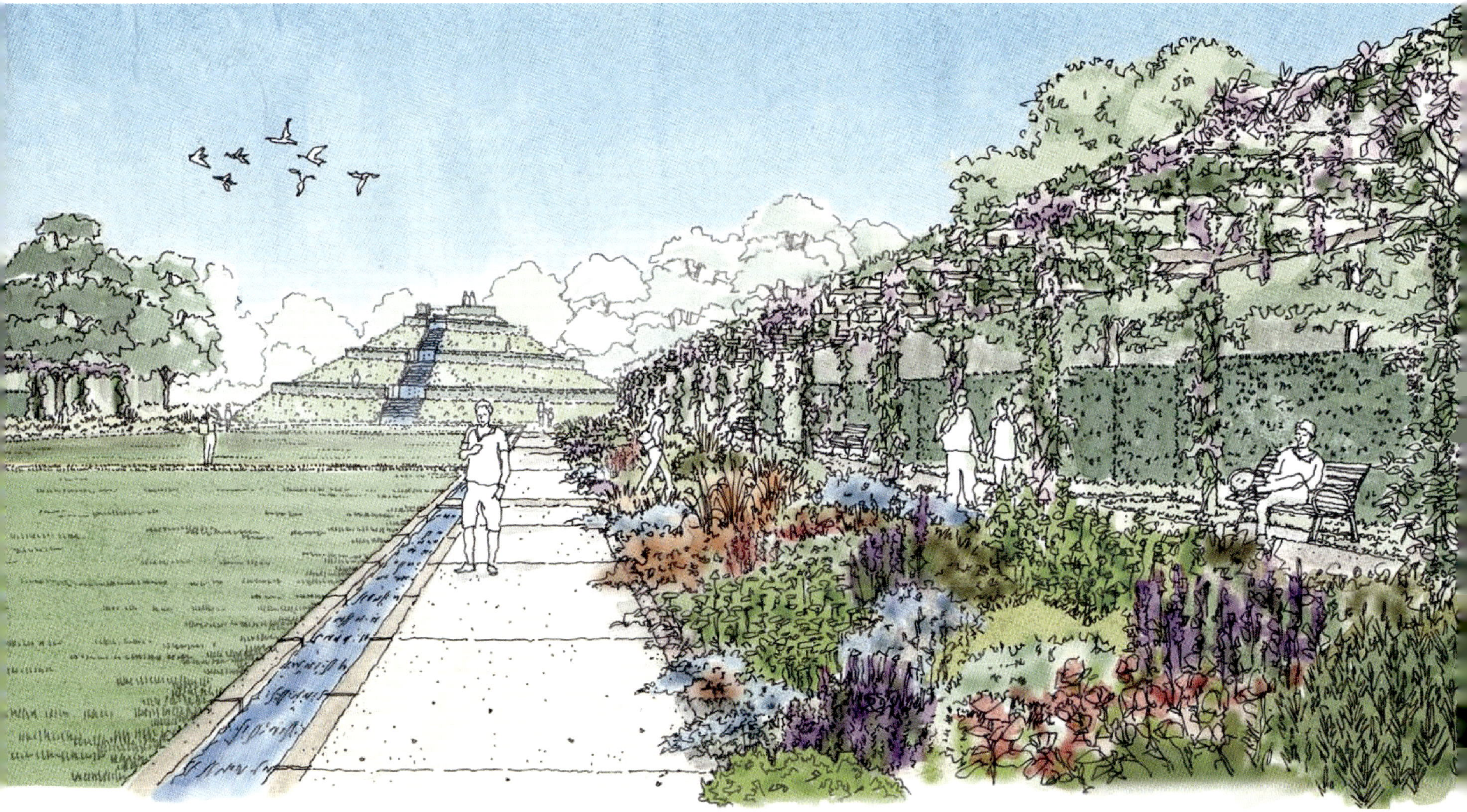

Centennial Green (2012, Hoerr Schaudt with White Oak Studio) looking west from the Entry Pavilion toward the Garden Mount with perennial garden borders and wisteria pergolas. Courtesy Hermann Park Conservancy.

the medical center come to soak up fresh air and sunshine, and golfers are spread over the historic Hermann Park golf course. Photographers find interesting natural subjects or use the natural beauty of the park for memorable pictures, such as bridal portraits. Moms with preschoolers feed the ducks, and birdwatchers count the birds in the early morning. Lovers hold hands by the lake in the evenings, and, on weekends, families ride the train, picnic, scoot pedal boats across the McGovern Lake, visit the zoo, celebrate birthdays, laugh, and play. This place, initially a gift of land from a very generous man, is still, a hundred years later, in the process of becoming. Stewards of the park know that to stand still is to go backward, and they have no intention of doing that. Private citizens, in an exemplary partnership with the City of Houston, plan to keep improving and maintaining Hermann Park's landscapes and services for another hundred years and beyond.

Afterword

The revitalization of Hermann Park is a miracle of community engagement. Determined to rejuvenate the park, supporters from the conservancy's early days wisely realized that a strong public/private partnership would be necessary to create a lasting transformation. At a time when few such partnerships existed in the United States, Houstonians joined with public agencies, especially the City of Houston Parks and Recreation Department, to renew the park project by project.

Twenty years later, Hermann Park has become a place not just loved by the Houston community, but also supported by it, through its institutions, corporations, and families. Thousands of people have given money and thousands more have given their time as volunteers working in the park and participants in public, board, and committee meetings to guide the park's future. It takes this level of personal commitment to sustain the successful public/private partnership we have in Hermann Park. This commitment also builds community — evident any pretty afternoon when you can hear a dozen different languages and see people of every age enjoying the park.

While this book captures Hermann Park's first hundred years, Hermann Park Conservancy is already planning for its next century. Immediate future plans for the park include an off-leash dog park and a healing garden, within park property, across the street from the Texas Medical Center. We will enhance educational programming as children in this increasingly dense city become more cut off from the natural world. We will continue to emphasize the health benefits of trees in an urban environment, the rich vitality found in a coastal prairie, and the magic of watching food come from the ground.

The park's centennial year, 2014, will bring many celebrations of the park: publication of this book, a kite festival, a bike ride along the new Brays Bayou trails to the Houston Ship Channel, and dedication of the Grand Gateway and the Centennial Gardens that will substantially complete the 1994 master plan. We will also host public art programs to bring people together to see both the art and the park in new ways. The Hermann Park Conservancy dares to dream of the rich, endless possibilities for the park's next hundred years. Join us!

Doreen Stoller
Executive Director, Hermann Park Conservancy

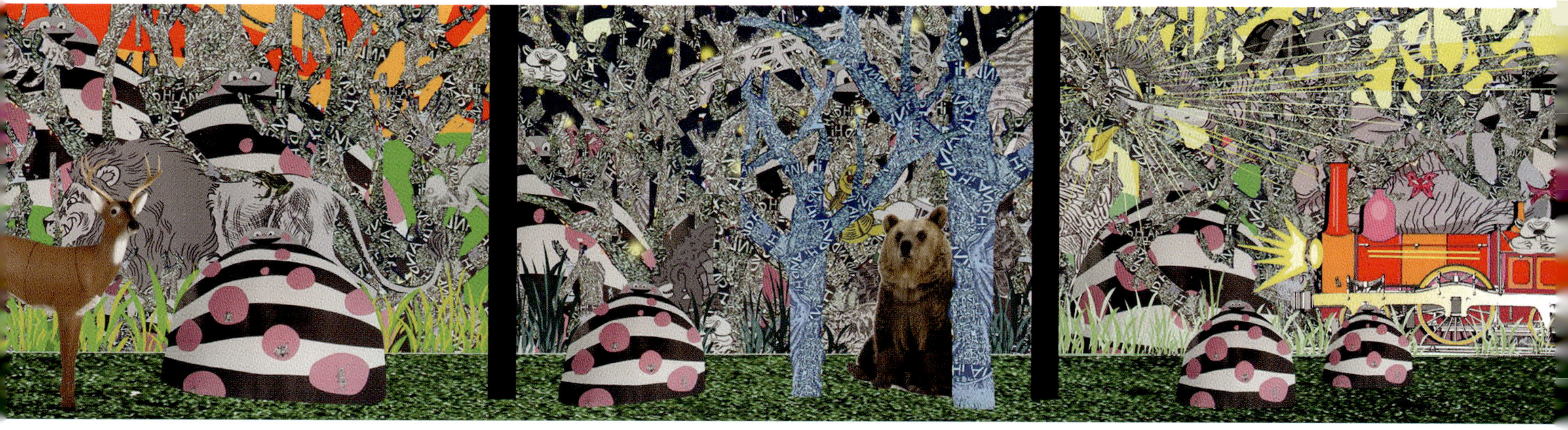

Train Tunnel Mural (2014, Trenton Doyle Hancock). Source: James Cohan Gallery, New York and Shanghai. Courtesy Hermann Park Conservancy.

APPENDIX ONE

Hermann Park and Houston Chronology of Significant Events

Year	Hermann Park	Houston
1910	Mayor H. Baldwin Rice appoints Board of Park Commissioners July 12: George H. Hermann signs Last Will and Testament leaving property for Hermann Park	Houston population: 78,800 (68th largest US city) surpasses Galveston Federal government agrees to pay one-half of the cost of building the Houston Ship Channel Mexican Revolution begins; displaced Mexicans begin to pour into Houston
1912	Arthur Coleman Comey retained to create a general plan for Houston	Classes begin at the Rice Institute
1913	March 1: Comey Report delivered	Ben Campbell elected mayor (1913–1917) Clarence Brock becomes first Park Superintendent. Houston Symphony established
1914	April: J. S. Cullinan meets George Kessler June 7: George Hermann formally donates land for Hermann Park October 21: George Hermann dies	Houston Ship Channel opens World War I begins in Europe Texas Company Building completed
1915	Maxcy Plan for Hermann Park published July 4: Dedication and Opening of Hermann Park George E. Kessler commissioned to plan Hermann Park	First deep water vessel docks in Houston
1916	Cullinan begins development of Shadyside Major roadways in Hermann Park built	March 15: Houston Department of Public Parks created *Titanic* sinks
1917	Shelter House built near entrance to Hermann Park—first structure in the park Sunken Garden at Main and Montrose built Site for Museum of Fine Arts secured	Joseph J. Pastoriza elected mayor (1917) Joseph C. Hutcheson elected mayor (1917–1918) US enters World War I Camp Logan and Ellington Field built
1918		A. E. Amerman elected mayor (1918–1921)

1919		18th Amendment to US Constitution institutes prohibition beginning in 1920 19th Amendment to US Constitution grants women's suffrage
1920	200 Memorial live oaks planted Earl the Buffalo donated to the City of Houston	Houston population: 138,276 (45th largest US city, 3rd largest city in Texas)
1921	Bridle and foot paths laid out and cleared William Ward Watkin commissioned to design new Miller Memorial Theatre	Oscar F. Holcombe elected mayor (1921–1929)
1922	Automobile Tourist Camp National Guard asks for property in park for armory Forty zoo animals move to Hermann Park Golf Course construction begun	Houston gets first motorized fire-fighting vehicles
1923	May 12: Miller Memorial Theatre opens	
1924	Central block of Museum of Fine Arts completed 133.5-acre Hogg Tract sold to city Hare & Hare landscaped Sunken Garden Golf Course completed	Port Terminal Railroad organized Parks Department budget is $216,604.22. The department's goal is to have a park within a 1/2 mile of every house. The Recreation Department believes a park should be within a 1/4 mile of every home. River Oaks lot sales begin
1925	Excavation of Grand Basin Hermann Hospital completed April: Sam Houston Monument installed	Houston–Dallas bus line begins KPRC, Houston's first radio station, begins broadcasting
1926	Flanking wings of Museum of Fine Arts completed Peggy MacGregor donates MacGregor Tract (108 acres) to the city	Warwick Hotel opens adjacent to Hermann Park
1927	Botanical Gardens planned	Niels Esperson Building completed Houston Junior College and its African American counterpart (forerunners of UH and Texas Southern University) open on separate campuses
1928		Bayou Bend completed Airmail service in Houston begins Democratic National Convention held in Houston
1929		Walter E. Monteith elected mayor (1929–1933) Gulf Building completed Stock Market Crash

1930	Hare & Hare General Plan Museum of Natural Science opens	Houston Population: 292,352 (26th largest US city, largest in Texas)
1933	Hermann Park Clubhouse constructed	Oscar F. Holcombe elected mayor (1933–1937) 21st Amendment to US Constitution repeals prohibition
1934		Intracoastal Canal system links Houston with the entire Mississippi River system of navigation Houston Junior College becomes a four-year institution and changes its name to the University of Houston
1935		Braniff Airways begins passenger air service in Houston Buffalo Bayou overflows, causing the worst flood in Houston history up to that time
1936	Pioneer Memorial Obelisk donated Pioneer Memorial Log Cabin donated	Texas and Houston Centennial celebrations
1937	Central Lions Club propose George Hermann Memorial Hermann Park has a donkey trail with fourteen donkeys at the zoo	R. H. Fonville elected mayor (1937–1938) Houston Municipal Airport (Hobby) opens Became illegal to pasture cows on city esplanades The Parks Department was re-created after the Depression with a board of six park commissioners
1938	2nd golf course proposed for Hogg Tract Houston Conservatory of Music asks for site on Main St. Houston Independent School District asks for site on Almeda for stadium W. W. Watkin designs Garden Center	
1939		Oscar F. Holcombe elected mayor (1939–1941) University of Houston moves to current campus
1940		Houston population: 384,514 (21st largest US city) Houston streetcar system dismantled, buses replace streetcars World War II begins
1941	Garden Center opens	C. A. Pickett elected mayor (1941–1943) Public Parks Department budget is $150,000
1942		Hare & Hare creates street and parks master plan for Houston
1943	Lion's Club commissions George Hermann Statue (Cerracchio) City of Houston initiated Summer Symphony Series at Miller Theatre	Otis Massey elected mayor (1943–1947) Parks Department and Recreation Department merged. C. C. "Pat" Flemming becomes first director. Budget of combined department $297,972.

1945	Hogg Tract sold to M. D. Anderson for Texas Medical Center	M. D. Anderson Foundation forms the Texas Medical Center World War II ends
1947	Hare & Hare Zoo expansion begins	Oscar F. Holcombe elected mayor (1947–1952) Foley's Department Store opens Alley Theatre begins productions First referendum on zoning defeated Texas Southern University founded University of St. Thomas founded
1948	Hare & Hare proposes museum on Cullinan house site in Shadyside Fannin cut through Hermann Park Miller Hill created with dirt for Fannin Street excavations	Gulf Freeway, the first freeway in Texas, opens
1949	$800,000 zoo expansion	KPRC (as KLEE), first TV station in Houston and 12th in US, begins broadcasting
1950	New zoo opens Beal v. Holcombe lawsuit filed protesting segregation of Hermann Park Golf Course	Houston population: 596,163 (14th largest US city)
1951	Jewish Community Center (now Judson Robinson, Jr., Community Center) constructed	Methodist Hospital opens in the Texas Medical Center Texas Children's Hospital opens
1953		Roy Hofheinz elected mayor (1953–1955)
1954	Miniature train begins operation, pulled by a tractor June 3: Hermann Park Golf Course racially integrated	
1955		Houston Ballet Academy opens Houston Grand Opera chartered
1956		Oscar F. Holcombe elected mayor (1956–1957)
1958		Lewis Cutrer elected mayor (1958–1963)
1959	Brays Bayou straightened and lined with concrete	
1960		Houston Population: 938,219 (7th largest US city) Houston Baptist University founded Houston Oilers founded

1961		Hurricane Carla hits Houston NASA selects Houston as headquarters for its manned space center Sharpstown Mall, the first indoor air-conditioned mall in Houston, opens
1962	Rose Garden approved	Zoning defeated for a second time Houston Astros baseball team founded
1963	Museum of Natural Science founded	NASA opens near Clear Lake on land donated by Rice University Humble Building completed, then the tallest building west of the Mississippi
1964	Mecom Fountain built in Sunken Garden Burke Baker Planetarium at Museum of Natural Science opens	Louie Welch elected mayor (1964–1973)
1965		Astrodome opens
1966		Barbara Jordan elected to US House of Representatives from Houston Jones Hall opens
1967		Houston Rockets basketball team founded
1968	Miller Memorial Theatre demolished Mecom Rockwell Colonnade built Museum of Natural Science's new building opens	
1969	Miller Outdoor Theatre opens Mecom–Rockwell Fountain installed	Houston Intercontinental Airport opens Houston Ballet Company formed
1970		Houston Population: 1,232,802 (6th largest US city) Galleria opens
1972	LAN/Cummins Master Plan submitted	Rice Design Alliance organized
1974		Fred Hofheinz elected mayor (1974–1977)
1975		Pennzoil Place completed
1978	Chinese Pavilion installed Exer-Trail opens	Jim McConn elected mayor (1978–1981) James S. Hart appointed Director of Houston Parks and Recreation Department Cultural Arts Council of Houston created to allocate hotel/motel taxes to promote tourism

Year	Hermann Park	Houston
1980	Cravens Walkway installed	Houston Population: 1,595,138 (5th largest US city)
1981	George Hermann statue installed	
1982	Kipp Aquarium opens	Kathryn Whitmire elected mayor (1982–1991) Texas Commerce Tower (tallest building west of the Mississippi) completed Trees for Houston founded as the Live Oak Society
1983	Charles Moore Plan submitted Bloch Cancer Survivors Plaza built	Don Olson appointed Director of Houston Parks and Recreation Department Hurricane Alicia strikes Houston Transco Tower completed
1985		Transco Fountain completed
1987	Hermann Park Joggers, Runners, and Walkers incorporated	Shamrock Hotel demolished George R. Brown Convention Center opens Wortham Center opens
1988	Pedal boats begin operation on McGovern Lake	
1989	Proposed site for George Bush Library Wortham IMAX Theatre opens at Museum of Natural Science Zoo reopens after renovation and begins to charge admission fees	Rick Dewees begins tenure with the Houston Parks and Recreation Department
1990	Neighbors of Hermann Park organized New entry plaza for Museum of Natural Science completed	Houston population: 1,630,553 (4th largest US city) Greater Houston population: 3,322,025 President George H. W. Bush hosts G7 Economic Summit in Houston
1991	Mecom–Rockwell Fountain and Colonnade landscaped	
1992	Friends of Hermann Park organized Heart of the Park Design Competition Japanese Garden opens	Bob Lanier elected mayor (1992–1997)
1993	Laurie Olin of Hanna/Olin retained for Master Plan Mary Anne Piacentini becomes executive director	Zoning defeated for the third time Bill Smith appointed Director of Houston Parks and Recreation Department
1994	Cockrell Butterfly Center at Museum of Natural Science opens	

1995	Olin Master Plan completed Carruth Playground for All Children opens	*Houston Post* ceases publication
1996	Zoo opens Wortham World of Primates Grant from the Lila Wallace–Reader's Digest Fund, a key gift that led to many others	Houston Oilers leave town
1997	City Council approves Master Plan and necessary funding arrangements in operating agreement with Hermann Park Conservancy	
1998	Miller Outdoor Theatre improvements completed Patricia Winn becomes executive director	Lee P. Brown elected mayor (1998–2004) Oliver Spellman, Jr., appointed Director of Houston Parks and Recreation Department
1999	Roksan Okan-Vick becomes executive director Bayou Parkland restored Bayou Parkland Pavilion built Golf Course renovation and new Golf Clubhouse constructed North MacGregor realigned	
2000	"Action 2000" strategic plan adopted New West Entrance to Zoo completed Bayou Parkland Pavilion constructed	Greater Houston Population: 4,177,646 Minute Maid park opens
2001	McGovern Lake opens Molly Ann Smith Plaza completed	World Trade Center twin towers destroyed on 9/11 Enron scandal Tropical Storm Allison devastates Houston area, flooding the Texas Medical Center
2002	Maintenance and Operations Plan by Ukeles and ETM Marvin Taylor Trail improvements Holiday Lights begins Kinder Station completed and the renewed Hermann Park Railroad begins operation Fannin Pavilion restored Bob's Fishing Pier opened	Houston Texans Football team founded
2003	Doreen Stoller becomes executive director Parking lot at Sam Houston Circle completed	Roksan Okan-Vick appointed Director of Houston Parks and Recreation Department Houston becomes fourth city to sign Urban Conservation Treaty for Migratory Birds

2004	Named changed to Hermann Park Conservancy from Friends of Hermann Park Urban Green formed Heart of the Park: Lindsey Plaza, Jones Reflection Pool, Mitchell Garden, Arbor in the Pines, and Smith Plaza completed Carousel installed at zoo	Bill White elected mayor (2004–2010) Joe Turner appointed Director of Houston Parks and Recreation Department METRORail Red Line opens Houston hosts the Super Bowl in new Reliant Stadium Houston hosts Major League All-star game in Minute Maid Park
2005	Heart of the Park wins national ASLA General Award for Design Excellence Rotary Picnic Grove completed	Houston welcomes more than 125,000 people displaced from Hurricane Katrina Houston Summit becomes Lakewood Church Houston Dynamo Soccer Team founded
2006	Pedestrian Greenway Trail through the golf course opened	
2007	Teronobu Nakai begins restoration of Japanese Garden	
2008	Train route expanded	Hurricane Ike strikes Houston
2009	Lake Plaza with Kinder Station opens Tiffany & Co. Foundation Bridge opens Jones Greenway completed Miller Theatre reopens after renovation and improvements Project Blazing Star	
2010	Bernar Venet Exhibition	Greater Houston Population: 5,946,800 Annise Parker elected mayor (2010–
2011	Pedestrian Trail renovated	Texas and Houston suffers catastrophic droughts Houston Ballet Center for Dance opens Houston celebrates 175th anniversary
2012	Ai Weiwei Exhibition *Circle of Animals/Zodiac Heads* Bill Coats Bridge completed Dan Duncan Wing of the Museum of Natural Science opens	BBV Compass Stadium for soccer completed
2014	Grand Gateway completed Hermann Park Centennial John P. and Kathrine G. McGovern Centennial Gardens completed Trenton Doyle Hancock Train Tunnel mural completed Cherie Flores Garden Pavilion completed	

APPENDIX TWO

Remarks of George H. Hermann

Sunday, June 7, 1914, City Auditorium

I am no talker, and I do not speak very loud, but I will try to make a short speech.

I am the son of a man who was born at Davos, Switzerland in 1791, who afterward went to France and served under Napoleon the First. When Napoleon called for troops, my father joined the army and fought at Waterloo, where he received a sabre wound. In 1821 he came to Norfolk, Va., but returned to Davos, where he married my mother. They came back to the country, went to Vera Cruz, and later returned to New Orleans.

My parents landed in Houston with five dollars and three children. My mother pawned her jewelry, and my father bought a little flour and sugar and established a bakery on Main Street, where the Postal telegraph office now is located. I guess he was the first baker in Houston. In 1842 he bought the block bounded by McKinney, Brazos, Smith and Walker, and built the house in which I was born. It was while living there that my mother taught me economy, which I have never forgotten. I served in the army when the war broke out, and there were two things that I learned there. Instead of "I won't" and "I can't," I learned "I will" and "I can."

When I returned from the army I found that both my parents were dead. I had to go to work. I had no experience. They say the old fogies don't know anything. But I went to the old fogies, Bagby, Fisher, Andrews, and others and got their advice. After listening to them, I did my own thinking and formed my own ideas and carried them out. Later I joined with W. J. and J. J. Settegast, and I would like to tell you a little story of how I worked a game on them.

John Huggins of Fulcher County met me one day and told me that he had $70,000 lying idle in a bank in New York. I said: "John, I would like to borrow $15,000, and I will give you good security but pay you very little interest."

"All right," said Huggins, and fixed the interest at 5 percent. Just then I remembered that my property was all mortgaged, but I couldn't tell him, and he wanted to see the security. So I carried him around and showed him the Dissen house. The property was not mine. It belonged to J. J. Settegast, so I hunted him up and said, "Jules, I've just mortgaged that property," and told him about it. "There's no way out," I said. "You've got to sign up with me."

Honesty and economy always go together. The man who will follow this idea will succeed. Always do your thinking before making your promises. Mr. Mayor, I want to present you this deed, as the representation of the people of the City of Houston, for the benefit of the poor and the rich, and, as their representative, you will see that its terms are complied with.

"Thousands Gather to Pay Tribute to Donor of City's Great New Park," *Houston Chronicle*, Monday, June 8, 1914.

APPENDIX THREE

Last Will and Testament of George H. Hermann
County Clerk's Office—Harris County Probate Court Records File # 6425

In the name of God Amen: I, George H. Hermann, a resident of the City of Houston, Harris County, Texas sound of mind and body, do make, publish and declare this to be my last will and testament, hereby revoking all former wills and codicils.

I.

It is my wish that the executors should pay all just debts, if any, that I may owe at the time of my death as soon after the probate of this will as it is convenient so to do.

II

I will bequeath to such of the children of W. J. Settegast deceased, that are living when this will takes effect the sum of Five Thousand ($5000.00) Dollars to be divided between them equally.

III.

I will and bequeath to my friend J. J. Settegast the sum of Five Thousand ($5000.00) Dollars. Should he not be living at the time this will takes effect then I will that the said sum of Five Thousand Dollars shall be divided equally among such of this other children as are living at that time.

IV.

I will and bequeath to Mrs. Mary Sherwine, and to Mrs. Henrietta Meineke, both formerly were Misses Ewing, to each the sum of One Thousand ($1000) Dollars.

V.

I will and bequeath to my friend T. J. Ewing, Sr. Lots Six (6) Seven (7) Eleven (11) and Twelve (12) in Block One Hundred and Forty Nine (149) on the South side of Buffalo Bayou in the City of Houston, Harris County, Texas, and also the sum of Six Thousand ($6000) Dollars in money. In addition thereto I will to the said T. J. Ewing Sr. the sum of Seventy-five ($75.00) Dollars per month, the same to be paid to him monthly by my executors and trustees as long as he shall live, and should his wife Martha survive him then I will that after his death the said sum of Seventy-five ($75.00) Dollars per month shall be paid to her during her life.

VI.

I will and bequeath to George H. Getchell, the son of Ellen Getchell a life estate in and to lot Number Nine (9) in Block Fifty-seven (57) on the South side of Buffalo Bayou in the City of Houston; also in 909 acres more or less in Fort Bend County, Texas, out of the Barnett & Shipman Survey, know as the Mulbery and White fields now rented to E. J. Williams, being all of the land owned by me in said survey; also my gold watch, the one usually worn by me, together with all the rents and revenues to be derived from said lands during his natural life. At his death, should he leave children surviving him, the fee simple title of said lot and lands to vest in his said children but in the event he leaves no children surviving him then said lot and lands above described shall become vested in the Hermann hospital hereinafter provided for in the Ninth paragraph.

VII.

I will and bequeath to the City of Houston Block 146 on the South Side of Buffalo Bayou, the same to be held in trust for the use of the public as a public park or breathing place and to be know as the "Hermann Square."

VIII.

I will and bequeath to the City of Houston to be held in trust for the public for a public park all of that portion of the lands I own in the following surveys to wit: The Joe Gamble, G.P. Forster, D.W.C. Harris and P.W. Rose, which lies west of Galveston, Harrisburg & San Antonio Railroad right of way and North of the Houston Belt and Terminal Railroad right of way and east of the prolongation of Caroline Street, including within said bounds several hundred acres of land, it being my intention to convey all of the land which I may own at the time of my death lying east of the prolongation of Caroline Street West of the

Galveston, Harrisburg & San Antonio Railroad right of way and North of the Houston Belt and Terminal Railroad right of way and South of the Joe Christy Survey, and I authorize my executors and trustees in their discretion at any time during their trusteeship to by [*sic*] any tracts of land lying within said bounds not owned by me at a price not exceeding Three Hundred ($300.00) Dollars per acre and include the same in said park making the necessary deeds to said City of Houston the said lands to be used as a Public park and to be known and called "The George Hermann Park", and I hereby authorize my executors to retain the said lands for ten years before conveying for Park purposes if they deem it necessary without they can purchase lands within the bounds of the tracts described above for park purposes, now owned by others at proper prices which if they can do so I then desire said property to be at once turned over to the City of Houston to be used for Public Park.

IX.

I will and bequeath to T. J. Ewing, Jr.[,] J. J. Settegast, Jr. and John S. Stewart in trust to be held, managed and operated by the as Trustees together with four other Trustees they are hereby authorized to appoint to act and co-operate with the for the purpose of maintaining a public charity hospital in the City of Houston, Harris County, Texas, for the benefit of the poor, indigent and infirm residents of the City of Houston all of Block One Hundred and fifty-two (152) owned by me on the South Side of Buffalo Bayou in said City and Lot One (1) of the Hathaway Addition adjoining the same and I authorize my executors and Trustees, to purchase Lot Number One (1) in said Block One Hundred and fifty-two (152) and Lots Three (3) and Five (5) and Seven (7) in the Hathaway Addition or any portion thereof if in their judgment the rice is reasonable, to be held and used by them in trust with other property devised herein for the purpose of a Hospital to be erected thereon to be known as the "Hermann Hospital," I also bequeath to said Trustees above named and their successors the sum of One Hundred Thousand ($100,000) Dollars to be used by them for the purpose of erecting suitable buildings on said lots for said Hospital, and I further will and bequeath unto the afore [s]aid trustees in trust as above stated all of the remainder of my property real, personal and mixed wherever located or situated in the United States of America that is not otherwise disposed of by my will or that is not disposed of by an codicil hereafter made by me the said Trustees are authorized and directed to keep the principal derived from such property well and securely invested either in real property or in notes, (bonds or other good securities and to use the rents), revenue and income there from solely for the maintenance, support, sustaining and operation of said Hospital. It is my will and I so instruct my Trustees that the indigent, sick and infirm of the City of Houston shall be taken care of in said Hospital in preference to any others but if there is at any time sufficient accommodation for others then that the indigent, sick and infirm of Harris County shall be accommodated in said Hospital. . . .

It is my desire that the Trustees act in the capacity named in this paragraph without compensation for their personal services, they having full power to employ such clerical assistance at a reasonable compensation as may be necessary in conducting the same, having from personal experience and observation become acquainted with the suffering and deprivation of the unfortunate, indigent, infirm and sick, and having great sympathy for them I desire that they shall receive the full benefit for the devise mentioned in this paragraph.

X.

In the event the City of Houston should decline to accept the devises and bequeaths contained in the seventh and eighth paragraphs of this will or either of them, or should fail in good faith to carry out the purposes for which they are so devised to said City as therein expressed, or having accepted the same the City of Houston should at any time thereafter fail to maintain either of the Parks as provided for in the Seventh and Eighth paragraphs of this will for the exclusive use of the Public as a Park, then in such even the property so devised in said paragraphs Seven and Eight of this will, which the City of Houston fails to maintain, keep up and operate for the purposes specified, shall revert to my estate and I now will it to the Trustees named in the preceding paragraph Number Nine in trust to be used by them as such Trustees for the benefit of the Hermann Hospital under the same terms, provisions and restrictions as named and set forth in said paragraph Nine of this will in reference to the other property therein devised. And should from any unforeseen cause the Trustees should fail to establish, maintain and operate the Hermann Hospital as provided for in Paragraph Nine and should said Trust named in said paragraph Nine fail from any cause and the property so devised and bequeathed to said Trustees should from any cause not be used for the purposes of maintaining and operation the Hermann Hospital for the indigent sick and infirm residents of the City of Houston in Harris County, Texas as provided for in the Ninth paragraph of said devised and bequests should lapse then in such event I will bequeath all of the property bequeathed to said Trustees in Paragraph Nine or that would have gone to said Trustees for the purposes named in said Paragraph Nine or any other provisions of my will, to my relatives who reside in Switzerland who are more particularly set forth and described in the Fourteenth paragraph of this will.

XI.

Such jewelry as I may have on hand when this will takes effect not otherwise disposed of by this will, I desire my executors to distribute as mementoes among J. J. Settegast and his children, the children of W. J. Settegast and the family of T. J. Ewing Sr.

XII.

I hereby name and appoint T. J. Ewing Jr.[,] J. J. Settegast Jr. and John S. Stewart executors of my will and estate and also trustees of my estate and it is my expressed wish that as such they shall hold and manage my estate so as to effectually carry out the purposes of my will as herein expressed without sacrificing any part thereof. . . .

I desire that such executors or those of them who qualify and act as such executors shall receive for the period that they so serve as executors the sum of Six Thousand ($6000) Dollars per year to be apportioned among said three executors or such of them acting as such.

XIII.

I will and bequeath to John McNew the West half of the property I own in what is known as the Moodymen tract of land near Washington Road West of the Southern Pacific Railroad in the City of Houston, being the tract of land I purchased from him several years since, it is my wish to devise to him the west one-half of the property I so purchased from him and his wife.

XIV.

It is my wish that my executors shall hold property not specially devised to individuals herein for a period of ten years if they consider it for the best interest so to do, but that is a matter that I leave entirely to their good judgment and by expressing this wish I do not want to limit the power of authority of my said executors to sell and convey any of said property at any time before the expiration of ten years if they deem it best so to do.

XV.

I hereby devise and set aside the sum of One Thousand ($1000) Dollars to be invested by my executors for the purpose of keeping in good condition property now owned by me and T. J. Ewing in Glenwood Cemetery in the City of Houston, Harris County, Texas, which property is all enclosed together as one piece and it is my will that only the revenues or interest from the investment of said One Thousand ($1000) Dollars to be used for this purpose so that a permanent fund devised from said revenues shall always be available for the purpose of keeping said lot in good condition.

XVI.

All of the property of whatever nature that I may be entitled to in Switzerland I will and bequeath to my nearest kin in Switzerland. In order that my Trustees may properly trace my relatives in Switzerland I state my mother's maiden name was Verina Michel, she was a native of Davos Canton, Granbanden. She was born about March 9th, 1805. Her mother was Mrs. Wisula, née Toos, she had a sister Sedonia who married Hans Bush. My mother's father was John Michel born in Davos County, Switzerland. He died about 1835 in New Orleans. My father was John Hermann who was born in 1791 in Davos, Doefle, Switzerland, his father was also named John Hermann. My father's mother was Christina née Niggle. My father had a brother whose name I think was George. He was a Colonel in the French Army; he died in . . . Switzerland. He had a son by the name of George who came to Texas along about 1849 but returned to Switzerland and died. He had another son by the name of John who died in Houston, Texas about 1857 or 1858.

In witness whereof I have hereunto signed my name in the presence of the subscribing witnesses who sign the same in my presence at my request and each in the presence of the other on the the 12 twelve day of July 1910.

G. H. Hermann

Witnesses Nat Ewing
A. J. Binz

John S. Stewart, attorney
James W. Lockett, attorney

APPENDIX FOUR

Trees of Hermann Park

Compiled by the Hermann Park Conservancy, 2012

Tree	Count
American Elm	77
American Holly	1
Arizona Ash	3
Arrowwood Viburnum	8
Bald Cypress	436
Big Tooth Maple	2
Black Cherry	18
Black Oak	6
Black Tupelo	5
Black Willow	11
BlackJack Oak	1
Bradford Pear	18
Bur Oak	92
Carolina Basswood	7
Carolina Buckthorn	1
Cedar Elm	327
Chalk Maple	1
Cherry Bark Oak	80
Chinese Elm	65
Chinese Pistache	29
Chinkapin Oak	15
Common Pear Tree	1
Common Persimmon	1
Cottonwood	1
Crepe Myrtle	685
Dahoon Holly	17
Eastern Red Cedar	58
Flowering Dogwood	8
Fringe Tree	17
Green Ash	22
Gum Bumelia	1
Hackberry	116
Honey Locust	1
Huisache	6
Italian Cypress	3
Japanese Apricot	6
Japanese Black Pine	5
Japanese Maple	12
Japanese Persimmon	3
Japanese Red Maple	2
Laurel Oak	39
Live Oak	1757
Loblolly Pine	1345
Long Leaf Pine	1
Loquat	9
Loquat Leaf Oak	2
Mesquite	2
Mexican Buckeye	2
Mexican Plum	150
Mexican Sycamore	27
Monterrey Oak	0
Northern Catalpa	4
Nuttall Oak	127
Overcup Oak	30
Parsley Hawthorn	7
Pecan	43
Petticoat Palm	5
Pin Oak	15
Pond Cypress	23
Possumhaw Holly	29
Possumhaw Holly	29
Post Oak	514
Red Bay	1
Red Maple	118
Red Osier Dogwood	2
Redbud	230
River Birch	56
Rough Leaf Dogwood	1
Rusty Blackhaw Viburnum	10
Sabel Palm	15
Sandjack Oak	1
Saucer Magnolia	6
Savannah Holly	20
Shagbark Hickory	1
Shumard Oak	229
Silver Maple	10
Slippery Elm	20
Southern Magnolia	77
Southern Red Oak	12
Sugar Maple	4
Swamp Chestnut Oak	40
Sweet Bay Magnolia	9
Sweet Gum	39
Sycamore	104
Taiwan Cherry	31
Texas Hawthorn	1
Toothache Tree	1
Trident Maple	1
Two-winged Silverbell	4
Washington Palm	4
Water Elm	9
Water Oak	215
Water Oak	215
Wax Myrtle	42
Weeping Willow	1
Western Soapberry	2
White Ash	61
White Oak	101
Willow Oak	469
Winged Elm	206
Winged Sumac	5
Witch Hazel	2
Yaupon Holly	110
Yellow-fruited Yaupon	1
Total	7366

APPENDIX FIVE

Birds of Hermann Park

Compiled by the Houston Audubon Society

Date	2/14/2011	3/14/2011	4/11/2011	5/9/2011	7/11/2011	8/8/2011	9/12/2011	10/10/2011
Time, Weather		8:00 a.m., rainy		78 deg., overcast	85+ deg., sunny	83+ deg.		69–80 deg., cloudy, wet
Number of Species	41	26	30	33	27	27	33	25
Species								
Black-bellied Whistling Duck	100+	100+	A	A	A*	24	A	50
Wood Duck				3		2		
Mallard	3	35						
Ring-necked Duck	20	30						
Lesser Scaup	1							
Pied-billed Grebe	4	11	2	2	2	3	3	1
Neotropic Cormorant			2	6				10
Double-crested Cormorant	19	12						13
Great Blue Heron	1	1	1	4	1	1		1
Great Egret	4	1	2	5		3		3
Snowy Egret	1		1	4	1	1	4	3
Little Blue Heron			1	2			1	
Green Heron			4	4	1	4		
Black-crowned Night-Heron			3	2	2*	4		
Yellow-crowned Night-Heron			5	13	12*	13*	2	2
White-faced Ibis			3					
Osprey			1					
Sharp-shinned Hawk	2							1
Cooper's Hawk	1						2	
Red-tailed Hawk	1		1	1	?	1	2	1
Crested Caracara								1
American Kestrel	1							
American Coot	100+	75+		1	2	5	3	9
Killdeer					1	1		
Ring-billed Gull	2							
Laughing Gull	1	18	A	8	5	11	2	
Rock Pigeonigeon	100+		A	A	A	A	A	A
Eurasian Collared-Dove					3			
Mourning Dove	7	4	6	10	3	40	2	2

(*continued*)

Date	2/14/2011	3/14/2011	4/11/2011	5/9/2011	7/11/2011	8/8/2011	9/12/2011	10/10/2011
Species (*continued*)								
White-winged Dove	3	6	A	12	13	24	A	A
Chimney Swifts				15	2			14
Common Nighthawk							1	
Ruby-throated Hummingbird					1		6	5
Downy Woodpecker	1						2	
Red-bellied Woodpecker	2	5	2	2	1	1	2	
Pileated Woodpecker							1	
Yellow-bellied Sapsucker		1						
Loggerhead Shrike				3		2		
Eastern Phoebe	2							
Eastern Wood-Pewee							1	
Great Crested Flycatcher							3	
Blue Jay	13	5	13	C	12	10	A	8
American Crow		1	1	1			2	1
Purple Martin		20	30	25				
Bank Swallow								
Cliff Swallow				20	4	1		
Cave Swallow								
Barn Swallow		8	1	19	5	5		
Carolina Chickadee		1					2	
Tufted Titmouse	2							
Brown Creeper	1							
Ruby-crowned Kinglet	5							
Golden-crowned Kinglet	1							
Blue-gray Gnatcatcher	2						3	
American Robin	4	2	12	4	4	2	1	
Northern Mockingbird	3	5		13	6	10	25	5

(*continued*)

Date	2/14/2011	3/14/2011	4/11/2011	5/9/2011	7/11/2011	8/8/2011	9/12/2011	10/10/2011
Species (*continued*)								
European Starling	13	6	A	A	8	A	A	
Pipit	1							
Orange-crowned Warbler	7	1					1	
Yellow-rumped Warbler	23	2	1					
Pine Warbler	6		1	3	2			
Common Yellowthroat								1
Wilson's Warbler	1							
Yellow Warbler							1	
American Redstart								1
Northern Waterthrush							1	
Swamp Sparrow	2							
Northern Cardinal	1	1	3	4		3	1	
Orchard Oriole					1			
Bronzed Cowbird					3			
Common Grackle			1				30	A
Great-tailed Grackle	31	11	A	A	A*	A*	10	20
Grackle species	A							
Brown-headed Cowbird				2				
House Sparrow	10	2	A	A	1	24	A	24
DOMESTICS								
Moscovy Duck								
Mallards						numerous		
Greylag Goose								

*Includes juveniles. Numerous juvenile Black-bellied Whistling Ducks and Great-tailed Grackles were found in July 2011. Eleven juvenile Yellow-crowned Night-Herons were found in August 2011.

Note: "A" stands for abundant or too many to count.

APPENDIX SIX

Hermann Park Conservancy Directors: 1992–2014

(Names in bold have served as Chairman of the Board.)

Natalye Appel, FAIA
Jana Arnoldy
Jay Baker, FAIA
John C. Beddow
David L. Benson
Lucia Benton
Kathryn Berg
Devinder Bhatia, M.D.
Sadie Gwin Blackburn
Jane Block
Louis A. Bodmer
S. Allison Bond
William G. Bowen, Jr.
Barrie Scardino Bradley
Kristy Bradshaw
Russell D. Brightwell
Larry Brown
Donna Buja
Zinetta A. Burney
John D. Burns
Richard W. Burr
Carol A. Butler
James C. Calaway
H. Mallory Caldwell
Alfred J. Calloway
Tony Canino
Roxanne Casscells
Raul Castillo
Gracie Cavnar
Jackson Chang
Yvette G. Chargois
John S. Chase, Sr.
William M. Coats
Estela Cockrell
Rev. D. Z. Cofield
Nellie Connally
Franci Crane
Sanford W. Criner, Jr.
Robert J. Cruikshank
Jane Anderson Curtis
Danny David
June Deadrick
Valerie Palmquist Dieterich
Terrell F. Dixon, Ph.D.
Sara Dodd
Steve Dolman
William R. Donovan
Scott Dorfman, M.D.
Thomas Downing
Milane Duncan-Frantz
Michael Easely
Yolande R. Eugere
Charlene T. Evans
R. Joan Fadden
Randall C. Falkenhagen
Cece Fowler
Ellie Francisco
Brent Friedman
J. Kent Friedman
Mel Gallagher
Steven J. Gibson
Audrey Gilbreath
John Michael Gonzalez
Lainie Gordon
Antonio M. Gotto, Jr., M.D.
Mike Gregorcyk
Scott K. Halliday
James B. Halter
Debbie Hanna
Jay David Hellums
Olive Hershey, Ph.D.
Catherine C. Hevrdejs
Leisa Holland-Nelson
Gregg Hollenberg
Steppie F. Holsclaw
Linda C. Hunsaker
Barbara Hurwitz
Yissel Ibarra
Donald E. Inman
Andrew L. Jefferson, Jr.
Al Jensen
Jill Jewett
Demetra C. Jones
Susan Booth Keeton
Ann Kennedy
Elizabeth W. Kidd
Christopher Lykes Knapp
Margaret L. Kripke, Ph.D.
David Langworthy
Elyse Lanier
Sharon Lay
Barry E. Leavitt
Ron Lerner
Barry M. Lewis
Diann L. Lewter
Carol Linn
Gene Locke
Marley Lott
Tommy Lott
Kathryn Louie, Ph.D.
Lyle Lovett
David R. Lummis
James R. Lykes
Rebecca Mark-Jusbasche
Jackie Wolens Mazow
Ryan McCord
Gerald W. McElvy
Anne C. Mendelsohn
Kunio Minami
O. Jack Mitchell
Melissa Mithoff
Kenneth A. Moffet
Jay Moore
Laurie Morian
M. Peter Morris
Lucian L. Morrison
Nancy Morrison
Terrylin G. Neale
H. Joe Nelson III
D. Patricia Nelson, Ph.D.
Warren R. Nicholson
Paula N. O'Neill
Judy Nyquist
Kathleen L. O'Reilly
Valerie Olsen
Carla Van Over
Dennis K. Peck, AIA
Didier F. Piot, M.D.
Gary Kenneth Porter
Linsay Radcliffe
Susan Raffle
Carolyn Redd

Christopher J. Reichert
Jay Riviere
James L. Robertson
Brian Rollins
Michael E. Rome
Karen A. Rozzell
Deborah Rylander
Manuel A. Sanchez III
Shirley B. Sanders
Mary Schiflett
Rand N. Schulman
Russell Scott, Jr., M.D.
Mariana Servitje
Carroll Shaddock
Donald W. Short
Louis Sklar
Holly A.N. Smith
Marcus Smith
Cassie B. Stinson
Nancy A. Stopper
Patrick Summers
Philip Patrick Sun
Marvin Taylor
Troy Thacker
Mariea Sibley Thomas
William Paul Thomas
Randell Thomas
Gary Tinterow
Melanie M. Trent
J. Michael Treviño
Phoebe Tudor
Kimberly A. Tutcher
Diana Untermeyer
Keith Watson Wade
Richard E. Wainerdi
Caro Ivy Walker
John E. Walsh, Jr.
Christine Y. Liang Wang
Dancie Perugini Ware
William Max Watson
Joe Weikerth
William H. Weiland
Randa Weiner
Ann Wheeler
Julie McClure Williams
Sheridan Williams
L. Burke Windham III
Brandy Wolf
Dan Wolterman
Lynn C. Woods, Jr.
Dennis Wright
George C. Yang
Sam M. (Trey) Yates III
Herbert H. Yuan

Ex-Officio

Rick Dewees
Roksan Okan-Vick, FAIA
Oliver B. Spellman
Joe Turner
Roy E. Wilson

APPENDIX SEVEN

The Institutions of Hermann Park

Hermann Park Conservancy
www.hermannpark.org
Doreen Stoller, Executive Director
6201-A Hermann Park Drive
Houston, TX 77030
713.524.5876

Houston Parks and Recreation Department
www.houstontx.gov/parks
Joe Turner, Director
2999 South Wayside Drive
Houston, TX 77023
832.395.7100

Houston Zoo
www.houstonzoo.org
Deborah Cannon, President
6200 Hermann Park Drive
Houston, TX 77030
713.533.6500

Miller Outdoor Theatre
www.milleroutdoortheatre.com
Cissy Segall Davis, Managing Director
6000 Hermann Park Drive
Houston, TX 77030
832.487.7102

Houston Museum of Natural Science
www.hmns.org
Joel A. Bartsch, President
5555 Hermann Park Drive
Houston, TX 77030–1799
713.639.4629

Notes

Chapter One

1. August Heckscher, "Open Spaces: A Metropolis Is Shaped by Them," in *Cities: The Forces that Shape Them*, ed. Lisa Taylor (New York: Rizzoli, 1982), 38.

2. *Daily Telegraph*, September 10, 1871.

3. Suzanne Turner and Joann Seale Wilson, *Houston's Silent Garden: Glenwood Cemetery, 1871–2009* (College Station: Texas A&M University Press, 2010).

4. *Houston Daily Post*, November 12, 1882.

5. "Primary Documents in American History," http://www.loc.gov/rr/program/bib/ourdocs/13thamendment.html. The 13th Amendment states: "Neither slavery nor involuntary servitude, except as a punishment for crime whereof the party shall have been duly convicted, shall exist within the United States, or any place subject to their jurisdiction." Lee surrendered, ending the Civil War on April 14, 1865, after which the Confederate states began to ratify the 13th Amendment. All states had ratified the amendment on December 6, 1865.

6. John Fenwick Dickson, an Irish immigrant, moved to Marshall, Texas, from Chicago in 1875 as superintendent of the Texas and Pacific Railway. In 1886 the Dicksons moved to Houston, where John F. Dickson founded the Dickson Car Wheel Co. with capital of $75,000. The rail car wheels produced by the company were sold throughout the United States and Mexico, making John Dickson a wealthy man. The family traveled widely and was the first in Houston to become serious art collectors. John's son, George M. Dickson (1865–1918), left his personal collection to the Houston Art League, and it became the nucleus for the Museum of Fine Arts. This information is from a "Chronology of the Museum of Fine Arts, Houston," http://prv.mfah.org/archives/pdf/mfah_chronology.pdf.

7. John F. Dickson, "The Emancipation Park: Should be Saved to the Negroes of Houston. An Appeal for Them," *Houston Daily Post*, July 3, 1910, 15.

8. Willie Parker Chestnutt, "Chapter VI: Emancipation Park," in "Recreation and the History of its Development among Negroes in Houston," an essay submitted to the faculty of Houston College for Negroes in candidacy for partial fulfillment of the degree of Bachelor of Science, June 1936: 20. Typescript found in vertical file "Emancipation Park," HMRC, HPL (Houston Metropolitan Research Center, Houston Public Library). Chestnutt's sources were all personal interviews.

9. Marshall Wellborn was a lawyer (*Houston City Directory* 1866:51 and 1867–68: 91, 173) and after 1872 a "produce commission merchant and grain dealer" (*Houston City Directory* 1873:21; 1877:202).

10. Chestnutt, "Chapter VI," 21. The first trustees were Milton Parker, Thomas Freeman, Rev. Jack Yates, Richard Brock, Richard Allen, and Alias Dibbrels.

11. "Emancipation Park," Texas Historical Marker, 2008.

12. Chris Moran, "Big Plans for Emancipation Park," *Houston Chronicle*, September 21, 2011.

13. *Galveston Daily News*, June 2, 1885, as reported in Turner and Wilson, *Houston's Silent Garden*, 72.

14. Sister M. Agatha, *The History of Houston Heights 1891–1918* (Houston: Premier Printing Company, 1956), 16.

15. Louis F. Aulbach, "Vick's Lake—A Popular Park on Buffalo Bayou," http://users.hal-pc.org/~lfa/BB35.html. Vick's Park is now called Spotts Park.

16. Marguerite Johnston, *Houston The Unknown City 1836–1946*. (College Station: Texas A&M University Press, 1991), 172–73. See also David G. McComb, *Houston: A History* (Austin: University of Texas Press, 1981), 43–44.

17. Sister Agatha, 95–96.

18. Ibid., 96.

19. Turner and Wilson, *Houston's Silent Garden*, 97.

20. Works Progress Administration (WPA), *Houston: A History and Guide* (Houston: Anson Jones Press, 1942), 218.

21. *Illustrated City Book of Houston*, 1908, 159–160.

22. *Illustrated City Book of Houston*, 1914, 280–83.

23. http://www.houstonzoo.org/history.

24. Elizabeth Barlow Rogers, *Landscape Design: A Cultural and Architectural History* (New York: Abrams, 2001).

25. http://www.livingplaces.com/people/Andrew_Jackson_Downing.html.

26. Melvin Kalfus, *Frederick Law Olmsted: The Passion of a Public Artist* (New York: New York University Press, 1990). Kalfus writes of the traumatic death of Olmsted's mother when he was only three years old, and his lifelong psychological troubles, numerous accidents, and increasingly painful sieges of insomnia. After the exhausting work at Biltmore in Asheville, NC, Olmsted "gradually slipped into a complete mental breakdown, signaled initially by losses of memory and paranoid suspicions." See also Michael Sperber, "Frederick Law Olmsted: Brief Life of the First Landscape Psycho-Architect 1822–1903," *Harvard Magazine*, July–August 2007. Sperber notes that Olmsted's medical records are sealed, so the exact nature of his mental illness is not known.

27. Witold Rybczynski, *A Clearing in the Distance: Frederick Law Olmsted and America in the Nineteenth Century* (New York: Scribner, 1999). See also Charles E. Beveridge and Paul Rocheleau, *Frederick Law Olmsted: Designing the American Landscape* (New York: Rizzoli, 1995).

28. Frederick Law Olmsted, *A Journey through Texas Or, a Saddle-Trip on the Southwestern Frontier* (Austin: University of Texas Press, 1978), a reprint of the 1857 edition (New York: Dix, Edwards), Fourth Paperback Printing, 1989, 361–62.

Chapter Two

1. George Hermann Diary, quoted in newspaper article (n.d., before 1980), vertical file "Hermann, George H.," HMRC, Houston Public Library. The Hermann diary was owned by the Hermann Hospital Estate Archives. The original diary and other Hermann records were destroyed in Tropical Storm Allison, 2001.

2. Thomas S. Hines, "American Writers and the City Beautiful Movement," in *Cities: The Forces That Shape Them,* ed. Lisa Taylor, 81–83.

3. Stephen Fox, "Big Park, Little Plans: A History of Hermann Park," in *Ephemeral City: Cite Looks at Houston*, ed. Barrie Scardino, William F. Stern, and Bruce Webb (Austin: University of Texas Press, 2003), 117–32. Originally published in *Cite 3: The Architecture and Design Review of Houston*, Spring 1983.

4. Dorothy Knox Houghton, Barrie Scardino, Sadie Gwin Blackburn, and Katherine Howe, *Houston's Forgotten Heritage: Landscape, Houses, Interiors 1824–1914* (Houston: Rice University Press, 1991), 186.

5. Ibid., 54–55. The Oaks, demolished in 1965, was sited at the curve of Oak Place near Baldwin and bound roughly by Webster, McGowan, Bagby, and Hadley. Townhouses occupy the midtown site today.

6. Ibid.

7. Ibid., 56.

8. *Houston,* July 1922. Wilson's photograph was on the cover.

9. Barrie Scardino, "Woodland Heights" brochure, *Houston Downtown Magazine*, 1987.

10. "Chapter I: Who Was George H. Hermann?" from "Hermann Hospital 1925–1975," typescript from "Hermann, George" vertical file HMRC, HPL.

11. "George H. Hermann, Philanthropist," Typescript from scrapbook, "Houston Art League 1900–1924," Museum of Fine Arts, Houston Library.

12. Augustus Koch, *Bird's Eye View of Houston*, 1873, shows the Hermann House with some outbuildings.

13. "Chapter I: Who Was George H. Hermann?" typescript from "Hermann, George" vertical file HMRC, HPL.

14. George Hermann Collection, Hermann Hospital Estate Archives, Memorial-Hermann Hospital.

15. Andrew Forest Muir, "HERMANN, GEORGE HENRY," *Handbook of Texas Online* (http://www.tshaonline.org/handbook/online/articles/fhe28), accessed February 18, 2012. Published by the Texas State Historical Association. See also Kate Sayen Kirkland, *The Hogg Family and Houston: Philanthropy and the Civic Ideal* (Austin: University of Texas Press, 2009), 51.

16. http://www.glenwoodcemetery.org/search/?name=&lastname=Hermann&date_from=&date_to. The Hermanns are buried in section C-1, lot 103.

17. Morrison and Fourmy, *Houston City Directory 1902–03*, 125.

18. "George Hermann," *Houston Chronicle*, n.d., from "Hermann, George" vertical file, HMRC, HPL.

19. George H. Hermann Diary.

20. "Incidents in Life of Mr. Hermann," *Houston Chronicle*, June 7, 1914.

21. Morrison and Fourmy, *Houston City Directory* 1894–1895, 1897–1898, 1900–1901, and 1902–1903. By the time the 1904–1905 city directory was published Hermann was listed as "capitalist," and both he and the large Ewing family had moved to 117 San Felipe where Hermann lived until he died. At this time Hermann also relocated his offices to the second floor of the Binz Building.

22. Olive Talley and Gordon Hunter, "Hermann Shared Fortune, But Trouble Stalks a Dream." *Houston Chronicle*, January 17, 1985.

23. Last Will and Testament of George H. Hermann, July 12, 1910. Probate File 6425, Harris County. Hermann left the two daughters of T. J. Ewing, Mary Ewing Sherwine and Henrietta Ewing Meineke, each $1,000. Lots 6, 7, 11, and 12 in Block 149 (site of Houston City Hall) and $6,000 were bequeathed to T. J. Ewing Sr. in addition to a provision for $75 per month for T. J. Ewing until his death, then to his wife Martha Ewing until her death. T. J. Ewing Jr. was an executor of Hermann's will as well as one of the original trustees of the Hermann Hospital Estate.

24. Morrison and Fourmy, *Houston City Directory* 1880–1881, 140.

25. *Houston Daily Post*, June 7, 1914.

26. WPA, *Houston: A History and Guide*, 315.

27. Fox, "Big Park, Little Plans," 126. In December 1943, a local referendum approved the sale of 133.5 acres of Hermann Park to the M. D. Anderson Foundation for $400,000.

28. John P. McGovern Historical Collections and Research Center. http://mcgovernhrc.wordpress.com/2011/04/08/candid-camera-george-h-hermann/.

29. Talley and Hunter, *Houston Chronicle*, January 27, 1984.

30. See the complete text of George H. Hermann's will in appendix 3.

31. "Story of Geo. H. Hermann Park in Word and Pictures: How One Good Citizen Has Found Joy in Presenting to Houston $500,000 Breathing Spot," *Houston Chronicle*, June 7, 1914.

32. "Mass Meeting to Accept Park of George Hermann," *Houston Daily Post*, June 7, 1914. See appendix 2 for text of the Hermann's speech.

33. "Story of Geo. H. Hermann Park," *Houston Chronicle*, June 7, 1914.

34. Arthur C. Comey, "Maximum Building Height Regulation," *Landscape Architecture* 3 (October 1912): 19–24. http://www.library.cornell.edu/Reps/DOCS/comey_12.htm, with biographical notes by John W. Reps, Cornell University.

35. Arthur Coleman Comey Collection, Frances Loeb Library Special Collections, Harvard University. This collection primarily contains typescripts of lectures, reprints of publications, and planning reports for his many projects from 1912 to 1954. From the contents it is clear that Houston was his first project.

36. Ibid. Comey's surviving 1912 photographs include many of the city's bayous, particularly Buffalo Bayou, one of a tree on E. B. Parker's estate, and one of William A. Wilson's house in Woodland Heights, indicating that he visited the homes of these two park commissioners.

37. Arthur Coleman Comey, *Houston Tentative Plans for its Development: Report to the Houston Park Commission* (Boston: Press of Geo. H. Ellis Co., 1913; Memphis: General Books, 2010).

38. Ibid., 5.

39. Ibid., 6.

40. Ibid., 20.

41. "Plans to Beautify the Park," *Houston Daily Post*, June 7, 1914.

42. Ibid.

43. *The Illustrated City Book of Houston*, 1915, HMRC, HPL. Master planner Laurie Olin described the Maxcy Plan as "marvelous," and more Olmstedian than the Kessler Plan that followed it. Laurie Olin, interview with author, April 11, 2012, Philadelphia, Pennsylvania.

44. St. Agnes Hospital was founded in 1862 by the Roman Catholic Daughters of Charity. It expanded in 1906 and became a full-service hospital. It was likely that Hermann received diagnostic and surgical care at Johns Hopkins, but stayed at St. Agnes for recuperation and rest. http://www.stagnes.org/index.php/about/overview/.

45. George H. Hermann to Will Powers, July 24, 1913 and September 12, 1912, George Hermann Collection, Hermann Hospital Estate Archives.

46. "Geo. H. Hermann Funeral May be Held Tuesday," *Houston Chronicle,* October 23, 1914.

47. "Several Thousand Attended Funeral of Geo. H. Hermann," *Houston Daily*

Post, October 28, 1914. This report includes the information that T. J. Ewing had been Hermann's "chief counsel in much of his business in late years."

48. "Plans Complete for Funeral of Geo. H. Hermann," *Houston Chronicle*, October 26, 1914.

49. "All Houston Pays Tribute to Geo. H. Hermann," *Houston Chronicle*, October 28, 1914.

Chapter Three

1. Fox, "Big Park, Little Plans," 120.

2. J. S. Cullinan to George Kessler, May 23, 1914, J. S. Cullinan Collection, HMRC, HPL.

3. Those copied on Cullinan's correspondence concerning the hiring of George Kessler were Will C. Hogg, Jesse H. Jones, Ben Campbell, William A. Wilson, H. T. D. Wilson, B. Gilmer, J. S. Rice, S. F. Carter, John T. Scott, John Henry Kirby, and John Wiley Link. Several of these responded to Cullinan expressing their support.

4. Lindsey H. Dunn to J. S. Cullinan, January 4, 1915. Cullinan Collection, HMRC, HPL. Dunn, a real estate man, concludes his letter saying: "Mayor Campbell states that this action was taken at your suggestion. . . . You are to be congratulated for pioneering along these lines, and I feel sure that much good will be accomplished by having Mr. Kessler come here."

5. Kirkland, *The Hogg Family*, 282, n35, says that family members remembered that Cullinan paid Kessler's consulting fees.

6. McComb, *Houston: A History* (Austin: University of Texas Press, 1981), 80.

7. John O. King, *Joseph Stephen Cullinan* (Nashville: Vanderbilt University Press, 1970).

8. April 12, 1919, Museum of Fine Arts Chronology. http://prv.mfah.org/archives/pdf/mfah_chronology.pdf.

9. David B. Warren, *Bayou Bend Gardens: A Southern Oasis* (Houston Scala Publishers in association with the Museum of Fine Arts, Houston, 2006), 10. Will Hogg placed an option on Lot Q in Shadyside, but when he asked for an extension because of his sister Ima's illness and hospitalization (for depression), Cullinan refused. "This was a great blow to Will Hogg and a disappointment that started him on an independent course that eventually led to establishing his own private enclave, River Oaks."

10. Joseph Stephen Cullinan Papers, HMRC, HPL. See also *Houston Architectural Survey*, vol. V, 1132.

11. "Shadyside," *Houston Architectural Survey*, vol. V: 1126–38. Cullinan possibly named Shadyside after the elite subdivision of that name in Pittsburgh, PA.

12. Edgar Odell Lovett, *Edgar Odell Lovett and the Creation of Rice University: The Meaning of the New Institution*. Reprint (Houston: Rice Historical Society, 2000). Original publication *The Rice Institute Pamphlets*, 1:1, April 1917, 45–132. http://archive.org/details/edgarodelllovettoolove.

13. Stephen Fox, *Rice University* (New York: Princeton Architectural Press, 2001), 6. See also Stephen Fox, "The General Plan of the William M. Rice Institute and Its Architectural Development (Houston: School of Architecture, Rice University, 1980).

14. "Houston Art League Contemplate Worth Project," *Houston*, December 1922, 5. This description of the new museum notes that the cost of the "first unit," the central section completed in 1926, would be $200,000.

15. "The Museum of Fine Arts, Houston," *Houston Architectural Survey*, vol. V: 1009.

16. Culbertson, Kurt, "Landscape of the American Renaissance: The Life and Work of George Edward Kessler," 2005. An unpublished biography available through the Kessler Society of Kansas City. kcsociety@georgekessler.org.

17. *Dallas City Directory*, various years 1879–1899.

18. Culbertson, "Landscape."

19. Ibid.

20. Ibid.

21. Ibid.

22. Ibid.

23. Ibid.

24. Culbertson, Kurt, "George E. Kessler: List of Projects," 1989. http://georgekessler.org.

25. Arthur Coleman Comey Collection, Harvard University. Comey taught at Harvard from 1928–1940, and, in addition to his landscape and planning practice, he wrote zoning laws for quite a few municipalities in New England. He also served on the United Nations site selection committee and prepared site plans for the UN headquarters to be located in Framingham, MA, and a feasibility study for another site in Sudbury. See also "Arthur Coleman Comey September 6, 1886–January 26, 1954: A Biographical Minute" in *Landscape Architecture*, vol. 44:3 (April 1954): 153–54.

26. Ibid.

27. WPA, *Houston, a History and Guide*, 314.

28. Mayor Ben Campbell to J. S. Cullinan, July 15, 1915. Cullinan Papers, HMRC, HPL.

29. Fox, "Big Park, Little Plans," 119.

30. Culbertson, "Landscape of the American Renaissance."

31. http://en.wikipedia.org/wiki/Houston_Police_Department.

32. Fox, "Big Park, Little Plans," 121.

33. William Bearden, *Images of America: Overton Park* (Charleston, SC: Arcadia Publishing, 2004).

34. "Clarence L. Brock, "Biographical Archive of *The Mineralogical Record*. http://www.minrec.org/labels.asp?colid=34.

35. Culbertson, "Landscape of the American Renaissance."

36. "History of Houston Parks." http://www.houstontx.gov/parks/history1.html.

37. H. A. Kipp, "Plan of Concrete Stairways for the Sunken Garden," January 1917. Ink on Linen. Hare & Hare Collection, HMRC, HPL.

38. "What About Hermann Park," *Houston*, April 1920, 8.

39. "Points of Interest in Houston," *Houston*, October 1920, 19.

40. Stan Redding, "Memorial Oaks Flourish Around Hermann Park," *Houston Chronicle*, February 10, 1957.

41. J. S. Cullinan to Craig F. Cullinan, October 21, 1921. Cullinan Papers, HMRC, HPL.

42. J. S. Cullinan to C. L. Brock, December 29, 1921. Cullinan Papers, HMRC, HPL.

43. Fox, "Big Park, Little Plans," 122.

44. Burion Davis, "Open Air Park Memorial," *Houston*, March 1922, 1–2.

45. Miller Outdoor Theatre, "Miller Outdoor Theatre Past and Present." http://milleroutdoortheatre.com/past-and-present.

46. Report of City Electrician, *Illustrated City Book of Houston, 1925*, 137.

47. Lee Pecht, "William Ward Watkin and Early Houston Architecture," Museum of Houston, a web-based project of the Greater Houston Preservation Alliance. http://www.museumofhouston.org/index.php/home/exhibits_watkin.

48. "The Museum of Fine Arts, Houston," *Houston Architectural Survey*, vol. V: 1008-1009. See also "Brochure of the Work of Wm. Ward Watkin," c. 1940 Woodson Research Center, Rice University.

49. "Tourist Camp Site," *Houston*, November 1921.

50. Fox, "Big Park, Little Plans," 122.

51. "The $29,011.49 Municipal Golf Course at Hermann Park Is Formally Opened," *Houston Post*, July 14, 1923.

52. "The History of Houston's Municipal Golf Course," *Illustrated City Book of Houston, 1925*, 149–52.

53. Alvin F. Jones, "Houston Exposition Will Be Great Annual Event," *Houston*, September 1922.

54. http://georgekessler.org/.

Chapter Four

1. S. Herbert Hare, *City of Houston Planning Commission Report*, 1929.

2. Cydney Millstein, "History of the Landscape Architecture Firm of Hare & Hare" (State Historical Society of Missouri), http://www.umkc.edu/whmckc/hare/hare%20history.htm. See also abstract "Hare and Hare Company Records (KC0206)," State Historical Society of Missouri Research Center-Kansas City, http://www.umkc.edu/whmckc/Collections/cframe.htm.

3. Millstein, "Hare & Hare."

4. Ibid., citing Bettina C. Van Dyke, "The Evolution of 19th and 20th Century Cemetery Landscape Types as Exemplified by Hare & Hare's Cemetery Design" (Manhattan, KS: Kansas State University, Master's Thesis, 1984).

5. Fox, "Big Park, Little Plans," 122.

6. S. Herbert Hare, " The New Zoological Garden at Houston, Texas," typescript, 1948, 1. Hare & Hare Collection, HMRC, HPL.

7. Report of the City Architect, W. A. Dowdy, *Illustrated City Book of Houston, 1925*, 161.

8. Kendall Curlee, "RODRIGUEZ, DIONICIO," *Handbook of Texas Online*, http://www.tshaonline.org/handbook/online/articles/frouw, accessed April 23, 2012. Published by the Texas State Historical Association.

9. "Aviary at the Houston Zoo," National Register Nomination, March 2005, ftp://ftp.thc.state.tx.us/nr_program/Houston%20Zoo%20Aviary%20NR.pdf.

10. *Civics for Houston*, June 1928. Davidson, a student of Emma Richardson Cherry, became known for her experimental modern paintings that influenced the Houston art community, including her student Robert Preusser. The June 1928 issue of *Civics for Houston* also included a poem called "The Bird Haunt" by Emily Langham.

11. "Houston Zoological Gardens," *Houston Architectural Survey*, vol. 5: 1005.

12. Hans Nagel Collection, 332, HMRC, HPL.

13. W. P. A., *Houston: A History and Guide*, 314 quoting the *Houston Chronicle and Herald*, January 11, 1925.

14. "Why Go to India to Look for Trouble with Wild Bengal Tigers When You Can Find It Right Here in Texas?" *The Bee*, Danville, Virginia, November 3, 1926, http://www.texasarchive.org/library/index.php?title=The_Sloane_Collection%2C_no._5_-_Houston_Zookeeper_Hans_Nagel_Breaks_a_Zebra.

15. Mrs. Fred P. Hodge, "Black Diamond," reprinted from the *Navarro County Scroll*, Volume xiv, 1969, http://www.rootsweb.ancestry.com/~txnavarr/biographies/b/black_diamond.htm.

16. "Bust of Zookeeper Nagel is Acquired by his Widow," *Houston Chronicle*, May 3, 1942.

17. "Grand Jury to Investigate Nagel Slaying by Officer: Zookeeper Tried 'to Pull Gun' Police Told," *Houston Press*, November 18, 1941. See also "Hans Nagel—Zookeeper," HAM Slice 3 video. Houston Arts and Media, January 2008, www.houstonartsandmedia.org.

18. W. P. A., *Houston: A History and Guide*, 312–14.

19. "Annual Report Parks and Recreation Department, City of Houston, 1944."

20. Hare, "The New Zoological Garden," 2.

21. "Mayor Favors Keeping Zoo in Hermann Park," *Houston Post*, December 19, 1947.

22. "Modernistic Monkey House Will Be Zoo's Focal Point," *Houston Chronicle*, June 20, 1948.

23. *Houston Chronicle*, March 1, 1917.

24. *Houston*, November 1923, vol. 1.

25. "Model for $75,000 Sam Houston Monument Submitted by Enrico Cerracchio Has Been Unanimously Adopted," *Houston Chronicle*, September 30, 1923. See also *Houston*, November 1923, vol. 1. The new monument was on the cover of *Houston* magazine. On the selection committee were Lynch Davidson, Denton Cooley, J. W. Bullock, R. C. Duff, John H. Hill, Jesse Jones, John H, Kirby, Judge Norman Kittrell, Mrs. Ernest Davis, and Julia Montgomery.

26. Cecilia Steinfeldt, *S. Seymour Thomas 1868–1956: A Texas Genius Rediscovered* (San Antonio: Witte Museum, 2005). Exhibition Catalog, February 12 to September 4, 2005. Following its exhibition at the fair, the huge equestrian portrait was shown in the Paris Salon in 1898, then presented in 1920 by Col. and Mrs. Francis Drake to the City of Houston; it now hangs in the San Jacinto Museum.

27. *Houston*, December 1919, vol. 4: 13.

28. Kendall Curlee, "CERRACCHIO, ENRICO FILIBERTO," *Handbook of Texas Online*, accessed February 14, 2012, http://www.tshaonline.org/handbook/online/articles/fce01. Published by the Texas State Historical Association.

29. Mrs. John Miles Stewart, typescript, March 13, 1962. HMRC, HPL. Waugh Transfer Company transported the statue and placed it atop the base, which was already in place.

30. W. P. A., *Houston: A History and Guide,* 311.

31. "TEICH, FRANK," *Handbook of Texas Online*, http://www.tshaonline.org/handbook/online/articles/fte05, accessed June 24, 2012. Published by the Texas State Historical Association.

32. "Harmonious Color Combinations Will Lend Beauty to Botanical Garden Planned for Hermann Park," *Houston Chronicle*, January 10, 1926.

33. Ibid.

34. Ibid.

35. *Houston Post*, February 1, 1923 (for 1921 and 1922), and *Houston Post*, December 27, 1923.

36. http://www.houstonhistory.com/decades/history5i.htm.

37. Fox, "Big Park, Little Plans," 125.

38. "Landscaping America: Beyond the Japanese Garden," an exhibition at the Japanese American Museum, Los Angeles, June 17 through October 21, 2007. Timeline and images from this exhibition available at http://www.discovernikkei.org/en/nikkeialbum/albums/142/.

39. William Bearden, *Overton Park* (Chicago: Arcadia Publishing, 2004). In San Antonio's Brackenridge Park the Japanese Tea Garden, established in 1917, was renamed the Chinese Tea garden in 1942 with the rise of anti-Japanese sentiment in World War II. San Antonio Parks and Recreation website: http://www.sanantonio.gov/parksandrec/directory_japanese.aspx.

40. Joan Ferry, "Autry House," *The Cornerstone: A Newsletter of the Rice Historical Society* (Winter 2008) 13:1, 3.

41. *Houston Press*, December 17, 1923. This article states that the city council authorized the mayor to purchase 133 1/2 acres of additional land for Hermann Park at a cost of $293,614, of which $33,614 was to be in cash and the rest to be paid over the next twenty years. See also Kirkland, *The Hogg Family*, 60. Kirkland points out that the Hoggs bought several tracts during the 1920s, including property around Hermann Square for a future civic center. The Hoggs' company, Varner Realty, held these sites until the city was ready to take them over.

42. Thomas D. Anderson, "ANDERSON, MONROE DUNAWAY," *Handbook of*

Texas Online, http://www.tshaonline.org/handbook/online/articles/fan09, accessed March 15, 2012. Published by the Texas State Historical Association.

43. Fox, "Big Park, Little Plans," 126.

44. Hanna/Olin Ltd., *Renewing Hermann Park: A Comprehensive Master Plan*, 1995, 26–27.

45. "Hermann Park Clubhouse," *Houston Architectural Survey*, vol. V: 996. Nutter's work still stands in Hermann, Mason, and MacGregor parks.

46. Mark W. Lambert, "SAN JACINTO CENTENNIAL ASSOCIATION," *Handbook of Texas Online*, http://www.tshaonline.org/handbook/online/articles/vts03, accessed March 17, 2012. Published by the Texas State Historical Association.

47. "Pioneer Memorial Log House Museum," http://www.sanjacintodrt.org/pioneer.htm.

48. Mark W. Lambert, "SAN JACINTO CENTENNIAL ASSOCIATION," *Handbook of Texas Online*, http://www.tshaonline.org/handbook/online/articles/vts03, accessed March 17, 2012. Published by the Texas State Historical Association.

49. http://en.wikipedia.org/wiki/Cleopatra's_Needle. Cleopatra's Needle is the popular name for each of three Ancient Egyptian obelisks re-erected in London, Paris, and New York City during the nineteenth century. The obelisks in New York and London are a pair from Heliopolis constructed around 1450 BCE. New York sought the Central Park obelisk after learning about the one given to London. The Paris obelisk, from the city of Luxor, was constructed about 1400 BCE. The Bunker Hill Monument (1827–1843) in Massachusetts, erected to commemorate the American Revolutionary Battle of Bunker Hill, is thought to be the first obelisk in the United States. Houston's San Jacinto Monument (1936–1939) is 567 feet high, and the Washington Monument (1848–1884) is 155 feet high.

50. Fox, "Big Park, Little Plans," 124.

51. Correspondence with David Boutros, State Historical Society of Missouri Research Center–Kansas City, March 14, 2012. This Kansas City research center houses a large Hare & Hare collection.

52. Ralph Ellifrit interview with Louis Marchiafava, September 26, 1979. Archive # OH 265_01, HMRC, HPL. Ellifrit graduated from the University of Illinois with a major in landscape architecture and worked for the National Park Service between 1933 and 1939.

53. Ibid.

54. Meda Wogan, "A History of the Houston Garden Center," typescript, October 24, 2007, 1. Hermann Park Conservancy archives.

55. "Proposed Hermann Park Garden Center," *Houston Chronicle*, February 11, 1938.

56. "Garden Center Plans Completed," *Houston*, June 1924, 29. "Ground Broken for City Garden Center," *Houston*, January 1941, 46.

57. Wogan, "A History of the Houston Garden Center," 3.

58. Hare & Hare Collection. HMRC, HPL.

Chapter Five

1. Fox, "Big Park, Little Plans," 125.

2. *Houston Post*, November 25, 1951.

3. "Two-Months-Old Museum of Natural History Lists Beautiful, Bizarre Items," *Houston Chronicle*, October 13. 1929. See also Diana J. Kleiner and Patricia Holm, "HOUSTON MUSEUM OF NATURAL SCIENCE," *Handbook of Texas Online*, http://www.tshaonline.org/handbook/online/articles/lbh02, accessed November 3, 2012. Published by the Texas State Historical Association. This article notes that in 1914 the city bought part of a natural history collection assembled by Henry Philemon Attwater, and in 1922 the remainder of the collection was bought by Sigmund J. Westheimer and given to the city.

4. Paige Allred Phillips, "C. C. Pat Fleming: Houston, Texas, Landscape Architect," thesis in partial completion of Master of Landscape Architecture, Louisiana State University and Agricultural and Mechanical College, December 2003. http://etd.lsu.edu/docs/available/etd-1112103-155132/unrestricted/Phillips_thesis.pdf

5. "$9000,000 Zoo and Museum Project Due," *Houston Chronicle*, September 12, 1943.

6. "Houston Museum of Natural History," *Houston Chronicle*, 1937. Vertical file, HMRC, HPL.

7. "Plans Are Made for New Nature Museum on Main Opposite Rice," *Houston Post*, March 24, 1946.

8. "The Warwick," *Houston Architectural Survey*, vol. V: 1119–21.

9. "Iconic Mecom Fountain Lights Hermann Park Entrance," Press Release, Houston Parks and Recreation Department, February 28, 2008.

10. "Program of the Museum of Natural History," n.d. This was a one-sheet brochure to solicit donations for the new museum. "Houston Museum of Natural History" vertical file, HMRC, HPL.

11. "Museum Bond Issue Is up Again," *Houston Post*, December 5, 1952.

12. "New Building Badly Needed for Museum," *Houston Chronicle*, February 28,1948.

13. "Dr. T. E. Pulley to Head Natural History Museum," *Houston Post*, August 2, 1957.

14. "New Natural Museum Planned for Memorial Park," *Houston Post*, February 8, 1958.

15. Sanjeev Baidyaroy, "Blacks, Golf, and the Emerging Civil Rights Movement, 1947–1954," 2011. Dietrich College Honors Thesis, Paper 116. Carnegie Mellon University, http://repository.cmu.edu/hsshonors/116, 2.

16. Baidyaroy, "Blacks, Golf, and the Emerging Civil Rights Movement," 6.

17. Ibid., 28–29.

18. George B. Kirsch, "Municipal Golf and Civil Rights in the United States, 1910–1965," *The Journal of African American History* (2007) 92: 3.

19. Chief Judge Thomas Kennerly, *103 F. Supp. 218 (1950)* Beal et al. v. Holcombe, Mayor, et al. Civ. A. No. 5407. United States District Court S. D., Texas, Houston Division, December 4, 1950. Mandell & Wright, Ben N. Ramey, of Houston, Texas, and W. J. Durham, of Dallas, Texas, for plaintiffs. Will Sears, City Atty., and Herman W. Mead, Asst. City Atty., of Houston, Texas, for defendants.

20. http://www.judicialview.com/Court-Cases/Constitutional_Law/Beal-v.-Holcombe/17/279623.

21. Kirsch, "Municipal Golf." http://secretinthedirt.com/index.php/forum/51-black-golfing-legends-in-america-group-forum/472-integration-of-public-golf-courses.

22. Ibid.

23. Marvin Taylor, interview with author, June 12, 2012.

24. Hanna/Olin, Ltd., "Renewing Hermann Park: A Comprehensive Master Plan," 1995, 28.

25. Stan Redding, "Out at the Zoo Is a Train That Goes Nowhere," *Houston Chronicle*, June 5, 1955.

26. "The New Lake Plaza Is Officially Open!" *Parkside: Hermann Park Conservancy Newsletter*, Fall 2009.

27. Ann Holmes, "Striking New Theatre Is Proposed for Park," *Houston Chronicle*, March 23, 1966.

28. Stephen Fox, *Houston Architectural Guide*, 3rd edition (Houston: American Institute of Architects, Houston Chapter, 2012), 164.

29. Houston Parks and Recreation Department, "Park Histories," http://www.houstontx.gov/parks/history1.html.

Chapter Six

1. "Hermann Park Consultant OKd for Master Plan," *Houston Post*, September 9, 1970.

2. LAN and James A. Cummins, "Hermann Park Master Plan," 1972. HMRC, HPL.

3. Ibid., 11.

4. Ibid., 4.

5. Ibid., 4–6.

6. Gary Christian, "Plan Urges Hermann Improvements," *Houston Post*, July 24, 1972.

7. Jim Asker, "Hermann Park to Get $4.5 million Facelift," *Houston Post*, April 20, 1978.

8. Hanna/Olin, Ltd., "Renewing Hermann Park: A Comprehensive Master Plan," 1995, 29.

9. Fox, "Big Park, Little Plans," 130.

10. "Teahouse Time," *Houston Chronicle*, March 14, 1978.

11. "Chinese Garden Proposed around Chinese Pavilion," *Houston Chronicle*, November 4, 1983.

12. Houston Taipei Society, http://www.sistercitiesofhouston.org/wp/houstons-sister-cities/?page_id=43/.

13. "Hermann Park Has a ew Exer-trail," *Houston Post*, June 23, 1978.

14. Betty Ewing, "City to Unveil Statue of Powerful Friend," *Houston Chronicle*, May 14, 1981.

15. "George Hermann," City of Houston, Municipal Art, http://www.houstontx.gov/municipalart/hermann.html.

16. http://www.houstonartsalliance.com/civic/general-information/recent-projects/george-hermann-sculpture/.

17. Fox, "Big Park, Little Plans," 128.

18. Drexel Turner, "From Less to Moore: New Proposals for Hermann Park," *Cite*, Spring 1983, 24.

19. http://www.wolfsonian.org/explore/collections/elephant-tower-portals-pacific-1939-golden-gate-international-exposition-san-fra.

20. Arthur Drexler, *Buildings for Best Products*, exhibition catalog (New York: Museum of Modern Art, 1979).

21. Invitation, "Proposals for Hermann Park, Charles Moore and the Urban Innovations Group." The exhibition was displayed February 8 through March 2, 1983. "Hermann Park" vertical file, HMRC, HPL.

22. Adolf Loos, trans. Michael Mitchell, and Adolf Opel, ed., *Ornament and Crime: Selected Essays* (Ariadne Press, 1997). The original essay "Crime and Ornament" was delivered in 1908 and can be found at http://www.gwu.edu/~art/Temporary_SL/177/pdfs/Loos.pdf.

23. Shivali Agnani, "Bernini's Elephant Obelisk," 2005, http://honorsaharchive.blogspot.com/2007/05/berninis-elephant-obelisk.html. After a 16-foot high ancient Egyptian obelisk was discovered in a Dominican monastery, Pope Alexander VII commissioned Bernini to create a sculptural base. One of Bernini's students, Ercole Ferrata, designed the elephant, inspired by the fifteenth-century novel, *Poliphil's Dream of the Love Battle*, in which Polophil encountered an elephant made of stone carrying an obelisk.

24. Ann Holmes, "Miller Theatre Needs Improving; Plans Are Afoot for That, and the Rest of Hermann Park too," *Houston Chronicle*, February 27, 1982.

25. "Sir Edwin Lutyens," Digital Archive of Architecture, Boston College," http://www.bc.edu/bc_org/avp/cas/fnart/arch/20_lutyens.html.

26. Holmes, "Miller Theatre Needs Improving,"1982.

27. Ibid.

28. Turner, "From Less to Moore," 24.

29. "Reclaiming Hermann Park," editorial, *Cite*, Spring 1983, 2.

30. Paul Hester, "Cite Seeing: Hermann Park Today," *Cite*, Spring 1983, 22.

Chapter Seven

1. William Johnson, recorded comments as a juror for Heart of the Park Competition, November 13, 1992. Johnson was a distinguished landscape architect from Ann Arbor, Michigan, and the 1986 winner of the prestigious ASLA Medal, the highest honor of the American Society of Landscape Architects. He was Professor of Landscape Architecture and Dean of the School of Natural Resources and Environment, University of Michigan.

2. Marvin Taylor, interview with David Goldstein, March, 6, 2008. Houston Public Library Digital Archives.

3. Marvin Taylor, interview with author, June 12, 2012.

4. "Hermann Park Has a New Exer-trail," *Houston Post*, June 23, 1978.

5. Gwen Lewis, "Hermann's Joggers Should Thank Taylor," *Houston Chronicle*, June 8, 1990.

6. Gwen Lewis, "Taylor's Effort Lit Hermann Trail," *Houston Chronicle*, November 19, 1992.

7. "Allan Turner, Park Trailblazer: Retired Postal Worker Cleared Way for Runners," *Houston Chronicle*, July 18, 2003.

8. Rick Dewees, interview with author, May 3, 2012, Houston, Texas.

9. "O. Jack Mitchell, 60, Professor of Architecture," *New York Times*, February 22, 1992.

10. "O. Jack Mitchell: A Testimonial," in *Heart of the Park Competition*, Jay Baker and Barrie Scardino (Houston: Rice Design Alliance, 1992), 10–11.

11. O. Jack Mitchell, FAIA, "Making a Public Realm," *Texas Architect* (March/April 1992) 42: 2, 36–43.

12. Susan Chadwick, "Design Contest Stirs Interest in Hermann Park," *Houston Post*, November 12, 1992.

13. Baker and Scardino, *Heart of the Park Competition*, 32–37.

14. Barrie Scardino, "Creating a Central Axis: Houston's Hermann Park," *Competitions*, v. 3, Spring 1993.

15. "Heart of the Park Design Competition Winners Announced at 1992 RDA Gala," *Cite 29*, Fall 1992–Winter 1993, 4–5.

16. Scardino, "Creating a Central Axis," 31–32.

17. Rick Dewees interview.

18. Ibid.

19. Hermann Park Conservancy executive director, Doreen Stoller, sits on the Board of Directors of the City Parks Alliance, whose membership has become primarily private, nonprofit park groups throughout the United States.

Chapter Eight

1. Information in this chapter, unless otherwise noted, is from the Hermann Park Conservancy Archives.

2. The logo, identity package, and, later, park signage, were created by Minor Design initially, in consultation with Peter Boyle.

3. Marley Lott, interview with author, May 15, 2012.

4. Ukeles Associates Inc. and ETM Associates, LLC, "Safeguarding Our Legacy: A Plan to Manage Maintenance and Operations in Hermann Park," September 2002. An electronic version is available by request from the Hermann Park Conservancy.

5. Exhibit 18: Allocation of Resources by Zone, "Safeguarding Our Legacy: A Plan to Manage Maintenance and Operations in Hermann Park," 49. The twelve zones are:

NW perimeter, Heart of the Park A, Heart of the Park B, Japanese Garden, Centennial Gardens, Miller Outdoor Theatre, Parking Lot and Park Administration area, Pavilion and Picnic Area, Jogging Trail, Wooded Picnic Area, Bayou Parkland B and the SW perimeter, and Bayou C.

6. Ibid., 42.

7. Ibid., 24.

8. Eric Berger, "Houston May Lose 66 Million Trees This Year," *Houston Chronicle*, September 22, 2011, http://blog.chron.com/sciguy/2011/09/houston-may-lose-66-million-trees-this-year-or-more-save-yours/.

9. Reed F. Noss, Edward T. LaRoe III, and J. Michel Scott, "Endangered Ecosystems of the United States: A Preliminary Assessment of Loss and Degradation," National Biological Service, US Geological Survey, 1995. Ecosystems listed as "endangered" have an 85 to 98 percent decline. See http://biology.usgs.gov/pubs/ecosys.htm.

10. Christopher Knapp, interview with author, June 15, 2012.

11. "From Generation to Generation," *Parkside*, Winter, 2011.

12. Texas Master Gardeners Association, http://txmg.org/.

13. Edward T. Cotham Jr., "Dick Dowling Statue: First Public Monument in Houston, Turns 100 on St. Patrick's Day," *Texas Escapes* Online Magazine, 2005, http://www.texasescapes.com/Houston/Dick-Dowling-Statue-Houston-Texas.htm.

14. James R. Ward, "DOWLING, RICHARD WILLIAM," *Handbook of Texas Online*, http://www.tshaonline.org/handbook/online/articles/fdo28, accessed June 20, 2012. Published by the Texas State Historical Association.

15. http://www.houstontx.gov/municipalart/elephant.html.

16. http://houston.cowparade.com.

17. Douglas Britt, "Public-Private Project Brings Sculptures to Hermann Park: Park Surprise: Steel Sculptures." *Houston Chronicle*, January 20, 2010.

18. http://www.aiweiweihouston.org/.

19. Christopher Knight, "Art Review: Ai Weiwei *Circle of Animals/Zodiac Heads* at LACMA," *Los Angeles Times*, August 31, 2011.

20. Jane Anderson Curtis, notes on manuscript, June 2012.

Chapter Nine

1. Hanna/Olin, Ltd., "Renewing Hermann Park: A Comprehensive Master Plan," April 1995.

2. Ibid.

3. Ibid., 1.

4. Ibid., 5.

5. Ibid.

6. Ibid., 7.

7. Ibid,. 9.

8. Ibid., 30.

9. Ibid., 33.

10. Ibid., 40.

11. Ibid.

12. Ibid., 41.

13. Ibid., 44.

14. Ibid., 48.

Chapter Ten

1. Jane Anderson Curtis, interview with author, April 5, 2012.

2. The approval/adoption of the master plan by the City of Houston came by language in the Recitals of the Hermann Park Development Agreement between the Hermann Park Conservancy and the City of Houston in 1997.

3. Rick Dewees interview.

4. "Cancer Survivor Parks," R. A. Bloch Cancer Foundation. http://blochcancer.org/about/cancer-survivors-parks/.

5. http://www.hmns.org/index.php?option=com_content&view=article&id=33&Itemid=37.

6. Allan Turner, "Dino Stampede: Paleontology Hall Will Be Home to a Herd of 26 Dinosaurs," *Houston Chronicle*, February 21, 2011.

7. Sara Lindsey, interview with author, June 15, 2012.

8. "General Design Award of Excellence, Heart of the Park at Hermann Park, Houston, TX. SWA Group Houston, Texas and Olin Partnership Ltd, Conceptual Design Collaboration Consultants, Philadelphia, PA." ASLA 2005 Professional Awards, http://www.asla.org/awards/2005/05winners/556.html.

9. Hermann Park Conservancy Annual Report, 2004, 8.

10. Kunio Minami, in an e-mail to Barbara Jo Harwell dated November 20, 2012, gives the following information on the founding of the Japanese Garden: "In 1988 Ysuo Hori, Consul General of Japan, began meetings with Mayor Kathy Whitmire on the possibility of constructing a Japanese Garden somewhere in Houston. The Japanese Business Association of Houston was consulted, and in 1989 the Japanese Garden Inc. was established, led by Robert Abboud, Chairman of First City Bancorporation of Texas, and Teruo Mitsuya, First Vice President of the Japanese Business Association. This nonprofit corporation was necessary to coordinate fund-raising for the design and construction. The Japanese businessmen associated with this project were rotating through Houston and were not consistently involved with the project. In 1991 the Japanese members of the Board of Japanese Garden Inc. were: Yoshio Mita, Senior VP of Mitsubishi Intl (Houston), Kinji Nakano, Senior VP of Mitsui & Co. (USA), Takahiro Hino, Executive VP of Nippon Steel USA, Katsuma Ohara, General Manager of Fuji Bank, Houston, and Shojiro Imanishi, Consul General of Japan (Houston)."

11. Kunio Minami, interview with author, Japanese Garden Teahouse, Houston, February 7, 2012.

12. Takeshi Nakajima, "Building a Japanese Garden at Hermann Park of Houston," translated by Yoshio Mita. Typescript, Hermann Park Conservancy archives, January 3, 199[illegible]

13. Rick Dewees, correspondence with author, May 12, 2012.

14. Ibid.

15. Nakajima, "Building a Japanese Garden," 3.

16. "Japanese Garden, "Houston Parks and Recreation Department," http://www.houstontx.gov/parks/ourparks/japanesegarden.html.

17. Nakajima, "Building a Japanese Garden," 4.

18. Kunio Minami interview.

19. "Japanese Landscape Architect Terunobu Nakai Returns to Houston's Japanese Tea Garden," http://www.houston.us.emb-japan.go.jp/en/archive/page20080305.htm.

20. Brenda Beust Smith, "Searching for Perfect Balance in Japanese Garden," *Houston Chronicle*, September 29, 2007.

21. "Terunobu Nakai Revisits the Japanese Garden," *Parkside*, Newsletter of the Hermann Park Conservancy, Spring 2011.

22. Aya Hashimoto, interview with author, Kunio Minami, translator, Japanese Garden, Houston, February 7, 2012.

23. Kunio Minami interview.

24. Kathrine McGovern, interview with author, June 15, 2012.

25. Hermann Park Birds, https://picasaweb.google.com/benhulsey3/HermannParkBirds.

26. Ben Hulsey, correspondence with author, June 28, 2012.

27. Lisa Gray, "Hermann Park: A Landscape Jewel," *Houston Chronicle*, October 6, 2008.

28. "Buddy Carruth Playground for All Children," Houston Parks Board website, www.houstonparksboard.org/projects/CarruthPlaygound.php.

29. http://www.houstonzoo.org.

30. *Zoo Crew Volunteer Handbook*, Houston Zoo Inc., 2005, 4.

31. "Houston, Texas," *Encyclopedia of Southern Jewish Communities*, Goldring/Woldenberg Institute of Southern Jewish Life, http://www.isjl.org/history/archive/tx/houston.html.

32. Sarah Gish, "Miller Outdoor Theater Opens Following Renovation," April 6, 2009, http://www.yourhoustonnews.com/greater_houston/entertainment/article_e1518d4b-effb-53cc-8491-8b0457ee17b7.html.

33. "Miller Outdoor Theatre, Past and Present," http://milleroutdoortheatre.com/past-and-present/.

34. "Art in Hermann Park," http://milleroutdoortheatre.com/art-in-hermann-park/.

35. International Sculpture Garden statues: Simon Bolivar (Venezuela), Mahatma Ghandi (India); Confucius (China); Benito Juarez (Mexico), Bernardo O'Higgins (Chile), Alvar Nunez Cabeza de Vaca (Spain), Field Marshall Ramon Castilla y Marquesado (Peru), Jose de San Martin (Argentina), Jose Marti (Cuba), Jose P. Rizal (Philippines), Robert Burns (Scotland), and Vincente Rocafuerte (Ecuador). http://www.houstontx.gov/municipalart/locator-garden.html.

36. "Great Confucius Statue: A Gift from China to Houston," http://www.confuciussculpture.org/news.htm.

Selected Bibliography

Agatha, Sister M. *The History of Houston Heights 1891–1918*. Houston: Premier Printing Company, 1956.

Baker, Jay, and Barrie Scardino. *Heart of the Park Competition*. Houston: Rice Design Alliance, 1992.

Bearden, William. *Images of America: Overton Park*. Charleston, SC: Arcadia Publishing, 2004.

Beveridge, Charles E., and Paul Rocheleau. *Frederick Law Olmsted: Designing the American Landscape*. New York: Rizzoli, 1995.

Comey, Arthur Coleman. *Houston; Tentative Plans for Its Development: Report to the Houston Park Commission*. Boston: Press of Geo. H. Ellis Co., 1913.

Downing, Andrew Jackson. *Victorian Cottage Residences*. New York: Dover Publications, 1981.

Fox, Stephen. *Braeswood: An Architectural History*. Houston: Anchorage Foundation of Texas and Old Braeswood Civic Club, 1988.

———. *The General Plan of the William M. Rice Institute and Its Architectural Development*. Architecture at Rice Monograph 29. Houston: School of Architecture, Rice University, 1980.

———. *Houston Architectural Guide*, 3rd edition. Houston: American Institute of Architects, Houston Chapter and Minor Design Group, 2012.

———. *The Museum of Fine Arts, Houston: An Architectural History 1924–1986*. Houston: The Museum of Fine Arts, Houston, 1992.

———. *Rice University*. New York: Princeton Architectural Press, 2001.

Hanna/Olin, Ltd. *Renewing Hermann Park: A Comprehensive Master Plan*. Houston: Friends of Hermann Park, 1995.

Harnik, Peter. *Inside City Parks*. Washington, DC: ULI–the Urban Land Institute, 2000.

Houghton, Dorothy Knox Howe, Barrie Scardino, Sadie Gwin Blackburn, and Katherine Howe. *Houston's Forgotten Heritage: Landscape, Houses, Interiors 1824–1914*. Houston: Rice University Press, 1991.

Houston Architectural Survey 6 vols. Project of the City of Houston, Texas Historical Commission, and Rice University School of Architecture. Houston: Southwest Center for Urban Research, 1981–1982.

Illustrated City Book of Houston, various years.

Johnston, Marguerite. *Houston The Unknown City 1836–1946*. College Station: Texas A&M University Press, 1991.

Kalfus, Melvin *Frederick Law Olmsted: The Passion of a Public Artist*. New York: New York University Press, 1990.

King, John O. *Joseph Stephen Cullinan*. Nashville: Vanderbilt University Press, 1970.

Kirkland, Kate Sayen. *The Hogg Family and Houston: Philanthropy and the Civic Ideal*. Austin: University of Texas Press, 2009.

———. *Captain James A. Baker of Houston, 1857–1941*. College Station: Texas A&M University Press, 2012.

McComb, David G. *Houston: A History*. Austin: University of Texas Press, 1981.

Miller, Sara Cedar. *Central Park, An American Masterpiece*. New York: Harry N. Abrams Inc., in association with the Central Park Conservancy, 2003.

Olmsted, Frederick Law. *A Journey through Texas, Or, a Saddle-Trip on the Southwestern Frontier*. Austin: University of Texas Press, 1978; reprint, New York, Dix, 1857.

Rogers, Elizabeth Barlow. *Landscape Design: A Cultural and Architectural History*. New York: Abrams, 2001.

———. *Rebuilding Central Park: A Management and Restoration Plan*. Cambridge, MA: MIT Press, 1987.

Rybczynski, Witold. *A Clearing in the Distance: Frederick Law Olmsted and America in the Nineteenth Century*. New York: Scribner, 1999.

Scardino, Barrie, William F. Stern, and Bruce Webb. *Ephemeral City. Cite Looks at Houston*. Austin: University of Texas Press, 2003.

Steinfeldt, Cecilia. *S. Seymour Thomas 1868–1956: A Texas Genius Rediscovered*. San Antonio: Witte Museum, 2005.

Taylor, Lisa, ed. *Cities: The Forces That Shape Them* New York: Rizzoli, 1982.

Turner, Suzanne, and Joann Seale Wilson. *Houston's Silent Garden: Glenwood Cemetery, 1871–2009*. College Station: Texas A&M University Press, 2010.

Warren, David B. *Bayou Bend Gardens: A Southern Oasis*. Houston: Scala Publishers in association with the Museum of Fine Arts, Houston, 2006.

Wolf, George E., Jr. *The Bend in the Bayou: History of Magnolia Park*. Self-published, 2011.

Work Projects Administration, Writers' Program. *Houston: A History and Guide*. American Guide Series. Houston: Anson Jones Press, 1942.

Special Collections

Arthur Coleman Comey Collection, Frances Loeb Library Special Collections, Harvard University.

Hare & Hare Collection, Houston Metropolitan Research Center, Houston Public Library.

Hare & Hare Collection, State Historical Society of Missouri, Research Center–Kansas City.

Houston History Archives, Special Collections, University of Houston.

John P. McGovern Historical Collections and Research Center, Houston Academy of Medicine, Texas Medical Center.

Joseph Cullinan Collection, Houston Metropolitan Research Center, Houston Public Library.

Various collections, Briscoe Center for History, University of Texas.

Various collections, Woodson Research Center, Rice University.

Index

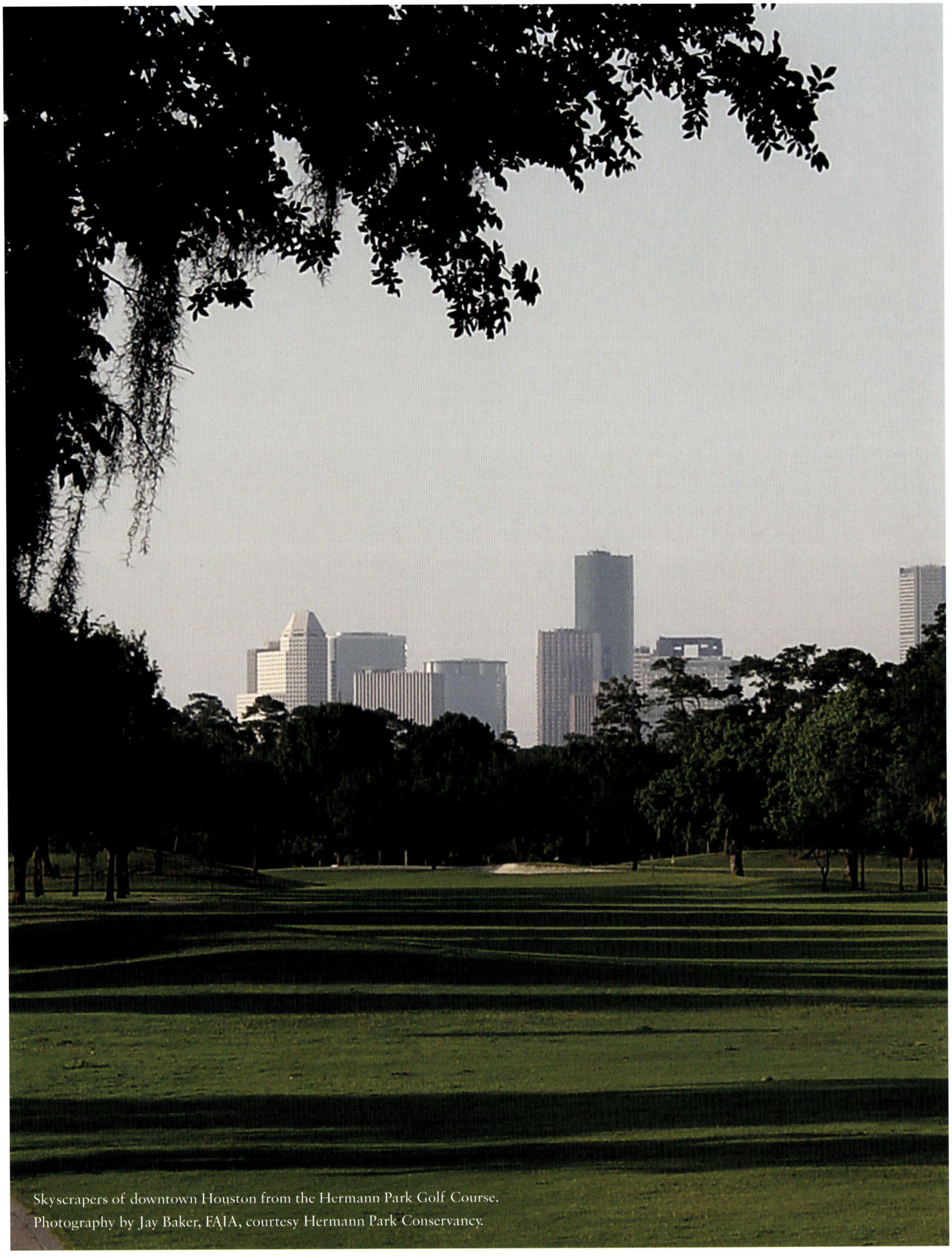

Skyscrapers of downtown Houston from the Hermann Park Golf Course.
Photography by Jay Baker, FAIA, courtesy Hermann Park Conservancy.